The Literary Works of Leonardo da Vinci; Volume 1

SCRITTI LETTERARI

DI

LEONARDO DA VINCI

cavati dagli Autografi e pubblicati

DA

J. P. RICHTER

IN DUE PARTI — PARTE I.

LONDRA:
SAMPSON LOW, MARSTON, SEARLE & RIVINGTON
188, FLEET STREET
1883

THE LITERARY WORKS

OF

LEONARDO DA VINCI

compiled and edited from the Original Manuscripts

BY

JEAN PAUL RICHTER, PH. DR.,

KNIGHT OF THE BAVARIAN ORDER OF ST. MICHAEL, &C.

IN TWO VOLUMES.—VOL. I.

LONDON:

SAMPSON LOW, MARSTON, SEARLE & RIVINGTON

188, FLEET STREET

1883

DEDICATED

BY PERMISSION

TO

HER MOST GRACIOUS MAJESTY

THE QUEEN

LIST OF SUBSCRIBERS.

H. R. H. THE PRINCE OF WALES.
H. I. H. THE CROWN PRINCE OF GERMANY.
H. R. H. THE DUKE OF ALBANY.
H. R. H. THE LANDGRÄFIN ANNA OF HESSE, PRINCESS OF PRUSSIA.

BERLIN, Industrial Museum (1 copy).
,, Ministry of Public Instruction (2 copies).
,, Royal Museum (1 copy).
BONN, Royal University (1 copy).
BOSTON, U. S., Boston Athenæum (1 copy).
BRESLAU, Provincial Museum (1 copy).
,, Royal University (1 copy).
BUDAPEST, Hungarian National Gallery (1 copy).
CAMBRIDGE, Fitzwilliam Museum (1 copy).
CASSEL, Royal Picture Gallery (1 copy).
COPENHAGEN, Royal Library (1 copy).
,, Royal Picture Gallery (1 copy).
DELFT, Polytechnic (1 copy).
DRESDEN, General Direction der Koenigl. Sammlungen &c. (1 copy).
DUBLIN, King's Inn Library (1 copy).
,, National Library of Ireland (1 copy).
HAGUE, the, Royal Library (1 copy).

HALLE, Royal University (1 copy)
HARROW, Vaughan Library (1 copy)
LONDON, Athenæum Club (1 copy)
„ Burlington Fine Arts Club (1 copy)
„ Fine Art Society (2 copies)
„ Guildhall Library (1 copy)
„ National Gallery (1 copy).
„ New University Club (1 copy)
„ Reform Club (1 copy)
„ Royal Academy of Arts (Subscription of one hundred Pounds).
„ South Kensington Museum (1 copy)
MUNICH, Royal Pinacoteca (1 copy)
NEW YORK, Brooklyn Library (1 copy)
OXFORD, Christ Church (1 copy).
PARIS, Bibliothèque Nationale des Beaux-arts (1 copy)
„ Musée du Louvre (1 copy).
PRAGUE, Imperial and Royal University (1 copy)
TURIN, Royal Library (1 copy)
VIENNA, the Albertina (1 copy)
„ Imperial and Royal University (1 copy)
„ Museum of Art and Industry (1 copy)
WEIMAR, Grand Ducal Museum (1 copy)
WINDSOR, Royal Library (1 copy)

Alma-Tadema, L. Esq., R. A., London (1 copy)
Amsler & Ruthardt, Berlin (2 copies)
Antinori, the Marquese, Senatore del Regno, Florence (1 copy)
Artom, Senatore del Regno, Asti (1 copy)
Asher & Co., London (4 copies)
Azeglio, the Marchese d', Senatore del Regno, Turin (1 copy)
Bain, James, London (4 copies).
Baring, Edw. Chas. Esq., M. P., London (1 copy)
Bartlett, W. H. and Co., London (1 copy).
Bell, Hugh Esq., London (1 copy)
Bickers and Sons, London (2 copies)
Birkett, The Revd. A. H., Bromham (1 copy)
Blacker, Louis, Esq. (1 copy)
Bode, Dr. W. Director of the Royal Museum, Berlin (1 copy)
Bower, R. M. Esq., London (1 copy).
Brambilla, Signor P., Milan (1 copy).
Bruins, Herr A., the Hague (1 copy)
Brioschi, Prof. Franc., Director of the Polytechnic, Milan (1 copy)

Brun, Herr Carl, Zürich (1 copy).
Bumpus, John, London (6 copies).
Bumpus, Edw., London (2 copies).
Bumpus, T. B., London (1 copy).
Burns and Oates, London (2 copies).
Bute, the Marquis of (1 copy).
Cagnola, Senatore del Regno, Milan (1 copy).
Campori, the Marchese G., Modena (1 copy).
Carter, Dr. F. A., Leamington (1 copy).
Clement, C. G. Esq., London (1 copy).
Christie, A. H. Esq., London (1 copy).
Civil Service Supply Association, London (3 copies).
Colvin, Prof. Sidney, Cambridge (1 copy).
Coomes's Regent Library, London (2 copies).
Coote, Walter, Esq., London (1 copy).
Cornish, Jos. and Sons, London (1 copy).
Cornish, J. E., Manchester (7 copies).
Cornish, Bros., Birmingham (1 copy).
Corsini, H. H. Prince Tommaso, Florence (1 copy).
Denny, A., London (1 copy).
Dawson, Bros., Montreal, Canada (2 copies).
Devonshire, the Duke of (1 copy).
Doetsch, Henry esq., London (1 copy).
Douglas and Foulis, Edinburgh (5 copies).
Downing and Co., Birmingham (1 copy).
Duguid, John Esq., Dover (1 copy).
Dumolard, Fratelli, Milan (3 copies).
Dunn, John, London (1 copy).
Ellis and White, London (1 copy).
Eastlake, Lady, London (1 copy).
Frizzoni, Dr. Gustavo, Milan (1 copy).
Fürstenberg, H. S. H., Prince Karl Egon zu (1 copy).
Gerold, L. C., Vienna (1 copy).
Gilbert and Field, London (1 copy).
Gill, M. H. and Son, Dublin (1 copy).
Giovannelli, H. H. Prince, Venice (1 copy).
Goode, Mrs., Baden (1 copy).
Graham, W. Esq., London (1 copy),
Grimm, Prof. Herman, Berlin (1 copy).
Gower, Lord Ronald (1 copy).
Habich, Herr Edw., Cassel (1 copy).
Haar and Steinert, Paris (1 copy).
Hamilton, Adams and Co., London (6 copies).
Hatchard, Messrs., London (2 copies).
Harrison and Sons, London (1 copy).

Heimbürger, Frl. N., Achern (1 copy).
Henderson and Co., J. T., Leghorn (1 copy).
Hertz, Frl. H., Northwich (1 copy).
Heseltine, J. P. Esq., London (1 copy).
Hichens, Andrew K., London (1 copy).
Hichens, J. K., London (1 copy).
Hodjes, Figgis, and Co., Dublin (1 copy).
Hodson, J. Stewart, Esq, Haslemere (1 copy).
Hoepli, Ulrico, Milan (8 copies).
Hollond, Mrs. Robt., London (1 copy)
James, F. H. Esq. M. D., Lancaster, U. S. (1 copy).
Jarrold and Sons, Norwich (1 copy).
Jersey, The Earl of (1 copy)
Joel, H. F. Esq., Dalston (1 copy).
Jordan, Geh. Rath, Dr. M, Berlin (1 copy).
Klincksick, C., Paris (2 copies).
Landriani, Signor C., Milan (1 copy)
Layard, Sir Henry A (1 copy).
Lehmann, Rudolph Esq, London (1 copy)
Leighton, Sir F, P. R. A, London (1 copy).
Leuchner and Lubensky, Graz (1 copy).
Levis, Dr. Giuseppe, Milan (1 copy).
Lippmann, Dr., Director of the Royal Museum, Berlin (1 copy).
Little, Brown and Co, Boston, U S. (3 copies).
Lockwood (Crosby) and Co, London (2 copies)
Löscher and Co, Rome (1 copy)
Mc Kelvie and Sons, Greenock (1 copy).
Maclehose and Sons, Glasgow (1 copy).
Marks, A. Esq., Long Ditton (1 copy).
Martin, Sir Theodore, K. C. B (1 copy).
Maxwell, Andrew, Esq, Glasgow (1 copy).
Menefee, R. J., Esq, Louisville, U. S. A. (1 copy)
Meyer, Dr., Director of the Royal Museum, Berlin (1 copy)
Mildmay, H. B. Esq, London (1 copy).
Minghetti, H E. Cav. Marco, Bologna (1 copy).
Molineux, R. J, Esq Guildford (1 copy).
Mongeri, Prof. Gius, Milan (1 copy).
Morelli, Comm Giov Senatore del Regno, Milan (1 copy).
Morison, Th. Esq, London (1 copy)
Morrison, Alfred Esq, London (1 copy).
Nast-Kolb, A. von, German Consul, Rome (1 copy).
Northbrook, the Earl of (1 copy)
Nunn, H. and Co, London (1 copy).
Papadopol, the Conti, Senatore del Regno, Venice (1 copy)
Parson, Edw. Esq, London (1 copy)

Petrie, Geo, Dundee (2 copies)
Philip, Son and Nephew, Liverpool (1 copy)
Ponti, Signor Andrea, Milan (1 copy).
Poynter, Edw. J. Esq., R. A, London (1 copy)
Powell, Francis Esq, Dunoon (1 copy)
Powerscourt, the Viscount (1 copy).
Prendergast, J. Esq, San Francisco (1 copy).
Prinetti, C, Senatore del Regno, Milan (1 copy).
Quaritch, Bernard, London (8 copies)
Radford, W. T. Esq, Sidmouth (1 copy)
Ramsden, Mrs. John, Godalming (1 copy)
Richmond, W B Esq, London (1 copy)
Robinson, J. C. Esq, London (1 copy)
Rose, J. Anderson Esq, London (1 copy)
Roth, Matthias, Esq M. D, London (1 copy)
Rotherham, L. and S. Society (1 copy)
Sartoris, E J Esq, London (1 copy)
Saunders, W., London (1 copy)
Schröder, Baron H, London (1 copy).
Scribner and Welford, New York (6 copies).
Serena, Arthur, Esq, London (1 copy).
Slopher, Th. Esq, Winchester (1 copy)
Siemens, C. W. Esq, London (1 copy).
Smith, A. Watson Esq, Stourbridge (1 copy)
Smith, W. H and Sons, London (2 copies)
Spaletti, the Conte V, Reggio (1 copy)
Sotheran, H and Co, London (11 copies).
Southampton Book Society (1 copy)
Spencer, the Earl of (1 copy)
Spithoever and Co, Rome (1 copy)
Stanford, E, London (1 copy)
Stevens, B F., London (2 copies)
Stubley, R, Boston (1 copy).
Stutfield, Marion, Brighton (1 copy).
Teano, H H. the Prince, Rome (1 copy)
Thibaudeau, A. W Esq., London (1 copy)
Thomson, J. A. Esq, Liverpool (1 copy)
Trivulzio, the Marchese G. G, Milan (1 copy).
Trübner and Co, London (4 copies)
Tubbs, Brooks and Chrystal, Manchester (2 copies)
Uzielli, Prof Gustavo, Turin (1 copy)
Venosta, H E. the Marchese Visconti, Milan (1 copy).
Wallace, Sir Richard, Bart., London (1 copy)
Wallis, Henry Esq, London (1 copy)
Walmsley, G. G, Liverpool (1 copy)

Wardle, George Esq., London (1 copy).
Waters, G. W., London (1 copy).
Wharncliffe, the Earl of (1 copy).
Westhorp, Sterling Esq., Ipswich (1 copy).
Wigan, Fred, Esq., London (1 copy).
Willett, Henry Esq., Brighton (1 copy).
Williams and Norgate, London (1 copy).
Woodgate, John, Esq., Colchester (1 copy).
Wyllie and Son, Aberdeen (1 copy).
Wyndham, Hon. Percy, London (1 copy).

PREFACE.

A singular fatality has ruled the destiny of nearly all the most famous of Leonardo da Vinci's works. Two of the three most important were never completed, obstacles having arisen during his life-time, which obliged him to leave them unfinished; namely the Sforza Monument and the Wall-painting of the Battle of Anghiari, while the third—the picture of the Last Supper at Milan—has suffered irremediable injury from decay and the repeated restorations to which it was recklessly subjected during the XVIIth and XVIIIth centuries. Nevertheless, no other picture of the Renaissance has become so wellknown and popular through copies of every description.

Vasari says, and rightly, in his Life of Leonardo, "that he laboured much more by his word than in fact or by deed", and the biographer evidently had in his mind the numerous works in Manuscript which have been preserved to this day. To us, now, it seems almost inexplicable that these valuable and interesting original texts should have remained so long unpublished, and indeed forgotten. It is certain that during the XVIth and XVIIth centuries their exceptional value was highly appreciated. This is proved not merely by the prices which they commanded, but also by the exceptional interest which has been attached to the change of ownership of merely a few pages of Manuscript.

That, notwithstanding this eagerness to possess the Manuscripts, their contents remained a mystery, can only be accounted for by the many and great difficulties attending the task of deciphering them. The handwriting is so peculiar that it requires considerable practice to read even a few detached phrases, much more to solve with any certainty the numerous difficulties of alternative readings, and to master the sense as a connected whole. Vasari observes with reference to Leonardo's writing: "he wrote backwards, in rude characters, and with the left hand, so that any one who is not practised in reading them, cannot understand them". The aid of a mirror in reading reversed handwriting appears to me available only for a first experimental reading. Speaking from my own experience, the persistent use of it is too fatiguing and inconvenient to be practically advisable, considering the enormous mass of Manuscripts to be deciphered. And as, after all, Leonardo's handwriting runs backwards just as all Oriental character runs backwards—that is to say from right to left—the difficulty of reading direct from the writing is not insuperable. This obvious peculiarity in the writing is not, however, by any means the only obstacle in the way of mastering the text. Leonardo made use of an orthography peculiar to himself; he had a fashion of amalgamating several short words into one long one, or, again, he would quite arbitrarily divide a long word into two separate halves; added to this there is no punctuation whatever to regulate the division and construction of the sentences, nor are there any accents—and the reader may imagine that such difficulties were almost sufficient to make the task seem a desperate one to a beginner. It is therefore not surprising that the good intentions of some of Leonardo's most reverent admirers should have failed.

Leonardo's literary labours in various departments both of Art and of Science were those essentially of an enquirer, hence the analytical method is that which he employs in arguing out his investigations and dissertations. The vast structure of his scientific theories is consequently built up of numerous separate researches, and it is much to be lamented that he should never have collated and arranged them. His love for detailed research—as it seems to me—was the reason that in almost all the Manuscripts, the different paragraphs appear to us to be in utter confusion; on one and the same page, observations on the most dissimilar subjects follow each other without any connection. A page, for instance, will begin with some principles of astronomy, or the motion of the earth; then come the laws of sound, and finally some precepts as to colour. Another page will begin with his investigations on the structure of the intestines, and end with philosophical remarks as to the relations of poetry to painting; and so forth.

Leonardo himself lamented this confusion, and for that reason I do not think that the publication of the texts in the order in which they occur in the originals would at all fulfil his intentions. No reader could find his way through such a labyrinth, Leonardo himself could not have done it.

Added to this, more than half of the five thousand manuscript pages which now remain to us, are written on loose leaves, and at present arranged in a manner which has no justification beyond the fancy of the collector who first brought them together to make volumes of more or less extent Nay, even in the volumes, the pages of which were numbered by Leonardo himself, their order, so far as the connection of the texts was concerned, was obviously a matter of indifference to him. The only point he seems to have kept in view, when first writing down his notes, was that each observation should be complete to the end on the page on which it was begun The exceptions to this rule are extremely few, and it is certainly noteworthy that we find in such cases, in bound volumes with his numbered pages, the written observations· "turn over", "This is the continuation of the previous page", and the like. Is not this sufficient to prove that it was only in quite exceptional cases that the writer intended the consecutive pages to remain connected, when he should, at last, carry out the often planned arrangement of his writings?

What this final arrangement was to be, Leonardo has in most cases indicated with considerable completeness. In other cases this authoritative clue is wanting, but the difficulties arising from this are not insuperable, for, as the subject of the separate paragraphs is always distinct and well defined in itself, it is quite possible to construct a well-planned whole, out of the scattered materials of his scientific system, and I may venture to state that I have devoted especial care and thought to the due execution of this responsible task.

The beginning of Leonardo's literary labours dates from about his thirty-seventh year, and he seems to have carried them on without any serious interruption till his death Thus the Manuscripts that remain represent a period of about thirty years Within this space of time his handwriting altered so little that it is impossible to judge from it of the date of any particular text. The exact dates, indeed, can only be assigned to certain note-books in which the year is incidentally indicated, and in which the order of the leaves has not been altered since Leonardo used them. The assistance these afford for a chronological arrangement of the Manuscripts is generally self evident. By this clue I have assigned to the original Manuscripts now scattered through England, Italy and France, the order of their production, as in many matters of detail it is highly important to be able to verify the time and place at which certain observations were made and registered. For this purpose the Bibliography of the Manuscripts given at the end of Vol. II, may be regarded as an Index, not far short of complete, of all Leonardo's literary works now extant. The consecutive numbers (from 1 to 1566) at the head of each passage in this work, indicate their logical sequence with reference to the subjects, while the letters and figures to the left of each paragraph refer to the original Manuscript and number of the page, on which that particular passage is to be found. Thus the reader, by referring to the List of Manuscripts at the beginning of Volume I, and to the Bibliography at the end of Volume II, can, in every instance, easily ascertain, not merely the period to which the passage belongs, but also exactly where it stood in the original document. Thus, too, by following the sequence of the numbers in the Bibliographical index, the reader may reconstruct the original order of the Manuscripts and recompose the various texts to be found on the original sheets—so much of it, that is to say, as by its subject-matter came within the scope of this work. It may, however, be here observed that Leonardo's Manuscripts contain, besides the passages here printed, a great number of notes and dissertations on Mechanics, Physics, and some other subjects, many of which could only be satisfactorily dealt with by specialists. I have given as complete a review of these writings as seemed necessary in the Bibliographical notes.

In 1651, Raphael Trichet Dufresne, of Paris, published a selection from Leonardo's writings on painting, and this treatise became so popular that it has since been reprinted about two-and-twenty times, and in six different languages. But none of these editions were derived from the original texts, which were supposed to have been lost, but from early copies, in which Leonardo's text had been more or less mutilated, and which were all fragmentary. The oldest and on the whole the best copy of Leonardo's essays and precepts on Painting is in the Vatican Library; this has been twice printed, first by Manzi, in 1817, and secondly by Ludwig, in 1882. Still, this ancient copy, and the published editions of it, contain much for which it would be rash to hold Leonardo responsible. and some portions—such as the very important rules for the proportions of the human figure—are wholly wanting; on the other hand they contain passages which, if they are genuine, cannot now be verified from any original Manuscript extant. These copies, at any rate neither give us the original order of the texts, as written by Leonardo, nor do they afford any substitute, by connecting them on a rational scheme; indeed, in their chaotic confusion they are anything rather than satisfactory reading. The fault, no doubt, rests with the compiler of the Vatican copy, which would seem to be the source whence all the published and extensively known texts were derived; for, instead of arranging the passages himself, he was satisfied with recording a suggestion for a final arrangement of them into eight distinct parts, without attempting to carry out his scheme. Under the mistaken idea that this plan of distribution might be that, not of the compiler, but of Leonardo himself, the various editors, down to the present day, have very injudiciously continued to adopt this order—or rather disorder.

I, like other enquirers, had given up the original Manuscript of the Trattato della Pittura for lost, till, in the beginning of 1880, *I was enabled, by the liberality of Lord Ashburnham, to inspect his Manuscripts, and was so happy as to discover among them the original text of the best-known portion of the Trattato in his magnificent library at Ashburnham Place. Though this discovery was of a fragment only—but a considerable fragment—inciting me to further search, it gave the key to the mystery which had so long enveloped the first origin of all the known copies of the Trattato. The extensive researches I was subsequently enabled to prosecute, and the results of which are combined in this work, were only rendered possible by the unrestricted permission granted me to investigate all the Manuscripts by Leonardo dispersed throughout Europe, and to reproduce the highly important original sketches they contain, by the process of "photogravure". Her Majesty the Queen graciously accorded me special permission to copy for publication the Manuscripts at the Royal Library at Windsor. The Commission Centrale Administrative de l'Institut de France, Paris, gave me, in the most liberal manner, in answer to an application from Sir Frederic Leighton, P. R. A., Corresponding member of the Institut, free permission to work for several months in their private collection at deciphering the Manuscripts preserved there. The same favour which Lord Ashburnham had already granted me was extended to me by the Earl of Leicester, the Marchese Trivulzi, and the Curators of the Ambrosian Library at Milan, by the Conte Manzoni at Rome and by other private owners of Manuscripts of Leonardo's; as also by the Directors of the Louvre at Paris; the Accademia at Venice; the Uffizi at Florence; the Royal Library at Turin; and the British Museum, and the South Kensington Museum. I am also greatly indebted to the Librarians of these various collections for much assistance in my labours; and more particularly to Monsieur Louis Lalanne, of the Institut de France, the Abbate Ceriani, of the Ambrosian Library, Mr. Maude Thompson, Keeper of Manuscripts at the British Museum, Mr. Holmes, the Queen's Librarian at Windsor, the Revd Vere Bayne, Librarian of Christ Church College at Oxford, and the Revd A. Napier, Librarian to the Earl of Leicester at Holkham Hall.*

In correcting the Italian text for the press, I have had the advantage of valuable advice from the Commendatore Giov. Morelli, Senatore del Regno, and from Signor Gustavo Frizzoni, of Milan. The translation, under many difficulties, of the Italian text into English, is mainly due to Mrs. R. C. Bell; while the rendering of several of the most puzzling and important passages, particularly in the second half of Vol. I, I owe to the indefatigable interest taken in this work by Mr. E. J. Poynter R. A. Finally I must express my thanks to Mr. Alfred Marks, of Long Ditton, who has most kindly assisted me throughout in the revision of the proof sheets.

The notes and dissertations on the texts on Architecture in Vol. II I owe to my friend Baron Henri de Geymüller, of Paris.

I may further mention with regard to the illustrations, that the negatives for the production of the "photo-gravures" by Monsieur Dujardin of Paris were all taken direct from the originals.

It is scarcely necessary to add that most of the drawings here reproduced in facsimile have never been published before. As I am now, on the termination of a work of several years' duration, in a position to review the general tenour of Leonardo's writings, I may perhaps be permitted to add a word as to my own estimate of the value of their contents. I have already shown that it is due to nothing but a fortuitous succession of unfortunate circumstances, that we should not, long since, have known Leonardo, not merely as a Painter, but as an Author, a Philosopher, and a Naturalist. There can be no doubt that in more than one department his principles and discoveries were infinitely more in accord with the teachings of modern science, than with the views of his contemporaries. For this reason his extraordinary gifts and merits are far more likely to be appreciated in our own time than they could have been during the preceding centuries. He has been unjustly accused of having squandered his powers, by beginning a variety of studies and then, having hardly begun, throwing them aside. The truth is that the labours of three centuries have hardly sufficed for the elucidation of some of the problems which occupied his mighty mind.

Alexander von Humboldt has borne witness that "he was the first to start on the road towards the point where all the impressions of our senses converge in the idea of the Unity of Nature." Nay, yet more may be said. The very words which are inscribed on the monument of Alexander von Humboldt himself, at Berlin, are perhaps the most appropriate in which we can sum up our estimate of Leonardo's genius:

"Majestati naturae par ingenium."

LONDON, April 1883.

J. P. R.

CONTENTS OF VOLUME I.

LIST OF ILLUSTRATIONS IN VOLUME I.

The reproductions of drawings are of the exact size of the originals; except that Plates I, XVIII and XLVI are slightly reduced. The colour and tone of the paper have in every case been faithfully imitated, in order to give to the facsimiles a perfect and complete resemblance to the originals, whether drawn in charcoal, red chalk or pen and ink. It is to be understood that all Drawings here reproduced are in pen-and-ink, unless otherwise stated.

ERRATA.

Italian text: page 44 *l.* 27 *for* luminosi se *read* luminosi; se.—*p.* 79 *l.* 23 *for* esse *read* e se.—*p.* 111 *l.* 4 *from the end for* c . d . e . *read* c .; d . e .—*p.* 146 *l.* 22 *for* i *read* ī.—*p.* 167 *l.* 9 *for* recto *read* resto.—*p.* 196 *l.* 4 *from the end for* Ĭi *read* Ĭi.—*p.* 228 *l.* 10 *for* il parte *read* parte.—*p.* 272 *l.* 20 *for* baso *read* baso.—*p.* 291 *l.* 6 *for* ī *read* i.

English text: page 48 *l.* 2 *from the end for* ever *read* over.—*p.* 65 *l.* 15 *for* tretragon *read* tetragon.—*p.* 81 *l.* 6 *for* WHICH WILL *read* WILL.—*p.* 109 *l.* 13 *for* on opposite *read* on the opposite.—*p.* 114 *ll.* 26, 27 *for* avelets . . . walways *read* wavelets . . . always.—*p.* 115 *l.* 7 *from the end for* as *read* at.—*p.* 135 *l.* 11 *for* holer *read* holes.—*p.* 153 *l.* 8 *from the end for* [on] *read* [at].—*p.* 164 *l.* 12 *for* each *read* at each.—*p.* 174 *l.* 9 *for* then-ose *read* the nose.—*p.* 182 *l.* 26 *for* length *read* teeth.—*p.* 188 *l.* 6 *for* And to *read* And do; *l.* 10 *for* a *read* and.—*p.* 200 *l.* 18 *for* it to out *read* it out.—*p.* 207 *l.* 5 *for* to with the *read* to the.—*p.* 238 *l.* 23 *for* as *read* as to.—*p.* 266 *l.* 16 *for* tla *read* flat.—*p.* 306 *l.* 30 *for* whirling *read* whirling.—*p.* 321 *l.* 4 *from the end for* thicker *read* thicken.—*p.* 329 *l.* 2 *for* farther *read* further.

Notes: page 201, *No.* 583 *l.* 5 *for* left *read* right.—*p.* 349 *l.* 1 *for* of the beginning *read* the beginning of.

I.

Prolegomena and General Introduction to the Book on Painting.

Clavis sigillorum.

1. *In the few instances in which Leonardo has written from left to right in the ordinary way this is stated in a note. In all other cases the writing is backwards.*

2. *The numbers printed above the line in the revised text:* [2], [3], [4] *&c. indicate the heads of the lines in the original MS. In many instances the breaking off of the lines in the original MS. accounts for peculiarities in the construction of Leonardo's sentences. In the translation the numbers refer only to the footnotes and they have been introduced in such passages, which require an explanation.*

3. *Clerical errors and obvious mistakes in spelling have been corrected in the text, but are given in the notes, so that all the peculiarities of the original text which are omitted in the revised text may be seen at a glance.*

4. *Leonardo frequently employs the following abbreviations:—*

for per *or* pr; *e. g.* che = perche; so a = sopra.

for di.

for br; *e. g.* eve = breve.

for ver; *e. g.* in so = inverso.

for ser; *e. g.* vo = servo.

These occur so constantly and are so unimportant that it has not been thought necessary to point them out. He also uses:

ì *for* uno.

î *for* una

5. *Such abbreviations as are common in familiar speech are retained in the text; e. g.* un sol punto.

6. *Leonardo's usual way of spelling*, ochio spechio *for* occhio specchio, *has also been left unaltered.*

7. *The combinations of two or three words into one, which Leonardo so frequently used, and which are so puzzling to the eye as to render reading difficult, though plain to the ear, have been separated in the revised text; e. g.* leforme ditutti = le forme di tutti. *These combinations were, however, intentional no doubt; in almost every case they indicate the author's desire of substituting a sort of phonetic writing for the rules in general use. This doubling of the letters—as, for instance in* chessia *for* che sia *and* essella *for* e se la—*is, I believe, clear evidence of what may be called the orthography of Leonardo da Vinci. The separation of the words has involved the loss of these doubled letters, but the original spelling has been given, for reference, in the foot notes.*

8. *Leonardo commonly wrote* ã ẽ ĩ õ ũ *or* ṽ *for* an, en, in, on, un. *This sign occasionally, but not often, represents* m. *It has been retained, as it was usual in printed type in the XVth and XVIth centuries.*

9. *Leonardo sometimes writes* j *for* i, *particularly where it is joined to* m, n *or* u; *e. g.* linje, tienj, mjnor. *As he never sets a dot over the ordinary* ı *(at any rate when he writes from right to left), it is plain that he uses* j *for* i *(he does not dot the* j*) simply to avoid confounding* ni *or* ui *with* m, *or* mi *with* nu. *As this difficulty cannot occur in print I have restored the usual spelling* i *for* j *without referring to it in the notes.*

10. *Accents and apostrophes are entirely lacking in the original manuscript, but it seemed necessary to introduce them into the printed text. The accent has also been added in those parts of the verb* avere *in which Leonardo had dropped the* h: *as* ò, ài, à, ànno.

11. | || ||| ( ) *In the MSS. there are no marks of punctuation but these, and they have been retained wherever they occur.* · *is always placed by Leonardo just above the line of writing and is never used as a full stop, but only to divide the words according to the sense; it very often occurs between every word, particularly in MSS. of about* 1490. *When a letter or number is placed between two points, as* . a ., *or* . 3 ., *it usually refers to a corresponding sign on a diagram or sketch.*

| || ||| *commonly serve to separate sentences which are entirely distinct.*

| . *This mark commonly indicates that words written above or below the line are to be inserted. In the revised text they have been simply inserted.*

In the notes these passages are distinguished by the following signs:—

« » *indicates that the words were written above the line.*

„ " *that the words were written below the line.*

( ) *This mark is used by Leonardo to mark off a digression, or parenthesis, or a quotation from some other work of his own; but it often takes the place of the colon:*

(*A simple bracket placed at the beginning of one or more lines serves to lay stress on particular sentences; it is also used to mark distinct sentences which have no connection with the rest of the text on the same page. In the printed text such sentences have been denoted by the mark* ¶.

— The last line of a section commonly ends with a horizontal line of variable length, making it of equal length with the preceding lines of writing.

12. *3, 4, 5. These figures, if written large, or some similar mark, are occasionally placed at the end of a page or at the beginning of a passage that has been crossed out; and this indicates that the continuation is to be sought for elsewhere, where the same sign is repeated.*

The sings ⊖ o, which occur in the passages on painting, have been added by some early copyist and have therefore not been reproduced in the notes.

13. , . : ; ! ? *These stops are never used in the original MSS. It seemed necessary however to insert such marks in order to render the text intelligible. A full stop is only used at the end of a section to avoid confusion with Leonardo's own use of points (see No. 11), for he never places one at the end of a section or paragraph. Wherever a full stop seemed wanting in the course of the text I have put a semi colon (;). The colon (:) is used instead of a full stop where, in the original, a point (.) occurs.*

14. [ ] *Passages between brackets are crossed out in the original.*

15. *When a word or passage of the revised text is printed in small type it indicates that the reading is doubtful in consequence of partial obliteration.*

16. \\\\\\ *indicates passages in which the original writing is entirely destroyed.*

17. R *indicates that the passage is written in red chalk.*

18. (R) *indicates that the original writing in red chalk has been written over in pen and ink.*

19. P *indicates that the original writing is in silverpoint.*

20. 1^a 2^a 3^a *&c. the front page*—recto—*of sheet* 1, 2, 3, *&c.*
1^b 2^b 3^b *&c. the back page*—verso—*of sheet* 1, 2, 3, *&c.*

The MSS. Tr. *and* S. K. M. I[2] *are the only ones in which the* pages *are numbered. In all other MSS. the* leaf *only is numbered. In referring to the Codex Atlanticus a double series of numbers has been used. The first apply only to the larger leaves of the Codex, on which two or more of the original leaves of the MS. have been mounted; the second series does not exist in the Codex itself; it refers to the original pages in the order in which they have been placed in it. By this second series of numbers the correspondence of the front and back pages has been verified. Wherever, in addition to the consecutive numbering, a different number occurs in Leonardo's writing it is quoted in a parenthesis, thus:*—C 27^b (3^a), *and this indicates that the back page of leaf* 27 *in the MS.* C *was originally numbered* 3.

21. *A Roman* II, *as* 26 II^a 26 II^b, *indicates that the same number* (26) *occurs twice. In the Codex Atlanticus* $\frac{1}{1}$ *is used for II.*

22. O', O'' *indicates that the passages so marked are originally notes written on the inside of the cover of the MS.;* O' *within the front or upper cover,* O'' *within the under cover.*

23. *The wood-cuts introduced into the text are facsimile-reproductions of Leonardo's own sketches and drawings which accompany the MSS. But the letters and numbers affixed to them have been inserted in ordinary writing.*

24 *The following is a list of Leonardo's letters and numbers, as they are found on those original drawings which are here reproduced by facsimile engravings. The reader will have to refer to this list, by which he will be enabled to identify the letters and numbers on the originals with the corresponding figures in the printed text.*

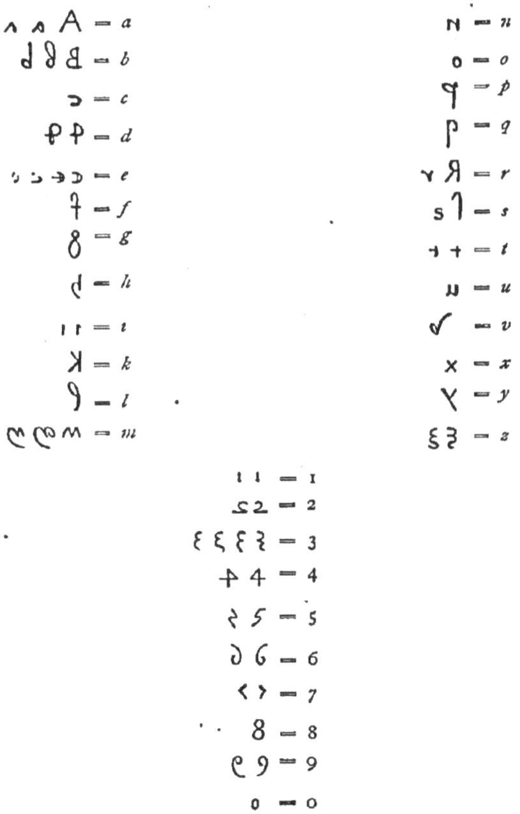

INDEX OF MANUSCRIPTS.

	MARK OF MANUSCRIPT	DESCRIPTION OF MANUSCRIPT	PLACE	TOTAL NUMBER OF PAGES	SIZE IN CENTIMÈTRES	DATE
1.	W. An. I.	Fragment of first treatise on Anatomy.	Royal Library, Windsor.	10	18,7×13,2	1489
2.	C.	Treatise on Light and Shade, bound, marked C.	Institut de France, Paris.	56	31×22	1490, 1491
3.	B.	Bound Volume, marked B.	Institut de France, Paris.	168	23,5×17	about 1490
4.	Ash. II.	Volume stitched in wrapper, marked $\frac{1875}{1}$, in the Library of Lord Ashburnham.	Ashburnham Place, Sussex.	26	24×17	about 1490
5.	Ash. I.	Fragment of the *Libro di Pittura*, marked $\frac{1875}{2}$, in the Library of Lord Ashburnham.	Ashburnham Place, Sussex.	68	21×11,5	1492
6.	A.	Fragment of MS., treating on various matters.	Institut de France, Paris.	126	21×14	1492
7.	S. K. M. III.	Notebook, marked III.	ForsterLibrary, South Kensington Museum, London.	176	9×6,7	1493
8.	H.3	Notebook, forming the third portion of the bound Volume, marked H.	Institut de France, Paris.	94	10,3×7,2	1493, 1494
9.	H.2	Notebook, forming the second portion of the bound Volume, marked H.	Institut de France, Paris.	92	10,3×7,2	1494, January
10.	H.1	Notebook, forming the first portion of the bound Volume, marked H.	Institut de France, Paris.	96	10,3×7,2	1494, March
11.	S. K. M. II.2	Notebook, forming the second part of the bound Volume, marked II.	ForsterLibrary, South Kensington Museum, London.	126	9,9×7,2	1493—1495
12.	S. K. M. II.1	Notebook, forming the first part of the bound Volume, marked II.	ForsterLibrary, South Kensington Museum, London.	190	9,9×7,2	1495
13.	I.2	Notebook, forming the second part of the bound Volume, marked I.	Institut de France, Paris.	182	10×7,2	1497
14.	I.1	Notebook, forming the first portion of the bound Volume, marked I.	Institut de France, Paris.	96	10×7,2	1497 ?
15.	W. P.	Studies on the Proportions of the Human Figure, loose sheets.	Royal Library, Windsor.	19	various large sizes	1490—1495
16.	W. H.	Treatise on the Anatomy of the Horse, loose sheets.	Royal Library, Windsor.	80	various sizes	1490—1495
17.	W. An. II.	Second treatise on Anatomy, loose sheets.	Royal Library, Windsor.	72	19×13,5	1490—1500

	MARK OF MANUSCRIPT	DESCRIPTION OF MANUSCRIPT	PLACE	TOTAL NUMBER OF PAGES	SIZE IN CENTIMÈTRES.	DATE
18	L.	Notebook, in original binding, marked L.	Institut de France, Paris.	188	10×7	1502
19.	W M.	Collection of Maps.	Royal Library, Windsor.	12	various large sizes	about 1502
20.	S. K. M. I.[1]	Treatise on Stereometry, first portion of a bound Volume, marked I.	Forster Library, South Kensington Museum, London.	76	14×10,5	1505
21.	S. K. M. I.[2]	Notebook, second portion of a bound Volume, marked I.	Forster Library, South Kensington Museum, London.	28	14×10,5	about 1505
22.	F.	Notebook, in original binding, marked F.	Institut de France, Paris	192	15×10,2	1508
23.	Br. M.	Collection of treatises and notes, bound Volume, marked Arundel 263.	British Museum, London.	566	19×12,5	about 1509
24.	W An. III.	Third treatise on Anatomy, loose sheets of greyish-blue colour.	Royal Library, Windsor.	46	29×21	1513
25.	E.	Notebook, in original binding, marked E.	Institut de France, Paris.	160	15,4×9,3	1513 and 1514
26.	G	Notebook, in original binding, marked G.	Institut de France, Paris	186	14×10	about 1515
27.	M.	Notebook, in original binding, marked M.	Institut de France, Paris	188	10×7	about 1515
28.	Tr.	Volume treating on various matters, bound, in possession of Marchese G. G. Trivulzio	Trivulzi Palace, Milan.	102	21×14	between 1497 and 1516
29.	Leic.	Bound Volume, containing chiefly scientific observations	Leicester Library, Holkham Hall, Norfolk.	72	30×22	between 1500 and 1516, 1510?
30.	Mz.	Volume treating on various subjects, in original binding.	In possession of Count Manzoni, Rome.	26	21,3×15,5	between 1490 and 1516
31.	D.	Treatise on the Eye, in original binding, marked D	Institut de France, Paris	20	25×16	between 1490 and 1516
32.	K.[1]	Notebook, forming the first part of a bound Volume, marked K.	Institut de France, Paris.	96	10×6,6	after 1504
33	K.[2]	Notebook, forming the second part of a bound Volume, marked K.	Institut de France, Paris	62	10×6,6	after 1504
34.	K.[3]	Notebook, forming the third part of a bound Volume, marked K.	Institut de France, Paris.	96	10×6,6	after 1504
35.	W. An. IV.	Fourth treatise on Anatomy, loose sheets.	Royal Library, Windsor.	138	29×22	about 1515
36.	W. L.	Collection of loose sheets in bound Volume (Fragment of Leoni's collection).	Royal Library, Windsor.	30	various large sizes	1490—1516
37.	W.	Loose sheets, partly mounted.	Royal Library, Windsor.	.	various sizes	about 1490—1516

	MARK OF MANUSCRIPT	DESCRIPTION OF MANUSCRIPT	PLACE	TOTAL NUMBER OF PAGES	SIZE IN CENTIMÈTRES	DATE
38.	C. A	Bound Volume, commonly called Codex Atlanticus, 395 folios, each containing one or more MS-sheets	Ambrosian Library, Milan.	1222	various sizes	about 1483—1518
39.	Trn	five loose sheets	Royal Library, Turin.	10	various sizes	uncertain
40.	F U.	two loose sheets.	Uffizi Gallery, Florence.	4	various sizes	1473 and 1478
41.	V.	five loose sheets	Academy, Venice	10	various sizes	uncertain
42.	Mi A.	one sheet	Gallery in the Ambrosian Library, Milan	2	20×14	uncertain
43.	Mi. A. R.	one sheet	Ambrosian Library, Cod Resta	2	8°	uncertain
44	Mch.	one sheet	Pinakothek, Munich	2	4°	uncertain
45.	P V	one sheet, marked N. 2260.	Cod Vallardi, Louvre, Paris.	2	4°	uncertain
46.	P. L.	one sheet (previously in the Collection of the King of Holland)	Collection of drawings, Louvre, Paris	2	27,7×21	about 1480—1500
47.	P. A.	one sheet.	Collection of drawings, M. Armand, Paris	2	26×18,5	uncertain
48.	Br M P.	two sheets.	British Museum, Printroom.	4	8° and 4°	uncertain
49	Th	one sheet	Collection of A. W. Thibaudeau, Esq London.	2	19,5×7,5	uncertain
50.	Mo	one sheet	Collection of A. Morrison, Esq	2	8°	uncertain
51.	P H. N	one sheet (previously in the Collection of Henry, Prince of Netherlands)	. . .	2	8°	uncertain
52.	B. H.	five sheets	Langton, Berkshire, seat of the Hon. Mr Baillie Hamilton	10	various sizes	uncertain
53	Ox.	two sheets	Library of Christ Church College, Oxford.	4	4° and 8°	uncertain
54.	Md.	one sheet.	Archivio Palatino, Modena.	2	. . .	1507
55.	Ash. III	Treatise on Mechanics, Architecture &c. by Francesco di Giorgio, with notes by Leonardo (on different pages)	Ashburnham Place, Sussex.	7	14,8×10	uncertain.

Contrary to the universal custom of western nations, Leonardo committed almost all his notes to paper in a handwriting that goes from right to left. This singular habit has sometimes been accounted for by supposing that Leonardo felt it necessary to put every difficulty in the way of the publication of his works. This assumption, however, seems to me to rest on no solid grounds, and is but an hypothesis at best. Perfectly explicit statements prove, on the contrary, that Leonardo wished to publish his writings, and that he cared greatly that they should be known and read; and any one who has taken the trouble, to make himself familiar with the Master's writing will, I think, hardly resist the conviction that even the character of the writing was expressly adapted to that view.

We know from the evidence of his friend Luca Paciolo that Leonardo drew with his left hand, and used it with perfect ease.[1] *In point of fact, in almost every drawing authentically known to be genuine—as those included in the texts of MSS. must be—wherever shading is introduced the strokes lie from left to right (downwards) as they would be drawn with the left hand.*[2]

The question as to why *Leonardo drew and wrote with his left hand is now probably a vain one. There is nothing to justify us in deciding whether accidental circumstance or mere caprice was the cause. It is worthy of remark, that the earliest notes, written in his twenty-first year, when he could hardly have had such reasons for caution as are attributed to him*[3], *are written backwards.*

The contents of Leonardo's MSS. sufficiently prove that he certainly intended them for publication, though the form is probably not always what he finally meant it to be.

The appeal or address 'tu', *which frequently occurs and more particularly in theoretical passages, is often no doubt meant for the reader, but in other cases it indicates rather the specially meditative character of the passage. Abstract speculations acquire a particular charm from this soliloquizing form—it is as if we overheard the mental process of the author.*

In the passages indicated below Leonardo expresses himself clearly as to the end and purpose of his literary labours.

In one passage in the MS. at Holkham (No. 1) he speaks of keeping a certain invention to himself, and not making it public. As he uses this reserve in no other instance, this exception sufficiently proves the rule.

1 "Scrivesi ancora alla rovescia e mancina che non si posson legere se non con lo specchio, ovvero guardando la carta dal suo rovescio contro alla luce, come so m'intendi senz' altro dica, e come fa il nostro Leonardo da Vinci, lume della pittura, quale è mancino, come più volte è detto" (L. PACIOLO, *Divina Proportione, Venezia,* 1509)

2 This was first pointed out in the '*Critical review of the drawings by the old Masters in the Dresden Gallery*' by Senatore GIOV MORELLI.

3 "Pour s'exprimer à peu près comme lui, des esprits étroits et routiniers d'une part, et de l'autre des aventuriers partant à cheval contre tout ce qui avait permis jusque-là d'établir ces règles qui, déterminant la limite du possible et de l'impossible, empêchent le chercheur de tomber dans le désespoir et la mélancolie, exagéraient à plaisir ce qu'il avait dit (?) pour réagir contre les abus et les paradoxes, et se servaient de ses propres expressions (?) pour le représenter comme un charlatan ou un fou Lorsqu'il parlait du moins, son éloquence persuasive donnait à ses idées toute leur valeur; mais *laisser voir* dans ses papiers des pensées incomplètement exprimées, des rédactions inachevées, des projets d'inventions de toutes sortes, *c'eût été s'exposer à la calomnie et au vol.*" (CH RAVAISSON-MOLLIEN, *Les Manuscrits de L. de Vinci, Paris* 1881, *p.* 2). *But we might suppose that Leonardo would have considered his papers and his instruments quite safe, by keeping them locked away in his own room*

In the passage from the MS. F (No. 2) the expression "mettere insieme" *is equally characteristic of his method of working and of the condition of the MSS. By it he means the classification of the separate details of his researches so as to make a connected whole, which could be done the more easily since it was his practice to write separate chapters on separate sheets.*

The MS. in the British Museum begins with an apology (No. 4) which is very interesting, for the self-evident disorder of the MS. This apology applies equally well to the notes on mathematics—where it is placed—and to all the branches of science on which Leonardo wrote.

The passages (Nos. 5—7*) are* soliloquies, *and refer to the arrangement of different MSS. as preparatory to publication in the form intended by Leonardo himself. From all this it was clearly not his intention that the notes should be printed as they lay, in confusion, under his hand.*

The schemes, which Leonardo himself proposed for the arrangement of the Book on Painting as well as of his other writings, give us a clue—as we shall presently see—which enables us perfectly to construct the whole work on the basis of his own rules and with some pretention to logical sequence.

We may conclude that the sections 9, 10 *and* 11 *headed* 'Proemio' *refer to the Book on Painting, and more particularly to the lessons on Perspective, because section* 21 *with its special title* "Proemio di prospettiva" *is, in the original (Cod. At.* 117^b; 561^b*), written on the same sheet.*

Sections 12 *to* 20 *give us the guiding idea of the general plan and of the object and purpose of the* Libro di Pittura.

No. 21 'Proemio di prospettiva, cioè dell' ufitio dell' ochio' *follows naturally after the other general introductions. Our acceptance of this introduction, it is true, wholly invalidates the arrangement of the materials which has been adopted by every editor of the old copies of the* Trattato *since* DUFRESNE; *but those, it must be remembered, contain only disconnected fragments of Leonardo's treatise on Perspective. His investigations in all the branches of optics do not, of course, come under consideration here. With regard to the physiology of the eye the reader will find, in Nos.* 24, 28—39, *passages which show that Leonardo understood the effect of the variation in the size of the pupil on the perception of objects. The insertion of these passages seemed indispensable because they form the basis of certain general principles of Perspective. The same may be said about his explanation of the difference between seeing with one eye and seeing with two (No.* 25—29*) as well as of his acute remarks as to the apparent variation in the size of objects according to the amount of light in which they are seen (No.* 30—39*).*

Leic 22*b*]

1.

Come molti stie[2]no con istrumēto alquāto sotto l'acque, Come e perchè io non scrivo il mio modo di [3]star sotto l'acqua, quāto io posso star sanza māgiare, e questo nō publico o diuolgo per le ma[4]le nature delli omini, li quali vserebono li assasinamēti ne' fondi de' mari col rompere [5]i navili in fondo e sommergierli insieme colli omini che ui son dentro, e benchè io insegni [6]delli altri, quelli nō son di pericolo, perchè di sopra all'acqua apparisce la bocca della canna, [7]onde alitano, posta sopra otri o sughero

The author's intention to publish his MSS

How by a certain machine many may stay some time under water And how and wherefore I do not describe my method of remaining under water and how long I can remain without eating And I do not publish nor divulge these, by reason of the evil nature of men, who would use them for assassinations at the bottom of the sea by destroying ships, and sinking them, together with the men in them Nevertheless I will impart others, which are not dangerous because the mouth of the tube through which you breathe is above the water, supported on air sacks or cork

F 2*b*]

2

Quādo tu metti insieme la scien[2]za de moti dell' acqua, ricordati di met[3]tere di sotto a ciascuna propositione [4]li sua giouamēti, acciochè tale scien[5]tia non sia inutile.

The preparation of the MSS for publication

When you put together the science of the motions of water, remember to include under each proposition its application and use, in order that this science may not be useless —

W An IV 163*b*]

3.

Nō mi legga, chi non è matematico, [2]nelli mia prīcipi

Admonition to readers

Let no man who is not a Mathematician read the elements of my work

1 2 isscrivo 3 quāto iposso māgrare ecquesto 5 soumergierli chi bēce 6 apariscie la bocha 7 otri ossugero
2 1 sscien 3 acciasscuna 4 gouamēti acco chettale
3 1 leggha matematicho

1 The leaf on which this passage is written, is headed with the words *Casi* 39, and most of these cases begin with the word '*Come*', like the two here given, which are the 26th and 27th 7 *Sughero* In the Codex Antlanticus 377[a], 1170[a] there is a sketch, drawn with the pen, representing a man with a tube in his mouth, and at the farther end of the tube a disk By the tube the word '*Channa*' is written, and by the disk the word '*sughero*'

2 A comparatively small portion of Leonardo's notes on water-power was published at Bologna in 1828, under the title "*Del moto e misura dell'Acqua, di L da Vinci*"

Br M 1 a]

4.

The disorder in the MSS

Comīciato in Firenze in casa Piero di Braccio Martelli addi 22 di [2]marzo 1508. e questo fia vn racolto sanza ordine, tratto di mol[3]te carte le quali io ho qui copiate sperando poi metterle per ordine alli lo-[4]chi loro, secondo le materie di che esse tratteranno, e credo che auāti ch'io [5]sia al fine di questo, io ci avrò a riplicare vna medesima cosa più volte, sī chè [6]lettore nō mi biasimare, perchè le cose son molte e la memoria nō le [7]può riseruare e dire, questa non voglio scriuere perchè dinanzi la scrissi, [8]e se io nō uolessi cadere in tale errore, sarebbe necessario che per ogni caso [9]ch'io uolessi copiare, sicchè per nō replicarlo, io auessi senpre a rilegere tutto [10]il passato, e massime stante co' lunghi interualli di tenpo allo scriuere [11]da una volta a un altra.

Begun at Florence, in the house of Piero di Braccio Martelli, on the 22nd day of March 1508. And this is to be a collection without order, taken from many papers which I have copied here, hoping to arrange them later each in its place, according to the subjects of which they may treat. But I believe that before I am at the end of this [task] I shall have to repeat the same things several times, for which, O reader! do not blame me, for the subjects are many and memory cannot retain them [all] and say: 'I will not write this because I wrote it before' And if I wished to avoid falling into this fault, it would be necessary in every case when I wanted to copy [a passage] that, not to repeat myself, I should read over all that had gone before, and all the more since the intervals are long between one time of writing and the next

F 23a]

5.

Suggestions for the arrangement of MSS treating of particular subjects (5—8)

Da profondare vn canale, [2]fa questo nel libro de giovamē[3]ti, e nel provarli allega le [4]propositioni prouate; e que[5]sto è il uero ordine, perchè se [6]tu volessi mostrare il giova[7]mēto a ogni propositione, [8]ti bisognerebbe anco[9]ra fare novi strumēti [10]per prouar tale utilità, e co[11]si cōfonderesti l'ordine de' [12]quarāta libri e cosi l'ordi[13]ne delle figurationi, cioè [14]avresti a mischiare pratica [15]con teorica, che sarebbe [16]cosa cōfusa e interrotta

Of digging a canal. Put this in the Book of useful inventions and in proving them bring forward the propositions already proved. And this is the proper order, since if you wished to show the usefulness of any plan you would be obliged again to devise new machines to prove its utility and thus would confuse the order of the forty Books and also the order of the diagrams; that is to say you would have to mix up practice with theory, which would produce a confused and incoherent work

Br M 32b]

6.

Non è da biasimare lo mostrare infra l'ordine del processo della scientia [2]alcuna regola generale nata dall' antidetta conclusione.

I am not to blame for putting forward, in the course of my work on science, any general rule derived from a previous conclusion.

4 1 Chomīciato in firenze piero di bracco martelli 2. ecquessto. 3. cqui 5 ciaro. 6. ella. 7. po . . scriuere [al] . . ascrissi 8 essio nō 9 repricarlo 10. collunghi.
5 2 cquesto . . govamē 3 allegha. 13 coe. 14 aresti a misciare 15 teoricha.
6 1 llordine

4 1. In the history of Florence in the early part of the XVIth century *Piero di Braccio Martelli* is frequently mentioned as *Commissario della Signoria*. He was famous for his learning and at his death left four books on Mathematics ready for the press; comp. LITTA, *Famiglie celebri Italiane, Famiglia Martelli di Firenze*.—In the Official Catalogue of MSS in the Brit. Mus., New Series Vol. I, where this passage is print[illegible]

2 *addi 22 di marzo* 1508. The Christian era was computed in Florence at that time from the Incarnation (Lady day, March 25th) Hence this should be 1509 by our reckoning

2. 3. *racolto tratto di molte carte le quali io ho qui copiate* We must suppose that Leonardo means that he has copied out his own MSS and not those of others. The first thirteen leaves of the MS. in the [illegible] on physics.

W An IV 107*a*]

7

Il libro della sciētia ²delle machine va inā³zi al libro de giovamēti, ⁴fa legare li tua libri di notomia'

The Book of the science of Mechanics must precede the Book of useful inventions — Have your books on anatomy bound! [4]

C A 146 II *a*, 436 *a*]

8.

La regola del tuo libro prociederà in questa ²forma prima l'aste senplice poi le sosten³ute di sotto poi le sospese in parte, poi tutte, ⁴poi esse aste fieno sostenitori d'altri pesi

The order of your book must proceed on this plan first simple beams, then (those) supported from below, then suspended in part, then wholly [suspended] Then beams as supporting other weights [4].

C A 117 *b*, 361 *b*]

9.

PROEMIO

²Vedendo io non potere pigliare materia di grāde vtilità o diletto, ³perchè li omini ināti a me nati ànno preso per loro tutte l'utili e ne⁴ciessari temi, farò come colui il quale per povertà ⁵giv̄gnie l'ultimo alla fiera, e nō potēdo d' altro fornirsi piglia ⁶tutte cose già da altri viste e non accettate ma rifiutate per la ⁷loro poca valitudine, io questa disprezata e rifiutata ⁸mercātia rimānēte de' molti cōpratori metterò sopra ⁹la mia debole soma, e con quella nō per le grosse città, ma pouere ¹⁰ville andro distribuendo, pigliādo tal premio qual merita ¹¹la cosa da me data

INTRODUCTION

General introductions to the book on Painting (9—13)

Seeing that I can find no subject specially useful or pleasing—since the men who have come before me have taken for their own every useful or necessary theme—I must do like one who, being poor, comes last to the fair, and can find no other way of providing himself than by taking all the things already seen by other buyers, and not taken but refused by reason of their lesser value I, then, will load my humble pack with this despised and rejected merchandise, the refuse of so many buyers, and will go about to distribute it, not indeed in great cities, but in the poorer towns, taking such a price as the wares I offer may be worth

C A 117 *b*, 361 *b*]

10

PROEMIO

³So che molti diranno questa essere opera invtile, ⁴e questi fieno quelli de quali Demetrio disse, nō facie⁵va conto

INTRODUCTION

I know that many will call this useless work [3], and they will be those of whom Demetrius [4] declared that he took no more

7 3 govamētı 4 libri di no "a

8 1 quessta 2 laste poi lossen 3 poi sosspese 4 asste sosstenitori

9 3 ano tutte luti [ube] ene 4 sciessari temi chome cholui 6 chose aciettate 7 pocha 8 merchātia chopratori 9 chon quela 10 dissiribuendo 11 chosa

10 2 naturalmente li omini boni disiderano sapere 3 dirano 4 ecquesti deometr \\\\\\ disse 5 chonto bocha

7 4 The numerous notes on anatomy written on loose leaves and now in the Royal collection at Windsor can best be classified in four Books, corresponding to the different character and size of the paper When Leonardo speaks of '*li tua libri di notomia*', he probably means the MSS which still exist; if this hypothesis is correct the present condition of these leaves might seem to prove that he only carried out his purpose with one of the Books on anatomy A borrowed book on Anatomy is mentioned in F,O'

8 4 Leonardo's notes on Mechanics are extraordinarily numerous, but, for the reasons assigned in my introduction, they have not been included in the present work

9 It need hardly be pointed out that there is in this '*Proemio*' a covert irony In the second and third prefaces, Leonardo characterises his rivals and opponents more closely His protest is directed against Neo latinism as professed by most of the humanists of his time, its futility is now no longer questioned

10 In the original, the *Proemio di prospettiva cioè dell' uffitio dell' occhio* (see No 21) stands between this and the preceding one, No 9

3 *questa essere opera inutile* By *opera* we must here understand *libro di pittura* and particularly the treatise on Perspective

4 *Demetrio* "With regard to the passage attributed to Demetrius", Dr H MULLER STRÜBING writes, "I know

piv · del uento · il quale nella lor bocca [6]causaua le parole, che del ueto ch' usciua delle parti [7]di sotto · vomini i quali · ànno · solamete desiderio di [8]corporal richezze, e interamete priui di quello della [9]sapiëtia · cibo · e veramete sicura richezza del' [10]anima; perchè quat' è piv degnia · l'anima · che 'l corpo, [11]tanto · piv · degni fie le richezze dell' anima · che del [12]corpo · e spesso · quãdo vedo · alcũ di questi pigliare [13]essa opera ĩ mano, dubito · no sia come fa la scimi[14]a, se 'l mettino al naso, o che mi domãdino, se è cosa [15]mãgiatiua.

account of the wind that came out their mouth in words, than of that they expelled from their lower parts: men who desire nothing but material riches and are absolutely devoid of that of wisdom, which is the food and the only true riches of the mind. For so much more worthy as the soul is than the body, so much more noble are the possessions of the soul than those of the body. And often, when I see one of these men take this work in his hand, I wonder that he does not put it to his nose, like a monkey, or ask me if it is something good to eat.

Proemio.

[17]So bene che per non essere · io literato, che alcuno [18]prosuntuoso gli parà ragionevolmente potermi [19]biasimare coll' allegare · jo · essere homo sanza lettere: [20]giẽte stolta! nõ sano questi · tali ch' io potrei si [21]come Mario · rispose contro a' patriti romani, io si [22]rispondere, diciendo · quelli che dell'altrui fatiche [23]se medesimi fanno · ornati · le mie a me mede[24]simo nõ uogliono · cõciedere: diranno che per non a[25]vere · io · lettere · non potere ben dire quello, di che [26]voglio trattare · or nõ sano · questi che le mie chose [27]son piv da esser tratte dalla sperietia, che d'altra pa[28]rola, la quale fu maestra di chi bene scrisse [29]e cosi per maestra la [30]in tutti casi allegherò.

Introduction.

I am fully concious that, not being a literary man, certain presumptuous persons will think that they may reasonably blame me; alleging that I am not a man of letters. Foolish folks! do they not know that I might retort as Marius did to the Roman Patricians [21] by saying: That they, who deck themselves out in the labours of others will not allow me my own. They will say that I, having no literary skill, cannot properly express that which I desire to treat of [26]; but they do not know that my subjects are to be dealt with by experience rather than by words [28]; and [experience] has been the mistress of those who wrote well. And so, as mistress, I will cite her in all cases.

6. chausaua. 7. vomini equali. 8. corporal richeze' diletta e priui. 9. sahara richeza de. 10. la uma chelchorpo. 11. fie . . richeze. 12. chorpo . alchũ. 13. imano . . . sichomelassimi. 15. domãdi . . chosa. 17. alchuno. 18. prosuntuoso. 19. biasimare choll alegare . . . esere. 21. chome mario . . . chontro. 22. quello. 23. amemenede. 24. chõciedere. 25. lettere. 26. chelle. 28. scrise. 29. [ma equel] e chosi per maestra la [illegible] nella. 30. chasi allegero.

not what to make of it. It is certainly not Demetrius Phalereus that is meant and it can hardly be Demetrius Poliorcetes. Who then can it be—for the name is a very common one? It may be a clerical error for Demades and the maxim is quite in the spirit of his writings; I have not however been able to find any corresponding passage either in the 'Fragments' (C. Müller, *Orat. Att.*, II. 441) nor in the Supplements collected by Dietz (*Rhein. Mus.*, vol. 29, p. 108)."

The same passage occurs as a simple Memorandum in the MS. Tr. 57, apparently as a note for this '*Proemio*' thus affording some data as to the time when these introductions were written.

21. *Come Mario disse ai patriti Romani.* "I am unable to find the words here attributed by Leonardo to Marius, either in Plutarch's Life of Marius or in the Apophthegmata (*Moralia*, p. 202). Nor do they occur in the writings of Valerius Maximus (who frequently mentions Marius) [illegible] to 43), Dio Cassius, Aulus Gellius, or Macrobius. Professor E. Mendelson of Dorpat, the editor of Herodian, assures me that no such passage is the found in that author" (communication from Dr. Müller Strübing). Leonardo evidently meant to allude to some well known incident in Roman history and the mention of Marius is the result probably of some confusion. We may perhaps read, for Marius, Menenius Agrippa, though in that case it is true we must alter Patriti to *Plebei*. The change is a serious one, but it would render the passage perfectly clear.

26—28. *le mie cose . . . . che d'altra parola.* This can hardly be reconciled with Mons. Ravaisson's estimate of L. da Vinci's learning. "*Léonard de Vinci était un admirateur et un disciple des anciens, aussi bien dans l'art que dans la science et il tenait à passer pour tel même aux yeux de la postérité.*" Gaz. des Beaux arts. Oct. 1877.

C. A. 115 *a*, 357 *a*]

11.

Se bene come loro nō sapessi allegare gli autori molto magiore e piv degnia cosa allegherò allegando [2]la speriētia maestra ai loro maestri, Costoro vanno sgonfiati e pōposi, vestiti e ornati [3]nō delle loro ma delle altrui fatiche, e le mie a me medesimo nō conciedono e se [4]me inventore disprezzeranno quāto magiormente loro non inventori, ma trōbetti e recita[5]tori dell' altrui opere potranno essere biasimati

Though I may not, like them, be able to quote other authors, I shall rely on that which is much greater and more worthy — on experience, the mistress of their Masters They go about puffed up and pompous, dressed and decorated with [the fruits], not of their own labours, but of those of others And they will not allow me my own They will scorn me as an inventor, but how much more might they—who are not inventors but vaunters and declaimers of the works of others—be blamed

Proemio

[7]E' ànno da essere givdicati e non altrementi stimati li omini [8]inventori interpetri tralla natura e gli omini a comparatione de recitatori e trōbetti dell' altrui opere, [9]quāt'è dall' obietto fori dello spechio alla similitudine d'esso obietto apparente nello spechio che l'u[10]no per se è qualche cosa, e l'altro è niēte giente poco obbligate alla natura, perchè sono sol' d'acidētal [11]vestiti sanza il quale potrei · aconpagnarli infra li armēti delle bestie

Introduction

And those men who are inventors and interpreters between Nature and Man, as compared with boasters and declaimers of the works of others, must be regarded and not otherwise esteemed than as the object in front of a mirror, when compared with its image seen in the mirror For the first is something in itself, and the other nothingness — Folks little indebted to Nature, since it is only by chance that they wear the human form and without it I might class them with the herds of beasts

C. A. 117 *b*, 361 *b*]

12.

Molti mi crederanno ragionevolmēte poteie riprēdere, [2]allegando le mie prove esser cōtro all' autorità [3]d'alquanti omini di grā reuerēza apresso de loro inesperti ivditi, [4]nō cōsiderādo le mie cose essere nate sotto la senplice e mera [5]sperientia la quale è maestra vera [6]Queste regole son cagione di farti conosciere il uero dal falso la [7]qual cosa fa che li omini si promettano le cose possibili e con piv moderanza, [8]e che tu non ti veli di ignoranza cosa tale che non avendo effetto, tu abbi [9]con disperatione a darti malinconia

Many will think they may reasonably blame me by alleging that my proofs are opposed to the authority of certain men held in the highest reverence by their inexperienced judgments, not considering that my works are the issue of pure and simple experience, who is the one true mistress These rules are sufficient to enable you to know the true from the false—and this aids men to look only for things that are possible and with due moderation—and not to wrap yourself in ignorance, a thing which can have no good result, so that in despair you would give yourself up to melancholy

C. A. 200 *a*, 594 *a*]

13

Intra li studi delle naturali cause e ragioni la luce diletta più i contēplanti, ītra le cose grandi [2]delle matematiche la cer-

Among all the studies of natural causes and reasons Light chiefly delights the beholder, and among the great features of Mathematics

11 1 4 sebene chome sapesi altori chosa allegere 2 schonfiati e pōpo si 3 elle mie conciedano [chostoro] esse 4 disprezzerano [da me] loro non inventore 5 tori [potrano] delli opere otrano esere 7 E da giv- 8 chonperatione 9 quāte dall obietto fori de dello dessobietto aparente chellu 10 chosa ellaltro he pocho obrigate 11 achonpgnarli

12 1 poter "e" 2 chōtro alturita [di qualche loro] 4 chōsiderādo chose 6 cagione chonossciere 7 chelli chose 'possibili e" chon 8 chettu nonti [per] "veli di' ignoranza chosa t abi 9 chon malinchonia

13 1 lisstudi chause rationi chontēplanti lle chose 2 matematice certera plecharamente investtighāti

tezza della dimostratione ĩalza piv preclaramente l'ingiegni dell' investigãti, [3]la prospectiva adunque à da essere preposta · a tutte le trattazioni e discipline vmane, nel campo · della quale [4]la linia radiosa è complicata dai modi delle dimostrationi, nella quale si truova la gloria nõ tãto [5]della matematica quanto della fisica, ornata cõ fiori dell' una e dell' altra le sentẽtie della quale [6]distese con gran circuitioni io le ,ristrignierò jn conclusiua breuità jntessendo secondo jl modo [7]della materia naturale e matematiche dimostrationi, alcuna volta conchiudendo gli effetti [8]per le cagioni e alcuna volta le cagioni per li effetti agivgniẽdo ancora alle mie cõclusioni alcuna [9]che nõ sono ĩ quelle nõ di meno di quelle · si tragano come si degnierà jl signiore luce d'ogni [10]cosa, illustrare me per trattare della luce per cui partirò la presente opera ĩ 3 parti

the certainty of its demonstrations is what preeminently (tends to) elevate the mind of the investigator Perspective, therefore, must be preferred to all the discourses and systems of human learning In this branch [of science] the beam of light is explained on those methods of demonstration which form the glory not so much of Mathematics as of Physics and are graced with the flowers of both [5] But its axioms being laid down at great length, I shall abridge them to a conclusive brevity, arranging them on the method both of their natural order and of mathematical demonstration, sometimes by deduction of the effects from the causes, and sometimes arguing the causes from the effects, adding also to my own conclusions some which, though not included in them, may nevertheless be inferred from them Thus, if the Lord—who is the light of all things—vouchsafe to enlighten me, I will treat of Light, wherefore I will divide the present work into 3 Parts [10]

Ash I 17*b*]

14.

Di tre nature prospettive

The plan of the book on Painting (14—17)

[2]Come sono di 3 nature prospectiue la prima s'astẽde ĩtorno alla [3]ragione del diminvire (e diciesi prospettiva diminvtiva) le cose che si allõtanano · dall'ochio, la secõda [4]cõtiene ĩ se il modo del uariare i colori · che si allõtanano dall'ochio, [5]la terza e vltima s'astẽde alla dichiaratione come le cose deuono [6]essere meno finite quanto piv s' alontanano | e nomi fieno questi

[7]prospetiva liniale
[8]prospetiva di colore
[9]prospetiva di speditione

On the three branches of perspective

There are three branches of perspective, the first deals with the reasons of the (apparent) diminution of objects as they recede from the eye, and is known as Diminishing Perspective —The second contains the way in which colours vary as they recede from the eye The third and last is concerned with the explanation of how the objects [in a picture] ought to be less finished in proportion as they are remote (and the names are as follows)

Linear Perspective
The Perspective of Colour.
The Perspective of Disappearance

3 "e' da preposta attutte le traduzioni champo 4 chomplichata inella grotia 5 matematicha fisicha chõ eddell 6 chom circhuitioni risstrigniero chonclusiua sechondo 7 dela matematice alchuna chonchiudendo 8 chagioni alchuna chagioni ancora chõclusi"o"ni alchuna 9 traghano chome 10. chosa [illuminare] ilustrare me trattare luce el quale parturo
14 1 prosspettire 2 alle 3 "(e diciesi prospettiva diminuetiva) le chose chessi 4 cholori chessi 5 diciaratione chome 6 mẽ finite qũto feno

13 From the character of the handwriting I infer that this passage was written before the year 1490

5 Such of Leonardo's notes on Optics or on Perspective as bear exclusively on Mathematics or Physics could not be included in the arrangement of the *libro di pittura* which is here presented to the reader They are however but few

10. In the middle ages—for instance, by ROGER BACON, by VITELLONE, with whose works Leonardo was certainly familiar, and by all the writers of the Renaissance—Perspective and Optics were not regard . . . is in its widest application the science of seeing. Although to Leonardo the two sciences were clearly separate, it is not so as to their names, thus we find axioms in Optics under the heading Perspective According to this arrangement of the materials for the theoretical portion of the *libro di pittura* propositions in Perspective and in Optics stand side by side or occur alternately Although this particular chapter deals only with Optics, it is not improbable that the words *partirò la presente opera in 3 parti* may refer to the same division into three sections which . . . in . . . 14 . . .

E 80 *b*]

15

De pictura e prospettiva

[2] 3 sono le parti della prospettiua di che si [3] serue la pictura, delle quali la prima s'astē[4]de alla diminutione delle quantità de' corpi oppachi, la [5] secōda è delle diminuitioni e perdimēti delli ter[6]mini d'essi corpi oppachi, La terza è della [7] diminuitione e perdimēti de' colori in lūga [8] distātia.

On painting and perspective

The divisions of Perspective are 3, as used in drawing, of these, the first includes the diminution in size of opaque objects, the second treats of the diminution and loss of outline in such opaque objects, the third, of the diminution and loss of colour at long distances

G 53 *b*]

16.

Discorso de pictura

[2] La perspectiva, la qual s'astende nella [3] pictura, si diuide in tre parti prīcipali, del[4]le quali la prima è della diminuitione che fan [5] le quātita de' corpi in diverse distantie, [6] La seconda parte è quella che tratta [7] della diminuitiō de colori di tali corpi, — [8] Terza è quella che diminuisce la notitia [9] delle figure e termini, che ànno essi corpi in varie distā[10]tie

The discourse on painting

Perspective, as bearing on drawing, is divided into three principal sections, of which the first treats of the diminution in the size of bodies at different distances The second part is that which treats of the diminution in colour in these objects The third [deals with] the diminished distinctness of the forms and outlines displayed by the objects at various distances

E 79 *b*]

17

Delle parti della pictura

[2] La prima parte della pittura è che li [3] corpi cō quella figurati si dimostrino [4] rilevati, e che li cāpi d'esse circūdatori, col[5]le lor distantie, si dimostrino ētrare [6] dentro alla pariete, doue tal pittura è giene[7]rata mediante le 3 prospective, cioè dimi[8]nuition delle figure de' corpi | diminui[9]tion delle magnitudini loro e dimi[10]nuitiō de' loro colori e di queste 3 prospec[11]tive la prima à origine dall' ochio, le altre due [12] ànno deriuatione dall' aria interposta infra l'occhio

On the sections of [the book on] painting

The first thing in painting is that the objects it represents should appear in relief, and that the grounds surrounding them at different distances shall appear within the vertical plane of the foreground of the picture by means of the 3 branches of Perspective, which are the diminution in the distinctness of the forms of the objects, the diminution in their magnitude, and the diminution in their colour And of these 3 classes of Perspective the first results from [the structure of] the eye, while the other two are caused by the atmosphere which intervenes between the eye and the objects seen

15 1 pressspectiva 2 parte prespectiua [che] di chessi 3 quale sasstē 4 "delle quantita" de chorpi 5 sechonda "he ' delle 7 decholori in lūgha 8 disstātia

16. 2 sasstende 3 parte 4 la p"a"he cheffan 5 chorpi in diuersi disstantie 6 sechonda hecquellachettracta 7 cholori chorpi 8 1 erza ecquella cheddiminuisscie 9 "ettermini' chorpi

17 1 parte 2 he chelli 3 chorpi fighurati si dimosstrino 4 chelli chāpi circhūdatori chol 5 disstantie si dimosstrino 6 alla he 8 chorpi 9 delle [quātita] magnitudine 10 cholori presspec 12 interpossta infralloc-

15 The division is here the same as in the previous chapter No 14, and this is worthy of note when we connect it with the fact that a space of about 20 years must have intervened between the writing of the two passages

17 This and the two foregoing chapters must have been written in 1513 to 1516. They undoubtedly indicate the scheme, which Leonardo wished to carry out in arranging his researches on Perspective as applied to Painting This is important because it is an evidence against the supposition of H LUDWIG and others, that Leonardo had collected his principles of Perspective in one book so early as before 1500, a Book which, according to the hypothesis, must have been lost at a very early period, or destroyed possibly, by the French (!) in 1500 (see H LUDWIG *L. da Vinci Das Buch von der Malerei* Vienna 1882 III, 7 and 8)

[13]e li obbietti da esso ochio veduti, La 2ª parte del[14]la pictura è li atti appropriati e variati nelle statu[15]re, si che li omini nō pajano fratelli ecc.

by it. The second essential in painting is appropriate action and a due variety in the figures, so that the men may not all look like brothers, &c.

C A 118*b*; 648*a*]

18.

The use of the book on Painting.

Queste · regole · sono da vsare solamēte per ripruova delle figure · jnperochè ogni omo nella prima cōpositione · fa qualche errore; [2]e chi nō li conoscie · nō li · raconcia · onde tu · per conosciere li errori · riprouerai l'opera tua, e dove trovi detti errori racō·ciali, [3]e tieni a mēte di mai piv ricaderci; Ma se tu volessi adoperare le regole nel cōporre non verresti mai acapo e fare[4]sti · confusione nelle · tue opere

[5]Queste regole fanno · che tu possiedi · uno libero · e bono · giuditio . jnperochè 'l bono · givditio · nascie · dal bene · intēdere ·, e 'l bene intēdere [6]diriua da ragione · tratta da bone · regole e le bone regole · sono figliole della · bona · sperietia · comvne madre · di tutte [7]le sciētie · e arti, Onde · avēdo tu · bene a mēte i precietti · delle mie regole · potrai · solamēte col racōcio givditio giv[8]dicare e conosciere · ogni · sproportionata · opera · cosi · in prospettiua · come in figure o altre cose.

These rules are of use only in correcting the figures; since every man makes some mistakes in his first compositions and he who knows them not, cannot amend them But you, knowing your errors, will correct your works and where you find mistakes amend them, and remember never to fall into them again. But if you try to apply these rules in composition you will never make an end, and will produce confusion in your works.

These rules will enable you to have a free and sound judgment; since good judgment is born of clear understanding, and a clear understanding comes of reasons derived from sound rules, and sound rules are the issue of sound experience—the common mother of all the sciences and arts. Hence, bearing in mind the precepts of my rules, you will be able, merely by your amended judgment, to criticise and recognise every thing that is out of proportion in a work, whether in the perspective or in the figures or any thing else

G 8*a*]

19.

Necessity of theoretical knowledge (19 20).

DELL' ERRORE DI QUELLI CHE VSANO LA PRATICA SANZA SCIĒTIA

[3]Quelli che s'inamorā di pratica [4]sāza sciētia, sō come 'l nochiere che ē[5]tra navilio sanza timone o bussola · [6]che mai à certezza dove si uada; [7]sēpre la pratica debbe esser edi[8]ficata sopra la bona teorica della [9]quale la prospettiva è guida e [10]porta, e sanza questa nulla si [11]fa bene ne' casi di pittura.

OF THE MISTAKES MADE BY THOSE WHO PRACTISE WITHOUT KNOWLEDGE.

Those who are in love with practice without knowledge are like the sailor who gets into a ship without rudder or compass and who never can be certain whether he is going. Practice must always be founded on sound theory, and to this Perspective is the guide and the gateway; and without this nothing can be done well in the matter of drawing.

C A 75*a*; 219*a*]

20.

Il pittore che ritrae per pratica e givditio d'ochio, sanza [2]ragione è come lo spechio, che in se imita tutte [3]le a se cō·traposte cose sanza cognitione d'esse.

The painter who draws merely by practice and by eye, without any reason, is like a mirror which copies every thing placed in front of it without being conscious of their existence.

chio 13 elli. 14 elli . apropiati nelli 15 recelli . nō paj

18 1. "solamēte" . . chōpositione 2 chonosscie nolli rachoncia . chonossciere erori . erori . rachōciali 3 richaderci Massettu . chōpore nōne veresti achapo effare 4 chonfusione 5 rego fanno chettu possiedi i . libero . . nasscie 6. elle bone . chomvne 7 chol rachōcio. 8 dichare echonossciere . . chosi . in prosspettiua chome . chose

19 1—11 R. 1. eror. 2 praticha 3 chessinamorā di praticha 4 nochieri 5 obbussola. 6 cierteza 8 teoricha. 9 qua la presspettiva 10. essānza

20 1. praticha 2 chome 3 assechōtra poste chose . . chognitione dese

C A 117*b*, 361*b*] **21**

PROEMIO DI PROSPETTIVA, CIOÈ DEL' UFITIO DELL' OCHIO

[3]Or', guarda lettore quello che non potremo [4]credere ai nostri antichi, i quali [5]ànno voluto difinire che cosa sia a[6]nima e uita cose inprovabili, quando [7]quelle (cose) che con isperiētia ogni ora si possono [8]chiaramēte conosciere e provare, sono [9]per tāti seculi igniorate o falsamēte cre[10]dute ! l'ochio, che così chiaramēte fa sperie[11]tia del suo ofitio, è insino ai mia tē[12]pi per infiniti autori stato difinito in ṽ mo[13]do trovo per isperiētia essere vn altro

INTRODUCTION TO PERSPECTIVE —THAT IS OF THE FUNCTION OF THE EYE

Behold here O reader! a thing concerning which we cannot trust our forefathers, the ancients, who tried to define what the Soul and Life are—which are beyond proof, whereas those things, which can at any time be clearly known and proved by experience, remained for many ages unknown or falsely understood The eye, whose function we so certainly know by experience, has, down to my own time, been defined by an infinite number of authors as one thing, but I find, by experience, that it is quite another[13] The function of the eye (21—23)

C A 337*b*, 1026*b*] **22**

Qui le figure, qui li colori, qui [2]tutte le spetie delle parti dell' u[3]niverso sō ridotte in ṽ punto, [4]e quel punto è di tāta mara[5]viglia ! [6]O mirabile, o stupēda neciessità tu costri[7]gni colla tua leggie tutti li effet[8]ti per breuissima [9]via a participare delle lor cau[10]se ! questi sono li miracoli

[17]in tanto minimo spatio pos[18]sa rinasciere e ricōpor[19]si nella sua dilatatione, [20]scriui nella tua notomia che proportione [21]ànno infra loro li diamitri di tutte [22]le spetie dell' ochio e che distantia [23]à da loro la spera cristallina

Here [in the eye] forms, here colours, here the character of every part of the universe are concentrated to a point, and that point is so marvellous a thing. Oh! marvellous, O stupendous Necessity—by thy laws thou dost compel every effect to be the direct result of its cause, by the shortest path These [indeed] are miracles,

In so small a space it can be reproduced and rearranged in its whole expanse Describe in your anatomy what proportion there is between the diameters of all the images in the eye and the distance from them of the crystalline lens.

Ash I 13*a*] **23**

DE' 10 · OFITI DELL' OCHIO TUTTI APARTENENTI ALLA PICTURA

[3]La pictura s'astēde in tutti i · 10 · ofiti dell' ochio cioè tenebre luce [4]corpo e colore figura e sito · remotione propīquita · moto e quiete, [5]de quali ofiti sarà intessuta questa mia piccola opera ricordādo [6]al pictore con che regola e modo debe imitare colla sua arte tutte [7]queste cose, opera di natura e ornamēto del mōdo

OF THE 10 ATTRIBUTES OF THE EYE, ALL CONCERNED IN PAINTING

Painting is concerned with all the 10 attributes of sight, which are —Darkness, Light, Solidity and Colour, Form and Position, Distance and Propinquity, Motion and Rest This little work of mine will be a tissue [of the studies] of these attributes, reminding the painter of the rules and methods by which he should use his art to imitate all the works of Nature which adorn the world

21 3 no 5 chosa s \\\\\\\ 6 chose inprovabili q \\\\\ 7 quelle che chon agniora sipossano 9 sechuli 10 locio chosi chosi 12 altori 13 nvnaltra

22 2 parte 6 "o stupēda chosstri 8 ti [a participare] per [v] 9 della lor chau 10 miracholi 11—16 *The leaf is here injured, only the following words at the beginning of the lines are preserved* —11 que stupēdo \\\! 12 col quale \\\\\ 13 quasi \\\\ 14 re \\\\ 15 finita \\\\ 16 gia per tute f \\\\\ 17 po 18 rinassciere 20 che 'pro"ne' 21 infralloroli 22 lesspetie 23 dalloro crisstallina

23 1 hofitu 2 apartenti 3 e 10 li ofiti 4 cholore essito 5 picholi richordādo 6 chon cholla 7 chose

21 In section 13 we already find it indicated that the study of Perspective and of Optics is to be based on that of the functions of the eye Leonardo also refers to the science of the eye, in his astronomical researches, for instance in MS. F 25b '*Ordine del provare la terra essere una stella Imprima difinisce l'occhio*', &c Compare also MS E 15b and F 60b The principles of astronomical perspective

13 Compare the note to No 70

E 17*b*]

24.

PICTURA.

Variability of the eye

[2] 1ª La popilla dell' ochio diminuiscie tanto la [3] sua quätita quäto crescie il luminoso che [4] in lei s'inprime. [5] 2ª Tanto crescie la popilla dell' ochio quäto di[6]minuiscie la chiarezza del giorno o d'altra lu[7]cie, che in lui s'inprime. [8] 3ª Tanto più intensiuamēte vede e cono[9]scie l'ochio le cose che li stanno per obbietto, [10] quäto la sua popilla più si dilata, e que[11]sto proviamo mediante li animali nocturni, [12] come nelle gatte e altri volatili, come il [13] gufo e simili, nei quali la popilla fa grā[14]dissima variatione da grāde a piccola ecc. [15] nelle tenebre o nell' alluminato. [16] 4ª L'ochio posto nell' aria alluminata ve[17]de tenebre dētro alle finestre delle abi[18]tationi alluminate, [19] 5ª tutti li colori posti in lochi onbrosi paiāo [20] essere d'equale oscurità infra loro. [21] 6ª Ma tutti li colori posti in lochi luminosi nō [22] si uariā mai della loro essentia.

ON PAINTING.

1st. The pupil of the eye contracts, in proportion to the increase of light which is reflected in it. 2nd The pupil of the eye expands in proportion to the diminution in the day light, or any other light, that is reflected in it. 3rd. [8] The eye perceives and recognises the objects of its vision with greater intensity in proportion as the pupil is more widely dilated; and this can be proved by the case of nocturnal animals, such as cats, and certain birds—as the owl and others—in which the pupil varies in a high degree from large to small, &c., when in the dark or in the light. 4th. The eye [out of doors] in an illuminated atmosphere sees darkness behind the windows of houses which [nevertheless] are light. 5th All colours when placed in the shade appear of an equal degree of darkness, among themselves 6th. But all colours when placed in a full light, never vary from their true and essential hue

C. A 136*b*, 412*b*]

25.

DELL' OCHIO

Focus of sight.

[2] Se l'ochio à a vedere · cosa · che sia tropo presso nō la può bē giudicare, come īteruiene [3] a quello · che si vol · vedere la pūta del naso, Onde per regola gienerale la natura [4] īsegnia che la cosa nō si vedrà mai perfettamēte se lo ītervallo che si trova tra l'ochio [5] e la cosa vista nō sarà almeno simile alla grādezza del uiso

OF THE EYE.

If the eye is required to look at an object placed too near to it, it cannot judge of it well—as happens to a man who tries to see the tip of his nose. Hence, as a general rule, Nature teaches us that an object can never be seen perfectly unless the space between it and the eye is equal, at least, to the length of the face.

C A 339*a*, 1033*a*]

26.

DELL' OCHIO.

Differences of perception by one eye and by both eyes (26—29)

[2] Quādo · i · 2 ochi · conduranno · la piramide · visuale · sopra l'obietto, [3] esso · obietto · fia dalli ochi · veduto · e bene conpreso.

OF THE EYE.

When both eyes direct the pyramid of sight to an object, that object becomes clearly seen and comprehended by the eyes.

H 3 85*a*]

27.

Le cose vedute da uno medesimo ochio [2] paranno alcuna volta · grāde alcuna [3] volta · picole.

Objects seen by one and the same eye appear sometimes large, and sometimes small.

24 2 ṗ La diminuiscie 3 cresscie 4 sinpreme 5 cresscie 6 minuisscie chiareza 7 sinprema 8 chonos 9 chose chelli 10 ecques 11 sto proviano 12 chome . ghatte . chome 13 ghufo essimili li quali 14 disima . appichola 15 ōnellaluminato 16 possto . . alluminato 17 finesstre 19 cholori . . inllochi. 20. [simi] essere osschurita infralloro 21 ttutti licholori possti

25 2 sellochioavedere chososa preso nolla po . giudichare chome 3. acquello chessi 4. chella chosa . . . sello . . . chessi . . . trallochio 5 ella sara il meno grādeza

26 1 de ochio 2 chondurano 3 chonpreso

27. 1—3 R 1 chose . da ị 3 pìchole

24. [illegible]

Tr. 74]

28.

Il movimẽto · della · cosa · visiua · alla cosa stabile · fa spesse [2]volte · essa · cosa · stabile · parere · trasmvtarsi in nel moto della [3]cosa · movẽte · e la cosa movẽte, parere · stabile e ferma.

The motion of a spectator who sees an object at rest often makes it seem as though the object at rest had acquired the motion of the moving body, while the moving person appears to be at rest.

Pittura.

[5]Le cose di rilievo da presso · viste con ũ sol' ochio parã simili [6]a vna · perfetta pittura; Se vederai · coll'ochio · · *a* · *b* · il pũto *c*, [7]parratti · esso · pũto · *c* · in · *d* · *f* [8]e se lo guardi col solo · ochio · *g* · parrà ti [9]*h* · in · *m* ◯ · e la pittura non avrà mai [10]in se queste · 2 · varietà.

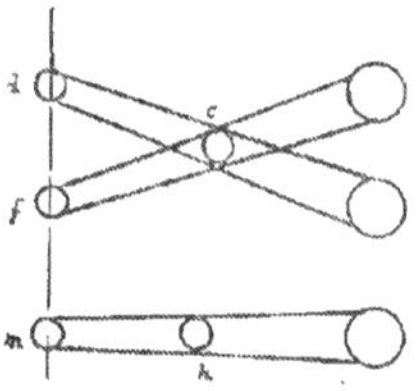

On painting.

Objects in relief, when seen from a short distance with one eye, look like a perfect picture. If you look with the eye *a*, *b* at the spot *c*, this point *c* will appear to be at *d*, *f*, and if you look at it with the eye *g*, *h* will appear to be at *m*. A picture can never contain in itself both aspects.

W. An. IV. 153 *b*]

29.

Sia il rilieuo *t* [2]veduto da due ochi; [3]volẽdo [4]te cõsiderare l'obbie[5]tto coll' ochio *m* destro, [6]tenẽdo chiuso il sinistro · *n* · [7]l'obbietto parrà overo occuperà lo spatio *a*; e se chiuderai il destro e aprirai il sinistro, l'obietto occuperà [8]lo spatio *b*; e se aprirai tutti e due li ochi esso obietto nõ occuperà più *a* *b*, ma lo spatio *e* *r* *f*; [9]perchè la pittura veduta cõ due ochi nõ fia [10]dimostratrice di tal relievo, come il rilieuo [11]veduto cõ due ochi, e perchè la pittu[12]ra veduta con ũ ochio parrà di rilievo, [13]come il propio rilievo, auẽte le medesime [14]qualità di lumi e d'õbre?

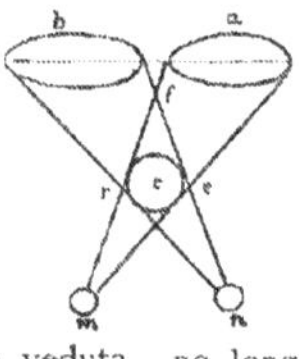

Let the object in relief *t* be seen by both eyes; if you will look at the object with the right eye *m*, keeping the left eye *n* shut, the object will appear, or fill up the space, at *a*; and if you shut the right eye and open the left, the object (will occupy the) space *b*; and if you open both eyes, the object will no longer appear at *a* or *b*, but at *e*, *r*, *f*. Why will not a picture seen by both eyes produce the effect of relief, as [real] relief does when seen by both eyes; and why should a picture seen with one eye give the same effect of relief as real relief would under the same conditions of light and shade?

C. 7 *b* (9)]

30.

L'ochio · piv terrà · e più riserberà · in se le similitudini delle cose luminose · che l'onbrose; la ragiõ si è : che l'ochio [2]in se è somma oscurita · e perchè il simile infra 'l simile nõ diuide, adũque la notte o altre cose oscure non possono essere riser[3]uate · o conosciute dall' ochio: il lume è interamẽte contrario · e piv divide ed è più detrimẽto e varietà alla cõsueta scurità [4]dell' ochio · onde di se lascia inpressa la sua similitudine.

The eye will hold and retain in itself the image of a luminous body better than that of a shaded object. The reason is that the eye is in itself perfectly dark and since two things that are alike cannot be distinguished, therefore the night, and other dark objects cannot be seen or recognised by the eye. Light is totally contrary and gives more distinctness, and counteracts and differs from the usual darkness of the eye, hence it leaves the impression of its image.

The comparative size of the image depends on the amount of light (30—39).

28. 1. chosa . . chosa. 2. inel. 3. ella . . . efferma. 5. chose . . chonũsolocio. 8. essella . . chol . . . paratti. 9. ella . . . ara.
29. 3. alli quali ochi vole. 4. te cõsiderare. 5. "m" desstro. 7. ochupera losspatio a esse . . . desstro . . . sinisstro l'obietto ||||||||. 8. |||| spatio besse apirai . . . due ochi lobietto esso obietto nõ ochupera . . . ma malo. 11. pittu[ra]. 12. porra.
30. 1. temera . . similitudine . . . chellochio. 2. essom'a osschurita . . . "adũque" . . . chose osschure po[sso]no "essere" riser. 3. ochonosciuti "dallochio" ilume e intera . mẽte chontrario . . . divide epi detrimẽto . . altala. 4. lasscia.

29. In the sketch, *m* is the left eye and *n* the right, while the text reverses this lettering. We must therefore suppose that the face in which the eyes *m* and *n* are placed is opposite to the spectator.

H[2] 38a]

31.

Tutte · le cose vedute parrãno [2]ma-gion · di mezza notte, che · di [3]mezzo · dì · e maggiori di mattina che [4]di mezzo dì

[5]Questo · accade · perchè · la pupilla [6]dell' ochio · è minore · assai di mezzo [7]dì · che di nessuno altro tenpo

Every object we see will appear larger at midnight than at midday, and larger in the morning than at midday.

This happens because the pupil of the eye is much smaller at midday than at any other time.

H[3] 40a]

32

¶Quella popilla che sarà maggiore, vederà [2]le cose di maggiore · figura ¶

[3]questo si dimostra nel uedere de' corpi lu[4]minosi e massime · de' celesti; quãdo [5]l'ochio escie delle tenebre e subito nsgu-[6]arda · essi corpi · li parirrãno [7]maggiori e poi diminuiscono, e se [8]riguarderai essi corpi per un picciolo [9]buso, li uederai minori · perchè mi[10]nore · parte d'essa (pupilla) s'adopera a tale ofitio.

The pupil which is largest will see objects the largest. This is evident when we look at luminous bodies, and particularly at those in the sky. When the eye comes out of darkness and suddenly looks up at these bodies, they at first appear larger and then diminish; and if you were to look at those bodies through a small opening, you would see them smaller still, because a smaller part of the pupil would exercise its function.

H[2] 43b]

33

Quell' ochio che uscendo dalle tenebre [2]vederà subito vn corpo luminoso, [3]li parrà assai maggiore nel primo is[4]guardo · che nel perseuerare il uederlo. [5]Il luminoso · corpo parrà · maggiore [6]e piv · luminoso · con due ochi · che [7]con ũ solo. [8]Quel luminoso · si dimostrerà · di minor [9]corpo · che per minore spiraculo [10]dall' ochio fia veduto [11]Quel corpo · luminoso · di lunga figura [12]si dimostrerà · di piv · rotõdo · corpo [13]che piv · distante · dall' ochio situato [14]fia

When the eye, coming out of darkness suddenly sees a luminous body, it will appear much larger at first sight than after long looking at it. The illuminated object will look larger and more brilliant, when seen with two eyes than with only one. A luminous object will appear smaller in size, when the eye sees it through a smaller opening. A luminous body of an oval form will appear rounder in proportion as it is farther from the eye.

Ash I 12a]

34.

Perchè l'ochio, visto la luce, il loco di mezzano [2]lume li pare tenebroso, e similmẽte [3]vscito dalle tenebre, il loco di mezzana luce, [4]gli pare chiarissimo?

Why when the eye has just seen the light, does the half light look dark to it, and in the same way if it turns from the darkness the half light look very bright?

L 41b]

35.

De pictura.

[1]L'ochio che sta · all' aria luminosa e vede il loco õbro[3]so, esso sito si dimostrerà di molta ma[4]ggiore oscurità che non è. [5]Questo · accade sol perchè l'ochio che sta [6]all' aria, diminuisce tanto piv la sua pu-

On painting.

If the eye, when [out of doors] in the luminous atmosphere, sees a place in shadow, this will look very much darker than it really is. This happens only because the eye when out in the air contracts the pupil in propor-

31. 1. tucte . le chose 2 meza 3 mezo . magiori 4 mezo. 5 acchade . mezo.

32 1—10 R. 1 "popilla" [chio] chessara magiore 2 chose "di" magiore 3 quessto dimosstra 4 ẽmassime cellessti quãdo lo. 5 escie . . . essubitorisgu 6. chorpi . li parirano [mino] 7. magiori . diminuisschano esse 8 chorpi 10 dessa sadopera attale

33 1 vsciẽdo delle tenebr 2 chorpo para . . magiore 5 chorpog 6 choa 7 choa 8 dimossterra. 9 "corpo" [forma] . spirachulo 11 chorpo 12 dimossterra . . . retõdo chorpo

34 1 ilocho mezano 3 ilocho . mezana.

35 2 chessta "luminosa'. locho 3 dimossterra 4 gore osscurita. 5 Quessto achade chessta 6 diminuisscie

32. 9 *buso* in the Lomb. dialect is the same as *buco*. sense of pupil of the eye as in no 51. C. A. 84b,

35

[7]pılla, quanto l'arıa, che ın se sı spechıa, è pı[8]ù lumınosa E quanto essa popılla pı[9]ù dımınuısce, manco la cosa da leı ve[10]duta sı dımostra lumınosa ¶Ma quando [11]l'ochıo entrerà ın alcuno loco onbroso, [12]subıto la oscurıtà dı tale onbroso parrà [13]dımınuıre ¶ Questo accade, perchè quā[14]to la luce entrerà ın aııa pıù tenebrosa, [15]pıù cresce sua figura, ıl quale accrescımē[16]to fa che la grande oscurıtà pare dımı[17]nuırsı

tıon as the atmosphere reflected ın ıt ıs more lumınous And the more the pupıl contracts, the less lumınous do the objects appear that ıt sees But as soon as the eye enters ınto a shady place the darkness of the shadow suddenly seems to dımınısh Thıs occurs because the greater the darkness ınto whıch the pupıl goes the more ıts sıze ıncreases, and thıs ıncrease makes the darkness seem less

S K M II 2 1a]

36.

De prospettiva

[2]L'ochıo, che sı parte dal bıanco allumınato dal [3]sole e va ın loco dı mınor luce, ognı cosa lı pa[4]rrà tenebrosa, E questo accade, perchè l'ochıo [5]che sta a esso bıāco allumınato o sı vıene a rıstrı[6]gnıere le sue popılle ī modo che se erano prıma [7]vna quātıtà vısıua esse mācano pıv che 'l 3/4 [8]dı sua quātıtà e mācādo dı [9]quātıtà esse mācano dı potētıa, benchè tu mı [10]potrestı dıre uno pıccolo vccello vederebbe all' a[11]venāte molto poco e per le pıccole sue popılle [12]ıl bıāco lı parebbe nero, a questa parte tı rıspō[13]dereı, che quı s'attende alla proportıone della sō[14]ma dı quella parte del cıervello, dedıcata alla vır[15]tụ̄ vısıua, e nō ad altra cosa, o per tornare questa [16]nostra popılla cresce e dımınvısce secōdo la [17]chıarıtà o scurıtà del suo obıetto e perchè cō qual[18]che tēpo fa esso cresciere e discresciere esso [19]nō vede cosı presto vscıēdo dal lume e andādo all' oscu[20]ro, e sımılmēte dallo scuro al lumınoso e questa [21]cosa gıà m'īgannò nel dıpıgnıere vn ochıo e dı lı l'ımparaı

On perspective

The eye whıch turns from a whıte object ın the lıght of the sun and goes ınto a less fully lıghted place wıll see everythıng as dark And thıs happens eıther because the pupıls of the eyes whıch have rested on thıs brıllıantly lıghted whıte object have contracted so much that, gıven at first a certaın extent of surface, they wıll have lost more than 3/4 of theır sıze, and, lackıng ın sıze, they are also deficıent ın [seeıng] power Though you mıght say to me A lıttle bırd (then) comıng down would see comparatıvely lıttle, and from the smallness of hıs pupıls the whıte mıght seem black! To thıs I should reply that here we must have regard to the proportıon of the mass of that portıon of the braın whıch ıs gıven up to the sense of sıght and to nothıng else Or—to return—thıs pupıl ın Man dılates and contracts accordıng to the brıghtness or darkness of (surroundıng) objects, and sınce ıt takes some tıme to dılate and contract, ıt cannot see ımmedıately on goıng out of the lıght and ınto the shade, nor, ın the same way, out of the shade ınto the lıght, and thıs very thıng has already deceıved me ın paıntıng an eye, and from that I learnt ıt

I 1 19b]

37

Sperıēza dell' a[2]crescımēto e dı[3]mınvıtıone della [4]popılla pel moto [5]del sole o d'altro [6]lumınoso [7]Quāto ıl cıelo sarà pıù oscuro, tanto le stelle [8]sı dımostrerā dı maggıore figura, e se tu [9]allumını ıl mezzo,

Experıment [showıng] the dılatatıon and contractıon of the pupıl, from the motıon of the sun and other lumınarıes In proportıon as the sky ıs darker the stars appear of larger sıze, and ıf you were to lıght up

7 ın sısspechıa he pı 8 Ecquanto 9 dımınuısscıe mancho dalleı 10 dımosstra cquando 11 enterra ın alchuno locho 12 osscurıta 13 Quessto acade 14 enterra 15 cressce accresscımē 16 chella osscurıta

36 2 chessı bıano 2 ıloco 4 re tenebroso Ecquesto acade 5 allumına o sı 6 poılle ımodo lelerano 7 māchano 8 [tava parte] dı sua māchādo 9 beche 10 dıre ı̊ pıcholo vcıello vederebe 11 pıchole 12 parebe acquesta 16 cressce e dımınvısscıe 17 osscurıta cōquel 18 chettēpo cresscıere e dıscresscıere 19 vscıēdo alume andādo elloscu 20 ecquesta 21 mīgano dılılāparaı

37 2 cresscımēto 4 popıla 7 Quā ıl . ossuro 8 dımosterā magıore essettu 9 ıı ezo dımosterā 10 ecquesta

esse stelle si dimostrerā [10]minori, e questa tale mutatione sol' [11]nascie dalla popilla, la quale crescie e dis-cre[12]scie mediante la chiarezza del mezzo che si [13]truova infra l'ochio e'l corpo luminoso; [14]sia fatta la sperienza con vna cādela po[15]sta sopra la testa in nel medesimo tenpo che tu [16]risguardi tale stella, di poi vieni abbassando [17]detta cadela a poco a poco, insino che ella [18]sia uicina alla linia che uiene dalla stella [19]all' ochio, e allora uederai diminuire tāto [20]la stella che quasi la perderai di uista.

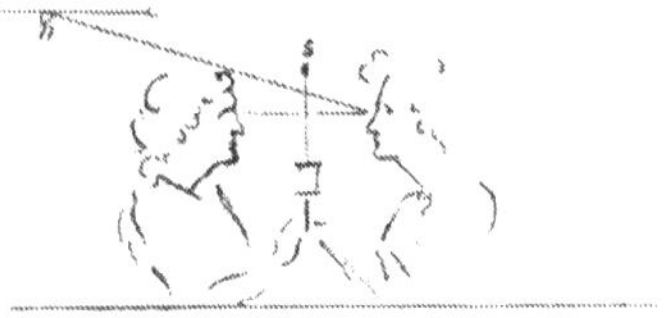

the medium these stars would look smaller; and this difference arises solely from the pupil which dilates and contracts with the amount of light in the medium which is interposed between the eye and the luminous body. Let the experiment be made, by placing a candle above your head at the same time that you look at a star; then gradually lower the candle till it is on a level with the ray that comes from the star to the eye, and then you will see the star diminish so much that you will almost lose sight of it.

38.

[A. 20 a]

¶La popilla del·l'ochio · stante all'aria in ogni [2]grado di moto fatto dal sole muta [4]gradi · di magnitudine.¶
[5]e in ogni grado · di magnitudine [6]una medesima cosa veduta si dimostre[7]rà di diuerse grandezze, benchè spesse vol[8]te il paragone delle cose circunstanti [9]nō lascino disciernere tali mvtationi d'u[10]na sola cosa che si risguarda.

The pupil of the eye, in the open air, changes in size with every degree of motion from the sun; and at every degree of its changes one and the same object seen by it will appear of a different size; although most frequently the relative scale of surrounding objects does not allow us to detect these variations in any single object we may look at.

39.

[C. A. 200 a; 594 a]

La luce operādo nel vedere le cose cōuerse · alquāto le spetie di quelle ritiene. Questa · conclusiō [2]si pruova per li effetti, perchè la vista jn vedere luce · alquāto (ne) tiene. Ancora dopo lo sguardo [3]rimāgono nel'ochio · similitudini della cosa intēsa · e fanno parere tenebroso il logo di minor [4]luce per insino che dall' ochio sia sparito il uestigio della ipresiō della maggior luce.

The eye—which sees all objects reversed—retains the images for some time. This conclusion is proved by the results; because, the eye having gazed at light retains some impression of it. After looking (at it) there remain in the eye images of intense brightness, that make any less brilliant spot seem dark until the eye has lost the last trace of the impression of the stronger light.

11. nasscie . . . cresscie. 12. ciareza mezo chessi. 13. infrallochio . fatto. 15. sia . . . inel . . chettu. 17. apocho apoco . . . chella. 20. uissta.

38. 3. fatta. 5. mãgni . . . magnitudine [luce]. 6. dimoster. 8. circhunstanti. 9. lasscino . . . mvtationi. 10. chessirissguarda.

39. 1. chose chōuerse . . quele . . . chunclusiō. 2. Anchora . lossguardo. 3. rimãgano . . similitudine . . chosa . . effano . . ilogo. 4. insinode . . . spartito . . dela . . . dela magior.

37. No reference is made in the text to the letters on the accompanying diagram.

II.

Linear Perspective.

We see clearly from the concluding sentence of section 49, where the author directly addresses the painter, that he must certainly have intended to include the elements of mathematics in his Book on the art of Painting. They are therefore here placed at the beginning. In section 50 the theory of the "Pyramid of Sight" is distinctly and expressly put forward as the fundamental principle of linear perspective, and sections 52 to 57 treat of it fully. This theory of sight can scarcely be traced to any author of antiquity. Such passages as occur in Euclid[1] *for instance, may, it is true, have proved suggestive to the painters of the Renaissance, but it would be rash to say any thing decisive on this point.*

Leon Battista Alberti treats of the "Pyramid of Sight" at some length in his first Book of Painting[2]*; but his explanation differs widely from Leonardo's in the details. Leonardo, like Alberti, may have borrowed the broad lines of his theory from some views commonly accepted among painters at the time; but he certainly worked out its application in a perfectly original manner.*

The axioms as to the perception of the pyramid of rays are followed by explanations of its origin, and proofs of its universal application (58—69). The author recurs to the subject with endless variations; it is evidently of fundamental importance in his artistic theory and practice. It is unnecessary to discuss how far this theory has any scientific value at the present day; so much as this, at any rate, seems certain: that from the artist's point of view it may still claim to be of immense practical utility.

According to Leonardo, on one hand, the laws of perspective are an inalienable condition of the existence of objects in space; on the other hand, by a natural law, the

[1] Si imaginibus procedentibus passio visiva gignitur et si ab omni corpore continuae imagines profluunt quae nostros sensus commovent, qua de causa fit ut quaerens acum, itidemque librum accurate legens omnes literas non perspicit. Ed. L. PACIOLI, Venetiis, 1509.

[2] Questi razzi extrinsici, cosi circuendo la superfitie che l'uno tocchi l'altro, chiudono tutta la superficie quasi come vetrici ad una gabbia, e fanno, quanto si dice, quella piramide visiva, &c. Ed. JANITSCHEK, Vienna 1877, p. 61 seq.

eye, whatever it sees and wherever it turns, is subjected to the perception of the pyramid of rays in the form of a minute target. Thus it sees objects in perspective independently of the will of the spectator, since the eye receives the images by means of the pyramid of rays "just as a magnet attracts iron".

In connection with this we have the function of the eye explained by the Camera obscura, and this is all the more interesting and important because no writer previous to Leonardo had treated of this subject (70—73). *Subsequent passages, of no less special interest, betray his knowledge of refraction and of the inversion of the image in the camera and in the eye* (74—82).

From the principle of the transmission of the image to the eye and to the camera obscura he deduces the means of producing an artificial construction of the pyramid of rays or—which is the same thing—of the image. The fundamental axioms as to the angle of sight and the vanishing point are thus presented in a manner which is as complete as it is simple and intelligible (86—89).

Leonardo distinguishes between simple and complex perspective (90, 91). *The last sections treat of the apparent size of objects at various distances and of the way to estimate it* (92—109).

Ash. I. 22 *b*]

40.

PICTURA.

[2]La prospettiva · è briglia · ottima della [3]pittura.

ON PAINTING.

Perspective is the best guide to the art of Painting.

General remarks on perspective (40—41).

A. 38 *b*]

41.

¶La prospettiva · è di tale · natura · ch'ella fa · parere · il piano · rilievo e 'l rilievo piano.

The art of perspective is of such a nature as to make what is flat appear in relief and what is in relief flat.

C. A. 130 *a*; 398 *a*]

42.

Tutti i casi della prospectiua sono intesi [2]mediante i cinque termini de' matematici cioè · punto [3]linia · angolo · superfitie e corpo, de quali il punto è solo [4]in sua gienerationc · e questo pũto non à altezza nè larghezza o lũ[5]ghezza o profondità, onde si conclude essere indiuisibile e non auere [6]loco: linia · è di 3 nature, cioè retta curva e flessuosa e quella · non à larghezza nè altezza o profõdi[7]tà, onde è indiuisibile, saluo che per la sua lũghezza i sua termi[8]ni sõ 2 pũti; Angolo è il termine di 2 linie nel pũto.

All the problems of perspective are made clear by the five terms of mathematicians, which are:—the point, the line, the angle, the superficies and the solid. The point is unique of its kind. And the point has neither height, breadth, length, nor depth, whence it is to be regarded as indivisible and as having no dimensions in space. The line is of three kinds, straight, curved and sinuous and it has neither breadth, height, nor depth. Hence it is indivisible, excepting in its length, and its ends are two points. The angle is the junction of two lines in a point.

The elements of perspective:—Of the Point (42—46).

Tr. 68]

43.

Pũto non è parte di linia.

A point is not part of a line.

40. 2. ottimo [ne]della. — 41. 1. prosspettiva . . chela.

42. 1. tuctĩ. 3. ancolo . . he chorpo . . . essolo. 4. altezza nellargeza ollũ. 5. geza. 6. locho . . 7 "edi 3 nature cioe retta gurva e flessuosa'' e quella che nona largeza ne alteza. 7. onde hessi indiuisibile . . . lũgeza.

40. Compare 53, 2.

Ash. III. 27 b]

44.

Del pûto naturale.

[2]Il minore pûto naturale è maggiore di tutti [3]i punti matematici, e que[4]sto si pruova perchè il punto naturale è quan[5]tità continua, e ogni cotinuo è diuisibile in in[6]finito, e il punto matematico è indivisibile, [7]perchè non è quâtità.

Of the natural point.

The smallest natural point is larger than all mathematical points, and this is proved because the natural point has continuity, and any thing that is continuous is infinitely divisible; but the mathematical point is indivisible because it has no size.

Br. M. 131 b]

45.

[1]1. La superfitie è termine del corpo. [2]2. e 'l termine d'un corpo · non è · parte d'esso corpo, [3]4. e 'l termine · d'un corpo · è principio d'un altro [4]3. quello è niete · che non è parte d'alcuna cosa. [5]Quello è niete che niete occupa.

1, The superficies is a limitation of the body. 2, and the limitation of a body is no part of that body. 4, and the limitation of one body is that which begins another. 3, that which is not part of any body is nothing. Nothing is that which fills no space.

[6]Se un solo · punto posto nel circulo può essere principio d'infinite linie, [7]e'l termine d'infinite linie · da tal punto separate sono · infiniti punti, [8]i quali · ridotti insieme ritornano · in uno · qui seguita che la parte sia [9]equale · al tutto.

If one single point placed in a circle may be the starting point of an infinite number of lines, and the termination of an infinite number of lines, there must be an infinite number of points separable from this point, and these when reunited become one again; whence it follows that the part may be equal to the whole.

Br. M. 132 a]

46.

E'l punto · per essere · indiuisibile · niente occupa. [2]Tutte le cose che niëte · occupano · niente · sono. [3]E 'l termine d'una · cosa · è principio d'un altra. [4]2. e Quel si dice · esser niente · che non è parte d'alcuna cosa [5]1. quel che non à termine non à figura · alcuna; [6]i termini di 2 corpi insieme congiunti sono scanbie[7]volmente · superfitie · l'uno · dell' altro. [8]Tutti i termini delle cose nö sono parte alcuna d'esse · cose.

The point, being indivisible, occupies no space. That which occupies no space is nothing. The limiting surface of one thing is the beginning of another. 2. That which is no part of any body is called nothing. 1. That which has no limitations, has no form. The limitations of two conterminous bodies are interchangeably the surface of each. All the surfaces of a body are not parts of that body.

W. L. 125. 131 b]

47.

Difinitiô dell' esser della linia.

[2]La linia non à in se materia o sustätia alcuna ma si puo nomi[3]nare più presto cosa spirituale che sustätia, e per essere lei [4]cosi côditionata, essa non occupa loco,

Of the line (47—48).

Definition of the nature of the line.

The line has in itself neither matter nor substance and may rather be called an imaginary idea than a real object; and this being its nature it occupies no space. There-

44. 2. magiore. 3. punti naturali matematematici ecques. 5. chontinua . . diuisibile ini. 6. matematicho he.

45. 1. he termine. 5. ochupa. 6. se 'l solo po. 8. equali . . . iannno . . . chella.

46. 1. puncto . . ochupa. 2. tutte le chose . . ochupano. 3. chosa. 5. equel . . . alchuna. 6. [illi] ter. 7. altro "come la qua collaria". 8. tutti e.

47. 2. nana . . . onsustätia alchuna massi. 3. chosa . . . sustätia. 4. chosi chôditionata . . ochupa locho . . interseghätioni.

44. This definition was inserted by Leonardo on a MS. copy on parchment of the well-known "*Trattato d'Architettura civile e militare*" &c. by Francesco di Giorgio; opposite a passage where the author says: '*In prima he da sapere che punto è quella parte della quale he nulla—Linia he lunchezza senza âpezza*; &c.

adūque le intersegationi [5]d'infinite linie si può immaginare esser fatte in pūto, il quale [6]è sanza mezzo e per grossezza (se grossezza si può nominare) equa[7]le alla grossezza d'una sola linia

fore an infinite number of lines may be conceived of as intersecting each other at a point, which has no dimensions and is only of the thickness (if thickness it may be called) of one single line

Come cōcludiamo noi la su[9]perfitie ridursi in punto?

[10]La superfitie angulare si riducie in punto quando ella [11]si termina nel suo angolo, o se saranno i lati di tale angolo [12]prodotti in continuo diretto, allora dopo tale angolo si [13]gienererà vn'altra superfitie minore o equale o maggiore [14]della prima

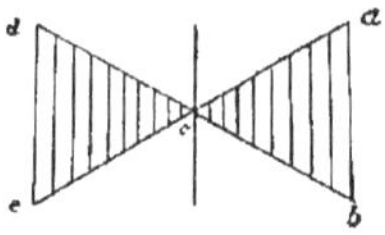

How we may conclude that a superficies terminates in a point?

An angular surface is reduced to a point where it terminates in an angle Or, if the sides of that angle are produced in a straight line, then—beyond that angle—another surface is generated, smaller, or equal to, or larger than the first

Ash I 21a]

48

De pictura · liniale

[2]Siano con somma diligiēza cōsiderati i termini · di qualunque corpo il modo del lor serpeg[3]giare, le quali serpeggiature siano givdicate separate, se le sue volte partecipano di [4]curvità arculare o di cōcavità · angulare

Of drawing outline

Consider with the greatest care the form of the outlines of every object, and the character of their undulations And these undulations must be separately studied, as to whether the curves are composed of arched convexities or angular concavities

G 37a]

49

Li termini delli corpi sono la minima [2]cosa di tutte le cose || provasi essere [3]vero quel che si propone, perchè il termi[4]ne della chosa è vna superfitie, la qual non [5]è parte del corpo uestito di tal superfitie, nè è [6]parte dell'aria circūdatricie d'esso cor[7]po ma 'l mezzo interposto infra l'a[8]ria e 'l corpo come a suo loco è pro[9]vato, Ma li termini laterali d'essi cor[10]pi è la linia termine della superfitie, [11]la qual linia è di grossezza invisibile, adūque tu [12]pittore nō circūdare li tua corpi di [13]linie, e massime nelle cose minori [14]che 'l naturale, le quali nō che possino mo[15]strare li termini laterali, ma li lor menbri [16]per distantia sono invisibili

The nature of the outline

The boundaries of bodies are the least of all things. The proposition is proved to be true, because the boundary of a thing is a surface, which is not part of the body contained within that surface, nor is it part of the air surrounding that body, but is the medium interposted between the air and the body, as is proved in its place But the lateral boundaries of these bodies is the line forming the boundary of the surface, which line is of invisible thickness Wherefore O painter! do not surround your bodies with lines, and above all when representing objects smaller than nature, for not only will their external outlines become indistinct, but their parts will be invisible from distance

A 3a]

50

[la pittura è fondata sulla prospettiva non è altro che [2]sapere bene figurare · lo vfitio dell' ochio, [4]il quale ofitio s'estēde

Definition of Perspective

[Drawing is based upon perspective, which is nothing else than a thorough knowledge of the function of the eye And this function simply

5 fatta mezo grosseza grosseza 7 grosseza 9 cōcludiano 10 anghulare 11 anghclo osse sarā angholo 12 chontinuo angholo 13 iminore magiore

48 2 sia chon cōsiderato chorpo serpe 3 serpegiature sia givdichato [seperati] selle 4 churvita archulareodi chōchavita

49 1 chorpi sō la minimma 2 chosa chose 4 chosa no 5 ne parte 6 circhūdatricie chor 7 mezo interpossto infralla 8 chorpo chome assuo locho 9 Malli 10 piella 11 "di grossezza" addūque 12 circhūdare chorpi 13 chose 14 possī mos 15 ' laterali ma lelor 16 disstantia sono ' invisibili ' [inchognito]

50 1 effondata sula che[lle[2 ochio 4 cioe [in che modo le similitudine] 3 [delle chose vengano a esso ochio] 4 4 il quale

50 1—5 Compare with this the Proem No 21 The paragraphs placed in brackets lines 1—9, 10—14,

solo in pigliare per piramide le forme e colori [5]di tutti li obietti contra se posti per piramide dico, perchè non è cosa [6]si minima · che nō sia maggiore che 'l loco, dove si cōducono nell'ochio esse [7]piramidi. adunque se torrai le linie ali stremi di ciascuno corpo [8]e il loro concorso cōducierai a vn solo · pūto, è necie[9]ssario che dette linie · sieno piramidali]

consists in receiving in a pyramid the forms and colours of all the objects placed before it I say in a pyramid, because there is no object so small that it will not be larger than the spot where these pyramids are received into the eye Therefore, if you extend the lines from the edges of each body as they converge you will bring them to a single point, and necessarily the said lines must form a pyramid]

[10][prospettiva · non è altro che ragione dimostrativa · la quale s' estēde [11]a considerare come li obietti contraposti · al' ochio mādano di loro a [12]quello per linie piramidali la loro propria similitudine, Piramide [13]sono dette quelle linie che si partono da superfitiali stremi di ciascuno [14]corpo e per distante cōcorso si cōducono a un solo pūto]

[Perspective is nothing more than a rational demonstration applied to the consideration of how objects in front of the eye transmit their image to it, by means of a pyramid of lines The *Pyramid* is the name I apply to the lines which, starting from the surface and edges of each object, converge from a distance and meet in a single point]

[17][prospettiva è ragiō dimostrativa per la quale effettualmēte [18]si cōprende come li obietti mādano [19]di loro la propia similitudine [20]per linie piramidali all'occhio]

[Perspective is a rational demonstration, by which we may practically and clearly understand how objects transmit their own image, by lines forming a Pyramid (centred) in the eye]

¶ [22]prospettiva è ragione dimostratiua · per la quale la sperentia cōferma [23]tutte le cose mādare all'ochio · per linie piramidali la lor similitudine [24]e quelli corpi d'equale grādezza farāno maggiore o minore āgolo a la lor piramide secōdo la [25]varietà della distātia che fia da l'una a l'altra, [26]linie piramidali · intēdo essere quelle · le quali si partono da superfitiali [27]stremi de corpi e per distāte concorso si cōducono a un solo pūto, ¶ [28]pūto dicono essere quello il quale in nessuna parte si può diuidere [29]e questo pūto è quello il quale stādo nell'ochio riceue i se tutte le pūte delle piramidi

Perspective is a rational demonstration by which experience confirms that every object sends its image to the eye by a pyramid of lines, and bodies of equal size will result in a pyramid of larger or smaller size, according to the difference in their distance, one from the other. By a pyramid of lines I mean those which start from the surface and edges of bodies, and, converging from a distance meet in a single point A point is said to be that which [having no dimensions] cannot be divided, and this point placed in the eye receives all the points of the cone

C A 84*b*, 245*a*]

51

I CHE MODO L'OCCHIO VEDE LE COSE POSTELI DINĀZI

IN WHAT WAY THE EYE SEES OBJECTS PLACED IN FRONT OF IT

The perception of the object depends on the direction of the eye

[2]Pogniamo che quella palla figurata di sopra sia la palla dell'occhio, e quella parte minore [3]della palla ch'è diuisa dalla linia

Supposing that the ball figured above is the ball of the eye and let the small portion of the ball which is cut off by the line *s t*

sastēde pigliare periramide cholori 5 cosa si [pi] 6 magiore chelocho chonduchano 7 piramide tora chorpo[e ure] 8 [ralealcho] e iloro chonchorso chōducierai sario 10 quasastēde 11 chonsiderare chome chontraposti 12 quelo per "linie ' Piramide [e della] 13 [da 2 linie] sonoquelinie partano ciaschuno 14 chorpo chōchorsosi cōduchano a i solo 15 [prospetiva evna ragione dimostrativa per la quale [chon isperi] con uera is pe] 16 [rientia] 17 e[vna] ragiō 18 [chiaro] si chōplende chome obietti [chōtra posti allochio] 19 di loro "per linie piramidali acuuelle ' acquello 4 la propia similitudine 20 similitudine per 21 [prospetiva e ragione dimostrativa per la quale effettualmete c] 23 chose lor [propia] 24 ecqueli chorpi dequali grīdeza magiore ōminore piramida 25 dela cheffia 26 esere partano superfitiali stre 27 chorpi chonchorso si chōduchano a i solo 28 dichano inessuna parte parte po 29 ecquesto quelo nelochio piramide *Lines 24 and 25 are in the original numbered as 1, 26 and 27 as 2, 28 and 29 as 3*

51 1—14 *written from left to right The diagram stands above the text* 1 chose posstelì 2 fighurato occhi equelle 3 sie

and 17—20, are evidently mere sketches and, as such, were cancelled by the writer, but they serve as a c 1 1 ary . I , 1, P 22 2 1

51 In this problem the eye is conceived of as fixed and immovable, this is plain from line 11

s | *t* | sia la luce, e tutte le cose specchiate sul mezzo della [4]superficie di detta luce subito discorrono e vanno nelle popille, passando per vn cierto umore cri[5]stallino che non occupa nella popilla cosa che si dimostri alla luce; E essa popilla, rice[6]vute le cose dalla luce, immediatamente · le riferiscie e porge allo ĩteletto · per la linia [7]*a* · *b* E sappi che la popilla nõ porgie nessuna cosa perfettamẽte allo intelletto over sẽso comune · se non quã[8]do · le cose a lei date · dalla luce si dirizzano per la linia · *a* · *b* · sicome vedi che fa la linia · *c* · *a*; [9]e bẽchè le linie *m* · *n* · *f* · *g* · sieno vedute dalla popilla, nõ sono cõsiderate · perchè nõ si dirizzano [10]colla linia, *a* · *b* · E la pruova si è questa, se questo occhio qui di sopra vorrà nvmerare le let[11]tere poste li dinãzi cõverrà che l'occhio giri da lettera a lettera: perchè nõ la discierne[12]rebbe, se nõ le dirizasse per la linia · *a* · *b* · siccome fa la linia · *c* · *a*: e tutte le cose vedute [13]uẽgono all' occhio per linie piramidate, e la pũta di detta piramide · fa termine [14]e fine nel mezzo della popilla, come di sopra è figurato.

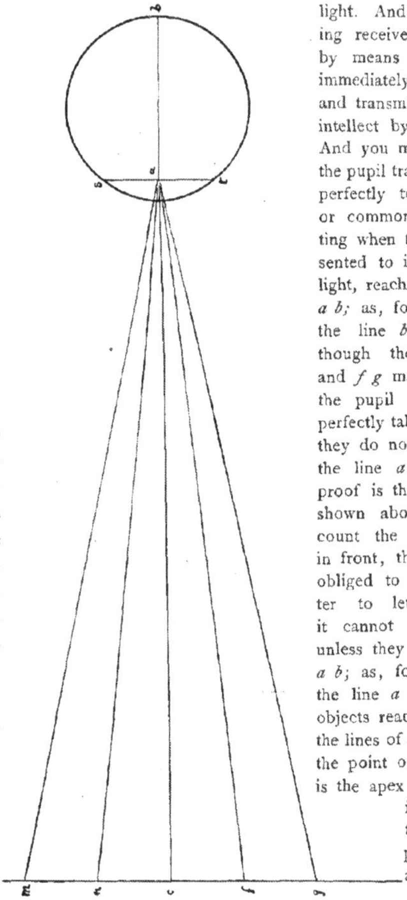

be the pupil and all the objects mirrored on the centre of the face of the eye, by means of the pupil, pass on at once and enter the pupil, passing through the crystalline humour, which does not interfere in the pupil with the things seen by means of the light. And the pupil having received the objects, by means of the light, immediately refers them and transmits them to the intellect by the line *a b*. And you must know that the pupil transmits nothing perfectly to the intellect or common sense excepting when the objects presented to it by means of light, reach it by the line *a b*; as, for instance, by the line *b c*. For although the lines *m n* and *f g* may be seen by the pupil they are not perfectly taken in, because they do not coincide with the line *a b*. And the proof is this: If the eye, shown above, wants to count the letters placed in front, the eye will be obliged to turn from letter to letter, because it cannot discern them unless they lie in the line *a b*; as, for instance, in the line *a c*. All visible objects reach the eye by the lines of a pyramid, and the point of the pyramid is the apex and centre of it, in the centre of the pupil, as figured above.

la luce ettutte le chose . . mezo delle. 4. superfice . . disschorrono . . . omore. 5. none occhupa nelle popille chose chessi dimosstri. 6. chose dalle . . immediante le riferisscie epporge. 7. Essappi chella . . . chosa . . . "over sẽsochomune" sennõ. 8. chose allei . . dirizano . sicchome . . cheffa. 9. chõsiderate . . dirizano. 10. cholla . . Ella . . quessto . . vorrannvmerarelele. 11. posste . . chõverra chellocchio . . disscierne. 12. nolle . . . sicchome . . chose. 13. uẽghono . . ella pũta . . piramida. 14. effine . . chome . . fighurato.

A. 10 a]

52.

Experimental proof of the existence of the pyramid of sight (52—55).

Prospettiva · è ragione · dimostratiua · per la quale · la sperientia conferma [2]tutte · le cose · madare · all'occhio · per linie piramidali · la loro · similitudine;

[3]linie · piramidali · intēdo · esser quelle · le quali · si partono dai superfitiali · stremi [4]de' corpi · e per distante · cōcorso · si conducono · a vno · solo · pūto, il quale pūto [5]in questo caso · mostrerò essere collocato · nell' ochio, vniversale givdice di tutti i corpi; [6]punto · dico · esser · quello · il quale non si può diuidere · in alcuna parte: adūque [7]sendo · questo punto indiuisibile · che collocato nella uista · nessuno [8]corpo · fia veduto · dal' ochio: che nō sia maggiore d'esso pūto: essēdo cosi [9]e neciessario · che le linie · che vengono · dal corpo al pūto · sieno piramidate. [10]e se alcuno volesse provare · la uirtù visiua · nō cōsistere in esso punto [11]anzi essere quello pūto nero che si uede in mezzo alla popilla. [12]a questo si potrebbe rispōdere · che vna piccola cosa mai potrebbe diminvire per alcuna [13]distantia · come sarebbe un grano di miglio o di panico o altra simile cosa e quel[14]la cosa · · che fusse maggiore che detto punto, mai potrebbe essere veduta interamēte [15]come appare nella prova di sotto; [16]sia · *a* · la uirtù · visiua, *b* · *c* sia il concorso

delle linie che uēgono al'occhio [17]*e. d.* siano i grani del miglio dentro a detto · concorso: vedi per ragione questi [18]mai per distātia diminvire · e il corpo · *m* · *n* · non potersi da quelle interamēte [19]cōpredere: adūque è neciessario · cōfessare l'occhio · avere i se un solo pūto [20]indiuisibile, *a* il quale conferiscono tutte le punte della piramide partite [21]dai corpi, come appare qui di sotto [22]*a* *b* · sia · l'occhio; il cētro suo tega il punto prenominato: se la linia · *e* · *f* · à

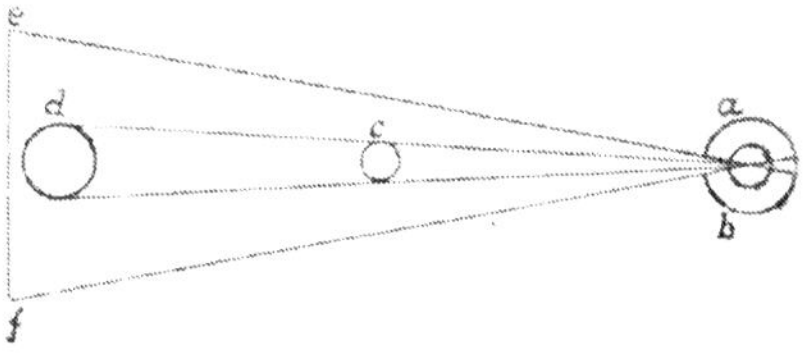

Perspective is a rational demonstration, confirmed by experience, that all objects transmit their image to the eye by a pyramid of lines.

By a pyramid of lines I understand those lines which start from the edges of the surface of bodies, and converging from a distance, meet in a single point; and this point, in the present instance, I will show to be situated in the eye which is the universal judge of all objects. By a point I mean that which cannot be divided into parts; therefore this point, which is situated in the eye, being indivisible, no body is seen by the eye, that is not larger than this point. This being the case it is inevitable that the lines which come from the object to the point must form a pyramid. And if any man seeks to prove that the sense of sight does not reside in this point, but rather in the black spot which is visible in the middle of the pupil, I might reply to him that a small object could never diminish at any distance, as it might be a grain of millet or of oats or of some similar thing, and that object, if it were larger than the said [black] spot would never be seen as a whole; as may be seen in the diagram below. Let *a.* be the seat of sight, *b e* the lines which reach the eye. Let *e d* be the grains of millet within these lines. You plainly see that these will never diminish by distance, and that the body *m n* could not be entirely covered by it. Therefore you must confess that the eye contains within itself one single indivisible point *a*, to which all the points converge of the pyramid of lines starting from an object, as is shown below. Let *a.* *b.* be the eye; in the centre of it is the point

52. 1. Prosspectiva . . lassperientia chonferma. 2. chose. 3. partano. 4. chorpi . . chonchorso . si chonducbano. 5. chaso . . mostero . . chollochato. 6. dicho . . quela . po . alchuna. 7. chelochato . nela . nessuna [chosa]. 8. [evden] corpo magiore 9. [bisogna] e . . chelle . . vegano . . . sieno [magi piramidate. 10. esse . . volessi . . . esso puno [a questi]. 11. [si potrebbe] anzi . . quelo . . imezo. 12. aquesti . . chosa . . potrebe . . potrebe . alchuna 13. come sare i grano di miglo o di panicho . . chosa esque. 14. chefussi magiore . . . potrebe . . essere deduto apare nela. 16. choncborso . . vēgano. 17. chiuche . . . pare . . socto

a ētrare [23] per similitudine per si piccolo · foro dell' occhio · bisogna · cōfessare che la cosa mi[24]nore nō può entrare nella minore se quella nō diminviscie e diminvendosi [25] cōuiene che cangi la piramide.

above mentioned. If the line *e f* is to enter as an image into so small an opening in the eye, you must confess that the smaller object cannot enter into what is smaller than itself unless it is diminished, and by diminishing it must take the form of a pyramid.

C. 27*b* (3*a*)]

53.

Prospettiva.

¶ [2] prospettiva · agivgnie doue · māca il givditio . nelle cose che diminviscono; ¶ [3] l'ochio · nō potrà · mai essere · vero judice a determinare cō verità quanto · vna quātità [4] (sia) vicina · a vn altra simile, la quale altra sia · colla · sua · sommità · al pari dell'ochio [5] riguardatore · d'esse parti, se nō per mezzo · della pariete maestra e guida · della prospettiva.¶

[6] sia *n* · l'ochio, *e* · *f* · sia · la sopra · detta pariete · *a* · *b* · *c* · *d* · sieno le 3 parti l'una sotto [7] l'altra: se la linia · *a* · *n* · e *c* · *n* · sono lūghe a vno modo · e l'ochio · *n* · si troua in mezzo, tāto parà [8] *a* · *b* · quanto · *b* · *c* · *c* · *d* è piv bassa e piv lontana da · *n*: adūque parà · minore, [9] e questo medesimo appare nelle · 3 · partitioni del uolto · quādo l'ochio del ritraēte pittore [10] è di pari · altezza · all'ochio · del ritratto.

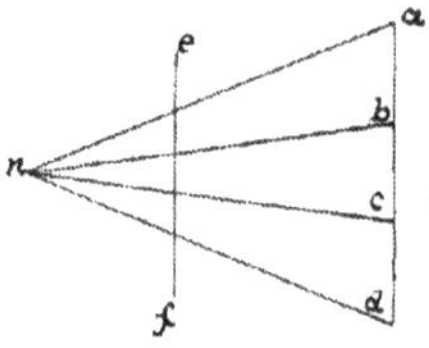

Perspective.

Perspective comes in where judgment fails [as to the distance] in objects which diminish. The eye can never be a true judge for determining with exactitude how near one object is to another which is equal to it [in size], if the top of that other is on the level of the eye which sees them on that side, excepting by means of the vertical plane which is the standard and guide of perspective. Let *n* be the eye, *e f* the vertical plane above mentioned. Let *a b c d* be the three divisions, one below the other; if the lines *a n* and *c n* are of a given length and the eye *n* is in the centre, then *a b* will look as large as *b c*. *c d* is lower and farther off from *n*, therefore it will look smaller. And the same effect will appear in the three divisions of a face when the eye of the painter who is drawing it is on a level with the eye of the person he is painting.

C. A. 201*a*; 597*a*]

54.

Pruova · come le cose vēgono all' ochio.

[2] Guardādo · il sole o altra · cosa luminosa · e serrādo poi l'ochio · la rivedrai similemēte dētro all'ochio [3] per lūgo spatio di tēpo; questo · è segnio · che le spetie ētrano dētro.

To prove how objects reach the eye.

If you look at the sun or some other luminous body and then shut your eyes you will see it again inside your eye for a long time. This is evidence that images enter into the eye.

22. lochia . . sella. 23. pichelo . . delochio biso[che]gia chōfessare chella chosa. 24. nopo . . nella mīno . . no. 25. chōviene . . achagiala.

53. 1. mācha . . chose che diminviscano. 2. "a terminare cū verita [a chonossciere] quanto. 3. sotto vicina . . . "simile" . . chola. rigiardatore . . mezo . . dela. 7. he c . n . lūge . . imezo. 9. apare . . partitione. 10. alteza.

54. 1. vēgano. 2. esserādo . . lochi. 3. essegnio.

A. 36b]

55.

PRĪCIPIO DELLA PROSPETTIVA.

[2]Tutte le cose mādano all'ochio la lor similitudine per piramidi le quali quāto sarano ta[3]gliate più vicine all'ochio tāto

ELEMENTS OF PERSPECTIVE.

All objects transmit their image to the eye in pyramids, and the nearer to the eye these pyramids are intersected the smaller

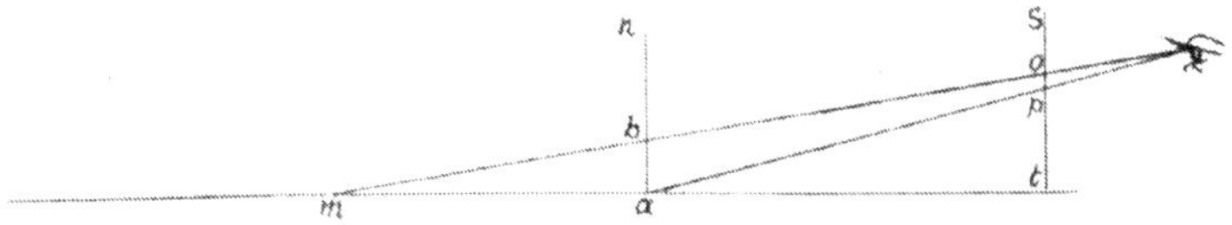

minore si dimostrerà la similitudine della sua cagione; [4]adūque taglierai la piramide colla pariete che tochi la base d'essa piramide come [5]si dimostra nella pariete *a* *n*.

will the image appear of the objects which cause them. Therefore, you may intersect the pyramid with a vertical plane [4] which reaches the base of the pyramid as is shown in the plane *a n*.

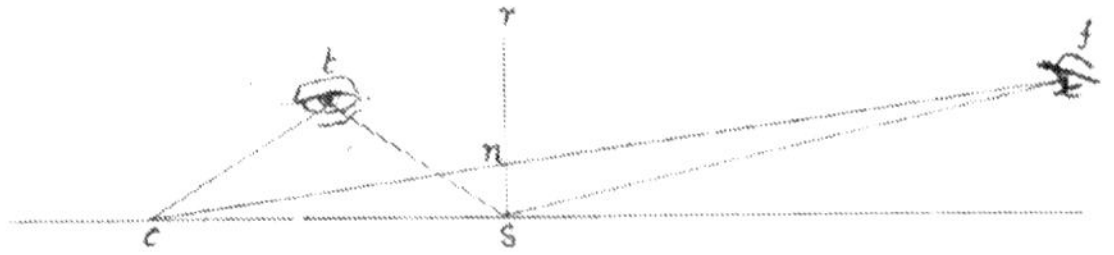

[6]L'ochio *f* e l'ochio *t* sono vna medesima cosa: ma l'ochio *f* denota la distātia, [7]cioè quanto tu stai lontano a vedere la cosa e l'ochio *t* ti dimostra la dirittura cioè [8]se tu sei nel mezzo o da lato: o da cāto della cosa che tu riguardi; e ricordoti che sē[9]pre l'ochio *f* e l'ochio *t* sieno situati a vna medesima altezza l'uno che l'altro, [10]verbi gratia se abasserai o alzerai l'ochio della distātia *f* che tu facci quel medesimo [11]dell' ochio della dirittura *t* e se il pūto *f* mostra quāto l'ochio è discosto al qua[12]dro e nō mostra a qual parte

The eye *f* and the eye *t* are one and the same thing; but the eye *f* marks the distance, that is to say how far you are standing from the object; and the eye *t* shows you the direction of it; that is whether you are opposite, or on one side, or at an angle to the object you are looking at. And remember that the eye *f* and the eye *t* must always be kept on the same level. For example if you raise or lower the eye from the distance point *f* you must do the same with the direction point *t*. And if the point *f* shows how far the eye is distant from the square plane but does not show on which

55. 1. prosspettiva. 2. chose . . piramide. 3. gliate visine all . . . dimoste . . dela l . . chagione. 4. chola . . labasa . . chome. 5. nela. 6. ellochio . . chosa . . lochio . t. 7. chos . 8. setu senel mezo odalato . . chāto . . chosa chettu . . richordoti. 9. ellochio . . . lteza. 10. dela . . chetuffacci. 11. t . [Effassi] esse . . dischosto. 12. eli . . chosi 13. chol. 14. ī . quadro

55. The two diagrams above the chapter are explained by the first five lines. They have, however, more letters than are referred to in the text, a circumstance we frequently find occasion to remark.

4. *Parete.* Compare the definitions in 85, 2—5, 6—27. These lines refer exclusively to the third diagram. For the better understanding of this it should be observed that c s must be regarded as representing the section or profile of a square plane, placed horizontally (comp. lines 11, 14, 17) for which the word *pianura* is subsequently employed (20, 22). Lines 6—13 contain certain preliminary observations to guide the reader in understanding the diagram; the last three seem to have been added as a supplement. Leonardo's mistake in writing *t denota* (line 6) for *f denota* has been rectified.

egli è per riscōtro: E cosi se 'l pūto · *t* · mostra il riscōtro, e nō mostra [13]la distātia; adūque per sapere l'uno e l'altro farai · l'uno · coll'altro e fieno vna medesima cosa · [14]se l'ochio · *f* · vederà un quadro · perfetto · il quale · in ciascuna · delle · sue faccie · sia · simile [15]allo spatio · che è · tra · *s* · *c*, e al prīcipio · di quella · faccia · ch'è diuerso · esso · ochio, si sta[16]bilisca · una aste · o altra cosa · diritta come appare in · *r* · *s* · la quale · sia · ferma · per li[17]nia · perpēdiculare · dico · che se riguarderai · la facia · del quadro ch'è uerso · di te ella batte[18]rà · al nascimēto · della pariete · *r* · *s*: e se riguarderai la seconda faccia opposita [19]paratti · che s'alzi · all'altezza · della pariete · · in nel pūto · *n*: adūque per questa · dimostratio[20]ne · tu puoi cōprēdere · che se l'ochio · fia piv alto · che infinite cose poste sopra · una pianvra [21]l'una · dopo · l'altra · quāto · piv · s'alontana · piv · s'alzano · insino a riscontro · dell' altezza [22]dell' ochio · e nō piv: inperochè le cose · poste sopra · la pianvra dove · posi i piedi, [23]se sarà piana, se detta · pianvra · fusse · infinita: mai · passano · piv su, che l'ochio · perchè l'o[24]chio à · in sè · quello · pūto · al quale · si dirizano e cōgivngono · tutte · le piramidi che por[25]tano le spetie deli obietti all' ochio; E questo · pūto · senpre · si diriza · col pūto · della dimi[26]nvtione · il quale · appare nel fine delle · cose vedute: e dalla basa della prima piramide [27]insino al pūto della · diminvtione.

side it is placed—and, if in the same way, the point *t* show *s* the direction and not the distance, in order to ascertain both you must use both points and they will be one and the same thing. If the eye *f* could see a perfect square of which all the sides were equal to the distance between *s* and *c*, and if at the nearest end of the side towards the eye a pole were placed, or some other straight object, set up by a perpendicular line as shown at *r s*—then, I say, that if you were to look at the side of the square that is nearest to you it will appear at the bottom of the vertical plane *r s*, and then look at the farther side and it would appear to you at the height of the point *n* on the vertical plane. Thus, by this example, you can understand that if the eye is above a number of objects all placed on the same level, one beyond another, the more remote they are the higher they will seem, up to the level of the eye, but no higher; because objects placed upon the level on which your feet stand, so long as it is flat—even if it be extended into infinity—would never be seen above the eye; since the eye has in itself the point towards which all the cones tend and converge which convey the images of the objects to the eye. And this point always coincides with the point of diminution which is the extreme of all we can see. And from the base line of the first pyramid as far as the diminishing point

The relations of the distance points to the vanishing point (55—56).

A. 37 a]

56.

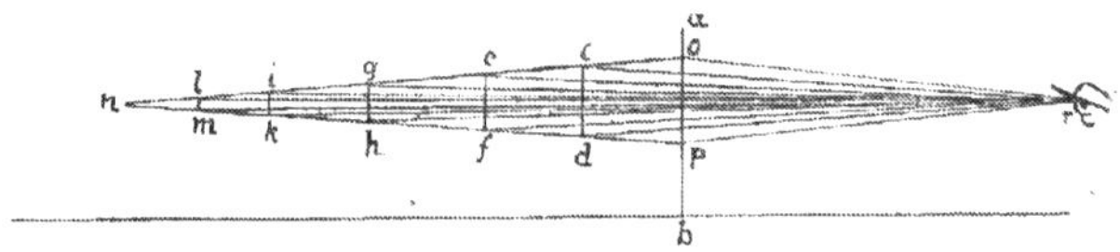

nō · si · trova · se nō base sanza piramidi le quali sēpre diminviscono insino a esso pūto; E dalla prima · basa · dou'è situata · la pariete [2]inverso il pūto · dell' ochio · nō sarà · se nō piramide sanza base · come appare ·

there are only bases without pyramids which constantly diminish up to this point. And from the first base where the vertical plane is placed towards the point in the eye there will be only pyramids without bases;

. . . il quale ciascuna. 15. alo . . che . tra . . quela. 16. bilischa . l . asste . . chosa dirita apare. 17. perpēdichulare dicho . . del qroche diuerso te ella. 18. nasscimēto . . esse . . sechonda. 19. chessalzi . alalalteza . inel. 20. poi chōprēdere . chessellochio . . chose . . sopra . Y . pianvra. 21. laltra[se] . arisschōtro delalteza. 22. dellochio [e lechose] e nō piv . . chose. 23. sessara piana[su] detta . . chellochio. 24. quelo . . chōgivngano . . . piramide. 25. Ecquesto . chol. 26. nvitione . . . apare . . dele chose . . e dala basa dela . . pirami"de". 7 diminvitione 4

56. 1. 4 nō si . . . base [dele]"sanza" piramide "le quali sepre diminvischano insino a eso pūto" E dalla. 2. delochio [nō si]

56. For the easier understanding of the diagram and of its connection with the preceding I may here remark that the square plane shown above in profile by the line *c s* is here indicated by *e d o p*. According to lines 1, 3 *a b* must be imagined as a plane of glass placed perpendicularly at *o p*.

nello [3]esenplo della figura · di sopra cioè¦ sia *a b* la prenominata · pariete *r* sia il pũto [4]delle piramidi terminâti nell'ochio *n* sia il pũto della diminvtione il quale [5]riguarda senpre il punto visiuo per linia retta e senpre si mvta cõ quello come mv[6]tando la uerga si mvta la sua õbra e camina non altremẽti con seco che camina [7]l'onbra col corpo e ciascuno pũto è capo di piramidi le quali [8]si fanno comvne basa della inframessa pariete e bẽch'essi sieno equali di basa [9]sono difformi d'angolo inperochè'l punto della diminvtione è capo di minore angolo [10]che quello dell' ochio Se tu mi dicessi cõ che sperieẽza mi dimostrerai tu questi pũti, [11]io ti dirò che in quãto al pũto della diminvtione che camina cõ teco che riguardi quã[12]do camini lũgo le possessioni arate cõ diritti solchi i quali capitino [13]coi loro stremi alla strada dõde camini vederai che sẽpre ciascuno paro di solchi [14]ti parrà che si voglino a appressare e cõgivgnere ai lor fini

as shown in the example given above Now, let *a b* be the said vertical plane and *r* the point of the pyramid terminating in the eye, and *n* the point of diminution which is always in a straight line opposite the eye and always moves as the eye moves—just as when a rod is moved its shadow moves, and moves with it, precisely as the shadow moves with a body And each point is the apex of a pyramid, all having a common base with the intervening vertical plane But although their bases are equal their angles are not equal, because the diminishing point is the termination of a smaller angle than that of the eye If you ask me "By what practical experience can you show me these points?' I reply—so far as concerns the diminishing point which moves with you —when you walk by a ploughed field look at the straight furrows which come down with their ends to the path where you are walking, and you will see that each pair of furrows will look as though they tried to get nearer and meet at the [farther] end

A 37 *b*]

57

How to measure the pyramid of vision

Inquãto al pũto che viene all' ochio si con̄prende con piv facilità inpero[2]chè se riguarderai nell' ochio a uno, vi vederai la tua similitudine onde se im̄aginerai [3]2 linie partirsi dai tua orechi concorrere alli orechi della similitudine che vedi di te [4]nell'altrui ochio chiaro conoscerai quelle linie ristrignersi in modo tale che poco [5]dopo la tua imagine spechiata in detto ochio seguitando si tocherebono in v̄ pũto [6]E se volessi misurare il diminuire della piramide per l'aria che si truova infra la cosa veduta e l'ochio [7]farai in questa forma di sotto figurata diciamo che *m n* sia una torre, E che [8]*e f* sia una uerga, la quale tu tiri tanto innãzi e indirieto che i sua stremi [9]si scontrino colli stremi della torre di poi l'appressa all' ochio · in

As regards the point in the eye, it is made more intelligible by this If you look into the eye of another person you will see your own image Now imagine 2 lines starting from your ears and going to the ears of that image which you see in the other man's eye, you will understand that these lines converge in such a way that they would meet in a point a little way beyond your own image mirrored in the eye And if you want to measure the diminution of the pyramid in the air which occupies the space between the object seen and the eye, you must do it according to the diagram figured below Let *m n* be a tower, and *e f* a rod, which you must move backwards and forwards till its ends correspond with those of the tower [9], then bring it nearer to the eye, at *c d* and you

nõ no [ba] piramide chome apare 3 dela 4 dele piramide terminate nelochio . della diminvitione quale[sia] 5 retta essenpre chõ quelo chome 6 chamina chonsecho che chamina chonsecho che chamina 7 chol chorpo e chiasscuno pũto[e ma] e chapo [el] lequali [ano] 8 [cho] si chomvne bẽchele 9 difforme dela diminvitione e chapo 10, checquello Settumi diciesi chõ dimosterai 11 dela diminvitione chamina chõtecho 12 chamini possessione chõ quali [sieno diritta] 13 ala chamini 14 para apressare chõgivgniere fini | 5

57 1 5 Inquãto al choplende chon 2 chesse nelochio 3 chochorere ali dela 4 nelaltrui chonossciérai risstrigniersi imodo pocho 5 seguitãto 6 Esse misurare | 'il diminuire dela piramide per laria chessi chosa *In the original Manuscript the words above the line are clearly marked as forming part of the text In Mons Ravaisson's Transcript however they are mistaken for a heading of the paragraph* 7 imquesta sia Ī torre Ecche 8 sia Ī verga

57 9 *I sua stremi . della torre* (its ends . of the tower) this is the case at *e f*

c · *d* · e vede[10]rai la similitudine della torre apparire minore come vedi in · *r* · *o* · poi l'appressa [11]all' ochio, e vederai la uerga avãzare fori della similitudine · della torre

will see that the image of the tower seems smaller, as at *r o*. Then [again] bring it closer to the eye and you will see the rod project far beyond the image of the tower

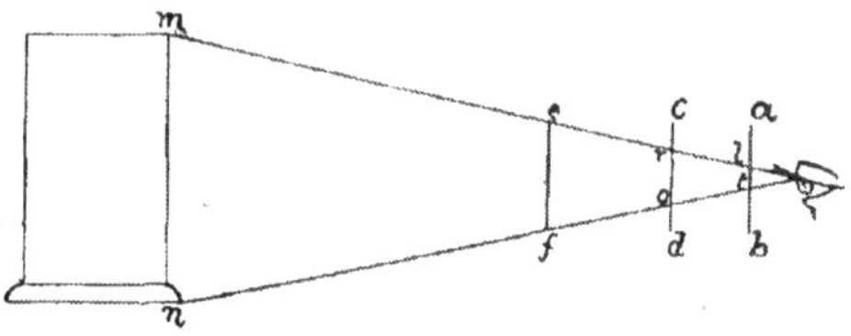

[12]da · *a* · *b* · et da *t* · *b* · e poi conoscerai che poco piv oltre [13]le linie cõcorrono al pũto.

from *a* to *b* and from *t* to *b*, and so you will discern that, a little farther within, the lines must converge in a point.

A. 27 *a*]

58.

Prospettiva.

[2]Subito · che l'aria · fia · alluminata · s'empierà · d'infinite spetie, le qua[3]li son cavsate da vari · corpi e colori, che infra essa sono collocati, [4]delle · quali · spetie · l'ochio · si fa · bersaglio · e calamita.

Perspective.

The instant the atmosphere is illuminated it will be filled with an infinite number of images which are produced by the various bodies and colours assembled in it. And the eye is the target, a loadstone, of these images.

The Production of pyramid of Vision (58—60).

W. 232 *b*]

59.

¶ tutta la superfitie de' corpi oppachi à tutto il simvlacro in tutta l'aria [2]alluminata che lo circunda per qualunche aspetto. ¶

The whole surface of opaque bodies displays its whole image in all the illuminated atmosphere which surrounds them on all sides.

C. A. 136 *b*; 412 *b*]

60.

Che l'aria · attragga · a se · come calamita tutte · le similitudini [2]delle · cose · che la · circũdano nõ che le forme de' corpi, ma ãncora le nature chiaramẽte · si vede · nel sole · il quale · è corpo · caldo e luminoso; [3]tutta · l'aria · che li è per obietto · tutta · per tutto · s'incorpora · di lume · e di calore e tutta [4]ricieve ĩ se la forma · della cagione del calore e splẽdore e in ogni minima parte · fa il simile; [5]la tramõtana dimostra per la calamita · fare · questo · medesimo: e la luna · e altri pianeti [6]sãza diminvtione di se fã il simile; ĩfra le cose terrestri è fatto il simile dal moscato [7]e altri odori.

That the atmosphere attracts to itself, like a loadstone, all the images of the objects that exist in it, and not their forms merely but their nature may be clearly seen by the sun, which is a hot and luminous body. All the atmosphere, which is the all-pervading matter, absorbs light and heat, and reflects in itself the image of the source of that heat and splendour and, in each minutest portion, does the same. The Northpole does the same as the loadstone shows; and the moon and the other planets, without suffering any diminution, do the same. Among terrestrial things musk does the same and other perfumes.

tuttiri . schontrino cholli . . lapressa alochio. 10. dela tore aparire [piv] . . pola. 11. alochio . . dela. 12. chonossciere poche. 13. chõcorano.

58. 2. chellaria . . senpiera. 3. chavsati . . chorpi e chonori . . esa . . chollocati. 4. berzaglio e chalamita.

59. 1. chorpi oppachi "actutto il simvlacro" in tucta. 2. chello circhunda . . asspecto.

60. 1. Che [ciasschuno chorpo . m] laria . siatraga . asse . chome chalamita . . similitudine. 2. chose chella . circhũdano . "ne che le forme de corpi ma ãncora le nature" chiaramẽte . . . chorp . caldo. 3. tuttutta . . sinchorpora . . chalore . . ettutta. 4. chagione . chalore einõni. 5. chalamita . . clluna. 6. diminvitione . . tereste effatto . . moscado.

Ash I. 22b]

61.

Tutti · i corpi · insieme · e ciascuno · per se empie la circũstãte · aria · d'ĩfinite [2]sua · similitudini · le quali son tutte per tutto e tutte nella parte · portãdo cõ lo[3]ro la qualità · del corpo · colore · e figura · della · loro cagione.

All bodies together, and each by itself, give off to the surrounding air an infinite number of images which are all-pervading and each complete, each conveying the nature, colour and form of the body which produces it.

[4]Che i corpi siano per similitudine · tutti per tutta la circũstãte aria · e tutti nella parte per corpo figura [5]e colore chiaramẽte si dimostra per le spetie di molti vari corpi, che si producono [6]a un solo · pũto perforato, doue con ĩtersegate linie portano per piramidi cõtrarie [7]le cose sotto sopra alla prima oscura pariete; [8]la ragione di questo si è—

It can clearly be shown that all bodies are, by their images, all-pervading in the surrounding atmosphere, and each complete in itself as to substance form and colour, this is seen by the images of the various bodies which are reproduced in one single perforation through which they transmit the objects by lines which intersect and cause reversed pyramids, from the objects, so that they are upside down on the dark plane where they are first reflected. The reason of this is —

W. L. 146a]

62.

Ogni pũto è capo d'ĩfinite linie le quali, givgniẽdo a fare basa [2]subito detta basa per le medesime linie tornano alla piramide [3]si per colore come per fazione. [4]immediate che la forma è creata o cõposta, subito [5]di se gienera ĩfiniti ãgoli e linie, le quali linie [6]ispargiẽdosi con ĩtersegazione per l'aria, ne resultano ĩfiniti [7]ãgoli, opposti l'uno all' altro, cõ ciascuno degli opposti angoli, [8]dato li basa, nitrarà triãgolo, e porterà ĩ se forma e proporzione [9]simile all'angolo magiore, e se la basa ẽtra 2 volte ĩ ciascheduna [10]delle 2 linie piramidali, quel medesimo farà piccolo triãgolo.

Every point is the termination of an infinite number of lines, which diverge to form a base, and immediately, from the base the same lines converge to a pyramid [imaging] both the colour and form. No sooner is a form created or compounded than suddenly infinite lines and angles are produced from it; and these lines, distributing themselves and intersecting each other in the air, give rise to an infinite number of angles opposite to each other Given a base, each opposite angle, will form a triangle having a form and proportion equal to the larger angle; and if the base goes twice into each of the 2 lines of the pyramid the smaller triangle will do the same.

61 1. ciaschuno . enpie . circhũstãte 2 similitudine . . pertutta ettutte nela . colo 3 la ["essentia"] qualita . effigura chagione *Between lines* 3 *and* 4 *stands the diagram given on Plate II, No* 1 4 "per similitudine" ettutti nela. 5 ciaramẽte chorpi chessi producano 6 a ĩ solo . . con . piramide 7 prime oscure pariete

62 chapo affare piramida 3 cholore chome *Here follow, in the original MS., ten lines bearing on geometry* 4 ['subito"] imediate chõpossto 5 ãgholi ellinie . quallinie 6 isspargiẽdosi chon ĩterseghazione . risulta 7 ãgholi cociaschuno . oposti angli 8 rinara triãgholo 9 alangholo basẽtra ciasscheduna 10. lini . picholo triãgholo

61. The diagram intended to illustrate the statement (Pl. II No 1) occurs in the original between lines 3 and 4. The three circles must be understood to represent three luminous bodies which transmit their images through perforations in a wall into a dark chamber, according to a law which is more fully explained in [illegible]. So far as concerns the present passage the diagram is only intended to explain that the images of the three bodies may be made to coalesce at any given spot. In the circles are written: *giallo*—yellow, *biãcho*—white, *rosso*—red.

The text breaks off at line 8 The paragraph No. 40 follows here in the original MS.

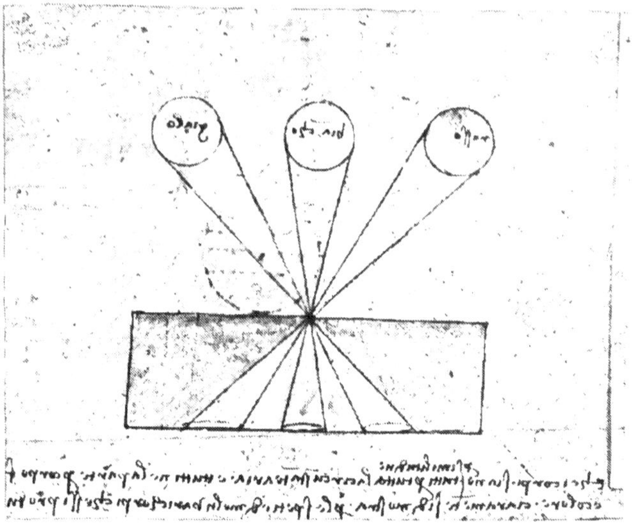

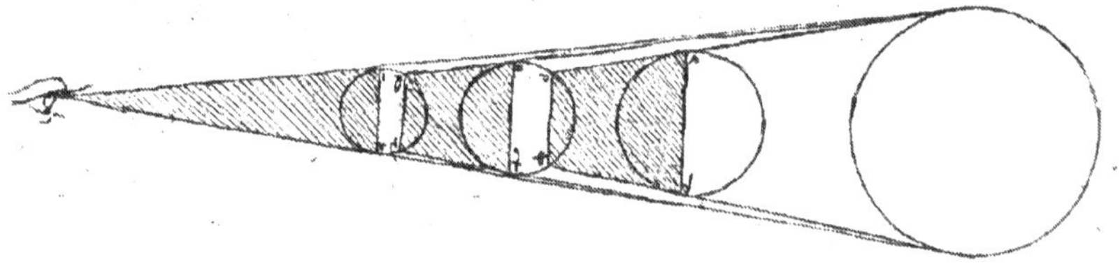

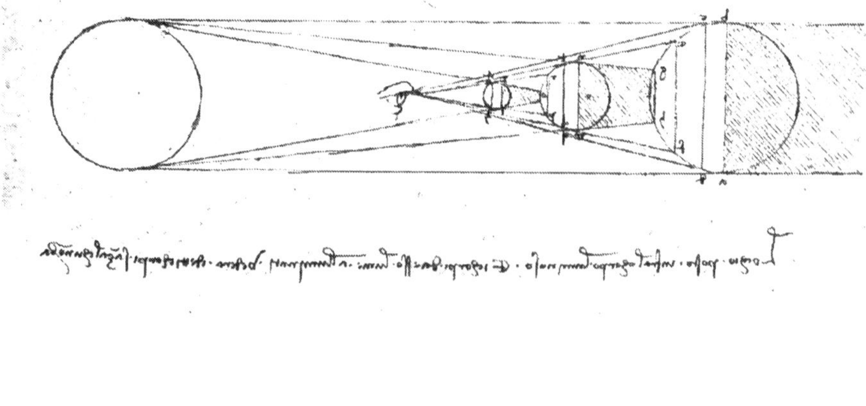

Ash. I. 27 II *a*]

63.

Ogni corpo · ōbroso · empie · la circūstāte · aria [2]d'infinite sue · similitudini · le quali da infinite pira[3]midi infuse per essa rappresentano esso corpo [4]tutto per tutto · e tutto · in ogni parte. [6]Ogni piramide cōposta da lū[7]go concorso · di razzi cōtiene [8]dētro a se · infinite · piramidi [9]e ciascuna · à potētia per tutte e tutte [10]per ciascuna; [11]l'equidistāte · circuito di pirami[12]dal cōcorso darà al suo obietto equa[13]le qualità · d'āgoli; e d'equale grādeza [14]fia ricievuto la cosa dall'obietto. [15]Il corpo · dell' aria · è pieno · d'infinite · piramidi · conposte da radiose e rette linie · le quali [16]si cavsano dai superfitiali · stremi · de' corpi · ombrosi · posti · in essa (aria) · e quāto piv s'alōta[17]nano dalla · loro · cagione · piv si fano acute: e benchè il loro cōcorso sia intersegato e in[18]tessuto, nō dimeno nō si cōfondono l'una con l'altra e cō disgregāte concorso si vāno āplifi[19]cādo e infondēdo per tutta la circūstante aria · e sono infra loro · d'equale potētia e tutte [20]quāto ciascuna · e ciascuna · quāto tutte · e per esse · la similitudine del corpo è portata [21]tutta · per tutto · e tutta nella · parte e ciascuna piramide · per se ricieve in ogni [22]minima · sua parte tutta · la forma della sua cagione.

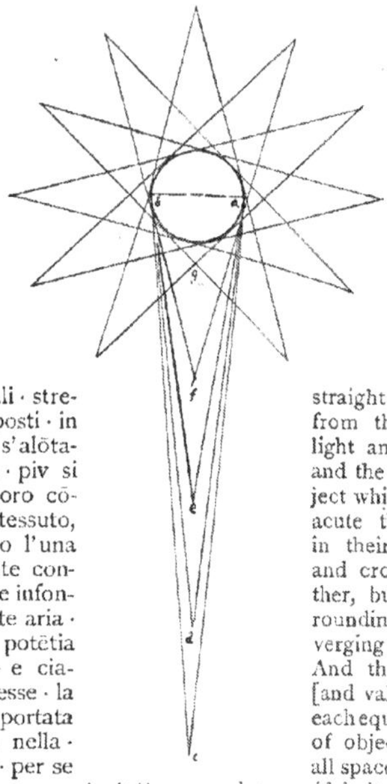

Every body in light and shade fills the surrounding air with infinite images of itself; and these, by infinite pyramids diffused in the air, represent this body throughout space and on every side. Each pyramid that is composed of a long assemblage of rays includes within itself an infinite number of pyramids and each has the same power as all, and all as each. A circle of equidistant pyramids of vision will give to their object angles of equal size; and an eye at each point will see the object of the same size. The body of the atmosphere is full of infinite pyramids composed of radiating straight lines, which are produced from the surface of the bodies in light and shade, existing in the air; and the farther they are from the object which produces them the more acute they become and although in their distribution they intersect and cross they never mingle together, but pass through all the surrounding air, independently converging, spreading, and diffused. And they are all of equal power [and value]; all equal to each, and each equal to all. By these the images of objects are transmitted through all space and in every direction, and each pyramid, in itself, includes, in each minutest part, the whole form of the body causing it.

C. A. 100 *b*; 313 *a*]

64.

Il corpo dell'aria è pieno d'īfinite piramidi radiose [2]cavsate dalla cosa posta · in essa, le quali intersegate [3]e intessute sanza occupatione · l'una dell'altra cō disgre[4]gante concorso s'infondono per tutta la circū[5]stāte aria, e sono d'equale potētia e tutte pos-

The body of the atmosphere is full of infinite radiating pyramids produced by the objects existing in it. These intersect and cross each other with independent convergence without interfering with each other and pass through all the surrounding atmosphere; and

63. 1. chorpo . . circhūstāte. 2. dinfine . . similitudine. 3. midi . . essa [aria] raprētano . . chorpo. 4. ettutto. 5. [Ogni radiosa piramide di lūgo]. 6. chōposta. 7. chonchorso . . chontiene. 8. asse . . pyramide. 9. ettutte. 11. lecquidistāte . circhuito. 12. chōchorso. *Lines 1—5 are written on the left side and lines 6—14 on the right side of the diagram. Below it is the rest of the text:* 15. chorpo . . piramide chonposte. 16. chavsano . . chorpi onbrosi poste . . [aria]. ecquāto. 17. chagione . . achute . . chōchorsia. 18. tesuto . . luna per laltra e chō . . chonchorso. 19. circhūstante . . essono . . ettutte. 20. ecciascuna. 21. e portata tutto . . ettutta. 22. chagione.

64. 1. piramide. 2. chavsate dala . . esa. 3. ochupatione . . chō. 4. chonchorso sinfondano [portādo] pertutta [lari]. 5. ettutte

sono quãto ciascuna, [6]e ciascuna quãto tutte e per esse la similitudine del corpo è porta[7]ta tutta per tutto e tutta ĩ nella parte, e ciascuna per se ricieve [8]in ogni minima parte tutta la sua cagione

are of equal force and value—all being equal to each, each to all And by means of these, images of the body are transmitted everywhere and on all sides, and each receives in itself every minutest portion of the object that produces it

C A 136a 412a]

65

Prospettiva

Proof by experiment (65—66)

[2]L'aria · è piena d'ĩfinite similitudini · delle cose le quali ĩfra quella sono distribuite [3]e tutte · si rapresẽtano in tutte e tutte in vna e tutte jn ciascuna õde accade che se sarãno [4]2 specchi volti ĩ modo che per linia retta si guardino l'uno l'altro jl primo si specchierà [5]nel secondo e 'l secondo nel primo il primo · che si specchia nel secondo porta cõ seco la similitudine di se cõ tutte le [6]similitudini che dentro vi si rapresẽtano ĩfra le quali è la spetie del secondo specchio e da simi[7]litudine ĩ similitudine se ne vanno in ĩfinito ĩ modo che ciascuno specchio à dẽtro in se li [8]specchi l'uno minore che l'altro e dentro l'uno all'altro [9]Onde per questo esemplo chiaramẽte · si pruova · ciascuna · cosa mãdare la similitudine [10]ĩ tutti quelli · lochi li quali possono vedere · detta cosa e cosi de cõuerso · detta · cosa essere capace [11]di pigliare in se tutte le similitudini delle cose che dinanzi se le rappresentano [12]Adũque l'ochio mãda ĩfra l'aria la sua · similitudine a tutti li obietti che li sono opposti e ĩ se [13]li ricieve cioè ĩ sulla sua superfi'ie dõde il sẽso comvne le piglia e le cõsidera e quelli [14]che piaciono le mãda alla memoria [15]Onde io givdico che la virtù spirituale delle spetie delli ochi si faccino ĩcõtro all'obietto come [16]le spetie dell'obietto all'ochio [17]Che le spetie di tutte le cose · sieno seminate ĩfra l'aria · lo esemplo si veda ĩ molti specchi [18]ĩn circolo e ĩfinite volte specchierãno l'uno l'altro e givto l'uno nell'altro risalta · dirieto [19]alla sua cagione e indi diminvẽdo risalta vn'altra volta all'obietto e poi ritorna e cosi fa ĩfinite [20]volte [21]Se metti un lume di notte ĩfra 2 specchi piani i quali abbino d'intervallo un braccio vedrai ĩ cias-

Perspective

The air is filled with endless images of the objects distributed in it, and all are represented in all, and all in one, and all in each, whence it happens that if two mirrors are placed in such a manner as to face each other exactly, the first will be reflected in the second and the second in the first The first being reflected in the second takes to it the image of itself with all the images represented in it, among which is the image of the second mirror, and so, image within image, they go on to infinity in such a manner as that each mirror has within it a mirror, each smaller than the last and one inside the other Thus, by this example, it is clearly proved that every object sends its image to every spot whence the object itself can be seen, and the converse· That the same object may receive in itself all the images of the objects that are in front of it Hence the eye transmits through the atmosphere its own image to all the objects that are in front of it and receives them into itself, that is to say on its surface, whence they are taken in by the common sense, which considers them and if they are pleasing commits them to the memory Whence I am of opinion That the invisible images in the eyes are produced towards the object, as the image of the object to the eye That the images of the objects must be disseminated through the air An instance may be seen in several mirrors placed in a circle, which will reflect each other endlessly When one has reached the other it is returned to the object that produced it, and thence—being diminished—it is returned again to the object and then comes back once more, and this happens endlessly If you put a light between two flat mirrors with a distance of 1 braccio between them you will see in each

possano quãte 7 to tutto per tutta ettutti inella

65 2 similitudine chose sono strebuite 3 ettutte si in tutte "ettutte in vna" ettutte jn ciasschuna acchade 4 recta sisghuardino spechier \\\ 5 nel 2° el 2° ne pr̊ nel 2° porta chõsecho chõ tutte \\\ 6 quale del 2° spechio e chõ si \\\ 7 vano ciaschuno dẽtro ĩs \\\\ 9 esenplo 10 possano chosa e chosi de chõuerso detta chosa chapa \\\\ 11 similitudine chose sili 12 attutti opositi e ĩ s \\\ 13 chomvne chõsidera e c \\\\\\ piaciano 15 chella ĩchõtro all obietto ch \\\ 17 Chelle chose llaria molti spe \\\\\ 18 circholo givta lũnel risalta e dirieto 19 chagione e dili diminvẽdo alobietto e po ritorna e chosi fa ĩf \\\\\\\\\\ 21 Si metti ĩ lume dintervallo ĩ br

cuno di quelli spec[22]chi ĩfiniti lumi · l'uno · minore che l'altro; [23]se di notte metterai vn lume · ǰfra le parieti d'una camera · tutte le parti d'essa · pariete rimarãno tĩte di [24]similitudini · d'esso lume · e tutte · quelle che saraño viste · dal lume, e 'l lume vederà similemẽte, [25]cioè quando ĩfra loro nõ fia · alcuna oppositione · che · rõpa · il cõcorso · delle spetie. [26]Questo medesimo · esẽplo · magiormẽte · appare in nel cõcorso de razzi solari, [27]i quali tutti per tutti, e ciascuno per se porta al suo obietto · la similitudine [28]della · cagione; [29]Che ciascũ · corpo · per se · solo empie tutta la cõtraposta · aria · delle · sue similitudini: e che · questa · medesima · aria fia capace. [30]ĩ quel medesimo · tẽpo di ricievere · ĩ se · le spetie d'ĩnfiniti · altri · corpi · che ĩfra quella fussino, chiaramente [31]si dimostra · per questi · esẽpli; E ciascuno · corpo · appare · tutto · per tutta la detta aria · e tutto in ogni minima [32]parte di quella; tutti · per tutta · e tutti in onj minima parte, [33]ciascuno per tutta · e tutti nella parte.

of them an infinite number of lights, one smaller than another, to the last. If at night you put a light between the walls of a room, all the parts of that wall will be tinted with the image of that light. And they will receive the light and the light will fall on them, mutually, that is to say, when there is no obstacle to interrupt the transmission of the images. This same example is seen in a greater degree in the distribution of the solar rays which all together, and each by itself, convey to the object the image of the body which causes it. That each body by itself alone fills with its images the atmosphere around it, and that the same air is able, at the same time, to receive the images of the endless other objects which are in it, this is clearly proved by these examples. And every object is everywhere visible in the whole of the atmosphere, and the whole in every smallest part of it; and all the objects in the whole, and all in each smallest part; each in all and all in every part.

W. L. 145 B. a]

66.

Sono le spetie de corpi tutte infuse per l'aria [2]che le vede e tutte in ogni parte di quella; provasi [3]siē *a c e* obbietti, le spetie de quali penetrano in loco oscuro [4]per li spiraculi *n p* e s'inpremono nella pariete *f i* cõtraposta a es[5]si spiracoli; le quali inpressioni sarā fatte in tāti lochi d'essa parie[6]te quāto sarà il numero delli predetti spiracoli.

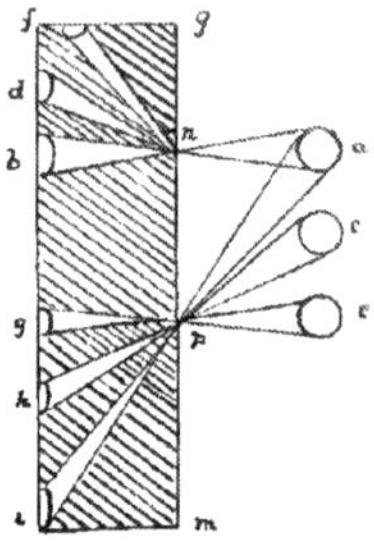

The images of objects are all diffused through the atmosphere which receives them; and all on every side in it. To prove this, let *a c e* be objects of which the images are admitted to a dark chamber by the small holes *n p* and thrown upon the plane *f i* opposite to these holes. As many images will be produced in the chamber on the plane as the number of the said holes.

C. A. 176 b; 531 b]

67.

Tutti ǰ corpi · ànno · infuse e miste tutte · loro · spetie · e similitudini [2]in tutta la quantità · dell'aria · a · se · contraposta; [3]La spetie di ciascun · punto · delle · corporee · superfitie · è in ciascũ punto [4]dell'aria; [5]Tutte · le spetie de' corpi · sono · in ciascũ

General conclusions.

All objects project their whole image and likeness, diffused and mingled in the whole of the atmosphere, opposite to themselves. The image of every point of the bodily surface, exists in every part of the atmosphere. All the images of the objects are

ciaschuno di |||||||||. 22. chelaltro elluna minore chellaltro. 23. se "di notte" . . ĩfralle pariete duna tutte le parti d'esse. 24. ettucte . . . chessarano . . da lume. 25. quā infralloro . . opositione . . chõchorso. 26. inel chõchorso . . "solari" [del sole]. 27. per tutti [ettu] o ciasciuno . . "li obietti ettala caione in oni minima parte dellobietto". 28. chagione. 29. ciassū. chorpo . . ēpia "tutta" la chõtraposta . . . [spetie] "similitudine" . . fia c||||||||||. 30. tēpo [di] . . chorpi . . . fussino chiar|||||||||||. 31. esēpli E ciascuno . . apare . . aria ettutto ĩonĩm||||||||||. 33. ettutti.

66. 1. lesspetie . . . chorpi [infuse per laria] tutte [infus] fure per laria. 2. chelle vede ettutte. 3. siē [*a b c*] *a c e* obbietti lesspetie . . illocho osscuro. 4. spirachuli . . *essinpremenano* . . contrapossta. 5. spiracholi. 6. quāto sarāno il . . spiracholi.

67. 1. chorpi . . infuso ēmisto "tutte", . e similitudine. 2. asse choutraposta. 3. la spetie di *is written on the margin.* La

pũto d'essa aria, [6]Tutta e la parte della similitudine dell'aria è in ciascuno pũto delle [7]superfitie · delli antiposti corpi, [8]Adunque la parte e 'l tutto delle spetie de' corpi appare in tutta [9]e nella parte della superfitie d'essi corpi [10]Onde chiaramente possiamo dire la similitudine di ciascũ corpo essere [11]tutto e in parte in ciascuna parte e nel tutto scanbievolmẽte [12]delli oppositi corpi, Come si uede nelli spechi l'uno all altro opposti

in every part of the atmosphere The whole, and each part of the image of the atmosphere is [reflected] in each point of the surface of the bodies presented to it Therefore both the part and the whole of the images of the objects exist, both in the whole and in the parts of the surface of these visible bodies. Whence we may evidently say that the image of each object exists, as a whole and in every part, in each part and in the whole interchangeably in every existing body As is seen in two mirrors placed opposite to each other.

Ash I 32*b*]

68

That the contrary is impossible

Ipossibile è che l'ochio mãdi fori di se per li razzi visuali · la uirtù visiua, [2]perchè nello suo aprire quella prima parte che desse prĩncipio all'uscita, [3]e auessi d'andare all'obietto nõ lo potrebbe fare sãza tẽpo, essẽdo cosi nõ [4]potrebbe caminare in ṽ mese all'altezza del sole, quãdo l'ochio lo uolesse [5]vedere e se la vi agivgniesse sarebbe neciessario ch'ella [6]fusse cõtinuata per tutta la uia ch'è dall' ochio al sole, e ch'e[7]lla sẽpre alargasse in modo che tra 'l sole e l'ochio cõponessino la basa [8]e la pũta d'una piramide essẽdo questo e'nõ basterebbe se l'ochio fusse [9]per un milione di mõdi che tutto nõ si cõsumasse ĩ detta virtù e se pure que[10]sta virtù avesse a caminare ĩfra l'aria come fa l'odore, i venti no [11]la torciereb-

It is impossible that the eye should project from itself, by visual rays, the visual virtue, since, as soon as it opens, that front portion [of the eye] which would give rise to this emanation would have to go forth to the object and this it could not do without time And this being so, it could not travel so high as the sun in a month's time when the eye wanted to see it And if it could reach the sun it would necessarily follow that it should perpetually remain in a continuous line from the eye to the sun and should always diverge in such a way as to form between the sun and the eye the base and the apex of a pyramid This being the case, if the eye consisted of a million worlds, it would not prevent its being consumed in the projection of its virtue, and if this virtue would have to travel through the air as perfumes do, the winds

Ciasc in he in 5 lesspetie dechorpi 6 ella he in 7 chorpi 8. chorpi apare 9 chorpi appare 10 dire | [11]la similitudine di ciaschũ chorpo 11 ciasscuna 12 opositi chorpi oppossto

68 1 chellochio razi 2 dessi prĩcipo all usita 3 auessiandare nollo potrebe 4 potrebe chaminare altera uolessi 5 essella [vi chaminasse] viagivgniessi sarebe chela 6 [sẽpre fa] fussi chotinuata tuta 7 lo alargassi imodo ellochio chõpcnessino 8 ella basterebe sellochio fussi 9 per ĩ milione chettutto cõnsumassi esse pure 10 avessi chome ivẽnto (?) 11 porterebbero no chõ 12 presteza vederemo ĩ distantia 13 dunobr alchuno accidente

68 The view here refuted by Leonardo was maintained among others by Bramantino, Leonardo's Milanese contemporary LOMAZZO writes as follows in his *Trattato dell' Arte della pittura* &c (*Milano* 1584 *Libr V cp XXI) Sovviemmi di aver gia letto in certi scritti alcune cose di Bramantino milanese, celebratissimo pittore, attenente alla prospettiva, le quali ho voluto riferire, e quasi intessere in questo luogo, affinchè sappiamo qual fosse l'opinione di cosi chiaro e famoso pittore intorno alla prospettiva Scrive Bramantino che la prospettiva è una cosa che contrafà il naturale, e che cio si fa in tre modi*

Circa il primo modo che si fa con ragione, per essere la cosa in poche parole conclusa da Bramantino in maniera che giudico non potersi dir meglio, contenendovi si tutta l'arte del principio al fine, io riferirò per appunto le proprie parole sue (cp XXII Prima prospettiva di Bramantino) La prima prospettiva fa le cose di punto, e l'altra non mai, e la terza più appresso Adunque la prima si dimanda prospettiva, cioè ragione, la quale fa l'effetto dell' occhio, facendo crescere e calare secondo gli effetti degli occhi Questo crescere e calare non procede della cosa propria, che in se per esser lontana, ovvero vicina, per quello effetto non può crescere e sminuire, ma procede dagli effetti degli occhi, i quali sono piccioli, e perciò volendo vedere tanto gran cosa, bisogna che mandino fuora la virtu visiva, *la quale si dilata in tanta larghezza, che piglia tutto quello che vuol vedere, ed* arrivando a quella cosa la vede dove è *e da lei agli occhi per quello circuito fino all' occhio, e tutto quello termine è pieno di quella cosa*

It is worthy of note that Leonardo had made his memorandum refuting this view at Milan in 1492 bono e porterebbero in altro loco; e noi vediamo cō quel[12]la medesima prestezza il corpo del sole · che noi vediamo una distantia [13]d'uno braccio e nō si mvta per sofiare de' uēti, nè per alcuno altro accidēte.

would bent it and carry it into another place. But we do [in fact] see the mass of the sun with the same rapidity as [an object] at the distance of a braccio, and the power of sight is not disturbed by the blowing of the winds nor by any other accident.

A. 9 *b*]

69.

Si come · la pietra · gittata · nell'acqua · si fa · ciētro · e cavsa · di uari circuli, [2]e 'l suono · fatto in nell' aria circularmente si spargie, [3]cosi ogni corpo posto · infra l'aria · luminosa circularmēte [4]spargie · e ēpie le circūstanti · parti · d'infinite sue similitudini · e appare tutto [5]per tutto · e tutto in ogni [minima] parte; [6]Questo si prova · per · isperiētia imperochè se serrerai una finestra volta a ponēte e farai uno buso . .

A parallel case.

Just as a stone flung into the water becomes the centre and cause of many circles, and as sound diffuses itself in circles in the air: so any object, placed in the luminous atmosphere, diffuses itself in circles, and fills the surrounding air with infinite images of itself. And is repeated, the whole every-where, and the whole in every smallest part. This can be proved by experiment, since if you shut a window that faces west and make a hole [6] · ·

C. A. 135 *b*; 404 *b*]

70.

Se la cosa cōtra · posta all' ochio · māda a quello di se la similitudine: ācora · l'ochio · māda la sua similitudine [2]alla cosa. E della cosa · per le partite · similitudini · nō si strema · parte alcuna d'alcuna ragione nè all'occhio nè alla cosa. [3]Adūque · possiamo · piv tosto credere · essere · natura e potētia di questa · aria · luminosa [4]che attrae e piglia · ī se · le spetie delle · cose che dētro vi sono che natura delle cose · in mādare · le spetie · ĭfra essa aria; [5]Se la cosa · cōtra · posta · all'ochio mādasse a quello di se · la similitudine: quel medesimo · avrebbe · a fare [6]l'ochio · alla cosa, onde · cōuerebbe che queste · spetie · fussino · virtù · spirituali: [7]essēdo · cosi · sarebbe [7]neciessario · che ciascuna cosa · presto · venisse meno, ĵperochè ciascuno · corpo · appare per similitudine [8]nella cōtraposta · aria; cioè tutto il corpo ī tutta · l'aria; e tutto nella parte, tutti i corpi ī tutta l'aria, [9]e tutti nella parte, parlādo di quell'aria ch'è capace · di ricieuere ī se le rette e radiose linie [10]delle spetie · mādate dalli

The function of the eye as explained by the camera obscura (70. 71).

If the object in front of the eye sends its image to the eye, the eye, on the other hand, sends its image to the object, and no portion whatever of the object is lost in the images it throws off, for any reason either in the eye or the object. Therefore we may rather believe it to be the nature and potency of our luminous atmosphere which absorbs the images of the objects existing in it, than the nature of the objects, to send their images through the air. If the object opposite to the eye were to send its image to the eye, the eye would have to do the same to the object, whence it might seem that these images were an emanation. But, if so, it would be necessary [to admit] that every object became rapidly smaller; because each object appears by its images in the surrounding atmosphere. That is: the whole object in the whole atmosphere, and in each part; and all the objects in the whole atmosphere and all of them in each part; speaking of that atmosphere which is able

69. 1. Si chome . . nellacqua . . chavsa . . circhuli. 2. el sono. fatto inellaria . . spargie [la sua voce Cosi]. 3. Cosi i [chorpi sparganoj ogni . . . 4. circhūstanti . . similitudine . capare 5. ettutto in ogni [minima] parte. 6. per . risperiētia in perochesse sererai ī finestra . effarai ī buso.

70. 1. māda | "aquello" di. 2. se . . cossa "e" per . . alchuna dalchuna rasione nea locho ne. 3. [quel medesimo fa locchio] Adūque posiamo . . natura "e potētia" di. 4. che | "altraee" piglia . . dele cose | "che dētro vi sono" che natura . . chose imādere . . ĭfra [l] "essa" aria. 5. Sella chosa chōtra . . . mādassi acquello . . . arebe . affare. 6. choso | ōnde chonuerebe . . chosi sarebe. 7. classchuna chosa . . venisi . . chorpo. 8. [inōni . parte della] "nella" chōtraposta . . tutto "il corpo" ī

69. Compare LIBRI, *Histoire des sciences mathématiques en Italie*. Tome III, p. 43.

6. Here the text breaks off.

obietti; Onde · per questo pare · neciessario · cõfessare · essere · natura di questa [11]aria che · si trova · infra · li obbietti · la quale · tiri come · calamita in se le similitudini delle cose [12]ĩfra quella · poste.

to contain in itself the straight and radiating lines of the images projected by the objects. From this it seems necessary to admit that it is in the nature of the atmosphere, which subsists between the objects, and which attracts the images of things to itself like a loadstone, being placed between them.

¶ PRUOVA · COME TUTTE LE COSE POSTE IN UN SITO · SONO TUTTE PER TUTTO [14]E TUTTE NELLA PARTE ¶

[15]Dico che, se vna faccia d'uno edifitio · o altra piazza · o cãpagnia che sia · illuminata dal sole [16]avrà al suo opposito vn'abitatione, e ĩ quella faccia che nõ uede il sole sia fatto un piccolo spiracolo [17]rotõdo: che tutte le alluminate cose mãderãno la loro · similitudine · per detto spiraculo e apparirãno [18]dentro all' abitatione · nella cõtraria faccia, la quale vuol essere biãca · e saranno li appunto e sotto sopra; [19]e se per molti lochi di detta · faccia faciessi · simili · buchi, simile effetto sarebbe ĩ ciascuno, Adũque le spetie [20]delle alluminate · cose · sono · tutte per tutta detta · faccia · e tutte in ogni minima parte di quella [21]la ragiõ si è: noi sappiamo · chiaro · che quello buco debe rẽdere alquãto di lume ĩ detta abitatione, e lume che [22]lui mezzano · rẽde è cavsato da vno · o da molti corpi luminosi se detti corpi fieno di vari colori e varie stãpe · di uari [23]colori e stãpe saranno i razzi delle spetie e di uari colori e stãpe fieno · le rappresẽtationi in nel mvro

PROVE HOW ALL OBJECTS, PLACED IN ONE POSITION, ARE ALL EVERYWHERE AND ALL IN EACH PART.

I say that if the front of a building—or any open piazza or field—which is illuminated by the sun has a dwelling opposite to it, and if, in the front which does not face the sun, you make a small round hole, all the illuminated objects will project their images through that hole and be visible inside the dwelling on the opposite wall which may be made white; and there, in fact, they will be upside down, and if you make similar openings in several places in the same wall you will have the same result from each. Hence the images of the illuminated objects are all everywhere on this wall and all in each minutest part of it The reason, as we clearly know, is that this hole must admit some light to the said dwelling, and the light admitted by it is derived from one or many luminous bodies. If these bodies are of various colours and shapes the rays forming the images are of various colours and shapes, and so will the representations be on the wall.

D 8 a]

71.

COME S'INTERSEGANO LE SPETIE DELLI OBBIETTI [2]RICEVUTI DALL OCHIO DENTRO AL OMORE ALBUGINO

[3]La speriẽtia che mostra come li obbietti mandino [4]le loro spetie over si-

HOW THE IMAGES OF OBJECTS RECEIVED BY THE EYE INTERSECT WITHIN THE CRYSTALLINE HUMOUR OF THE EYE.

An experiment, showing how objects transmit their images or pictures, inter-

tutta ettutto . tuttutti 9 ettutti nella pare . chapace . "ĩ se" le rette [lime de radira] e radiose. 10. pare [essere] . . chõfessare 11 aria [la quale] "che". si chome chalamita . similitudine 12 ĩ fracquella 13 chome tutti le chose poste nvn sito 14 ettutte. 15 dicho chesse . facia piatao chãpagnia chessia 16. ara al suo oposito . . fatto ĩ picholo spiracholo 17 retõdo . . chose . . siraculo 18. chõtraria . . viol esere biãcha e sarano lapunto essotto 19. esse per . . busi simile sarebe ĩ ciaschuno 20. chose facia ettutte inognimminima 21 sapiano . quello buso 22 merano . . chavsata da [molti] corpi chorpi . cholori , "e varie stãpe" di uari 23 cholori | "e stãpe" sarano irazi . . cholori | "e stãpe" fieno le rapresentatione inel mvro [osscuro]

70. 15—23. This section has already been published in the "*Saggio delle Opere di Leonardo da Vinci.*" Milan 1872, pp. 13, 14. G GOVI observes upon it, that Leonardo is not to be regarded as the inventor of the Camera obscura, but that he was the first to explain by it the structure of the eye An account of the Camera obscura first occurs in CESARE CESARINI'S Italian version of Vitruvius, pub 1523, four years names Benedettino Don Papnutio as the inventor of the Camera obscura. In his explanation of the function of the eye by a comparison with the Camera obscura Leonardo was the precursor of G. CARDANO, Professor of Medicine at Bologna (died 1576) and it appears highly probable that this is, in fact, the very discovery which Leonardo ascribes to himself in section 21 without giving any further

militudini intersegate dentro all' o[5]chio nello umore albugino si dimostra quando [6]per alcuno piccolo spiraculo rotōdo penetrāno le [7]spetie delli obbietti alluminati in abitatione for[8]temente oscura; allora tu riceverai tale spetie in v[9]na carta bianca posta dentro a tale a[10]bitatione alquāto vicina a esso spiraculo e ve[11]drai tutti li predetti obbietti in essa carta colle lor [12]propie figure e colori, ma sarā minori e fieno sot[13]to sopra per causa della detta intersegatione li qua[14]li simulacri se nascierāno di loco alluminato dal [15]sole parā propio dipīti in essa carta, la qual' uole [16]essere sottilissima e veduta da riverscio, e lo spira[17]colo detto sia fatto in piastra sottilissima di ferro; [18]*a b c d e* sieno li detti obietti alluminati dal sole, *o r* [19]sia la faccia della abitatione oscura, nella quale è lo spi[20]racolo detto in *n m*, *s t* sia la detta carta dove si ta[21]gliano li razzi delle spetie d'essi obietti sotto sopra perchè essē[22]do li lor razzi diritti, *a* destro si fa sinistro in *k* e lo *e* si[23]nistro si fa destro in ·*f*·, e cosi fa dentro alla popilla.

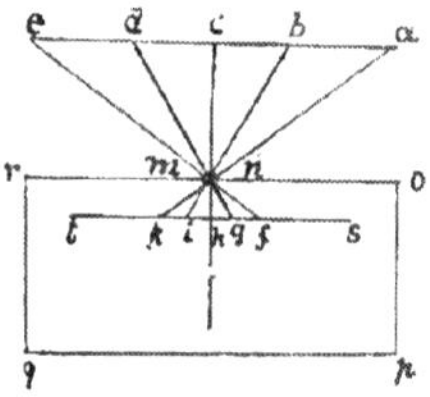

secting within the eye in the crystalline humour, is seen when by some small round hole penetrate the images of illuminated objects into a very dark chamber. Then, receive these images on a white paper placed within this dark room and rather near to the hole and you will see all the objects on the paper in their proper forms and colours, but much smaller; and they will be upside down by reason of that very intersection. These images being transmitted from a place illuminated by the sun will seem actually painted on this paper which must be extremely thin and looked at from behind. And let the little perforation be made in a very thin plate of iron. Let *a b c d e* be the object illuminated by the sun and *o r* the front of the dark chamber in which is the said hole at *n m*. Let *s t* be the sheet of paper intercepting the rays of the images of these objects upside down, because the rays being straight, *a* on the right hand becomes *k* on the left, and *e* on the left becomes *f* on the right; and the same takes place inside the pupil.

C. A. 201*b*; 598*b*]

72.

Il lume nel ufitio della prospettiva [2]non à alcuna differēza coll'ochio.

In the practice of perspective the same rules apply to light and to the eye. The practice of perspective (72. 73).

W. L. 145; D.*b*]

73.

Ciò che vede la lucie dell' ochio [2]è veduto da essa lucie, [3]e ciò che vede la lucie è [4]veduto dalla sua popilla.

The object which is opposite to the pupil of the eye is seen by that pupil and that which is opposite to the eye is seen by the pupil.

Br. M. 221*b*]

74.

Il concorso · delle linie create dalle spetie delli obbietti antiposti all' ochio nō concorro[2]no in punte dentro a esso ochio per linie rette.

The lines sent forth by the image of an object to the eye do not reach the point within the eye in straight lines. Refraction of the rays falling upon the eye (74. 75).

71. 3. Lassperientia . . mosstra. 5. omore. 6. picholo . . retōdo peneterāno. 8. te osscura alora . . spetie nv. 9. biancha [depola] posta . . attale. 10. spirachulo. 12. . effieno so. 13. chausa . . interseghatione li q"a". 14. nasscierāno dillocho. 16. ello spira. 17. cholo . . inpiasstra. 19. fachia . . osscura . . nel . . ello spi. 20. racol. 21. razi. 22. razi . . desstro . . sinisstro . , hello *e*. 23. desstro.

72. 1. ufio della. 2. differēza chol.

73. 3. eccio . . lucie he.

74. linie crete . . antiposssti . . concorra.

71. This chapter is already known through a translation into French by VENTURI. Compare his '*Essai sur les ouvrages physico-mathématiques de L. da Vinci avec des fragments tirés de ses Manuscrits, apportés de l'Italie. Lu à la première classe de l'Institut national des Sciences et Arts.*' *Paris, An V* (1797).

Br. M. 220b]

75.

Se 'l giuditio dell'ochio è dentro di lui, le linie rette delle spetie [2] si rompono · insulla superfitie sua perchè uanno dal raro al denso; [3] se tu sia sotto l'aqua e riguardi la cosa infrall'aria · tu vedrai essa cosa [4] fori del suo sito, e cosi fa la cosa infrall'acqua veduta dall'aria.

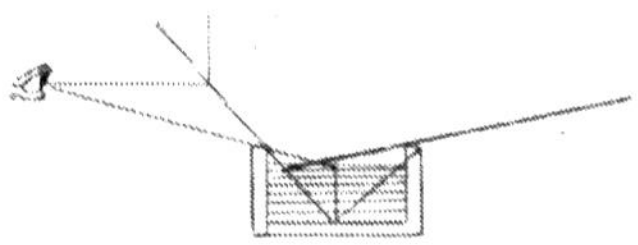

If the judgment of the eye is situated within it, the straight lines of the images are refracted on its surface because they pass through the rarer to the denser medium. If, when you are under water, you look at objects in the air you will see them out of their true place; and the same with objects under water seen from the air.

Br. M. 171b]

76.

The inversion of the images.

Tutte le similitudini delle cose che passano per finestra [2] dall' aria libera all' aria costretta da pariete, sono viste [3] i cōtrario sito, e quella cosa che nella libera aria [4] si moverà da oriēte a occidēte apparirà, per ōbra nelle parie[5]te · alluminate dalla cōstretta aria di cōtrario movimēto.

All the images of objects which pass through a window [glass pane] from the free outer air to the air confined within walls, are seen on the opposite side; and an object which moves in the outer air from east to west will seem in its shadow, on the wall which is lighted by this confined air, to have an opposite motion.

W. L. 145, B.b]

77.

PRINCIPIO COME LE SPETIE DE' CORPI S'INTER[2]SEGANO NELLI LABRI DELLI SPIRACULI DA LOR PENETRATI.

The intersection of the rays (76—82).

[3] Che diferētia è dalla penetra[4]tione delle spetie che passano [5] in spiraculi stretti a quelle [6] che passā per larghi spiracoli [7] o da quelle che passan' ne' la[8]ti de corpi onbrosi? [9] Movansi le spetie delli obbietti inmobili, movendosi li labri di quello [10] spiracolo donde li razzi delle spetie penetrano [11] e questo accade per la 9ª che dicie ¶le spetie di qualunche cor[12]po son tutte per tutto e tutte in ogni parte del sito a lor circūstāte¶ [13] seguita che movēdo vn delli labri dello spiracolo, donde tali spetie pe[14]netrano in loco oscuro, esso lascia li razzi delle spetie che li era[15]no in cōtatto e si congiūgono con altri razzi d'esse spetie che li erā [16] remoti ecc.

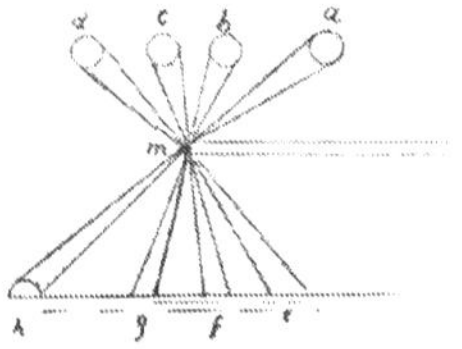

THE PRINCIPLE ON WHICH THE IMAGES OF BODIES PASS IN BETWEEN THE MARGINS OF THE OPENINGS BY WHICH THEY ENTER.

What difference is there in the way in which images pass through narrow openings and through large openings, or in those which pass by the sides of shaded bodies? By moving the edges of the opening through which the images are admitted, the images of immovable objects are made to move. And this happens, as is shown in the 9th which demonstrates[11]: the images of any object are all everywhere, and all in each part of the surrounding air. It follows that if one of the edges of the hole by which the images are admitted to a dark chamber is moved it cuts off those rays of the image that were in contact with it and gets nearer to other rays which previously were remote from it &c.

75. 1. adi. 2. ronpano. 3. settu . . lac q. . esa cosa. 4. infrallacq . . dellaria.
76. 1. simılitudine. 2. dalaria. 3. chososa . . nellalbra. 4. ocidēte aparira "per ōbra" nelle.
77. 1. chome . . chorpi. 2. seghano . . spirachuli dallor. 3. he dalla. 5. isspirachuli . . acquelle. 6. cheppassā . . spricacholi. 8. chorpi. 9. lesspetie . . movenli labri. 10. spircholo donte . razi. 11. ecquesto achade . . cheddicie lesspetie. 12. son tucte . . etturte in . . allor circūsstāte. 13. spiracholo donte. 14. locho osscchuro e lasscia . razi . chelli. 15. chōtacto essi

77. 2. In the first of the three diagrams Leonardo had drawn only one of the two margins, at *m*.

11. *per la 9ª che dicie.* When Leonardo refers thus t[illegible] indicate marginal diagrams; this can in some instances be distinctly proved. The ninth sketch on the page W. L. 145 b corresponds to the middle sketch of the three reproduced.

DEL MOTO DEL LABRO DESTRO O SINISTRO, O SUPERIORE, [18]O INFERIORE.

[19] Se moverai il lato destro dello spiracolo, allora si moverà la inpres[20]sione sinistra dell'obbietto destro, che penetrava per esso spiracolo, [21]e 'l simile farà tutti li altri lati di tale spiracolo e questo si pro[22]va coll'aiuto

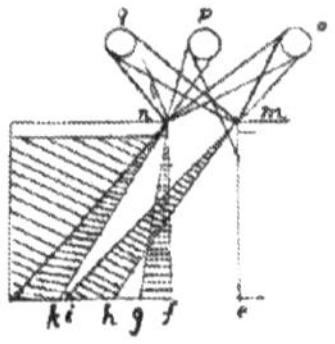

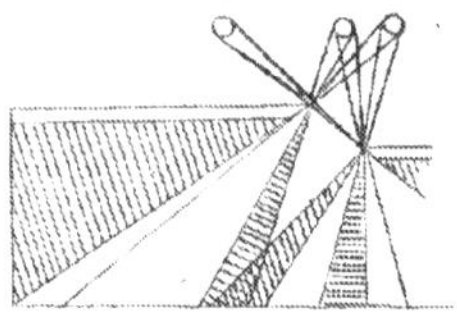

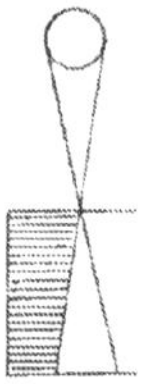

della seconda di questo che dicie ¶tutti li razzi che portā le spe[23]tie de corpi per l'aria son retti lini¶; adunque, avendo a passare le spe[24]tie delli corpi massimi per li minimi spiraculi e dopo tale spiraco[25]lo ricōporsi alla massima dilatatione, egli è neciessario gienerar[26]si la intersegatione.

OF THE MOVEMENT OF THE EDGE AT THE RIGHT OR LEFT, OR THE UPPER, OR LOWER EDGE.

If you move the right side of the opening the image on the left will move [being that] of the object which entered on the right side of the opening; and the same result will happen with all the other sides of the opening. This can be proved by the 2nd of this which shows: all the rays which convey the images of objects through the air are straight lines. Hence, if the images of very large bodies have to pass through very small holes, and beyond these holes recover their large size, the lines must necessarily intersect.

W. L. 145; B. a] **78.**

Neciessità à proveduto che tutte le spetie de corpi antiposti all'och[2]io s'interseghino in due lochi, delle quali l'una intersegatio[3]ne si gienera dentro alla popilla l'altra dentro alla spera cris[4]tallina, il che se così nō si faciesse, l'ochio nō potrebbe vedere [5]si grā numero di cose quāto esso vede; [6]pruovasi perchè tutte le linie che s'interseg[a]no gienerā tale in[7]tersegatione in punto, cōciosiachè de corpi nō ci si dimostra se[8]nō le loro superfitie, li termini delle quali sō linie per la cō[9]versa della difinitiō delle superfitie, e ogni minima parte della linia [10]è equale al pūto, perchè minima è detta quella cosa della quale nessu[11]na altra può essere minore, e questa tal difinitione è simile al[12]la difinitione del pūto; adunque è pos[13]sibile che tutta la circūferentia d'un cierchio mandi la sua similitu[14]dine alla sua intersegatione come mostra la quarta di que[15]sto che

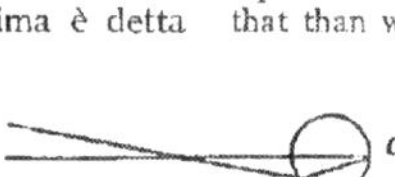

Necessity has provided that all the images of objects in front of the eye shall intersect in two places. One of these intersections is in the pupil, the other in the crystalline lens; and if this were not the case the eye could not see so great a number of objects as it does. This can be proved, since all the lines which intersect do so in a point. Because nothing is seen of objects excepting their surface; and their edges are lines, in contradistinction to the definition of a surface. And each minute part of a line is equal to a point; for *smallest* is said of that than which nothing can be smaller, and this definition is equivalent to the definition of the point. Hence it is possible for the whole circumference of a circle to transmit its image to the point of intersection, as is shown in the 4th of this which shows: all the smallest parts of the images cross each

chongiugnie chon . . chelli. 17. desstro ossini o. 19. desstro . . sirachολo. 20. sinisstra . . desstro . . spiracholo. 21. spiracholo equesto . . 22. choll . . a[?]di. 23. chorpi . . recti . . appassare. 24. chorpi . . spirachuli eddopo . . spiracho. 26. interseghatione.

78. 1. chettutte . . chorpi antiposstī. 2. interseghatio. 4. stallina . . chosi . . faciessi . . vedere se. 5. [il nvmero delle chose che] si . . chose. 6. tutte [le ch] le . . chessinterseghano. 7. terseghatione . . ciossiache dimosstrasē. 8. li termini delle qua li termini. 10. chosa . . nesu. 11. equesta . . essimile al. 12. lla difini[?] . . adunque eppos. 13. chettutta la circhū-

dicie ¶tutte le parti minime delle spetie penetrá una l'altra sanza [16]occupatione l'una dell'altra.¶ [17]Queste dimostrationi [18]son per esẽplo dell'ochio; [19]nessuna spetie di

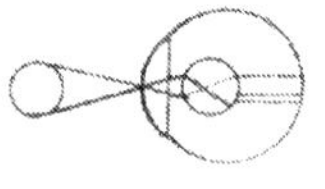

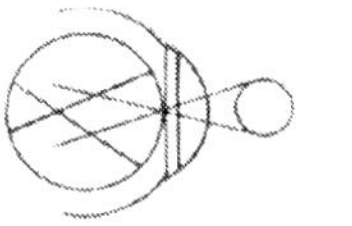

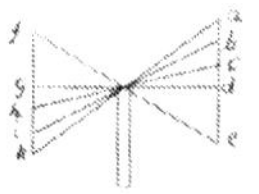

si minimo [20]corpo penetra nell'ochio [21]che non si volti sotto sopra, [22]e nel penetrare la spe[23]ra cristallina an cora [24]si rivolta sotto sopra, e co[25]si ritorna diritta la spe[26]tie dentro all'ochio co[27]me era l'obbietto di fori [28]dell'ochio.

other without interfering with each other. These demonstrations are to illustrate the eye. No image, even of the smallest object, enters the eye without being turned upside down; but as it penetrates into the crystalline lens it is once more reversed and thus the image is restored to the same position within the eye as that of the object outside the eye.

W. L. 145; D. 8]

79

Della linia cĕtrale dell'ochio.

[2]Solamĕte vna linia è quella infra le spetie [3]che penetrano alla virtù visiva che nŏ si intersega, e questa [4]non à virtù sensibile perchè è linia matematica la [5]quale à origine dal pŭto matematico il quale non à mezzo.

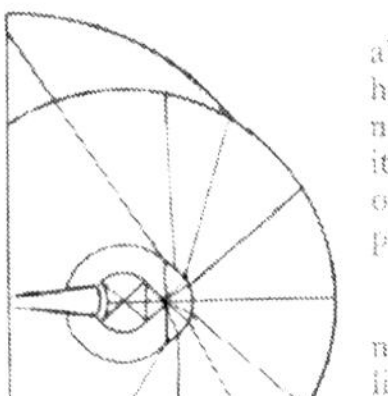

[6]Neciessità vole secŏdo l'avversa[7]rio che la linia ciĕtrale di tut[8]te le spetie che ĕtrā per li sottili [9]e stretti spiraculi in loco oscu[10]ro sia volta sotto sopra insieme [11]cŏ tutte le spetie de corpi che la [12]vestano.

Of the central line of the eye.

Only one line of the image, of all those that reach the visual virtue, has no intersection; and this has no sensible dimensions because it is a mathematical line which originates from a mathematical point, which has no dimensions.

According to my adversary, necessity requires that the central line of every image that enters by small and narrow openings into a dark chamber shall be turned upside down, together with the images of the bodies that surround it.

Windl. L. 146. C. 7]

80.

Se la linia ciĕtrale delle spetie si può in se intersegare dĕtro allo spiracolo o no?

[3]Inposibile è che la linia in se si possa intersegare cioè che 'l [4]lato destro d'una delle sua fronti passi al lato sinistro del lato [5]della frŏte opposita, e cosi il suo lato si-

As to whether the central line of the image can be intersected, or not, within the opening.

It is impossible that the line should intersect itself; that is, that its right should cross ever to its left side, and so, its left side become its right side. Because such

ferentia. 14. intersseghatione [perche] . . la 3ª di . . parte. 16. ochupatione. 17. Quesste dimosstrationi. 20. chorpo. 21. socto. 22. penetrare [pia]. 23. cristallina anchora. 24. sotto . . che. 26. cho.

79. 2. equella infralle. 3. visiva nŏ si intersegha equesta. 4. perche [nasscie dal] ellinia matematicha. 5. matematicho. 6. sechŏdo laversa. 7. chella . . di tu. 8. lesspetie. 9. esstretti spirachuli illocho oscu. 10. so volta. 11. lesspetie . . chorpi chella. 12. vestano.

80. 1. sella . . no. 2. intersseghare . . . 3. he chella . intersseghare . 4. desstro . sinisstro . e chosi . sinisstro.

nistro passi al lato de[6]stro, perchè tale intersegatione richiede due linie per li due det[7]ti lati, delli quali nō si può dar moto da destra e sinistra e da sini[8]stra a destra in se medesimo, se nō v'è spatio di grossezza, il quale sia ca[9]pacie di tal moto: e se v'è spatio, essa non è linia, āzi è superfitie, e [10]noi cierchiamo la natura della linia e nō

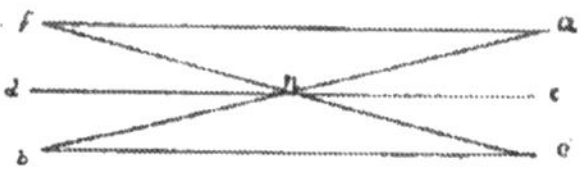

d'essa superfitie, e perchè la [11]linia non avendo mezzo nella sua grossezza essa nō si pvò diuidere; [12]adunque cōcludiamo la linia nō potere aver lati inter[13]segabili infra loro; pruovasi nel moto della linia *a f* [14]in *a b*, e della linia *e b* in *e f*, le quali sō lati della super[15]fitie *a f e b*; Ma se tu moverai la linia *a b* e la linia [16]*e f* colle fronti *a e* al sito *c*, tu avrai mosso li oppositi [17]stremi *f b* l'uno inverso l'altro al punto *d*, e avrai di due li[18]nie fatto la linia retta *c d*, la quale risiede in mezzo al[19]la intersegatione d'esse due linie nel pūto *n*, sanza alcuna [20]intersegatione, perchè se tu immaginerai tali due linie [21]essere corporee, egli è necessario mediāte il detto mo[22]to che l'una copra integralmēte l'altra, essendo equali sanza [23]alcuna intersegatione nel sito *c d*, e questo basta a pro[23]vare il nostro proposito.

an intersection demands two lines, one from each side; for there can be no motion from right to left or from left to right in itself without such extension and thickness as admit of such motion. And if there is extension it is no longer a line but a surface, and we are investigating the properties of a line, and not of a surface. And as the line, having no centre of thickness cannot be divided, we must conclude that the line can have no sides to intersect each other. This is proved by the movement of the line *a f* to *a b* and of the line *e b* to *e f*, which are the sides of the surface *a f e b*. But if you move the line *a b* and the line *e f*, with the frontends *a e*, to the spot *c*, you will have moved the opposite ends *f b* towards each other at the point *d*. And from the two lines you will have drawn the straight line *c d* which cuts the middle of the intersection of these two lines at the point *n* without any intersection. For, you imagine these two lines as having breadth, it is evident that by this motion the first will entirely cover the other—being equal with it—without any intersection, in the position *c d*. And this is sufficient to prove our proposition.

W. L. 145; D. *b*]

81.

Come innvmerabili razzi delle innvme[2]rabili spetie si possā ridurre in un sol pūto.

[3]Siccome ī un punto passā tutte le linie sanza occupatione [4]l'una dell'altra per essere incorporee, cosi possono passarvi [5]tutte le spetie delle superfitie, e siccome o[6]gni dato punto vede ogni antiposto obbietto, e ogni obiet[7]to vede l'antiposto punto naturale, ancora per esso punto possono [8]transire i diminviti razzi di tali spetie, dopo il transito del[9]le quali si riformeranno, e ricresceranno le quātità di tali

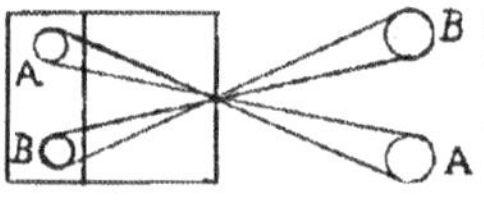

How the innumerable rays from innumerable images can converge to a point.

Just as all lines can meet at a point without interfering with each other—being without breadth or thickness—in the same way all the images of surfaces can meet there; and as each given point faces the object opposite to it and each object faces an opposite point, the converging rays of the image can pass through the point and diverge again beyond it to reproduce and re-magnify the real size of that image. But their impressions will

. des. 6. interseghatione . . due . . dec. 7. desstro essinistro . . ssinis. 8. stro a desstro . . grosseza . . qual . . . cha. 9. esse cie mezo . . grosseza. 12. cōcludiano. 13. seghabili infralloro II. 15. Massetu . . ella lini. 16. arai. 17. arai. 19. lla interseghatione . . alchuna. 20. interseghatione . . settu inmaginerai tale. 21. chorporee . . neclessario che mediāte. 22. chellala copra. 23. alchuna interseghatione . . ecquesto bassta. 24. nosstro.
81. 1. Chome . . invme. 2. nū sol. 3. sichome . . ochupatione. 4. chosi possā. 5. essichome [in ogni] ho. 6. obiec. 7. au-

81. On the original diagram at the beginning of this chapter Leonardo has written "*azurro*" (blue) where in the facsimile I have marked *A*, and "*giallo*" (yellow) where *B* stands.

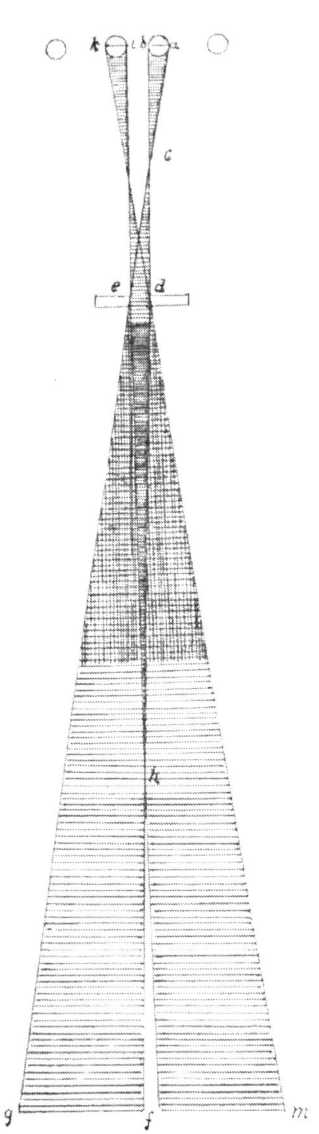

Fig. I.

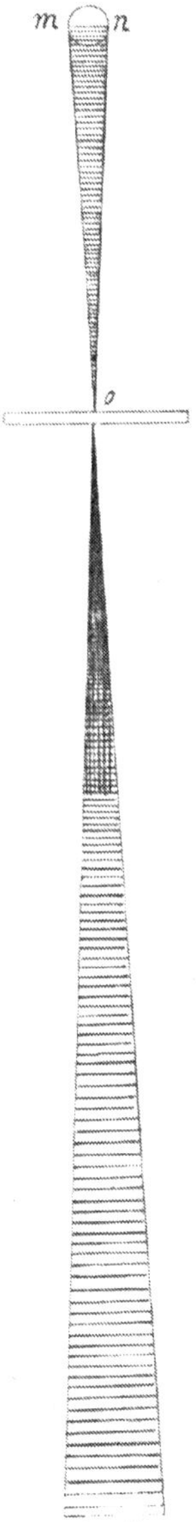

Fig. II.

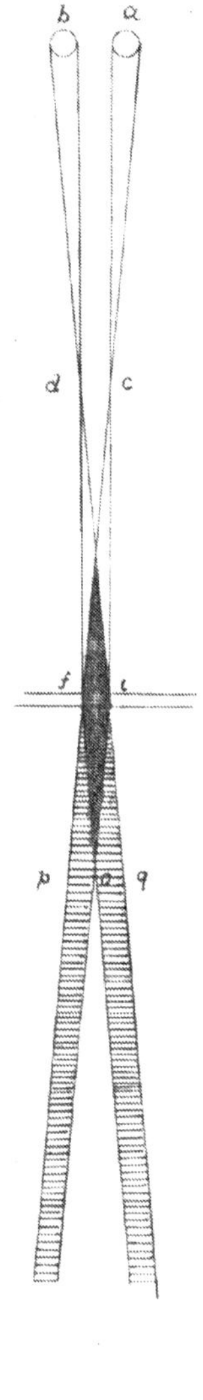

Fig. III.

spetie; Ma le loro inpressioni sarà riverscie, come è provato nella prima di sopra, dove dicie che ogni spetie s'intersega nello introito delli stretti spiraculi fatti in materia di minima grossezza.

appear reversed—as is shown in the first, above; where it is said that every image intersects as it enters the narrow openings made in a very thin substance.

Leggi a riscōtro in margine

Read the marginal text on the other side.

W. L. 145; D. a]

Quanto lo spiracolo è minore del corpo ōbroso, tanto meno le spetie penetrate in esso spiracolo penetrano l'una nell' altra.

In proportion as the opening is smaller than the shaded body, so much less will the images transmitted through this opening intersect each other.

Li simulacri che passano per spiracoli in loco oscuro intersegano li lor lati tanto più vicino allo spiraculo quāto esso spiracolo fia di minore larghezza; pruovasi, e sia *a b* il corpo ōbroso il quale, nō l'onbra, ma il simulacro della sua oscurità e figura manda per lo spiracolo · *d e* · il quale è della larghezza d'esso corpo ōbroso, e li sua lati *a b* essendo rettilini (com' è provato) è neciessario che s'interseghino infra 'l corpo ōbroso e lo spiracolo, ma tāto piv vicino allo spiracolo, qvanto esso spiracolo è di minor larghezza che il corpo ōbroso, come si dimostra dal lato tuo destro e dal lato sinistro nelle due figure *a b c n m o*, dove essendo lo spiracolo destro · *d e* eguale in larghezza al corpo ōbroso *a b*, la intersegatione de lati di tale ōbroso si ferma in mezzo infra lo spiracolo e 'l corpo onbroso nel punto *c*, il che far nō può la figura sinistra per essere lo spiracolo *o* assai minore del corpo ōbroso *n m*.

The sides of images which pass through openings into a dark room intersect at a point which is nearer to the opening in proportion as the opening is narrower. To prove this let *a b* be an object in light and shade which sends not its shadow but the image of its darkened form through the opening *d e* which is as wide as this shaded body; and its sides *a b*, being straight lines (as has been proved) must intersect between the shaded object and the opening; but nearer to the opening in proportion as it is smaller than the object in shade. As is shown, on your right hand and your left hand, in the two diagrams *a b c n m o* where, the right opening *d e*, being equal in width to the shaded object *a b*, the intersection of the sides of the said shaded object occurs half way between the opening and the shaded object at the point *c*. But this cannot happen in the left hand figure, the opening *o* being much smaller than the shaded object *n m*.

Ĵpossibile è che le spetie de'corpi si possino vedere infra li corpi e

It is impossible that the images of objects should be seen between the objects and the

chora . . . puo. 8. le . . tale. 9. ricresscierāno. 10. Malie . . chome. 11. sintersegha. 12. spirachuli. 14. Legge. 15. los. 16. pirachₒlo. 19. lesspe. 21. spiracho. 25. per isspiracholi illocho osschuro. 26. interseghano. 27. spirachulo. 28. spiracholo. 29. larghe . . essia. 30. chorpo. 31. osscurita. 32. fighura . . spiracho. 34. chorpo . . elli. 35. pr"o". 37. ello. 38. racholo mattanto . . allos. 39. spiracholo . . spiracho. 41. chome . . da. 42. tuo [sin] desstro. 43. fighure. 44. spiracholo. 45. desstro . . equale illarghezza. 46. intersegha. 48. mezo infrallo spiracholo. 49. chorpo. 51. stra . . losspiracholo.

15—23. These lines stand between the diagrams I and III.

24—53. These lines stand between the diagrams I and II.

li spiracoli, per li quali penetrano li simulacri d'essi corpi; e questo si manifesta perchè doue l'aria è alluminata, tali simulacri nō si gienerano evidēti.

Li simulacri radoppiati per la penetratio che scanbievolmēte è fatta dall'uno nell'altro, senpre radoppia la loro oscurità; provasi e sia tal radoppiamēto *d e h*, il quale ancora che esso nō ueda se nō dentro allo spatio de' corpi in *b i*, e nō resta che esso nō sia veduto da *f g* e dal *f m*, il quale è conposto delli simulacri *a b i k*, li quali in *d e h* s'infondano l'un nell'altro.

openings through which the images of these bodies are admitted; and this is plain, because where the atmosphere is illuminated these images are not formed visibly.

When the images are made double by mutually crossing each other they are invariably doubly as dark in tone. To prove this let *d e h* be such a doubling which although it is only seen within the space between the bodies in *b* and *i* this will not hinder its being seen from *f g* or from *f m*; being composed of the images *a b i k* which run together in *d e h*.

C. A. 123 *b*; 380 *b*]

82.

Sperīezia come nō movēdo [2]la pupilla del suo sito le cose [3]viste da quella paiono moversi [4]fori del suo loco.

[5]Se riguarderai · vna cosa alquāto distāte da te [6]la quale sia piv bassa · che l'ochio, e fermerai i quella [7]le tue due popille, e coll'una · delle mani apri e tieni [8]fermo · il coperchio di sopra e coll'altra · alzerai [9]in

An experiment showing that though the pupil may not be moved from its position the objects seen by it may appear to move from their places.

If you look at an object at some distance from you and which is below the eye, and fix both your eyes upon it and with one hand firmly hold the upper lid open while

52. chorpi. 54. be. 55. chelle. 56. chorpi. 58. fralli corpi ci. 59. spiracholi. 62. cre . . chorpi. 63. eequesto. 66. laria al. 72. cÎte. 76. oschurita. 77. essia. 80. anchora. 81. sen. 82. ē dentro allos. 87. eddal. 94. si. 95. fondan'"o".
82. 1. chome. 2. la pupila . . chose. 3. dacquella pare. 4. locho. 5. chosa . . datte. 6. effermersi. 7. chollūna . . tuni.

54—97 are written along the left side of diagram I.

alto il coperchio di sotto, senpre tenēdo ferme le luci [10]nella cosa riguardata, vederai essa cosa [11]diuidersi in due e l'una sta ferma, l'altra si mo[12]ve in cōtrario moto, a quello che fai fare col dito [13]al coperchio di sotto; — [14]Com'è falsa l'openione di quegli [15]che dicono · questo accadere perchè [16]la lucie escie fori · di suo · sito.

[17]Come per le sopra dette cose [18]si dimostra la popilla operare [19]sotto, sopra il suo vedere.

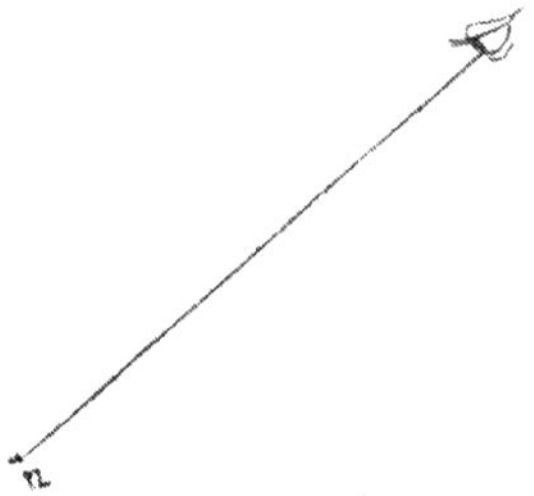

with the other you push up the under lid—still keeping your eyes fixed on the object gazed at—you will see that object double; one [image] remaining steady, and the other moving in a contrary direction to the pressure of your finger on the lower eyelid. How false the opinion is of those who say that this happens because the pupil of the eye is displaced from its position.

How the above mentioned facts prove that the pupil acts upside down in seeing.

A. 1 b.]

83.

PARIETE DI VETRO.

[2]Prospettiva · non è altro · che vedere [3]uno sito dirieto uno vetro piano [4]e ben' transparēte, sulla superfitie del [5]quale · siano · segniate · tutte le cose · che [6]sono da esso · vetro · ĩdirieto: le qua[7]li si possono cōdurre per piramidi [8]al pūto dell'ochio e esse piramidi si [9]tagliano su detto vetro.

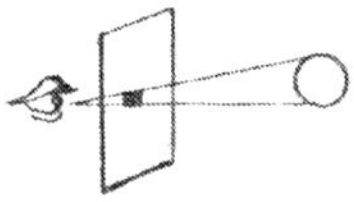

OF THE PLANE OF GLASS.

Perspective is nothing else than seeing a place [or objects] behind a plane of glass, quite transparent, on the surface of which the objects behind that glass are to be drawn. These can be traced in pyramids to the point in the eye, and these pyramids are intersected on the glass plane.

Demonstration of perspective by means of a vertical glass plane (83—85).

Br. M. 220 a]

84

Mai la prospettiva de' pittori in pa[2]ri distantia mostrerà [3]la cosa di quella grandezza [4]che si mostra all'ochio — [5]vedi la piramide *f c d* essere colla [6]sua punta tanto

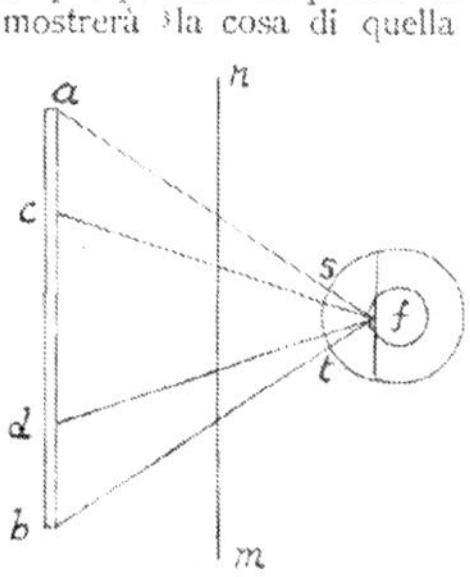

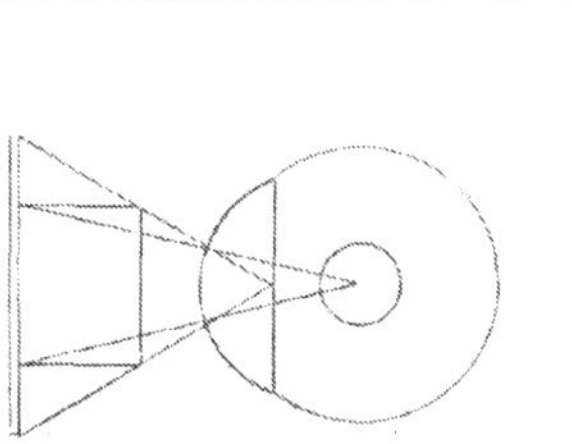

Pictorial perspective can never make an object at the same distance, look of the same size as it appears to the eye. You see that the apex of the pyramid *f c d* is as far

8. choperchio . . choll. 9. choperchio . . luce. 10. chosa . . chosa. 11. elluna. 12. chōtrario . . cheffai . . chel. 13. coperchio. 14. chome falso. 15. dichano . . achadere. 16. esscie. 17. chome . . chose. 18. popila.
83. 3. ĩno . . ĩno vetro. 4. pen transsparēte sula. 5. sia . segnato . . chose. 7. posano ghondure . . piramide. 8. piramide.
84. 1. prosspettiva. 2. disstantia mōsterra [in pari distā]. 3. [na la cos] la grandeza. 4. chessi mosstra alochio 6. disstante .

82. 14—17. The subject indicated by these two headings is fully discussed in the two chapters that follow them in the original; but it did not seem to me appropriate to include them here.

distante all' obbietto [7] *c d*, quanto il medesimo punto *f* all' obbi[8]etto · *a b*, e non dimeno · *c d* basa [9] fatta dal punto de' pictori è minore [10] che *a b* · basa fatta dalle linie delle spetie concorrēti all' occhio e ronpendo[11] si in · *s t* · superfitie dell' ochio, [12] di questo farà esperienza · colle linie [13] uisuali e poi colle linie del filo de pictori [14] tagliando esse linie visuali e essentiali so[15]pra una medesima pariete, sopra la quale [16] si misuri · vn medesimo obbietto.

from the object *c d* as the same point *f* is from the object *a b*; and yet *c d*, which is the base made by the painter's point, is smaller than *a b* which is the base of the lines from the objects converging in the eye and refracted at *s t*, the surface of the eye. This may be proved by experiment, by the lines of vision and then by the lines of the painter's plumbline by cutting the real lines of vision on one and the same plane and measuring on it one and the same object.

A 10 *b*]

85.

Prospettiva.

[2] Pariete è · vna linia · perpēdiculare · la quale · si figura dināzi · al pūto comvne, doue [3] si cōgivgnie · il concorso · delle · piramidi; E fa questa · pariete col detto pūto, [4] quello · medesimo · ofitio, che farebbe · un vetro · piano per lo quale in riguardādo [5] varie cose sù ve le disegniasse; E sarebbero le cose disegniate tanto mi[6]nori che l'origine: quāto · lo spatio · che sta tra 'l uetro e l'ochio fusse minore [7] che quello · che dal vetro alla cosa.

Perspective

The vertical plane is a perpendicular line, imagined as in front of the central point where the apex of the pyramids converge. And this plane bears the same relation to this point as a plane of glass would, through which you might see the various objects and draw them on it. And the objects thus drawn would be smaller than the originals, in proportion as the distance between the glass and the eye was smaller than that between the glass and the objects.

Prospettiva.

[9] Il cōcorso · delle piramidi cavsate da corpi · mostreranno sulla pariete [10] la uarietà delle grādezze · e distāzie della loro · cagione.

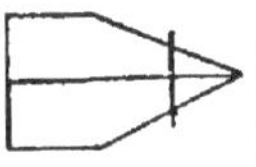

Perspective.

The different converging pyramids produced by the objects, will show, on the plane, the various sizes and remoteness of the objects causing them.

Prospettiva.

[13] Tutti · quelli · piani che i loro stremi · si cōgivgneranno con linie · perpēdiculari [14] cavsando angoli · retti, E neciessario che, essendo di pari larghezza, che quāto piv [15] s'alzano all'ochio meno si uegga e quāto piv lo passa piv si vegga la uera grādezza.

Perspective.

All those horizontal planes of which the extremes are met by perpendicular lines forming right angles, if they are of equal width the more they rise to the level of eye the less this is seen, and the more the eye is above them the more will their real width be seen.

Prospettiva.

[17] Quāto piv s'allontana dall'ochio il corpo sperico piv ne vedi.

Perspective.

The farther a spherical body is from the eye the more you will see of it.

A 38 *a*]

86.

The angle of sight varies with the distance (86—88)

Modo · senplice · e naturale · cioè come le cose sanza altro [2] mezzo appariscono · all' ochio.

A simple and natural method; showing how objects appear to the eye without any other medium.

obbiecto 8 basa]emi] 9 fatto ēminore 10. concorēti 12 quessto . . essperienza 15 prī medesima.

85 1 pro *is used here—as in lines* 8, 11, 16 *as a title, and is an abbreviation for* Prospettiva. *The word is written at full length at the head of the first chapter on this page (see no* 94) 2 perpēdichulare 3 chōgivgnie . . conchorso . . piramideEffa. 4 cheffarebbe ī vetro . . per | "lo" quale 5 chose . disegniassi Essarebouo le chose 6 fussi 7 quelo chosa. 9. chōchorso piramide chavsate . chorpi . mosterano sula. 10 grādeze chagione 12 [tutti . quelli piani situati in varie altere e di par] 13 chōgivgneranno chollinie . perpendichulare 14 chavsando . . largeza. 15 salza alochio mēsi uega . . veg

[3]Quella · cosa · ch'è · piv · presso · all'ochio · senpre · apparisscie maggiore che vn altra [4]di pari qualità · che sia · piv · distante.

[5]l'ochio · *m* che vede · li spati · *o* · *v* · *x* · nō conoscie · quasi · differentia · dall'uno · all'altro [6]e questo · nascie · per esser · visino · a loro, e se li leverai detti spati · sulla pariete [7]*n* · *o*: lo spatio · *o* · *v* · apparirà nella · parte della · pariete · *o* · *r* · e cosi lo spatio [8]*v* · *x* · apparirà · in · *r* · *q*: e se tu · mettessi · questo · in opera · in qualche loco che vi si [9]potesse andare · attorno · ti parebbe una · cosa · discordante · per la grā varietà ch'è da [10]lo spatio · *o* · *r* · e da · *r* · *q*: e questo diriva · che l'ochio è tanto · sotto · alla · pariete [11]che la pariete · li scorta: Onde se pure volessi · metterlo in opera, ti bisogniere[12]bbe · che essa prospettiva · si uedesse da uno · solo buso il quale fusse [13]nel loco . *m* · o veramēte stessi lontano · al meno · 3 volte · la grādezza della cosa che vedi; [14]la pariete: *o* · *p* · per l'essere sempre equidistante all'ochio a vno modo renderà [15]le cose bene · e atte a essere vedute da loco a loco.

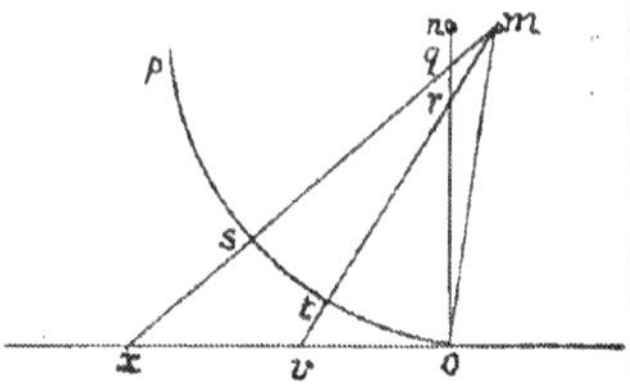

The object that is nearest to the eye always seems larger than another of the same size at greater distance.

The eye *m*, seeing the spaces *o v x*, hardly detects the difference between them, and the reason of this is that it is close to them [6]; but if these spaces are marked on the vertical plane *n o* the space *o v* will be seen at *o r*, and in the same way the space *v x* will appear at *r q*. And if you carry this out in any place where you can walk round, it will look out of proportion by reason of the great difference in the spaces *o r* and *r q*. And this proceeds from the eye being so much below [near] the plane that the plane is foreshortened. Hence, if you wanted to carry it out, you would have [to arrange] to see the perspective through a single hole which must be at the point *m*, or else you must go to a distance of at least 3 times the height of the object you see. The plane *o p* being always equally remote from the eye will reproduce the objects in a satisfactory way, so that they may be seen from place to place.

W. L. 145. C. *b*]

87.

Come ogni grā quātità manda [2]fuor di se le sua spetie, le quali sono [3]in potentia di diminuire in infinito.

[4]Le spetie d'ogni grā quātità essendo diuisibili in īfinito son di[5]minuitive in īfinito.

How every large mass sends forth its images, which may diminish through infinity.

The images of any large mass being infinitely divisible may be infinitely diminished.

A. 9 *b*]

88.

quelli · corpi d'equale · grādezza · situati ī uarj [2]lochi fieno veduti · per diuerse · piramidi : le qua[3]li saranno tanto · piv · strette [5]quāto piv · lontana · fia · la sua · cagione.

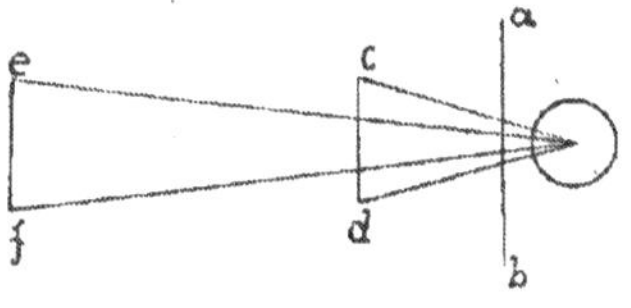

Objects of equal size, situated in various places, will be seen by different pyramids which will each be smaller in proportion as the object is farther off.

86. 1. chome le chose. 2. mezo apparischano. 3. chosa . . apparisscie magiore. 4. chessia. 5. lochio . "m" che . . lisspati . . chonosscie . quassi . . diferentia. 6. ecquesto . nascie . . alloro esseli leuera . idetti. 7. losspatio . . aparira nela . . chosi. 8. aparira . . essettu . . locho. 9. potessi . . parebbe . ī . chosa . dischordante. 10. losspatio . . ecquesto . . ettanto. 11. schorta. 12. be . . essa [dipintura si] prossprettiva si vedessi da ī solo . . 13. nelocho . . il mē . . grādeza dela. 14. . . equi"di"stante alochio. 15. chose . . assere . . dallocho allocho.

87. 4. Lesspetie . . diuisibile. 5. ifinite.

88. 1. chorpi . . grādeza . . uarie. 2. [distantie] "lochi" . . piramide. 3. li [vienchta] sarano . . strette luna [chella]. 4. tra quanto fia piv lontano luno chorpo che laltro]. 5. chagione.

86. 6. It is quite inconceivable to me why M. RAVAISSON, in a note to his French translation of this simple passage should have remarked: *Il est clair que c'est par erreur que Léonard a écrit* per esser visino *au lieu de* per non esser visino. (See his printed ed. of MS. A, p. 38.)

89.

G. 53b]

Opposite pyramids in juxtaposition.

La prospectiva adopera nelle distatie [2]due contrarie piramidi, delle quali l'u[3]na à l'angolo nell'ochio e la basa re[4]mota insino all'orizzōte, La secōda [5]a la basa diuerso l'ochio e l'angolo [6]all'orizzōte; Ma la prima attēde allo [7]vniversale, abracciādosi tutte le qua[8]tità delli corpi antiposti all'ochio, co[9]me sarebbe vn grā paese veduto per [10]istretto spiracolo, che tāto maggiore [11]numero di cose per tale spiracolo si uede, [12]quāto esse cose sō più remote da tal' [13]ochio, e cosi si gienera la basa all'orizzō[14]te e l'āgolo nell'ochio, come di sopra dissi; [15]La 2ª piramide s'astende in un particu[16]lare, il qual si dimostra tanto minore [17]quāto più si remove dall'ochio, e questa [18]2ª prospectiva nascie dalla prima.

Perspective, in dealing with distances, makes use of two opposite pyramids, one of which has its apex in the eye and the base as distant as the horizon. The other has the base towards the eye and the apex on the horizon. Now, the first includes the [visible] universe, embracing all the mass of the objects that lie in front of the eye; as it might be a vast landscape seen through a very small opening; for the more remote the objects are from the eye, the greater number can be seen through the opening, and thus the pyramid is constructed with the base on the horizon and the apex in the eye, as has been said. The second pyramid is extended to a spot which is smaller in proportion as it is farther from the eye; and this second perspective [= pyramid] results from the first.

90.

G. 13b]

Perspectiva senplice.

On simple and complex perspective.

[2]La sēplicie prospettiua è quella che è fat[3]ta dall'arte sopra sito equalmente distante [4]dall'ochio con [5]ogni sua parte,—[5]prospettiua conposta è quella che è fatta [6]sopra sito il quale cō nessuna sua parte è equal[7]mente distante dall'ochio.

Simple perspective.

Simple perspective is that which is constructed by art on a vertical plane which is equally distant from the eye in every part. Complex perspective is that which is constructed on a ground-plan in which none of the parts are equally distant from the eye.

91.

H.[3] 33a]

Prospettiva.

The proper distance of objects from the eye (91—92).

[2]Nessuna superfitie si dimostrerà · perfetta, [3]se l'ochio risguardator di quella nō [4]sarà equalmēte distāte ai sua stre[5]mi.

Perspective.

No surface can be seen exactly as it is, if the eye that sees it is not equally remote from all its edges.

92.

Ash. I. 12a]

Perchè · la cosa · posta vicina · all'ochio lascia i sua termini īdiscernibili.

[3]Tutte quelle · cose opposte all'ochio · che fieno troppo a quello uicine [4]cōuerrà che · sua termini · sieno cōfusi a disciernere, come aca[5]de delle cose uicine a lume, che fanno ōbra grāde cōfusa, e cosi [6]fa quest' ochio col gividicare le cose ī fori; ī tutti i casi di prospettiva liniale [7]l'ochio è simile

Why when an object is placed close to the eye its edges are indistinct.

When an object opposite the eye is brought too close to it, its edges must become too confused to be distinguished; as it happens with objects close to a light, which cast a large and indistinct shadow, so is it with an eye which estimates objects opposite to it; in all cases of linear per-

89. 1. presspectiva . . disstantie. 2. piramide. 3. allanghelo . . ella. 4. orizōte . . sechōta. 5. alla . . ellanghelo. 6. Malla 8. antiposste . . cho. 10. isstretto spirachole chetāto. 11. chose . . spirachol. 12. chose . . dattale. 13. chosi. 14. ellāgholo . . chome. 15. sastende nūparticha. 16. dimosstra. 17. dellochio equesta. 18. presspectiva nasscie.

90. 2. presspectiua equello . . effac. 3. eequalmente disstante. 4. choa. 5. presspectiua chonpossta equella cheffacta. 6. quale chō . . equal. 7. disstante dell.

91. 2. perfecta. 3. sellochio.

92. [illegible] estochi dal

al lume, e la ragiō si è che l'ochio · fa · una · linia maestra, la qua[8]le per distātia igrossa e abbraccia cō uera cognitione le cose gradi [9]da lontano come le piccole da presso: ma perchè l'ochio māda moltitudi[10]ne di linie che circūdano questa prī-cipale di mezzo, le quali quando le cose si [11]trovano piv lontane dal cietro in essa circulatione sono meno potēti [12]a conosciere · il uero: accade che la cosa posta presso all'ochio, nō [13]sendo in quella distātia, si uicina alla linia maestra capace di cōprēdere i ter[14]mini d'essa cosa; onde cōuiene a essi termini capitare in nelle linie di debole [15]cō · prēsione, le quali sono al'ufitio dell'ochio come i brachi alle caccie, [16]che leuā la preda e nō la · possō pigliare: cosi queste nō possono pigliare · ma sono [17]cagione che la linia maestra si uolta alle cose leuate da esse linie, [18]onde le cose, delle quali i termini sono [19]givdicati da esse linie, sō cōfuse.

spective, the eye acts in the same way as the light. And the reason is that the eye has one leading line (of vision) which dilates with distance and embraces with true discernment large objects at a distance as well as small ones that are close. But since the eye sends out a multitude of lines which surround this chief central one and since these which are farthest from the centre in this cone of lines are less able to discern with accuracy, it follows that an object brought close to the eye is not at a due distance, but is too near for the central line to be able to discern the outlines of the object. So the edges fall within the lines of weaker discerning power, and these are to the function of the eye like dogs in the chase which can put up the game but cannot take it. Thus these cannot take in the objects, but induce the central line of sight to turn upon them when they have put them up. Hence the objects which are seen with these lines of sight have confused outlines.

A. 8 b]

93.

The relative size of objects with regard to their distance from the eye (93—98).

Prospettiva.

[2]La cosa · piccola · da presso · e la grāde · da lontano, essendo · viste dentro · a equali [3]angoli ·, apparirāno · d'equale · grandezza.

Perspective.

Small objects close at hand and large ones at a distance, being seen within equal angles, will appear of the same size.

A. 10 b]

94.

Prospettiva.

[2]Nessuno · corpo · fia di tāta · magnitudine · che per lunga distantia al-l'ochio non apparisca [3]minore · che'l minore · obietto piv · vicino.

Perspective.

There is no object so large but that at a great distance from the eye it does not appear smaller than a smaller object near.

C. A. 1 a, 1 b]

95.

Infra le cose d'equal grandezza quella che [2]fia più distante dall'ochio si dimostrerà di minor [3]figura.

Among objects of equal size that which is most remote from the eye will look the smallest.

givdícare . . chasi. 7. l'ochio essimile . . ella . . fa . ī . linia. 8. abracia chō . . chose. 9. chome le pichole. 10. circhū-dano . . meza . . quā le chessi 11. dietro . . circhulatione. 12. vero . onde achade chella chosa. 13. uisina la . . cōplēdere. 14. cosa cōuieue . . inele. 15. cōplēsione . . chome . . ale chaccie. 16. posono pigliare . . maso. 18. 19. *These two lines are written lengthways on the margin.* 18. delle. 19. cōfusi.

93. 2. chosa pichola . . ella . . dallontano . . acqali. 3. angholi apatirano . . grandeza.

94. 1. prosspettiva. 2. distantia | "alochio" nōn aparisca.

95. 1. Infralle chose . . grandeza . . chef. 2. disstante . . dimossterra.

95. This axiom, sufficiently clear in itself, is in the original illustrated by a very large diagram, constructed like that here reproduced under No. 108. The same idea is repeated in C. A. 1 a; 1 a, stated as follows: *Infra le cose d'equal grandeza quella si dimostra di minor figura che sarà più distante dall' ochio.*—

C. A 142*b*; 425*b*]

96.

Perchè la cosa quanto · piv s'auisina · all'ochio · meno si conosce ·, e perchè gli ochiali e perchè l'ochio nō ben vede da presso ²o da lontano.

Why an object is less distinct when brought near to the eye, and why with spectacles, or without the naked eye sees badly either close or far off [as the case may be]

S. K. M. II² 63*a*]

97.

PROSPETTIVA.

¹Infra le cose d'equal grandezza ³quella che sarà piv distante dall'o⁴chio si di- mostrerà di minore ⁵figura.

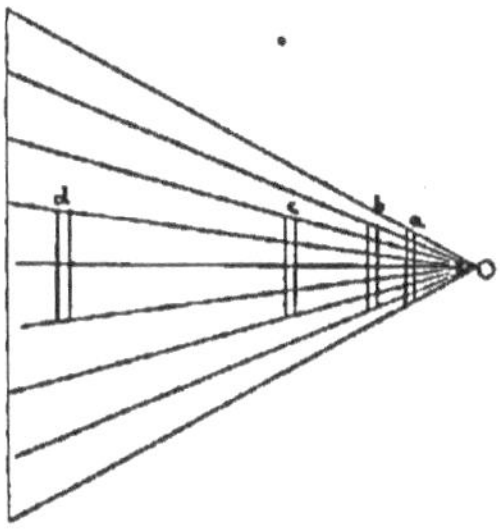

PERSPECTIVE.

Among objects of equal size, that which is most remote from the eye will look the smallest.

A 11*a*]

98.

PROSPETTIVA.

²Nessuna · secōda · cosa fia tanto · piv bassa · che la · prima | che, stādo ³l'ochio · di sopra · la secōda nō li paia piv alta.

PERSPECTIVE.

No second object can be so much lower than the first as that the eye will not see it higher than the first, if the eye is above the second.

PROSPETTIVA.

⁵E · quella · cosa · secōda · nō fia mai · tāto · piv · alta · che la prima | che, stādo ⁶l'ochio · di sotto, nō paia · la secōda sotto · la prima.

PERSPECTIVE.

And this second object will never be so much higher than the first as that the eye, being below them, will not see the second as lower than the first.

PROSPETTIVA.

⁸Se l'ochio riguarderà il secōdo quadrato · per lo ciētro del minore piv uisino ⁹apparirà li il secōdo · maggiore esser circūdato · dal minore ·

PERSPECTIVE.

If the eye sees a second square through the centre of a smaller one, that is nearer, the second, larger square will appear to be surrounded by the smaller one.

PROSPECTIVA—PROPOSITIONE.

¹¹Le cose · seconde · nō fieno · mai di tāta · grādezza che le prime minori ¹²nō le · occupino · o circūdino.

PERSPECTIVE—PROPOSITION.

Objects that are farther off can never be so large but that those in front, though smaller, will conceal or surround them.

96. 1. chosa . mesi chonosscie
97 2 Infralle . . grandeza 3 chessara 4 dimossterra
98 1 pro 2 sechōda chosa . chella 3 sechōda . paia "di" [sopra la prima] "piv alta". 4. pro. 5 cqella . chella
6 [illegible] 11 chose

Definitione.

[14]Questa · propositione si proua · per isperiē-tia · inperochè, se riguarderai [15]per uno · piccolo · spiraculo non sarà · si grā cosa [16]che per quello nō si vegga [17]e la cosa veduta parrà circūdata e terminata [18]dalli stremi lati · d'esso spiraculo ·, e se tu lo stopperai, quello piccolo [19]stoppamēto fia quello che occuperà la ueduta della cosa grāde.

Definition.

This proposition can be proved by experiment. For if you look through a small hole there is nothing so large that it cannot be seen through it and the object so seen appears surrounded and enclosed by the outline of the sides of the hole. And if you stop it up, this small stopping will conceal the view of the largest object.

Ash. I. 12*b*]

99.

Della prospettiva liniale.

[2]La prospectiva liniale s'astēde · nello ofitio delle linie visuali a provare [3]per misura quanto la cosa secōda è minore che la prima; e quāto la terza [4]è minore che la seconda, e cosi di grado ī grado insino al fine delle cose [5]vedute: truovo per isperiēza che la cosa seconda se sarà tāto distāte dalla · [6]prima · quāto la prima · è distāte da · l'ochio tuo, che bēchè ifra loro [7]sieno di pari grādezza ·, che la 2ª fia altrettāto minore che la prima, e se [8]la terza cosa di pari grādezza alla · 2ª e 3ª inanzi a essa fia lontana dalla 2ª [9]quāto la 2ª dalla terza ·, fia di metà grādezza della 2ª e cosi di grado in gra[10]do per pari distāzia farāno sempre diminutione per metà la secōda dalla prima [11]pure che lo ītervallo nō passi dentro al numero di 20 braccia e īfra 20 dette braccia la [12]figvra simile a te perderà i ²/₄ di sua grādezza e īfra 40 · perderà i ⁹/₁₀ [13]e poi i ¹⁹/₂₀ ī · 60 braccia, e così di mano ī mano farà sua diminutione, facendo [14]la pariete lōtana da te · 2 · volte · tua grādezza; che'l fare una sola fa grā diffe[15]rēzia dalle prime braccia alle 2ᵉ.

Of linear perspective.

The apparent size of objects defined by calculation (99—106).

Linear Perspective deals with the action of the lines of sight, in proving by measurement how much smaller is a second object than the first, and how much the third is smaller than the second; and so on by degrees to the end of things visible. I find by experience that if a second object is as far beyond the first as the first is from the eye, although they are of the same size, the second will seem half the size of the first and if the third object is of the same size as the 2nd, and the 3rd is as far beyond the second as the 2nd from the first, it will appear of half the size of the second; and so on by degrees, at equal distances, the next farthest will be half the size of the former object. So long as the space does not exceed the length of 20 braccia. But, beyond 20 braccia figures of equal size will lose $^2/_4$ and at 40 braccia they will lose $^9/_{10}$, and $^{19}/_{20}$ at 60 braccia, and so on diminishing by degrees. This is if the picture plane is distant from you twice your own height. If it is only as far off as your own height, there will be a great difference between the first braccia and the second.

sechōde . . grādeza. 12. ochupino . o circhūdino. 13. difinitione. 15. pichojo spirachulo . . chosa [chosa di la da esso]. 16. si "vegha" [possa vedere esso stoperaí detto spircolo quello]. 17. [stopamēto ti ochu] ella . . para. 18. spirachulo . essettu . . stoperai . . picholo. 19. ochupera [tutte] la.

99. 2. nelo. 3. quā la cosa . . ecquāto. 4. sechōda ecchosi. 5. chosa sechonda sessara. 7. grādeza chella . esse. 8. grādeza ala. 9. dala . . grādeza . . ecossi. 10. diminvitione . . sechōda. 11. 20 br . . dette br . la. 12. atte . i $4/_2$ di . . grādeza. 13. 60 br ecossi . . diminvitione. 14. parieta . . datte . . grādeza . . fare ī sola . . dife . 15. 2.

99. This chapter is included in DUFRESNE's and MANZI's editions of the Treatise on Painting. H. LUDWIG, in his commentary, calls this chapter "*eines der wichtigsten im ganzen Tractat*", but at the same time he asserts that its substance has been so completely disfigured in the best M.S. copies that we ought not to regard Leonardo as responsible for it. However, in the case of this chapter, the old M.S. copies agree with the original as it is reproduced above. From the chapters given later in this edition, which were written at a subsequent date, it would appear that Leonardo corrected himself on these points.

A. 8a]

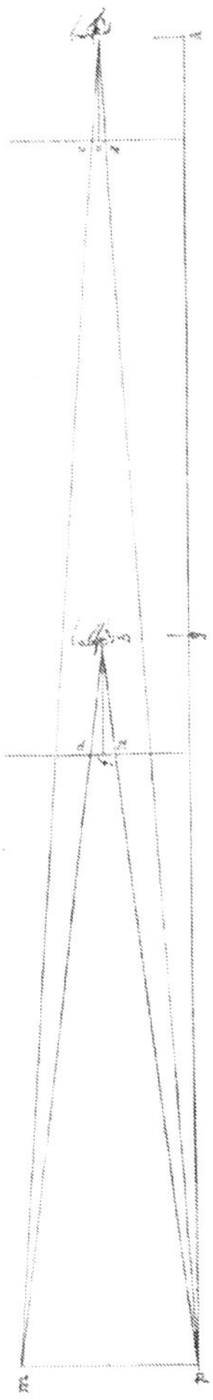

100.

Della diminutione delle · cose per varie distātie.

[1]La cosa · 2[a] che sia · lontana · dalla prima · quāto · la prima · dall'ochio · apparirà la metà minore che la · prima · benchè infra loro · sieno di pari grandezza.

Of the diminution of objects at various distances.

A second object as far distant from the first as the first is from the eye will appear half the size of the first, though they be of the same size really.

De' gradi del diminvire.

[5]Se tu · porrai · la pariete · vicina · all'ochio · uno braccio la prima · cosa · che fia · lontana dal tuo [6]ochio · 4 · braccia diminvirà · j · 3/4 della sua · altezza in detta · pariete; E se fia lōtana [7]dall'ochio · 8 · braccia, diminvirà · j 7/8 · e se fia lontona · 16 · braccia diminvirà · j 15/16 di sua [8]altezza ·, e cosi · farà · di mano · in mano · raddoppiādo il passato spatio, raddoppierà [9]la diminvitione.

Of the degrees of diminution.

If you place the vertical plane at one braccio from the eye, the first object, being at a distance of 4 braccia from your eye will diminish to 3/4 of its height at that plane; and if it is 8 braccia from the eye, to 7/8; and if it is 16 braccia off, it will diminish to 15/16 of its height and so on by degrees, as the space doubles the diminution will double.

C. A. 3[?] [?]

101.

Comicia prima dalla linia | *m f* coll'ochio di sotto [2]poi alza e colla linia *n · f* · | rifa il medesimo | po'fa coll'ochio di sopra e riscōtra le [3]2 mire atte attera cicc j · *m · n* · e quāto · *c · m* · entra · j · *m · n* · tanto · *n · m* · ētra j · · j *n · s*.

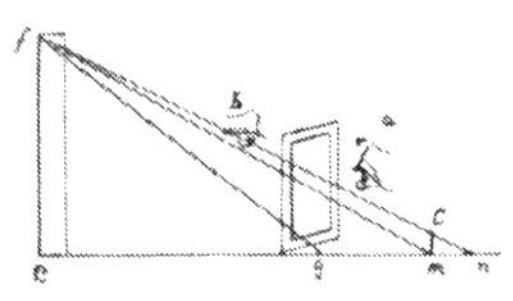

[4]se *a · n* · entra · 3 · volte j *f · b* · *m · p* · farà quel medesimo j *p · g* ·, di poi ti tira tāto j drieto che [5] *c · d* · | entri · 2 · volte jn · *a · n* · e tāto sarà da · *p · g* · quanto · da · *g · h* · e quāto *d · c* entra [6]j · *o · p* ·, tanto · *m · p* · entra j · *h · p* ·

Begin from the line *m f* with the eye below; then go up and do the same with the line *n f*, then with the eye above and close to the 2 gauges on the ground look at *m n*; then as *c m* is to *m n* so will *n m* be to *n s*.

If *a n* goes 3 times into *f b*, *m p* will do the same into *p g*. Then go backwards so far as that *c d* goes twice into *a n* and *p g* will be equal to *g h*. And *m p* will go into *h p* as often as *d c* into *o p*.

Ash. I. 28]

102.

Io do i gradi delle cose opposte all'ochio [2]come il mvsico quelli delle uoci opposte all'orechio.

[3]Benchè · le cose opposte all'ochio · si tocchino l'una l'altra di mano ī mano, nō [4]di meno farò · la mia regola di 20 in 20 braccia

I give the degrees of the objects seen by the eye as the musician does the notes heard by the ear.

Although the objects seen by the eye do, in fact, touch each other as they recede, I will nevertheless found my rule on spaces of 20

100. 1. dimmvitione . . chose 2. chosa 2a chessia . aparira. 3. chella . . [che] infralloro . grandeza. 5. Setu porai . . i br la . . chosa cheffia 6. 4 br . . altera . . Esseffia. 7. . 8 . br . . esseffia. . . 16 . br. 8. alteza . . choṡi . . inmano . radopiādo . . radopiera.

101. 1. chomīcia . . oposte al . . ch.d. 2. chola . . fa chol . . risschōtra.

102. 1. dala 2. chome il mvsicho delle. 3. oposte . tocino. 4. 20 br . affatto il mvsicho. 5. apichata. 6. quele . . echosi. 7. ale.

101. The first three lines are unfortunately very obscure.

come à fatto il mvsico īfra [5]le voci che, benchè la sia vnita e appiccata isieme, nōdimeno à posti gra[6]di di uocie in uocie · domādādo quello prima e 2ª 3ª 4ª e 5ª e cosi di grado [7]i grado à posto nomi alle varietà d'alzare e bassare la voce.

braccia each; as a musician does with notes, which, though they can be carried on one into the next, he divides into degrees from note to note calling them 1st, 2nd, 3rd, 4th, 5th; and has affixed a name to each degree in raising or lowering the voice.

S. K. M. IIª. 16*b*]

103.

PROSPETTIVA.

[2]*f* sia l'altezza e distantia dell'ochio, [3]*a* sia la pariete dell'altezza d'un omo [4]*e* sia vn omo; dico cotale fia sulla [5]pariete la distātia che dalla parie[6]te al 2° homo.

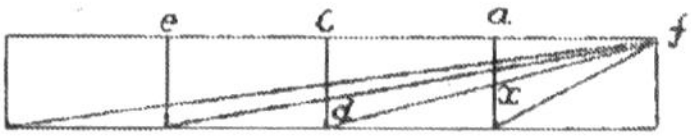

PERSPECTIVE.

Let *f* be the level and distance of the eye; and *a* the vertical plane, as high as a man; let *e* be a man, then I say that on the plane this will be the distance from the plane to the 2nd man.

C. A. 130*b*; 398*b*]

104.

Li ecciessi della diminutione che fanno le cose equali per essere cō [2]uarie distātie dallo occhio remote; āno infra loro le medesime propor[3]tioni ·, quali son quelle delli spazi che infra l'ochio e le cose s'i[4]terpongono.

The differences in the diminution of objects of equal size in consequence of their various remoteness from the eye will bear among themselves the same proportions as those of the spaces between the eye and the different objects.

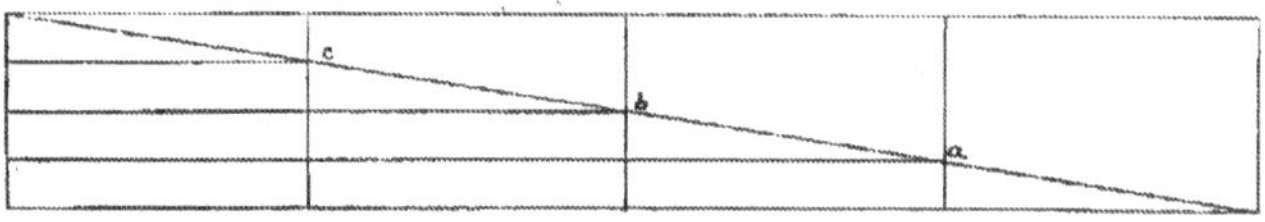

[5]Cierca quādo vn omo diminviscie in tāta distātia quāto [6]è la sua lūghezza, e poi in 2 lūghezze e poi in 3, e così fa [7]tua regola gienerale.

Find out how much a man diminishes at a certain distance and what its length is; and then at twice that distance and at 3 times, and so make your general rule.

H.³ 28*b*]

105.

¶L'ochio nō può giudicare [2]doue la cosa alta debe [3]disciēdere.¶

The eye cannot judge where an object high up ought to descend.

G. 29*b*]

106.

PROSPETTIVA.

[2]Infra le due cose simili e equali [3]poste l'una dopo l'altra con una data [4]distantia si dimostrerà maggiore [5]differētia in nelle loro grādezze, quādo [6]esse sarā più vicine

PERSPECTIVE.

If two similar and equal objects are placed one beyond the other at a given distance the difference in their size will appear greater in proportion as they are

103. 2. lalteza he. 3. alteza. 4. chotale.

104. 1. delle diminuitioni cheffauno. 2. infralloro. 3. spati che infrallochio elle. 4. terpongano. 5. ciercha . . diminviscie. 6. he la sua lūgeza . . lūgeze.

105. 1—3 R. 1. po. 3. dissciēdere.

106. 1. presspecctiva. 2. Infralle due chose. 3. posste . . chon. 4. disstantia . . dimossterra magiore. 5. diferēti . . inelle lor . . quā.

all'ochio che le [7]vede ‖ E cosi de cõverso [8]si dimostrerà infra loro meno [9]varietà di gradezza quato esse sõ [10]più remote dal predetto ochio.

[11]Prouasi mediante le proportioni che ànno [12]infra loro le lor distantie, perchè se fra [13]essi due corpi sarà tanta distantia [14]dall'ochio alla prima quãto dalla pri[15]ma alla 2a, questa si dimãda 2a [16]proportione, perchè se la prima è discosta vn braccio dall'oc[17]chio e la 2a e discosta 2 braccia, il 2 è do[18]pio all'uno e per questo il primo corpo si di[19]mostrerà doppio al 2o E se tu [20]rimoverai da te cento braccia la prima è cento uno braccio [21]la secoda, tu troverai la prima essere [22]maggiore della secõda quato cen[23]to è minore di cẽto uno e questa per cõversa; [24]E ãcora il medesimo si proua per la 4a di questo [25]che dicie delle cose equali tal proportione è da grãdezza [26]a grandezza qua[27]le è da distãtia [28]a distantia [29]dell'ochio che le [30]vede.

nearer to the eye that sees them. And conversely there will seem to be less difference in their size in proportion as they are remote from the eye.

This is proved by the proportions of their distances among themselves; for, if the first of these two objects were as far from the eye, as the 2nd from the first this would be called the second proportion: since, if the first is at 1 braccia from the eye and the 2nd at two braccia, two being twice as much as one, the first object will look twice as large as the second. But if you place the first at a hundred braccia from you and the second at a hundred and one, you will find that the first is only so much larger than the second as 100 is less than 101; and the converse is equally true. And again, the same thing is proved by the 4th of this book which shows that among objects that are equal, there is the same proportion in the diminution of the size as in the increase in the distance from the eye of the spectator.

E. 16 b]

107.

Pa [1]DELLE COSE EQUALI LA PIÙ REMOTA PAR MINORE.[2]

On natural perspective (107—109).

[3]La pratica della prospettiva si diuide [4]in . . . parti, delle quali la prima figura tut[5]te le cose vedute dall'ochio in qualunche [6]distantia e questa in se mostra tutte esse [7]cose come l'ochio le uede diminuite, e non [8]è obbligato l'omo a stare più in un sito [9]che in un'altro, pure che il muro non [10]la riscorti la secõda volta.

[11]Ma la 2a pratica è vna mistione [12]di prospettiva fatta in parte dall'arte e in par[13]te dalla natura, e l'opera fatta [14]colle sua regole non à

OF EQUAL OBJECTS THE MOST REMOTE LOOK THE SMALLEST.

The practice of perspective may be divided into . . . parts[4], of which the first treats of objects seen by the eye at any distance; and it shows all these objects just as the eye sees them diminished, without obliging a man to stand in one place rather than another so long as the plane does not produce a second foreshortening.

But the second practice is a combination of perspective derived partly from art and partly from nature and the work done by its rules is in

6. chelle. 7. chosi . . cõverso [si dime]. 8. [sterã] si dimosstera infralloromẽ. 11. le pro "ne" che. 12. infralloro . . disstantie . . seffra. 13. disstantia 15. quessta. 16. pro "ne" perche sella p.a e disscossta vnbr. 17. ella . . disscossta 2 br. do. 18. il p.o 19. mosstrra . . . Esse . 20. "datte" certo br . . cento ĩ br . 21 . troverrai [lultima] "la prima" essere [ma]. 22. [uore] magiore. 23. cẽto ĩ e equessta p "uo" cõversa . . 24. 4 di quessto. 25. tal pro "ne". 27. disstãtia. 28. addisstantia. 29. chelle.
107. 1. chose. 3. praticha . . prosspectiva. 4. in . . . parte . . p.a figura tuc. 5. dele chose. 6. equesta . . mosstra. 7. chose chome . diminute e ne. 8. ne obbrighato . . asstare piu nũn sito. 9. nol. 10. rissccorti . . sechõda. 11. Malla 2a praticha . . misstione. 12. prosspettiva facta dall . . *As a marginal note* "in parte". 13. natura [e nonam] elloperа. 14. reghole.

107. 4. *in . . . parti*. The space for the number is left blank in the original.

parte al[15]cuna che nõ sia mista colla prospet-[16]tiva naturale ę colla prospettiva [17]accidentale ‖ colla prospettiva na[18]turale intendo essere la pariete pia[19]na dove tale prospettiva è figura[20]ta, la qual pariete ancora ch'e[21]lla sia di lunghezza e altezza paralella, [22]ella è costretta a diminuire le parti [23]remote più che le sua parti prime, e que[24]sto si prova per la prima di sopra e la sua diminu[25]tione è naturale; e la prospettiva accidẽ[26]tale cioè quella ch'è fatta dall'arte fa il cõtra[27]rio in se, perchè crescie nella pariete scorta[28]ta tanto più li corpi che ĩ lor sono equali, [29]quãto l'ochio è più naturale e più vicino al[30]la pariete e quanto la parte d'essa pariete, [31]dove si figura è più remota dall'ochio;

every portion of it, influenced by natural perspective and artificial perspective. By natural perspective I mean that the plane on which this perspective is represented is a flat surface, and this plane, although it is parallel both in length and height, is forced to diminish in its remoter parts more than in its nearer ones. And this is proved by the first of what has been said above, and its diminution is natural. But artificial perspective, that is that which is devised by art, does the contrary; for objects equal in size increase on the plane where it is foreshortened in proportion as the eye is more natural and nearer to the plane, and as the part of the plane on which it is figured is farther from the eye.

[32]e questta tal pari-[33]ete sia *d e* nel-[34]la qual si figv-[35]rã 3 circoli equa-[36]li che son dopo [37]esso *d e*, cioè [38]li circoli *a b c*; ora [39]tu vedi che l'ochi-[40]o · *h* · vede sulla [41]pariete retti [42]linia li tagli del-[43]le spetie maggio-[44]ri nelle maggiori [45]distantie o mi-[46]nori nelle vicine.

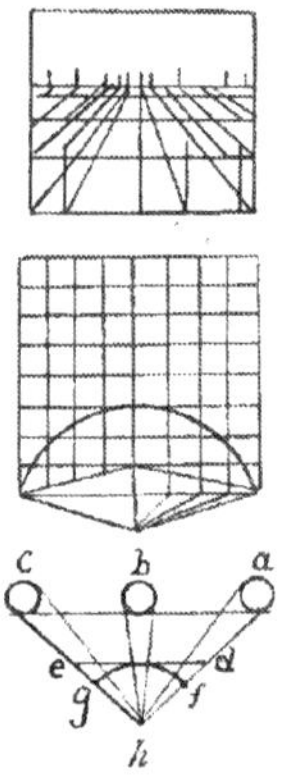

And let this plane be *d e* on which are seen 3 equal circles which are beyond this plane *d e*, that is the circles *a b c*. Now you see that the eye *h* sees on the vertical plane the sections of the images, largest of those that are farthest and smallest of the nearest.

E. 16 *a*]

108.

Qui seguita quel che manca in margine, [2]da piedi dirieto a questa faccia.

[3]Il che natura nella sua prospectiva [4]adopera in coņtrario con ciosiachè nelle [5]maggiori distantie la cosa veduta · si dimo[6]stra minore e nella distantia minore [7]la cosa par maggiore; Ma questa ta[8]le inuencione costrignie

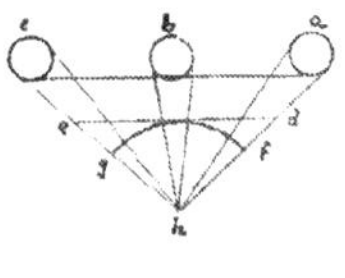

Here follows what is wanting in the margin at the foot on the other side of this page.

Natural perspective acts in a contrary way; for, at greater distances the object seen appears smaller, and at a smaller distance the object appears larger. But this said invention requires the spectator to stand with his eye at a

15. chuna . . . missta cholla prespec. 16. cholle presspettiva. 17. cholla presspettiva. 19. presspettiva effighura. 20. pariete [in se] anchora. 21. alteza. 22. chostretta . . parterte. 23. chelle . . parte . . ecq. 24. lap°di . . . elia sua diminui. 26. cheffatta dallaltre. 27. cresscie. 28. illcrsono. 30. ecquanto. 31. fighura eppiu. 32. ecquesta. 34. fighv. 35. ro 3 cl equa. 36. chesson sop. 38. li cl a. 39. chellochi. 43. magio. 44. magior. 46. nor.

108. 1. mancha. 2. [dir] dappiedi . . acquesta. 3. prosspectiva. 4. inchontrario chon . . chẽnel. 5. magior distantie . . . vedita, si dimos. 7. Macquesta. 8. chosstrignie . . ueditore as. 9. chollochio . . piracholo. 10. dattale spiracholo si dimossterra.

24. *la prima di sopra* i. e. the first of the three diagrams which, in the original MS., are placed in the margin at the beginning of this chapter.

il ueditore a [9]stare coll'ochio a vno spiracolo e [10]allora da tale spiracolo si dimostrerà [11]bene; Ma perchè molti occhi s'ab[12]battono a vedere a un medesimo tenpo vna [13]medesima opera fatta con tale arte e so[14]lo vn di quelli vede bene l'ufitio di tal pro[15]spectiua e li altri tutti restā confu[16]si; Egli è dunque da fuggire tal pro[17]spettiva conposta e a tenersi alla sē[18]plicie. la qual no uol uedere pariete in i[19]scorto, ma più in propia forma che sia [20]possibile; E di questa prospettiua [21]senplicie. della quale la pariete taglia le [22]piramidi portatricie delle spetie all'ochio [23]equalmente distanti dalla virtù visiua [24]ci ne dà sperietia la curva lucie del[25]l'ochio sopra la quale tali piramidi si ta[26]gliano equalmēte distanti dalla virtù [27]visiua ecc.

small hole and then, at that small hole, it will be very plain. But since many (men's) eyes endeavour at the same time to see one and the same picture produced by this artifice only one can see clearly the effect of this perspective and all the others will see confusion. It is well therefore to avoid such complex perspective and hold to simple perspective which does not regard planes as foreshortened, but as much as possible in their proper form. This simple perspective, in which the plane intersects the pyramids by which the images are conveyed to the eye at an equal distance from the eye is our constant experience, from the curved form of the pupil of the eye on which the pyramids are intersected at an equal distance from the visual virtue.

Br. M. 62a]

109.

Della prospettiva naturale mista colla prospettiva accidētale.

[1]Questa dimostratione divide la prospettiva naturale dalla accidētale, [2]ma auanti che più oltre proceda difinirai quale è naturale e quale accidētale; prospettiva naturale dicie così [4]delle cose d'equal magnitudine [5]la più remota si dimostra minore; E de converso la più propinqua si dimo[6]stra maggiore, e tal proportione è da diminutione a diminutione qua[7]le è da distantia a distantia Ma la prospettiua accidētale pone le co[8]se inequali in varie distantie, riservādo la minore più vicina all'ochio che la maggiore, cō tal distantia che essa maggiore si dimostra essere minore di tutte [10]l'altre, e di questo è causa il mvro doue tal dimostratione è figurata, il quale [11]à distantia inequale dall'ochio in ogni

Of a mixture of natural and artificial perspective.

This diagram distinguishes natural from artificial perspective. But before proceeding any farther I will define what is natural and what is artificial perspective. Natural perspective says that the more remote of a series of objects of equal size will look the smaller, and conversely, the nearer will look the larger and the apparent size will diminish in proportion to the distance. But in artificial perspective when objects of unequal size are placed at various distances the smallest is nearer to the eye than the largest and the greatest distance looks as though it were the least of all; and the cause of this is the plane on which the objects are represented; and which is at unequal distances from the eye throughout its length. And this diminution

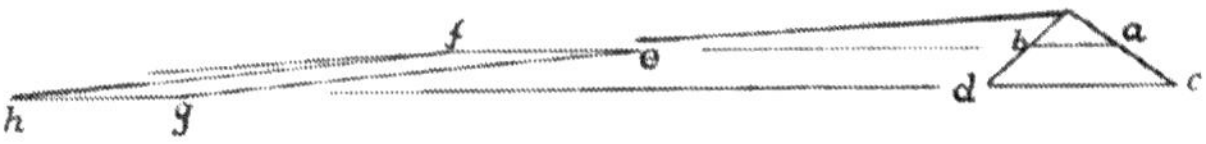

11. molti (omi) occhi [p]sa. 12. battano aumedesimo. 13. chon . . arte esso. 14. lo vn di megli vede . . pres 15. elli . . restā. 16. daffuggire . . pre. 17. chonposta e attenersi. 19. chessia. 20. presspectiva. 22. piramide portatricie. 23. distante. 24. cienela sperietia. 25. tale piramide. 26. distante.

109. 1. presspectiua . . chella presspectiva. 2. presspectiva. 3. proceeds difinira . . ennaturale eequale. 4. presspectiua . . chosi. 5. dimostra . . chonverso . . dimos. 6. etal . . diminuitione addiminuitione. 7. dissantia addistantia Malla presspectiua . . el [illegible] questo è chausa . .

parte della sua lūghezza e questa tal [12] diminutione del muro è naturale, ma la prospettiua in esso figurata è accidē[13]tale, perchè in nessuna parte non si accorda colla vera diminutione del det[14]to muro; onde ne resulta che, removendosi alquāto l'ochio d'essa prospetti[15]va risguardatore, ogni cosa figurata apparisce mostruosa, il che nō [16]interviene nella prospettiua naturale, la quale è difinita di sopra ecc. [17]adunque diremo il quadrato *a b c d* figurato di sopra essere un □ in iscor[18]to, veduto dall'ochio situato in mezzo della larghezza che à la sua fronte; Ma [19]la · prospettiva accidētale mista colla naturale fia trovata nel quadra[20]to detto el main, cioè *e f g h*, il quale à a parere all'ochio che lo vede simile [21]al *a b c d* stāte l'ochio fermo nel primo sito infra *c d*, e questo si [22]dimostrerà fare buono effetto: perchè la prospettiua naturale del muro fa [23]che tal muro occulterà il mancamēto di tal mostruosità.

of the plane is natural, but the perspective shown upon it is artificial since it nowhere agrees with the true diminution of the said plane. Whence it follows, that when the eye is somewhat removed from the [station point of the] perspective that it has been gazing at, all the objects represented look monstrous, and this does not occur in natural perspective, which has been defined above. Let us say then, that the square *a b c d* figured above is foreshortened being seen by the eye situated in the centre of the side which is in front. But a mixture of artificial and natural perspective will be seen in this tetragon called *el main*, that is to say *e f g h* which must appear to the eye of the spectator to be equal to *a b c d* so long as the eye remains in its first position between *c* and *d*. And this will be seen to have a good effect, because the natural perspective of the plane will conceal the defects which would [otherwise] seem monstrous.

dimosstratione e fighurata. 11. disstantia . . ecquesta. 12. diminuitione . . malla presspectiua. 13. acchorda cholla . . diminuitione del dec. 14. cherremovendosi . . presspecti. 15. rissghuardatore . . chosa fighurata apparisscie mōsstruoso. 16. ne interviene . . presspectiua . . eddifinita. 17. addunque direno . . fighurato . . innissco "r". 18. largheza . . froncte. 19. lla . presspectiva . . missta cholla. 20. decto . . apparere . . chello. 21. ecquesto. 22. dimossterra . . presspectiua. 23. chettal . . ochulture il manchamēto . . musstrvosita.

109. 20. *el main* is quite legibly written in the original; the meaning and derivation of the word are equally doubtful.

III.

Six books on Light and Shade.

Linear Perspective cannot be immediately followed by either the "prospettiva de' perdimenti" *or the* "prospettiva de' colori" *or the aerial perspective; since these branches of the subject presuppose a knowledge of the principles of Light and Shade. No apology, therefore, is here needed for placing these immediately after Linear Perspective.*

We have various plans suggested by Leonardo for the arrangement of the mass of materials treating of this subject. Among these I have given the preference to a scheme propounded in No. III, *because, in all probability, we have here a final and definite purpose expressed. Several authors have expressed it as their opinion that the Paris Manuscript* C *is a complete and finished treatise on Light and Shade. Certainly, the Principles of Light and Shade form by far the larger portion of this MS. which consists of two separate parts; still, the materials are far from being finally arranged. It is also evident that he here investigates the subject from the point of view of the Physicist rather than from that of the Painter.*

The plan of a scheme of arrangement suggested in No. III *and adopted by me has been strictly adhered to for the first four Books. For the three last, however, few materials have come down to us; and it must be admitted that these three Books would find a far more appropriate place in a work on Physics than in a treatise on Painting. For this reason I have collected in Book V all the chapters on Reflections, and in Book VI I have put together and arranged all the sections of MS.* C *that belong to the book on Painting, so far as they relate to Light and Shade, while the sections of the same MS. which treat of the* "Prospettiva de' perdimenti" *have, of course, been excluded from the series on Light and Shade.*

GENERAL INTRODUCTION.

Br. M. 171 a]

110.

Bisognia ti descrivere la teorica e poi. [2]la pratica; [3]discriuerai primo de ōbra e lumi de' corpi [4]densi e poi de' corpi trasparenti.

Prolegomena.

You must first explain the theory and then the practice. First you must describe the shadows and lights on opaque objects, and then on transparent bodies.

C. A. 246 a; 733 a]

111.

PROEMIA.

[2][Auēdo · io trattato della natura · de' ōbre · e loro · percussione, Ora · tratterò · de lochi, i quali da esse ōbre · tochi · fieno, [3]E di loro curuità, obbliquità · o dirittura o di qualunque qualità trovare per me si potrà.]

[4]Ōbra · è privatione di luce; [5]Parendo a me le ōbre · essere di somma neciessità · in nella prospettiva, perochè sanza quelle i corpi opachi e cubi · male sieno [6]intesi; quello che dētro · a' sua termini collocato · fia, e male i sua cōfini ītesi fieno · se essi nō terminano ī cāpo di uario [7]colore da quello · del corpo; E per questo jo propōgo nella prima propositione dell' ōbre, dico ī questa forma come ogni corpo [8]opaco .fia circū-

Scheme of the books on Light and Shade.

INTRODUCTION.

[Having already treated of the nature of shadows and the way in which they are cast, I will now consider the places on which they fall; and their curvature, obliquity, flatness or, in short, any character I may be able to detect in them.]

Shadow is the obstruction of light. Shadows appear to me to be of supreme importance in perspective, because, without them opaque and solid bodies will be ill defined; that which is contained within their outlines and their boundaries themselves will be ill-understood unless they are shown against a background of a different tone from themselves. And therefore in my first proposition concerning shadow I state that every opaque body is surrounded and its whole surface enveloped in shadow and light. And on

110. 1. teoricha. 2. praticha. 3. ellume. 4. chorpi trāpareti.

111. 1. tractato delle nature . . elloro . perchussione. 2. choruita . . diritti. 3. Obra . he. 5. āme . . inella prosspettiva . . chorpi | "oppachi e" chubi. 6. malle esua chōfini . . chāpo. 7. dacquello . . chorpo . . allōbre | "dicho īquesta forma" chome . .

111. This text has already been published with some slight variations in Dozio's pamphlet *Degli scritti e disegni di Leonardo da Vinci*, Milan 1871, pp. 30—31. Dozio did not transcribe it from the original MS. which seems to have remained unknown to him, but from an old copy (MS. H. 227 in the Ambrosian Library).

2. *Avendo io tractato.*—We may suppose that he here refers to some particular MS., possibly Paris C.

dato e superfitialmēte vestito d'ōbre · e di lumi, e sopra questo · edifico · il primo libro; Oltre a di questo [9]esse ōbre sono in se di uarie qualità d'oscurità · perchè da varie quātità di razzi luminosi abbādonate sono, e queste domado ōbre originali, [10]perchè sono le prime ōbre, che uestono i corpi doue appiccate sono, e sopra questo · edificherò il 2° libro; [11]da queste ōbre originali ne resultano · razzi ōbrosi · i quali si uāno dilatando per l'aria, e sono di tante qualità, quāte [12]sono le uarietà dell'onbre originali, donde essi derivano · e per questo io chiamo esse ōbre ōbre diriuatiue, perchè da altre ōbre [13]nascono, e sopra di questo jo farò il 3° libro; Ancora · queste onbre diriuative nelle loro percussioni fanno [14]tanti vari · effetti · quāto · son vari i lochi dove esse percuotono, e qui farò . il quarto libro; E perchè la [15]percussione della diriuativa ōbra è senpre circūdata da percussione di luminosi razzi · la quale per reflesso cōcorso [16]risaltando indirieto uerso la sua cagione trova l'onbra originale · e si mischia e si cōuerte in quella alquāto variādola di sua [17]natura e sopra questo edificherò · il quīto libro; Oltr'a di questo farò il sesto libro, nel quale si cōterrà le uarie [18]e molte diuersificationi · delli risultanti razzi reflessi, i quali uarierāno la originale di tanti vari colori quā[19]to fiē vari i lochi ōde essi reflessi razzi luminosi deriuano ¶ancora farò la settima diuisione delle uarie [20]distantie, che fiā infra la percussione del razo reflesso al loco dōde nasce; quāto fiē uarie le similitudini de co[21]lori che esso nella percussione al corpo opaco appicca.

this proposition I build up the first Book. Besides this, shadows have in themselves various degrees of darkness, because they are caused by the absence of a variable amount of the luminous rays; and these I call Primary shadows because they are the first, and inseparable from the object to which they belong. And on this I will found my second Book. From these primary shadows there result certain shaded rays which are diffused through the atmosphere and these vary in character according to that of the primary shadows whence they are derived. I shall therefore call these shadows Derived shadows because they are produced by other shadows; and the third Book will treat of these. Again these derived shadows, where they are intercepted by various objects, produce effects as various as the places where they are cast and of this I will treat in the fourth Book. And since all round the derived shadows, where the derived shadows are intercepted, there is always a space where the light falls and by reflected dispersion is thrown back towards its cause, it meets the original shadow and mingles with it and modifies it somewhat in its nature; and on this I will compose my fifth Book. Besides this, in the sixth Book I will investigate the many and various diversities of reflections resulting from these rays which will modify the original [shadow] by [imparting] some of the various colours from the different objects whence these reflected rays are derived. Again, the seventh Book will treat of the various distances that may exist between the spot where the reflected rays fall and that where they originate, and the various shades of colour which they will acquire in falling on opaque bodies.

Ash. I. 6b]

112.

Different principles and plans of treatment (112—116).

¶ Tratterai · prima · de' · lumi · fatti dalle . finestre · ai quali porrai nome [2]aria cōstretta; poi tratterai de lumi della cāpagnia, ai quali porai nome lume [3]libero · di poi tratterai del lume de corpi luminosi.¶

First I will treat of light falling through windows which I will call Restricted [Light] and then I will treat of light in the open country, to which I will give the name of diffused Light. Then I will treat of the light of luminous bodies.

chorpo oppacho . . circhūdato . . vessito . . edificho. 9. dosschurita . . vari [razi] "quātita dirazzi" lumīuosi [sono] abbādonate | "sono" ecqueste. 10. vestano i chorpi . . apichate . . libro [dopo questo]. 11. dacqueste . . resulta razi e quali siuano . . laria [i quali] e. 12. originale essi ōbre "ōbre" diriuatiue. 13. naschano . . ibro Anchora . . porchussioni. 14. effe effetti . . dove | "essa" perchotano . . perche [dintorno alla]. 15. perchussione . . circhūdata . . perchussione . . chōchorso. 16. essimista essi chōuerte. 17. essopra . . chotera. 18. diuersifichationi . . risaltanti razi refressi . . cholori. 19. refressi . . anchora. 20. cheffia infralla perchussione . . alloch . . nasscie . . similitudine. 21. perchussione . . chorpo oppacho appicha.

112. 1. per[illegible] 2. [illegible] 3. [illegible] libro dipo trare.

K.3, 25*b*]

113.

De pittura.

[2]Li aspetti dell'onbre e lumi [3]coll'ochio sono 3, de quali [4]l'uno è quãdo l'ochio e 'l lu[5]me son da un medesimo [6]lato del corpo veduti; [7]2° è quando l'ochio è dinã[8]ti al-l'obietto e 'l lume è do[9]po esso obbietto; 3° è [10]quel che l'ochio dinãti al[11]l'obbietto e 'l lume è da lato [12]ĩ modo che la linia che s'astẽ[13]de dall'obbietto all'ochio, e da es[14]so obbietto al lume, giugnẽ[15]dosi la cõgiũtiõ sarà rettãgulare.

Of painting.

The conditions of shadow and light [as seen] by the eye are 3. Of these the first is when the eye and the light are on the same side of the object seen; the 2nd is when the eye is in front of the object and the light is behind it. The 3rd is when the eye is in front of the object and the light is on one side, in such a way as that a line drawn from the object to the eye and one from the object to the light should form a right angle where they meet.

K.3, 26*a*]

114.

De pittura.

[2]Ecci vn altra partitione, [3]cioè della natura dell'ob[4]bietto riflesso posto ĩ[5]fra l'ochio e'l lu[6]me per diuersi aspetti.

Of painting.

This is another section: that is, of the nature of a reflection (from) an object placed between the eye and the light under various aspects.

M. 80*a*]

115.

De pictura.

[2]Di tutte le cose vedute si à a cõsiderare [3]·3· cose cioè il sito dell'ochio che [4]vede, e 'l sito della cosa veduta e'l lume, [5]el sito del lume che allumina [6]tal corpo;

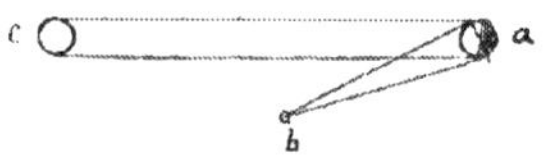

[7]*b*. è l'ochio · *a* · è la cosa veduta · *c* è il lume;

[8]*a* · è l'ochio · *b* · è la cosa che allumina, [9]*c* è il corpo ch'è alluminato.

Of painting.

As regards all visible objects 3 things must be considered. These are the position of the eye which sees: that of the object seen [with regard] to the light, and the position of the light which illuminates the object. *b* is the eye, *a* the object seen, *c* the light. *a* is the eye, *b* the illuminating body, *c* is the illuminated object.

M. 79*b*]

116.

a · sia il lume · *b* · l'ochio · *c* è la cosa [2]veduta dall'ochio e dal lume; [3]Queste dan vna volta l'ochio fra 'l

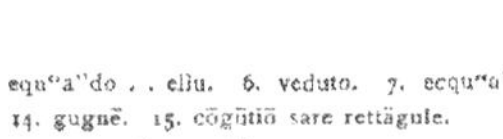

Let *a* be the light, *b* the eye, *c* the object seen by the eye and in the light. These show, first, the eye between

113. 1—15 R. 2. asspetti . . ellumi. 4. equ"a"do . . ellu. 6. veduto. 7. ecqu"a"ndo locho. 10. chellochio. 11. dallato. 12. chella . . chessastẽ. 13. e da e. 14. gugnẽ. 15. cõgũtiõ sare rettãgule.

114. 1—6 R. 2. partione. 3. coe. 4. rẽfresso posto. 6. asspetti.

115. 2. chose . . siaha chõsiderare. 3. [la]. 3. cose coe [lochio] il. 5. [che a] el. 7. *b*. hellochio a ella . . c ellume. 8. ellochio . 6. ella cosa [veduta] che allũma.

lume e'l corpo [4]la 2ª il lume fra l'ochio e'l corpo, 3ª il corpo fra [5]l'ochio e'l lume [6]*a* · è l'ochio *b* · la cosa alluminata · *c* · è il lume.

the light and the body; the 2nd, the light between the eye and the body; the 3rd the body between the eye and the light. *a* is the eye, *b* the illuminated object, *c* the light.

E. 3*b*]

117.

PICTURA.

DELLE 3 SORTE DE' LUMI CHE ALLUMINANO [3]LI CORPI OPACHI

[4]Il primo de lumi colli quali s'alluminano li cor[5]pi opachi è detto particulare · e questo è [6]il sole o altro lume di finestra o fuoco: Il [7]secondo è vniversale come accade ne'tēpi nu[8]bolosi o di nebbia e simili, Il 3° è cōpo[9]sto, cioè quando il sole da sera o da mattina [10]è integralmēte sotto l'orizonte

Different sorts of Light (117 118).

OF PAINTING.

OF THE THREE KINDS OF LIGHT THAT ILLUMINATE OPAQUE BODIES.

The first kind of Light which may illuminate opaque bodies is called Direct light—as that of the sun or any other light from a window or flame The second is Diffused [universal] light, such as we see in cloudy weather or in mist and the like. The 3rd is Subdued light, that is when the sun is entirely below the horizon, either in the evening or morning.

G 3*b*]

118.

DE' LUMI

[2]I lumi che alluminano li corpi opachi sono [3]di 4 sorti, cioè vniversale come quello del'aria ch'è [4]dentro al nostro orizzonte | e particolare com'è [5]quello del sole o d'una finestra o porta o altro spa[6]tio, e'l terzo è il lume riflesso ed ecce ne vn [7]4°, il quale passa per cose trasparēti, come tela [8]o carta o simili, ma nō trasparēti come vetri, [9]o cristali o altri corpi diafani, li quali fan il mede[10]simo effetto come se nulla fusse interposto ī[11]fra'l corpo ōbroso e'l lume che l'allumina, e di que[12]sti parleremo distintamēte nel nostro discorso.

OF LIGHT.

The lights which may illuminate opaque bodies are of 4 kinds. These are: diffused light as that of the atmosphere, within our horizon And Direct, as that of the sun, or of a window or door or other opening. The third is Reflected light, and there is a 4th which is that which passes through [semi] transparent bodies, as linen or paper or the like, but not transparent like glass, or crystal, or other diaphanous bodies, which produce the same effect as though nothing intervened between the shaded object and the light that falls upon it, and this we will discuss fully in our discourse.

Ash I 13*b*]

119

CHE COSA È ŌBRA E LUME.

[2]Ōbra è priuatiō di luce e sola oppositione de' corpi dēsi opposti a razzi luminosi: ōbra è di natu[3]ra delle tenebre: lume è di natura della luce; l'una [4]ciela e l'altro dimostra: sono sēpre ī cōpagnia cōgivti · ai corpi, e l'onbra è di maggiore potētia che

Definition of the nature of shadows (119—122).

WHAT LIGHT AND SHADOW ARE.

Shadow is the absence of light, merely the obstruction of the luminous rays by an opaque body. Shadow is of the nature of darkness. Light [on an object] is of the nature of a luminous body, one conceals and the other reveals. They are always associated and inseparable from all objects. But shadow

116 1 c ella 4 ilume frallochio 7 ellochio
117 2 oppachi 3 chorpi oppachi 4 cholli li chor 5 oppachi he detto partichulare ecquesto he. 6. offuocho 7 sechondo he achade 8 3ª he chōpo 9 dassera
118 3 di [3] "4" sorte coe quel 4 nosstro orizonte 5 quel 6. refresso 7 trassparēti. 8. charta ossimili . trassparēti. 9. crisstali. 10 chome . fussi 12 parlerē nosstrodisscorso
119 ellume 2 Ōbra "e priuatiō di luce" e sola oposittione opostia razi. 3 luna [e privatione e laltro] 4 [di mo] ciela ellaltro . magiore 5 proibissce 6 luce ella luche . . chaciare

'l lume ïpero·chè quella proibisce e priva [6]ïteramëte · i corpi · della · luce, e la luce nö può mai cacciare ï tutto [7]l'öbra de' corpi · cioè corpi dësi.

is a more powerful agent than light, for it can impede and entirely deprive bodies of their light, while light can never entirely expel shadow from a body, that is from an opaque body.

W. L. 145; Da] **120.**

¶Öbra è lume diminuito [2]mediante l'oppositiö dell'opaco¶. [3]¶Öbra è 'l suppliomë[4]to del razzo luminoso ta[5]gliato dallo opaco¶.

[6]Pruovasi, perchè il razzo [7]öbroso è della medesima [8]figura e quä-tità che era [9]il razzo luminoso nel quale [10]essa öbra si träsmuta.

Shadow is the diminution of light by the intervention of an opaque body. Shadow is the counterpart of the luminous rays which are cut off by an opaque body.

This is proved because the shadow cast is the same in shape and size as the luminous rays were which are transformed into a shadow.

W. 232b] **121.**

L'öbra è diminutione di lucie e di tenebre [2]ed è interposta infra esse tenebre e lucie;

[3]L'onbra è d'infinita oscurità e d'infinita di[4]minutione d'essa oscurità;

[5]Li principi e fini dell'onbra s'astëdono infra [6]la lucie e le tenebre ed è d'infinita dimi[7]nuitione e d'ïfinita aumëtatione.

L'onbra è pronütiatione de' corpi delle lor [9]figure.

[10]Le figure de corpi nö darä notitia delle lo[11]ro qualità sanza l'onbra.

Shadow is the diminution alike of light and of darkness, and stands between darkness and light.

A shadow may be infinitely dark, and also of infinite degrees of absence of darkness.

The beginnings and ends of shadow lie between the light and darkness and may be infinitely diminished and infinitely increased. Shadow is the means by which bodies display their form.

The forms of bodies could not be understood in detail but for shadow.

Ash. I. 14a] **122.**

Del'essere del'öbra per se.

[2]L'öbra · è della natura · delle cose · vniversali · che tutte sono piv [3]potëti · nel prïcipio · e iuerso il fine ïdeboliscono; dico nel principio · [4]d'ogni forma e qualità · evidëte ed inevidëte · e nö delle cose cödotte [5]di piccol prïcipio ï molto accrescimëto dal tëpo, come sarebbe una gran [6]quercia che à debole prïcipio per una piccola ghiäda; äzi dirò la quer[7]cia essere piv potëte al nascimëto ch'ella fa della terra, cioè nella [8]maggiore sua grosseza, adunque le tenebre sono il primo [9]grado del'onbra · e la · luce · è l'ultimo: adüque · tu · pittore farai l'ö[10]bra · piv scura appresso alla · sua · cagione e il fine fa che si cöverta in luce, cioè che paia säza fine.

Of the nature of shadow.

Shadow partakes of the nature of universal matter. All such matters are more powerful in their beginning and grow weaker towards the end, I say at the beginning, whatever their form or condition may be and whether visible or invisible. And it is not from small beginnings that they grow to a great size in time; as it might be a great oak which has a feeble beginning from a small acorn. Yet I may say that the oak is most powerful at its beginning, that is where it springs from the earth, which is where it is largest—(To return:) Darkness, then, is the strongest degree of shadow and light is its least. Therefore, O Painter, make your shadow darkest close to the object that casts it, and make the end of it fading into light, seeming to have no end.

120. 1. ellume. 2. oppacho. 3. Öbra [ellume]. 4. te del. 5. oppacho. 8. ecquatita.

121. 1. diminuitione . . eddi. 2. ellucie. 3. osschurita. 4. minuitione . . osscurita. 5. effini . . sasstëdano infral. 6. elle tenebr. . nuitione. 8. chorpi. 10. chorpi . . no dara.

122. 2. dela . . chose . . chettutte. 3. ïdeboliscano. 4. ecqualita. 5. pichol . . ïmolt . . sarebe ï gra. 6. che he debole . . per pichola. 7. cie essere . . chela fa dela tera. 8. magiore . . grosseza adunq le tenebre e. 9. ella luce. 10. apresso . chagione . . cöverti.

123.

C. 11 b]

Of the various kinds of shadows (123—125).

*|Tenebre è privatiō di luce; ²ōbra è diminutiō di luce; ³obra primitiva · è quella che è appiccata a corpi ōbrosi; ⁴ōbra dirivativa è quella che si spicca da corpi obrosi e scorre per l'aria; ⁵obra ripercossa è quella che è circōdata da luminata pariete; ⁶l'ōbra senplice è quella che no uede alcuna parte del lume che la causa *|⁷l'obra senplice comïcia in nella linia che si parte da'termini de' corpi luminosi · *a* · *b*.

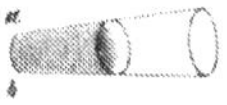

Darkness is absence of light. Shadow is diminution of light. Primitive shadow is that which is inseparable from a body not in the light. Derived shadow is that which is disengaged from a body in shadow and pervades the air. A cast transparent shadow is that which is surrounded by an illuminated surface. A simple shadow is one which receives no light from the luminous body which causes it. A simple shadow begins within the line which starts from the edge of the luminous body *a b*.

124.

Br. M. 248 b]

|Onbra senplice è quella che nō vede alcu lumi²noso|

³onbra composta è quella che da vno o più lu⁴minosi è alluminata.

A simple shadow is one where no light at all interferes with it.

A compound shadow is one which is somewhat illuminated by one or more lights.

125.

Ash. I. 13 b]

Che differētia · è da ōbra cōgiūta coi corpi a' ōbra separata?

³Ōbra · cōgivnta · è quella · che mai · si parte · dai corpi alluminati, ⁴come sarebbe una palla · la quale · stāte al lume · sēpre à una parte di se ⁵occupata dall'ōbra, la quale mai si diuide per mvtatiō di sito fatto da essa ⁶palla; Ombra · separata · può · essere · e non essere creata dal corpo; ⁷poniamo che essa palla sia distāte a uno muro uno braccio e dal'opposita parte sia ⁸il lume; il detto lume · mādera i detto mvro · appūto tanta dilatazione di ō⁹bra quāt'è quella che si troua sulla · parte della palla ch'è volta · a detto ¹⁰muro · Quella parte · dell'ōbra separata · che non appare fia quādo il lume ¹¹fia di sotto alla palla che la sua ōbra ne va inverso il cielo e no trovādo resi¹²stētia pel camino si perde.

What is the difference between a shadow that is inseparable from a body and a cast shadow?

An inseparable shadow is that which is never absent from the illuminated body. As, for instance a ball, which so long as it is in the light always has one side in shadow which never leaves it for any movement or change of position in the ball. A separate shadow may be and may not be produced by the body itself. Suppose the ball to be one braccia distant from a wall with a light on the opposite side of it; this light will throw upon the wall exactly as broad a shadow as is to be seen on the side of the ball that is turned towards the wall. That portion of the cast shadow will not be visible when the light is below the ball and the shadow is thrown up towards the sky and finding no obstruction on its way is lost.

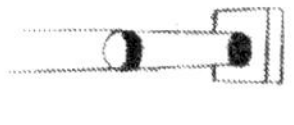

ōbra separata e cōgiūta
(separate and inseparable shadow).

ōbra separata inevidēte
(separate invisible shadow).

123. 1—7 R. 2. ōbra he diminutiō. 3. he quella . . che he appichata achorpi. 4. he quella . . spicha . . escore. 5. eequella che he . . dallumunata. 6. he senplice he . . chella. 7. inella . . chessiparte.

124. 1. eequela . . alchū. 3. chonposta e quella . oppiu.

125. 3. eequella. 4. chome sarebe ī . . a ī parte. 5. ochupata. 6. po . . corpo. 7. a ī muro ī br e . . oposita. 8. detta . . apūto dāta. 9. chessi troua. 10. Quela . . seperata . apare . ilume. 11. ala pala. 12. chamino.

Br. M. 171 a]

126.

COME SON DI 2 RAGIONI LUMI [2] L'UNO SEPARATO E L'ALTRO CŌGIVTO · [3] AI CORPI.

[4] Separato · è quello che illumina [5] il corpo: cōgivnto · è quella par[6]te del corpo alluminato da esso lu[7]me; l'uno lume si dimāda primi[8]tiuo e l'altro dirivatiuo; [9] e cosi sono di 2 nature ōbre, [10] l'una primitiva e ōbra dirivatiua; [11] primitiva è quella · ch'è appiccata ai [12] corpi, dirivatiua è quella [13] che si separa dai corpi, portādo [14] ī se alle parieti de' mvri la forma [15] della sua cagione.

HOW THERE ARE 2 KINDS OF LIGHT, ONE SEPARABLE FROM, AND THE OTHER INSEPARABLE FROM BODIES.

Separate light is that which falls upon the body. Inseparable light is the side of the body that is illuminated by that light. One is called primary, the other derived. And, in the same way there are two kinds of shadow:—One primary and the other derived. The primary is that which is inseparable from the body, the derived is that which proceeds from the body conveying to the surface of the wall the form of the body causing it.

Of the various kinds of light (126. 127).

Br. M. 170 b]

127.

Come sono 2 differenti lumi [2] l'uno si chiama libero e l'altro cōstretto, [3] il libero è quello che libero allumina i corpi, [4] costretto è quello

How there are 2 different kinds of light; one being called diffused, the other restricted. The diffused is that which freely illuminates

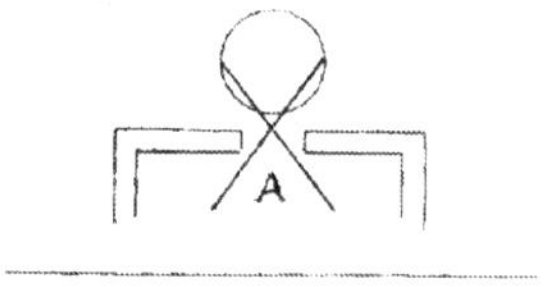

che per qualche [5] spiracolo o finestra allumina [6] medesimamēte i corpi.

objects. The restricted is that which being admitted through an opening or window illuminates them on that side only.

C. A. 114 1/11 355 a]

128.

Lucie è discacciatore di tenebre, [2] onbra è priuatione di luce, [3] lume primitiuo · è quello [4] il quale è cagione d'allumina[5]re i corpi ōbrosi; [6] e li diriuatiui · lumi sō quelle [7] parti de' corpi [8] dal primo lume alluminate; [9] Onbra primitiva è quella [10] parte de' corpi che dal lume [11] veduta esser nō può;

Light is the chaser away of darkness. Shade is the obstruction of light. Primary light is that which falls on objects and causes light and shade. And derived lights are those portions of a body which are illuminated by the primary light. A primary shadow is that side of a body on which the light cannot fall.

General remarks (128. 129).

126. 2. seperato elalto. 4. [seperato ecquello] seperato ecquello chellumina. 5. ecquella. 8. ellaltro. 11. e que che apicata. 12. ecquella. 13. chessi sepera. 14. ale pariete. 15. chagione.
127. 1. difentu. 2. ciama libro. 3. i libre ecquello . . alumina. 4. costeto ecquelo. 5. alumina. 6. chorpi.
128. 1. discaciatore. 3. ecquello. 4. chagione. 6. el diriuatiui. 7. parte . . corpi [alluminate]. 9. hecquella. 10. chorpi . . da-

127. At the spot marked *A* in the first diagram Leonardo wrote *lume cōstretto* (restricted light). At the spot *B* on the second diagram he wrote *lume libera* (diffused light).

[12]Cõcorso õbroso e luminoso [13]è quella soma de'razzi che da [14]corpo õbroso o luminoso si parto[15]no scorrendo per l'arie sanza [16]percussione õbrosa o luminosa [17]e quel loco che inpediscie e sopra se taglia [18]il concorso de'razzi õbrosi e lumi[19]nosi.

[20]E quell'ochio meglio conoscierà [21]le figure de' corpi che infra le parti [22]onbrose e luminose · situato fia.

The general distribution of shadow and light is that sum total of the rays thrown off by a shaded or illuminated body passing through the air without any interference and the spot which intercepts and cuts off the distribution of the dark and light rays.

And the eye can best distinguish the forms of objects when it is placed between the shaded and the illuminated parts.

A. 8*b*]

129.

MÊTIONE DELLE CHOSE · LE QUALI IO DIMANDO · CHE MI SIANO CÕCIEDUTE [2]IN NELLE · PROVE DI QUESTA · MIA · PROSPECTIUA.

MEMORANDUM OF THINGS I REQUIRE TO HAVE GRANTED [AS AXIOMS] IN MY EXPLANATION OF PERSPECTIVE.

[1]Io dimãdo che mi sia cõceduto lo · affermare che ciascuno razzo [3]passando · per aria che sia · d'equale · sottilità scorrino per retta linia · dalla [5]loro cagione · all'obbiecto o percussione.

I ask to have this much granted me— to assert that every ray passing through air of equal density throughout, travels in a straight line from its cause to the object or place it falls upon.

lume. 11. po. 12. elluminoso. 13. equalla soma . . razi. 14. elluminoso si parta. 15. scorrendo . . sanza percussione. 16. perchussione. 17. equelloch . . inpediascie essopra. 18. chonchorso . . razi. 20. equellochio . . chonosciera. 21. de corpi infralle.

129. 1. chose . . sia chõciedute. 2. Inelle. 3. chõcieduto lo . affermare [che i razi visuali . e razi luminosi] [2]che ciascuno razo". 4. aria [duna] chessia . . soctilita scorino . . dala. 5. chagione.

FIRST BOOK ON LIGHT AND SHADE.

W. L. 146 *a*]

130.

On the nature of light (130. 131).

La ragione perchè il lume à ĩ se vn solo ciẽtro si è questa; [2]noi conosciamo chiaramente vn lume grãde avãza[3]re molte volte vna cosa piccola, il quale niẽte di meno, [4]benchè lui cõ sua razzi la circũdi molto più che mezza, [5]senpre l'onbra apparisce nella prima pariete e senpre si vede;

[6]Poniamo che *c* | *f* sia il lume grãde [7]e che | *n* sia la cosa opposta gli che genera [8]l'õbra nella pariete, e che | *a* · *b* sia la pariete; [9]chiaro apparisce che il grã lume nõ cõducerebbe [10]l'onbra *n* · alla pariete; ma perchè il lume à ĩ se [11]ciẽtro, provo sperimẽtãdo, l'onbra si cõduce alla [12]pariete, come lo figura | *m* | *o* | *t* *r*.

The reason by which we know that a light radiates from a single centre is this: We plainly see that a large light is often much broader than some small object which nevertheless—and although the rays [of the large light] are much more than twice the extent [of the small body]—always has its shadow cast on the nearest surface very visibly.

Let *c f* be a broad light and *n* be the object in front of it, casting a shadow on the plane, and let *a b* be the plane. It is clear that it is not the broad light that will cast the shadow *n* on the plane, but that the light has within it a centre is shown by this experiment. The shadow falls on the plane as is shown at *m o t r*.

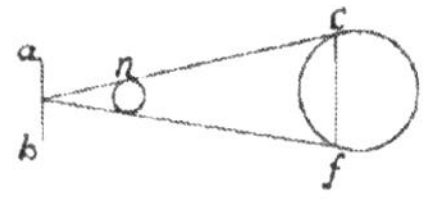

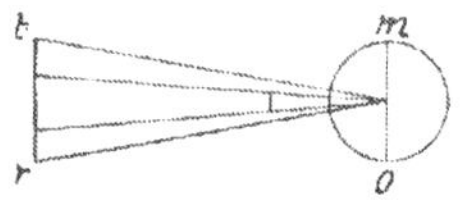

[13]Perchè ĩ due o dinãzi ai dua occhi, [14]rappresentatovi 3 cose si faño 2.

[15]Perchè liuellãdo vna dirittura cõ 2 mire la prima apparisce [16]falsa: dico

[13] Why, to two [eyes] or in front of two eyes do 3 objects appear as two?

Why, when you estimate the direction of an object with two sights the nearer

130. 1. ilume. 2. noi choi chogniossiamo. 3. chosa . . mene. 4. beneche lui cho . . razi . . circhudi . . m[ezaj. 5. apparissce. 7. e che | n | sia la chosa . . gienerare. 9. aparirebe il . . chonducerebe. 11. ciẽtro pro sperimẽtãdo lonbra schõduce. 12. chomel fighura. 13. duco odinãza ai dua. 14. rapresentatovi . . chose. 15. chõ . . apparisscie. 16. dicho chellochio . .

130. 13. In the original MS. no explanatory text is placed after this title-line; but a space is left for it and the text beginning at line 15 comes next.

che l'ochio portãdo con seco ĩfinite linie le quali sono appiccate overo vnite cō le sopravenienti che si partono dalle cose vedute e solo la linia di mezzo d'essa sẽsuale è quella che conosce e givdica ĩ corpi e colori, tutte l'altre sono false e bugiarde; e quãdo tu porrai 2 cose distanti vno gomito l'una dall'altra e che la prima sia appresso all'ochio, la superfizie della prima rimarrà in alto piv cõfusa che la secõda, la ragiõ si è che la prima è vinta da maggior nvmero di linie false che la secõda, però è piv dubbiosa.

appears confused. I say that the eye projects an infinite number of lines which mingle or join those reaching it which come to it from the object looked at. And it is only the central and sensible line that can discern and discriminate colours and objects; all the others are false and illusory. And if you place 2 objects at half an arm's length apart if the nearer of the two is close to the eye its form will remain far more confused than that of the second; the reason is that the first is overcome by a greater number of false lines than the second and so is rendered vague.

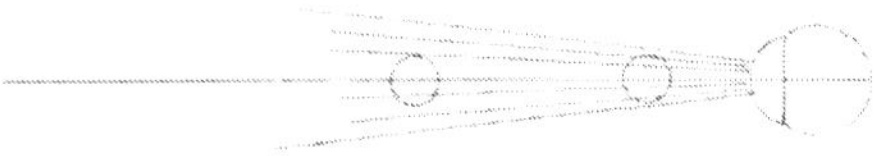

Il lume fa questo medesimo, perchè negli effetti delle sue linie e massime nell'opere di prospettiva è molto simile all'occhio; e 'l suo cẽtro porta il uero nella ripruova dell'onbre · e quãdo la cosa posta gli dinãzi sarà troppo presta vĩta da' razzi tristi mostrerà õbra grãde e sproporzionata e mal terminata; ma quãdo la cosa che à a gienerare l'õbra taglierà i razzi del lume e sarà apresso alla percussione allora l'ombra s'aviene buona e massime quãdo il lume sarà discosto, perchè il razzo del cẽtro nella lunga distãzia à meno compagnia de' razzi falsi · perchè le linie dell'ochio, e solari e altre linie luminose, scorrẽdo per l'aria cõuiene a loro osservare retta dirittura; se già nõ fussino ĩpedite per l'aria piv spessa o piv rara rimarebbero in alcuna parte torte; ma se l'aria è netta di grossezze o di umidità quelle osserueranno la loro retta natura, senpre portando ĩ dirieto alla lor derivazione la cagione del lor rõpimento, e se sarà l'occhio li sarà givdicato 'l ronpimẽto per colore come per fazione o grãdezza; Ma se la pariete di detto rõpimẽto avrà ĩ se alcuno piccolo foro il quale ẽtri in abitazione oscura nõ per tĩtura ma per privazziõ di lume: vedrai le linie entrare per detto forame li portano nella secõda pariete tutta la forma del lor nascimẽto, sì per colore come per fazione;

Light acts in the same manner, for in the effects of its lines (=rays), and particularly in perspective, it much resembles the eye; and its central rays are what cast the true shadow. When the object in front of it is too quickly overcome with dim rays it will cast a broad and disproportionate shadow, ill defined; but when the object which is to cast the shadow and cuts off the rays near to the place where the shadow falls, then the shadow is distinct; and the more so in proportion as the light is far off, because at a long distance the central ray is less overcome by false rays; because the lines from the eye and the solar and other luminous rays passing through the atmosphere are obliged to travel in straight lines. Unless they are deflected by a denser or rarer air, when they will be bent at some point, but so long as the air is free from grossness or moisture they will preserve their direct course, always carrying the image of the object that intercepts them back to their point of origin. And if this is the eye, the intercepting object will be seen by its colour, as well as by form and size. But if the intercepting plane has in it some small perforation opening into a darker chamber—not darker in colour, but by absence of light—you will see the rays enter through this hole and transmitting to the plane beyond all the details of the

chonsecho. 18. apichate . . . che [quelle] "le sopravenenti" chessi partano . . . chose. 18. mezo . . . [illegible] 19. givdicha; i chorpe cholori. 20. porai . . . chose distan vn ghomito. 21. chella . . . apresso. 22. rimara . . . chōfusa chella sechōda. 23. chella . . . magior. 24. sechōda. 25. questo. 26. prospettiva e molto. 28. chosa posta. 29. presta vita . . . razi trissti mostera . . . e sproporr. 30. ziona e mai terminata . . . chosa. 31. razi [illegible]. 32. perchussione [illegible] saviene buona. 33. [illegible] . . . razo . . . cietro. 34. [illegible] . . . chōpagnia . . . razi. 35. [illegible] . . . chōuiene [illegible] . . . diri. 37. ipedita. 38. aro rimarebono in alchuna . . . sellaria ene. 39. grossezze . . . osserueranno loro retta. 41. cagione [illegible]. 42. givdichato . . . cholore chome . . . gradeza. 43. Masselle . . . ara . . . alchuno [piccolo] foro. 44. oschura. 45. [illegible] "portano. 46. nella

Ma ogni cosa sarà sotto sopra; [48]Ma quado e' sarà tāto dal forame al' ultima percussione delle [49]linie, quāto è da lor nascimēto, sarà la percussione per grandezza a [50]rinascimēto delle linie, [52]ītersegarsi e gie[53]nerare 2 piramidi [54]colle pūte īsieme [55]e le basi opposite; [56]sia · *a* · *b* il nascimento delle linie, [57]sia · *d* · *e* la prima pariete; sia *c* · [58]il forame dov'è la intersegazione [59]delle linie; sia · *f* · *g* · l'ultima pariete: [60]troverai 'l *a* nell'ultima pariete a percussione [61]rimanere di sotto nel luogo del *g* e 'l · *b* · di sotto [62]risalire di sopra nel luogo del *f*; [63]chiaro apparirà ali sperimētatori che ogni [64]corpo luminoso à per se una virtù recōdita che è ciētro, dal [65]quale e al quale capitano tutte le linie [66]gienerate dalla luminosa superficie e di li [67]ritornano o risaltano ī fuori, esse non āño īpedimento [68]si spargeranno per l'aria.

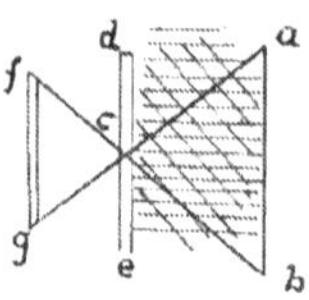

object they proceed from both as to colour and form; only every thing will be upside down. But the size [of the image] where the lines are reconstructed will be in proportion to the relative distance of the aperture from the plane on which the lines fall [on one hand] and from their origin [on the other]. There they intersect and form 2 pyramids with their point meeting [a common apex] and their bases opposite. Let *a b* be the point of origin of the lines, *d e* the first plane, and *c* the aperture with the intersection of the lines; *f g* is the inner plane. You will find that *a* falls upon the inner plane below at *g*, and *b* which is below will go up to the spot *f*; it will be quite evident to experimenters that every luminous body has in itself a core or centre, from which and to which all the lines radiate which are sent forth by the surface of the luminous body and reflected back to it; or which, having been thrown out and not intercepted, are dispersed in the air.

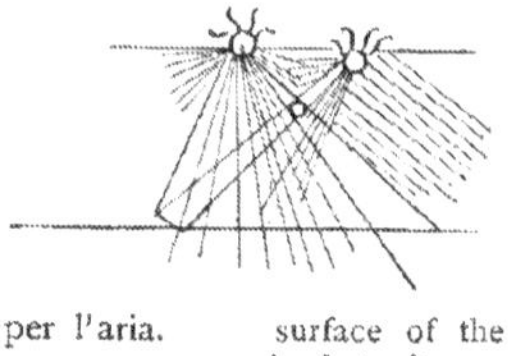

C. 8*a*]

131.

I RAZZI ONBROSI E LUMINOSI · SONO · DI MAGGIORE · POTENTIA · E VALITUDINE · NELLE · PUNTE LORO CHE NE' LATI.

[2]Benchè le punte delle luminose piramidi s'astēdino in ōbro sisiti e quelle delle [3]piramidi ōbrose discorrino ī luminosi lochi, e che infra le luminose [4]egli nasca da maggiore basa l'una che l'altra, nō di meno, se per cagiō di uarie [5]lunghezze esse luminose piramidi pervengono a equale grossezze d'āgoli saran[6]no di pari lume infra loro e il simile farāno le piramidi ōbrose, come [7]si dimostra nelle tagliate piramidi *a* · *b* · *c* e così *d e f* che benchè elle nascano [8]da uarie grādezze di base · pur son simili di grādezza e di lume.

THE RAYS WHETHER SHADED OR LUMINOUS HAVE GREATER STRENGTH AND EFFECT AT THEIR POINTS THAN AT THEIR SIDES.

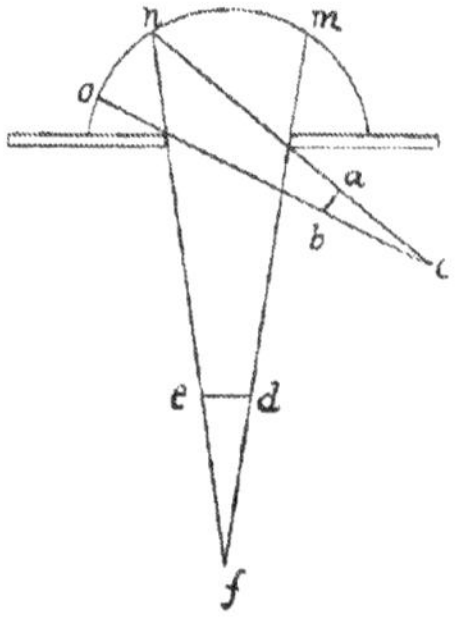

Although the points of luminous pyramids may extend into shaded places and those of pyramids of shadow into illuminated places, and though among the luminous pyramids one may start from a broader base than another; nevertheless, if by reason of their various length these luminous pyramids acquire angles of equal size their light will be equal; and the case will be the same with the pyramids of shadow; as may be seen in the intersected pyramids *a b c* and *d e f*, which though their bases differ in size are equal as to breadth and light.

sechōda . . nasscimēto. 47. cholore chome . . chosa. 48. Mquāda . . perchussione. 49. nasscimēto . . perchusione per ghandeza. 50. a rianassimēto. 51. + li +. 52. ītersegharsi. 53. piramida. 54. chole. 55. elle base. 56. nassimēto. 58. dove lāterseghazione. 60. perchussione. 61. luogho. 62. luogho. 63. aparira alissperimētatori. 64. chorpo . . ape secēōdita eccīētro. 65. chapitano. 67. esse nonāno īpe. 68. sessparghā per laria.

131. 1. razi . . elluminosi . . magiore. 2. benchelle . . piramide . . ecquelle. 3. piramide . . dischorrino . . infral[loro]eluminose. 4. enascha . . magiore . . chellaltra . . chagiò. 5. lungeze . . piramide peruegino . . grosseze. 6. infralloro ellsimile . . piramide . . chome. 7. piramide . . echosi . . benchelle nasscino. 9. di uarie . . simile . . grādeza.

51—55. This supplementary paragraph is indicated as being a continuation of line 45, by two small crosses.

Ash. I. 3a]

132.

The difference between light and lustre (132—135).

Che differētia · è da lumi [2]a lustri e come i lustri [3]nō sono in nel nvmero de co[4]lori ed è saziare di bianco [5]e nascie ne'stremi de [6]bagniati corpi; Il lume è [7]del colore della cosa doue [8]nascie come oro o arieto o [9]simile cosa.

Of the difference between light and lustre; and that lustre is not included among colours, but is saturation of whiteness, and derived from the surface of wet bodies; light partakes of the colour of the object which reflects it (to the eye) as gold or silver or the like.

Ash. I. 3b]

133.

De'colmi · de lumi che si voltano e tras-mutano [2]secondo · che si trasmuta · l'ochio veditore d'esso corpo.

[3]Poniamo · che 'l corpo detto sia questo tōdo qui d'acato · figurato, e che il lume [4]sia · il pūto *a* · e che la parte del corpo · alluminata sia · *b* · *c*, e che l'ochio [5]sia nel pūto *d*: dico che 'l lustro perchè è tutto · per tutto e tutto nella parte [6]che stādo nel pūto *d*, che il lustro · parrà nel pūto · *c* · e tāto quāto l'ochio si tras[7]mvterà da · *d* · all' · *a* tanto il lustro si trasmuterà da *c* · a · *n*.

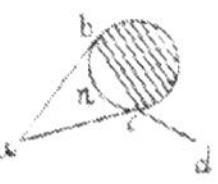

Of the highest lights which turn and move as the eye moves which sees the object.

Suppose the body to be the round object figured here and let the light be at the point *a*, and let the illuminated side of the object be *b c* and the eye at the point *d*: I say that, as lustre is every where and complete in each part, if you stand at the point *d* the lustre will appear at *c*, and in proportion as the eye moves from *d* to *a*, the lustre will move from *c* to *n*.

H.[3] 32b]

134.

De pictura.

[2]I lumi de' lumi cioè il lustro di qualūque [3]cosa non sarà situato · nel mezzo [4]della · parte · alluminata ·, āzi farà tā[5]te · mutazioni · quāte · farà · l'ochio ri[6]guardatore · di quello.

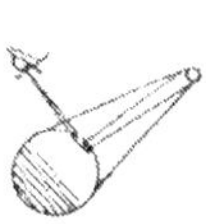

Of painting.

Heigh light or lustre on any object is not situated [necessarily] in the middle of an illuminated object, but moves as and where the eye moves in looking at it.

E. 31b]

135.

Del lume e lustro.

[2]Che differētia è dal lume al lustro [3]che si dimostra nella superfitie [4]tersa delli corpi opachi?

[5]Li lumi che si gienerāno nelle super-[6]fitie terse delli corpi opachi sa[7]ranno inmobili ne' corpi inmo[8]bili, ācora che l'ochio d'essi vedito[9]re si · mvova; Ma li lustri sa-[10]ran sopra li medesimi corpi in tāti [11]lochi della sua superfitie quāti sono [12]li siti dove l'ochio si move.

Of light and lustre.

What is the difference between light and the lustre which is seen on the polished surface of opaque bodies?

The lights which are produced from the polished surface of opaque bodies will be stationary on stationary objects even if the eye on which they strike moves. But reflected lights will, on those same objects, appear in as many different places on the surface as different positions are taken by the eye.

132. 2. lustri echeme ilusstri. 3. inei . . decho. 4. saziaredi *doubtful.* 6. chorpi Ilume. 7. cholore dela chosa. 8. chome. 9. chosa.

133. 1. chessi . . trassmutano. 2. sechondo chessi trassmuta. 3. dachāto. 4. chella . . chorpo . . chellochio. 5. dicho. 6. che lustro para . . entāto . . distra. 7. trassmutera.

134. 2. lusstro. 3. chosa . . mezo. 5. quāto.

135. 1. ellustro. 2. differētia . . lustro se. 3. [p] che si dimosstra nella superfitie [del]. 4. [li [l] che] terse . . chorppi oppachi. 5. chessi. 6. chorpi oppachi. 7. chorpi. 8. Schora chellochio. 9. Malliilustri. 10. chorpi. 12. dove lliio si move. 13. chorpi.

QUALI CORPI SON QUEL[14]LI CHE HANNO LUME SÃZA LUSTRO?

[15]Li corpi opachi che avrã superfitie densa [16]e àspra nõ gienerãno mai lustro [17]in alcuno loco della sua parte al[18]luminata.

WHAT BODIES HAVE LIGHT UPON THEM WITHOUT LUSTRE?

Opaque bodies which have a hard and rough surface never display any lustre in any portion of the side on which the light falls.

QUALI CORPI SÕ QUELGLI [20]CHE AVRÃ LUSTRO E NÕ PAR[21]TE LUMINOSA?

[22]Li corpi opachi densi con dësa [23]superfitie son quelgli che ànno tutto il lustro in [24]tanti lochi della · parte alluminata quãti [25]sono li siti che possino ricievere l'ango[26]lo della incidentia del lume e dell'ochio; ma [27]perchè tale superfitie spechia tutte le cose cir[28]custãti, la alluminata nõ si cono[29]scie in tal parte del corpo alluminato.

WHAT BODIES WHICH WILL DISPLAY LUSTRE BUT NOT LOOK ILLUMINATED?

Those bodies which are opaque and hard with a hard surface reflect light [lustre] from every spot on the illuminated side which is in a position to receive light at the same angle of incidence as they occupy with regard to the eye; but, as the surface mirrors all the surrounding objects, the illuminated [body] is not recognisable in these portions of the illuminated body.

Br. M. 171 a]

136.

Ogni [1]/[2] d'õbra e lume cõgiũ[2]to a' corpi õbrosi si dirizza al [3]mezzo del suo lume primitiuo. [4]Ogni lume e õbre si ritrae [5]a linie pirimidali; [6]è neciessario che il mezzo [7]di ciascuna · õbra risguardi il mezzo [8]del suo lume per linia retta che passi il ciẽtro [10]d'esso corpo; [11]il mezo del lume sarà *a*, [12]dell'õbra fia · *b*. [13][ancora i corpi õbrosi circũscritti [14]da õbre e lume conviẽ · che 'l mez[15]zo di ciascuno si dirizzi al ciẽtro d'esso corpo [16]e sia linia retta dal-l'uno all'altro mezzo passã[17]do al ciẽtro].

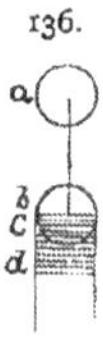

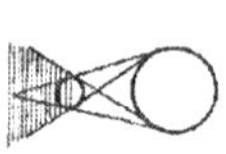

The relations of luminous to illuminated bodies.

The middle of the light and shade on an object in light and shade is opposite to the middle of the primary light. All light and shadow expresses itself in pyramidal lines. The middle of the shadow on any object must necessarily be opposite the middle of its light, with a direct line passing through the centre of the body. The middle of the light will be at *a*, that of the shadow at *b*. [Again, in bodies shown in light and shade the middle of each must coincide with the centre of the body, and a straight line will pass through both and through that centre.]

W. I.

137.

PRUOVA COME OGNI [2]PARTE DI LUME FA UNO [3]PŨTO.

[4]Benchè le palle · *a* · *b* · *c* [5]abĩ lume da vna finestra [6]niẽte di meno se seguiterai [7]le linie delle sue õbre vedrai [8]a quelle fare ĩtersegatione [9]e pũto · nel angolo · *n* ·

SHOWS HOW LIGHT FROM ANY SIDE CONVERGES TO ONE POINT.

Experiments on the relation of light and shadow within a room (137—140).

Although the balls *a b c* are lighted from one window, nevertheless, if you follow the lines of their shadows you will see they intersect at a point forming the angle *n*.

14. chaã lume saza lusstro. 15. chorpi "oppachi" che arã. 16. casspra no . . lusstro. 17. alchuna [po] locho. 20. arã lusstro. 21. luminoso. 22. chorpi oppachi [chonass] chon. 23. cheantutto. 24. quãto. 25. cheppossino . . langho. 27. chose. 28. chusstãte [la allume] lo . . nõ si chon.

136. 1. ellume. 2. accorpi . . diriza. 3. mezo. 4. lumeme. 5. allinie piramidale. 6. mezo. 7. mezo. 13. circhũscritti. 14. õbrel-lume convie chõuie chel me. 15. dirizi. 16. essia . . dalluno alaltro mezo.

137. 1. chome. 2. fa ĩ. 3. benchelle balle. 6. seghuiteral. 7. õbr"e". 8. acquele . . ĩterseghatione.

136. In the original MS., at the spot marked *a* of the first diagram Leonardo wrote *primitiuo*, and at the spot marked *c*—*primitiva* (primary); at the spot marked *b* he wrote *dirivatiuo* and at *d deriuatiua* (derived).

137. The diagram belonging to this passage is slightly sketched on Pl. XXXII; a square with three balls below it. The first three lines of the text belonging to it are written above the sketch and the six others below it.

Ash. I. 20*b*]

138.

Ogni öbra fatta da'corpi si dirizza colla linia del mezzo [2]a vn solo · [3]punto · fatto per itersegatione di linie luminose [4]in nel mezzo dello spatio e grossezza · della · finestra; [5]la ragione promessa · di sopra · chiaramẽte appare per isperiëza, iperochè [6]se figurerai vno · sito colla · finestra a tramõtana la quale · sia · *s* · *f* · [7]vederai all'orizzõte di levãte produrre vna · linia che toccãdo li 2 ãgoli del[8]la finestra · *o* · *f* · capiterà in · *d* · e l'orizzõte di ponẽte · produrrà la sua [9]linia toccando li altri 2 ãgoli della finestra · *r* · *s* · e finirà in · *c* · e questa [10]intersegatione viene appũto · nel · mezzo dello spatio e della grossezza della [11]finestra; ãcora ti cõfermerai meglio questa ragione a porre due basto[12]ni · come nel loco di · *g* · *h* · vi vederai la linia fatta dal mezzo del' obra [13]reale · dirizzarsi al cietro · *m* || e coll'orizzõte · *n* · *f*.

Every shadow cast by a body has a central line directed to a single point produced by the intersection of luminous lines in the middle of the opening and thickness of the window. The proposition stated above, is plainly seen by experiment. Thus if you draw a place with a window looking northwards, and let this be *s f*, you will see a line starting from the horizon to the east, which, touching the 2 angles of the window *o f*, reaches *d*; and from the horizon on the west another line, touching the other 2 angles *r s*, and ending at *c*; and their intersection falls exactly in the middle of the opening and thickness of the window. Again, you can still better confirm this proof by placing two sticks, as shown at *g h*; and you will see the line drawn from the centre of the shadow directed to the centre *m* and prolonged to the horizon *n f*.

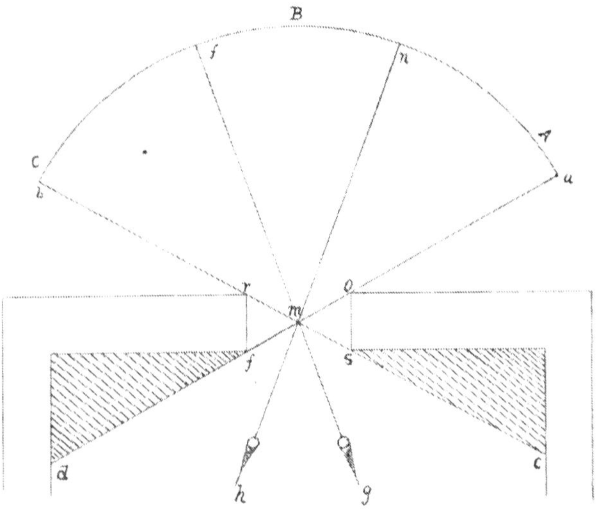

138. 1 driza . . mezo. 4. inel mezo . . grosseza. 5. apare. 6. figurerai . . cola. 7. aloriadte . . produre . . tochãdo . . de. 8. i. d. elloriżõte . . prodora. 9. tochando li ãtri 2 . . effinira . . ecquesta. 10. mezo . . grosseza. 11. ãchora . . meglo . . apare. 12. lochо . . linia [del me] fatta . . mezo. 13. dirizarsi . . lorizõte.

138. *B* here stands for *cerchio del' orizonte tramontane* on the original diagram (the circle of the horizon towards the North); *A* for *levante* (East) and *C* for *ponẽte* (West).

Ash. I. 20 *a*]

139.

Ogni õbra cõ tutte sue varietà che per distãtia cresce [2]per larghezza piv · che la · sua · cagione, le sue linee esteriori [3]si cõgivngono · insieme · ĩfra il lume · e 'l corpo õbroso. [4]Questa propositione · chiaramẽte appare e si cõferma [5]dalla · esperiẽza, ĩperochè se *a* · *b* · fia una finestra sãza alcuna tramezzatura, [6]l'aria · luminosa · che sta da destra · in · *a* · è vista, da sinistra in · *d* ·. e l'a[7]ria che sta · da · sinistra allumina da destra nel punto · *c* e dette linie s'inter[8]secano · nel pũto *m*.

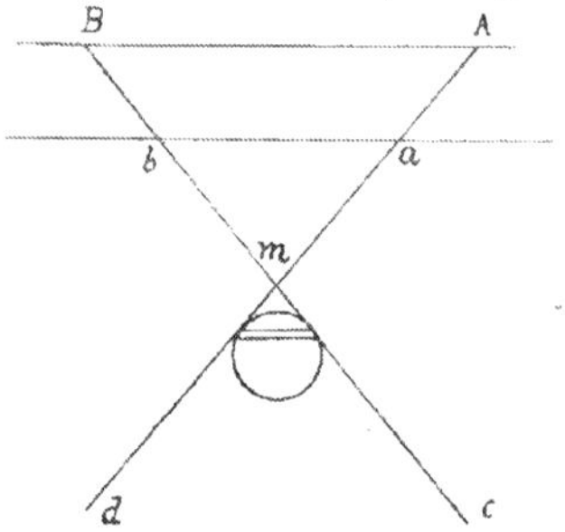

Every shadow with all its variations, which becomes larger as its distance from the object is greater, has its external lines intersecting in the middle, between the light and the object. This proposition is very evident and is confirmed by experience. For, if *a b* is a window without any object interposed, the luminous atmosphere to the right hand at *a* is seen to the left at *d*. And the atmosphere at the left illuminates on the right at *c*, and the lines intersect at the point *m*.

Ash. I. 20 *a*]

140.

Ogni corpo õbroso si truova ĩfra · 2 · piramidi [2]vna scura e l'altra luminosa, l'una si uede e l'altra no, [3]e questo solo accade ·

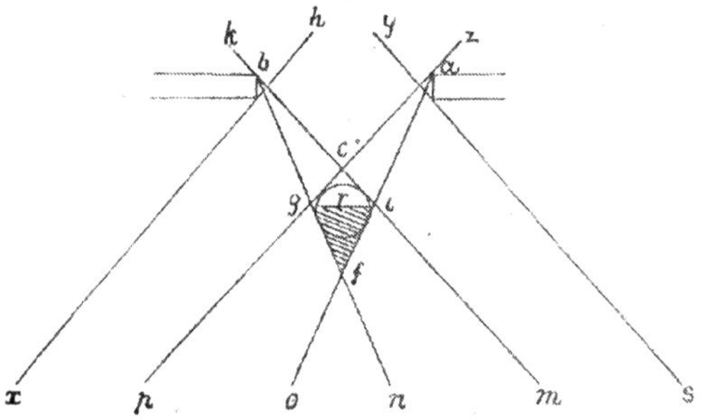

quãdo il lume ẽtra per una finestra; [4]fa cõto · che · *a* · *b* · sia la finestra e che · *r* · sia il corpo õbroso il lume [5]destro *z* · passa il corpo da lato sinistro del corpo õbroso · in · *g* · e va in · *p* ·, il lume [6]sinistro · *k* passa a detto corpo nel lato · destro · in · *i* · e va ·

Every body in light and shade is situated between 2 pyramids one dark and the other luminous, one is visible the other is not. But this only happens when the light enters by a window. Supposing *a b* to be the window and *r* the body in light and shade, the light to the right hand *z* will pass the object to the left and go on to *p*; the light to the left at *k* will pass to the right of the object at *i* and

139. 1. chõ . . chresscie. 2. largeza . . chella. 3. cõgivngauo . . chorpo. 4. Questa [cosa chiaramente] propositione . . apare . . essi. 5. dala . . fia ĩ finestra . . tramézatura. 6. in . d . ella.

140. 1. piramide. 2. uno scuro e laltro luminoso luno . . ellaltro. 3. ecquesto . . achade . . ilume . . per ĩ finestra. 4. chorpo

139. *A* here stands for *levante* (East), *B* for *ponente* (West).

in · *m* · e queste 2 linie s'iter'segano î · *c* · e li faño piramide · dipoi *a* · *b* · tocca il corpo obroso in · *i* · *g* · e fa sua [7]piramide · in · *f*; *i* · *g* · *f* fia oscuro · perchè mai egli può vedere il lume · *a* · *b*; [9] · *i* · *g* · *c* · sepre fia luminoso perchè egli uede · il lume.

go on to *m* and the two lines will intersect at *c* and form a pyramid. Then again *a b* falls on the shaded body at *i g* and forms a pyramid *f i g*. *f* will be dark because the light *a b* can never fall there; *i g c* will be illuminated because the light falls upon it.

C. 20 *a*]

141.

Light and shadow with regard to the position of the eye (141—145).

Tutti · i corpi ōbrosi di maggior grādezza che la · popilla · i quali s'interporranno · infra l'occhio · e'l corpo · luminoso · si dimo'streranno d'oscura · qualità.

[3]L'ochio · posto · infra 'l · corpo · luminoso · E i corpi · da esso · lume · alluminati · vedrà i detti corpi · sāza alcun ōbra.

Every shaded body that is larger than the pupil and that interposes between the luminous body and the eye will be seen dark.

When the eye is placed between the luminous body and the objects illuminated by it, these objects will be seen without any shadow.

Ash. I. 22 *a*]

142.

Come i 2 lumi che mettino in mezzo [2]vno corpo da 2 lati piramidato di basse [3]piramidi lo lasciano saza obra.

Why the 2 lights one on each side of a body having two pyramidal sides of an obtuse apex leave it devoid of shadow.

Br. M. 171 *a*]

143.

Il corpo obroso situato [2]infra il lume e l'ochio nō mo[3]strerà mai di se parte luminosa se l'ochio nō uede tutto il [5]lume originale.

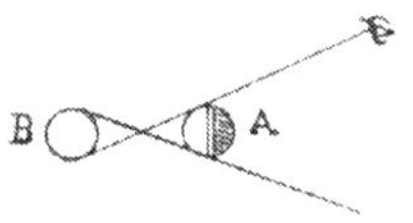

A body in shadow situated between the light and the eye can never display its illuminated portion unless the eye can see the whole of the primary light.

Tr. 20]

144.

L'ochio · che si troverà · in mezzo fra l'onbra e i lumi circūda'tori · delli · ōbrosi ·

The eye which looks (at a spot) half way between the shadow and the light which

[luminoso] ōbroso ilume. 8. 2555 . . ecque 2. 7. piramida . . effa. 8. piramida . . oschuro . . mailipo . . ilume. 9. perchelli uede.

141. 1. Tutti i chorpi "ōbrosi" di magior grādeza chella . . quali [saranno situati] "sinterporanno" infralochio el chorpo. 2. steranno dosschura. 3. chorpo . . chorpi . . vedera . . chorpi . . sanzalchun.

142. 1. comeme i 2 . . imezo. 2. chorpo. 3. piramide.

143. 2. infralome. 3. sstra. 5. lume [primitu] originale.

144. 1. chessi . . mezo . . ellumi circhūda. 2. chorpi . . . vedera . . chorpi . . magiore. 3. sieno . rischōtarsi . chōsecho.

141. The diagram which in the original stands above line 1 is given on Plate II, No 2. Then, after a blank space of about eight lines, the diagram Plate II No 3 is placed in the original. There is no explanation of it beyond the one line written under it.

142. The sketch illustrating this is on Plate XLI No 1.

143. *A* stands for *corpo* (body), *B* for *lume* (light).

144. In both these diagrams *A* stands for *lume* (light) *B* for *ombra* (shadow).

corpi · vedrà · in essi corpi le maggiori ōbre [3]che in esse · sieno · a riscōtrarsi · cō seco · infra equali āgoli [4]cioè della incidētia visuale.

surrounds the body in shadow will see that the deepest shadows on that body will meet the eye at equal angles, that is at the same angle as that of sight.

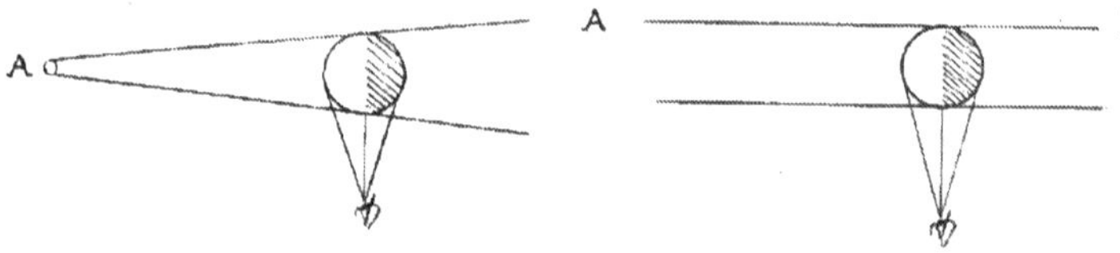

Ash. I. 17 *a*]

145.

DELLA DISCRETIONE DEL'ONBRE DE' SITI [2]E DELLE COSE POSTE Ī QUELLI.

[3]Se il sole fia · nel'oriēte e guarderai īuerso · occidēte · vedrai [4]tutte le cose luminate essere īteramēte private d'ōbra perchè vedi ciò che vede 'l sole, e se riguar[5]di a mezzodì e tramōtana · vedrai tutt'i corpi essere circūdati da [6]ōbra · e lume perchè vedi quello che nō vede · e vede il sole e se riguarderai īverso il cāmino del sole, tutti [7]i corpi ti mostreranno la loro parte aῡbrata, perchè quella parte [8]nō può essere veduta dal sole.

OF THE DIFFERENT LIGHT AND SHADE IN VARIOUS ASPECTS AND OF OBJECTS PLACED IN THEM.

If the sun is in the East and you look towards the West you will see every thing in full light and totally without shadow because you see them from the same side as the sun: and if you look towards the South or North you will see all objects in light and shade, because you see both the side towards the sun and the side away from it; and if you look towards the coming of the sun all objects will show you their shaded side, because on that side the sun cannot fall upon them.

Tr. 29]

146.

¶J labri della finestra · che sieno · alluminati · da 2 · vari · lumi [2]d'equale · chiarezza · nō metteranno · lume dētro · all'abitatione [3]d'equale qualità. ¶

[4]Se · *b* · fia · vna · cādela · e *a · c* sia · il nostro · emisperio; [5]l'uno · e l'altro allumina i labri · della · finestra · *m · n* · ma il lu[6]me · *b* · non allumina · se nō · *f · g* · e lo emisperio · *a · c* · alluminerà [7]insino in · *d · e*.

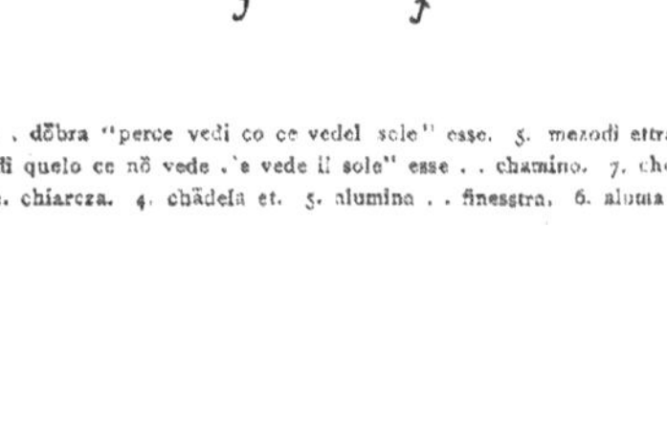

The law of the incidence of light.

The edges of a window which are illuminated by 2 lights of equal degrees of brightness will not reflect light of equal brightness into the chamber within.

If *b* is a candle and *a c* our hemisphere both will illuminate the edges of the window *m n*, but light *b* will only illuminate *f g* and the hemisphere *a* will light all of *d e*.

145. 3. vederai. 4. tute lecosse . . dōbra "perce vedi co ce vedel sole" esse. 5. mezodi ettramōtana vederai . . chorpi . . circhūdati. 6. lume "perce vedi quelo ce nō vede . 'e vede il sole" esse . . chamino. 7. chorpi . . mostreranc . . quela. 8. po.
146. 1. finesstra . . lumi [che]. 2. chiarcza. 4. chādela et. 5. alumina . . finesstra. 6. aluma . . cilo emissperio.

Ash. I. 28b]

147.

Pittura.

¶Quella · parte · dell' obietto · che ricieve sopra se il razzo luminoso · infra equali · angoli · Quella · fia · più ch' altra parte d' esso obbietto · luminosa.¶

¶E quella parte che fia ferita da luminoso · razzo infra angoli · piv · disequali · quà apparirà mè luminosa.¶

Of painting.

That part of a body which receives the luminous rays at equal angles will be in a higher light than any other part of it.

And the part which the luminous rays strike between less equal angles will be less strongly illuminated.

147. 2. [Il lume che ferissce lobietto infra equeliangoli]. 3. soprse . . razo. 6. Ecquella . . chefia . . razo . . aparira.

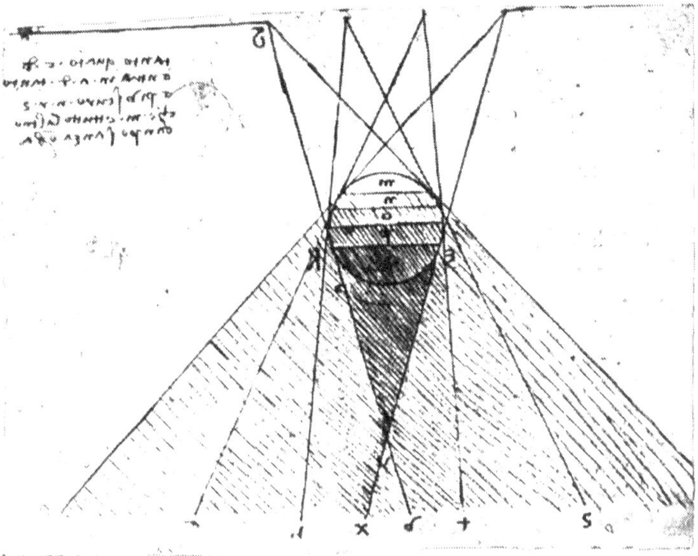

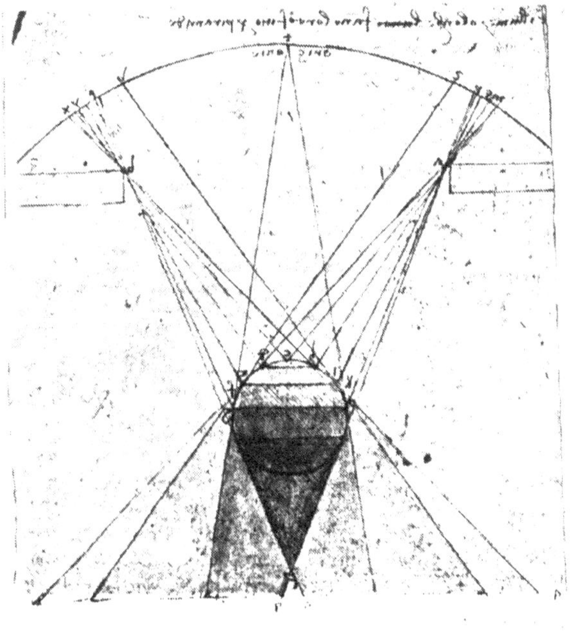

SECOND BOOK ON LIGHT AND SHADE.

Ash. I. 22 *a*]

148.

QUELLA PARTE DEL CORPO ŌBROSO FIA · MENO LUMINOSA [2] CHE FIA VEDUTA DA MINORE QUĀTITA DI LUME.

[3] La parte del corpo · *m* è primo grado di lume perchè lì vede tutta la finestra · *a* · *d* · [4] per la linia · *a* · *f* ·, *n* è'l secōdo grado perchè lì uede il lume · *b* · *d* · per la · linia · *b* · *e* ·, *o* è 'l ter[5]zo grado perchè lì vede il lume · *c* · *d* · per la linia · *c* · *h* · | *p* è 'l penoltimo perchè lì ue[6]de · *c* · *d* per la linea · *d* · *v* · | *q* è l'ultimo grado perchè lì non uede nessuna parte [7] della finestra ·

[8] Tanto quāto · *c* · *d* · [9] entra in · *a* · *d* · tanto [10] è piv scuro · *n* · *r* · *s* [11] che · *m* · e tutto l' altro [12] canpo sanza ōbra.

THAT PORTION OF A BODY IN LIGHT AND SHADE WILL BE LEAST LUMINOUS WHICH IS SEEN UNDER THE LEAST AMOUNT OF LIGHT.

That part of the object which is marked *m* is in the highest light because it faces the window *a d* by the line *a f*; *n* is in the second grade because the light *b d* strikes it by the line *b e*; *o* is in the third grade, as the light falls on it from *c d* by the line *c h*; *p* is the lowest light but one as *c d* falls on it by the line *d v*; *q* is the deepest shadow for no light falls on it from any part of the window. Gradations of strength in the shadows (148, 149).

In proportion as *c d* goes into *a d* so will *n r s* be darker than *m*, and all the rest is space without shadow.

Ash. I. 21 *b*]

149.

Ogni · lume · che cade · sopra · ai corpi ōbrosi · īfra equali · āgoli tiene il primo [2] grado · di chiarezza · e quello fia piv scuro che ricieve l'āgoli meno · equali [3] e il lume · o l'onbre faño loro · ofitio per piramide; [4] l'angolo · *c* · tiene · jl primo · grado · di chiarezza ·

The light which falls on a shaded body at the acutest angle receives the highest light, and the darkest portion is that which receives it at an obtuse angle and both the light and the shadow form pyramids. The angle *c* receives the highest grade of light because it is directly in

148. 1. Quela . . chorpo . . luminoso. 2. cheffia. 4. . a . f . el secōdo. 6. novede. 11. ettutto.

149. 1. chade . . chorpi. 2. chiareza ecquelo. 3. ollonbre. 4. chiareza. 5. ettutto lorizōte . . pocha diferētia mettano. 6. socto .

148. The diagram belonging to this chapter is No 1 on Plate III. The letters *a b c d* and *r* are not reproduced in facsimile of the original, but have been replaced by ordinary type in the margin.

5—12. The original text of these lines is reproduced within the diagram.—Compare No 275.

149. The diagram belonging to this chapter is No 2 on Plate III. In the original it is placed between lines 3 and 4, and in the reproduction these are shown in part. The semi circle above is marked *orizonte* (horizon). The number 6 at the left hand side, outside the facsimile, is in the place of a figure which has become indistinct in the original.

perchè gli uede · tutta · la finestra · *a* · *b* · [5]e tutto l'orizzote del cielo · *m* · *x* ·, l'angolo · *d* · fa poca · differetia da · *c* · perchè li agoli che lo mettono [6]i mezzo · no sono tato difformi di proportione · quato li altri · di sotto · e macagli solamēte quella [7]parte dell'orizzōte · ch'è tra · *y* · *x* · bench'eli acquisti altrettato dall'opposito lato · nodimeno la sua linia è di po[c]ca poteza perchè il suo angolo · è minore · che'l suo cōpagno, l'angoli · *e* · *i* · fia di minore lume [8]perchè · egli · non vede manco · il lume · *m* · *s* · e 'l lume *v* · *x* · e i loro agoli sono assai disformi: l'angolo [10]· *k* · e l'angolo · *f* · sono messi in mezzo ciascū · per se · da agoli · molto diformi l'uno dal'altro e però fieno [11]di poco lume · perchè in · *k* · vede solamēte il lume · *p* · *t* · e in · *f*; no uede se nō *t* · *q* · ; *o* · *g* · fia l'ultimo [12]grado di lume perchè li no uede nessuna parte del lume del'orizzōte · e sono quelle le linie che vn altra [13]volta ricōpogono una · piramide · simile · alla piramide · *c* · la quale piramide · *l* si troverà [14]nel primo grado · d'obra. perchè acora lei cade ifra · equali agoli e essi agoli · si dirizzano [15]e si sguardano per una · linia retta che passa dal cientro del corpo ōbroso e capita al mezzo del lume: [16]le spetie luminose mvltiplicate · ne' termini della · finestra ne' pūti · *a* · *b* · fāno [17]chiarore · che circūda l'obra diriuativa creata dal corpo ōbroso ne' lochi 4 · e 6 · [18]le spetie oscure si mvltiplicano · jn · *o* · *g* e finiscono · in · 7 · e 8.

front of the window *a b* and the whole horizon of the sky *m x*. The angle *d* differs but little from *c* because the angles which divide it are not so unequal as those below, and only that portion of the horizon is intercepted which lies between *y* and *x*. Although it gains as much on the other side its line is nevertheless not very strong because one angle is smaller than its fellow. The angles *e i* will have less light because they do not see much of the light *m s* and the light *v x* and their angles are very unequal. The angle *k* and the angle *f* are each placed between very unequal angles and therefore have but little light, because at *k* it has only the light *p t*, and at *f* only *t q*; *o g* is the lowest grade of light because this part has no light at all from the sky; and thence come the lines which will reconstruct a pyramid that is the counterpart of the pyramid *c*; and this pyramid *l* is in the first grade of shadow; for this too is placed between equal angles directly opposite to each other on either side of a straight line which passes through the centre of the body and goes to the centre of the light. The several luminous images cast within the frame of the window at the points *a* and *b* make a light which surrounds the derived shadow cast by the solid body at the points 4 and 6. The shaded images increase from *o g* and end at 7 and 8.

150.

C. A. 92 *b*; 339 *d*]

On the intensity of shadows as dependent on the distance from the light (150-151).

Quel corpo si dimostra più ōbroso che sia alluminato da minor luminoso [2]e quel luminoso alluminerà minor parte del corpo ōbroso il quale [3]li fia più vicino; per la couersa tanto maggior quātità n'allu[4]minerà quāto egli fia più lontano.

[5]Quel lume che sia minore dell'obroso n'alluminerà tanto minor quātità quan[6]to li fia più vicino e per la cōuersa farà essendo più remoto; Ma [7]quando il lume sarà maggiore che l'ōbroso allor tanto più ne vedrà [8]dell'ombroso quāto esso fia più vicino e per il contrario farà essēdo pi[u] remoto.

The smaller the light that falls upon an object the more shadow it will display. And the light will illuminate a smaller portion of the object in proportion as it is nearer to it; and conversely, a larger extent of it in proportion as it is farther off.

A light which is smaller than the object on which it falls will light up a smaller extent of it in proportion as it is nearer to it, and the converse, as it is farther from it. But when the light is larger than the object illuminated it will light a larger extent of the object in proportion as it is nearer and the converse when they are farther apart.

5. e tutto l'orizzōte ... dalopposito. 8. cha potēza ... chōpagno langolo. 9. mancha ilume. 10. ellangolo ... imezo. 12. ilume ... orizōte ... quele. 13. volto ... piramide ... alsa. 14. chade ... equali ... dirizano. 15. essi ... per ... linia ... chapita ... mezo. 18. efiniscano.

150. 1. dimostra. 2. e quel. 3. [fia] lifia piu ... magior. 4. quāto eli fia. 5. Quelume chesia ... quātita ā. 7. equando ... chellōbroso ... tanta.

C. A. 130 b, 398 b]

151

¶Quella parte della cosa [2]alluminata sarà piv lumi[3]nosa, la qual fia piv vici[4]na alla cavsa del suo lume ¶

That portion of an illuminated object which is nearest to the source of light will be the most strongly illuminated.

H.[3] 18 a]

152

Quella parte dell' ōbra primitiva [2]sarà meno oscura che fia piv [3]lōtana dai sua stremi.

[4]L'ōbra dirivativa che cōfi[5]na colla primitiua fia piv [6]oscura d'essa primitiva.

That portion of the primary shadow will be least dark which is farthest from the edges.

The derived shadow will be darker than the primary shadow where it is contiguous with it.

E. 17 a]

153

Quella parte del corpo opaco sa[2]rà più aōbrato o allumināta che fia [3]più vicina all'ōbroso che la oscura [4]o luminoso che l'alumina.

[5]Le cose vedute infra lume e l'ōbre si di[6]mostrerā di maggiore rilievo che quelle [7]che sō nel lume o nell'ōbre.

That portion of an opaque body will be more in shade or more in light, which is nearer to the dark body, by which it is shaded, or to the light that illuminates it.

On the proportion of light and shade (153—157).

Objects seen in light and shade show in greater relief than those which are wholly in light or in shadow.

S. K. M. II.[2] 76 b]

154

DE PROSPETTIVA.

OF PERSPECTIVE.

[3]Le parti aōbrate e alluminate de' corpi [4]opachi saraño nella medesima [5]proportione di chiarezza e oscurità [6]qual fiē quelle de' loro obbietti.

The shaded and illuminated sides of opaque objects will display the same proportion of light and darkness as their objects [6].

G. 32 a]

155

DE PICTURA.

OF PAINTING.

[2]Li termini e figura di qualunche [3]parte de' corpi ōbrosi male si conos[4]cono nelle ōbre e ne' lumi loro, ma [5]nelle parti interposte infra li lumi [6]e l'onbre le parti d'essi corpi sono ī[7]primo grado di notitia.

The outlines and form of any part of a body in light and shade are indistinct in the shadows and in the high lights; but in the portions between the light and the shadows they are highly conspicuous.

E. 15 a]

156

PICTURA.

OF PAINTING.

[2]Ĵfra li corpi di uarie oscurità, pri[3]vati d'un medesimo lume, tal proportione [4]fia

Among objects in various degrees of shade, when the light proceeds from a single source,

151. 1—4 R.
152. 2 osschura. 3 dasua. 4 chōfi. 5 cholla. 6 oschura.
153. 1 chorpo oppacho. 2 cheffia. 3 chella oscura. 4 olluminoso chellalumina. 5 chose infrallume ellōbre. 6 mossterra.
7 chessō.
154. 2 [le parte obrose elluminose]. 3 parte. 5 ciareza e osscurita.
155. 2 effigura. 3 chorpi. 4 chōnelle. 5 interposste infralli. 6 ellonbre le parte. chorpi.
156. 2 Ĵfralli chorpi. osschurita. 3 proportio. 4 infralle. 5 osscurita.

154. 6. The meaning of *obbietti* (objects) is explained in no 153, lines 1—4. —Between the title-line and the next there is, in the original, a small diagram representing a circle described round a square.

infra le loro õbre qual fia la pro[5]portione delle loro naturali oscurità [6]e il medesimo ài ad intendere delli lor lumi.

there will be the same proportion in their shadows as in the natural diminution of the light and the same must be understood of the degrees of light.

E. 32 *a*]

157.

Il lume particulare è causa di dare [2]migliore rilievo alli corpi onbrosi che [3]lo vniversale come si mostra il para[4]gone d'una parte di campagnia alluminata [5]dal sole e vna aõbrata dal nuvolo che sol si [6]allumina del lume vniversale dell'aria.

A single and distinct luminous body causes stronger relief in the object than a diffused light; as may be seen by comparing one side of a landscape illuminated by the sun, and one overshadowed by clouds, and so illuminated only by the diffused light of the atmosphere.

157. 1. llume partichulare e chausa. 2. chorpi . . chel. 3. chome si mosstra. 4. ghone . . chanpagnia. 5. delume.

THIRD BOOK ON LIGHT AND SHADE.

W. 232 *b*]

158.

Onbra diriuativa non. è in essere sanza [2]lume primitivo; pruovasi per la prima [3]di questo che dicie¶ tenebre essere integrale pri[4]vatiõ di lucie, e õbra è alleuiation di te[5]nebre e di lucie, e tanto participa più [6]o mẽ delle tenebre che della lucie, quãto la [7]tenebra è in se corrotta da essa lucie.

Derived shadow cannot exist without primary shadow. This is proved by the first of this which says: Darkness is the total absence of light, and shadow is an alleviation of darkness and of light, and it is more or less dark or light in proportion as the darkness is modified by the light.

Definition of derived shadow (158. 159).

E. 32 *b*]

159.

Onbra è diminuitiõ di lume.
[2]Tenebre è privatione di lucie.
[3]L'onbra si diuide in due parti delle [4]quali la prima è detta onbra pri[5]mitiva, la secõda è l'onbra diriuativa; [6]senpre l'onbra primitiva si fa basa [7]dell'onbra diriuativa.
[8]Li termini dell'onbre dirivative [9]son retti linii.

Shadow is diminution of light.
Darkness is absence of light.
Shadow is divided into two kinds, of which the first is called primary shadow, the second is derived shadow. The primary shadow is always the basis of the derived shadow.
The edges of the derived shadow are straight lines.

158. 1. non [po] "e in" essere. 2. per la p[a]. 3. essere ingral pri. 5. eddi . . ettanto. 6. õmẽ delle. 7. tenebre . . conrocta.
159. 1. honbra. 3. parte. 4. he decta. 5. ellonbra. 8. dirivativi. 10. diminuisscie la osscu. 12. eppiu.

158. The theory of the *ombra dirivativa*—a technical expression for which there is no precise English equivalent is elaborately treated by Leonardo. But both text and diagrams (as Pl. IV, 1—3 and Pl. V) must at once convince the student that the distinction he makes between *ombra primitiva* and *ombra dirivativa* is not merely justifiable but scientific. *Ombra dirivativa* is by no means a mere abstract idea. This is easily proved by repeating the experiment made by Leonardo, and by filling with smoke the room in which the existence of the *ombra dirivativa* is investigated, when the shadow becomes visible. Nor is it difficult to perceive how much of Leonardo's teaching depended on this theory. The recognised, but extremely complicated science of cast shadows—*percussione dell'ombre dirivative* as Leonardo calls them—is thus rendered more intelligible if not actually simpler, and we must assume this theory as our chief guide through the investigations which follow.

[10]Tanto più diminuisce la oscu[11]rità dell'onbra diriuativa, quáto essa [12]è più remota dall'óbra primitiva.

The darkness of the derived shadow diminishes in proportion as it is remote from the primary shadow.

160.

C. 7 A]

Onbra e lume.

Shadow and light.

Different sorts of derived shadows (160—162).

[2]Tre · sono · le figure · dell'óbre · inperochè · se la · materia che fa · l'onbra · è pari · al lume ·, l'ombra è simile a vna co-

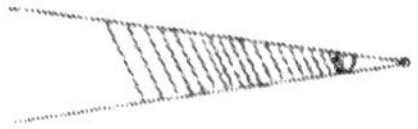

[3]lonna · nè à · termine alcuno. [4]Se la · materia é maggiore · che 'l lume: l'onbra · sua · è simile · a vna · retrosa e contraria piramide e la sua longitudine [5]è sanza alcuno termine; [6]Ma se la materia · è minore · che la · lucie · l'ombra fia simile a vna · piramide · ed è finita come si dimostra [7]nelle · eclissi della luna.

The forms of shadows are three: inasmuch as if the solid body which casts the shadow is equal (in size) to the light, the shadow resembles a column without any termination (in length). If the body is larger than the light the shadow resembles a truncated and inverted pyramid, and its length has also no defined termination. But if the body is smaller than the light, the shadow will resemble a pyramid and come to an end, as is seen in eclipses of the moon.

161.

E. 31 a]

Delle óbre dirivative [2]senplici.

Of simple derived shadows.

[3]La senplicie óbra dirivativa è [4]di due sorti cioè vna finita in [5]lunghezza e due in-

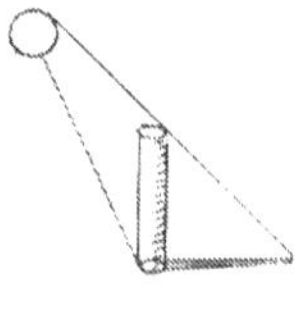

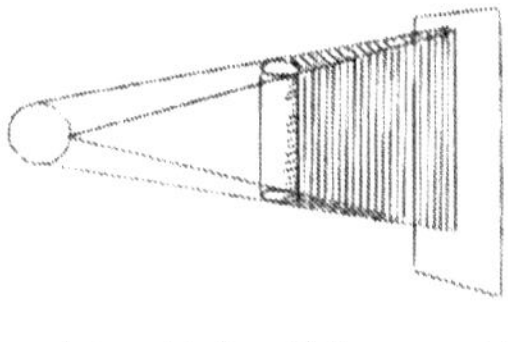

finite [6]e la finita è piramidale [7]e delle infi[8]nite vna ve n'è colonnale e [9]l'altra dilatabile, e tutte tre son [10]di lati rettilini; Ma l'onbra cō[11]corrēte cioè piramidale na[12]sci[12]e dall'onbroso minore del lumino[13]so, e la colōnale nasce da on[14]broso equale al luminoso, e la dila[15]tabile da obroso maggiore del lu[16]minoso ecc.

The simple derived shadow is of two kinds: one kind which has its length defined, and two kinds which are undefined; and the defined shadow is pyramidal. Of the two undefined, one is a column and the other spreads out; and all three have rectilinear outlines. But the converging, that is the pyramidal, shadow proceeds from a body that is smaller than the light, and the columnar from a body equal in size to the light, and the spreading shadow from a body larger than the light; &c.

160. 2. óbr . . sella . . cheffa . . lume [lonbra] l'ombra essimile . . cho. 3. alchuna. 4. Sella materia . . magiore . . essimile . . chontraria . . ella. 5. alchuno. 6. Massella . . chella . . chome. 7. nello.

161. 3. he. 4. sorte cioe. 5. lunghezza eddue. 6. ella . . he. 8. cholonnale e el. 9. ettutte. 10. rectilini [Mallonbra] cō. 11. chorrète . . nassci. 13. ella cholōnale nassce. 14. ella. 17. chō. 18. posste. 19. onbra . . conposste. 20. sortti . . cholūnali. 21. tabile.

92'

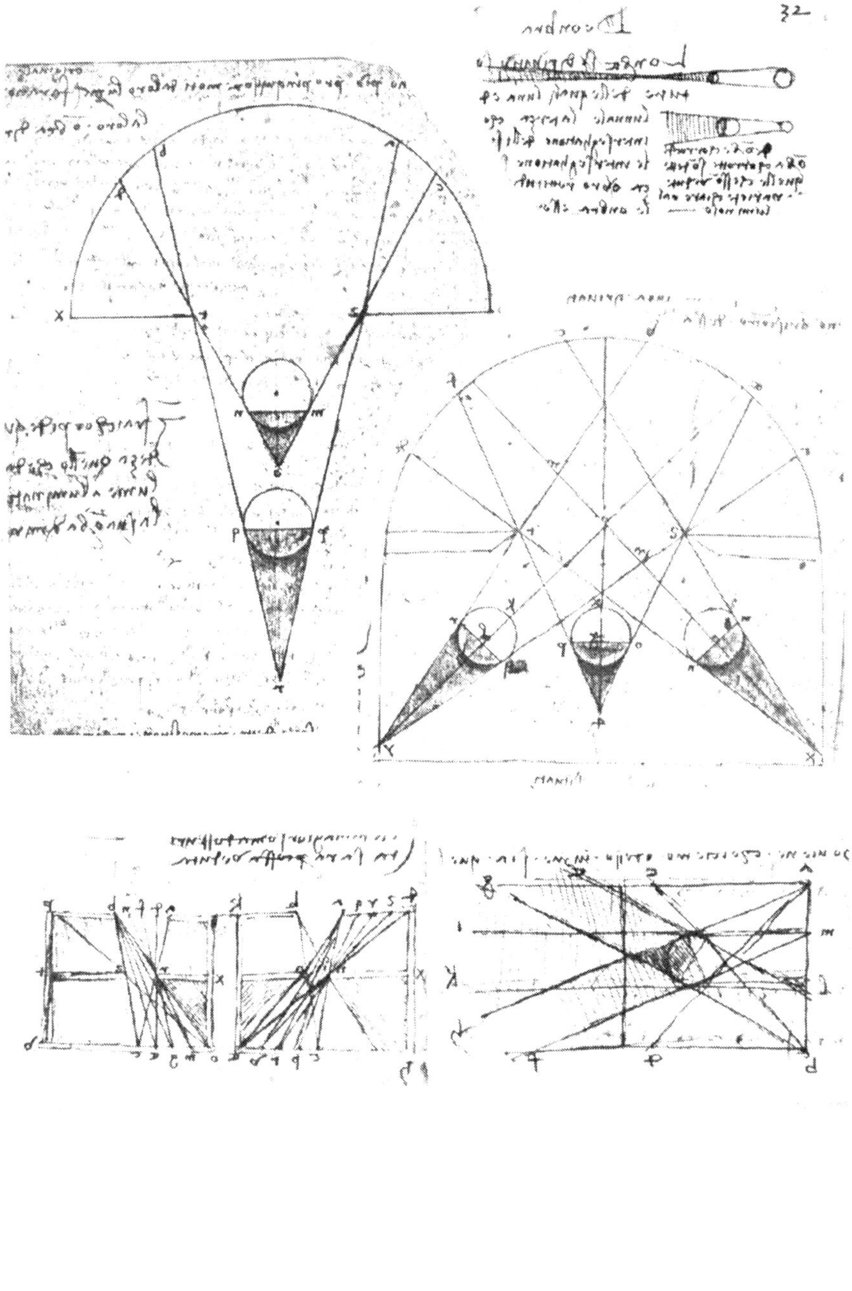

DELLE ÕBRE DIRIUATIVE CÕ[18]POSTE.

[19]Le onbre deriuative conposte sono [20]di due sorti cioè colõnali e dila[21]tabili.

OF COMPOUND DERIVED SHADOWS.

Compound derived shadows are of two kinds; that is columnar and spreading.

E. 32*a*]

162.

DE ONBRA.

[2]L'onbre dirivative sono di tre na[3]ture, delle quali l'una è dilatabile, l'altra co[4]lunnale, la terza concorrẽte al sito della [5]intersegatione delli sua lati, li quali dopo ta[6]le intersegatione sono d'ĩfinita lunghez[7]za overo rettitudine; E se tu diciessi ta[8]le onbra essere terminata nell'angolo [9]della congiũtione de sua lati e nõ passare piv oltre, questo si ni[10]ega · perchè nella prima dell'onbre sopra ò pro[11]vato ¶quella cosa essere interamente termi[12]nata della qual parte alcuna non eccede [13]li sua termini¶ il che qui in tale onbra si ve[14]de il contrario conciosiachè mediante che [15]nascie tale onbra dirivativa nascie manife[16]stamẽte la figura di due piramidi õbrose, le quali nel[17]li sua angoli son congiũte; addunque [18]se per l'aversario la prima piramide õbrosa è ter[19]minatricie dell'onbra dirivativa col suo ango[20]lo donde nascie, addunque la seconda pira[21]mide õbrosa · dicie l'aversario esser cavsa[22]ta dall'angolo e nõ dal corpo õbroso; e questo si [23]niega coll'aiuto della 2ª di questo che [24]dicie ¶l'õbra essere vn'accidẽte creato dalli cor[25]pi õbrosi interposti infra 'l sito d'essa õbra [26]e 'l corpo luminoso¶, e per questo è chia[27]rito l'onbra nõ dal angolo dell'onbra dirivativa [28]esser gienerata, ma sol dal corpo õbroso ecc. [29]Se lo sperico õbroso fia alluminato dal lumi[30]noso di lũga figura, l'onbra che si gienera dalla [31]parte più lunga d'esso luminoso fia di termini [32]men noti che è quella che si gienera dalla larghez[33]za del medesimo lume; E questo si prova per la pas[34]sata che disse quell'õbra essere di termini mẽ noti [35]ch'è creata da maggiore luminoso e de cõverso, quel[36]la essere di termini più noti che s'allumina da minor luminoso.

OF SHADOW.

Derived shadows are of three kinds of which one is spreading, the second columnar, the third converging to the point where the two sides meet and intersect, and beyond this intersection the sides are infinitely prolonged or straight lines. And if you say, this shadow must terminate at the angle where the sides meet and extend no farther, I deny this, because above in the first on shadow I have proved: that a thing is completely terminated when no portion of it goes beyond its terminating lines. Now here, in this shadow, we see the converse of this, in as much as where this derived shadow originates we obviously have the figures of two pyramids of shadow which meet at their angles. Hence, if, as [my] opponent says, the first pyramid of shadow terminates the derivative shadow at the angle whence it starts, then the second pyramid of shadow —so says the adversary—must be caused by the angle and not from the body in shadow; and this is disproved with the help of the 2nd of this which says: Shadow is a condition produced by a body casting a shadow, and interposed between this shadow and the luminous body. By this it is made clear that the shadow is not produced by the angle of the derived shadow but only by the body casting the shadow; &c. If a spherical solid body is illuminated by a light of elongated form the shadow produced by the longest portion of this light will have less defined outlines than that which is produced by the breadth of the same light. And this is proved by what was said before, which is: That a shadow will have less defined outlines in proportion as the light which causes it is larger, and conversely, the outlines are clearer in proportion as it is smaller.

162. 2. [si] dirivativ. 3. cho. 4. choncorrẽte. 5. intersegliatione. 6. interseghatione . . dĩfinita "righor" lunghe. 7. Essettu "di" ciessi [chella] ta. 8. anghelo. 9. della [interseghatione] "congiũtione" de sua ati. Questo. *The following occurs in the margin* e nõ passare piv oltre. 10. egha . perche [terminata] nella pª dellonbre so pro. 11. chosa. 12. alchuna . . eciede. 13. qui [no] in "t" ale onbra sivi. 14. chontrario chonciossiache. 15. nasscie . . nasscie. 16. piramide "õbrose". 17. angholi son chongiũte [ella]. 18. etter. 19. chol suo angho. 20. nasscie . . sechonda. 21. õbrosa [perche] . dicie . . chavsa. 22. anghola . . quessto. 23. niegha [medi] choll . . chẽd. 24. chor. 26. chorpo luminoso) [addunque] e . . quessto. 27. angholo. 29. Sello spericho. 30. lũgha fighura . . chessi. 31. [parte piu] lungha. 32. [chen] "men" noti che ecquella chessi. 33. Ecquesto. 34. cheddisse. 35. magiore. 36. termini mẽnoti chessalumina dãminor.

162. The two diagrams to this chapter are on Plate IV, No. I.

163.

B.¹ 28 a]

On the relation of derived and primary shadow (163—165).

¶ L'onbra diriuatiua nõ fia mai simile al corpo dove nascie se il lume no sarà della figura e gradezza del corpo obroso¶

¶ L'obra dirivativa nõ può essere simile per figura alla primitiva, se essa nõ percuote fra equali angoli.¶

The derived shadow can never resemble the body from which it proceeds unless the light is of the same form and size as the body causing the shadow.

The derived shadow cannot be of the same form as the primary shadow unless it is intercepted by a plane parallel to it.

164.

Ash. I. 6 a]

Come l'õbra separata nõ fia mai simile per grãdezza alla sua cagione.

How a cast shadow can never be of the same size as the body that casts it.

Se li razzi luminosi sono, come sperïeza coferma, cavsati da uno solo püto e i corso circulare al suo püto si vanno disgregãdo e spargẽdo per l'aria, quato piv s'alontanano piv s'alargano e sẽpre la cosa posta fra lume e la pariete è portata per õbra maggiore perchè i razzi che la toccano givnto lor cõcorso alla pariete è fatto piv largo.

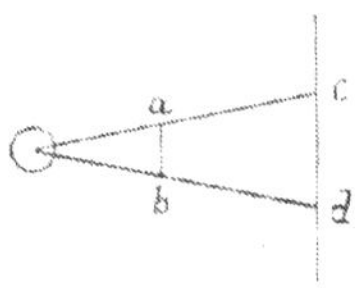

If the rays of light proceed, as experience shows, from a single point and are diffused in a sphere round this point, radiating and dispersed through the air, the farther they spread the wider they must spread; and an object placed between the light and a wall is always imaged larger in its shadow, because the rays that strike it[7] would, by the time they have reached the wall, have become larger.

165.

Br. M. 170 a]

Ogni õbra separata dal corpo õbroso è tutta della natura e qualità di quella ch'è cõgivnta a esso corpo; il mezzo della lughezza di ciascuna õbra sẽpre si dirizza al mezzo del corpo luminoso; neciessario è che ogni õbra risguardi col suo mezzo il mezzo del suo lume.

Any shadow cast by a body in light and shade is of the same nature and character as that which is inseparable from the body. The centre of the length of a shadow always corresponds to that of the luminous body [6]. It is inevitable that every shadow must have its centre in a line with the centre of the light.

166.

E. 31 a]

On the shape of derived shadows (166—174).

Del'õbra piramidale.

Of the pyramidal shadow.

L'onbra piramidale gienerata dal corpo parallelo sarà tanto più strettta che 'l corpo õbroso, quato la sẽplice onbra deriuativa fia tagliata più distante al suo corpo obroso.

The pyramidal shadow produced by a columnar body will be narrower than the body itself in proportion as the simple derived shadow is intersected farther from the body which casts it.

163. 1—6 R. . . nasscie sellume. 3. figura e grãdera. 4. dirivativ . . po. 5. percote.
164. . . grãdeza. 3. razi . . da i solo. 4. circhulare . . vãu. 5. essẽpre. 6. magiore perche 4. 7. 4 i razi . . tocano.
165. 1. õbr. . . etutta . . quela. 3. chorpo. 4. mezo . . lügeza. 5. diriza . . mezo. 6. [Egli e] neciessario è cheo. 7. gni obra [si dirizi al mezo del suo]. 8. [lume] risguardi . . mezo. 9. mezo.
166. 3. chorpo . . strec. 4. chel chorpo. 6. disstante . . chorpo.

164. 7. The following lines are wanting to complete the logical connection.

165. 6. This second statement of the same idea as in the former sentence, but in different words, does not, in the original, come next to the foregoing; sections 172 and [illegible] are placed between them.

166. Compare the first diagram to No. 161. If we here conceive of the outlines of the pyramid of shadow on the ground as prolonged beyond its apex this gives rise to a second pyramid; this is what is spoken of at the beginning of No. 166.

B. M. 170*b*]

167.

Quel'onbra separata [2]fia piv lūga · che avrà il lume [3]piv basso.

The cast shadow will be longest when the light is lowest.

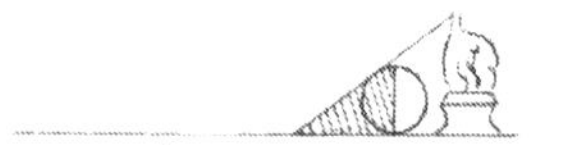

[4]Quell'ōbra separata [5]fia piv brieve, la quale avrà [6]il lume piv alto.

The cast shadow will be shortest when the light is highest.

Tr. 28]

168.

¶L'onbra primitiva · e dirivativa fia [2]maggiore a essere · cavsata da lume [3]di cādela · che quello dell'aria¶ [4]tāto quāto [5]l'ōbra diriva[6]tiva · entra [7]la maggiore nella [8]minor tāto la [9]cavsa della mi[10]nore è piv [11]luminosa che la [12]maggiore.

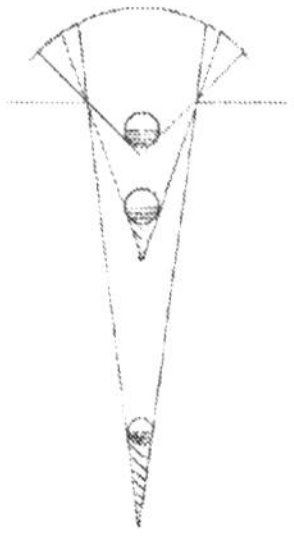

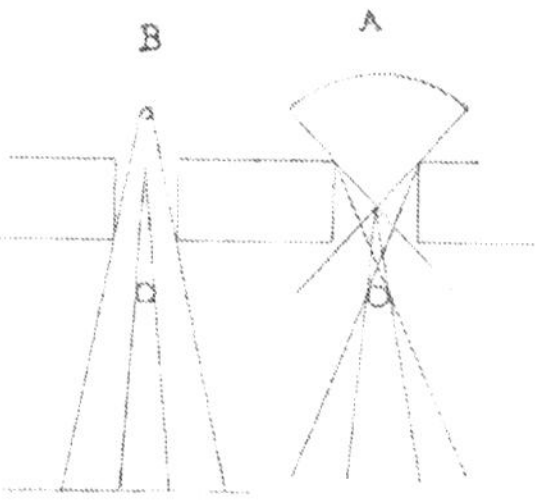

Both the primary and derived shadow will be larger when caused by the light of a candle than by diffused light. The difference between the larger and smaller shadows will be in inverse proportion to the larger and smaller lights causing them.

Ash. I. 25*a*]

169.

QUELLI CORPI · CHE FIENO PIV PROPINQUI O REMOTI DAL LORO LUME ORIGINALE · FARĀNO PIV [2]O MENO BRIEVE LA LORO · ŌBRA DERIVATIVA.

[3]Jfra i corpi d'equal grā[4]dezza quello che da maggior [5]lume alluminato fia avrà [6]la sua ōbra di minore lūghezza; [7]Nello sperimētare · s'afferma · la sopra detta · propositione · per cagione · che 'l corpo [8]*m · n* · è

ALL BODIES, IN PROPORTION AS THEY ARE NEARER TO, OR FARTHER FROM THE SOURCE OF LIGHT, WILL PRODUCE LONGER OR SHORTER DERIVED SHADOWS.

Among bodies of equal size, that one which is illuminated by the largest light will have the shortest shadow. Experiment confirms this proposition. Thus the body *m n* is surrounded by a larger amount of light

167. 1. ombra [sia] separata. 2. ara ilume. 4. Quello ōbra [fia piv] separata. 5. ara. 6. ilume.
168. 2. magiore . . chausata. 3. chādela. 7. magiore nela. 11. chella. 12. magiore.
169. 1. chorpi cheffiano. 3—6 R. 3. chorpi. 4. dera . . magior. 5. ara. 6. lungeza. 7. chagione. 8. abraciato. 9. cheffa . .

168. In the diagrams *A* stands for *celo* (sky), *B* for *cādela* (candle).

169. The diagram, given on Pl. IV, No. 2, stands in the original between lines 2 and 7, while the text of lines 3 to 6 is written on its left side. In the reproduction of this diagram the letter *v* at the outer right-hand end has been omitted.

abbracciato da piv · parte di lume · che 'l corpo · *p · q* · come di sopra si dimostra; [9]Diciamo · che *v · c · a · b · d · x* · sia il cielo che fa il lume originale · e che · *s · t* · sia una [10]finestra dōde ētri le spetie luminose · e cosi · *m · n* · *p · q* · sieno i corpi ōbrosi [11]cōtraposti · a detto · lume; *m · n* sarà di minore ōbra deriuativa perchè la sua ōbra ori[12]ginale fia · poca e il lume diriuatiuo fia · grāde perchè ancora fia grande [13]il lume originale *c · d* · *p · q* · avrà piv ōbra diriuativa perchè la sua · ōbra [14]originale · fia maggiore; il lume suo derivativo · fia minore · che quello del corpo [15]*m · n* · perchè quella · parte dell' emisperio *a · b* · che l'allumina è minore [16]che l'emisperio *c · d* alluminatore del corpo · *m · n*.

than the body *p q*, as is shown above. Let us say that *v c a b d x* is the sky, the source of light, and that *s t* is a window by which the luminous rays enter, and so *m n* and *p q* are bodies in light and shade as exposed to this light; *m n* will have a small derived shadow, because its original shadow will be small; and the derivative light will be large, again, because the original light *c d* will be large and *p q* will have more derived shadow because its original shadow will be larger, and its derived light will be smaller than that of the body *m n* because that portion of the hemisphere *a b* which illuminates it is smaller than the hemisphere *c d* which illuminates the body *m n*.

W. II.]

170.

Quella proportione che à la linia *b c* [2]colla linia *f c* tale avrà la scurità [3]*m* colla oscurità *n*.

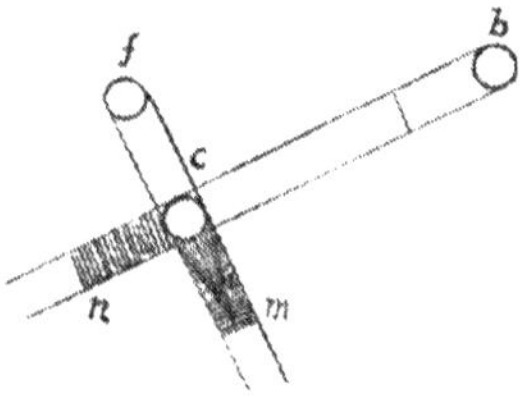

The shadow *m* bears the same proportion to the shadow *n* as the line *b c* to the line *f c*.

Ash. I. 25 b.]

171.

Pittura.

Infra l'onbre · di pari · qualita · quella che sia · piv · visina · all'ochio [3]apparirà · di minore oscurità.

[4]Perchè l'onbra · *e · a · b* è in primo · grado di scurita [5]*b · c* · è in secōdo, *c · d* è in terzo? La ragione · si è che [6]*e · a · b* · non vede il cielo in alcuna parte · adūque [7]nessuna · parte · del cielo · uede · lui · e per questo è priva[8]to del lume originale · · *b · c* · vede la parte

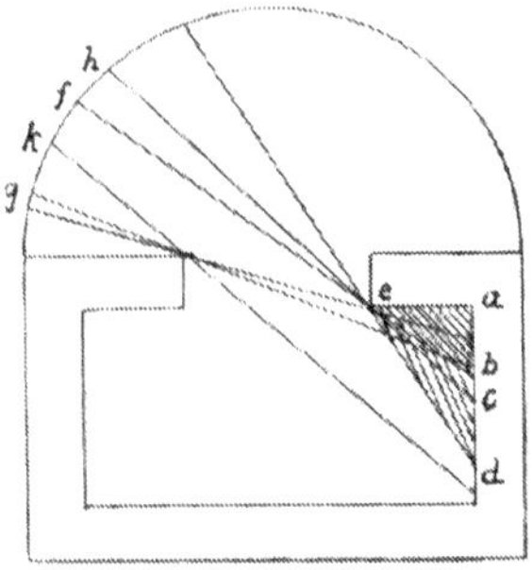

Of painting.

Of different shadows of equal strength that which is nearest the eye will seem the least strong.

Why is the shadow *e a b* in the first grade of strength, *b c* in the second; *c d* in the third? The reason is that as from *e a b* the sky is nowhere visible, it gets no light whatever from the sky, and so has no direct [primary] light. *b c* faces the portion of the sky *f*

sia 8. 10. dōdētri . . echosi. 12. pocha ellume . . anchora. 13. c . d . [A] p . q . ara. 14. magiore ilume . . chorpo. 15. perche [lemisper] quella . . chellalumina. 16. chorpo.
170. 2. ara. 3. oscurita.
171. ... quela. 10. ma-

del cielo [9]*f g* e da quella è alluminata *c d* vede il cielo [10]*h k*, essendo visto *c d* da maggiore soma di cielo [11]che non è *b c*, e ragione vole che sia piv luminoso, [12]e cosi insino · a cierta distantia il muro *a d* senpre [13]rischiarerà per le dette ragioni insino a tāto che la [14]scurità del'abitatione vīcierà il lume della finestra

g and is illuminated by it *c d* faces the sky at *h k c d*, being exposed to a larger extent of sky than *b c*, it is reasonable that it should be more lighted And thus, up to a certain distance, the wall *a d* will grow lighter for the reasons here given, until the darkness of the room overpowers the light from the window

Br M 170*b*]

172

[2]Quādo il lume dell'aria [3]sarà costretto a luminare i corpi [4]ōbrosi, essēdo essi corpi equidistāti [5]dal cietro d'essa finestra, quello che si [6]troverà piv traverso farà maggiore [7]ōbra dopo se.

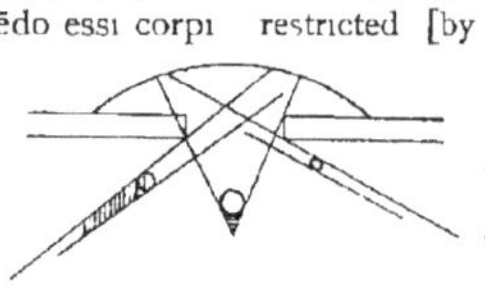

When the light of the atmosphere is restricted [by an opening] and illuminates bodies which cast shadows, these bodies being equally distant from the centre of the window, that which is most obliquely placed will cast the largest shadow beyond it

Ash I 24*b*]

173

Quelli corpi sparsi situati in abitatione alluminãta [2]da una sola · finestra faranno l'ōbra diriuativa piv o meno brieue secōdo [3]che fia piv o meno a riscōtro d'essa finestra [4]¶ Jfra l'onbre fatte [5]da equali corpi [6]e ī disequali distātie [7]dallo spiraculo lo[8]ro alluminatore quel[9]la fia piv lūga che [10]à il suo corpo meno [11]luminoso e tāto fia [12]più luminoso l'ū [13]che l'altro corpo, quā[14]to l'ombra sua fia [15]piv corta che l'al[16]tra ¶ [17]Quella proportione [18]che à in se *n m e v* [19]*k* cō *r t* et *v x*, [20]tale avrà onbra *x* cō[21] 4 *y*

[23]La ragione che i corpi ōbrosi, che si trovano situati piv dritti al mezzo della finestra, [24]fanno l'obre piv brievi che quelli situati ī trauerso sito si è, che vedono mag[25]giore la finestra ī propia forma, e i corpi traversi la uederanno in iscorto, a quello [26]di mezzo la finestra pare grāde, ai traversi pare piccola, quel di mezzo vede

These bodies standing apart in a room lighted by a single window will have derivative shadows more or less short according as they are more or less opposite to the window Among the shadows cast by bodies of equal mass but at unequal distances from the opening by which they are illuminated, that shadow will be the longest of the body which is least in the light And in proportion as one body is better illuminated than another its shadow will be shorter than another The proportion *n m* and *e v k* bear to *r t* and *v x* corresponds with that of the shadow *x* to 4 and *y*

The reason why those bodies which are placed most in front of the middle of the window throw shorter shadows than those obliquely situated is —That the window appears in its proper form and to the obliquely placed ones it appears foreshortened, to those in the middle, the window shows its full size, to the oblique ones it appears smaller, the one in the middle faces the whole hemisphere that is *e f* and those on the side have only a strip, that is *q r* faces *a b*,

giore soma 12 chosi 13 risciarera attāto 14 surita ilume
172 1 [lōbra reale sia piv lūga quāto piv] 2 [si trova] Quādo ilume 3 cosstreto 5 al chessi magiore
173 1 chorpi [separati chessi trōueranno] sparsi 2 da ī sola ōmeno sechōdo 3 cheffia 4 īfrallonbre 5 ecquali 6 e īdisegli 7 spirachulo 8 alumatore que 9 la effia piv lūga 10 fia il suo chorpo m̄ 11 ettāto fi''a' 13 chellaltro chorpo qu''a 15 chorta 18 n m ∞ ''e' v 19 k chō 1 20 ara onbra + c''ō 22 [situati] 23 chessi . mezo 24 lōbra queli sie [questa] che vede ma 25 propia uechano acquelo 26 mezo picola

173 Compare the diagram on Pl IV, No 3 In the original this drawing is placed between lines 3 and 22, the rest, from line 4 to line 21, is written on the left hand margin

l'emisperio [27]grãde cioè · *e* · *f* · e quelli da lato lo uedono piccolo cioè *q* · *r* · vede *a* · *b* · e cosi *m* · *n* · vede [28]*c* · *d*: il corpo di mezzo perchè à maggiore quãtità di lume che quelli da cãto, è allumi-[29]nato assai piv basso che'l suo cientro, e però · l'obra è piv breve, e tãto quãto *a* · *b* · entra [30]in · *e* · *f* · tanto la piramide *g* · 4 · entra in · *l* · *y* · appunto. [31]Ogni mezzo · d'obra dirivativa passa per 6½, e si dirizza col mezzo dell'obra [32]originale e col cietro del corpo õbroso e del lume deriuatiuo [33]e col mezzo della finestra · e in vltimo col mezzo di quella [34]parte del lume originale fatto dal'emispe[35]rio cieleste; [36] · *y* · *h* · è il mezzo dell'obra · diriuatiua · *l* · *h* · del'õbra originale · *l* · sia il mezzo del corpo õbroso [37]*l* · *k* del lume deriuatiuo · *v* sia il mezzo della finestra · *e* · sia l'ultimo mezzo del lume [38]originale fatto da quella parte dell'emisperio del cielo che lumina il corpo obroso.

and *m n* faces *c d*; the body in the middle having a larger quantity of light than those at the sides is lighted from a point much below its centre, and thus the shadow is shorter. And the pyramid *g* 4 goes into *l y* exactly as often as *a b* goes into *e f*. The axis of every derivative shadow passes through 6½ [31] and is in a straight line with the centre of the primary shadow, with the centre of the body casting it and of the derivative light and with the centre of the window and, finally, with the centre of that portion of the source of light which is the celestial hemisphere. *y h* is the centre of the derived shade, *l h* of the primary shadow, *l* of the body throwing it, *l k* of the derived light. *v* is the centre of the window, *e* is the final centre of the original light afforded by that portion of the hemisphere of the sky which illuminates the solid body.

174.

C. 21 a]

QUANTO PIÙ L'ONBRA · DIRIVATIUA S'ALLONTANA · DELLA PRIMITIUA · TANTO [2]PIÙ · PARTICIPA · DI CHIAREZZA.

[3]Tal proportione quale à il diamitro · dell'onbra · diriuatiua [4]con quello della · primitiua, · tale · trouerai · nella oscurità dell'õbra [5]primitiua · con quello · della · diriuatiua.

[6]*a* · *b* · sia il diamitro dell'onbra primitiua · *c* · *d* · sia · quello della · di[7]riuatiua ·, dico che ẽtrando come vedi *a* · *b* · 3 · volte in · *d* · *c* · [8]che l'onbra · *d* · *c* · fia · 3 · volte · piv · chiara che quella di *a* · *b*.

[9]se la grandezza del corpo · alluminãte · supera · quella · del corpo [10]alluminato · accaderà · onbrosa · intersegatione · dopo la quale

THE FARTHER THE DERIVED SHADOW IS PROLONGED THE LIGHTER IT BECOMES.

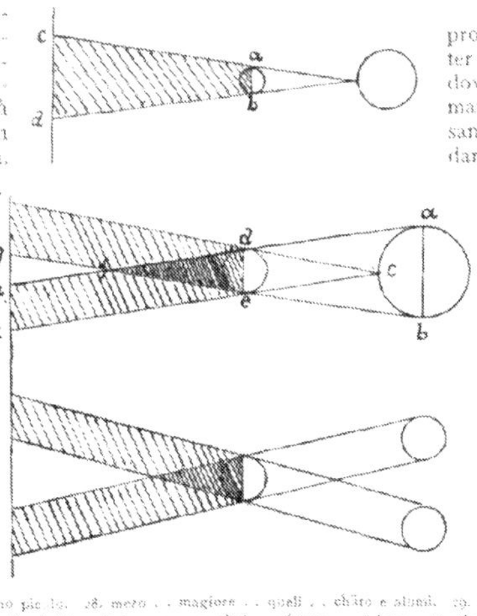

You will find that the proportion of the diameter of the derived shadow to that of the primary shadow will be the same as that between the darkness of the primary shadow and that of the derived shadow.

[6] Let *a b* be the diameter of the primary shadow and *c d* that of the derived shadow, I say that *a b* going, as you see, three times into *d c*, the shadow *d c* will be three times as light as the shadow *a b*. [8]

If the size of the illuminating body is larger than that of

mezo. 27. equelli . . vedano pic lo. 28. mezo . . magiore . . queli . . chãto e alumi. 29. asai. 30. piramida. 31. mezo . . dirivativa ["passa per 6½"] esi diriza chol mezo. 32. chol . . chorpo . . delume. 33. chol [nacho] mezo . . chol mezo. 34. del in [emisperio lume] me. 35. mezo . . sie . . mezo. 37. sie . . mezo . . sie . . mezo. 38. dacquella.

174. 2. chiareza. 3. [Quanto quella] tal proportione "quale" cha il. 4. chon quello . . talle osscurità ta. 5. chonquello. 6. dela. 8. chella quella. 9. grandeza . . chorpo . . del chorpo. 10. achadera. 11. cho chorreranno . . . chonchorsicho.

31. *passa per* 6½ (passes through 6½). The meaning of these words is probably this: Each of the three axes of the derived shadow intersects the centre (*mezzo*) of the primary shadow (*ombra originale*) and, by prolongation upwards crosses six lines. This is self evident only in the middle diagram; but it is equally true of the side figures if we conceive of the lines 4 *f*, *x n v m*, *y l k v*, and 4 *e*, as prolonged beyond the semicircle of the horizon.

174. 6—8. Compare No. 177.

[11]l'onbre correranno · in due diuersi · concorsi ·, co[12]me · se · da · due · diuersi · lumi diriuassino.

the illuminated body an intersection of shadow will occur, beyond which the shadows will run off in two opposite directions as if they were caused by two separate lights.

K.[2] 31 *b*]

175.

Pittura.

[2]L'onbra diriuatiua [3]è tāto più potēte quan[4]to ell'è piv vicina [5]alli sua principi.

On painting.

The derived shadow is stronger in proportion as it is nearer to its place of origin. On the relative intensity of derived shadows (175—179).

Ash. I. 15 *a*]

176.

Come l'ōbre per lūga distātia si perdono.

[2]L'onbre · si perdono ī lūnga distātia · perchè · la grā quātità · dell'aria luminosa, [3]che si truova īfra l'ochio · e la · cosa · veduta ·, tigne le sue ōbre d'essa cosa nel suo colore.

How shadows fade away at long distances.

Shadows fade and are lost at long distances because the larger quantity of illuminated air which lies between the eye and the object seen tints the shadow with its own colour.

Tr. 22]

177.

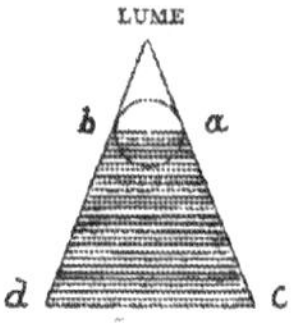

Quāte volte · *a* · *b* · ētra in [2]*c* *b* · tāto fia piv scuro [3]*a* *b* · che · *c* · *d*.

a b will be darker than *c d* in proportion as *c d* is broader than *a b*.

C. A. 36 *a*; 115 *a*]

178.

Pruovasi perchè l'onbra *o p c h* è tanto piv oscura, [2]quanto ella più s'avicina alla liniā *p* · *h*, ed è tanto più [3]chiara quāto essa più s'avicina alla linia *o c*, e sia il [4]lume *a b* finestra, e la pariete oscura, dove tale finestra [5]è collocata, sia *b s* cioè vn de lati d'essa pariete.

[6]Addunque diremo la linia *p h* essere più oscura che [7]altra parte dello spatio · *o p c h*, perchè essa linia ve[8]de ed è veduta da tutto lo spatio ōbroso

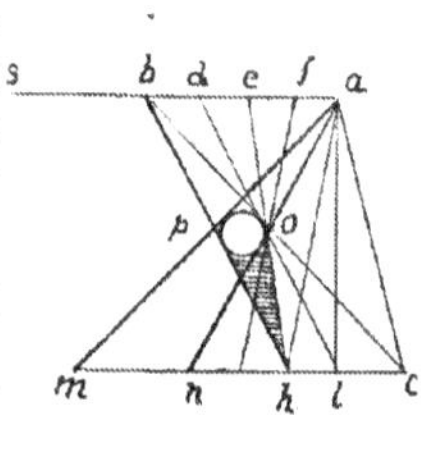

It can be proved why the shadow *o p c h* is darker in proportion as it is nearer to the line *p h* and is lighter in proportion as it is nearer to the line *o c*. Let the light *a b*, be a window, and let the dark wall in which this window is, be *b s*, that is, one of the sides of the wall.

Then we may say that the line *p h* is darker than any other part of the space *o p c h*, because this line faces the whole surface in shadow of

175. 1—4 R. 3. ettāto . . . potēte q[ta]".
176. 1. come [son] lōbre . . distātia *si perdono*. 2. illūnga . . dellaire luminoso. 3. chessi . . ella . . le sue ōbre d'essa cosa.
177. 2. suro.
178. 1. op c h e ettanto . . osscura . . tanto pi. 3. essia. 4. ella . . osschura . . tal finesstra. 5. e cholochata. 6. direno . .

177. In the original MS. the word *lume* (light) is written at the apex of the pyramid.

178. In the original the diagram is placed between lines 27 and 28.

della pariete *b s*, ma la linia *o c* è piv chiara che altra parte d'esso spatio *o p c h* perchè essa linia vede lo spatio luminoso *a b*.

[Doue l'obra è maggiore o minore o equale al corpo obroso sua origine.]

[Di prima della qualità de lumi divisi.

the wall *b s*. The line *o c* is lighter than the other part of this space *o p c h*, because this line faces the luminous space *a b*.

Where the shadow is larger, or smaller, or equal the body which casts it.

[First of the character of divided lights [14].

DELL'ONBRA COMPOSTA *F, R, C, H* NATA DAL LUME PARTICULARE.

L'onbra composta *f r c h* è in tal modo conditionata che quanto ella si fa più remota dal suo lato intrinsico, tanto perde della sua oscurità; pruovasi:

Sia adunque il luminoso *d a* e l'ōbroso *f n*, e sia *a e* vna delle parieti laterali della finestra cioè *d a*; Dico per la 2ª, la superfitie d'ogni corpo participa del color del suo obbietto, adunque il lato *r c*, ch'è veduto dalla oscurità *a e*, participa d'essa oscurità e similmēte il lato estrinsico ch'è veduto dal lume *d a* participa d'esso lume e cosi abiā definito tale stremo del mezzo cōtenuto dalli stremi]

Questa si diuide in 4 parti prima delli stremi cōtenēti l'onbra conposita, seconda, Dell'onbra cōposita dentro alli sua stremi.

OF THE COMPOUND SHADOW *F, R, C, H* CAUSED BY A SINGLE LIGHT.

The shadow *f r c h* is under such conditions as that where it is farthest from its inner side it loses depth in proportion. To prove this:

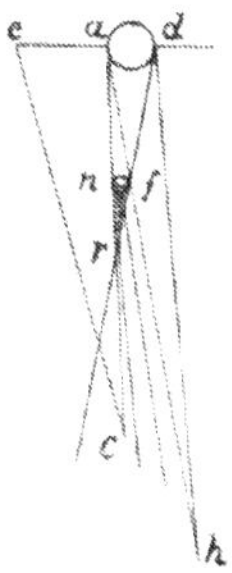

Let *d a*, be the light and *f n* the solid body, and let *a e* be one of the side walls of the window that is *d a*. Then I say—according to the 2nd [proposition]: that the surface of any body is affected by the tone of the objects surrounding it,—that the side *r c*, which faces the dark wall *a e* must participate of its darkness and, in the same way that the outer surface which faces the light *d a* participates of the light; thus we get the outlines of the extremes on each side of the centre included between them.]

This is divided into four parts. The first the extremes, which include the compound shadow, secondly the compound shadow between these extremes.

C. A. 201 a; 597 a]

179.

L'OPERATIONE · DEL LUME · COL SUO · CIĒTRO.

Se tutto · il lume · fusse · quello che cavsasse · l'onbre · dopo i corpi a quello · cōtraposti ·, converebbe, che quello · corpo ·, ch'è molto · minore che'l lume ·, facesse · dopo se vn ōbra · piramidale ·, e la spetrièza non lo mostrādo · côuiene · che'l cietro d'esso lume sia · quello che facci · tale ofitio.

THE ACTION OF THE LIGHT AS FROM ITS CENTRE.

If it were the whole of the light that caused the shadows beyond the bodies placed in front of it, it would follow that any body much smaller than the light would cast a pyramidal shadow; but experience not showing this, it must be the centre of the light that produces this effect.

oschura. 8. dsemite losspatio. 9. [losspatio] la linia. 10. 11. [perche] o p c h . vede [[[12. magiore ominor. 13. chorpo. 15. chonposte. 16. partichulare. 17. chonposta. 19. cho . . osschurita. 20. ellōbroso . . essia. 21. pariete . . finesstra. 22. Dicho . . dongni chorpo. 23. cholor . . ilato. 24. veduta . . osschurita . . osschurit. 25. esstrinsicho che veduta. 26. chosi . . stre "mo". 29. 4 p"a" p"a" delli. 31. 2 "a" De Dellonbra chonposita.

179. 1. lume . chosuo. 2. esstutto . . fussi . . charsassi . . aquello . . chonverebe. 3. chorpo . . facessi . . ella. 4. rièza nol

14. *lumi divisi.* The text here breaks off abruptly.

179. The diagram belonging to this passage is between lines 4 and 5 in the original. Comp. the reproduction Pl. IV, No. 4. The text and drawing of this chapter have already been published with tolerable accuracy. See M. JORDAN: *"Das Malerbuch des Leonardo da Vinci"*. Leipzig 1873, p. 90.

PRUOVA.

[6] *a* · *b* · sia la grãdezza · del lume · d'una · finestra ·, la quale dia · il lume · a vno · bastone ritto · ĩ piè [7] da · *a* · *c* · e da · *a* · *d* · sia dove la finestra .tutta · ĩteramẽte da il suo · lume · · Jn · *c* · *e* · nõ può vedere · quella · parte [8] della · finestra ·, ch'è ĩfra · *l* · *b* · · E simil · mẽte · *d* · *f* · nõ uede · *a* · *m* · e per questa · cagione ĩ questi · 2 · lochi co°mĩcia · a stremare · il lume.

PROOF.

Let *a b* be the width of the light from a window, which falls on a stick set up at one foot from *a c* [6]. And let *a d* be the space where all the light from the window is visible. At *c e* that part of the window which is between *l b* cannot be seen. In the same way *a m* cannot be seen from *d f* and therefore in these two portions the light begins to fail.

C. 8 *b*]

180.

Shadow as produced by two lights of different size (180. 181).

[2] Quel corpo · õbroso · che infra equali lumi collocato fia, farà tãte õbre quã tĩ fieno i lumi, le quali õbre fieno tãto piv scure l'una che l'altra, quãto il lume [4] che fia dall'opposita parte fia piv visino a esso corpo · che li altri.

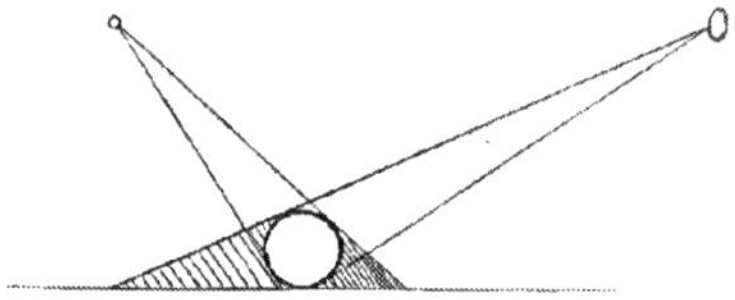

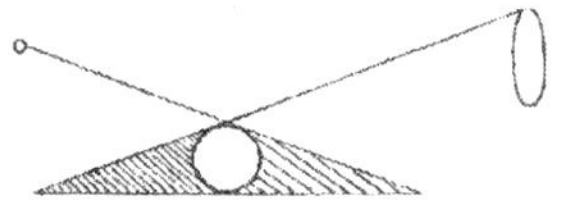

[5] Quel corpo onbroso che equalmẽte distãte infra 2 lumi situato sia, farà [6] due õbre tanto piv oscure l'una · che l'altra · quãto · i lumi d'esso cagiõ siẽ maggiori [7] l'una · che l'altra.

A body in light and shade placed between two equal lights side by side will cast shadows in proportion to the [amount of] light. And the shadows will be one darker than the other in proportion as one light is nearer to the said body than the other on the opposite side.

A body placed at an equal distance between two lights will cast two shadows, one deeper than the other in proportion, as the light which causes it is brighter than the other.

Br. M. 170 *b*]

181.

Il lume minore che corpo õbroso [2] fa l'ombre terminare in esso corpo [3] e fa poca õbra · mista, e lo vede [4] meno di mezzo; [5] il lume maggiore · che'l corpo õbroso [6] lo vede piv di mezzo e fa molta õbra mista.

A light which is smaller than the body it illuminates produces shadows of which the outlines end within [the surface of] the body, and not much compound shadow; and falls on less than half of it. A light which is larger than the body it illuminates, falls on more than half of it, and produces much compound shadow.

mostrãdo chõuiene . . cheffacci. 6. grãdeza . . pie [c d]. 7. sie . . ĩtera mẽta . . po. 8. Essimil . mẽte . . chagione . . iochl cho. 9. ilu ne.

180. 1—7 R. 1. ĩnfrae. 2. Quel chorpo . . chollochato . chellaltra. 4. cheffia . . oposita . . chorpo piv chelli. 5. chorpo . . lumi [ch] situato. 6. osschure . . chellaltra . quãto . elumi . . chagiõ . magiori 7. chelialtra.

181. 1. ilume . . õbrso. 3. effa pocha . . mezo. 5. magiore chel chorpo. 6. mezo effa.

6. *bastone* (stick). The diagram has a sphere in place of a stick.

180. In the MS. the larger diagram is placed above the first line; the smaller one between l. 4 & 5.

Ash I 5*b*]

182.

DEL'ÕBRA FATTA DA UNO CORPO SITUATO . ĨFRA 2 EQUALI LUMI.

The effect of light at different distances.

Quello corpo che si troverà collocato · Ĩfra 2 equali lumi moverà da se 2 õbre le quali si dirizzerãno per linia a 2 lumi e se rimoverai detto corpo e farai lo più presso all'uno · de'lumi, l'ombra sua, che si dirizzerà al più propĩquo lume, fia di minore oscurità, che quella che si dirizzerà al più lõtano lume.

OF THE SHADOW CAST BY A BODY PLACED BETWEEN 2 EQUAL LIGHTS

A body placed between 2 equal lights will cast 2 shadows of itself in the direction of the lines of the 2 lights, and if you move this body placing it nearer to one of the lights the shadow cast towards the nearer light will be less deep than that which falls towards the more distant one.

W L 145 A*a*]

183.

Further complications in the derived shadows (183—187).

La massima oscurità delle õbre è la sẽplice onbra dirivatiua, perchè essa nõ vede nessun de'due lumi *a b, c d*.

La secõda di minore oscurità è l'õbra dirivativa *e f n*, e questa è la oscurità minore la metà perchè da vn sol lume è rischiarata cioè *c d*.

E questa è d'uniforme oscurità naturale, perchè per tutto vn sol de'due luminosi la vede; Ma si varia colla oscurità accidentale, perchè quãto più si scosta da tale lume, mẽ participa della sua chiarezza.

La terza oscurità è l'onbra media, ma questa non è di vniforme oscurità naturale, perchè quãto più s'avicina alla senplice õbra dirivativa, tanto si fa più oscura, e la uniformità vniformemẽte difforme accidentale è quella che la corronpe cioè che quãto più si discosta dalli due luminosi si fa più oscura.

La quarta è l'onbra *k r s*, e questa si fa tanto più oscura di scurità naturale, quanto essa s'avicina al *k s*, perchè mẽ vede del lume *a b*, ma per accidentale più perde d'oscurità, perchè più s'avicina al lume *c d*, e questa sẽpre vede li due lumi.

The greatest depth of shadow is in the simple derived shadow because it is not lighted by either of the two lights *a b, c d*.

The next less deep shadow is the derived shadow *e f n*; and in this the shadow is less by half, because it is illuminated by a single light, that is *c d*.

This is uniform in natural tone because it is lighted throughout by one only of the two luminous bodies [10] But it varies with the conditions of shadow, inasmuch as the farther it is away from the light the less it is illuminated by it [13]

The third degree of depth is the middle shadow [15]. But this is not uniform in natural tone, because the nearer it gets to the simple derived shadow the deeper it is [18], and it is the uniformly gradual diminution by increase of distance which is what modifies it [20]. that is to say the depth of a shadow increases in proportion to the distance from the two lights.

The fourth is the shadow *k r s* and this is all the darker in natural tone in proportion as it is nearer to *k s*, because it gets less of the light *a b*, but by the accident [of distance] it is rendered less deep, because it is nearer to the light *c d*, and thus is always exposed to both lights.

182 1. da ĩ corpo. 3 quelo chorpo chessi chollochato 4. muvera õbre che quali. 5. esse . detto ||| corpo effara 6 de lumi [che allaltro] lombra . chessi dirizera 7 oschurita chessi dirizera.

183 1. osschurita , ella 4 sechõda . osschurita ello 5 he *c/n* ecquessta ella. 6 osscurita 7 risschiarata. 8 ecquesta 9 osschurita 10 Massi cholla osscurita 11 sisschossta 12 dattale lume [pi] mẽ 14 osschurita ellonbra 15 macquessta e di 16 osschurita . . quẽto pi 18 osscura ella unifor 20 quela chella . . cioe cheq"ua" 21 disschosta. 22 osschura 23 hellonbra ecquessta. 24. osschura. 26. acidentale . dosscu 27 cd ecq 29 osschurita. 30. ciasscuna.

183. The diagram to this section is given on Pl. V. To the left is the facsimile of the beginning of the text belonging to it.

15. We gather from what follows that *q g r* here means *ombra media* (the middle shadow).

18—20 Compare lines 10—13

[29]La quĩta è di minore oscurità [30]che ciascuna delle altre perchè sen[31]pre vede ũ de due lumi interi e tutto [32]o parte dell'altro, e questa tanto [33]più perde d'oscurità quanto [34]ella più s'avicina alli due lu[35]mi, e tanto più quanto più [36]s'avicina al lato esteriore *x t*, [37]perchè più vede del secõdo lume [38]*a b*.

The fifth is less deep in shadow than either of the others because it is always entirely exposed to one of the lights and to the whole or part of the other; and it is less deep in proportion as it is nearer to the two lights, and in proportion as it is turned towards the outer side *x t*; because it is more exposed to the second light *a b*.

C. A. 174 *a*; 523 *a*]

184.

DELL'ONBRA SENPLICIE.

Perchè nelle intersegationi *a·b* delle due õbre cõposte [3]*e f*, *m c*, si gienera l'onbra senplicie e cosi in *e h* e *m g*, [4]e nõ si gienera tale õbra senplicie nelle due altre intersega[5]tioni *c d*, fatte dalle medesime õbre composte dette di sopra?

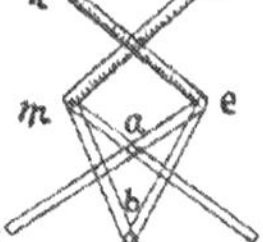

RISPOSTA.

[7]Le õbre conposte son miste di chiaro e di scuro, e [8]le senplici sõ di senplicie oscurità; adũque delli [9]due lumi *n o* l'uno vede l'õbre cõposte da vn lato e l'altro [10]vede l'onbre conposte dall'altro, ma nessũ lume vede le inter[11]segationi *a b* e però è senplicie õbra, ma nell'õbra cõposta [12]vede l'uno o l'altro lume; e qui nasce vn dubbio [13]per l'aversario, perchè dicie nelle intersegatiõ dell'onbre cõpo[14]ste per neciessità vedi li due lumi causa d'esse õbre, e per [15]questo tali onbre si debbono annullare; concio[16]siachè dove nõ vede li due lumi, noi diciamo l'õbra essere [17]senplicie, e dove vede ṽ solo de' due lumi diremo tal'onbra [18]esser cõposta, e dove vede li due lumi, essere õbra [19]annullata, perchè dove vede li due lumi, nõ si gienera [20]õbra di nessuna sorte, ma solo cõpone la chiarezza del cãpo [21]circũdatore delle õbre; Qui si rispõde esser vero [22]il detto d'esso aversario, il quale sol fa mentione di quella veri[23]tà ch'è ĩ suo fauore, ma se vi agivgnie il rimanẽte, egli cõcluderà [24]esser vera la mia proposta, e questo è [25]che, se vedendo li due lumi in tale interse[26]gatione, tali õbre sarebbono annullate;

OF SIMPLE SHADOWS.

Why, at the intersections *a*, *b* of the two compound shadows *e f* and *m c*, is a simple shadow produced as at *e h* and *m g*, while no such simple shadow is produced at the other two intersections *c d* made by the very same compound shadows?

ANSWER.

Compound shadow are a mixture of light and shade and simple shadows are simply darkness. Hence, of the two lights *n* and *o*, one falls on the compound shadow from one side, and the other on the compound shadow from the other side, but where they intersect no light falls, as at *a b*; therefore it is a simple shadow. Where there is a compound shadow one light or the other falls; and here a difficulty arises for my adversary since he says that, where the compound shadows intersect, both the lights which produce the shadows must of necessity fall and therefore these shadows ought to be neutralised; inasmuch as the two lights do not fall there, we say that the shadow is a simple one and where only one of the two lights falls, we say the shadow is compound, and where both the lights fall the shadow is neutralised; for where both lights fall, no shadow of any kind is produced, but only a light background limiting the shadow. Here I shall say that what my adversary said was true: but he only mentions such truths as are in his favour; and if we go on to the rest he must conclude that my proposition is true. And that is: That if both lights fell on the

31. ettutto. 32. dellaltro ecqua tanto. 33. dosschurita. 35. ettanto. 36. allato seriore. 37. sechõdo.

184. 2. interseghatione . . cõposste. 3. chosi in a h he m g. 4. interseghа. 5. composste. 6. rissposста. 7. composste son misste . . edidisscuro. 8. osscurita addũque. 9. ellaltro. 10. conposste. 11. seghationi . . essenplicie. 12. ollaltro . . nasscie. 13. interseghatiõ . . chõpo. 14. sta . . chausa. 15. annulare [sima] concio. 16. novede . . noi diciã. 17. senplicie eduve vedi vsol de due lumi dirietal. 18. chõpossta . . 20. soli . . ciarezza del chãpo. 21. circhũdatore. 23. se nagivgnie il rimanẽte e chõcludera. 24. ecquesto. 25. chesse. 26. ghatione . . tale. 27. Quando. 28. vedessino. 29. vedo.

[27]questo cōfesso esser vero, quando [28]le due ōbre nō vedessimo nel medesimo [29]sito, perchè se dove vedi vn'ōbra e vn [30]lume, si gienera ōbra cōposta, e dove [31]vedi due obre e due lumi simili, no si pu[32]ò variare in parte alcuna essa ōbra, [33]essendo le ōbre equali e equali li lu[34]mi, e questo si prova nell'ottava de [35]proportione dove dicie, tal proportio[36]ne à senplicie potētia cō senplicie resistē[37]tia quale à duplicata potētia cō duplicata resistētia.

point of intersection, the shadows would be neutralised. This I confess to be true if [neither of] the two shadows fell in the same spot; because, where a shadow and a light fall, a compound shadow is produced, and wherever two shadows or two equal lights fall, the shadow cannot vary in any part of it, the shadows and the lights both being equal. And this is proved in the eighth [proposition] on proportion where it is said that if a given quantity has a single unit of force and resistance, a double quantity will have double force and double resistance.

Br. M. 232a]

185.

Definitione.

[2]La intersegatione *n* è fatta dall'onbre create dal lume [3]*b*, perchè tale lume *b* gienera l'onbra *x b* e l'ōbra *s b*, ma [4]la intersegatione *m* è fatta dal lume *a* che gienera [5]l'ōbra *s a* e l'ōbra *x a*.

[6]Ma se tu scopri li due lumi *a b*, allora si generà le due ōbre *n m* [7]in ū medesimo tēpo, e oltre a di questo se ne generà due altre di [8]senplicie onbre cioè *r o*, nelle quali nō uede nessū de due luminosi. [9][10]tanto sono li gradi della oscurità che acquista l'onbre copo[11]ste, quanto saran minori li numeri de' luminosi che la vedono.

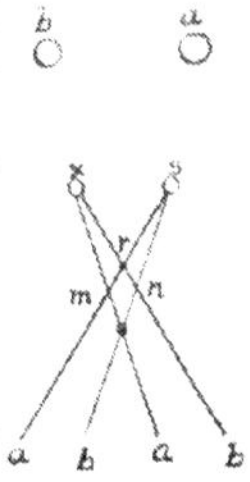

Definition.

The intersection *n* is produced by the shadows caused by the light *b*, because this light *b* produces the shadow *x b*, and the shadow *s b*, but the intersection *m* is produced by the light *a* which causes the shadow *s a*, and the shadow *x a*.

But if you uncover both the lights *a b*, then you get the two shadows *n m* both at once, and besides these, two other, simple shadows are produced at *r o* where neither of the two lights falls at all. The grades of depth in compound shadows are fewer in proportion as the lights falling on, and crossing them are less numerous.

Br. M. 248a]

186.

Perchè la intersegatione *n* essendo cōposta di due cō'poste ōbre diriuatiue gie-

Why the intersections at *n* being composed of two compound derived shadows,

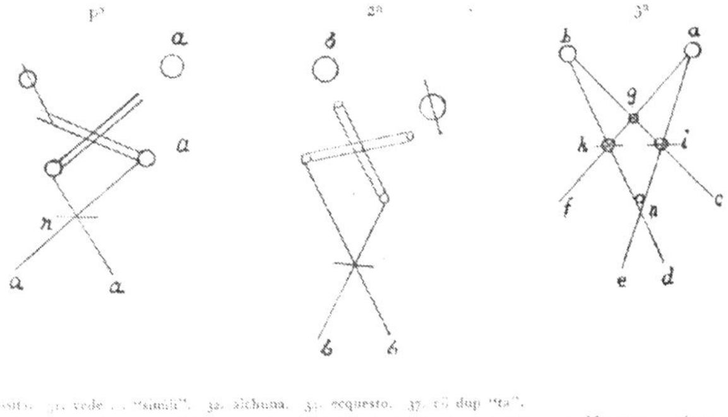

30. cōposita. 31. vede . . "simili". 32. alchuna. 33. equesto. 37. cō dup "ta".
185. 2. intersegthatione n effatta. 3. elōbra. 4. intersegthatione m effatta. 5. lo he lōbra. 6. Massetu . . gienera. 7. nū me-

nera onbra cōposta [3]e nō senplicie come fan l'altre intersegationi dell ōbre cōpos[4]te. [5]Questo accade per la 2ª di questo che dicie ¶ [6]La intersegatione dell'ōbre dirivative· nata · dalla [7]intersegatione delli ōbrosi collūnali alluminati da ū sol lu[8]minoso non gienera onbra sēplicie¶; e questo nascie [9]per la prima che dicie: la intersegatione delle senplici [10]onbre diriuatiue mai acquista oscurità | perchè [11]tutte le somme oscurità insieme giunte non ac[12]quistano maggiore oscurità che vna sola, perchè se le mol[13]te somme oscurità crescessino oscurità nelle lor dup[14]plicationi, esse non si potrebbino nominare oscurità sō[15]me ma parte di oscurità; Ma se tali interse[16]gationi sarā alluminate da un secondo lume po[17]sto infra l'ochio e li corpi intersegati, allora tali [18]ōbre sarā ōbre conposte e avrā vniforme oscurità [19]cosi nella intersegatione come nel rimanēte; [20]per la prima e seconda di sopra le intersegationi *i k* nō [21]si raddoppiano · di oscurità come elle si raddoppiano di quā[22]tità, ma in questa 3ª le intersegationi *g n* si rad[23]doppiā di oscurità e di quantità.

forms a compound shadow and not a simple one, as happens with other intersections of compound shadows. This occurs, according to the 2nd [diagram] of this [prop.] which says:—The intersection of derived shadows when produced by the intersection of columnar shadows caused by a single light does not produce a simple shadow. And this is the corollary of the 1st [prop.] which says:—The intersection of simple derived shadows never results in a deeper shadow, because the deepest shadows all added together cannot be darker than one by itself. Since, if many deepest shadows increased in depth by their duplication, they could not be called the *deepest* shadows, but only part-shadows. But if such intersections are illuminated by a second light placed between the eye and the intersecting bodies, then those shadows would become compound shadows and be uniformly dark just as much at the intersection as throughout the rest. In the 1st and 2nd above, the intersections *i k* will not be doubled in depth as it is doubled in quantity. But in this 3rd, at the intersections *g n* they will be double in depth and in quantity.

C. A. 187 II *a*; 562 *a*]

187.

COME E DOVE L'OBIETTO OSCURO [2]SI MISCHIA [3]COL LUME DIRIUATIVO DEL CORPO LUMINOSO.

[4]L'onbre diriuative delle parieti oscure [5]cōlaterali dello splendore della finestra son quel[6]le che colle lor varie oscurità si mischiano col [7]lume diriuativo d'essa finestra · e cō uarie oscu[8]rità tutto lo tingono ecciètto nel lume massi[9]mo · *c*: provasi e sia *d · a* l'onbra primiti[10]va la quale tutta vede e fa oscuro colla sua ōbra [11]diriuatiua il pūto *e*, come si dimostra per il △ [12]*a e d* del quale l'angolo *e* vede tutta la basa [13]oscura *d a e*, il pūto *v* è veduto dalla oscur[14]ità *a s*, parte del *a d* e per esser più il tutto che

HOW AND WHEN THE SURROUNDINGS IN SHADOW MINGLE THEIR DERIVED SHADOW WITH THE LIGHT DERIVED FROM THE LUMINOUS BODY.

The derived shadow of the dark walls on each side of the bright light of the window are what mingle their various degrees of shade with the light derived from the window; and these various depths of shade modify every portion of the light, except where it is strongest, at *c*. To prove this let *d a* be the primary shadow which is turned towards the point *e*, and darkens it by its derived shadow; as may be seen by the triangle △ *a e d*, in which the angle *e* faces the darkened base *d a e*; the point *v* faces the dark shadow *a s* which is part of *a d*, and as the whole is greater than a part, *e*

186. 1. interseghatione . . chōposta . . chō. 2. posste . . chōposta. 3. interseghatiō . . chōpo. 4. site. 5. achade. 6. interseghation. 7. interseghation chollūnali. 9. la p^a che . . interseghatione. 10. osschurita. 11. some osschurita. 12. magiore osschurita . . selle. 13. some osschurita cresściessino osschurita. 14. plichationi . . osscurita. 15. disschurita Massettale. 16. ghatione . . sechondo. 17. infrallochio elli chorpi interseghati . . tale. 18. arā . . osscurita. 19. chosi . . interseghation chome. 20. per la p^a e 2^a disopra . . interseghatio. 21. radoppiano disscurita chomelle se radoppiā. 22. quessta . . interseghationi . . ra. 24. disschurita eddi.

187. come [l] e dove lobbietto osscuro. 2. si missta colla suōbra diriuatiua. 3. chol . . lumi "noso". 4. lonbra diriuativa . . osscure [chesō la]. 5. finesstra. 6. cholle . . misstaro. 8. tinghano. 9. essia. 10. effa. 12. laughulo. 14. eser . . chelia. 15. osscu.

187. The diagram on Pl. IV, No. 5 belongs to this passage; but it must be noted that the text explains only the figure on the right-hand side.

[15]parte *e*, che vede il tutto della basa, sarà più oscu[16]ro che *v* che ne vede parte; mediāte la cōclusio[17]ne di sopra alla figura, *t* sarà meno os[18]curo che 'l *v*, perchè la basa del *t* △ è parte della [19]basa del △ *v*, e similmēte succede *p* meno o[20]scuro del *t*, perchè la basa del △ *p* è parte della ba[21]sa del △ *t*·e'l *c* è termine del'ōbra dirivatiua e pri[22]cipio massimo della massima parte alluminata.

which faces the whole base [of the triangle], will be in deeper shadow than *v* which only faces part of it. In consequence of the conclusion [shown] in the above diagram, *t* will be less darkened than *v*, because the base of the △ *t* is part of the base of the △ *v*; and in the same way it follows that *p* is less in shadow than *t*, because the base of the △ *p* is part of the base of the △ *t*. And *c* is the terminal point of the derived shadow and the chief beginning of the highest light.

17. fighura . . t [e piu] sara . 18. chiaro . 19. essimilmēte suciede meno os.

FOURTH BOOK ON LIGHT AND SHADE.

On the shape of cast shadows (188—191).

I.[2] 37 *b*]

188.

La stanpa dell'onbra di qualuque cor[2]po di uniforme grossezza mai sarà simile [3]al corpo donde ella nasce.

The form of the shadow cast by any body of uniform density can never be the same as that of the body producing it.

C. A. 184 *b*; 555 *b*]

189.

Nessuna ōbra separata potrà stampare sulla pariete la uera forma del corpo ōbroso, [2]se il ciētro del lume nō fia equidistāte dalli stremi d'esso corpo.

No cast shadow can produce the true image of the body which casts it on a vertical plane unless the centre of the light is equally distant from all the edges of that body.

A. 1 *a*]

190.

Se la finestra · *a* · *b* · māda · per se · in casa il sole ·, cresscierà codesto sole la grā[2]dezza della · finestra · e diminvirà l'onbra dell'omo · in modo · che quādo detto omo acco[3]sterà quella ōbra · di se persa · a quella che porta la uera grādezza della finestra, vedrà [4]in sul contatto dell'onbre · perse e cō-fuse dalla potētia della luce chiudere e nō la[5]sciare passare i razzi solari, e farà l'onbra fatta dall'omo sul detto cōtatto [6]lo effetto che qui di sopra · è figurato appūto.

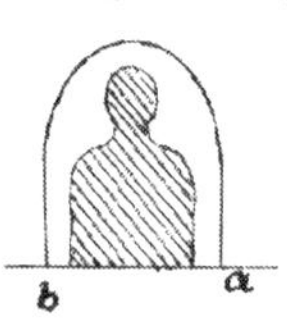

If a window *a b* admits the sunlight into a room, the sunlight will magnify the size of the window and diminish the shadow of a man in such a way as that when the man makes that dim shadow of himself, approach to that which defines the real size of the window, he will see the shadows where they come into contact, dim and confused from the strength of the light, shutting off and not allowing the solar rays to pass; the effect of the shadow of the man cast by this contact will be exactly that figured above.

188. 2. grosseza. 3. nassciesi.

189. 1 stāpire suli. 2. sel . alli.

190. 1. sella . . chasa . . desto sole. 2. deza . . imodo chequādo . . acho. 3. acquella . grādeza . . vedera. 4. chontatto . . ciudere e nō [po] la. 5. razi solari [chome acjeffara. 6. effigurato apūto.

188. Comp. the drawing on Pl. XXVIII, No. 5.

190. It is scarcely possible to render the meaning of this sentence with strict accuracy; mainly because the grammatical construction is defective in the most important part—line 4. In the very slight original sketch the shadow touches the upper arch of the window and the correction, here given is perhaps not justified.

191.

C. A. 232 b; 715 b]

L'onbra nō si dimostrerà mai d'uniforme oscurità nel [2]loco dove essa si taglia se tale loco non è equidistante dal [3]corpo luminoso; provasi per la 7ª che dice: quell'ōbra si [4]dimostrerà più chiara o più oscura che fia circunda[5]ta da cāpo più oscuro o più chiaro, per la ottava di [6]questo: quel campo avrà le sua parti tanto più [7]scure o più chiare quāto egli sarà piv remoto o più vicino [8]al corpo luminoso · e: infra li siti d'equal distan[9]tia dal luminoso quel si dimostrerà più allu- minato [10]che ricieve li razzi luminosi infra angoli più equali, [11]senpre: l'onbra seguata in qualunche inequalità di sito [12]si dimo- trerà colli sua vari termini equali al corpo [13]onbroso, se l'ochio si pone dove fū il cētro del luminoso.

[14]Quell' onbra si dimostra più oscura che è più remota [15]dal suo corpo ōbroso, [16]l'ōbra *c d*, nata dallo [17]a se equidistāte corpo ō[18]broso *a b*, nō si dimostra [19]equale in oscurità per esse[20]re in capo di uarie chia- re[21]zze.

A shadow is never seen as of uniform depth on the surface which intercepts it unless every portion of that surface is equidistant from the luminous body. This is proved by the 7th which says:—The shadow will appear lighter or stronger as it is surrounded by a darker or a lighter background. And by the 8th of this:—The background will be in parts darker or lighter, in proportion as it is farther from or nearer to the luminous body. And:—Of various spots equally distant from the luminous body those will always be in the highest light on which the rays fall at the smallest angles: The outline of the shadow as it falls on inequalities in the surface will be seen with all the contours similar to those of the body that casts it, if the eye is placed just where the centre of the light was.

The shadow will look darkest where it is farthest from the body that casts it. The shadow *c d*, cast by the body in shadow *a b*, which is equally distant in all parts, is not of equal depth because it is seen on a back ground of varying brightness.

192.

C. A. 121 a; 383 a]

I termini · di quella · ōbra · diriuativa · sa- rāno · più · distinti, della · quale · la sua per- cussione · fia piv propiqua [2]all'ombra ori- ginale.

The edges of a derived shadow will be most distinct where it is cast nearest to the primary shadow.

193.

C. A. 363 a; 1136 a]

Quāto più l'onbra diriuativa si remove dall'ōbra [2]primitiva, più si uaria da essa primitiva col[3]li sua termini.

As the derived shadow gets more distant from the primary shadow, the more the cast shadow differs from the primary shadow.

194.

C. A. 146 b; 431 a]

DE ŌBRE CHE MAI SŌ TERMINATE.

[2]Quāto il lume sarà maggiore [3]del corpo ōbroso, tanto li ter[4]mini dell'onbre di tal corpo [5]sarā più confusi.

OF SHADOWS WHICH NEVER COME TO AN END.

The greater the difference between a light and the body lighted by it, the light being the larger, the more vague will be the outlines of the shadow of that object.

191. 1. dimossterra mai [de] duniforme osscurita. 2. lecho . . settale lecho . . al. 3. chorpo. 4. dimossterra . . chiarata oppiu osschura chefia circhunda. 5. chāpo . . osschuro oppiu chiaro [ecqual] per la 8ª. 6. quessto . . chanpo[sia] . ara . . parte. 7. oppiu . . escura "piv remoto o" piu vicino [orremo]. 8. to al . . infralli . . disstan. 9. tia al . . dimossterra. 10. angholi. 12. dimossterra cholli. 13. seliochio si pō. 14. dimossatra . . osscura. 15. chorpo. 17. ass. equidisstāte chorpo. 19. iscurita. 20. chapo.

192. 1. disstinti.

193. 1. dellōbra. 2. chol.

194. 2. magore. 5. ara. 7. cofusi termini . . percu.

191. Compare the three diagrams on Pl. VI, no 1 which, in the original accompany this section.

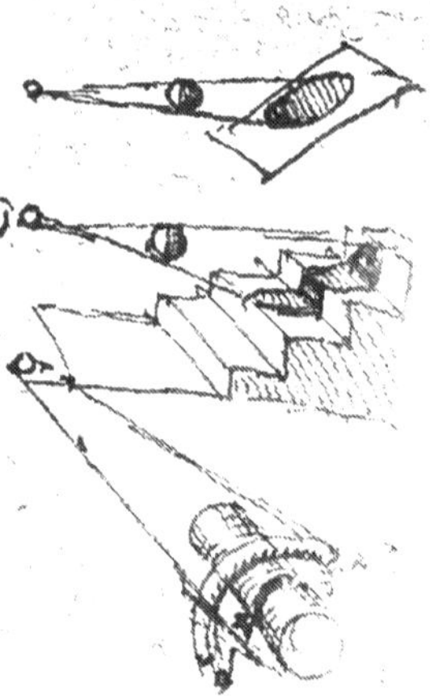

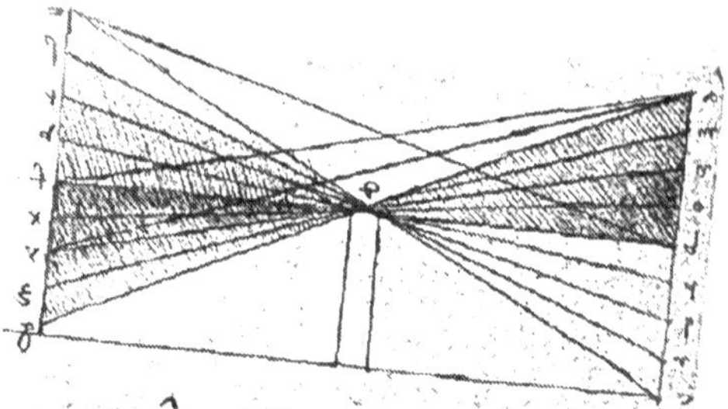

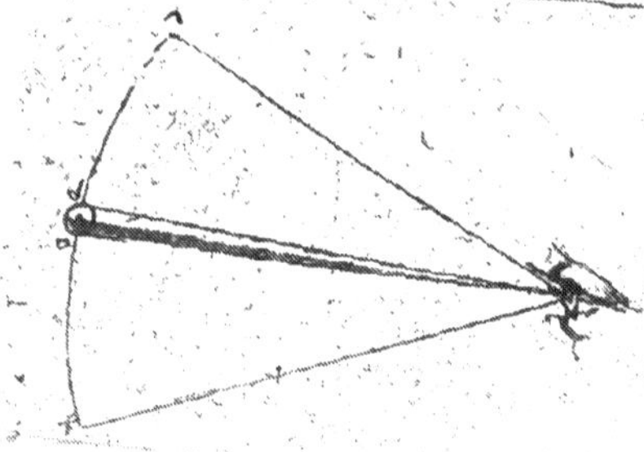

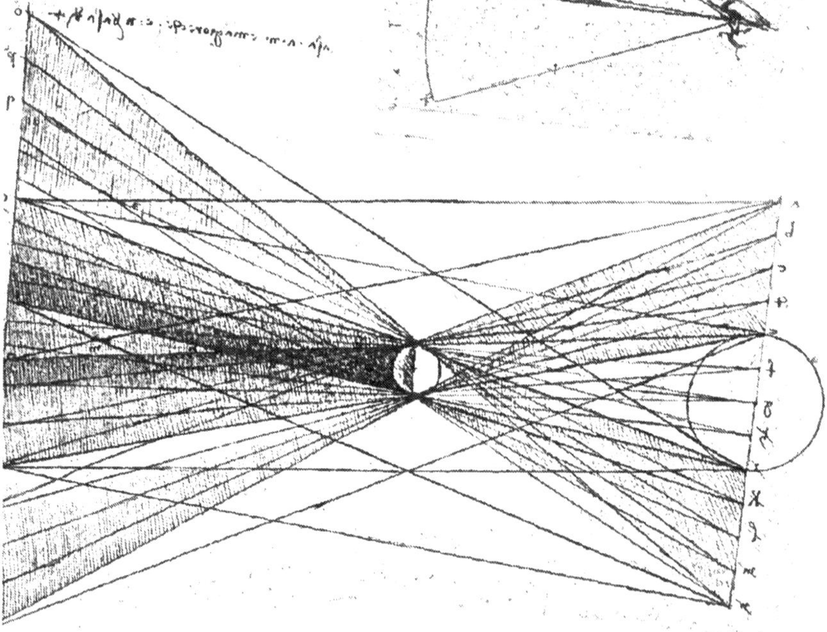

[6]Quell' ōbra dirivatiua avrà più [7]cōfusi li termini della sua percus[8]sione nella pariete, la quale [9]è più remota dal suo corpo ōbroso.

The derived shadow will be most confused towards the edges of its interception by a plane, where it is remotest from the body casting it.

W. 232*b*]

195.

Che causa è quella che fa li [2]termini dell' ōbra cōfusi e in[3]gnoti?

[4]Se' l' è possibile di dare termi[5]ni spediti e noti alli cōfini [6]delle ōbre.

What is the cause which makes the outlines of the shadow vague and confused?

Whether it is possible to give clear and definite outlines to the edges of shadows.

Ash. I. 5*b*]

196.

QUEL CORPO CHE È PIV PROPĪQUO [2]AL LUME FA MAGGIORE ŌBRA, E PERCHÈ?

[3]Se uno obietto · antiposto a uno particulare · lume fia di propīqua vi[4]cinità ·, vedrai a quello fare obra gradissima nella cōtra[5]posta · pariete: e quāto · piv allōtanerai detto obbietto dal lu[6]me, tāto si diminvirà la forma d' essa ōbra.

PERCHÈ · L' ONBRA MAGGIORE CHE LA SUA [8]CAGIONE SI FA DI DISCORDĀTE PROPORTIONE.

[9]La discordantia della proportione dell' ōbra grāde piv che la sua [10]cagione nascie, perchè il lume ·, sendo · minore · che l' obietto, nō può esse[11]re di equale distātia alle stremità · d' esso obbietto, e quella parte ch' è piv [12]distāte piv cresce che le propīque, e però piv cresce ...

PERCHÈ L' ONBRA MAGGIORE CHE LA SUA CAGIONE [14]À TERMINI CŌFUSI.

[15]Quell' aria che circūscrive il lume è quasi di natura d' esso lume per chia[16]rezza

THE BODY WHICH IS NEAREST TO THE LIGHT CASTS THE LARGEST SHADOW, AND WHY?

If an object placed in front of a single light is very close to it you will see that it casts a very large shadow on opposite wall, and the farther you remove the object from the light the smaller will the image of the shadow become. On the relative size of cast shadows (196. 197).

WHY A SHADOW LARGER THAN THE BODY THAT PRODUCES IT BECOMES OUT OF PROPORTION.

The disproportion of a shadow which is larger than the body producing it, results from the light being smaller than the body, so that it cannot be at an equal distance from the edges of the body[11]; and the portions which are most remote are made larger than the nearer portions for this reason[12].

WHY A SHADOW WHICH IS LARGER THAN THE BODY CAUSING IT HAS ILL-DEFINED OUTLINES.

The atmosphere which surrounds a light is almost like light itself for brightness and

195. 1. chausa ecquella cheffa. 2. chōfusi. 4. selle. 5. ennot.
196. 1. che piv. 2. alume . . magiore. 3. se ī . . a ī partichulare. 4. acquelo . . chotra. 5. ecquāto. 7. magiore chella. 8. chagione . . dischordāte. 9. dischordantia. 10. chagione . . ilume . . po. 11. ecquella. 13. magiore. 15. circhūscriue

196. 11. 12. H. LUDWIG in his edition of the old copies, in the Vatican library—in which this chapter is included under Nos. 612, 613 and 614 alters this passage as follows: *quella parte ch'è piu propinqua piu cresce che le distanti*, although the Vatican copy agrees with the original MS. in having *distante* in the former and *propinque* in the latter place. This supposed amendment seems to me to invert the facts. Supposing for instance, that on Pl. XXXI No. 3. *f* is the spot where the light is that illuminates the figure there represented, and that the line behind the figure represents a wall on which the shadow of the figure is thrown. It is evident, that in that case the nearest portion, in this case the under part of the thigh, is very little magnified in the shadow, and the remoter parts, for instance the head, are more magnified.

e per colore, e quato piv si allotana, piv perde sua similitudine, e la [17]cosa che fa grande obra è vicina al lume e truovasi alluminata • dal lume [18]e dal'aria luminosa, ōde quest'aria lascia i termini • confusi del'ōbra.

colour; but the farther off it is the more it loses this resemblance. An object which casts a large shadow and is near to the light, is illuminated both by that light by the luminous atmosphere; hence this diffused light gives the shadow ill-defined edges.

E. 31 r]

197

Quel luminoso di lunga [2]e stretta figura fa [3]li termini dell'obra diri[4]vativa piv confusi [5]che il lume sperico, e [6]questo è quel che co[7]tradicie alla propo[8]sitione sequete: Quel[9]l'obra avrà li termini [10]più noti che fia più [11]vicina all'onbra pri[12]mitiva, o voi dire il [13]corpo obroso, ma [14]di questo è cavsa la [15]figura luga del [16]luminoso *a c* ecc.

A luminous body which is long and narrow in shape gives more confused outlines to the derived shadow than a spherical light, and this contradicts the proposition next following: A shadow will have its outlines more clearly defined in proportion as it is nearer to the primary shadow or, I should say, the body casting the shadow; [14]the cause of this is the elongated form of the luminous body *a c*, &c.[16].

E. 32 r]

198.

De ōbre corrotte.

Effects on cast shadows by the tone of the back ground.

[1]Ōbre corrotte sō dette [2]quelle che sō vedute [3]da parieti chiare o al[4]tro luminoso.

¶[6]Quell'ōbra si dimostra [7]più oscura che è in [8]canpo più biaco. ¶[9]Li termini di quell'o[10]bra diriuatiua sara più noti [11]che fien più vici[12]ni all'ōbra primitiva.¶ [13]L'ōbra dirivativa [14]avrà li termini del[15]la sua impressione pi[16]v noti, li quali si ta[17]gliano infra ango[18]li più equali nella [19]sua pariete.

[20]Quella parte d'u-
[21]na medesima ōbra
[22]si dimostrerà piv
[23]oscura che avrà co-
[24]tra se più oscuri
[25]obietti; E si dimo-
[26]strerà me-
[27]no oscura che fia
[28]veduta da obbiet-
[29]to più chiaro; E
[30]quello obietto chia-
[31]ro che fia maggiore, pi-
[32]v rischiarerà;

[34]e quello
[35]obietto
[36]oscuro
[37]che fia
[38]di mag-
[39]giore qu-
[40]atità, più
[41]oscure-
[42]rà l'ōbra
[43]diriuati-
[44]va nel
[45]sito della
[46]sua percus-
[47]sione.

Of modified shadows.

Modified shadows are those which are cast on light walls or other illuminated objects.

A shadow looks darkest against a light background. The outlines of a derived shadow will be clearer as they are nearer to the primary shadow. A derived shadow will be most defined in shape where it is intercepted, where the plane intercepts it at the most equal angle.

Those parts of a shadow
will appear
darkest which have
darker objects opposite
to them. And they
will appear less
dark when they face
lighter objects.
And the larger
the light object
opposite, the more
the shadow will
be lightened.

And the
larger
the
surface
of the
dark
object
the more
it will darken
the derived
shadow
where it is
inter-
cepted.

[illegible] perdia. 16. reza [illegible] chedare cequāte [illegible] alla. 17. alume [illegible] aluminata da. 18. chonfusi.

197. 1. longha. 2. estretta fighura. [illegible] chonfusi. 5. sperichо. 6. questo equel [illegible] cho. 7. traddicie. [illegible] 13. chorpo. 15. questo [illegible] 15. fighura lugha.

198. 1. cherrotte. 2. ōbra chorrotte. 3. chessō. 4. pariete. 6. dimosstra. 7. osscura. 8. chanpo [illegible] biancho. 10. bra [illegible] sara. 14. ara. 15. [illegible]pressione. 17. angho. [illegible] pari[illegible]ete. 22. dimosstera. 23. osschura che ara. 24. tra se [illegible] osscuri. 25. E si. 26. sterra [piu] me. 27. osschura. 30. equello. 31. chefia magiore. 32. risciarera. 33. [echi]. 35. osschuro. 37. chefia. 38. ma. 39. givre [illegible] 41. osscure. 45. percha.

197. [illegible]

Ash. I. 13*b*]

199.

OPENIONE D'ALCUNI CHE UN TRIÃGOLO NÕ FACCI IN VNA PARIETE ALCUN' ÕBRA.

[3]Sono stati alcuni · matematici · che ànno · tenvto per fermo che uno triãgolo, che abbia [4]la basa volta · verso el lume, nõ facci in vna pariete · alcuna õbra ·, la qual [5]cosa prouano diciẽdo: così, nessuno corpo sperico minore [6]che lume può givgnere alla metà · col'õbra: le linie · radiose sono rette, [7]adunque poniamo · il lume sia *g* · *h* · e 'l triãgolo sia *l* · *m n*; e la pariete sia · *i* · *k*: dica[8]no il lume · *g* · vedere · la faccia del triãgolo · *l* · *n* · e la parte della pariete · *i* · *q* ·, [9]e così · *h* · vede · come · *g* · la faccia · *l* · *m* · e poi vede · *m* · *n* · e la pariete · *p* · *k* ·, e se [10]essa tutta la pariete è vista dal lume · *g* · *h* · cõuiene essere il triãgolo sãza õbra, e che [11]non à õbra · nõ la può dare: la qual cosa pare ĩ questo caso credibile se'l triãgolo [12]*n* · *p* · *g* · nõ fusse visto da 2 lumi · *g* · *h* ·, ma · *i* · *p* · e così *g* · *k* · nõn è ciasuno per se [13]visto se nõ da uno solo · lume ·, cioè *i* · *p* · nõ può esser visto da · *h* · *g*; *k* · nõ sarà mai [14]visto da · *g* · adũque · *p* · *q* · fia piv chiaro il doppio che dua visiui spati che tẽgã d'õbra.

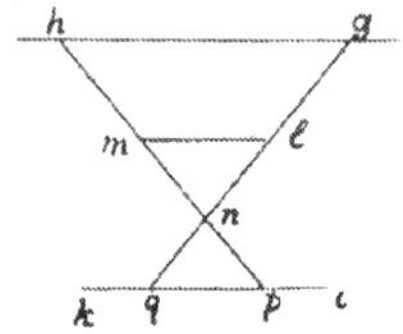

OF THE OPINION OF SOME THAT A TRIANGLE CASTS NO SHADOW ON A PLANE SURFACE.

A disputed proposition.

Certain mathematicians have maintained that a triangle, of which the base is turned to the light, casts no shadow on a plane; and this they prove by saying [5] that no spherical body smaller than the light can reach the middle with the shadow. The lines of radiant light are straight lines [6]; therefore, suppose the light to be *g h* and the triangle *l m n*, and let the plane be *i k*; they say the light *g* falls on the side of the triangle *l n*, and the portion of the plane *i q*. Thus again *h* like *g* falls on the side *l m*, and then on *m n* and the plane *p k*; and if the whole plane thus faces the lights *g h*, it is evident that the triangle has no shadow; and that which has no shadow can cast none. This, in this case appears credible. But if the triangle *n p g* were not illuminated by the two lights *g* and *h*, but by *i p* and *g* and *k* neither side is lighted by more than one single light; that is *i p* is invisible to *h g* and *k* will never be lighted by *g*; hence *p q* will be twice as light as the two visible portions that are in shadow.

C. A. 30*b*; 96*a*]

200.

¶[3]Quel loco è piv õbroso che da mag[4]gior soma di razzi õbrosi veduto fia ¶[5]quel loco · che sarà [6]percosso da piv g[7]rosso angolo fat[8]to da razzi õbrosi, [9]fia piv scuro; [10]*a* · fia di doppia osc[11]urità · che · *b* · perch[12]è da doppia base [13]nascie in pari dist[14]ãtia ¶ [15]quel · loco sarà piv luminoso · che da mag[16]gior somma di razzi luminosi ripercosso fia¶ [17]*d* · è il principio dell'onbra · *d* · *f* ·, e tignie poco [18]in · *c* · *d* · *e* · è mezza · l'onbra · *d* · *f*; e piv tignie [19]nella percussione · *b* · di · *f* e tutto lo intervallo [20]õbroso *e* interamẽte tignie di se il loco *a*.

A spot is most in the shade when a large number of darkened rays fall upon it. The spot which receives the rays at the widest angle and by darkened rays will be most in the dark; *a* will be twice as dark as *b*, because it originates from twice as large a base at an equal distance. A spot is most illuminated when a large number of luminous rays fall upon it. *d* is the beginning of the shadow *d f*, and tinges *c* but a little; *d e* is half of the shadow *d f* and gives a deeper tone where it is cast at *b* than at *f*. And the whole shaded space *e* gives its tone to the spot *a*.

On the relative depth of cast shadows (200—202).

199. 1. dalchuni cun . . faci. 3. Estati alchuni . . che ĩ triãgolo cheabi. 4. facinvna. 5. cosa [riprouo i questa forma] prouano. 6. po [avere] givgnere. 7. ilume. 8. facia . . dela. 9. facia . . esse. 10. esse . . dalume . . õbreche. 11. nona õbr . . po. 12. fussi. 13. da ĩ solo . po. 14. vsto da . . charo . . dopio . . spatio.

120 1. ettinta [del cholore] delli chontra se posti chorpi õbrosi e luminosi. 2. della chiareza osscurita. 3. Qualocho . ma. 4. razi. 5. qel locho . . chessara. 6. perchosso. 7. fa. 8. razi. 9. schuro. 10. dopia ossc. 12. dopia ossc. 13. nasscie. 15. locho . . ma. 16. razi . . riperchosso. 17. pocho. 18. d . e . he . *mezza*. 19. perchossione . . ettutto. 20. illocho.

199. 5—6. This passage is so obscure that it would be rash to offer an explanation. Several words seem to have been omitted.

200. The diagram here referred to is on Pl. XLI, No. 2.

Tr. 201

201.

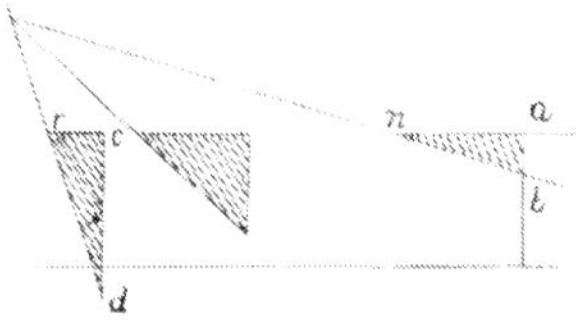

[1] Tāto · quāto · *a* · *b* · ētra in · *c* · *d* [2] tanto · *a* *n* · fia piv scuro che [3] *c* · *r*.

A n will be darker than *c r* in proportion to the number of times that *a b* goes into *c d*.

Ash. I. 28 *b*

202.

[1] Quanto · l'onbra fatta dall'obbietto · sopra la pariete [2] sarà minore · che la sua cagione, tanto esso obbietto [3] fia · alluminato · da piv deboli razzi · luminosi. [4] *d* · *e* · è l'obietto · *d* · *e* si è la pariete tanto · quāto · *d* · *e* · entra [5] in · *f* · *g* · tante volte · fia · piv lume in · *f* · *h* · che in · *d* · *e*. [6] Quanto il razzo · luminoso · fia · piv debole, tāto [7] fia piv lontano · dal suo · spiracolo.

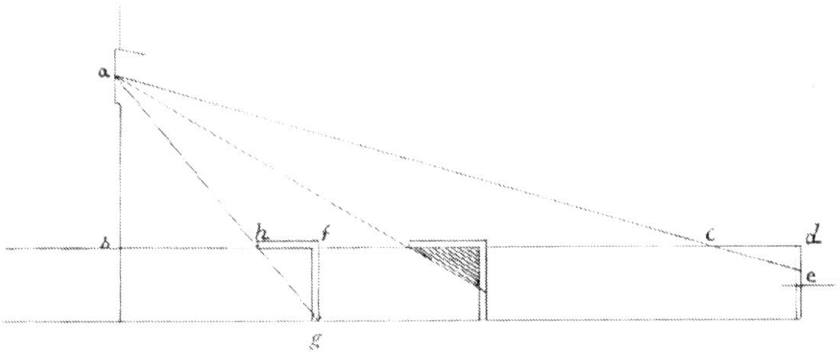

The shadow cast by an object on a plane will be smaller in proportion as that object is lighted by feebler rays. Let *d e* be the object and *d c* the plane surface; the number of times that *d e* will go into *f g* gives the proportion of light at *f h* to *d e*. The ray of light will be weaker in proportion to its distance from the hole through which it falls.

202. 1. [tanto] Quanto. 2. chella sua chagione. 3. razi. 4. qui . d . e. 5. pivlume. 6. razo. 7. spirachol(o).

FIFTH BOOK ON LIGHT AND SHADE.

Ash. I. 3*a*]

203.

MODO · DOVE · DEBBONO TERMI[2]NARE · L'ONBRE · FATTE DALI OBBIETTI.

[3] Se l'obietto · fia · questa mõtagna · qui · figurata · e'l lume fusse il pũto · *a* ·, [4] dico che · da · *b* · *d* · e similmẽte da · *c* · *f* · nõ fia lume · se nõ per ra[5]zzi · reflessi ·, e questo · nasce · che i razzi · luminosi · nõ s'adoprano se · non per [6] linia · recta: e quel · medesimo fanno i secondi · razzi · che sono · reflessi.

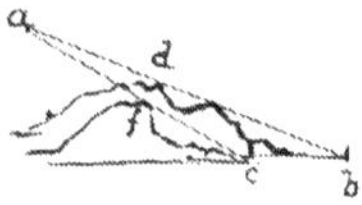

OF THE WAY IN WHICH THE SHADOWS CAST BY OBJECTS OUGHT TO BE DEFINED.

If the object is the mountain here figured, and the light is at the point *a*, I say that from *b d* and also from *c f* there will be no light but from reflected rays. And this results from the fact that rays of light can only act in straight lines; and the same is the case with the secondary or reflected rays. Principles of reflection (203. 204).

W. 232 *b*]

204.

Li termini dell'onbra dirivativa son [2] circundati dai colori delli obbietti allumi[3]nati circũstãti [4] al corpo luminoso, causatore di essa [5] õbra.

The edges of the derived shadow are defined by the hues of the illuminated objects surrounding the luminous body which produces the shadow.

Ash. I. 21 *a*]

205.

DE RIVERBERATIONE.

[2] Le riverberationi · sono cavsate · da corpi di chiara qualità · di piana e semidẽsa . superfitie, le [3] quali, percosse dal lume a similitudine · del balzo · della palla, lo ripercuotono · nel primo · obbietto.

OF REVERBERATION.

Reverberation is caused by bodies of a bright nature with a flat and semi opaque surface which, when the light strikes upon them, throw it back again, like the rebound of a ball, to the former object. On reverberation.

203. 3. fussi. 4. essimilmẽte. 5. nasscie. 6. fano . . razi chessono.
204. 2. circhundad de. 3. nati li [quali circũdano] circhũsstãti. 4. chausatore dessa.
205. 2. chavsate . . chorpi. 3. perchossa dal lume quelo assimilitudine dei bazo . . riperchuotano. 5. chorpi dẽsi . si vestano

Dove nô può · essere riverberatione luminosa.

[5]Tutti i corpi dêsi · rivestono · le loro superfitie di uarie qualità di lume · e ôbre; [6]i lumi · sono · di due nature ·, l'uno · si domada originale · l'altro · derivatiuo; [7]originale · dico · essere quello · che diriva da vapa · di foco o dal lume · del sole [8]o d'aria: lume · dirivatiuo · fia il lume · reflesso; ma per tornare alla [9]promessa · difinizione · dico · che riverberatione luminosa · nô fia da quella [10]parte del corpo · che fia · volta a corpi ôbrosi, come lochi scuri ·, prati [11]di varie altezze d'erbe ·, boschi · verdi · o secchi · i quali ·, benchè la parte di ciascu[12]no ramo volta al lume originale · si veste della qualità · d'esso lume ·, niête [13]di meno · e' sono · tâte l'onbre fatte da ciascuno · ramo · per se · e tâte l'onbre fatte dal[14]l'uno · ramo sull'altro che in soña ne risulta · tale · oscurità che il lume v'è [15]per niête ·, onde nô possono · simili obbietti · dare · a corpi oppositi · alcuno lume [16]riflesso.

Where there can be no reflected lights.

All dense bodies have their surfaces occupied by various degrees of light and shade. The lights are of two kinds, one called original, the other borrowed. Original light is that which is inherent in the flame of fire or the light of the sun or of the atmosphere. Borrowed light will be reflected light; but to return to the promised definition: I say that this luminous reverberation is not produced by those portions of a body which are turned towards darkened objects, such as shaded spots, fields with grass of various height, woods whether green or bare; in which, though that side of each branch which is turned towards the original light has a share of that light, nevertheless the shadows cast by each branch separately are so numerous, as well as those cast by one branch on the others, that finally so much shadow is the result that the light counts for nothing. Hence objects of this kind cannot throw any reflected light on opposite objects.

206.

H.[3] 28 *b*]

Reflection on water (206. 207).

Prospectiva.

[2]L'onbre over · le cose [3]spechiate nell'acqu[4]a movête, cioè co[5]n'onde piccole, sê[6]pre sarâ · maggiori [7]che la cosa di fo[8]ri, donde nasce.

Perspective.

The shadow or object mirrored in water in motion, that is to say in small avelets, will always be larger than the external object producing it.

207.

Br. M. 93 *b*]

Inpossibile è · che la cosa · spechiata sopra [2]dell'acqua · sia simile in figura al-

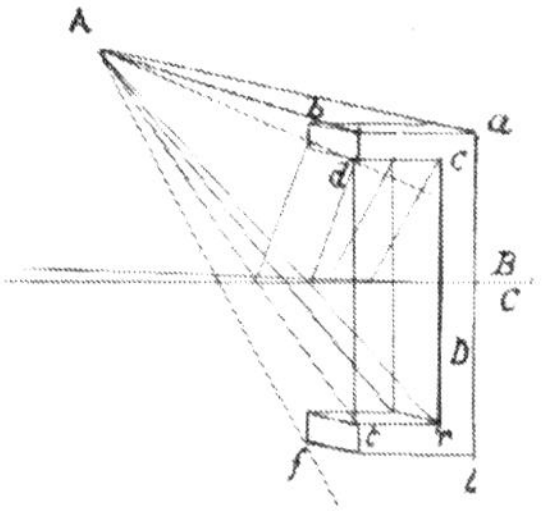

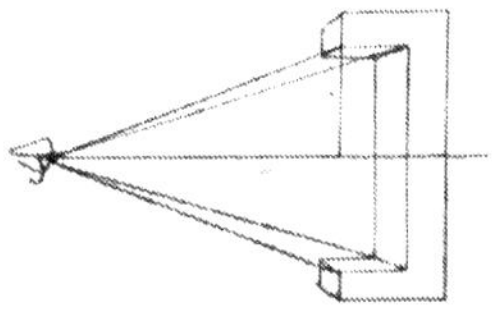

l'obbietto che [3]si spechia, essendo il centro dell'ochio sopra [4]la superfitie dell'acqua.

It is impossible that an object mirrored on water should correspond in form to the object mirrored, since the centre of the eye is above the surface of the water.

le loro. 7. dicho . . fecho o dalume. 8. ilume . refresso. 9. dicho . . dacquella. 10. cherpo cheffia . . achorpi . . chome. 11. altere . . boschi . verdi essecchi . . ciascun. 12. vessta. 13. ciasscuno . . ettante. 14. isscurita che lume. 15. [illegible] simili . . chorpi . . alchuno. 16. refresso.

206. 2. chose. 3. achu. 4. picholo. 6. magiore. 7. chella chosa. 8. nasscie.

207. *A* stands for *ochio* [eye], *B* for *aria* [air], *C* for *acqua* [water], *D* for *cateto* [cathetus].—In the original MS. the second diagram is placed below line 13.

[5]Quel che di sopra si manifesta nella figura [6]fatta qui da parte, nella quale si uede l'oc[7]chio uedere la superfitie · *a · b*, e non la può [8]poi vedere in · *l f* · e in *r t*, vede [9]la superfitie del simulacro in *r t* e non la [10]vede nella cosa · reale *c d*: adunque [11]è inpossibile vedere quel ch'è detto di sopra, [12]se l'ochio non è situato nella superfitie dell'a[13]cqua, come si mostra qui di sotto.

This is made plain in the figure here given, which demonstrates that the eye sees the surface *a b*, and cannot see it at *l f*, and at *r t*; it sees the surface of the image at *r t*, and does not see it in the real object *c d*. Hence it is impossible to see it, as has been said above unless the eye itself is situated on the surface of the water as is shown below[13].

S. K. M. III. 37*b*]

208.

Spechio.

[2]Se la alluminata fia della [3]grādezza della cosa allumi[4]nāte e di quella dou'esso lu[5]me si reflette · tal propor[6]tione avrà la qualità del lume [7]reflesso · col lume mezzano, [8]quale · avrà esso · lume secōdo [9]col primo, essēdo essi corpi [10]piani e biāchi.

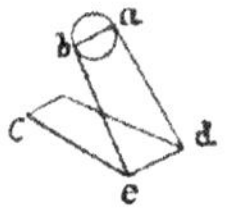

The mirror.

Experiments with the mirror (208—210).

If the illuminated object is of the same size as the luminous body and as that in which the light is reflected, the amount of the reflected light will bear the same proportion to the intermediate light as this second light will bear to the first, if both bodies are smooth and white.

W. 232*b*]

209.

Descrivi come nessū corpo in se è terminato nello [2]spechio ma lo termina l'ochio, che dētro a tale spechio [3]lo vede, inperochè, se tu rappresenti il tuo viso nel[4]lo spechio, la parte è simile al tutto, [5]conciossiachè la parte è tutta per tutto lo spechio, ed è [5]tutta in ogni parte del medesimo spechio, e il simile ac[7]cade di tutto il simulacro di tutto l'obietto cōtra po[8]sto a quello spechio ecc.

Describe how it is that no object has its limitation in the mirror but in the eye which sees it in the mirror. For if you look at your face in the mirror, the part resembles the whole in as much as the part is everywhere in the mirror, and the whole is in every part of the same mirror; and the same is true of the whole image of any object placed opposite to this mirror, &c.

C. A. 137*b*; 419*b*]

210.

Nessuno omo vedrà la similitudine [2]dell'altr'omo sopra lo specchio nel propio [3]loco · dove si riferiscie, perchè ciascuno [4]obietto cade sopra [5]lo spechio ifra equali [6]angoli, e se l'omo, che vede l'altro nello specchio, [7]non è posto colla linia delle spetie, nō lo vedrà [8]nel loco dove cade, e s'egli entra nelle linie, [9]egli occupa l'altr'omo e mette · se medesimo [10]sopra la sua similitudine: [11]*n o* sia lo spechio · *b* · sia

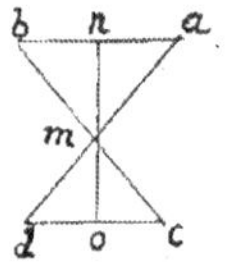

No man can see the image of another man in a mirror in its proper place with regard to the objects; because every object falls on [the surface of] the mirror as equal angles. And if the one man, who sees the other in the mirror, is not in a direct line with the image he will not see it in the place where it really falls; and if he gets into the line, he covers the other man and puts himself in the place occupied

207. 1. chella chosa. 2. infigra. 3. sisspechia. 4. dellacq "a". 5. manifessta. 6. dapparte. 7. po. 9. nolla. 12. sellochio. 13. qua . . mossstra.

208. 2. sella. 3. grādeza. 4. edidi quella douessolu. 5. rifretta. 6. ara. 7. refresso . . mezano. 8. ara. 10. ebbianchi.

209. 1. desscriui . . etterminato. 2. mallo . . attale. 3. inperochessettu rapresenti. 4. spechio [il tutto ettutta] la . . essimile al tuchō. 5. chonciossia chella . . ettutta . . losspechio. 7. chade di tutto il il simulacro . . cōtrappos. 8. sta acquale.

210. 1. vedera. 3. locho. 4. chade. 6. nelo. 7. cola . . vedera. 8. nelocho . . esseli. 9. elli ochupa. 16. tocha. 17. tochera

l'ochio dell'amico tuo · [12] *d* · sia il tuo ochio; [13] l'ochio del tuo amico ti pare in · *a* : e all'amico par [14] che'l tuo sia in *c* [15] e la ïter-[16]segatione delle linee visuali · si fa in · *m* · e qualüque tocca [17] in *m* · toccherà l'ochio del-l'altro omo che fia aperto; [18] Se toccherai l'ochio [19] dell'altr'omo sopra [20] lo spechio parrà al' [21] altro che tocchi il tuo.

by his image. Let *n o* be the mirror, *b* the eye of your friend and *d* your own eye. Your friend's eye will appear to you at *a*, and to him it will seem that yours is at *c*, and the intersection of the visual rays will occur at *m*, so that either of you touching *m* will touch the eye of the other man which shall be open. And if you touch the eye of the other man in the mirror it will seem to him that you are touching your own.

E. 2 *b*]

211.

Dell'onbra o suo moto.

Appendix — On shadows in movement (211. 212).

[2] Se li 2 öbrosi che l'ü dopo l'altro son in[3]fra la finestra e la pariete con alquä[4]to spatio s'interponghino, [5] l'onbra dell'onbroso, che sarà vicina alla [6] pariete del muro, sarà mobile, se l'ö[7]broso propinquo alla finestra fia in [8] moto traversale a essa finestra; prova[9]si e siä li due öbrosi *a b* interpo[10]sti infra la finestra *n m* e la pari[11]ete *o p*, con alquanto spatio interpo[12]sto infra loro il quale è lo spatio *a b*; [13] dico che se l'öbroso *a* si moverà in[14]verso *s* che l'öbra dello öbroso *b*, la qua[15]le è *c*, si moverà in · *d*.

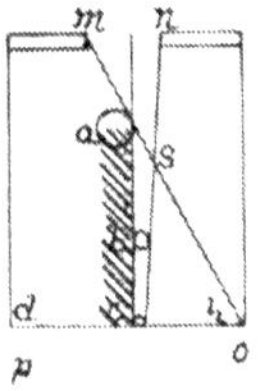

Of the shadow and its motion.

When two bodies casting shadows, and one in front of the other, are between a window and the wall with some space between them, the shadow of the body which is nearest to the plane of the wall will move if the body nearest to the window is put in transverse motion across the window. To prove this let *a* and *b* be two bodies placed between the window *n m* and the plane surface *o p* with sufficient space between them as shown by the space *a b*. I say that if the body *a* is moved towards *s* the shadow of the body *b* which is at *c* will move towards *d*.

E. 30 *b*]

212.

Del moto della öbra.

[2] Senpre il moto della öbra è più [3] velocie che il moto del corpo, che [4] la genera, essëdo il luminoso ïmobile; provasi e sia il lumi[5]noso *a* e l'öbroso *b* e l'öbra *d*; [6] Dico che in pari tëpo si moue l'onbro[7]so *b* in *c*, che il *d* onbra si move i [8] *e*, e quella proportione è da ve[9]locità a velocità fatta in medesi[10]mo tëpo, quale è da lunghezza [11] di moto a lunghezza di moto; a[12]düque pella proportione che à la [13] lüghezza del moto fatto dall'öbro[14]so *b* ïnsino in *c* colla lüghezza [15] del moto fatto dall'öbra *d* in *e*,

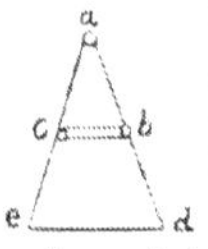

Of the motion of shadows.

The motion of a shadow is always more rapid than that of the body which produces it if the light is stationary. To prove this let *a* be the luminous body, and *b* the body casting the shadow, and *d* the shadow. Then I say that in the time while the solid body moves from *b* to *c*, the shadow *d* will move to *e*; and this proportion in the rapidity of the movements made in the same space of time, is equal to that in the length of the space moved over. Thus, given the proportion of the space moved over by the

. . chelfia. *Lines 18—21, are placed in the margin opposite lines 3—5.* 20. spechi. 21. tochi.

211. 1. ossuo. 2. delli. 3. fralla finesstra ella. 4. sinterponghino [disellonbra]. 5. chessara. 6. mobile sello. 8. finesstra 9. essia. 10. infralla finesstra n m ella. 11. interpos. 12. infrallor. il quale he. 13. dicho chessellöbroso. 14. chellobra. 15. le he c.

212. 2. eppiu. 3. chorpo chel. 4. gienera "essëdo il luminoso ï mobile" provasi essia. 5. ellöbroso *b* ellobra. 6. Dicho. 8. ecquella . . he da. 10. dallunghezza. 11. allunghezza. 14. cholla lughezza. 16. tredecete. 18. Masse. 19. all moto.

[16]tale ànno infra loro le predette ve[17]locità de' moti.

[18]Ma se il luminoso sarà equale in ve[19]locità al moto dello ōbroso, allora l'onbra [20]e l'onbroso fieno infra loro di moti · equali; [21]E se il luminoso sarà più velocie dello ō[22]broso ·, allora il moto del-l'ōbra sarà più tar[23]do che'l moto dello ōbroso.

[24]Ma se il luminoso fia più tardo che l'onbroso, [25]allora l'ōbra sarà più velocie che l'ōbroso.

body *b* to *c*, to that moved over by the shadow *d* to *e*, the proportion in the rapidity of their movements will be the same.

But if the luminous body is also in movement with a velocity equal to that of the solid body, then the shadow and the body that casts it will move with equal speed. And if the luminous body moves more rapidly than the solid body, the motion of the shadow will be slower than that of the body casting it.

But if the luminous body moves more slowly than the solid body, then the shadow will move more rapidly than that body.

20. ellonbroso fiē infralloro . . equali. 21. Essellumınoso. 23. da chel. 24. Masse . . chelionbroso. 25. alora . chellōbroso.

SIXTH BOOK ON LIGHT AND SHADE.

C. 7a (26)]

213.

The effect of rays passing through holes (213. 214).

PROSPETTIVA.

[1]Se farai passare i razzi del sole per lo spiracolo in forma di stella · vedrai belli effetti di prospettiua [3]in nella percussione fatta dal passato sole.

PERSPECTIVE.

If you transmit the rays of the sun through a hole in the shape of a star you will see a beautiful effect of perspective in the spot where the sun's rays fall.

A. 94b]

214.

[1]Nessuno · spiraculo · può trasmutare · il concorso · de razzi · luminosi i modo che per lunga [3]distantia · non porgino · all'obietto la similitudine della · lor cagione; [4]inpossibile · e · che i razzi · luminosi · passati · per paralello · non dimostrino nell'obbietto · la forma [5]della · loro · cagione; [6]perchè tutti li effetti · de' corpi · luminosi · son dimostratori · delle · loro · cagioni; la luna di forma [7]naviculare · passata dallo spiracolo figurerà nell'obietto uno corpo naviculare.

[8]Perchè l'ochio vede le cose distati maggiori [9]che no le misura · sulla · pariete?

No small hole can so modify the convergence of rays of light as to prevent, at a long distance, the transmission of the true form of the luminous body causing them. It is impossible that rays of light passing through a parallel [slit], should not display the form of the body causing them, since all the effects produced by a luminous body are [in fact] the reflection of that body: The moon, shaped like a boat, if transmitted through a hole is figured in the surface [it falls on] as a boat-shaped object. [8]Why the eye sees bodies at a distance, larger than they measure on the vertical plane?

213. 2. seffarai . . razi . . spirachulo . . vederai . . prosspetiua [in esso sole]. 3. inella perchussione.

214. 1. [ogni spirachulo per lunga distantia . porgie allobietto la forma]. 2. spirachulo potrassmutare . il chonchorso . . modo. 3. disstantia . . porghino allobietto [la forma] la . . chagione. 4. razi. 5. non *is wanting in the original*. chagione. 6. chorpi . . chagioni. 7. navichulare . . spirachulo [alo] figurera . . î corpo. 8. chose.

213. In this and the following chapters of MS. C the order of the original paging has been adhered to, and is shown in parenthesis. Leonardo himself has but rarely worked out the subject of these propositions. The space left for the purpose has occasionally been made use of for quite different matter. Even the numerous diagrams, most of them very delicately sketched, lettered and numbered, which occur on these pages, are hardly ever explained, with the exception of those few which are here given.

214. This chapter, taken from another MS. may, as an exception, be placed here, as it refers to the same subject as the preceding section.

8. In the MS. a blank space is left after this question.

C. 5 *a* (11 *b*)]

215.

La larghezza · e lunghezza · dell'onbra · e del lume ·, benchè per li scorti · si facci · piv stretta · e più · corta, [2]non diminuirà · nè crescierà · la qualità · e quantità · di sua chiarezza o scurità.

[3]L'ofitio · dell'onbra · e del lume · diminvito · per li scorti · sarà · da onbrare e l'altro · da luminare [4]jl contraposto · corpo secondo · la qualità · e quātità che a esso · corpo · appare.

[5]Quanto · piv · l'onbra · diriuatiua s'auicinerà · ai sua penvltimi · stremi ·, di tanta maggiore · scurezza · apparirà: [6]*g* · *z* · è dopo la intersegatione · sol ueduto · dalla parte dell'onbra · *y* · *z* · che piglia · per ĩtersegatione l'onbra · *m* · *n* · [7]e per dirittura · l'onbra · *a* · *m*: onde ha · due tanti più · ōbra · che *g* · *z* ·: *y* · *x* uede · per intersegatione · *n* · *o* · e per [8]diretto · *n* · *m* · *a* ·, onde *x* · *y* si dimostra · auere · 3 · tanti · più · ōbra · che *z* · *g*: *x* · *f* · vede per ĩtersegatione [9] · *o* · *b* · e per diretto · vede *o* · *n* · *m* · *a*; onde · diremo adunque · che l'onbra ch'è tra · *f* · *x* sarà 4 tanti piv [10]scura · che · l'onbra · *z* · *g* · perch'è vista da 4 tanti piv obra˙

[11]*a* · *b* · sia la parte del'onbra primitiua,· *b* · *c* fia il lume primitiuo,· *d* sia · il loco della intersegatione, [12]*f* · *g* · sia l'onbra diriuatiua · *f* · *e* · il lume diriuatiuo.

[13]E questo · uole essere nel principio · della dimostratione.

On gradation of shadows (215. 216).

Although the breadth and length of lights and shadow will be narrower and shorter in foreshortening, the quality and quantity of the light and shade is not increased nor diminished.

[3]The function of shade and light when diminished by foreshortening, will be to give shadow and to illuminate an object opposite, according to the quality and quantity in which they fall on the body.

[5]In proportion as a derived shadow is nearer to its penultimate extremities the deeper it will appear. *g z* beyond the intersection faces only the part of the shadow [marked] *y z*; this by intersection takes the shadow from *m n* but by direct line it takes the shadow *a m* hence it is twice as deep as *g z*. *Y x*, by intersection takes the shadow *n o*, but by direct line the shadow *n m a*, therefore *x y* is three times as dark as *z g*; *x f*, by intersection faces *o b* and by direct line *o n m a*, therefore we must say that the shadow between *f x* will be four times as dark as the shadow *z g*, because it faces four times as much shadow.

Let *a b* be the side where the primary shadow is, and *b c* the primary light, *d* will be the spot where it is intercepted, *f g* the derived shadow and *f e* the derived light.

And this must be at the beginning of the explanation.

C. 4 *b* (12 *a*)]

216.

Quella parte della superfitie · de' corpi · che fia · percossa da maggiore · angolo delle spetie de' contra se posti corpi · piv si tignierà [2]in nel color di quelle: 8 di sotto · è maggiore āgolo che · 4, perchè la sua basa · *a* · *n* · è maggiore che · *e* · *n* basa di 4 [3]Questa figura di sotto vol'essere terminata · da · *a* · *n* · e · 4 · e · 8. [4]Quella parte · dell'alluminato ·

That part of the surface of a body on which the images [reflection] from other bodies placed opposite fall at the largest angle will assume their hue most strongly. In the diagram below, 8 is a larger angle than 4, since its base *a n* is larger than *e n* the base of 4. This diagram below should end at *a n* 4 8. [4]That portion of the

215. 1. largeza . ellungeza . . schorti . . piv strecta . eppiu . chorta. 2. cressciera . . osschurita. 3. lisschorti . . . e[llaltro] dalluminare. 4. chontrapossto chorpo sechondo . . chorpo. 5. "pen" vltimi . . magiore scureza. 6. dellonbra [z] . y . z piglia. 9. adumque . . sara. 10. schura . che. 11. lume [diriuatiuo] "primitiuo". 13. ecquesto.

216. 1. chorpi . cheffia . perchossa da magiore . . chontra . . chorpi. 2. inel cholor diquele . . magiore . . magiore. 3. a . n . he . 4 . he 8. 4. circhunda la perchussione . . percusiō.

215. In the original MS. the text of No. 252 precedes the one given here. In the text of No. 215 there is a blank space of about four lines between the lines 2 and 3. The diagram given on Pl. VI, No. 2 is placed between lines 4 and 5. Between lines 5 and 6 there is another space of about three lines and one line left blank between lines 8 and 9. The reader will find the meaning of the whole passage much clearer if he first reads the final lines 11—13. Compare also line 4 of No. 270.

216. The diagram originally placed between lines 3 and 4 is on Pl. VI, No. 3. In the diagram given above line 14 of the original, and here printed in the text, the words *corpo luminoso* [luminous body] are written in the circle *m*, *luminoso* in the circle *b* and *ombroso* [body in shadow] in the circle *o*.

che circunda · la percussione dell'onbra fia · piv · luminosa, la quale · sarà · più a essa percussione uicina. [5]Siccome vna · cosa toccata · da maggior soma · di razzi luminosi · si fa piv chiara, cosi quella si farà · piv scura che da maggior [6]soma di razzi obrosi sia percossa.

[7]4 Sia la parte dell'alluminato · 4 · 8 · che circūda la percussione dell'onbra · *g* · *e* · 4, e fia esso [8]loco · 4 · piv luminoso · perchè li uede minor soma d'onbra che no fa · nel loco · 8 ·, perchè 4 [9]vede solamete l'obra · *i* · *n* ·, e · 8 · vede ed è percosso dall'onbra · *a* · *e* · e dal'obra [10]*i* · *n* · ch'è 2 tāti piv scura, e questo medesimo accade quādo [11]l'aria col sole metterai in loco dell'obra · e del lume.

On relative proportion of light and shadows (216—221).

[12]Il concorso · dell'onbra, nata · e terminata · infra propinque · et piane · superfitie di pari · qualità · e retta oppositione, [13]avrà più scuro fine che principio · jl quale · terminerà · infra la · percussione de'luminosi razzi.

[14]Quella proportione troverai di oscurità infra l'ōbre diriuatiue · *a* · *n* ·, quale fia quella della vicinità de' corpi luminosi *m* · *b*, che le cavsano, [15]e se essi corpi luminosi fieno di pari grandezza ancora troverai tal proportione delle percussioni de' cierchi luminosi e l'obre qual'è quella della distantia d'essi corpi luminosi.

illuminated surface on which a shadow is cast will be brightest which lies contiguous to the cast shadow. Just as an object which is lighted up by a greater quantity of luminous rays becomes brighter, so one on which a greater quantity of shadow falls, will be darker.

Let 4 be the side of an illuminated surface 4 8, surrounding the cast shadow *g e* 4. And this spot 4 will be lighter than 8, because less shadow falls on it than on 8. Since 4 faces only the shadow *i n*; and 8 faces and receives the shadow *a e* as well as *i n* which makes it twice as dark. And the same thing happens when you put the atmosphere and the sun in the place of shade and light.

[12]The distribution of shadow, originating in, and limited by, plane surfaces placed near to each other, equal in tone and directly opposite, will be darker at the ends than at the beginning, which will be determined by the incidence of the luminous rays.

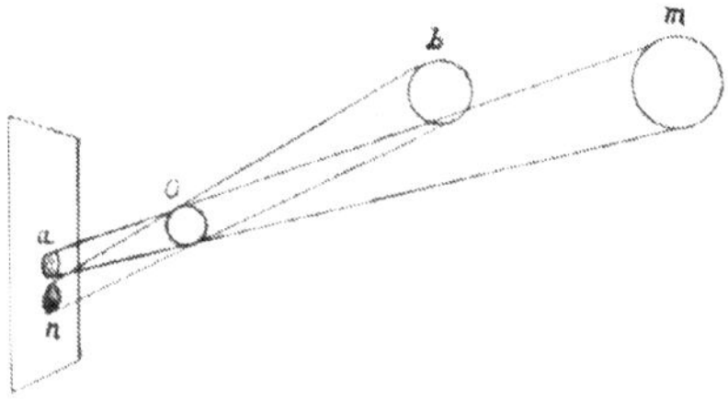

You will find the same proportion in the depth of the derived shadows *a n* as in the nearness of the luminous bodies *m b*, which cause them; and if the luminous bodies were of equal size you would still farther find the same proportion in the light cast by the luminous circles and their shadows as in the distance of the said luminous bodies.

217.

C. 4a [12a]

QUELLA · PARTE · DEL REFLESSO · FIA · PIV · CHIARA · DELLA QUALE I RAZZI · DELLA REFLESSIONE FIEN PIÙ CORTI.

[2]La oscurità · fatta · nella percussione · dell'onbroso · concorso · avrà · conformità · col suo principio, la quale [3]fia · nata · e finita · infra · propinque e piane · superfitie · di pari · qualità e retta · oppositione.

THAT PART OF THE REFLECTION WILL BE BRIGHTEST WHERE THE REFLECTED RAYS ARE SHORTEST.

[2]The darkness occasioned by the casting of combined shadows will be in conformity with its cause, which will originate and terminate between two plane surfaces near together, alike in tone and directly opposite each other.

5. Sichome . . chosa tocha da magior . . razi . Chosi . . pivsschura . . magior. 6. razi . . perchossa. 7. circhūda la perchussione . . effia. 8. locho . . locho. 9. i . n . he . 8 . . perchoso . . a . e . he dallōbra. 10. schuro . . achade. 11. chol sole meterai illocho. 12. choncorso . . etterminata. 13. ara . . infraila . perchussione. 14. troverai di oschurita infrallōbre . . luminosi "m. b." chelle chavsano. 15. essehessi . . grandeza anchora . . perchussiom luminosi delle. 16. bri quale quella.
217. 1. refresso . razi . chorti. 2. osscurita facta per'ne'la perchussione . . comchorsso . ara . chonformita . chol. 3. effinita . .

217. Diagrams are inserted before lines 2 and 4.

[4]Quanto maggiore fia · il corpo · luminoso · tanto più 'l corso delli onbrosi e luminosi razzi · fia insieme misto; [5]l'effetto · della · sopra detta propositione · accade · perchè · doue · si truoua · essere · maggiore · somma · di razzi · luminosi [6]li si è · maggior · lume · e doue · n'è meno ·, mĩnor lume · ne resulta · onde i razzi õbrosi · si uẽgono a mischiarsi ĩsieme.

[4]In proportion as the source of light is larger, the luminous and shadow rays will be more mixed together. This result is produced because wherever there is a larger quantity of luminous rays, there is most light, but where there are fewer there is least light, consequently the shadow rays come in and mingle with them.

C. 3*b* (13*a*)]

218.

Di tutte · le proportioni · ch'io farò s'intende · che 'l mezzo che si trova · infra corpi · sia per se equale; [2]Quanto · minore · fia · il corpo · luminoso · tanto · più · distinto · fia il concorso · dell'onbroso.

[3]Quando · due õbre · opposte, nascienti · da ũ medesimo · corpo fieno l'una all'altra · per oscurità duplicate [4]e per figura · simili i due lumi ·, causa · di quelle ·, fieno · infra loro · di dupplicato diametro e distantia da esso corpo [5]onbroso · l'uno all'altro duplice; [6]Se l'obietto fia mosso cõ tardità dinãzi al corpo luminoso e la percussione dell'onbra d'esso obbietto sia lontana da esso obbi[7]etto: tal proportione avrà · il moto dell'õbra diriuativa · col moto della primitiva · quale · avrà lo spatio che tra l'obbietto [8]e lume · con quello che tra l'obbietto · e la percussione dell'onbra ĩ modo che movẽdosi l'obietto cõ tardità, l'õbra fia veloce.

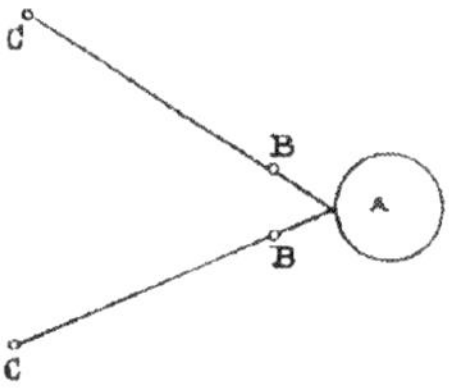

In all the proportions I lay down it must be understood that the medium between the bodies is always the same. [2]The smaller the luminous body the more distinct will the transmission of the shadows be.

[3]When of two opposite shadows, produced by the same body, one is twice as dark as the other though similar in form, one of the two lights causing them must have twice the diameter that the other has and be at twice the distance from the opaque body. If the object is lowly moved across the luminous body, and the shadow is intercepted at some distance from the object, there will be the same relative proportion between the motion of the derived shadow and the motion of the primary shadow, as between the distance from the object to the light, and that from the object to the spot where the shadow is intercepted; so that though the object is moved slowly the shadow moves fast.

C. 3*a* (13*b*)]

219.

Quel corpo luminoso · parrà di minore splendore jl quale · da piv · luminoso · campo · circundato fia.

[2]Ho trovato · che quelle stelle che sõ piv · presso all'orizõte appariscã di maggiore figura che l'altre perchè esse vedono e sõ vedute [3]da maggior sõma del corpo solare che quãdo esse sõ sopra di noi ·, e per ueder piv sole esse ãño maggior lume e 'l corpo che

A luminous body will appear less brilliant when surrounded by a bright background.

[2]I have found that the stars which are nearest to the horizon look larger than the others because light falls upon them from a larger proportion of the solar body than when they are above us; and having more light from the sun they give more light, and the bodies

ecpiaue . . errecta. 4. chorpo . . chorso . . missto. 5. decta . . achade . . razi. 6. magior . . razi siuẽgano a mistícharsi.
218. 1. proportioue . . mezo del chessi. 2. chorpo . . disstinto . . fiel chonchorso dal!. 3. due "õbre" oposite nasscienti . . chorpo [onbroso] fia . . Iscurita duplicata. 4. infralloro di dupplichoto diamitro . . chorpo. 6. obiecto chõ . . ella perchussione . . obbiecto. 7. eto . . ara il . . chol . . ara . . trallobietto. 8. trallobbiecto ella perchussione . . chõ.
219. 1. chorpo . . chanpo circhundato. 2. chessõ . . aparisscã di magiore . . chellaltre hesse vegano essõ. 3. hesse . . hesse ano

218. There are diagrams inserted before lines 2 and 3 but they are not reproduced here. The diagram above line 6 is written upon as follows: at *A lume* (light), at *B obbietto* (body), at *C ombra d'obbietto* (shadow of the object).

219. Between lines 1 and 2 there is in the original a large diagram which does not refer to this text.

[4] sarà piv luminoso si dimostra di maggiore figura, come si mostra il sole nella nebbia sopra di noi che par maggiore, [5] essedo sanza nebbia, e colla nebbia diminvisce; [6] Nessuna · parte del corpo · luminoso · mai · fia · veduta dalla · piramidal pura ombra diriuativa.

which are most luminous appear the largest. As may be seen by the sun through a mist, and overhead; it appears larger where there is no mist and diminished through mist. No portion of the luminous body is ever visible from any spot within the pyramid of pure derived shadow.

C. 22 (140)]

220.

Il corpo che riceve i razzi solari · passati · infra le sottili ramificationi delle piante, a lungo andare · nõ farà piv d'un' obra. [2] Se'l corpo onbroso · e luminoso fieno di sperica retondità ·, tal proportione · avrà la basa · della · luminosa · [3] piramide col suo · corpo ·, quale · à · la basa dell' onbrosa · piramide · col suo · corpo onbroso. [4] Quanto · la percussione ·, fatta dall' onbroso · concorso · nella · contra se posta · pariete, fia più distante al corpo · luminoso e piv [5] propinqua · a sua · diriuatione, tanto · più scure · e di termini · più distinti appariranno.

A body on which the solar rays fall between the thin branches of trees far apart will cast but a single shadow.

[2] If an opaque body and a luminous one are (both) spherical the base of the pyramid of rays will bear the same proportion to the luminous body as the base of the pyramid of shade to the opaque body.

[4] When the transmitted shadow is intercepted by a plane surface placed opposite to it and farther away from the luminous body than from the object [which casts it] it will appear proportionately darker and the edges more distinct.

C. 22 (14 b)]

221.

Il corpo alluminato · dai solari · razzi · passati · per le grosse ramificationi delle piãte · farà tãte õbre · quãt' è il nvmero de' rami che infra 'l sole [2] e esse interposti · sono.

¶ [3] La percussione · delli onbrosi · razzi nati da piramidal corpo õbroso ·, sarà di biforcata figura · e uaria oscurità nelle sue pũte ¶ [4] jl lume · che sarà maggior della pũta · e minor della basa · del contra se · posto

A body illuminated by the solar rays passing between the thick branches of trees will produce as many shadows as there are branches between the sun and itself.

Where the shadow-rays from an opaque pyramidal body are intercepted they will cast a shadow of bifurcate outline and various depth at the points. A light which is broader than the apex but narrower than the base

magior . . el [lume] chorpo. 4. magiore figura [Macq] come . . magiore. 5. cholla . . diminvisscie. 6. chorpo.

220. 1. "il chorpo che ricie[ono] "e"" [razi . . infralle . . ramifichatione . . allongo. 2. elluminose . . sperícha . . ara. 3. chol . . chorpo . . chol . . chorpo. 4. perchussione facta . . chonchorso . . chontrasseposta . . disstante alchorpo . . eppav. 5. essua . . schure . . termĩ piu disstinti.

221. 1. chorpo . . razi . . per"le" grosse ramifichatione . . piãte fara . . in fral sole esse interpossdi. 3. perchussione . . razi . . chorpo . . biforchata . . osscurita propĩ. 4. chessara magior . . ẽminor . . chontrasse . posto . . chorpo . . chellonbroso

220. The diagram which, in the original, is placed above line 2, is similar to the one, here given on page 73 (section 120). — The diagram here given in the margin stands, in the original, between lines 3 and 4.

221. Between lines 2 and 3 there are in the original two large diagrams.

piramidal · corpo · onbroso ·, farà · che l'onbroso · cavserà [5]in sua percussione ōbra · di biforcata · figura · e uaria · qualità di scurezza.

[6]Se 'l corpo · onbroso ·, minor del luminoso ·, fa due · onbre · e il corpo · ōbroso ·, simile al luminoso, e il maggiore · ne fa vna, è cōue?niēte cosa · che 'l corpo piramidale ·, che à parte · di se · minore · parte pari e parte maggiore dal luminoso, faccia ōbra biforcata.

of an opaque pyramidal body placed in front of it, will cause that pyramid to cast a shadow of bifurcate form and various degrees of depth.

If an opaque body, smaller than the light, casts two shadows and if it is the same size or larger, casts but one, it follows that a pyramidal body, of which part is smaller, part equal to, and part larger than, the luminous body, will cast a bifurcate shadow.

. chausera. *Here in the margin:* propō (proposition). 5. perchussione . . biforchata . . disscurezza. 6. chorpo . . onbre e hel chorpo . . luminoso e hel magiore . . vna cchōua. *Here in the margin:* come. 7. chosa chel.chorpo . . magiore dal . . faccōbra biforchata.

IV.

Perspective of Disappearance.

The theory of the "Prospettiva de' perdimenti" *would, in many important details, be quite unintelligible if it had not been led up by the principles of light and shade on which it is based. The word* "Prospettiva" *in the language of the time included the principles of optics; what Leonardo understood by* "Perdimenti" *will be clearly seen in the early chapters, Nos.* 222—224. *It is in the very nature of the case that the farther explanations given in the subsequent chapters must be limited to general rules. The sections given as* 227—231 *"On indistinctness at short distances" have, it is true, only an indirect bearing on the subject; but on the other hand, the following chapters,* 232—234, *"On indistinctness at great distances," go fully into the matter, and in chapters* 235—239, *which treat "Of the importance of light and shade in the Perspective of Disappearance", the practical issues are distinctly insisted on in their relation to the theory. This is naturally followed by the statements as to "the effect of light or dark backgrounds on the apparent size of bodies"* (*Nos.* 240—250). *At the end I have placed, in the order of the original, those sections from the MS.* C *which treat of the "Perspective of Disappearance" and serve to some extent to complete the treatment of the subject* (251—262).

E. 80 *a*]

222.

PERSPECTIVA DE' PERDIMĒTI [2]CHE FĀ LI STREMI DE' CORPI O[3]PACHI.

[4]Se inuisibili son li veri stremi de' corpi opachi [5]in qualunche minima distantia, maggiormente [6]sarā invisibili nelle lūghe distātie; ¶e se [7]per li termini si cognosce la uera figura di cias[8]cū corpo opaco e mācādo per distantia la [9]cognitiō d'esso tutto, maggiormēte mancherà [10]la cognitione delle sue parti e termini.

OF THE DIMINISHED DISTINCTNESS OF THE OUTLINES OF OPAQUE BODIES.

Definition (222. 223).

If the real outlines of opaque bodies are indistinguishable at even a very short distance, they will be more so at long distances; and, since it is by its outlines that we are able to know the real form of any opaque body, when by its remoteness we fail to discern it as a whole, much more must we fail to discern its parts and outlines.

E. 80 *b*]

223.

DELLA PROSPETTIVA DIMINUTRICE [2]DELLI CORPI OPACHI.

[3]Infra li corpi opachi d'equal magnitudine [4]tal fia la diminutione delle lor figure in ap[5]parētia qual'è quella delle lor distantie dal[6]l'ochio che le vede, ma tale proportione è [7]cōuersa¶ perchè dove la distantia è mag[8]giore, il corpo opaco si dimostra minore [9]e dove la distantia è minore, esso corpo si [10]dimostrerà maggiore, e di qui nasce la pro[11]spectiva liniale e in seguito converrà ¶ogni [12]corpo per lunga distātia perde prima quel[13]la parte di quel corpo, la quale in se è più [14]sottile come dire: d'un cavallo si perderā pri[15]ma le ganbe che la testa, perchè le gā[16]be son più sottili d'essa testa, e prima si per[17]derà il collo che il busto, per la medesima ragio[18]ne detta; adūque seguita che l'ultima parte

OF THE DIMINUTION IN PERSPECTIVE OF OPAQUE OBJECTS.

Among opaque objects of equal size the apparent diminution of size will be in proportion to their distance from the eye of the spectator; but it is an inverse proportion, since, where the distance is greater, the opaque body will appear smaller, and the less the distance the larger will the object appear. And this is the fundamental principle of linear perspective and it follows:—[11]every object as it becomes more remote loses first those parts which are smallest. Thus of a horse, we should lose the legs before the head, because the legs are thinner than the head; and the neck before the body for the same reason. Hence it follows that the last part of the horse which would be discernible by the eye would be the mass of the body in an oval

222. 2. cheffālisstremi de chorpi op. 4. chorpi oppachi. 5. disstantia. 6. disstātie esse. 7. chognosscie . . fighura. 8. chū . . oppacho e māchādo. 9. magiormēte. 10. chognitione . . parte || "ettermini" adunque.

223. 1. prosspectiva diminuitrice. 3. Infralli chorpi oppachi . . magnitudi. 4. diminuitione. 5. Quale "qu'lla delle. 6. chelle. 7. chonversa. 8. chorpo oppacho si dimosstra. 9. chorpo. 10. dimossterra . . nasscie. 11. seguita chonve "ra" (?) ogni. 12. chorpo . . lungha. 14. chome . . chavallo. 15. ghanbe [che il cho] chella tessta. 16. sottile dessa tessta. 17. chollo . .

[19]che della cõgnitione del cavallo fia al-l'ochio riser[20]vata sarà il busto restato in forma ovale, [21] ma più tosto traente al colonnale e perderas[22]si prima la grossezza che la lunghezza per la anti[23]detta 2ª conclusione ecc.

[24]Se l'ochio è in[25]mobile, la prospet[26]tiva termina [27] la sua distanti[28]a in punto; [29]ma se l'ochio [30]si move per ret[31]ta linia la pro[32]spettiva ter[33]mina in linia, [34]perchè è prova[35]to la linia es[36]sere gienera[37]ta dal moto del [38]pũto e il no[39]stro vedere ··· [41]e per [42]questo seguita [43]che chi move il ve[44]dere, move il pũ[45]to e chi mo[46]ve il pũto, giene[47]ra la linia ecc.

form, or rather in a cylindrical form and this would lose its apparent thickness before its length—according to the 2nd rule given above, &c. [23].

If the eye remains stationary the perspective terminates in the distance in a point. But if the eye moves in a straight [horizontal] line the perspective terminates in a line and the reason is that this line is generated by the motion of the point and our sight; therefore it follows that as we move our sight [eye], the point moves, and as we move the point, the line is generated, &c.

Ash. I. 23a]

224.

[2]Ogni · forma · corporea ·, ĩ quãto · allo ofitio · dell'ochio ·, si divide · in 3 parti · cioè [3]corpo · figura · e colore: la similitudine · corporea s'astẽde piv lontana dalla [4]sua · origine ·, che nõ fa il colore · o la figura ·, di poi · il colore s'astẽde piv che la figura, [5]ma questa regola nõ si osserua da corpi luminosi.

Every visible body, in so far as it affects the eye, includes three attributes; that is to say: mass, form and colour; and the mass is recognisable at a greater distance from the place of its actual existence than either colour or form. Again, colour is discernible at a greater distance than form, but this law does not apply to luminous bodies.

An illustration by experiment.

[6]La propositione · di sopra · è molto bene dimostrata · e cõfermata · dalla sperięza, inpero[7]chè, se tu · vedrai uno · uomo · da presso ·, tu conoscerai · la qualità · del corpo ·, la qualità della [8]figura, e similmẽte · del colore ·, e, se quello s'allontana da te alquãto spatio, tu nõ conoscierai [9]chi quello · si sia · perchè mãca · la qualità · della figura: se s'astẽderà ãcora · piv lõtano [10]nõ potrai disciernere · il colore suo: anzi ti parrà uno corpo oscuro · di piv lontano ti parà [11]un minimo corpo retõdo · e scuro retõdo parrà · perchè · la distãtia diminv[12]isce tanto le particulari mẽbra · che non ne · apparisce se non la maggiore · massa; [13]la ragione è questa · Noi sappiamo chiaro · che tutte · le similitudini · delle cose ẽtrano [14]nella inpressiua per uno · piccolo · spiracolo · dell'ochio: aduque · se tutto · l'orizzõte *a* · *d* [15]ẽtra per simile · spiracolo ·, sendo · il corpo · *b* · *c* · una minimissima parte d'esso orizzõte, [16]che parte avrà

The above proposition is plainly shown and proved by experiment; because: if you see a man close to you, you discern the exact appearance of the mass and of the form and also of the colouring; if he goes to some distance you will not recognise who he is, because the character of the details will disappear, if he goes still farther you will not be able to distinguish his colouring, but he will appear as a dark object, and still farther he will appear as a very small dark rounded object. It appears rounded because distance so greatly diminishes the various details that nothing remains visible but the larger mass. And the reason is this: We know very well that all the images of objects reach the senses by a small aperture in the eye; hence, if the whole horizon *a d* is admitted through such an aperture, the object *b c* being but a very small fraction of this horizon what space can it fill in that

busto. 18. challiulúma. 21. tosato . . cholonale e perdera. 22. grossaza chella . . perle anti. 24. sellochio he. 25. la perspe. 27. disstanu . . puncto. 29. Masellochio . . sec. 30. sstre. 40. [ecc]. 41. elnpĩito e per. 42. quessto. 45. [li quai] e chi.

224. 1. [le similitudine delle chorpi f]. 2. chorporea. 3. chulore. 5. marquesta. 6. chõfermata. 7. chessetu . vederai . ĩ . homo . . chonoscierai. 8. essimilmẽte . . essa quelo . . datte. 9. chiequello . . mãcha. 10. cholore . . para ĩ chorpo . . para. 11. in minimo chorpo . . escuro [di forma quasi] retõdo para. 12. isscie . . none apariscie . . magiore. 13. eequesta . . sapiamo . .

223. 2[illegible] No. 4

224. [illegible]

egli · a occupare della minima rappresētatione di si grāde emisperio; [17]e perchè i corpi luminosi · sono · piv · potēti · īfra · le tenebre · che nessun altro · corpo, [18]è neciessario che ·, essendo lo spiracolo della vista assai tenebroso, com'è la natura [19]di tutti i busi ·, che le spetie de' corpi lōtani si cōfondino īfra tāta luce del [20]cielo, e se pure appariscano, che paiano oscure e nere come fa ogni corpo piccolo [21]visto nel chiarore dell'aria.

minute image of so vast a hemisphere? And because luminous bodies have more power in darkness than any others, it is evident that, as the chamber of the eye is very dark, as is the nature of all colored cavities, the images of distant objects are confused and lost in the great light of the sky; and if they are visible at all, appear dark and black, as every small body must when seen in the diffused light of the atmosphere.

E. 79*b*]

225.

Dell'aria ĩterposta ĩfra l'ochio e l'obietto visibile.

[3]L'obbietto si dimostrerà tanto più o meno [4]noto in una medesima distātia, quāto l'ari[5]a, interposta infra l'ochio e esso obbietto, [6]sarà più o mē rara; Adunque conoscē[7]do io che la maggiore o minore quantità del[8]l'aria interposta infra l'ochio e l'obietto rē[9]de all'ochio più o mē confusi li termi[10]ni · d'essi corpi, tu farai li perdimēti [11]delle notitie d'essi corpi tanto nella me[12]desima proportione infra loro quale è [13]quella delle loro distātie dall'ochio d'esso [14]risguardatore.

Of the atmosphere that interposes between the eye and visible objects.

A guiding rule.

An object will appear more or less distinct at the same distance, in proportion as the atmosphere existing between the eye and that object is more or less clear. Hence, as I know that the greater or less quantity of the air that lies between the eye and the object makes the outlines of that object more or less indistinct, you must diminish the definiteness of outline of those objects in proportion to their increasing distance from the eye of the spectator.

L. 77*b*]

226.

Quando io fussi in vn sito di mare [2]equalmēte distante infra la spiaggia [3]e'l mōte, molto piv lūgo mostra essere [4]quello della spiaggia che quello del mōte.

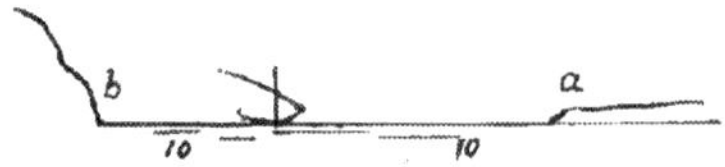

An experiment.

When I was once in a place on the sea, at an equal distance from the shore and the mountains, the distance from the shore looked much greater than that from the mountains.

Br. M. 115*a*]

227.

Se ti porrai uno corpo [2]ōbroso dināti alli ochi per spatio di 4 dita, [3]e ch' egli · sia · minore che non è dall'una all'al[4]tra · luce, · non occuperà il uedere d'alcuna [5]cosa che sia dopo quella; [6]nessuna cosa situata dopo il uisiuo [7]obietto dell'ochio nō può essere occupa[8]ta · da esso obbietto, se sarà mino[9]re che lo spatio che sta · infra le luci.

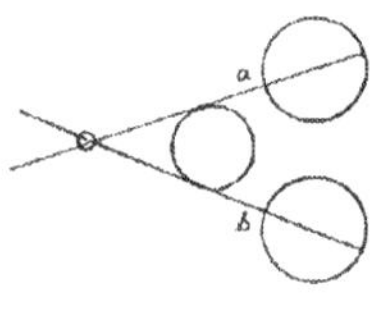

On indistinctness at short distances (227—231).

If you place an opaque object in front of your eye at a distance of four fingers' breadth, if it is smaller than the space between the two eyes it will not interfere with your seeing any thing that may be beyond it. No object situated beyond another object seen by the eye can be concealed by this [nearer] object if it is smaller than the space from eye to eye.

chettutte . le similitudine . delle chose. 14. ala inpresina . . pichofo . . settutto lorizōte. 15. b . c . ĩ . . orizōte. 16. ara . . ochupare dela . . rapresētatione. 17. chorpo. 18. spiracho. 19. chelle . . chōfondino infrattāta. 20. esse . . apariseano. . . paino ēhere.

225. 1. infrallochio. 2. ellobietto. 3. dimossterra . . ōmeno. 4. noto nuna . . disstātia. 5. interpossta . . obbiecto. 6. chonossiē 7. chella. 8. interpossta . . ellobietto. 9. chonfusi. 11. chorpi. 12. infralloro quale he. 13. disstātie. 14. risghuardatore.

226. 2. disstante infralla spiagga. 3. mosstra.

227. 1. setti porai ĩ chorpo. 2. ispatio. 3. echella . sia . . alla. 4. ochupera. 5. chosa chessia. 6. chosa. 7. ochupa. 9. chello ispatio.

B.[3] 23a]

228.

L'ochio nõ conprende il propi-[2]quo · angolo luminoso.

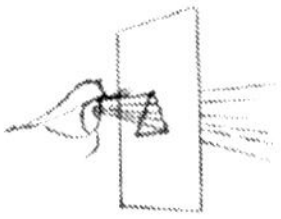

The eye cannot take in a luminous angle which is too close to it.

C. 12a]

229.

Quella · parte · della pariete · alluminata · fia · piv · luminosa [2]che da piv · grosso angolo luminoso alluminata fia; E quel loco da detti razzi osseruerà meno [3]la conveniēte qualità · del lume che da piv grosso · angolo obroso adombrata fia.

That part of a surface will be better lighted on which the light falls at the greater angle. And that part, on which the shadow falls at the greatest angle, will receive from those rays least of the benefit of the light.

E. 15a]

230.

Dell'ochio.

[2]Li termini di quel corpo antiposto alla pu[3]pilla dell'ochio si dimostrerà tanto meno noti [4]quanto e' sarāno più vicini a essa popilla; [5]provasi per lo stremo del corpo *n* antiposto [6]alla popilla *d*, la quale popilla nel uedere es[7]so termine vede ancora tutto lo spatio *a c*, [8]che è di là da esso termine, e le spetie che vengono [9]da esso spatio · si mischiano colle spetie di tal ter[10]mine e così l'una spetie cōfonde l'altra[11]e tale cōfusione priva la popilla della notitia di tal termine.

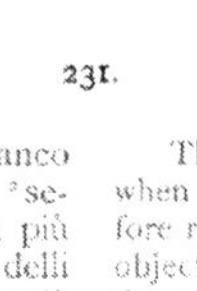

Of the eye.

The edges of an object placed in front of the pupil of the eye will be less distinct in proportion as they are closer to the eye. This is shown by the edge of the object *n* placed in front of the pupil *d*; in looking at this edge the pupil also sees all the space *a c* which is beyond the edge; and the images the eye receives from that space are mingled with the images of the edge, so that one image confuses the other, and this confusion hinders the pupil from distinguishing the edge.

Br. M. 188a]

231.

I termini di quella cosa saranno manco noti li quali sarà più vicini agli ochi, [2]seguita che gli termini più remoti saran più noti; [3]infra li corpi minori della popilla delli ochi [4]quelli sarâ mãco noti, che sarà più vicini [5]a essa lucie.

The outlines of objects will be least clear when they are nearest to the eye, and therefore remoter outlines will be clearer. Among objects which are smaller than the pupil of the eye those will be less distinct which are nearer to the eye.

228. 1. 2. R.
229. 1. piv . [luminosa] . lominosa [che da magiore soma]. 2. Equel locho. . razi . 3. chosvemiete.
230. 2. chorpo antiposto. 3. dimostterrà. 5. chorpo n antiposto. 7. anchora . . lospatio. 8. lespetie che vengh[o]n[o]. 9. mistano cholle. 10. chosi . . chōfonde. 11. attal chofusione . . termi[n]e.
231. 1—5. *The writing runs from left to right.* 1. qlla cosa seran mancho note. . qual sera piu vicina. 2. seran. 3. infralli chorpi. 4. sara macho noti chessera . . vicina.

H.[3] 1 a]

232.

On indistinctness at great distances (232—234).

Le cose vicine all'ochio pare[2]rāno di maggiore obbietto che le di[3]stāti.

[4]Le cose vedute cō du'ochi parirāno [5]piv rotonde, che quelle che cō uno [6]ochio vedute fieno.

[7]Le cose vedute īfra il lume [8]e l'ōbra parirāno di maggior relie[9]vo.

Objects near to the eye will appear larger than those at a distance.

Objects seen with two eyes will appear rounder than if they are seen with only one.

Objects seen between light and shadow will show the most relief.

C. A. 173 b; 520 b]

233.

De pictura.

[2]Tanto si perde · della uera cognitione della figura, quanto per distantia [3]diminvisce della sua grandezza.

Of painting.

Our true perception of an object diminishes in proportion as its size is diminished by distance.

A. 8 b]

234.

Prospettiva.

[2]Perchè le cose da lontano paiono · al'ochio · grandi e la ripruova fatta · nella [3]pariete le dimostra piccole.

Perspective.

Why objects seen at a distance appear large to the eye and in the image on the vertical plane they appear small.

Prospettiva.

[5]Domādo quāto · l'ochio · può vedere lontano · un corpo · che nō sia · luminoso [6]come dire una mōtagnia; vedrassi assai, se 'l sole fia · di là · da lei e vedrassi [7]più · o meno · lontana · secōdo · dove fia il sole · nel cielo.

Perspective.

I ask how far away the eye can discern a non-luminous body, as, for instance, a mountain. It will be very plainly visible if the sun is behind it; and could be seen at a greater or less distance according to the sun's place in the sky.

A. 2 a]

235.

The importance of light and shade in the perspective of disappearance (235—239).

Il corpo ōbroso ·, che fia · veduto · per la linia · della incidētia del lume, nō dimostrerà [2]di se · all'ochio · alcuna eminēte parte; [3]esenpli gratia · sia · il corpo · ōbroso · *a* ·, *c* · sia il lume ·, *c* · *m* · e cosi · *c* · *n* siano [4]le linie incidēti luminose, cioè quelle · linie · che trāsferiscono · il lume al corpo [5]*a*: l'ochio sia in

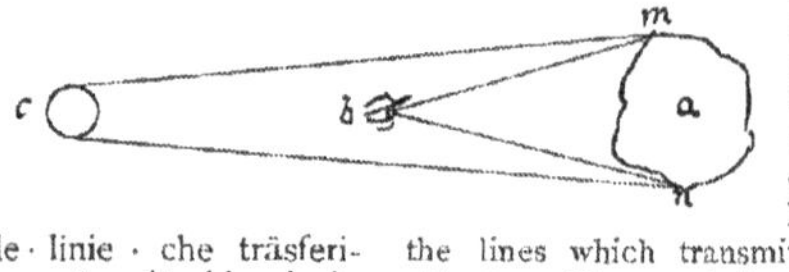

An opaque body seen in a line in which the light falls will reveal no prominences to the eye. For instance, let *a* be the solid body and *c* the light; *c m* and *c n* will be the lines of incidence of the light, that is to say the lines which transmit the light to the object *a*. The eye being at the point *b*, I say

232. 1—6 R. 2. magiore . . chelle dis. 4. la chosa veduta . . chō. 5. retonde checquelle chochō. 6. ochi. 7. chose . . infralume. 8. ellōbra . . magior.

233. 2. cognitione "dela figura" della cosa Quanto. 3. diminvisscie . . sua [propia] grandezza.

234. 2. chose dallontano paiano . . grande. 3. pichole. 5. po . . chorpo. 6. chome dire ī montagnia vederassi . . dallei evederassi. 7. sechōdo.

235. 1. chorpo . . cheffia . . dimostera. 2. alchuna. 3. chorpo . . echosi. 4. Incidēte luminosa . . trāsferisschano . . chorpo.

234. The clue to the solution of this problem (lines 1—3) is given in lines 4—6, No. 232. Objects seen with both eyes appear solid since they are seen from two distinct points of sight separated by the distance between the eyes, but this solidity cannot be represented in a flat drawing. Compare No. 535.

nel pũto · *b* ·, dico che vedẽdo il lume · *c* tutta la parte *m* · *n* che quelli rilieui che ui sono sarãno tutti alluminati: adũque l'ochio posto ĩ *c* nõ ui potrà vedere obra · e lume ·, nõ la vedẽdo ogni parte li parà d'uno colore õde le differẽtie delle parti emineti e globose non apariràno.

that since the light *c* falls on the whole part *m n* the portions in relief on that side will all be illuminated. Hence the eye placed at *c* cannot see any light and shade and, not seeing it, every portion will appear of the same tone, therefore the relief in the prominent or rounded parts will not be visible.

Ash. I. 21 *a*]

236.

DE PITTURA.

L'onbre · le quali · tu discernerai · con dificultà e · i loro · termini · nõ puoi · conosciere anzi con cõfuso · givditio · lo pigli · e trascrivi in nella · tua · opera, nõ le farai finite overo terminate, che la · tua · opera · fia di legniosa · resultatione.

OF PAINTING.

When you represent in your work shadows which you can only discern with difficulty, and of which you cannot distinguish the edges so that you apprehend them confusedly, you must not make them sharp or definite lest your work should have a wooden effect.

E. 17 *a*]

237.

PITTURA.

Noterai nel tuo ritrarre come infra le õbre sono õbre insẽsibili d'oscurità e di figura e questo si prova per la 3ª che dicie le superfitie globulenti sõ di tante varie oscurità e chiarezza, quãte sõ le uarietà delle oscurità e chiarezze che le stan per obbietto.

OF PAINTING.

You will observe in drawing that among the shadows some are of undistinguishable gradation and form, as is shown in the 3rd [proposition] which says: Rounded surfaces display as many degrees of light and shade as there are varieties of brightness and darkness reflected from the surrounding objects.

E. 3 *a*]

238.

DE ÕBRE E LUME.

Vedi tu che ritrai dell'opere di natura, le quãtità le qualità e le figure de' lumi e onbre di ciascun muscolo e nota nelle lũghezze della lor figura a qual muscolo si dirizzano colla rettitudine delle lor linie ciẽtrali.

OF LIGHT AND SHADE.

You who draw from nature, look (carefully) at the extent, the degree, and the form of the lights and shadows on each muscle; and in their position lengthwise observe towards which muscle the axis of the central line is directed.

Ash. I. 25 *b*]

239.

Quella · cosa ·, che per chiarezza fia · piv · simile alla · luce ·, fia veduta · piv · da lontano e di maggiore · forma che non si richiede alla qualità del corpo · in detta · distãtia.

An object which is [so brilliantly illuminated as to be] almost as bright as light will be visible at a greater distance, and of larger apparent size than is natural to objects so remote.

5. inel . . dicho. 6. chequelli . . alluminate . . [[ejo. 7. ellume nolla. 8. chilore. 9. diferẽtie. 10. globbose.

236. 2. dissciernerai chon difichulta . . poi [disciernere] "chonosciere" anzi chon cho. 2. ettrasscrivi innella . . nolle. 3. chella

237. 2. chome infrai. 3. dosscurita. 4. fighura cequesto. 5. chedicie . . globbulenti. 6. osschurita 7. tanto . . osschurita. 8. chelle.

238. 1. ellume. 3. elle 4. fighure. 5. scun muscholo. 6. gheze. 7. dirizano chelle.

239. 1. chosa . . chiareza. 2. dallontano . . magiore. 3. chorpo.

E. 32 *b*]

240.

Quell' onbra si dimostrerà più oscu[2]ra che fia circundata da più [3]splendida biãchezza e de conver[4]so sarà meno evidẽte dov' ella è giene[5]rata in più oscuro canpo.

A shadow will appear dark in proportion to the brilliancy of the light surrounding it and conversely it will be less conspicuous where it is seen against a darker background.

The effect of light or dark backgrounds on the apparent size of objects (240—250).

I.[1] 17 *b*]

241.

De prospettiva comune.

¶ [2]Quella cosa d' uniforme grossezza [3]e colore che sarà veduta in cã[4]po di disuniforme colore si dimos[5]trerà di disuniforme grossezza ¶

[6]E se una cosa d' uniforme grossezza [7]e di uarii colori sarà veduta in cã[8]po d' uniforme colore, essa cosa [9]si dimostrerà di uaria grossezza, [10]e quanto i colori del canpo o della cosa [11]nel canpo veduta sarà di colori ch' abbino [12]maggiore varietà, allora le grossezze par[13]rãno · piv varie, ancora che le cose [14]nel canpo vedute sieno di pari grossezza.

Of ordinary perspective.

An object of equal breadth and colour throughout, seen against a background of various colours will appear unequal in breadth.

And if an object of equal breadth throughout, but of various colours, is seen against a background of uniform colour, that object will appear of various breadth. And the more the colours of the background or of the object seen against the ground vary, the greater will the apparent variations in the breadth be though the objects seen against the ground be of equal breadth [throughout].

J.[1] 18 *a*]

242.

¶ Quella cosa oscura che fia veduta in cãpo [2]chiaro · essa si dimostrerà minore ch' essa [3]non è ¶

[4]Quella cosa chiara [5]si dimostrerà di maggiore figura [6]che sarà veduta in canpo di piv oscuro [7]colore.

A dark object seen against a bright background will appear smaller than it is.

A light object will look larger when it is seen against a background darker than itself.

C. A. 124 *b*; 383 *b*]

243.

Del lume.

[2]Quel corpo luminoso, che si trouerà essere occupato [3]da piv grossa aria, apparirà di minore grãdezza, [4]come si dimostra nella luna o sole occupati dalla [5]nebbia.

Of light.

A luminous body when obscured by a dense atmosphere will appear smaller; as may be seen by the moon or sun veiled by mists.

Del lume.

[7]Infra i corpi luminosi d' equal grandezza distantia e splẽdore quello [8]si dimostrerà di maggiore · forma ·, il quale da più oscuro · canpo circhũ[9]dato · fia.

Of light.

Of several luminous bodies of equal size and brilliancy and at an equal distance, that will look the largest which is surrounded by the darkest background.

Del lume.

[11]Jo trouo · che ciascuno · corpo luminoso, veduto · nella folta · e spessa [12]nebbia ·,

Of light.

I find that any luminous body when seen through a dense and thick mist diminishes

240. 1. dimosstera piu oscu. 2. cheffia circhundata dappiu. 3. biãchezza [e de chon ver]. 4. dovella giene. 5. osschuro chanpo.

241. 1. prosspectiva. 2. grosseza. 3. chessara. 5. tera . . grosseza. 6. esse . . grosseza. 7. vari[a] colore. 8. cholore. 9. dimosterra . . grosseza. 11. colori cabino. 12. magiore . . grosseze pa. 13. chelle. 14. grosseza.

242. 1. Quala . . oscura fia . . chãpo. 2. dimossterra. 4. Quala . . chiara [sara veduta in]. 5. [canpo di] si dimosterra . . magiore. 6. chessara . . chanpo . . osscuro. 7. cholore.

243. 2. chorpo . . chessi troverra . . ochupato. 3—5 R. 3. arie aparira. 5. cheme si dimosstra . . ossole ochupati. 7. chorpi . . essprẽdore. 8. dimossterra di magiore . . dappiu osschuro chanpo circhu. 11. checciasscuno chorpo . . esspessa. 12. dimi-

quanto più · s'allontana dall'occhio · più · diminuisce, e così [13]fa · il sole di dì come la luna · e li altri immortali lumi di notte. E quā[14]do l'aria · è pura quanto · essi lumi · più · s'allontanano · dall'occhio, [15]più pare si faccino · di maggiore · forma.

in proportion to its distance from the eye. Thus it is with the sun by day, as well as the moon and the other eternal lights by night And when the air is clear, these luminaries appear larger in proportion as they are farther from the eye

F. 22 a]

244.

Quella parte dello obbietto oscuro d'uniforme grosse[2]zza si dimostrerà più sottile che fia veduta in cāpo [3]più luminoso.

[4]*e* è il corpo dato oscuro in se e d'uniforme gros[5]sezza, *a b* e *c d* son cāpi oscuri più l'uno che l'altro, [6]*b c* è canpo luminoso come se fusse vn loco percosso [7]da vno spiracolo di sole in una camera oscura; dico, [8]che l'obietto *e g* parrà più grosso in · [9]*e f* che in *g h* perchè *e f* à 'l canpo più oscuro che esso [10]*g h*; ancora la parte *f g* parrà sottile per esse[11]re veduta dall'ochio *o* in campo *b c* che è chiaro [12]La parte del corpo luminoso d'uniforme grossezza [13]e splendore parrà esser piu grossa che fia veduta [14]in canpo più oscuro e questo luminoso essere ĩfocato

That portion of a body of uniform breadth which is against a lighter background will look narrower [than the rest].

[4] *e* is a given object, itself dark and of uniform breadth, *a b* and *c d* are two backgrounds one darker than the other, *b c* is a bright background, as it might be a spot lighted by the sun through an aperture in a dark room. Then I say that the object *e g* will appear larger at *e f* than at *g h*, because *e f* has a darker background than *g h*; and again at *f g* it will look narrower from being seen by the eye *o*, on the light background *b c*. [12] That part of a luminous body, of equal breadth and brilliancy throughout, will look largest which is seen against the darkest background; and the luminous body will seem on fire.

Ash I. 3 b]

245.

COME · I CORPI ACCOMPAGNATI DA ONBRA E LUME [2]SEMPRE · VARIANO · I LOR TERMINI DAL COLORE E LUME [3]DI QUELLA COSA CHE CŌFINA · COLLA SUA SUPERFITIE

WHY BODIES IN LIGHT AND SHADE HAVE THEIR OUTLINES ALTERED BY THE COLOUR AND BRIGHTNESS OF THE OBJECTS SERVING AS A BACKGROUND TO THEM.

[4]Se vedrai · uno corpo · che la · parte alluminata · campeggi e termini ĩ campo oscuro [5]la parte d'esso · lume che parrà · di maggiore · chiarezza · fia · quella [6]che terminerà coll'oscuro in *d* E se detta · parte · alluminata · cõfina col [7]canpo chiaro ·, il termine d'esso · corpo · alluminato parrà men chiaro che prima [8]e la · sua · soma chiarezza apparirà ĩfra al termine del campo *m* · *f* · e l'onbra; E questo [9]medesimo accade all'ōbra, imperochè 'l termine di quella parte del corpo

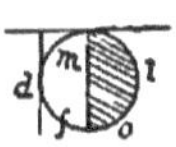

If you look at a body of which the illuminated portion lies and ends against a dark background, that part of the light which will look brightest will be that which lies against the dark [background] at *d*. But if this brighter part lies against a light background, the edge of the object, which is itself light, will be less distinct than before, and the highest light will appear to be between the limit of the background *m f* and the shadow. The same thing is seen with regard to the dark [side],

nuisscie e chosi 13 chome . altrimortali . . Ecquā. 14 eppura.

244. 1 barte . . obbiecto osscuro 2 seza . dimosterra . . cheffia veduto 4 e he il duniforma 5 seza ab he . osscuri piu lūcellaltro 6 fussi . percoso 7 spiracol di sole nuna . osscura 8 chellobietto 11 veduto . chia"ro' 13 essplendore eser. 14 osscuro ecquesto esere I "focato"

245 1 achompagniati ellume. 2 cholore ellume. 3 chosa . cholle. 4 ĩ chorpo chella champegi ettermini oschuro 5 parira . . chiareza 6 chetterminera cholloschuro Esse . col. 7 chanpo para 8 chiareza. champo 9 achade

244 The diagram to which the text, lines 1—11, refers, is placed in the original between lines 3 and 4, and is given on Pl. XLI, No 3. Lines 12 to 14 are explained by the lower of the two diagrams on Pl. XLI, No 4. In the original these are placed after line 14

245 In the original diagram *o* is inside the shaded surface at the level of *d*

aonbrato che [10] cāpeggia in loco chiaro in *l*, parrà di molta maggiore oscurità che 'l resto, E se [11] detta ōbra termina in campo oscuro, il termine dell'onbra parrà [12] piv chiaro che prima e la soma sua scurezza fia infra detto termine e'l lume [13] nel punto *o*

inasmuch as that edge of the shaded portion of the object which lies against a light background, as at *l*, looks much darker than the rest But if this shadow lies against a dark background the edge of the shaded part will appear lighter than before, and the deepest shade will appear between the edge and the light at the point *o*

C A 124*a*, 383*a*]

246

Quel corpo ōbroso si dimostrerà di minore grādezza, il quale da più luminoso cāpo fia circūdato, [2] e quel luminoso si dimostrerà maggiore che cōfinerà cō piv oscuro cāpo [3] come si dimostra nell'altezze degli edifiti la notte, quādo dirieto a quelli vāpeggia che subito par [4] che 'l vāpeggiado diminvisca l'edifitio di sua altezza e di qui nasce che essi [5] edifizi paiono maggiori quādo è nebbia o notte che quādo l'aria è purificata e alluminata

An opaque body will appear smaller when it is surrounded by a highly luminous background, and a light body will appear larger when it is seen against a darker background This may be seen in the height of buildings at night, when lightning flashes behind them, it suddenly seems, when it lightens, as though the height of the building were diminished For the same reason such buildings look larger in a mist, or by night than when the atmosphere is clear and light

G 12*b*]

247

De' lumi infra l'ōbre

[2] Quando ritrai alcuno corpo, [3] ricordati quando fai paragō [4] della potētia de' lumi delle sua [5] parti alluminate che spesso l'o[6]chio s'inganna, parēdogli più chi[7]aro quello ch'è mē chiaro, e la [8] cavsa nascie mediante li pa[9]ragoni delle parti che cōfinano [10] con loro, perchè se avrā due par[11]ti di chiarezza ine[12]guali e che la mē chiara confi[13]ni con parti oscure e la pi[14]v chiara cōfini cō parti chia[15]re chom'è il celo o simili chiarez[16]ze allora quella ch'è mē chi[17]ara o vo dire lucida, parà pi[18]v lucida e la più lucida parrà [19] più oscura

On light between shadows

When you are drawing any object, remember, in comparing the grades of light in the illuminated portions, that the eye is often deceived by seeing things lighter than they are And the reason lies in our comparing those parts with the contiguous parts Since if two [separate] parts are in different grades of light and if the less bright is conterminous with a dark portion and the brighter is conterminous with a light background—as the sky or something equally bright—, then that which is less light, or I should say less radiant, will look the brighter and the brighter will seem the darker

C A 124*a*, 383*a*]

248

Infra le cose di pari oscurità che dopo lunga e pari distantia situate sieno, quella apparirà più oscura, che piv alta da terra [2] collocata fia

Of objects equally dark in themselves and situated at a considerable and equal distance, that will look the darkest which is farthest above the earth

10 chāpegia illocho para magiore ischurita Esse 11 jn champo oschuro parira 12 ella scureza
246 1 dimosterra grādeza 2 dimosterra magiore osscuro 3 alteze vīpegia 4 che vāpegiādo diminvisca alteza nasscie 5 paiano magiori
247 5 parte 6 parendoli 7 ara quelle ella 9 parte 10 colloro arā 11 ti d[equale] di chiareza inne 12 chella 13 parte osscure ella 14 parte 15 ossimili 17 chiare 18 ella piu lucia 19 osscura
248 1 Infralle chose osschurita eppari disstantia hoschura datterra 2 chollochata

A. 91 b]

249.

PRUOVA · COME I CORPI LUMINOSI [2]PAIONO DI LONTANO · MAGGIORI · CHE NÕ SONO.

[3]Se porrai · 2 · candele acciese · appresso · l'una · all'altra ½ · braccio · e allontanerati da esse 200 · braccia vedrai [4]per l'accrescimẽto · di ciascuno · farsi · uno · solo · corpo luminoso · de' due lumi · e parrà uno solo [5]lume · grande · uno braccio.

PRUOVA A VEDERE · LA UERA GRÃDEZZA [7]DE' CORPI LUMINOSI.

[8]Se vuoi · vedere la vera grãdezza · d'essi corpi luminosi · abbi una assetta · sottile e fauі uno buso quãto sareb·be uno piccolo pũtale · di striga · e ponitela · tãto · presso · all'ochio · quãto · puoi · ĩ modo che riguardãdo [10]per esso buso · il sopra · detto · lume · tu gli vegga · assai · spatio · d'aria · dintorno e cosí leuãdo · e ponẽdo [11]cõ prestezza essa · asse · dal tuo · ochio · cosi cho prestezza vedrai · cresciere · esso · lume.

TO PROVE HOW IT IS THAT LUMINOUS BODIES APPEAR LARGER, AT A DISTANCE, THAN THEY ARE.

If you place two lighted candles side by side half a braccio apart, and go from them to a distance 200 braccia you will see that by the increased size of each they will appear as a single luminous body with the light of the two flames, one braccio wide.

TO PROVE HOW YOU MAY SEE THE REAL SIZE OF LUMINOUS BODIES.

If you wish to see the real size of these luminous bodies take a very thin board and make in it a hole no bigger than the tag of a lace and place it as close to your eye as possible, so that when you look through this hole, at the said light, you can see a large space of air round it. Then by rapidly moving this board backwards and forwards before your eye you will see the light increase [and diminish].

C. 21 a (53)]

250.

Propositions on perspective of disappearance from MS. C. (250—262).

Infra i corpi di pari qualità che sien dall'occhio equalmẽte · distanti, quello · apparirà di minor figura [2]che da piv luminoso · campo circundato fia.

¶ [3]Ogni corpo evidẽte fia da lume e obra circũdato.¶ ¶ [4]Quel corpo d'equale rotõdità, che da lume [5]e obra circũdato fia, parrà avere tanto piv [6]grande l'una parte che l'altra quãto fia piv [7]alluminata l'una che l'altra.¶

Of several bodies of equal size and equally distant from the eye, those will look the smallest which are against the lightest background.

Every visible object must be surrounded by light and shade. A perfectly spherical body surrounded by light and shade will appear to have one side larger than the other in proportion as one is more highly lighted than the other.

C. 23 a (78)]

251.

PROSPETTIVA.

[2]Nessuno evidẽte corpo · può dagli umani · ochi · essere ben conpreso · e ben giudicato [3]se nõ per la uarietà del canpo · doue · li stremi · d'essi · corpi · terminano e cõfinano, [4]e nessuna cosa · inquãto · a liniamẽti · de' sua · stremi · apparirà · essere · da essi cãpi diuisa; [5]la luna benchè · sia molto · distante ·

PERSPECTIVE.

No visible object can be well understood and comprehended by the human eye excepting from the difference of the background against which the edges of the object terminate and by which they are bounded, and no object will appear [to stand out] separate from that background so far as the outlines of its borders are concerned. The moon,

249. 1. chome i chorpi . . 2. paiano . . . magiori. 3. porai . . chandele . . . apresso . ½a . br. e alontanerati 200 br. vederai. 4. lacresscimẽto . . . no solo chorpo [de] luminoso . . . parra ĩ solo. 5. grande . ĩ . br [esse]. 6. grãdeza. 7. chorpi. 8. se volli vedere . grãdeza . chorpi . . abbi ĩ assetta . . effaui ĩ buso . . sare 9. be ĩ pich

olo . . . põsla. 10. tulli vega . . chosi. 11. cho presteza . . choso chõ . . presteza vederai cresciere.

250. 1. Chessien. 2. dapoi . . circhundato. 3. Omi . . dallume . . circhũdato. 4. chorpo . . rotõdita . . dallume. 5. circhũdato. 6. chelaltra. 7. aluminata . . chelaltra.

251 . . . chonpreso. 2. chanpo . . liastremi . . chorpi . . chõfinano. 4. chosa . . alma-

dal corpo del sole quã[6]do per le eclissi si truovi infra li ochi nostri e'l sole, perchè essa lu[7]na danpeggia sopra il sole, appare ali ochi vmani congivnta e appiccata con esso [8]sole

though it is at a great distance from the sun, when, in an eclipse, it comes between our eyes and the sun, appears to the eyes of men to be close to the sun and affixed to it, because the sun is then the background to the moon

C 5a (11b)]

252

Quel corpo luminoso parrà piv splendido il quale da più oscure tenebre circundato fia

A luminous body will appear more brilliant in proportion as it is surrounded by deeper shadow

C 1b (15a)]

253

I retti termini de' corpi parrãno rotti che termineranno in loco tenebroso rigato da percussione di luminosi razzi

The straight edges of a body will appear broken when they are conterminous with a dark space streaked with rays of light

C 1a (15b)]

254

Infra i corpi d'equal grãdezza e distãtia quello che fia piv alluminato parrà all'ochio piv propĩquo e maggiore

Of several bodies, all equally large and equally distant, that which is most brightly illuminated will appear to the eye nearest and largest

C 14b (16a)]

255

Se molti corpi luminosi fieno veduti di lontan paese, benchè infra loro sien diuisi parranno insieme vniti e cõgivnti

If several luminous bodies are seen from a great distance although they are really separate they will appear united as one body

C 14a (16b)]

256.

Se molti corpi õbrosi di quasi congiunta vicinità fieno veduti in cãpo luminoso in lunga distãtia parrãno separati da grãde intervallo.

If several objects in shadow, standing very close together, are seen against a bright background they will appear separated by wide intervals

C 21b (17a)]

257

Infra le cose d'equal grãdezza e colore quella che fia piv lontana parrà piv chiara e di minore figura

Of several bodies of equal size and tone, that which is farthest will appear the lightest and smallest

mẽti aparira 5 [Il sole lume ealtre ste] la luna chorpo b pe''r le clissi 6 nosstri sole [e che essa luna chãpe] perche 7 chãpegia apare chongivnta e appichata chon esso

252 1 chorpo parra [di magiore] piv splendido [che] il osschure circhundato

253 1 chorpi Chetterminneranno illocho tenebroso [umato] rigato'' da perchussione razi

254 1 chorpi grãdeza Quello cheffia para magiore

255 1 chorpi paesse infralloro parano vnite e chõgivnte

256 1 chorpi chongiunta chãpo illunga

257 1 Jfralle chose grãdeza cholore cheffia

252 The diagram which, in the original, is placed after this text, has no connection with it

253 254. Here again the diagrams in the original have no connection with the text

258.

C. 22a]

Infra le cose d'equal grandezza · bianchezza di căpo e longitudine · quella · che fia · di più · chiara superfitie apparirà · di maggior figura; [2]Il ferro d'equal grossezza · mezzo ifocato · ne fa proua, ‡peroche essa parte · ifocata · pare · più · grossa che 'l resto.

Of several objects equal in size, brightness of background and length that which has the flattest surface will look the largest. A bar of iron equally thick throughout and of which half is red hot, affords an example, for the red hot part looks thicker than the rest.

259.

C. 85]

Infra i corpi · d'equale · grandezza · e longitudine · e d'equale · figura · e oscurità · quella apparirà [2]di minor grandeza · che da più · luminoso · canpo · circundata fia.

Of several bodies of equal size and length, and alike in form and in depth of shade, that will appear smallest which is surrounded by the most luminous background.

260.

C. 85]

QUELLA · PARTE · DELLA PARIETE · FIA · PIV OSCURA · O LUMINOSA · CHE DA PIV · GROSSO · ANGOLO · OSCURO O LUMINOSO FIA PERCOSSO.

DIFFERENT PORTIONS OF A WALL SURFACE WILL BE DARKER OR BRIGHTER IN PROPORTION AS THE LIGHT OR SHADOW FALLS ON THEM AT A LARGER ANGLE.

[2]La sopra detta · propositione · chiaramēte in questa · forma · si pruova: diciamo *m* · *q* · essere il corpo luminoso e cosi [3]*f* · *g* ·

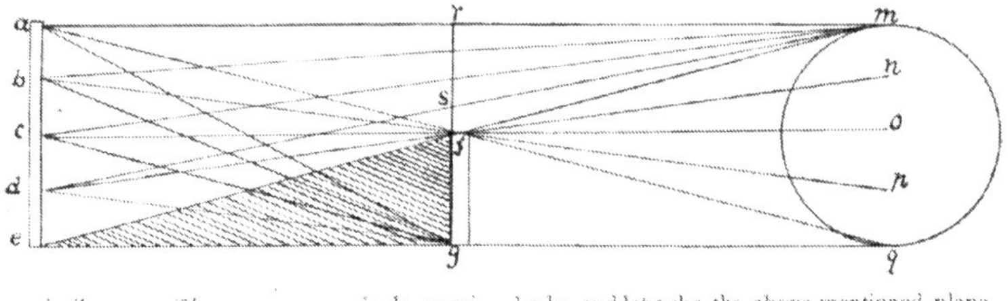

sarà · il corpo ōbroso: e *a* · *e* · sia la nominata pariete, doue sopra detti āgoli percuotono, li rappresentādo la natura [4]e qualità di loro base: ora · ¶*a* · fia piv luminoso che *b* · la basa dell'angolo · *a* · è piv . grossa che quella [5]di · *b* · e però fa piv · grosso āgolo, il quale · fia · *a* · *m* · *q*; e la piramide · *b* · *p* · *m* fia piv stretta, e più sottille sia [6]quella · *m* · *o* · *c* e cosi di mano in mano, quāto piv s'appressa a *e* fieno le piramidi piv strette e piu oscure; [7]Quel pūto della pariete · fia · di minore chiarezza nel quale la grossezza

The foregoing proposition can be clearly proved in this way. Let us say that *m q* is the luminous body, then *f g* will be the opaque body; and let *a e* be the above-mentioned plane on which the said angles fall, showing [plainly] the nature and character of their bases. Then: *a* will be more luminous than *b*; the base of the angle *a* is larger than that of *b* and it therefore makes a greater angle which will be *a m q*; and the pyramid *b p m* will be narrower and *m o c* will be still finer, and so on by degrees, in proportion as they are nearer to *e*, the pyramids will become narrower and darker. That portion of the wall will be the darkest where the breadth of the

258. 1. Infralle chose . . grandeza bianchezza | "chāpo" ellongitudine. Quella chellia . di piu . piana superfitie aparira . . magior. 2. fero . . grossezza . mezo ifochato . . ifochata.

259. 1. chorpi . . grandeza ellongitudine . . osschurita. Quella [chellia] apparira. 2. grandeza . . dappiu . . chanpo circhundata.

260. 1. osschura olluminosa . . dappiu . . oscuro olluminoso [fia perchosso]. 2. chorpo . . chosi. 3. chorpo . . douessopra . . perc[illegible] . piramide

della piramide ōbrosa supera la grossez[8]za della luminosa.

[9]Nel pūto · *a* · fia di tāta · potētia la piramide luminosa quāto la ōbrosa, perchè la basa · *f* · *g* · è simile alla basa · *r* · *f*; E nel pūto [10]*d* · la piramide luminosa fia tanto piv · sottile che la obrosa ·, quāto la basa · *s* · *f* · è minore che la basa · *f* · *g*.

[11]Diuidi la sopra detta propositione in due figure cioè una colle piramidi ōbrose e luminose e l'altra colle [12]luminose.

pyramid of shadow is greater than the breadth of the pyramid of light.

At the point *a* the pyramid of light is equal in strength to the pyramid of shadow, because the base *f g* is equal to the base *r f*. At the point *d* the pyramid of light is narrower than the pyramid of shadow by so much as the base *s f* is less than the base *f g*.

Divide the foregoing proposition into two diagrams, one with the pyramids of light and shadow, the other with the pyramids of light [only].

C. 13b]

261.

Infra l'onbre · di pari qualità · Quella che fia · piv · propinqua · all'ochio apparirà · di minore · oscurità.

Among shadows of equal depth those which are nearest to the eye will look least deep.

C. 10a]

262.

Quanto · di maggiore splendore fia · il corpo · luminoso · di tanta maggiore oscurità · fieno · l'onbre · fatte da'corpi da esso alluminati.

The more brilliant the light given by a luminous body, the deeper will the shadows be cast by the objects it illuminates.

. . osschure. 7. chiareza . . quale [la piramide] la grosseza . . grosse. 9. essimile. 10. chella ōbrosa. 11. cioe ĩ chole piramide . . ellaltra chole.

261. 1. Infrallonbre . . cheffia . . Apparira . . hosscurita.

262. 1. magiore [“splendore” . . . chorpo . . magiore osschurita . . lonbr . . chorpi.

V.

Theory of colours.

Leonardo's theory of colours is even more intimately connected with his principles of light and shade than his Perspective of Disappearance and is in fact merely an appendix or supplement to those principles, as we gather from the titles to sections 264, 267, *and* 276, *while others again* (*Nos.* 281, 282) *are headed* Prospettiva.

A very few of these chapters are to be found in the oldest copies and editions of the Treatise on Painting, and although the material they afford is but meager and the connection between them but slight, we must still attribute to them a special theoretical value as well as practical utility—all the more so because our knowledge of the theory and use of colours at the time of the Renaissance is still extremely limited.

The reciprocal effects of colours on objects placed opposite each other (263—272).

G. 37 a]

263.

DE PICTURA.

[2]Il colore dello alluminato participa [3]del colore dello alluminante.

OF PAINTING.

The hue of an illuminated object is affected by that of the luminous body.

E. 32 b]

264.

DE ONBRA.

¶[2]La superfitie d'ogni opaco participa [3]del colore del suo obbietto¶.

OF SHADOW.

The surface of any opaque body is affected by the colour of surrounding objects.

W. 232 b]

265.

L'onbra participa sēpre del color del suo obbietto.

A shadow is always affected by the colour of the surface on which it is cast.

Br. M. 211 b]

266.

Il simvlacro inpresso nello spechio participa del co[2]lore del predetto specchio.

An image produced in a mirror is affected by the colour of the mirror.

Ash. I. 2 a]

267.

DE ŌBRA E LUME.

[2]Ogni · parte · della · superfitie ·, che · circūda · i corpi, [3]si trasmuta ī parte del colore · di quella · cosa · che gl'è posta per obietto.

OF LIGHT AND SHADE.

Every portion of the surface of a body is varied [in hue] by the [reflected] colour of the object that may be opposite to it.

263. 2. cholore . . 3. cholore . . alluminancte.
264. 2. oppacho. 3. cholore . . obbieto.
265. obbiecto.
266. 1. delcho.
267. 1. ellume. 2. circhūda . i chorpi. 3. trassmuta . . cholore . . chelle posta. 5. settu porai uno[palla da] uno chorpo . speri-

ESẼPLO.

[5]Se tu porrai · uno corpo · sperico · i mezzo a vari obietti, [6]cioè che da una · parte · sia · lume · del · sol' e · dall' opposita parte sia · uno · muro [7]alluminato dal sole ·, il quale · sia verde o d'altro colore, il piano dove si posa [8]sia · rosso ·, dai 2 · lati · traversi · sia scuro: vedrai il natura[9]le colore · di detto corpo participare de' colori · che li sono per obietto; [10]Il più potẽte fia il luminoso; Il secondo fia quello · della pariete allumina[11]ta ·, Il terzo quello · dell' obra ·, Rimane poi una quãtità, che participa del colo[12]re delli · stremi.

EXAMPLE.

If you place a spherical body between various objects that is to say with [direct] sunlight on one side of it, and on the other a wall illuminated by the sun, which wall may be green or of any other colour, while the surface on which it is placed may be red, and the two lateral sides are in shadow, you will see that the natural colour of that body will assume something of the hue reflected from those objects. The strongest will be [given by] the luminous body; the second by the illuminated wall, the third by the shadows. There will still be a portion which will take a tint from the colour of the edges.

E. 17 a]

268.

La superfitie d'ogni corpo opaco [2]participa del colore del suo obbietto [3]Ma cõ tanta maggiore o minore [4]impressione quãto esso obietto · [5]fia più vicino o remoto o di [6]maggiore o minore potẽtia.

The surface of every opaque body is affected by the colour of the objects surrounding it. But this effect will be strong or weak in proportion as those objects are more or less remote and more or less strongly [coloured].

W. 240 f]

269.

PITTURA.

[2]La superfitie d'ogni corpo opaco participa del [3]colore del suo obbietto.

[4]Cõ tanta maggiore potẽtia si tignie la superfitie del corpo [5]opaco · del color del suo obbietto quãto li razzi [6]delle spetie di tali obbietti feriscono essi corpi [7]infra angoli più equali.

[8]E tanto più si tigne la superfitie de' corpi opachi del colore [9]del suo obietto quãto tal superfitie è più biãca e'l colore dello [10]obietto più luminoso o alluminato.

OF PAINTING.

The surface of every opaque body assumes the hues reflected from surrounding objects.

The surface of an opaque body assumes the hues of surrounding objects more strongly in proportion as the rays that form the images of those objects strike the surface at more equal angles.

And the surface of an opaque body assumes a stronger hue from the surrounding objects in proportion as that surface is whiter and the colour of the object brighter or more highly illuminated.

W. L. 145. Ba]

270.

DELLI RAZZI CHE PORTÃ PER L'ARIA LE SPETIE DE' CORPI.

¶[2]Tutte le parti minime delle spetie penetra [3]l'una l'altra sanza occupatione l'una

OF THE RAYS WHICH CONVEY THROUGH THE AIR THE IMAGES OF OBJECTS.

All the minutest parts of the image intersect each other without interfering with

cho imezo . . sia i muro. 7. cholore. 8. schuro . vederai [detto chorpo] al natura. 9. cholore . . chorpo . . cholori. 10. iluminoso . . sechondo.

268. 1 chorpooppacho. 2. del cholore del cholore del suo obbietto. 3. Ma[cqua] tanta . . ominore. *In the margin:* 4. chẽ. 5. orremoto. 6. ominore.

269. 2. oppacho. 4. magiore. 5. oppacho . . razi. 6. feriscano. 8. Ettanto. 9. biãcha. 10. aluminato.

270. 1. razi . . lesspetie de chorpi. 3. ochupatione. 4. essia . . spirachulo. 5. risseũtro. 6. losstremo. 7. la[spema nõ po . . attaie.

270. 13. This probably refers to the diagram given under No. 66.

dell'altra;¶ [4]pruovasi e sia *r* l'un de'lati dello spiracolo [5]a riscōtro del quale sia *s* ochio, il quale ve[6]de lo stremo inferiore *o* della linia *n o*, il qua[7]le stremo nō può mādare la similitudine di se a tale [8]ochio · *s* · ch'ello nō tocchi esso stremo *r*, e' l si[9]mile fa *m* mezzo d'essa linia e cosi accade allo [10]stremo superiore *n* all'ochio · *u* ·, e se lo stremo *n* [11]è rosso *u* ochio nō vedrà in tal labro di spira[12]colo *r* il colore verde di *o*, ma solo il rosso [13]di *n* per la 7ª di questo, dove dicie ogni simula[14]cro māda fori di se spetie sue per linia bre[15]vissima ¶la quale per neciessità è retta ecc.

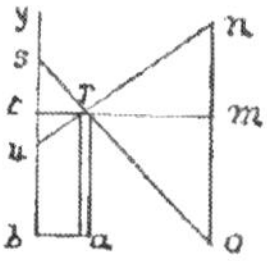

each other. To prove this let *r* be one of the sides of the hole, opposite to which let *s* be the eye which sees the lower end *o* of the line *n o*. The other extremity cannot transmit its image to the eye *s* as it has to strike the end *r* and it is the same with regard to *m* at the middle of the line. The case is the same with the upper extremity *n* and the eye *u*. And if the end *n* is red the eye *u* on that side of the holer will not see the green colour of *o*, but only the red of *n* according to the 7th of this where it is said: Every form projects images from itself by the shortest line, which necessarily is a straight line, &c.

C. A. 178 *a*; 536 *a*]

271.

Pictura.

[2]La superfitie d'ogni corpo participa del colore del suo obbietto. [3]Li colori delli obbietti alluminati s'imprimono nelle superfitie l'ū del'altro [4]in tāti vari siti quāte son le uarietà delle situationi di tali ob[5]bietti; [6]*o* è l'obbietto azzurro alluminato e vede solo sanza altra [7]conpagnia lo spatio *b c* della spera biā[8]ca *a b c d e f*, e la tignie di colore azzurro; [9]*m* è l obbietto giallo il quale allumina [10]lo spatio *a b* in cōpagnia dello *o* azzur[11]ro e lo tigne in colore verde ¶per la 2ª [12]di questo che prova lo azzurro e giallo fa[13]re verde bellissimo ecc¶ · e'l rimanēte si dirà [14]nel libro della pictura; E in questo libro si pro[15]verà faccïēdo penetrare la spetie de' corpi e co[16]lori delle cose alluminate dal sole per piccolo [17]spiracolo rotondo in loco oscuro ī pa[18]riete piana in se bianca ecc.

[19]Ma ogni cosa fia sotto sopra.

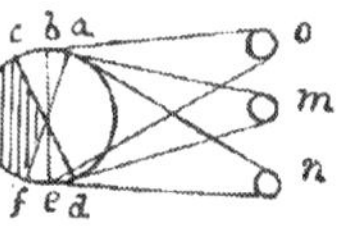

Of painting.

The surface of a body assumes in some degree the hue of those around it. The colours of illuminated objects are reflected from the surfaces of one to the other in various spots, according to the various positions of those objects. Let *o* be a blue object in full light, facing all by itself the space *b c* on the white sphere *a b c d e f*, and it will give it a blue tinge. *m* is a yellow body reflected onto the space *a b* at the same time as *o* the blue body, and they give it a green colour (by the 2nd [proposition] of this which shows that blue and yellow make a beautiful green &c.) And the rest will be set forth in the Book on Painting. In that Book it will be shown, that, by transmitting the images of objects and the colours of bodies illuminated by sunlight through a small round perforation and into a dark chamber onto a plane surface, which itself is quite white, &c.

But every thing will be upside down.

C. A. 44 *b*; 137 *b*]

272.

Quel che [2]fa l'ōbra [3]nō la ue[4]de.

[5]Perchè l'ōbre [6]son fatte [7]da lumino[8]so gignitor'e [9]circūdato[10]re del'ōbre. [11]L'onbra fatta dal luminoso *e* che è [12]giallo,

That which casts the shadow does not face it, because the shadows are produced by the light which causes and surrounds the shadows. The shadow caused by the light *e*, Combination of different colours in cast shadows.

8. chella g nō tochi . . stremo [o]r. 9. chosi achade. 10. essello. 11. errosso . . la [pr]bro. 12. cholo . . ongni.

271. 2. obbiecto. 3. obbiecti "alluminati" inpremano. 4. quāto. 5. bietta. 6. ellobbietto azurro "alluminato". 7. Losspatio bc dulla. 8. cha . . ella. 9. ellobbietto gialloiquale. 10. losspatio. 11. ello tugnie in cholore. 12. azurro egualle. 15. chorpiecho. 16. picholo. 17. spiracholo retondo ilocho osschuro. 18. biancha. 19. ōnchosa.

viene a essere [13]azzurra perchè è l'onbra del corpo [14]*a* fatta sopra il pauimēto in *b*, nel[15]la quale è veduta dal luminoso azzur[16]ro, e cosi l'onbra fatta dal lumi[17]noso *d* che è azzurro fia gialla nel [18]sito *c* per essere veduta dal lumi[19]noso giallo, e 'l canpo circudatore [20]d'esse onbre *b c* sarà (oltre al suo [21]natural colore) tinto d'un colore mi[22]sto di giallo e d'azzurro perchè è vedu[23]to e alluminato da luminoso giallo [24]e da luminoso azzurro in u medesimo [25]tenpo.

[26]Onbre di uari co[27]lori secondo i lu[28]mi da loro veduti. [29]Quel lume che fa l'öbra nö [30]la [31]uede.

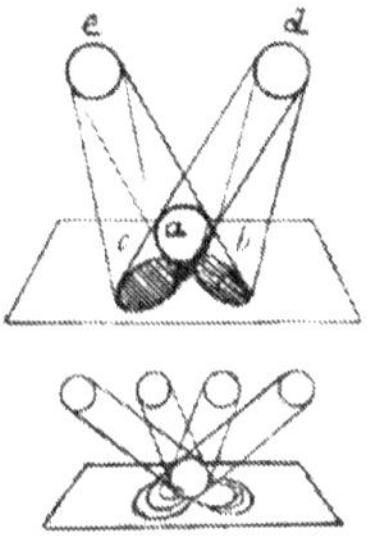

which is yellow, has a blue tinge, because the shadow of the body *a* is cast upon the pavement at *b*, where the blue light falls; and the shadow produced by the light *d*, which is blue, will be yellow at *c*, because the yellow light falls there and the surrounding background to these shadows *b c* will, besides its natural colour, assume a hue compounded of yellow and blue, because it is lighted by the yellow light and by the blue light both at once.

Shadows of various colours, as affected by the lights falling on them. That light which causes the shadow does not face it.

C. A. 187 II a; 562a]

273.

The effect of colours in the camera obscura (273. 274).

Li termini d'ogni color che [2]passa per spiracoli sö più [3]evidēti che i loro mezzi.

[4]Li termini delle spetie [5]di qualūche colore che per stretto [6]spiraculo penetrano i loco o[7]scuro fien sēpre di più potē[8]te colore che il suo mezzo.

The edges of a colour(ed object) transmitted through a small hole are more conspicuous than the central portions.

The edges of the images, of whatever colour, which are transmitted through a small aperture into a dark chamber will always be stronger than the middle portions.

W. L. 145; D.]

274.

DELLA INTERSEGATIONE DELLE SPETIE [2]NELLA POPILLA DELL'OCHIO.

[1]La intersegatione delle spetie nello introito della popilla [3]nō s'infondono l'una nell'altra in quello spatio dove tale interseg[5]tione le vniscie, e questo si manifesta perchè se li razzi [6]del sole passā per li dua vetri che sieno infra loro in cōtatto, de [7]quali uetri l'un sia azzurro e l'altro giallo, allora il razzo [8]in esso penetrato non si tignierà d'azzurro nè di giallo, ma di [9]bellissimo verde, e il medesimo accaderebbe al-l'ochio se le spe[10]tie de' colori giallo e verde nella intersegatiō da lor fatta in[11]fra se nello introito della popilla s'avessino a infondere l'una ne[12]l'altra, la qual cosa non accadendo tal mistione noñ è in essere.

OF THE INTERSECTIONS OF THE IMAGES IN THE PUPIL OF THE EYE.

The intersections of the images as they enter the pupil do not mingle in confusion in the space where that intersection unites them; as is evident, since, if the rays of the sun pass through two panes of glass in close contact, of which one is blue and the other yellow, the rays, in penetrating them, do not become blue or yellow but a beautiful green. And the same thing would happen in the eye, if the images which were yellow or green should mingle where they [meet and] intersect as they enter the pupil. As this does not happen such a mingling does not exist.

272. 6. tacta. 11. dei. 12. giallo vede lonbre viene a essere. 13. azurra. 15. del . . azur. 16. chosi. 17. azurro. 21. natural colore. 22. edazurro. 26. cho. 27. sechondo. 28. dallore. 29. Quellume chella.

273. 1. aspiracoli. 3. illoro. 5. cholore . . istretto. 6. spirachulo . . illocho os.

274. 1. interseghatione. 3. interseghatione. 4. sinfondono . . interseghu. 5. ecquessto . . selli razi [solari]. 6. passa . . inchotacto. 7. asurro ellaltro . . il raz. 8. azurro. 9. achaderebbe . . selle. 10. cholori gialli . . interseghatiō dallor. 11. frasse

272. In the original diagram we find in the circle *e* "*giallo*" (yellow) and the cirle *d* "*azurro*" (blue) and also under the circle of shadow to the left "*giallo*" is written and under that to the right "*azurro*". In the second diagram where four circles are placed in a row we find written, beginning at the left hand, "*giallo*" (yellow), "*azurro*" (blue), "*verde*" (green), "*rosso*" (red).

NATURA DELLI RAZZI CHE SI CŌPŌGONO [14]DELLE SPETIE DE' CORPI E LORO ĪTERSEGATIONE

[15]La rettitudine delli razzi che portā per l'aria la figura [16]e color de' corpi donde si partono nō tingono di se l'aria, nè ancora possono tignie[17]re l'uno l'altro nel cōtatto della loro intersecatione, ma sol tin[18]gono il loco dove eglino perdono il loro essere perchè tale loco ve[19]de ed è veduto dal'origine d'essi razzi, e nessuna altra cosa che circuisca [20]essa origine può essere veduta da loco dove tale razzo taglian[21]dosi resta destrutto, quivi lasciādo la preda da lui portata

[22]E questo si prova per la 4ª de colori de' corpi dove dicie la su[23]perfitie d'ogni corpo opaco participa del colore del suo obbi[24]etto, adūque è concluso che il loco che mediāte il razzo [25]che porta le spetie vede ed è veduto dall'origine di tale [26]spetie si tinga del colore d'esso obbietto

OF THE NATURE OF THE RAYS COMPOSED OF THE IMAGES OF OBJECTS, AND OF THEIR INTERSECTIONS

The directness of the rays which transmit the forms and colours of the bodies whence they proceed does not tinge the air nor can they affect each other by contact where they intersect. They affect only the spot where they vanish and cease to exist, because that spot faces and is faced by the original source of these rays, and no other object, which surrounds that original source can be seen by the eye where these rays are cut off and destroyed, leaving there the spoil they have conveyed to it

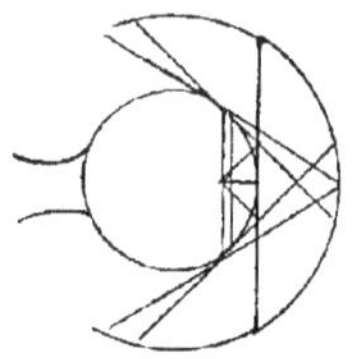

And this is proved by the 4th [proposition], on the colour of bodies, which says The surface of every opaque body is affected by the colour of surrounding objects, hence we may conclude that the spot which, by means of the rays which convey the image, faces—and is faced by the cause of the image, assumes the colour of that object

Ash I, 22a]

275

OGNI ŌBRA FATTA DAL CORPO ŌBROSO MINORE DEL LUME ORIGINALE [2]MĀDERA LE ŌBRE DIRIVATIVE TĪTE DEL COLORE DELLA LORO ORIGINE.

[3]L'origine · dell'ōbra *e f* sia *n*, e fia tīta in suo colore ‖ l'origine di *h e* sia | *o* [4]e fia similmēte tīta ī suo colore, e così il colore di *v h* fia tīto nel colore di · *p* [5]perchè nascie da lui ‖ e l'ōbra del triāgolo *z · k y* fia tīta nel colore di *q* perchè [6]diriva da lui , [7]Tanto quāto *c d* [8]entra in *a d* tanto [9]è piv scuro *n r s* [10]che *m* e tutto l'altro [11]canpo sanza ōbra, *f g* · è 'l primo grado di lume perchè quivi allumina tutta la finestra *a d* [12]e così nel corpo ōbroso *m e* è di simil chiarezza, *z k y* è vno triāgolo [13]che cōtiene in se il primo

ANY SHADOW CAST BY AN OPAQUE BODY SMALLER THAN THE LIGHT CAUSING THE SHADOW WILL THROW A DERIVED SHADOW WHICH IS TINGED BY THE COLOUR OF THE LIGHT

On the colours of derived shadows (275 276)

Let *n* be the source of the shadow *e f*, it will assume its hue Let *o* be the source of *h e* which will in the same way be tinged by its hue and so also the colour of *v h* will be affected by *p* which causes it, and the shadow of the triangle *z k y* will be affected by the colour of *q*, because it is produced by it [7] In proportion as *c d* goes into *a d*, will *n r s* be darker than *m*, and the rest of the space will be shadowless [11] *f g* is the highest light, because here the whole light of the window *a d* falls, and thus on the opaque body *m e* is in equally high light, *z k y* is a triangle which includes the

popila 12 chosa non achadendo tal [fusione] "mistione" 13 razi chessi cōpōghano 14 chorpi elloro interseghatione 15 fighura 16 e cholor de chorpi "donde si partano nō si tinghano anchora possā 17 intersechatione Massol 18 ghano il locho dove e perdano illoro locho 19 de 'ede veduto da" lorigine razi e nessussuna chosa che circhuissca 20 dallocho do tale razo 21 ressta desstrutto "quivi" lassciādo dallui 22 equesto cholori de chorpi 23 chorpo oppacho cholore 24 ecto choncluso ilocho 25 veduta 26 tingha

275 1 delume 3 sic n effia sic 4 effia nel cholore 10 ettutto 11 alumina tucta 12 chiareza f z k

275 The diagram Pl III, No 1 belongs to this chapter as well as the text given in No 148 Lines 7—11 (compare lines 8—12 of No 148) which are written within the diagram, evidently apply to both sections and have therefore been inserted in both

grado d'onbra, perchè in esso triãgolo nõ capita [14]il lume *a d*; *a h* è 'l 2° grado d'õbra perchè egli non allumina se non ⅓ [15]della finestra cioè *c d*; *h e* fia il terzo grado d'õbra perchè egli uede [16]i dua terzi della finestra *b d c f* fia l'ultimo grado d'õbra perchè [17]l'ultimo grado di lume della finestra allumina nel loco di *f*.

deepest shadow, because the light *a d* cannot reach any part of it. *a h* is the 2nd grade of shadow, because it receives only ⅓ of the light from the window, that is *c d*. The third grade of shadow is *h e*, where two thirds of the light from the window is visible. The last grade of shadow is *b d e f*, because the highest grade of light from the window falls at *f*.

W. L. 145; Ca]

276.

Delli colori dell'õbre dirivative [2]senplici.

[3]Li colori dell'õbre diriuative fie [4]senpre participanti delli colori de cor[5]pi che le rischiarano: pruovasi [6]e sia il corpo onbroso interposto [10]infra la pariete *s c t d* e li lu[11]minosi *d e* azzurro e *a b* rosso; [12]dico *d e* luminoso azzurro ve[13]de tutta la pariete *s c t d* ecciet[14]to *o p*, il quale occupa l'onbra del [15]corpo õbroso *q r*, come mostrã [16]le linie rette *d q o*, *e r p*; E il simi[17]le accade del luminoso *a b*, il quale [18]vede tutta la pariete *s c t d* ecciet[19]to il loco occupato dall' õbroso *q r* co[20]me mostrã le linie *d q o e e r p*; [21]adũque si cõclude che l'onbra *n m* [22]vede il luminoso azzurro *d e* e nõ [23]potendo vedere il luminoso *a b* rosso [24]*n m* resta vn'õbra azzurra in càpo [25]rosso misto d'azzurro, perchè in campo [26]*s c t d* vede l'uno e l'altro luminoso, [27]ma nell'õbre nõ vede se nõ vn sol lu[28]minoso e per questo tale õbra è õbra me[29]zzana, perchè se tale õbra nõ fusse veduta [30]da nessun luminoso essa sarebbe õbra [31]massima ecc.; Ma nell'onbra *o p* nõ ve[32]de il luminoso azzurro, perchè il corpo *q r* [33]colla sua interpositione

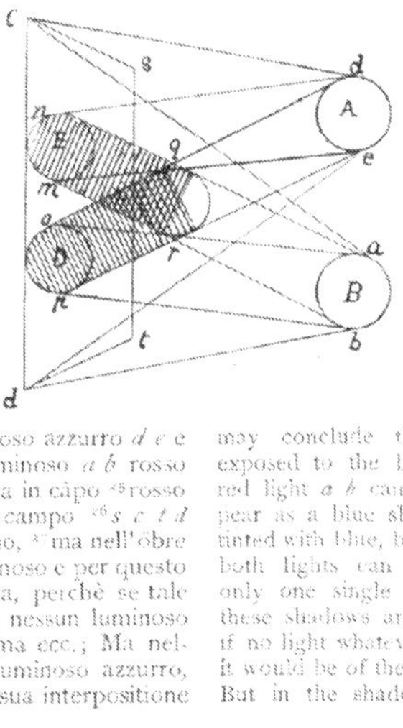

Of the colours of simple derived shadows.

The colour of derived shadows is always affected by that of the body towards which they are cast. To prove this: let an opaque body be placed between the plane *s c t d* and the blue light *d e* and the red light *a b*, then I say that *d e*, the blue light, will fall on the whole surface *s c t d* excepting at *o p* which is covered by the shadow of the body *q r*, as is shown by the straight lines *d q o e r p*. And the same occurs with the light *a b* which falls on the whole surface *s c t d* excepting at the spot obscured by the shadow *q r*; as is shown by the lines *d q o*, and *e r p*. Hence we may conclude that the shadow *n m* is exposed to the blue light *d e*; but, as the red light *a b* cannot fall there, *n m* will appear as a blue shadow on a red background tinted with blue, because on the surface *s c t d* both lights can fall. But in the shadows only one single light falls: for this reason these shadows are of medium depth, since, if no light whatever mingled with the shadow, it would be of the first degree of darkness &c. But in the shadow at *o p* the blue light

13. chõliena. 14. alume . . dõbra perchele . . alumina. 15. dela . . perchelì . . dela. 17. dela . . alumina . . locuo.
276. 1. cholori. 3. choIori. 4. cholori. 5. chelle risciarano. 6. [essia il luminoso azurro de il qual] 7. [le alumina il chanp la pariete sc.] 8. [t d cholla dilatatione a b c d d e c d]. 9. essia il chorpo . . interposto. 10. infralla . . ella. 11. azurro he . . ab. 12. dicho. 14. echapto. 15. chorpo . . chome mosstrã. 19. locho ochupato . . cho. 20. mostra . . e bec. 21. adũque si chõclude chellonbra. 22. luminoso. 24. ressta . . chãpo. 25. missto da dazurro . . charpo. 26. ellaltro. 29. settale . . fussi. 30. sarabe. 32. iluminoso. 33. ilelo. 35. figugme . . tal. 30. ressta inchãpo. 37. dazurro errosso. 38. del

276. In the original diagram Leonardo has written within the circle *q r corpo õbroso* (body in shadow); at the spot marked *A*, *luminoso azzurro* (blue luminous body); at *B*, *luminoso rosso* (red luminous body). At *E* we read *ombra azzurra* (blue tinted shadow) and at *D ombra rossa* (red tinted shadow).

ghelo proibi[34]scie, Ma sol ui vede il lume rosso *a b* il [35]quale lo tignie di color rosso e così ta[36]le ōbra rosseggiāte resta incāpo mi[37]sta d'azzurro e rosso

[38]L'onbra del *q r* in *o p* [39]mediante il luminoso azzurro *d e* [40]è rossa e l'ōbra d'esso *q r* mediā[41]te il rosso luminoso *a b* è azzurra [42]in *ō p̄*, adunque diremo che [43]il lume azzurro fa in questo caso [44]fare l'onbra dirivativa rossa al cor[45]po onbroso *q̄ r̄* e che'l lume rosso [46]fa fare al medesimo ōbroso l'ōbra [47]dirivativa azzurra, ma l'onbra [48]primitiva nō fia d'esso colore ma [49]fia mista di rosso e azzurro

[50]Le ōbre dirivative sarā d'equal [51]oscurità se le nascono da [52]lumi d'equale potētia e distā[53]tia, pruova

does not fall, because the body *q r* interposes and intercepts it there Only the red light *a b* falls there and tinges the shadow of a red hue and so a ruddy shadow appears on the background of mingled red and blue

The shadow of *q r* at *o p* is red, being caused by the blue light *d e*, and the shadow of *q r* at *o' p'* is blue being caused by the red light *a b* Hence we say that the blue light in this instance causes a red derived shadow from the opaque body *q' r'*, while the red light causes the same body to cast a blue derived shadow, but the primary shadow [on the dark side of the body itself] is not of either of those hues, but a mixture of red and blue

The derived shadows will be equal in depth if they are produced by lights of equal strength and at an equal distance, this is proved [53]

F 23 a]

277

Nessū bianco o nero [2]è trāsparēte

No white or black is transparent

On the nature of colours (277 278)

F 75 a]

278

Pictura

[2]Perchè il bianco non è colore, ma è inpotentia ricettiva [3]d'ogni colore, quando esso è in cāpagna alta tutte le su[4]e ōbre sono azzurre, e questo nasce per la 4ª che [5]dice la superfitie d'ogni opaco participa del colo[6]re del suo obbietto, Adūque tal bianco essendo pri[7]vato del lume del sole per interpositiō di qualche obbietto [8]infra messo infra'l sole e esso biāco, resta adunque [9]tutto il biāco che vede il sole e l'aria participante [10]del colore del sole e dell'aria, e quella parte che non ue[11]de il sole, resta onbrosa participante del colore dell'aria, e se [12]tal biāco non vedesse la verdura della cāpagnia i[13]sino all'orizzonte, nè ancora vedesse la biāchezza di tale [14]orizzōte, sanza dubbio esso biāco parrebbe essere [15]del semplice colore del quale si mostra essere l'aria

Of painting

[2] Since white is not a colour but the neutral recipient of every colour [3], when it is seen in the open air and high up, all its shadows are bluish, and this is caused, according to the 4th [prop], which says the surface of every opaque body assumes the hue of the surrounding objects Now this white [body] being deprived of the light of the sun by the interposition of some body between the sun and itself, all that portion of it which is exposed to the sun and atmosphere assumes the colour of the sun and atmosphere, the side on which the sun does not fall remains in shadow and assumes the hue of the atmosphere And if this white object did not reflect the green of the fields all the way to the horizon nor get the brightness of the horizon itself, it would certainly appear simply of the same hue as the atmosphere

[dea]qr[m]in 40 errosso ellōbra 42 direno 43 llume inquessto chaso 44 lonbra [azzu] "dirivativa ' rossa al chor 48 cholore 49 missta 51 osschurita selle nasschano 52 eddisstā
277 2 he
278 4 azzurro ecquessto nassce 5 oppaco 6 biancho 7 interpositiode 8 biācho 9 ellaria 10 ecquella parte che ue 11 resta "onbrosa dellaria esse 12 biācho vedessi 13 orizonte neacora vedesse biācheza 14 orizōte biācho parebbe

53 The text is unfinished in the original

278 2 3 *il bianco non è colore ma e inpotentia ricettiva d'ogni colore* (white is not a colour, but the neutral recipient of every colour) Leon Batt Alberti "*Della pittura*" libro I, asserts on the contrary "*Il bianco e 'l nero non sono veri colori, ma sono alteratione delli altri colori*" (ed Janitschek, p 67, Vienna 1877)

279.

C. A. 102b; 371b]

On gradations in the depth of colours (279. 280).

Perchè il nero dipinto in cõfine del biãco [2]nõ mostra piv nero che dove confina col [3]nero, nè il biacho nõ mostra più biã[4]co in cõfine del nero che del biãco, co[5]me fan le spetie passate per ispiraculo [6]o per termine d'alcuno ostaculo opaco . . .

Since black, when painted next to white, looks no blacker than when next to black; and white when next to black looks no whiter than white, as is seen by the images transmitted through a small hole or by the edges of any opaque screen. . .

280.

C. A. 181b; 536b]

De colori.

[2]De colori d'equal bianchezza quel si mostrerà [3]più candido che sarà in campo più oscuro; [4]E 'l nero si mostrerà più tenebroso che fia in cã[5]po di maggior bianchezza.

[6]E'l rosso si dimostrerà più focoso che sarà [7]in căpo più giallo, e così farã tutti li colori cir[8]cundati da loro retti · contrari colori.

Of colours.

Of several colours, all equally white, that will look whitest which is against the darkest background. And black will look intensest against the whitest background.

And red will look most vivid against the yellowest background; and the same is the case with all colours when surrounded by their strongest contrasts.

281.

A. 19b]

On the reflection of colours (281—283).

Prospettiva.

[2]Ogni corpo · sanza colore · si colorisce tutto · o in parte · in nel colore cõtra se [3]posto; [4]questo · si uede per isperiēza · impero · chè ogni · corpo · che spechia · si tignie nel co[5]lore che gli è per obbietto; E quel corpo che si tignie in parte · si è il bianco, e quella [6]parte che fia luminata da rosso parrà rossa ed ogni altro colore luminoso o õbroso.

Perspective.

Every object devoid of colour in itself is more or less tinged by the colour [of the object] placed opposite. This may be seen by experience, inasmuch as any object which mirrors another assumes the colour of the object mirrored in it. And if the surface thus partially coloured is white the portion which has a red reflection will appear red, or any other colour, whether bright or dark.

Prospettiva.

[8]Ogni · corpo · opaco · sanza · colore partícipa · di quel colore ch'egli à · per obietto; [9]questo · accade a uno mvro biãco.

Perspective.

Every opaque and colourless body assumes the hue of the colour reflected on it; as happens with a white wall.

279. 1. biacho. 3. cho . . biãcho. 5. pasate. 6. ostachulo oppacho.

280. 2. bianchezza cholori . . mosstera. 3. chandido . . chanpopiu osschuro. 4. mosstera . . chetfia. 5. magior. 6. dimosstera . . fochoso. 7. chosi . . cholori. 8. chundati . . cholori.

281. 1. pro. 2. cholore . . colorisscie . . inel cholore chõtra. 4. [ogni] questo . si . . chorpo chesspechia . . nel cho. 5. chorpo chessi . . biancho checquela. 6. para. 7. pro. 8. chorpo oppacho . . cholore . . cholore chelli. 9. questo achade a 1 muro biãcho.

281. 282. The title line of these chapters is in the original simply "*pro*", which may be an abbreviation for either *Propositione* or *Prospettiva*—taking Prospettiva of course in its widest sense, as we often find it used in Leonardo's writings. The title "*pro*" has here been understood to mean *Prospettiva*, in accordance with the suggestion afforded by page 10b of this same MS., where the first section is headed *Prospettiva* in full (see No. 94), while the four following sections are headed merely "*pro*" (see No. 85).

A. 20 *a*]

282.

PROSPETTIVA.

[2]Quella · parte del corpo · ōbroso · che fia · alluminata · mãderà · all' ochio la similitudine delle [3]sue particule · piv · disciernibili · e spedite · che quella che si troverà nell' onbra.

PERSPECTIVE.

That side of an object in light and shade which is towards the light transmits the images of its details more distinctly and immediately to the eye than the side which is in shadow.

PROSPETTIVA.

[5]I razzi · solari ripercossi · sopra · lo spechio · quadro · risalterãno nel distãte obbietto di rotõda forma.

PERSPECTIVE.

The solar rays reflected on a square mirror will be thrown back to distant objects in a circular form.

PROSPETTIVA.

[7]Ogni corpo biãco e opaco · si tignie in parte della similitudine de colori che li sono per obbietto.

PERSPECTIVE.

Any white and opaque surface will be partially coloured by reflections from surrounding objects.

Ash. I. 3 *a*]

283.

QUAL PARTE DEL COLORE [2]RAGIONEVOLMÊTE DEVE ESSERE [3]PIÙ BELLA.

[4]Se · *a* · fia · il lume · *b* fia · alluminato · per linia · da esso lume, [5]*c* che nō può vedere esso lume ·, vede solo · la parte alluminata [6]la quale parte diciamo che sia rossa ·; Essendo così il lume ch'ella [7]gitterà alla parte somiglierà alla sua cagione e tignierà ĩ rosso [8]la faccia · *c* · e se · *c* fia ancora · lui rosso · vedrai essere molto [9]piv bello · che · *b* · e se · c · fusse giallo · vedrai lì crearsi · uno · colo[10]re cãgiãte ĵfra · giallo · e rosso.

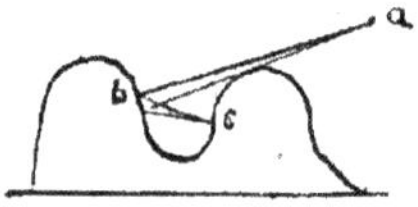

WHAT PORTION OF A COLOURED SURFACE OUGHT IN REASON TO BE THE MOST INTENSE.

If *a* is the light, and *b* illuminated by it in a direct line, *c*, on which the light cannot fall, is lighted only by reflection from *b* which, let us say, is red. Hence the light reflected from it, will be affected by the hue of the surface causing it and will tinge the surface *c* with red. And if *c* is also red you will see it much more intense than *b*; and if it were yellow you would see there a colour between yellow and red.

Ash. I. 2 *b*]

284.

COME IL BELLO DEL COLORE [2]DEVE ESSERE JN SU LUMI.

[3]Se noi · vediamo · la qualità · de' colori · essere · conoscivta · mediãte [3]il lume · è da giudicare · che dov'è · piv lume · quivi si vegga piv la vera [4]qualità · del colore · alluminato ·, e dov'è · più tenebre il colore tignersi [5]nel colore d'esse tenebre, · adũque · tu · pittore ricordãti · dimostrare [5]la verità de' colori ĩ su le · parti · alluminate.

WHY BEAUTIFUL COLOURS MUST BE IN THE [HIGHEST] LIGHT.

Since we see that the quality of colour is known [only] by means of light, it is to be supposed that where there is most light the true character of a colour in light will be best seen; and where there is most shadow the colour will be affected by the tone of that. Hence, O Painter! remember to show the true quality of colours in bright lights. On the use of dark and light colours in painting (284—286).

282. 1. pro. 2. chorpo . . cheffia. 3. partichule . piv . [spe] . . esspedite . . chessi. 4. pro. 5. razi . . riperchossi . . losspechio . . retõda. 6. pro. 7. chorpo biãcho e opacho . . cholori.

283. 1. cholore. 2. deessere. 3. belle. 4. ilume. 6. chessia. 7. gitera . . sumigliera . . ettigniera. 8. esse . c fiachora . . vederai. 9. esse . e . fussi gialo vedra . . crearsi . ĩ . cholo. 10. re chãgiãte.

284. 2. deessere. 4. giudichare . . vega. 6. richordati. 7. cholori . . parte.

Ash. I. 9a]

285.

Quella · cosa · che fia · dipinta di biāco . [2]cō nero · apparirà di migliore rilievo · [3]che alcun'altra ·, e però ricordo a te · pictore · che vesti le tue figure di colori piu chiari · che puoi che se le farai di colore oscuro sieno di poco rilievo e [5]di poca evidētia da lōtano — e quest'è per l'onbre di tutte le cose che sono · scure ; [6]e se farai una vesta scura poco ci vario · fia da lumi · al'obre e ne colori chiari vi fia grāde vario.

An object represented in white and black will display stronger relief than in any other way; hence I would remind you O Painter! to dress your figures in the lightest colours you can, since, if you put them in dark colours, they will be in too slight relief and inconspicuous from a distance. And the reason is that the shadows of all objects are dark. And if you make a dress dark there is little variety in the lights and shadows, while in light colours there are many grades.

E. 18a]

286.

Pictura.

[2]Li colori posti nelle onbre parteciperā[3]no tanto più o meno della lor natural [4]bellezza quanto essi sarāno in minore o in maggio[5]re oscurità.

[6]Ma se li colori sarā situati in [7]spatio luminoso, allora essi si mostrerā di [8]tanto maggiore bellezza quanto il luminoso fia [9]di maggiore splēdore.

Aversario.

[11]Tante sono le varietà de' colori delle ōbre quāto sono [12]le uarietà de' colori che ànno le cose aōbrate.

Risposta.

[14]Li colori posti nell'onbre mostrerāno [15]infra loro tanta minor varietà, quato l'ō[16]bre che vi son situate fieno più oscure, [17]e di questo è testimonio quelli che dalle pi[18]azze riguardano dentro alle porte delli tē[19]pi onbrosi, doue le pitture vestite di [20]vari colori appariscono tutte uesti[21]te di tenebre.

[22]Adunque in lunga distantia tutte l'ō[23]bre delli vari colori appariscono d'una [24]medesima oscurità.

[25]Delli corpi vestiti d'ōbra e lume la parte [26]luminata mostra il suo vero colore.

Of painting.

Colours seen in shadow will display more or less of their natural brilliancy in proportion as they are in fainter or deeper shadow.

But if these same colours are situated in a well-lighted place, they will appear brighter in proportion as the light is more brilliant.

The adversary.

The variety of colours in shadow must be as great as that of the colours in the objects in that shadow.

The answer.

Colours seen in shadow will display less variety in proportion as the shadows in which they lie are deeper. And evidence of this is to be had by looking from an open space into the doorways of dark and shadowy churches, where the pictures which are painted in various colours all look of uniform darkness.

Hence at a considerable distance all the shadows of different colours will appear of the same darkness.

It is the light side of an object in light and shade which shows the true colour.

W. An. IV. 232a]

287.

On the colours of the rainbow (287. 288).

Fa l'arco cieleste nell'ultimo libro della pictura ma fa [2]prima il libro delli colori nati dalla mistiō nelli altri colori, [3]acciò che tu possa provare mediante essi colori de' pictori [4]la gieneratiō de' colori del'arco.

Treat of the rainbow in the last book on Painting, but first write the book on colours produced by the mixture of other colours, so as to be able to prove by those painters' colours how the colours of the rainbow are produced.

285. 1. quela chossa chefia . . biāche. 2. aparira. 3. dchunaltra . . richordo atte . . cholori 4. chesse . . cholore osschuro . . pocho. 5. pocha . . ecquesto . . chose sono . scure. 6. esse fara ī vesta . . pocho . . gradi.

286. 2. cholori possti. 4. belleza . . [illegible] o in maggi[illegible]. 5. osschurita. 6. Masselli [medesimi] cholori. 7. mosstrerā. 8. magiore . . lluminoso. 9. maggiore [chiarezza] splēdore. 11. cholori. 12. cholori che ā lechose. 14. cholori . . mosterrāno. 15. infralloro . . 16. eve son . . osschure. 17. ettestumonio. Queli che delle. 18. dellte. 20. cholori aparisschō. 22. lungha disstantia. 23. cholori aparisschano. 24. osschurita. 25. chorpi . . ellume. 26. cholore.

287. 1. fallarcho . . mafa. 2. cholori nati della . . cholori. 3. acio chettu . . 4. cholori delarcho

W. L. 145; A *b*.]

288.

SE LI COLORI DELL'ARCO NASCONO DAL SOLE.

[2]Li colori dell'arco nō nascō [dal sole, perchè ī molti modi si gienerā [3]tali colori sanza sole come accade nell'accostare al-l'ochio il bicchiere dell'acqua, [4]nel uetro del quale siā le minute vesciche che esser sogliono nelli vetri mal pur[5]gati; le quali vesciche, ancora-chè nō si veda il sole, gienerā da vno de' sua [6]lati tutti li colori dell'arco, e questo vedrai nel metter tale bicchiere in[7]fra l'aria e l'ochio tuo in modo che sia in cōtatto con esso ochio e che tale bi-[8]cchiere abbia vna parte per la qual penetri el lume dell'aria e dall'altra l'ō[9]bra della pariete laterale di tal finestra destra o si-nistra, che nō fa ca[10]so qual lato si sia, e cosi voltando tal bicchiere intorno vedrai li detti [11]colori intorno a esse vesciche del uetro ecc., e li altri modi diremo a suo [12]loco.

WHETHER THE COLOURS OF THE RAINBOW ARE PRODUCED BY THE SUN.

The colours of the rainbow are not produced by the sun, for they occur in many ways without the sunshine; as may be seen by holding a glass of water up to the eye; when, in the glass—where there are those minute bubbles always seen in coarse glass—each bubble, even though the sun does not fall on it, will produce on one side all the colours of the rainbow; as you may see by placing the glass between the day light and your eye in such a way as that it is close to the eye, while on one side the glass admits the [diffused] light of the atmosphere, and on the other side the shadow of the wall on one side of the window; either left or right, it matters not which. Then, by turning the glass round you will see these colours all round the bubbles in the glass &c. And the rest shall be said in its place.

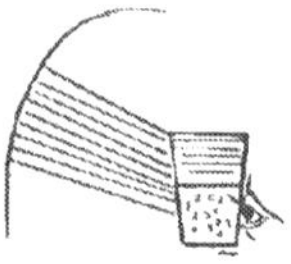

COME L'OCHIO NON À PARTICIPATIONE [14]ALLA GIENERATIŌ DE' COLORI DELL'ARCO.

[15]L'ochio nella sopra detta esperiētia pare auer participatione al[16]li colori dell'arco perchè esse vesciche del uetro nō mostrā da se tali [17]colori se non me-diante l'aspetto dell'ochio; Ma se tu poni tal bicchi[18]ere pieno d'acqua sul piano della finestra in modo che dall'opposita par[19]te lo fe-rischino li razzi solari, allora tu vedrai li predetti colori gie-[20]nerarsi nella inpressiō fatta dalli razzi solari penetrati per esso bi[21]cchiere e terminati so-pra il pavimēto in loco oscuro a piedi d'essa finestra, e per-chè [22]qui nō s'adopera l'ochio, possiā cō ciertezza mani-festamēte dire tali co[23]lori non avere parte alcuna dall'ochio.

THAT THE EYE HAS NO PART IN PRODUCING THE COLOURS OF THE RAINBOW.

In the experiment just described, the eye would seem to have some share in the colours of the rainbow, since these bubbles in the glass do not display the colours except through the medium of the eye. But, if you place the glass full of water on the window sill, in such a position as that the outer side is exposed to the sun's rays, you will see the same colours produced in the spot of light thrown through the glass and upon the floor, in a dark place, below the window; and as the eye is not here concerned in it, we may evidently, and with certainty pronounce that the eye has no share in producing them.

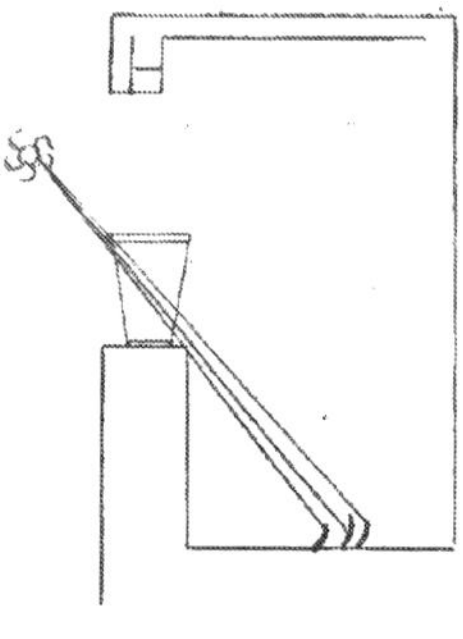

288. 1. selli . . archo nasschā. 2. cholori dellarcho nōnasschā. 3. cholori san"za sole" chome achade nell'achostare . . bichieri . . acqu"a". 4. sia . vessciche . esser sole nelli. 5. ghati . . vesciche anchora . vadesua. 6. cholori dell'archo acquesto vedera . . bichieri. 7. fralaria ellochio . . chessia in chōtatto a esso. 8. chieri . . peritri. 9. lateral . . finesstra desstra ossinistre . . cha. 10. chosi . . bichieri . . vederai. 11. cholori . vessciche . . [elli altri modi direno assuo]. 12. locho. 13. chome. 14. cholori . . archo. 15. essperiētia. 16. cholori . . archo . . vessciche . . mosstrā dasse. 17. cholori sennō . . lasspecto . . Massettu . . bichi. 18. eri . . dacq"a" . . finesstra. 19. ferisschino . . cholorigi. 20. facta . . penetrata. 21. chieri etterminata . . "in locho osscuro" . . finesstra. 22. ciertexa cho. 23. alchuna. 24. dalchuno. 26. quali si. 27. cholori.

Delli colori posti nelle peñe d'alcuno [25]vccello.

[26]Molti sono li veccelli nelle varie regiō del modo, nelle penne de' quali [27]si vede bellissimi colori gienerarsi nelli lor diuersi movimēti, [28]come far si vede infra noi alle penne delli pagoni o nelli colli del[29]l'anitre o delle colonbe ecc.

[30]Ancora nelle superfitie delli antichi vetri trovati sotto terra e in ne[31]le radici de' ravanelli stati lūgo tēpo ne' fondi delle fonti o altre ac[32]que inmobili, che ciascuna di tal radici è circūdata da tali archi si[33]mili al cieleste; vedesi nell'ūtuosità sparsa sopra l'acqua, ancora [34]nelli razzi solari reflessi dalla superfitie del diamāte o berillo, a[35]cora nell'angolo fatto dal berillo ogni cosa oscura la [36]qual termini coll'aria o altra cosa chiara è circhūdata da [37]tale arco interposto infra l'aria e detta cosa oscura, e cosi mol[38]ti altri modi li quali lascio perchè questi sō bastāti a tal discorso.

Of the colours in the feathers of certain birds.

There are many birds in various regions of the world on whose feathers we see the most splendid colours produced as they move, as we see in our own country in the feathers of peacocks or on the necks of ducks or pigeons, &c.

Again, on the surface of antique glass found underground and on the roots of turnips kept for some time at the bottom of wells or other stagnant waters [we see] that each root displays colours similar to those of the real rainbow. They may also be seen when oil has been placed on the top of water and in the solar rays reflected from the surface of a diamond or beryl; again, through the angular facet of a beryl every dark object against a background of the atmosphere or any thing else equally pale-coloured is surrounded by these rainbow colours between the atmosphere and the dark body; and in many other circumstances which I will not mention, as these suffice for my purpose.

28. paghoni. 29. oddelle cholonbe. 31. lūghe . . fondi delle fonte . . altra. 32. eque . . ciascuna . . cecirchūdata dattali. 33. cielesste . . ūduosita . . anchora. 34. reflessi . . ollberillo. 35. chora . . anghelo . . chosa osscura. 36. qual [chanpegi] termini chollaria . . chosa . . ecirchūdata. 37. archo . . infradiaria eddetta . . osschura ecchosi. 38. lasscio . . basstā attal disscorso.

VI.

'Prospettiva de' colori' (Perspective of Colour)

and

'Prospettiva aerea' (Aerial Perspective).

Leonardo distinctly separates these branches of his subject, as may be seen in the beginning of No. 295. Attempts have been made to cast doubts on the results which Leonardo arrived at by experiment on the perspective of colour, but not with justice, as may be seen from the original text of section 294.

The question as to the composition of the atmosphere, which is inseparable from a discussion on Aerial Perspective, forms a separate theory which is treated at considerable length. Indeed the author enters into it so fully that we cannot escape the conviction that he must have dwelt with particular pleasure on this part of his subject, and that he attached great importance to giving it a character of general applicability.

C. 12 b]

289.

La uarietà · de' colori de' corpi · nõ fia in lunga · distantia · conosciuta · se nõ in quelle · parti · che dai soli razzi percosse fieno.

The variety of colour in objects cannot be discerned at a great distance, excepting in those parts which are directly lighted up by the solar rays.

General rules (289—291).

C. 13 a]

290.

Infra i colori · de' corpi nõ fia · differentia · in lunga · distantia · nelle · loro · parti onbrose.

As to the colours of objects: at long distances no difference is perceptible in the parts in shadow.

Ash. I. 17 b]

291.

DELLA EVIDÊTIA DE' COLORI.

[2] Quale colore è piv evidête? quella cosa ch'è piv chiara piv appariscie [3] di lontano; e la · piv scura fa il cõtrario.

OF THE VISIBILITY OF COLOURS.

Which colour strikes most? An object at a distance is most conspicuous, when it is lightest, and the darkest is least visible.

W. 232 b]

292.

Delli termini dell'õbre; alcu[2]ni sõ fumosi d'insẽsibile termine, altri [3] di termini noti.

[4] Nessu corpo opaco è sanza õbra o lumi se [5] non è nella nebbia, sopra terra coperta di neve, e el [6] simile fa quãdo fiocca in canpagnia essa fia [7] sanza lume e sarà circũdata dalle tenebre.

Of the edges [outlines] of shadows. Some have misty and ill defined edges, others distinct ones.

No opaque body can be devoid of light and shade, except it is in a mist, on ground covered with snow, or when snow is falling on the open country which has no light on it and is surrounded with darkness.

An exceptional case.

289. 1. cholori de chorpi . . illunga . . nõ "in" quele . [lor] parti che [fieno] dai sola razi perchosse.
290. 1. choluri de chorpi . diferentia . llunga.
291. 1. della . . cholori. 2. cholore . . chosa . . aparisscie. 3. lontano [allo] ella pivschura . . chõtrario.
292. 2. õbre [in che alchu]. 2. nisõ. 4. nessũ chorpo oppacho . . ollumi. 5. nelanebia. 6. fiocha in chanpagniaessa. 7. circhũdata. 8. ecquesto achade neli.

E questo accade ne' corpi sperici, perchè nelli al[9]tri corpi, che ànno mēbrificatione, le parti [10]delle mēbra riguardatrici l'una del-l'altra tingo[11]no l'una l'altra dell'accidēte della sua superfitie.

And this occurs [only] in spherical bodies, because in other bodies which have limbs and parts, those sides of limbs which face each other reflect on each other the accidental [hue and tone] of their surface.

Ash I 25 b]

293

TUTTI I · COLORI NELLE LONTANE · ŌBRE SONO IGNIORATI E INDISCERNIBILI.

An experiment

[2]Tutti · i colori · in lontano · fieno · nel-l'ōbre · igniorati; perchè la cosa; che non è tocca dal principale [3]lume, non è potēte · a mandare · di se · all'occhio per l'aria piv · luminosa · la sua similitudine, perchè il minore [4]lume · è vīnto · dal maggiore, Esenplo: · Noi · vediamo · essendo in vna · casa · che tutti [5]i colori · i quali sono nelle · pareti delle · mvra · si ueggono chiaro e speditamēte, · quādo le finestre [6]di detta abitatione · fieno · aperte, e se noi · usciremo · fori · d'essa casa · e riguardaremo vn poco di [7]lontano · per dette · finestre · di rivedere · le pitture · fatte sù dette mura · in iscambio d'esse picture [8]vedremo · vna cōtinvata · oscurità

ALL COLOURS ARE AT A DISTANCE UNDISTINGUISHABLE AND UNDISCERNIBLE.

All colours at a distance are undistinguishable in shadow, because an object which is not in the highest light is incapable of transmitting its image to the eye through an atmosphere more luminous than itself; since the lesser brightness must be absorbed by the greater. For instance · We, in a house, can see that all the colours on the surface of the walls are clearly and instantly visible when the windows of the house are open; but if we were to go out of the house and look in at the windows from a little distance to see the paintings on those walls, instead of the paintings we should see an uniform deep and colourless shadow.

Ash I 13 a]

294.

COME IL PITTORE DEBE METTERE [2]IN PRATICA LA PROSPETTIVA DE' COLORI

The practice of the prospettiva de' colori

[3]A volere · mettere questa · prospettiva del uariare e perdere over diminvire la [4]propia · essētia de' colori · piglerai di ciēto ī ciento braccia cose poste īfra [5]la cāpagnia come sono · albori case, omini e siti, e ī quāto al [6]primo albore avrai uno uetro fermo bene e così sia fermo l'ochio tuo, e ī detto [7]vetro disegnerai uno albero sopra

HOW A PAINTER SHOULD CARRY OUT THE PERSPECTIVE OF COLOUR IN PRACTICE.

In order to put into practice this perspective of the variation and loss or diminution of the essential character of colours, observe at every hundred braccia some objects standing in the landscape, such as trees, houses, men and particular places. Then in front of the first tree have a very steady plate of glass and keep your eye very steady, and then, on this plate of glass, draw a tree, tracing it over the form of that tree Then move it on one

chorpi 9 mēbrifichatione parte 10 riguardatricie tingha 11 nolluna
293 1 cholori . indisscierinibili 2 cholorinllontano nell ōbre chosa tocha 3 sua [forma] similitudine 4 essendo nvna chasa chetutti 5 icholori uegono esspeditamēte 6 essenō usciremo . chasa e riguardareno vn poche di 7 ischanbio 8 vederemo chōtinvata oschurita
294 2 praticha. 4 cholori . . ciento br chose 5 omini [e pianv] essiti 6 arai ī uetro 7 vetro [colorisai ī albero p] di-

294. This chapter is one of those copied in the Manuscript of the Vatican library Urbinas 1270, and the original text is rendered here with no other alterations, but in the orthography. H. LUDWIG, in his edition of this copy translates lines 14 and 15 thus. "*Ich finde aber als Regel, dass der zweite um vier Fünftel des ersten abnimmt, wenn er nämlich zwanzig Ellen vom ersten entfernt ist* (?)". He adds in his commentary. "*Das Ende der Nummer ist wohl jedenfalls verstümmelt*" However the translation given above shows that it admits of a different rendering.

la forma di quello, di poi [8]scosta tàto per traverso che l'albero naturale · cõfini quasi col tuo disegnia[9]to; poi colorisci il tuo · disegnio in modo che per colore e forma stia a paragone [10] l'uno dell'altro e che tutti e 2, chivdẽdo uno ochio, paino dipĩti sul detto vetro d'una [11]medesima distãtia; e questa regola medesima fa degli alberi secõdi [12]e de' terzi di ciẽto ĩ ciẽto braccia di mano ĩ mano; e questi ti servã · come tua auto[13]ri e maestri, sẽpre operãdo nelle tua opere doue s'appartẽgono, e faranno [14]bene fuggir l'opera; ma io trovo per regola · che'l secõdo diminviscie $^4/_5$ del primo [15]quãdo fusse lõtano 20 · braccia dal primo.

side so far as that the real tree is close by the side of the tree you have drawn; then colour your drawing in such a way as that in colour and form the two may be alike, and that both, if you close one eye, seem to be painted on the glass and at the same distance. Then, by the same method, represent a second tree, and a third, with a distance of a hundred braccia between each. And these will serve as a standard and guide whenever you work on your own pictures, wherever they may apply, and will enable you to give due distance in those works. [14] But I have found that as a rule the second is $^4/_5$ of the first when it is 20 braccia beyond it.

Ash. I. 10a]

295.

Della prospettiva aerea.

[2]E ci una altra · prospectiva · la quale chiamo aerea, ĩperochè per la uarietà [3]dell'aria · si può conosciere le diverse distãtie [4]di uari edifiti, terminati ne' lor nascimẽti da una sola linia, come sa[5]rebbe il uedere molti edifiti di là da uno muro, che tutti apparischino sopra [6]alla stremità di detto mvro d'una medesima grãdezza, e tu vo[7]lessi in pittura · fare parere piv lontano l'uno che l'altro e da figura[8]re una aria vn poco grossa; Tu sai che ĩ simili arie l'ultime cose viste [9]ĩ quella, come sono le mõtagnie · per la grã quãtità dell'aria · che si truova infra l'ochio [10] tuo · e la mõtagnia · quella pare azzurra quasi del colore dell'aria quãdo il sole [11]è per leuãte; Adũque farai sopra · detto mvro il primo edificio del suo colore, [12]il · piv lõtano fa lo meno profilato e piv azzurro; quello · che tu vuo che sia piv [13]in là · altrettãto ·, fa lo · altrettãto · piv · azzuro: quello che voi che sia cĩque volte [14]piv lõtano ·, fallo · 5 volte più azzuro; e questa regola farà che li edifiti [15]che sopra una linia paiono d'una · medesima grãdezza, ·chiaramẽte si conoscierà [16]qual è piv distãte e quale è maggiore che li altri.

Of aerial perspective.

The rules of aerial perspective (295—297).

There is another kind of perspective which I call Aerial Perspective, because by the atmosphere we are able to distinguish the variations in distance of different buildings, which appear placed on a single line; as, for instance, when we see several buildings beyond a wall, all of which, as they appear above the top of the wall, look of the same size, while you wish to represent them in a picture as more remote one than another and to give the effect of a somewhat dense atmosphere. You know that in an atmosphere of equal density the remotest objects seen through it, as mountains, in consequence of the great quantity of atmosphere between your eye and them—appear blue and almost of the same hue as the atmosphere itself [10] when the sun is in the East [11]. Hence you must make the nearest building above the wall of its real colour, but the more distant ones make less defined and bluer. Those you wish should look farthest away you must make proportionately bluer; thus, if one is to be five times as distant, make it five times bluer. And by this rule the buildings which above a [given] line appear of the same size, will plainly be distinguished as to which are the more remote and which larger than the others.

segnia ĩ albero. 8. chol. 9. Colorisci tuo . . imodo . . cholore efforma. 10. chivdẽdo ĩ ochio . . di piti si detto vetro luna. 11. ecquesta . . dela 12. ciento br . . ecquesti . . serbã . . tua alto. 13. sapartẽgano effarano.

295. 2. Ecci ĩ altra. 3. conosciere [la distãtia di] le diuersa. 4. da ĩ sola. 5. rebe . . da ĩ muro chettutti apariscino. 6. alla [distãti] stremita . . grãdeza echettu. 8. re ĩ aria vn pocho . . Tussai che ĩsimile . . chose. 9. ĩ quella *these two words written beyond the margin have apparently later been added by Leonardo* . . chessi. 10. ella . . azurra . . cholore. 12. priffilato . . azurro . . chettu voi chessia. 13. fallo . . azzuro . . voi chessia. 14. azuro . . ecquesta. 15. sopra ĩ linia paiano . . grãdeza . . chonosciera. 16. ecquale.

295. 10. 11. *quãdo il sole è per leuante* (when the sun is in the East). Apparently the author refers here to morning light in general. H. LUDWIG however translates this passage from the Vatican copy *"wenn nämlich die Sonne* (dahinter) *im Osten steht"*.

Tr. 75]

296.

Il mezzo ch'è infra l'ochio e la cosa vista · trasmuta essa [2] cosa · in nel suo · colore, come l'aria azzura fa che le lõtane [3] motagnie paiono azzure; il uetro rosso fa che ciò che l'ochio [4] vede dopo · lui · pare · rosso: jl lume che fanno le stelle [5] d'intorno ase · è occupato per la tenebrosità della notte che si [6] truova infra l'ochio · e la luminatione d'essa stella.

The medium lying between the eye and the object seen, tinges that object with its colour, as the blueness of the atmosphere makes the distant mountains appear blue and red glass makes objects seen beyond it, look red. The light shed round them by the stars is obscured by the darkness of the night which lies between the eye and the radiant light of the stars.

W. 3]

297.

Fa che la prospettiua de' [2] colori non si discordi [3] dalle grandezze di qualu[4]che cosa cioè che li [5] colori diminuischino [6] tanto della lor natu[7]ra quãto diminuisco[8]no li corpi in diuerse [9] distantie della loro [10] naturale quãtità.

Take care that the perspective of colour does not disagree with the size of your objects, hat is to say: that the colours diminish from their natural [vividness] in proportion as the objects at various distances diminish from their natural size.

Ash. I. 17a]

298.

Come l'aria si debe piv fare [2] chiara quãto piv la fai finire bassa.

On the relative density of the atmosphere (298—299).

[3] Perchè quest' aria è grossa presso alla terra · e quãto piv si leua piv [4] s'assottiglia; quãdo · il sole · è per leuãte, e tu riguarderai il ponẽte [5] participãte di mezzodì e tramõtana, vedrai quel'aria grossa [6] ricievere piv lume dal sole che la sottile, perchè i razzi trovano più resistẽtia; [7] e se il cielo a la vista tua terminerà colla bassa pianvra, quella [8] parte vltima del cielo · fia veduta per quella aria · piv grossa e piv [9] bianca, la quale · corromperà la verità del colore che si vedrà [10] pel suo · mezzo, e parrà lì · il cielo piv biãco che sopra te, che la linia visuale [11] passa · per meno quãtità d'aria corrotta da grossi umori; e se riguarde[12]rai inverso · leuãte ·, l'aria ti parrà piv scura, quãto piv s'abbassa, perchè [13] in detta aria bassa i razzi luminosi meno passano.

Why the atmosphere must be represented as paler towards the lower portion.

Because the atmosphere is dense near the earth, and the higher it is the rarer it becomes. When the sun is in the East if you look towards the West and a little way to the South and North, you will see that this dense atmosphere receives more light from the sun than the rarer; because the rays meet with greater resistance. And if the sky, as you see it, ends on a low plain, that lowest portion of the sky will be seen through a denser and whiter atmosphere, which will weaken its true colour as seen through that medium, and there the sky will look whiter than it is above you, where the line of sight travels through a smaller space of air charged with heavy vapour. And if you turn to the East, the atmosphere will appear darker as you look lower down because the luminous rays pass less freely through the lower atmosphere.

Ash. I. 17b]

299.

Del modo del cõducere [2] in pittura le cose lõtane.

[3] Chiaro si uede · essere una aria grossa piv che l'altre, la quale cõfina [4] colla · terra ·

Of the mode of treating remote objects in painting.

It is easy to perceive that the atmosphere which lies closest to the level ground is denser

296. 1. infrallochio . . chosa. 2. inel . . chomelaria azura . . chelle. 3. parano azure . . chellochio. 4. lume cheffano 5. asse echo chupato . . dela . . chessi. 6. ella.

297. 1. chella persspectiua. 2. cholori . . disscordi grandezze. 4. chosa . . chelli. 5. cholori diminuisschino. 7. diminuisca. 8. chorpi . . diversi. 9. disstantie.

298. 3. equãto . . sassotiglia. 4. etta. 5. mezodi . . ettramõtana . . vederaia. 6. "dal sole" chella . . razi. 7. esse . . chella. 9. biancha [di quale] la . . corompera . . chessi. 10. mezo . parali il . . chella. 11. corotta . . omori esse riguharde. 12. para . . schura . . sabassa. 13. razi.

299. 3. easserere î aria . . chellaltre . . chõfina. 4. tera . . equãto . . essottile. 5. chose [che fiens] eleuate . . dacte. 6. bassezza i

piana, e quãto piv si leua ĩ alto, piv è sottile e trãsparẽte, [5]le cose eleuate e grãdi, che fieno da te lontane, la lor [6]bassezza poco fia veduta perchè la uedi per una linia che passa infra [7]l'aria piv grossa, e cõtinvata, la sõmità di dette altezze si trova [8]essere veduta per una linia, la quale benchè dal cãto dell'ochio tuo [9]si cavsi in nel'aria grossa nõdimeno terminãdo nella sõma altezza [10]della cosa vista, viene a terminare in aria molto piv sottile che [11]nõ fia la sua bassezza, e per questa ragione questa linia quãto piv s'allõtana [12]da te, di pũto ĩ punto sẽpre mvta qualità di sottile ĩ sottile aria, adũ[13]que tu pittore, quãdo fai le mõtagnie, fa che di colle ĩ colle sẽpre le bassezze sie[14]no piv chiare che l'altezze e quãto vi farai piv lontana l'una da l'altra fa le basse[15]ze piv chiare, [16]e quãto piv se leverà in alto, piv most[17]rerà la verità della forma e colore

than the rest, and that where it is higher up, it is rarer and more transparent The lower portions of large and lofty objects which are at a distance are not much seen, because you see them along a line which passes through a denser and thicker section of the atmosphere The summits of such heights are seen along a line which, though it starts from your eye in a dense atmosphere, still, as it ends at the top of those lofty objects, ceases in a much rarer atmosphere than exists at their base, for this reason the farther this line extends from your eye, from point to point the atmosphere becomes more and more rare Hence, O Painter! when you represent mountains, see that from hill to hill the bases are paler than the summits, and in proportion as they recede beyond each other make the bases paler than the summits, while, the higher they are the more you must show of their true form and colour

I etc 4a]

300

Del colore dell'aria

[2]Dico l'azzuro in che si mostra l'aria non essere suo propio colore, ma è cavsato da vmidità cal[3]da vaporata in minvtissimi e insensibili attomi, la quale piglia dopo se la percussiõ de' razzi solari e fassi luminosa [4]sotto la oscurità delle immẽse tenebre della regione del fuoco che di sopra le fa coperchio, e questo vedrà, come vid'io, chi ãdrà so[5]pra Mõboso, giogo dell' alpi che diuidono la Francia dalla Italia, la qual montagnia à la sua basa che parturisce [6]li 4 fiumi che rigã per 4 aspetti contrari tutta l'Europa, e nessuna montagnia à le sue base in simile al[7]tezza, questa si leua in tanta altura che quasi passa tutti li nuvoli e rare volte vi cade neve, ma sol grãdi[8]ne d'istate quando li nvvoli sono nella maggiore altezza, e questa grandine vi si cõserua in modo che se nõ [9]fusse la retà del cadervi e del montarvi nvuoli, che non accade 2 volte in vna età, egli ui sarebbe altissima quãtità di

Of the colour of the atmosphere

On the colour of the atmosphere (300—307)

I say that the blueness we see in the atmosphere is not intrinsic colour, but is caused by warm vapour evaporated in minute and insensible atoms on which the solar rays fall, rendering them luminous against the infinite darkness of the fiery sphere which lies beyond and includes it And this may be seen, as I saw it by any one going up [5] Monboso, a peak of the Alps which divide France from Italy The base of this mountain gives birth to the four rivers which flow in four different directions through the whole of Europe And no mountain has its base at so great a height as this, which lifts itself almost above the clouds, and snow seldom falls there, but only hail in the summer, when the clouds are highest And this hail lies [unmelted] there, so that if it were not for the absorption of the rising and falling clouds, which does not happen twice in an age, an enormous mass of ice would

7 chõtinvata lassomita alteze 8 chãto 9 chavsi inel some alteza 10 atterminare 11 basseza 12 datte qualita [daria] di sottile 13 basseze 14 lalteze ecquãto 15 ze piv chiare + 16 *The two last lines which are headed by +, are written on the margin* 17 stera dela

300 2 dicho lazuro inchessi cholore chavsato chal 3 attimi pigla perchussiõ razi effassi 4 osscurita fuocho "che di sopra le facoperchio" ecquesto 5 gogo diuitano la francia alla patrurissce 6 aspeti alle 7 teza nvuoli chade 8 magore alteza ecquesta imodo chesse 9- fussi "la reta del caderui e del montarui nvuoli' che non achade [del s] 2 volte vna eui sarebbe di diacco inalzato 'da li gradi della grãndine il

300, 5 With regard to the place spoken of as *M'obọso* (compare No 301 line 20) its identity will be discussed under Leonardo's Topographical notes in Vol II

7 *reta* here has the sense of *malanno*

diaccio inalzato da li gradi della grâdine il qua[10]le di mezzo luglio vi trovai grossissimo e vidi l'aria sopra di me tenebrosa e'l sole che percotea la möta[11]gnia essere piv luminoso quiui assai che nelle basse pianure, perchè minor grossezza d'aria s'interponea in[12]fra la cima d'esso möte e 'l sole; Ancora per esenplo del colore dell'aria allegheremo il fumo nato di legne [13]secche e vecchie il quale vscendo de' camini pare forte azzureggiare quädo si trova infra l'ochio e 'l loco [14]oscuro, ma quädo monta in alto e s'interpone infra l'ochio e l'aria alluminata, inmediate si dimostra [15]di colore cenerognolo, e questo accade perchè non à piv oscurità dopo se, ma in loco di quella aria lu[16]minosa; e se tal fumo sarà di legne verdi e giovani allora non penderà in azzurro, perchè nö [17]sendo trasparente e piē di superchia vmidità, esso fa vfitio di condensata nvuo lache piglia in se lumi e öbre ter[18]minate, come se solido corpo fusse; El simile fa l'aria che la troppa vmidità rende biäca e la [19]poca infusa col caldo la rēde oscura, di color di scuro azzurro, e questo ci basta in quäto alla di[20]finitione del colore dell'aria; Benchè si potrebbe ancora dire che se l'aria avesse per suo naturale colo[21]re esso azzurro transparente, seguirebbe che doue s' interponesse maggior quantità d'aria infra [22]l'ochio e l'elemēto del foco, che quiui si comporrebbe il suo azzurro con maggiore oscurità, come si vede [23]nelli vetri azzurri e ne' zaffiri li quali si mostrā tanto piv oscuri, quäto essi son piv grossi; E l'a[24]ria in questo caso adopera in retto contrario, conciosiachè dove piv in quätità s'in[25]terpone infra l'ochio e la spera del foco, quiui ci si mostra più biancheggiante; e questo accade [26]inverso l' orizzonte; equäto minor soma d'aria s'interpone infra l'ochio e la spera del foco tanto piv [27]oscuro azzurro, ci si mostra, ancorachè noi stiamo nelle basse pianvre; Adunque segue pur quel che io di[28]co che l'aria piglia l'azzurro mediante li corpuscoli dell'umidità che pigliano li razzi luminosi del sole; [29]vedesi ancora la differētia nelli attomi di poluere o nelli attomi del fumo ne' razzi solari, che passā per li [30]spiraculi delle parieti in lochi oscuri, che l'un razzo pare essere cenerino

be piled up there by the hail, and in the middle of July I found it very considerable. There I saw above me the dark sky, and the sun as it fell on the mountain was far brighter here than in the plains below, because a smaller extent of atmosphere lay between the summit of the mountain and the sun. Again as an illustration of the colour of the atmosphere I will mention the smoke of old and dry wood, which, as it comes out of a chimney, appears to turn very blue, when seen between the eye and the dark distance. But as it rises, and comes between the eye and the bright atmosphere, it at once shows of an ashy grey colour; and this happens because it no longer has darkness beyond it, but this bright and luminous space. If the smoke is from young, green wood, it will not appear blue, because, not being transparent and being full of superabundant moisture, it has the effect of condensed clouds which take distinct lights and shadows like a solid body. The same occurs with the atmosphere, which, when overcharged with moisture appears white, and the small amount of heated moisture makes it dark, of a dark blue colour; and this will suffice us so far as concerns the colour of the atmosphere; though it might be added that, if this transparent blue were the natural colour of the atmosphere, it would follow that wherever a larger mass air intervened between the eye and the element of fire, the azure colour would be more intense; as we see in blue glass and in sapphires, which are darker in proportion as they are larger. But the atmosphere in such circumstances behaves in an opposite manner, inasmuch as where a greater quantity of it lies between the eye and the sphere of fire, it is seen much whiter. This occurs towards the horizon. And the less the extent of atmosphere between the eye and the sphere of fire, the deeper is the blue colour, as may be seen even on low plains. Hence itfollows, as I say, that the atmosphere assumes this azure hue by reason of the particles of moisture which catch the rays of the sun. Again, we may note the difference in particles of dust, or particles of smoke, in the sun beams admitted through holes into a dark chamber, when the former will look ash grey

10. mezo . . grossimo . . tenenebrosa ellsole. 11. luminosi . . grossezza. 12. allegereno. 13. seche e vechie le quale vsciendo . . azuregiare . . locho. 14. osscuro macquãdo . . essinterpone . . ellaria. 15. ecquesto achade . . osscurita . . il locho. 16. essendo . . govane alora . . azzuro. 17. trassparente . . contensata . . biglia. 18. chome . . chorpo fussi . . chella tropa vmidita la rende biācha ella. 19. pocha . . chaldo . . osscura . . ecquesto . . bassta inquādo. 20. finition . . chessel-faria avessi. 21. azurro . . sinterponessi magor. 22. ellamēto del focho . . magore osscurita. 23. azurri . . osscuri . . Ella. 24. concosia. 25. nterpone . . ella . . focho . . mostra . . bianchegiante . . ecquesto achade. 26. lorizonte ecquãto . . soma . . ella . . focho. 27. osscuro azzuro . . stiano. 28. cho chellaria . . lazurro . . corpusscoli . . razi. 29. anchora

e l'altro del fumo [31]sottile pare essere di bellissimo azzurro; Vedesi ancora nell'ōbre oscure delle mōtagne remote [32]dall'ochio, l'aria che si trova infra l'ochio, e tale ōbra parere molto azzurra e nella parte luminosa di [33]tal mōtagnie nō uariarsi troppo dal primo colore; ma chi ne vol uedere le vltime prove tin[34]ga vna asse di diuersi colori fra li quali sia messo bellissimo nero e sopra tutti sia data sottile [35]e transparēte biacca, allora si uedrà la chiarezza di tal biacca non si mostrare sopra nessun [36]colore di piv bello azzurro che sopra il nero, ma diasi sottile e ben macinata.

and the thin smoke will appear of a most beautiful blue; and it may be seen again in in the dark shadows of distant mountains when the air between the eye and those shadows will look very blue, though the brightest parts of those mountains will not differ much from their true colour. But if any one wishes for a final proof let him paint a board with various colours, among them an intense black; and over all let him lay a very thin and transparent [coating of] white. He will then see that this transparent white will nowhere show a more beautiful blue than over the black —but it must be very thin and finely ground.

Leic. 36a]

301.

È sperienza che mostra, come l'aria à dopo se tenebre e però pare azzurra; [2]sia fatto fumo di legnie secche in poca quantità sopra il quale fumo [3]percotā li razzi solari, e dopo questo fumo poni vna pezza di uellu[4]to nero che nō sia visto dal sole, e uedrai tutto quel fumo [5]che s'oppone infra l'ochio e la oscurità mostrarsi in co[6]lor di bellissimo azzurro, e se in loco del ueluto metti panno biāco, el fumo, cioè [7]el tropofu[8]mo, inpedi[9]sce e'l poco nō forma la perfezione d'e[10]sso azzurro · [11]onde la me[12]diocre [13]dispo[14]sitione [15]di fu[16]mo forma bello azzurro; [17]come l'acqua soffiata a uso d'attomi in loco scuro doue passi la spera del sole fa esso razzo azzurro [18]e massime essendo tale acqva destillata e'l fumo sottile fa azzurro; quest'è detto per mostrare che [19]l'azzurro · dell'aria è causato di oscurità che è sopra di lei, e dannosi li predetti esempli a chi nō confermasse [20]la sperietia di Mōboso.

Experience shows us that the air must have darkness beyond it and yet it appears blue. If you produce a small quantity of smoke from dry wood and the rays of the sun fall on this smoke, and if you then place behind the smoke a piece of black velvet on which the sun does not shine, you will see that all the smoke which is between the eye and the black stuff will appear of a beautiful blue colour. And if instead of the velvet you place a white cloth smoke, that is too thick smoke, hinders, and too thin smoke does not produce, the perfection of this blue colour. Hence a moderate amount of smoke produces the finest blue. Water violently ejected in a fine spray and in a dark chamber where the sun beams are admitted produces these blue rays and the more vividly if it is distilled water, and thin smoke looks blue. This I mention in order to show that the blueness of the atmosphere is caused by the darkness beyond it, and these instances are given for those who cannot confirm [on] my experience on Monboso.

F. 18a]

302.

Quando il fumo di legne secche si troua [2]infra l'ochio di chi lo vede e altro loco oscuro [3]esso pare azzurro; [4]adunque l'aria si fa azzurra per le tene[5]bre che essa à dopo se; E se tu guardi inver[6]so l'orizzonte

When the smoke from dry wood is seen between the eye of the spectator and some dark space [or object], it will look blue. Thus the sky looks blue by reason of the darkness beyond it. And if you look towards the horizon of the sky, you will see the atmo-

la diucretia attimi . . attimi . . razi. 30. parlete illochi osscuri che lun "razo" pare essere cenenereo elfaltro. 31. accurro . . nellobre osscure. 32. chessi . . tale ōbr . . molta azzurro. 33. del. 34. fralli . . essopra. 35. eltrausparēte biacha . . chiareza . . biacha. 36. chessopra . . ebben.

301. 1. mostra. 2. seche pocha. 3. perchota . . razi . . peza. 4. vissto. 5. chessoppone infrallochio ella osscurita. 6. azuro essellocho . . meti pano biācho effumo coe. 9. el pocho . . de. 10. so azurro. 13. dispo. 16. azurro. 17. dattimi ilocho . . accurro. 18. masime . . desstillata . . accurro. 19. lazurro . . e chaussato da osscurita . . dassi . . essenpli . . confermassi. 20. essperiētia.

302. 2. di cillo vede . . locho. 3. azzurro [ettāto piu quāte piu scuro]. 5. Essettu. 6. lorizonte . . non es. 7. ecquesto nasscie.

del celo, tu vedrai l'aria non esse[7]re azzurra, e questo nascie per la sua gros[8]sezza; e così in ogni grado che tu [9]alzi l'ochio sopra esso orizzonte insino al [10]celo che ti sta di sopra, tu troverai l'aria [11]farsi più oscura, e questo è che mĕ somma [12]d'aria s'interpone infra l'ochio tuo e esse [13]tenebre; E se tu ti troverai sopra vn al[14]to mōte, l'aria si farà tanto più oscura [15]sopra di te, quanto essa è fatta più sottile [16]infra te e dette tenebre, e così seguiterà in [17]ogni grado d'altezza tanto che al fine re[18]sterà tenebrosa.

[19]Quel fumo parrà più azzurro che nasce[20]rà da più secche legne e che sarà più presso al[21]la sua cagione, e che è veduto in più oscu[22]ro canpo, dandovi sù il lume del sole.

sphere is not blue, and this is caused by its density. And thus at each degree, as you raise your eyes above the horizon up to the sky over your head, you will see the atmosphere look darker [blue] and this is because a smaller density of air lies between your eye and the [outer] darkness. And if you go to the top of a high mountain the sky will look proportionately darker above you as the atmosphere becomes rarer between you and the [outer] darkness; andthis will be more visible each degree of increasing height till at last we should find darkness.

That smoke will look bluest which rises from the driest wood and which is nearest to the fire and is seen against the darkest background, and with the sunlight upon it.

C. 18 a]

303.

Quella · cosa · tenebrosa · parrà · più azzurra · che infra se · e l'ochio · maggior somma d'aria luminosa interposta · fia, [2]come · per el color · del cielo dimostrar si può.

A dark object will appear bluest in proportion as it has a greater mass of luminous atmosphere between it and the eye. As may be seen in the colour of the sky.

H.[3] 29 b]

304.

L'aria è azzurra per le tenebre che à di [2]sopra, perchè nero e biāco fà azzurro.

The atmosphere is blue by reason of the darkness above it because black and white make blue.

Br. M. 169 a]

305

La mattina la nebbia è piv folta inverso l'altezza che nella [2]sua bassezza, perchè il sole l'attrae in alto, onde li edifiti grā[3]di, ancora che ti sia lontana la cima quāto il fondamēto, essa [4]cima ti fia ignota; E per questo il celo si dimostra più oscu[5]ro inverso l'altezza e inver l'orizzonte e non azzurreggia, anzi è tra [6]fumo e poluere.

[7]L'aria infusa colle nebbie è interamēte privata d'azzurro, ma solo [8]pare di quel colore de' nvgoli che biācheggiano quādo 'l tēpo è sereno; e quā[9]to piv rigvardi verso l'occidēte tu la troverai [10]piv oscura e piv lucida e chiara verso l'oriēte; E le verdure de[11]lle cāpagnie in mezzana nebbia azzurreggiano alquāto, ma ne[12]greggiano nella piv grossa.

In the morning the mist is denser above than below, because the sun draws it upwards; hence tall buildings, even if the summit is at the same distance as the base have the summit invisible. Therefore, also, the sky looks darkest [in colour] overhead, and towards the horizon it is not blue but rather between smoke and dust colour.

The atmosphere, when full of mist, is quite devoid of blueness, and only appears of the colour of clouds, which shine white when the weather is fine. And the more you turn to the west the darker it will be, and the brighter as you look to the east. And the verdure of the fields is bluish in a thin mist, but grows grey in a dense one.

8. serra [Esse] e cosi . . chettu. 9. [le] alzi orizonte. 10. chetti . . troverai. 11. osscuro esequesto. 13. Esetu . . troverrai. 14. osscura. 15. effatta. 16. infratte. 17. nogni*. . dalteza. 19. para . . azurro . . nassca. 20. ra di piu seche. 21. cagone . . osscu.

303. 1. chosa . . azurra . . in frasse . eliochio . . magior . . interpossta. 2. chome . . chelor . . dimosstrar.

304. 1—2. R. 2. sapra . . biācho . . azurro.

305. 1. lalteza. 2. bāsseza. 4. ingnota . . osscu. 5. lalteza . . lorizonte . . azuregia . . ettra. 7. dasurro. 8. biācheggano . . sereno ecoua. 9. rissgvadi . . troverai 10. osscura . . ciara . Elle. 11. mezana . . azzurreqiano. 12. gregiano.

[13]Li edifizi inver ponẽte sol ci dimostrã la lor parte lumino[14]sa, poichè'l sole si scopre, e'l resto le nebbi lo occultano; [15]Quãdo il sol s'inalza e caccia le nebbie e si comĩcia a rischiarare i colli da quel[16]la parte donde esse si partono, e' fansi azzurri e fumano inver[17]so le nebbi fuggieti e li edifiti mostrano lumi e õbre,· e nelle nebbie [18]mẽ folte mostrã solo i lumi e nelle piv folte niẽte; e questo è [19]quãdo il moto della nebbia si parte traversalmẽte, e allora i ter[20]mini d'essa nebbia saranno poco evidenti coll'azzurro dell'aria [21]e inverso la terra parrà quasi poluere che s'iñalzi; [22]Quanto l'aria sarà piv grossa, li edifiti delle città · e li alberi [23]delle cãpagnie parraño piv rari, perchè sol si mo[24]streranno i piv eminẽti e grossi.

[25]Le tenebre [26]tingono o[27]gni cosa [28]del lor colore, [29]e quãto piv [30]la cosa si par[31]te da esse tene[32]bre piv si uede [33]del suo vero e natural co[34]lore. [35]I mõti fieno rari, perchè sol si dimostrã quelli che ànno mag[36]giore intervalli, perchè in tal ispatio la grossezza mvltiplica in [37]modo che fa chiarezza tale che la oscurità de' collisi diuide e si [38]spedisce bene inverso la sua altezza: ne'colli piccoli e vicini non [39]se ne interpone tãta e però mãco si discernono e mẽ nelle lor bassezze.

The buildings in the west will only show their illuminated side, where the sun shines, and the mist hides the rest. When the sun rises and chases away the haze, the hills on the side where it lifts begin to grow clearer, and look blue, and seem to smoke with the vanishing mists; and the buildings reveal their lights and shadows; through the thinner vapour they show only their lights and through the thicker air nothing at all. This is when the movement of the mist makes it part horizontally, and then the edges of the mist will be indistinct against the blue of the sky, and towards the earth it will look almost like dust blown up. In proportion as the atmosphere is dense the buildings of a city and the trees in a landscape will look fewer, because only the tallest and largest will be seen.

Darkness affects every thing with its hue, and the more an object differs from darkness, the more we see its real and natural colour. The mountains will look few, because only those will be seen which are farthest apart; since, at such a distance, the density increases to such a degree that it causes a brightness by which the darkness of the hills becomes divided and vanishes indeed towards the top. There is less [mist] between lower and nearer hills and yet little is to be distinguished, and least towards the bottom.

G. 53*b*]

306.

La superfitie d'õgni [2]corpo participa [3]del color [4]che l'allumina,—[5]e del color dell'a[6]ria che infra l'oc[7]chio e esso corpo [8]s'interpone, cioè [9]del color del mez[10]zo transpa[11]rẽte interposto [12]ĩfra la cosa e l'occhio, e [13]ĩfra li colori di me[14]desima qualità [15]il secondo sarà del [16]medesimo colore [17]del primo, e ques[18]to nascie per la mul[19]tiplicatione del color [20]del mezzo interpo[21]sto infra la cosa e [22]l'ochio.

The surface of an object partakes of the colour of the light which illuminates it; and of the colour of the atmosphere which lies between the eye and that object, that is of the colour of the transparent medium lying between the object and the eye; and among colours of a similar character the second will be of the same tone as the first, and this is caused by the increased thickness of the colour of the medium lying between the object and the eye.

13. sol si dimosstra. 14. sisscopre, el ressto . . nebie ochultano. 15. sol "sinalza" caccia . . rissciarare e colli dacq. 16. partano effarsi azzuri effumano. 17. nebiefugiẽti elli . . nebie. 18. solo e lumi . . ecquesto. 19. e ter. 20. sarano pochi . . chol azurro. 21. para . . chessiñalzi. 22. elli. 23. parano. 24. sterrannoe. 26. tingano. 33. vero "e natural" co. 35. E mõti . . sol s dimostra quelgli . . ma. 36. ispati . . grosseza. 37. cheffa ciareza . . chella osscurita . . vi diuide essi. 38. spedissce . . alteza . . picholi . . no. 39. discernano. *On the margin between lines* 35 *and* 36: mera purifi catione.

306. 2. chorpo. 3. del color del color. 4. chellalumina. 6. infralloc. 7. chorpo. 10. zo [chessi] transpa. 11. interpossto. 12. ĩfralla . . ellocchio. 13. infralli color. 14. qualita ma. 15. sechondo. 16. cholore. 17. ecques. 18. nasscie. 20. mezo. 21. ssto infralla.

L. 75 b]

307.

De pictura.

Infra i colori che nō sono azzurri quello in lūga distantia participerà · più d'azzurro il quale sarà piv vicino al nero e così de converso si mostrerà per lūga distantia nel suo propio colore, il quale sarà piv dis simile a detto nero.

Adunque il uerde delle campagnie si transmvterà piv in azzurro che nō fa il giallo o biāco e così de couerso il giallo e 'l biāco māco si transmuta che lo verde, e 'l rosso māco.

Of painting.

Of various colours which are none of them blue that which at a great distance will look bluest is the nearest to black; and so, conversely, the colour which is least like black will at a great distance best preserve its own colour.

Hence the green of fields will assume a bluer hue than yellow or white will, and conversely yellow or white will change less than green, and red still less.

307. 2. azurri . . illū. 3. dazurro. 5. montera . . disstantia. 6. cholore . . di. 7. dicto. 9. azuro. 10. biācho māc 11. chello . . mācho.

VII.

On the Proportions and on the Movements of the Human Figure.

Leonardo's researches on the proportions and movements of the human figure must have been for the most part completed and written before the year 1498; *for* LUCA PACIOLO *writes, in the dedication to Ludovico il Moro, of his book* Divina Proportione, *which was published in that year:* "Leonardo da venci . . . hauẽdo gia cõ tutta diligẽtia al degno libro de pictura e movimenti humani posto fine".

The selection of Leonardo's axioms contained in the Vatican copy attributes these words to the author: "e il recto si dirà nella universale misura del huomo". (MANZI, *p.* 147; LUDWIG, *No.* 264). LOMAZZO, *again, in his* Idea del Tempio della Pittura Milano 1590, cap. IV), *says:* "Lionardo Vinci . . . dimostrò anco in figura tutte le proporzioni dei membri del corpo umano".

The Vatican copy includes but very few sections of the "Universale misura del huomo" *and until now nothing has been made known of the original MSS. on the subject which have supplied the very extensive materials for this portion of the work. The collection at Windsor, belonging to her Majesty the Queen, includes by far the most important part of Leonardo's investigations on this subject, constituting about half of the whole of the materials here published; and the large number of original drawings adds greatly to the interest which the subject itself must command. Luca Paciolo would seem to have had these MSS. (which I have distinguished by the initials* W. P.) *in his mind when he wrote the passage quoted above. Still, certain notes of a later date—such as Nos.* 360,

362 *and* 363, *from MS. E, written in* 1513—14, *sufficiently prove that Leonardo did not consider his earlier studies on the Proportions and Movements of the Human Figure final and complete, as we might suppose from Luca Paciolo's statement. Or else he took the subject up again at a subsequent period, since his former researches had been carried on at Milan between* 1490 *and* 1500. *Indeed it is highly probable that the anatomical studies which he was pursuing with so much zeal between* 1510—16 *should have led him to reconsider the subject of Proportion.*

H I 31 b]

308

Ciascuno homo nel terzo año [2] è la metà della sua altezza ultima.

Every man, at three years old is half the full height he will grow to at last. Preliminary observations (308 309)

C A 157 a; 463 a]

309.

Se l'omo · di · 2 braccia è piccolo · quello di quattro è troppo grãde · essendo la uia [2] di mezzo laudabile ·; il mezzo ĩfra · 2 e 4 · si è · 3 : adũque piglia · un omo [3] di 3 · braccia · e quello · misura · colla regola ch'io ti darò, se tu mi diciessi, io mi potrei [4] ĩgãnare, givdicãdo · vno bene proportionato · che sarebbe · il cõtrario, a questa [5] parte io rispõdo · che tu debi vedere molti omini di 3 · braccia e quella maggiore quã[6]tità · che sono · cõformi di mẽbra: sopra uno di quelli di migliore gratia · piglia tue misure, [7] la lũghezza · della mano è $^1/_3$ di braccio e ẽtra 9 volte nell'omo · e così la testa · e dalla fõtanella [8] della gola alla spalla · e dalla spalla alla tetta · e dal'una all'altra tetta · e da ciascuna [9] tetta · alla fontanella

If a man 2 braccia high is too small, one of four is too tall, the medium being what is admirable Between 2 and 4 comes 3; therefore take a man of 3 braccia in height and measure him by the rule I will give you. If you tell me that I may be mistaken, and judge a man to be well proportioned who does not conform to this division, I answer that you must look at many men of 3 braccia, and out of the larger number who are alike in their limbs choose one of those who are most graceful and take your measurements. The length of the hand is $^1/_3$ of a braccio [8 inches] and this is found 9 times in man And the face [7] is the same, and from the pit of the throat to the shoulder, and from the shoulder to the nipple, and from one nipple to the other, and from each nipple to the pit of the throat.

308 1 homo he nel 2 ella meta alteza "ultima"
309 1 2 br e picholo ettropo 2 mezo laldabile il mezo pigha ĩ omo 3 di 3 br ecquello . cioti . . settu 4 giudichãdo . . sarebe . acquesta 5 irispõdo chettu . di 3 br ecquella . settu 6. chessono chõformi di mẽbrisopra ĩ di 7 lũgeza . $^1/_3$ di br e dala 8 ala ; dala spala ala 9 teza alla

309 7. The account here given of the *braccio* is of importance in understanding some of the succeeding chapters.

Testa must here be understood to mean the face The statements in this section are illustrated in part on Pl. XI

W. P. 22]

310.

Proportions of the head and face (310—318)

Lo spatio ch'è infra 'l taglio della bocca e 'l prĩcipio · del naso è la settima · parte del uolto; [2]lo spatio · ch'è dalla bocca al di sotto · del mẽto · *c d*, fia · la quarta · parte · del uolto; e simile alla larghezza della bocca; [3]lo spatio ch'è dal mẽto · al principio di sotto del naso *e f*, fia la terza · parte del uolto; e simile al naso · e alla fronte, [4]lo spatio · ch'è dal mezzo · del naso al di sotto · del mẽto *g h*, fia · la metà · del volto, [5]lo spatio ch'è dal principio di sopra del naso, dove prĩcipiano le ciglia, *i k*, al di sotto del mento, fia i due terzi del uolto; [6]lo spatio · ch'è · infra 'l taglio della bocca e 'l prĩcipio del mento di sopra *l m*, cioè dou'esso mẽto finiscie terminãdo col labro di sotto[7] della bocca, fia la terza parte dello spatio ch'è dal taglio d'essa bocca al di sotto del mẽto e la dodecima parte del uolto, [8]dal di sopra · al di sotto · del mẽto *m n* fia la · sesta · parte del uolto, e fia la cinquãta quatroesima parte dell'omo, [9]dallo ultimo sporto del mẽto alla gola *o p* fia simile allo spatio, ch'è dalla bocca al di sotto del mẽto e la quarta parte del uolto; [10]lo spatio · ch'è dal di sopra della gola al prĩcipio di sotto *q r*, fia la metà · del uolto · e la diciottesima parte dell'omo, [11]dal mento · al dineto del collo *s t* è quel medesimo · spatio · ch'è infra la bocca · e 'l nascimẽto · de' capegli cioè [12]i tre quarti · della · testa; [13]dal mẽto alla ganascia *v x* è mezza testa ed è simile alla grossezza del collo · in proffilo; [14]la grossezza del collo entra vna volta · e 3/4 dal ciglio · alla nuca

The space between the parting of the lips [the mouth] and the base of the nose is one-seventh of the face.

The space from the mouth to the bottom of the chin *c d* is the fourth part of the face and equal to the width of the mouth.

The space from the chin to the base of the nose *e f* is the third part of the face and equal to the length of the nose and to the forehead

The distance from the middle of the nose to the bottom of the chin *g h*, is half the length of the face

The distance from the top of the nose, where the eyebrows begin, to the bottom of the chin, *i k*, is two thirds of the face.

The space from the parting of the lips to the top of the chin *l m*, that is where the chin ends and passes into the lower lip of the mouth, is the third of the distance from the parting of the lips to the bottom of the chin and is the twelfth part of the face. From the top to the bottom of the chin *m n* is the sixth part of the face and is the fifty fourth part of a man's height

From the farthest projection of the chin to the throat *o p* is equal to the space between the mouth and the bottom of the chin, and a fourth of the face.

The distance from the top of the throat to the pit of the throat below *q r* is half the length of the face and the eighteenth part of a man's height.

From the chin to the back of the neck *s t*, is the same distance as between the mouth and the roots of the hair, that is three quarters of the head.

From the chin to the jaw bone *v x* is half the head and equal to the thickness of the neck in profile

The thickness of the head from the brow to the nape is once and 3/4 that of the neck.

310 1 in fral [la bocha] taglio . . bocha. 2 bocha . mẽto "cd ' fia . uolto" e simile alla largeza della bocha". 3 naso "e f" fia uolto "essimile al naso ella [testa] fronte". 4 mezo . mẽto "g h ' fia 5 ciglia "i k" al 6. bocha . d sopra "l m ' cioe cholabro 7 bocha . bocha mẽto "ella [vẽtunesima] dodecima parte del uolto". 8 mẽto "m n ' fia . uolto "effia la cinquãta, quatrocsima parte, dellomo" 9 dalo gola "o p ' fia alo . bocca . ella. 10 sotto "q r" fia ella di sollesima. 11 dinecto del chollo "s t ' e quel . infralla bocha il nassimẽto del chapegli. 13 alla ganasscia "v x" . e meza testa eddissimile chollo 14 chollo . . nucha.

310. The drawings to this text, lines 1—10 are on Pl. VII, No. 1. The two upper sketches of heads, Pl. VII, No. 2, belong to lines 11—14, and in the original are placed immediately below the sketches reproduced on Pl. VII, No. 1.

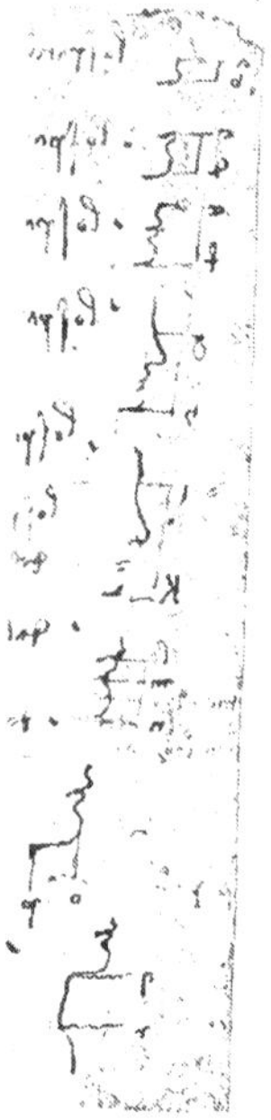

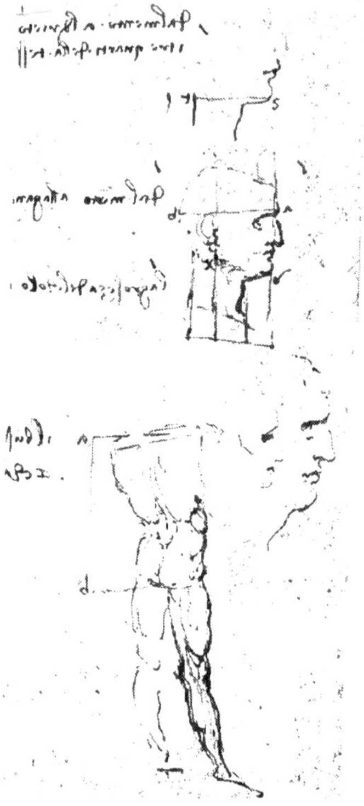

3

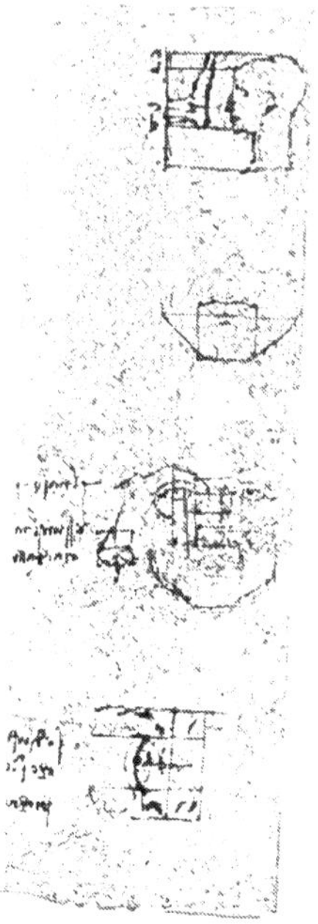

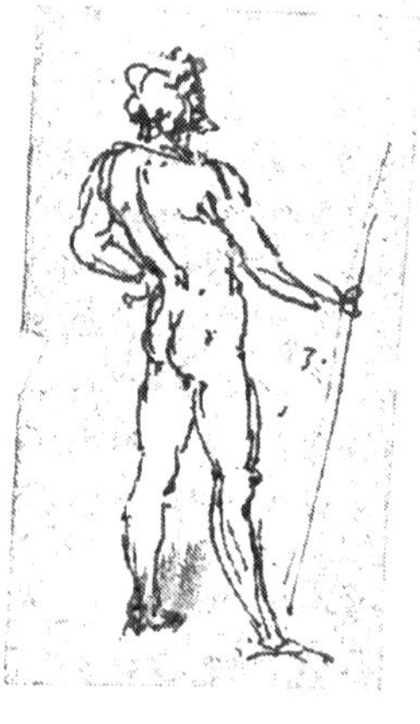

5

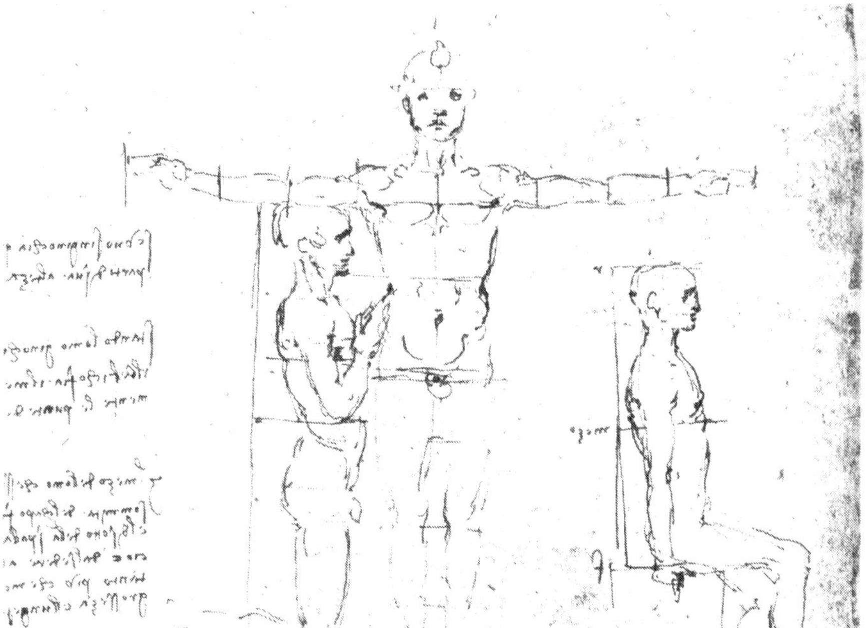

A. 62 *b*]

311.

Tanto è dall' una · appiccatura · dell' orechio · all' altra ·, quãto è dalle givnture delle ciglia al mẽto; [2]tanto · è grãde la bocca d' ũ bel uolto, quãto è dalla diuisiõ de' labri al di sotto del mẽto.

The distance from the attachment of one ear to the other is equal to that from the meeting of the eyebrows to the chin, and in a fine face the width of the mouth is equal to the length from the parting of the lips to the bottom of the chin.

A. 63 *a*]

312.

Il taglio overo spigolo del labro [2]di sotto · della · bocca · è il mezzo ĩfra [3]il di sotto del naso · e 'l di sotto del mẽto.

[5]Il uiso fa ĩ se uno quadro, cioè [6]la sua larghezza è da l'uno al'altro [7]stremo del ochio, e la sua altezza [8]è da il fine di sopra del naso [9]al di sotto del labro di sotto [10]della bocca, poi ciò che resta [11]di sopra e di sotto a esso quadro [12]fa l'altezza d'ũ simile quadro [13]¶*a* · *b* è simile allo spatio · ch'è · infra · *c* · *d* · [14]*d* · *n* · e cosi *n* · *c* · e similmẽte · *s* · *r* ‖ *q* · *p* · ‖ [15]*h* · *k* · sono · infra loro simili.¶

[16]Tãto è da *m* · *s* · quãto è dal di sotto del naso · al mẽto; [17]l' orechio · è appũto tãto lũgo, quãto il naso; [18]tãto è da *x* · *s* quãto dal naso al mẽto; [19]il taglio della bocca ĩ proffilo si dirizza all' ãgolo della mascella; [20]tãto deb' essere alto l' orechio, quãt' è dal di sotto del naso [21]al di sopra del coperchio · dell' ochio; [22]tanto è lo spatio · ch' è infra li ochi, quãto la grãdezza d'un ochio; [23]l' orechio cade nel mezzo · del collo · in proffilo; [24]tanto · è · da 4 · a 5 · quãto · è da · *s* · a · *r*.

The cut or depression below the lower lip of the mouth is half way between the bottom of the nose and the bottom of the chin.

The face forms a square in itself; that is its width is from the outer corner of one eye to the other, and its height is from the very top of the nose to the bottom of the lower lip of the mouth; then what remains above and below this square amounts to the height of such another square. *a b* is equal to the space between *c d*; *d n* in the same way to *n c*, and likewise *s r*, *q p*, *h k* are equal to each other.

It is as far between *m* and *s* as from the bottom of the nose to the chin. The ear is exactly as long as the nose. It is as far from *x* to *s* as from the nose to the chin. The parting of the mouth seen in profile slopes to the angle of the jaw. The ear should be as high as from the bottom of the nose to the top of the eye-lid. The space between the eyes is equal to the width of an eye. The ear is over the middle of the neck, when seen in profile. The distance from 4 to 5 is equal to that from *s* to *r*.

W. P. 119 *a*]

313.

(*a* · *b*) è simile a (*c* · *d*).

(*a b*) is equal to (*c d*).

311. 1. apichatura . . da [pi] le . . dele. 2. bocha . . dala.
312. 1. delabro. 2. bocha . . mezo. 4. [la large]. 5. se ĩ quadro. 6. largeza. 7. alteza. 9. delabro. 10. dela bocha. 13. essimile alo. 14. essimilmente. 16. tãto [te] e. 17. apũto . . lugo quãto. 19. bocha . . diriza al . . masscella. 20. esere. 21. choperchio. 22. ellosspatio . . quãda la grãdelza. 23. chade . . mezo . . chollo.
313. essimile.

312. See Pl. VIII, No. 1, where the text of lines 3—13 is also given in facsimile.

313. See Pl. VII, No. 3. Reference may also be made here to two pen and ink drawings of heads in profile with figured measurements, of which there is no description in the MS. These are given on Pl. XVII, No. 2.—A head, to the left, with part of the torso [W. P. 5[a]], No. 1 on the same plate is from MS. A 2[b] and in the original occurs on a page with wholly irrelevant text on matters of natural history. M. RAVAISSON in his edition of the Paris MS. A has reproduced this head and discussed it fully [note on page 12]; he has however somewhat altered the original measurements. The complicated calculations which M. RAVAISSON has given appear to me in no way justified. The sketch, as we see it, can hardly have been intended for any thing more than an experimental attempt to ascertain relative proportions. We do not find that Leonardo made use of circular lines in any other study of the proportions of the human head. At the same time we see that the proportions of this sketch are not in accordance with the rules which he usually observed (see for instance No. 310).

W. P. 7a]

314.

Il capo *a f* · è $^1/_6$ · maggiore · che *n* · *f*.

The head *a f* $^1/_6$ larger than *n f*.

V IV. 16]

315.

Dal ciglio alla cōgiuntione del labro col mēto · e la punta della · masciella · e 'l fine di sopra dello orecchio · colla · tenpia · fia uno quadrato · perfetto; E ciascuna faccia per se · è mezza · testa

E'l cauo · dell'osso · della · guancia si truova · ī mezzo fralla punta del naso · e 'l confine · della · masciella ·, ch'è la · punta · di sotto · dello · orecchio in nella · figurata · stella;

dal cantone dell'osso · dell'ochio allo' orecchio · è tanto · spatio quanto è la lunghezza · dello · orecchio ·, o vuoi · il terzo · della testa.

From the eyebrow to the junction of the lip with the chin, and the angle of the jaw and the upper angle where the ear joins the temple will be a perfect square And each side by itself is half the head.

The hollow of the cheek bone occurs half way between the tip of the nose and the top of the jaw bone, which is the lower angle of the setting on of the ear, in the frame here represented.

From the angle of the eye-socket to the ear is as far as the length of the ear, or the third of the face -

W Pr. 12]

316

Tanto · dev'essere · da · *a b* cioè dal nascimēto dinãzi · de' capelli alla linia · della · sõmita · del capo, quãto è da · *c* · *d* · cioè dal · fine di sotto · del naso · alla · cõgiũtiõ de' labbri dinãzi della bocca; tanto è dal lagrimatoio dell'occhio · *m* · alla sõmita · del capo · *a* · quãto è da | *m* | al di sotto del mēto · *s* · *s* · *c* · *f* · *b* · sono · simili per spatio l'uno · all'altro.

From *a* to *b*—that is to say from the roots of the hair in front to the top of the head—ought to be equal to *c d*,—that is from the bottom of the nose to the meeting of the lips in the middle of the mouth. From the inner corner of the eye *m* to the top of the head *a* is as far as from *m* down to the chin *s*. *s c f b* are all at equal distances from each other.

W P 5a]

317.

Dalla sommità del capo al di sotto del mēto $^1/_8$, dal nascimēto de' capelli al mento è $^1/_9$ dello spatio ch'è da esso nascimēto a terra. La maggior larghezza del uolto

From the top of the head to the bottom of the chin is $^1/_8$, and from the roots of the hair to the chin is $^1/_9$ of the distance from the roots of the hair to the ground. The greatest width of the face is equal to the

314. Il capo [v q] a f $^1/_6$ magiore.
315. 1. cõgiunctione. 2 chol ella. 3 massciella. 4 cholla . fia I qua. 5 perfecto Ecciascuna 6. meza teasta 7 chauo. 8 Imezo 9. chonfine della massciella 10 lla . . disocto . orechio 11 issella. 12 chantone 13 ettanto . ella. 14 lungeza 15 teasta.
316 1. deessere 2 nasscimēto 3 chapo 4. diso. 5. dela. 6. bocha 7. ochio. 8. chapo 10. simile perispatio
317 1. dalasomita del chapo. 2. chapelliti ella mento 3 nasscimēto atterra 4. magior largeza . essimile. 5 dala bocha al

315. See Pl. IX. The text, in the original is written behind the head The handwriting would seem to indicate a date earlier than 1480. On the same leaf there is a drawing in red chalk of two horsemen of which only a portion of the upper figure is here visible The whole leaf measures $22^1/_2$ centimetres wide by 29 long, and is numbered 127 in the top right-hand corner.

316 The drawing in silver-point on bluish tinted paper—Pl. X—which belongs to this chapter has been partly drawn over in ink by Leonardo himself

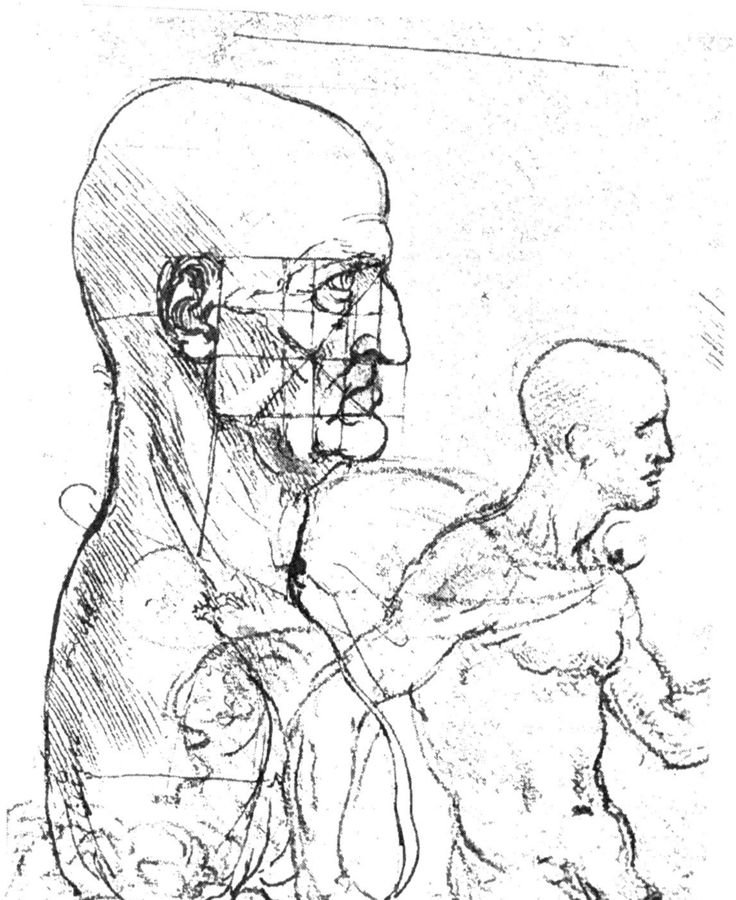

è simile allo spatio [5]ch'è dalla bocca al nascimẽto de' capelli ed è [6] $1/12$ del tutto [7]Dalla sommità dell'orechio alla sommità del capo fia [8]simile allo spatio ch'è dal di sotto del mento al lagrima[9]tojo delli occhi, E simile allo spatio ch'è dalla punta [10]del mento a quella della mascella ed è la $1/16$ [11]parte del tutto [12]Il picciuolo che si trova infra 'l buso dell'orecchio [13]inverso il naso fia mezzo infra la nuca e 'l ciglio, [14]La grossezza del collo in profilo è simile [15]allo spatio ch'è dal mẽto alli occhi e simile allo [16]spatio ch'è dal mẽto alla mascella e ẽtra [17]15 volte in tutto l'omo

space between the mouth and the roots of the hair and is $1/12$ of the whole height. From the top of the ear to the top of the head is equal to the distance from the bottom of the chin to the lachrymatory duct of the eye, and also equal to the distance from the angle of the chin to that of the jaw, that is the $1/16$ of the whole The small cartilage which projects over the opening of the ear towards the nose is half-way between the nape and the eyebrow, the thickness of the neck in profile is equal to the space between the chin and the eyes, and to the space between the chin and the jaw, and it is $1/15$ of the height of the man

W P 3, 1a]

318.

a b , c d , e f , g h , i k infra loro ànno similitudine [2]di grãdezza saluo che *d f* ch'è libero

a b, c d, e f, g h, i k are equal to each other in size excepting that *d f* is accidental

Tur 7].

319

¶*a n o f* son simili [2]alla bocca ¶ [3]¶*a c* e *a f* sõ simili [4]allo spatio ch'è fra l'uno [5]ochio e l'altro ¶ [6]*n m o p · q r* [7]son simili alla [8]metà della grossezza [9]de labri dell'ochio, cioè [10]da lagrimatojo dell'o[11]chio alla sua coda, [12]e similmẽte la diui[13]sione ch'è fra 'l mẽto e la [14]bocca, e similmẽte [15]la piv stretta parte che [16]à il naso, infra l'uno o[17]chio e l'altro, e que[18]sti tali spati ciascũ per se [19]è la n° parte della testa, [20]*n o* è simile alla lũ[21]ghezza dell'ochio ovvero lo [22]spatio ch'è infra li ochi, [23]*m c* è $1/3$ di *n m*, [24]misurãdo dal taglio [25]di fori del labro dell'ochio [26]al segnio · *c* , [27]*b s* fia simile alla [28]larghezza delle nari del [29]naso

Proportions of the head seen in front (319—321)

a n o f are equal to the mouth

a c and *a f* are equal to the space between one eye and the other

n m o p q r are equal to half the width of the eye lids, that is from the inner [lachrymatory] corner of the eye to its outer corner, and in like manner the division between the chin and the mouth, and in the same way the narrowest part of the nose between the eyes And these spaces, each in itself, is the 19th part of the head. *n o* is equal to the length of the eye or of the space between the eyes

m c is $1/3$ of *n m* measuring from the outer corner of the eyelids to the letter *c* *b s* will be equal to the width of the nostril

Tur 11]

320

Lo spatio ch'è infra i ciẽtri delle [2]popille dell'ochio è $1/3$ del uolto, [3]lo spatio, ch'è infra li stremi del[4]li ochi inver li orechi,

The distance between the centres of the pupils of the eyes is $1/3$ of the face. The space between the outer corners of the eyes,

nasimẽto elechapelli. 7 della somita somita del chapo 9 ochi 10 acquella masscella 12 pincierolo chessi 13 mezo infralla nuchi 14 grosseza chollo inproffilo essimile 15 alosspatio ochi essimile 16 maschiella

318 1 ano 2 grãdeza

319 2 ala bocha 3 *c* he *a* 4 fralluno 5 ellaltro 6 simile 7 simili a alla 8 dela grosseza 10 lagrimatoro 11 coda ne 12 essimilmẽte 13 ella 14 bocha essimilmẽte 16 infralluno 17 ellaltro 18 ciascũ 19 ellan° 20 *n m* essimile 21 gezo dellochio ovolo 23 *c* he $1/3$ 28 largheza dellanari

320 2 popille 3 infralli de 5 cholla 6 chello riciéve poste 7 vmezo 8 magiore largeza abia 10 apichatura

318 See Pl XI
319 See Pl XII

19 *la n° parte* This singular notation seems to mean *decima nona*(nineteenth)

cioè dove [5]l'ochio termina colla cassa dell'osso [6]che lo ricieve, le code di fori, fia [7]ẽ mezzo volto.

[8]La maggiore larghezza, che abbia [9]il uolto per la linia degli ochi, fia [10]quãt'è dall'appiccatura dinãzi de' ca[11]pegli al taglio della bocca.

that is where the eye ends in the eye socket which contains it, thus the outer corners, is half the face.

The greatest width of the face at the line of the eyes is equal to the distance from the roots of the hair in front to the parting of the lips.

W. P. 5a (B)]

321.

Il naso farà · 2 · quadrati ·, cioè · la larghezza · del naso nelle narici entra · 2 · volte · dalla punta · del · naso · al principio · delle ciglia, [2]e similmẽte i profilo tãto · fia · dalla · strema · parte della narice, doue si cõgivgnie · colla · guãcia ·, alla pũta · d'esso · naso ·, quãto il naso è largo in faccia da l'una · al'altra · narice; [4]se diuiderai · in 4 · parti · equali · tutta la lunghezza · del naso, cioè dalla · sua · pũta · all'appiccatura delle ciglia: tu · troverai · [5]che una delle parti ẽtra dal di sopra delle narici al di sotto della · pũta · del naso e la superiore · parte ẽtra · dal lagrimatojo dell'ochio all'a[6]ppiccatura · delle · ciglia: e le · 2 parti di mezzo · fieno tãto grãdi quãto · è · l'ochio · dal lagrimatojo · alla · coda · d'esso · ochio.

The nose will make a double square; that is the width of the nose at the nostrils goes twice into the length from the tip of the nose to the eyebrows. And, in the same way, in profile the distance from the extreme side of the nostril where it joins the cheek to the tip of the nose is equal to the width of the nose in front from one nostril to the other. If you divide the whole length of the nose—that is from the tip to the insertion of the eyebrows, into 4 equal parts, you will find that one of these parts extends from the tip of the nostrils to the base of the nose, and the upper division lies between the inner corner of the eye and the insertion of the eyebrows; and the two middle parts [together] are equal to the length of the eye from the inner to the outer corner.

W. P. 5 b]

322.

Il dito grosso del piè è la sesta · parte · d'esso piè, tolgliendo · la misura in profilo di detro dode esso dito nascie [2]dalla polpa del petto del piè · insino alla · sua stremità *a* · *b*; ed è simile allo spatio ch'è dalla bocca · al di sotto del mẽto; [3]se fai · il piè · in profilo di fora ·, fa nasciere · il piccolo · dito · ai tre quarti della · lunghezza d'esso piè, e troverai lo spatio [4]ch'è dal principio d'esso dito insino all'ultimo sporto del dito grosso.

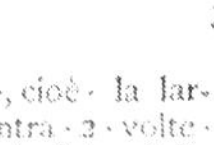

The great toe is the sixth part of the foot, taking the measure in profile, on the inside of the foot, from where this toe springs from the ball of the sole of the foot to its tip *a b*; and it is equal to the distance from the mouth to the bottom of the chin. If you draw the foot in profile from the outside, make the little toe begin at three quarters of the length of the foot, and you will find the same distance from the insertion of this toe as to the farthest prominence of the great toe.

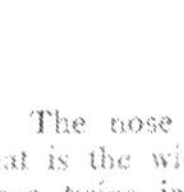

. . de cha. 11. bocha.

321. 1. quatrati . . lungheza . . nelle narise entra . . dala pũta. 2. essimilmẽte ["i profilo"] tanto . . naria . . chõgivgnie chola. 3. dalluna alaltra nanrsa. 4. dimiderai . . parte . . lungeza . . apichatura. 5. che i dele . . narise . . ella lagrimatoro. 6. pichatura . . elle . . mezo . . lagrimatoro . alla . chodo.

322. 1. ella . . dito [si po] nascie. 2. bocha. 3. seffai . . nasciere . il pichololo . . lungeza. 4. allultimo [spatio] sporto . . gro.

320. There are, with this section, two sketches of eyes, not reproduced here.

321. The two bottom sketches on Pl. VII, No. 4 face the six lines of this section.—With regard to the proportions of the head in profile see No. 312.

W. P. 8*a*]

323.

Tāto è ī v̄ medesimo [2]homo lo spatio · che è īfra [3] · *a* · *b* · quāto · *c* · *d*.

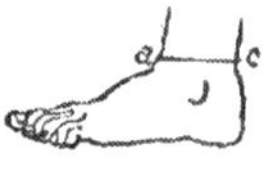

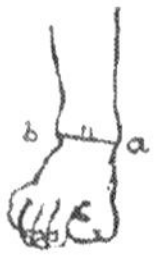

For each man respectively the distance between *a b* is equal to *c d*.

W. P. 1*a*]

324.

Il piè · è · tanto · piv · lungo · che la · mano ·, quanto · è la grossezza · del bracio · alla · givntura · della · mano · cioè dou' eli è piv · sottile, [2]stando in faccia; [3]Ancora · troverai · il piè · essere · tanto · maggiore · della · mano · quanto · è dall' appiccatura · di dentro · del piccolo · dito del piè · all' ultimo [4]sportamento · del dito grosso ·, togliendo la misura · per la lunga · dirittura · del piè; [5]La palma · della mano · sanza · le dita · entra · due · volte · nel piè · sanza le sue dita; [6]Se tu terrai · la mano · coi sua diti · diritti e stretti · insieme ·, trouerai · quella · essere larga · quāto la maggior larghezza · del piede cioè doue [7]si cōgiugnie coi sua · diti; [8]E se tu · misuri dalla · pūta · della nocca del piè di dētro · alla · pūta del dito · grosso · trouerai questa misura · essere · grāde [9]quāto · è tutta · la mano; [10]Dalla givntura del piè · di sopra · all' appiccatura · de' sua diti di sopra · è tanto · quāto dal' appiccatura della · mano · alla pūta [11]del suo · dito · grosso; [12]La minore · larghezza della mano · è simile · alla minore · larghezza del piè · infra la sua appiccatura · colla gāba e 'l pricipio de' diti sua. [13]La larghezza del calcagnio · nel suo · disotto · è simile alla grossezza dello bracio, dove · si givgnie colla mano di dentro,

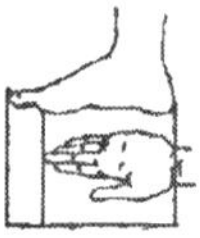

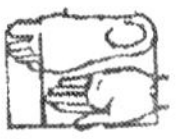

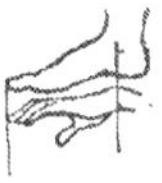

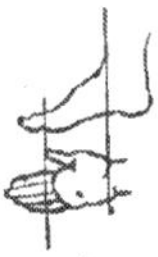

Relative proportions of the hand and foot.

The foot is as much longer than the hand as the thickness of the arm at the wrist where it is thinnest seen facing.

Again, you will find that the foot is as much longer than the hand as the space between the inner angle of the little toe to the last projection of the big toe, if you measure along the length of the foot.

The palm of the hand without the fingers goes twice into the length of the foot without the toes.

If you hold your hand with the fingers straight out and close together you will find it to be of the same width as the widest part of the foot, that is where it is joined onto the toes.

And if you measure from the prominence of the inner ancle to the end of the great toe you will find this measure to be as long as the whole hand.

From the top angle of the foot to the insertion of the toes is equal to the hand from wrist joint to the tip of the thumb.

The smallest width of the hand is equal to the smallest width of the foot between its joint into the leg and the insertion of the toes.

The width of the heel at the lower part is equal to that of the arm where it joins the hand; and also to the leg

324. 1. ettanto piv . lung . chella . . ella grosseza. 3. magiore . . apichatura . . pichholo. 4. tollendo. 6. settutterrai . . choi . . esstretti . . magiore largeza del piedi. 7. cho sua. 8. essettu . . pūta [del pie] . della noce. 9. ettutta. 10. apichatura . . apichatura. 12. largeza [del pie] "della mano" . essimile . . largeza . . infralla sua apichatura cholla. 13. largeza del chalchagnio . . grosseza essimile . . givgnie chol suo bracio di dentro Essimile. 14. facia. 16. mezo . . grādeza . . bocha

E simile [14]dove la ganba in faccia è piv sottile;

[15]Lo spatio · che à · il piv · lungo · dito del piè infra 'l principio · della · sua diuisione dal dito grosso · alla sua · stremità è la quarta parte del piè, [16]ciòè dal mezzo · del suo · polo di dētro · alla sua · punta, Ed è simile alla grādezza della bocca: E lo spatio ch'è infra la bocca e 'l mento; [17]è simile · allo spatio ch'è infra le nocche e delle 3 dita di mezzo e le prime givnture d'esse, stando la mā distesa, [18]e simile allo nodo del dito grosso della mano al pricipio della . sua · vnghia, stādo disteso, ed è la quarta parte [19]della mano e del uolto;

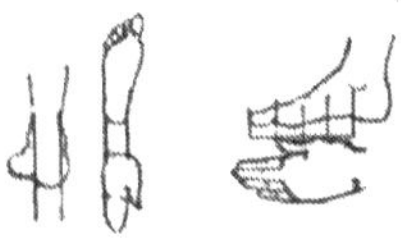

[20]Lo spatio ch'è infra li stremi de' poli dentro e fori de' piedi, detti talloni ouero nocche · o burelle del piè *a b* fia simile alto [21]spatio · ch'è infra la bocca e 'l lagrimatojo del-l'ochio.

where it is thinnest when viewed in front.

The length of the longest toe, from its first division from the great toe to its tip is the fourth of the foot from the centre of the ancle bone to the tip, and it is equal to the width of the mouth. The distance between the mouth and the chin is equal to that of the knuckles and of the three middle fingers and to the length of their first joints if the hand is spread, and equal to the distance from the joint of the thumb to the outset of the nails, that is the fourth part of the hand and of the face.

The space between the extreme poles inside and outside the foot called the ancle or ancle bone *a b* is equal to the space between the mouth and the inner corner of the eye.

W. P. 4 *b*]

325.

Relative proportions of the foot and of the face (325—327).

Il piè dal suo · nascimēto · colla ganba insino · alla stremità del dito · grosso · è simile allo spatio [2]ch'è infra 'l principio di sopra del mēto, al nascimēto de' capegli *a · b*, e simile a cinque sesti del uolto.

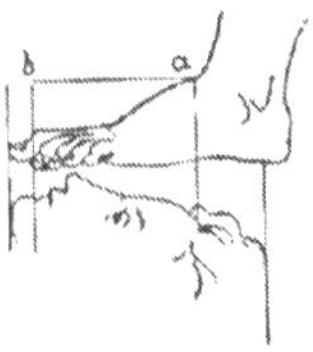

The foot, from where it is attached to the leg, to the tip of the great toe is as long as the space between the upper part of the chin and the roots of the hair *a b*; and equal to five sixths of the face.

W. P. 7 *a*]

326.

a d è vna testa, [2]*c b* è vna testa, [3]i quatro minori diti son dal di sopra dell'unghie al di sotto grossi a v̄ modo e sono $^1/_{13}$ del piè.

a d is a head's length, *c b* is a head's length. The four smaller toes are all equally thick from the nail at the top to the bottom, and are $^1/_{13}$ of the foot.

W. P. 3. II]

327.

Tutto il piè · entra dal gomito · alla givntura della mano · e · dal gomito all'appiccatura di dētro del braccio · diuerso la poppa,

The whole length of the foot will lie between the elbow and the wrist and between the elbow and the inner angle of the arm

. Ello . . infralla bocha. 17. Essimile . noche . . dimezo della cile . . lama. 18. essimile alla nocha . . vaghia. 20. infralli . . effori . . ouero noci [di] . o bu relle de pie "a b". 21. la boga el lagrimatorio.

325. 1. nassciměto . cholla . . essimile alla allosspatio. 2. nassciměto de chapeglis. 6 esimia.

326. 3. minor . . son grossi dal . . ungie.

327. 1. apichatura . . bracio diuer la popa. 2. ettanto . . chapo magiore altesa . chapo . . effigurato il pie entra 3 volte. *Here the text breaks off.*

326. See Pl. XIV, No. 1, a drawing of a foot with the text in three lines below it.

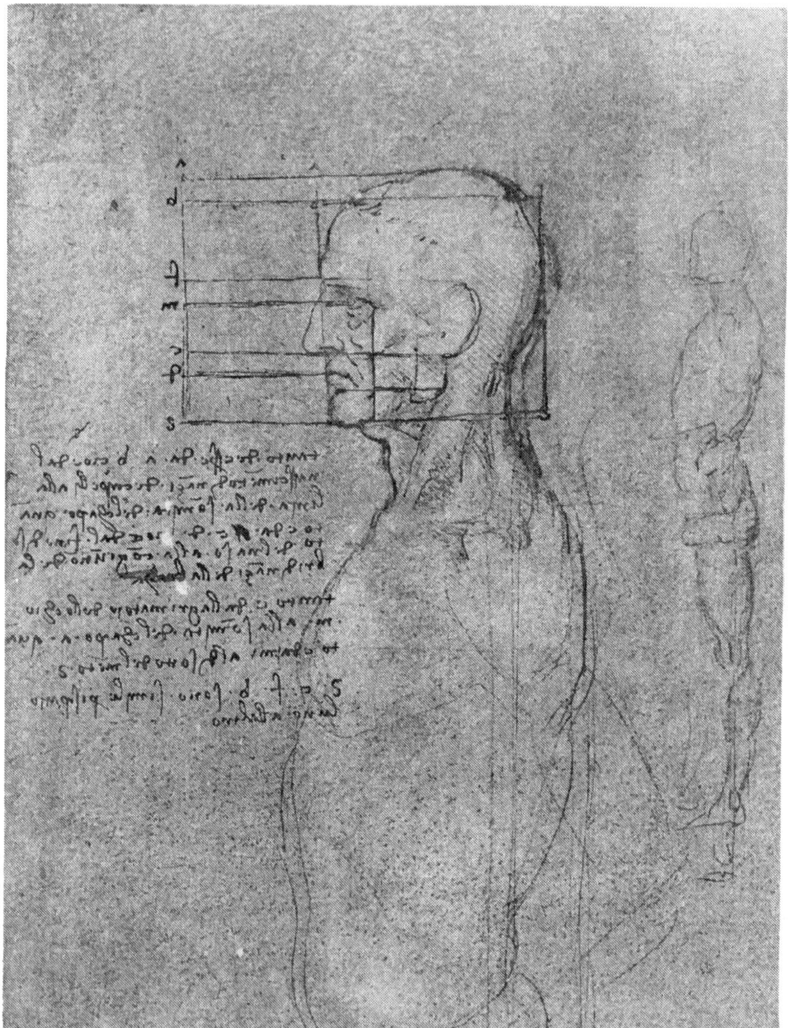

Héliog. Dujardin

Imp. Eudes

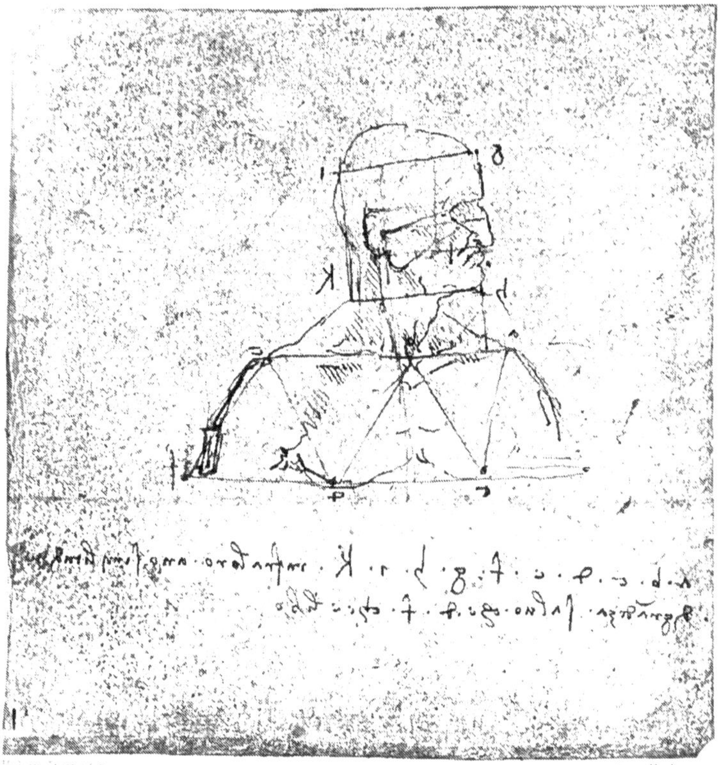

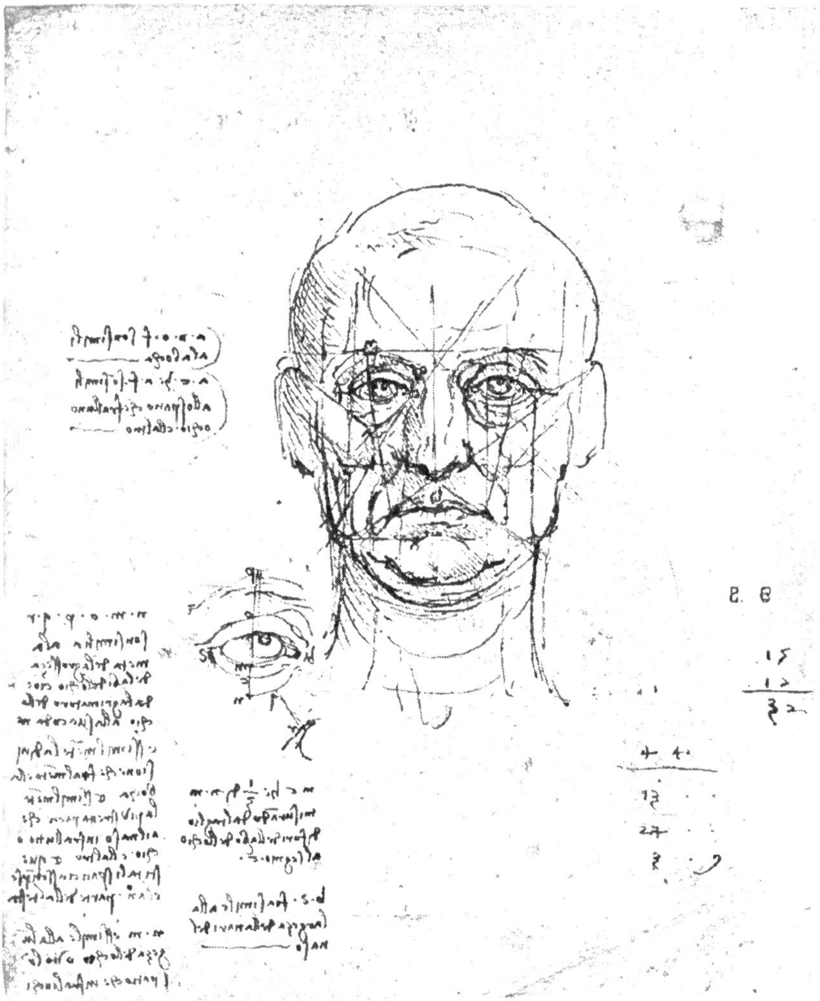

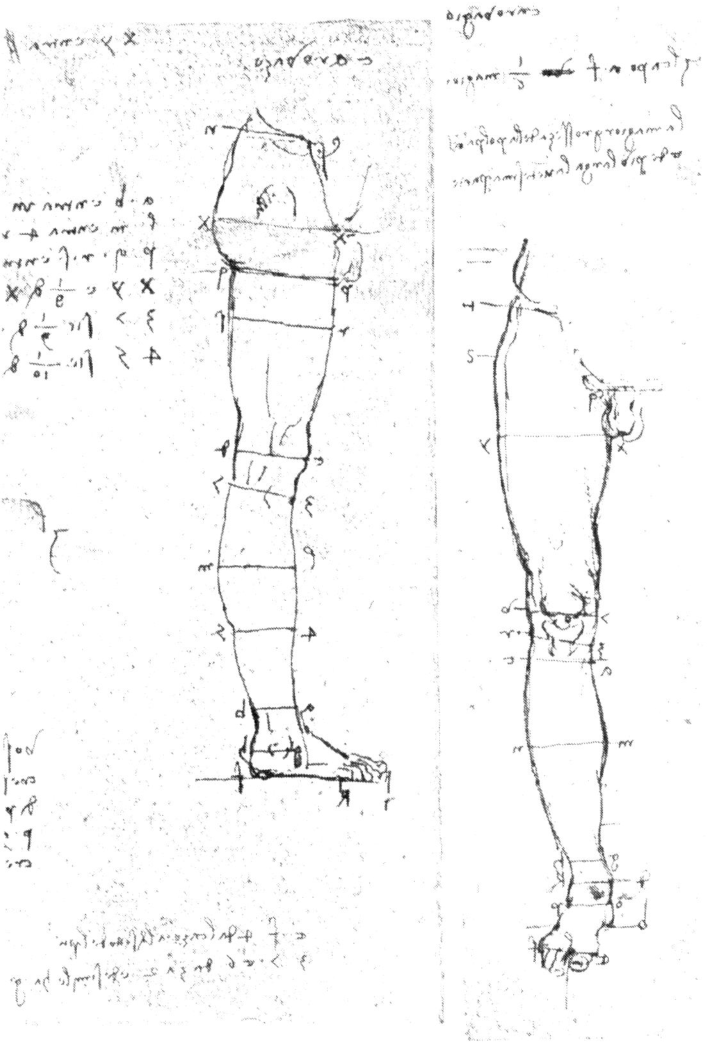

quādo · il braccio sta piegato; [2]Il piè è tanto grāde quāto tutto · il capo · dell'omo, cioè dal di sotto del mēto alla maggiore altezza del capo nel modo che qui è figurato.

towards the breast when the arm is folded. The foot is as long as the whole head of a man, that is from under the chin to the topmost part of the head[2] in the way here figured.

W. P. 7a]

328.

La maggior grossezza della polpa della gāba è nel terzo della sua altezza *a b* [2]ed è piv larga la uētesima parte che la maggiore larghezza del piè.

[3]*a c* è mezza testa, ed è simile a *d b* e all'appiccatura de' [4]cinque diti · *e f*, [6]*d k* diminviscie il sesto · in nella gāba *g* · *h* · [7]*g h* è $^{1}/_{3}$ della testa; [8]*m n* crescie il sesto di *a* · *e* ed è $^{7}/_{12}$ della testa; [9]*o* · *p* è minore $^{1}/_{10}$ di *d* · *k* ed è $^{6}/_{17}$ della testa, [10]*a* si è il mezzo infra *b q* ed è $^{1}/_{4}$ dell'omo, [11]*r* si è mezzo infra *s* · *b*; [12]il cauo del ginochio di fori *r* è piv · alto che 'l cavo di dētro · *a*, [13]la metà della grossezza della gāba da piè, [14]*r* si trova in mezzo infra il gobbo *s* · e il piano *b*; [15]*v* è in mezzo infra *t* · *b* · [16]la grossezza della coscia ī faccia è simile alla maggiore [17]larghezza della faccia del uiso cioè $^{2}/_{3}$ dello spatio ch'è [18]dal mēto alla sōmità del capo; [19]*z* · *r* è $^{5}/_{6}$ di 7 · *v*. [20]*m n* è simile a · 7 · *v* ed è $^{1}/_{4}$ di *r b*, [21]*x y* entra · 3 · in *r* · *b* · e in *r* · *s*;

[22]*a* · *b* entra in *c* · *f* 6, e 6 in *c* · *n* ed è simile a *g* · *h* · *i k*, [23]*l m* entra 4 in *d* · *f*, e 4 in · *d* · *n*, ed è $^{3}/_{7}$ del piè, [24]*p q* · *r* · *s* · entra 3 in *d* · *f* e 3 in *b n*, [25]*x y* è $^{1}/_{8}$ di *x f* ed è simile a | *n* · *q*, [26]3 7 si è $^{1}/_{9}$ di *n f*, [27]4 5 si è $^{1}/_{10}$ di *n f*;

Proportions of the leg (328—331). The greatest thickness of the calf of the leg is at a third of its height *a b*, and is a twentieth part thicker than the greatest thickness of the foot.

a c is half of the head, and equal to *d b* and to the insertion of the five toes *e f*. *d k* diminishes one sixth in the leg *g h*. *g h* is $^{1}/_{3}$ of the head; *m n* increases one sixth from *a e* and is $^{7}/_{12}$ of the head. *o p* is $^{1}/_{10}$ less than *d k* and is $^{6}/_{17}$ of the head. *a* is at half the distance between *b q*, and is $^{1}/_{4}$ of the man. *r* is half way between *s* and *b*[11]. The concavity of the knee outside *r* is higher than that inside *a*. The half of the whole height of the leg from the foot *r*, is half way between the prominence *s* and the ground *b*. *v* is half way between *t* and *b*. The thickness of the thigh seen in front is equal to the greatest width of the face, that is $^{2}/_{3}$ of the length from the chin to the top of the head; *z r* is $^{5}/_{6}$ of 7 to *v*; *m n* is equal to 7 *v* and is $^{1}/_{4}$ of *r b*, *x y* goes 3 times into *r b*, and into *r s*.

[22]*a b* goes six times into *c f* and six times into *c n* and is equal to *g h*; *i k l m* goes 4 times into *d f*, and 4 times into *d n* and is $^{3}/_{7}$ of the foot; *p q r s* goes 3 times into *d f*, and 3 times into *b n*; [25]*x y* is $^{1}/_{8}$ of *x f* and is equal to *n q*. 3 7 is $^{1}/_{9}$ of *n f*; 4 5 is $^{1}/_{10}$ of *n f*[27].

328. 1. magior grosseza . . alteza. 2. parte [del] chella magiore largeza. 3. meza T ed esimile ha . . apichatura. 5. g h l. 8. cresscie. 9. della T. 10. infra b ede $^{1}/_{4}$. 10. mezo. 11. mezo. 12. difori "r" e . . chelchavo. 13. grosseza. 14. mezo . . gobo. 15. imezo. 16. grosseza cosscia . . facia essimile magiore. 17. largezza . . facia. 18. somita del chapo. 20. essimile ha. 22. entra [6]. 3 . in. c . f . "6 e 6 in c . n" ed e simile ha g. 25. h . ha. 28. [Il]. 31. cinarsi. 33. chosi. 34. cazo.

327. 2. *nel modo che qui è figurato.* See Pl. VII, No. 4, the upper figure. The text breaks off at the end of line 2 and the text given under No. 321 follows below. It may be here remarked that the second sketch on W. P. 311 has in the original no explanatory text.

328. The drawing of a leg seen in front Pl. XIII, No. 1 belongs to the text from lines 3—21. The measurements in this section should be compared with the text No. 331, lines 1—13, and the sketch of a leg seen in front on Pl. XV.

11. *b* is here and later on measured on the right side of the foot as seen by the spectator.

22—35. The sketch illustrating these lines is on Pl. XIII, No. 2.

22. a b *entra in* c f 6 *e* 6 *in* c n. Accurate measurement however obliges us to read 7 for 6.

25. *y* is not to be found on the diagram and *x* occurs twice; this makes the passage very obscure.

22—27. Compare with this lines 18—24 of No. 331, and the sketch of a leg in profile Pl. XV.

[30]Vo sapere quãto vno [31]crescie leuãdosi in pũta [31]di piè, e nel chinarsi quãto [32]*p*·*g* diminviscie e quãto *n q* [33]cresca e così la piega del piè;

[34]*e f* 4 dal cazzo al di sotto del piè [35]3 7 è 6 da 3 a 2 ed è simile a *g*·*h*·et *i*·*k*.

I want to know how much a man increases in height by standing on tip-toe and how much *p g* diminishes by stooping; and how much it increases at *n q* likewise in bending the foot.

[34]*e f* is four times in the distance between the genitals and the sole of the foot; [35]3 7 is six times from 3 to 2 and is equal to *g h* and *i k*.

B. 3]

329.

Il piè dalla · punta al calcagnio ẽtra 2 volte [2]dal calcagnio al ginochio, cioè dove l'osso della [3]ganba si cõgivgnie con quello della coscia.

The length of the foot from the end of the toes to the heel goes twice into that from the heel to the knee, that is where the leg bone [fibula] joins the thigh bone [femur].

W. P. 7a]

330.

a n b son simili, [2]*c n d* son simili · *n* · *c* fia 2 piè; [3]*n d* fia 2 piè.

a n b are equal; *c n d* are equal; *n c* makes two feet; *n d* makes 2 feet.

W. P. 8a]

331.

m · *n* · *o* sono simili; [2]la minore grossezza [3]della gãba ĩ faccia ẽtra [4]8 volte dal di sotto del piè [5]alla givntura del ginochio, [6]e à similitudine col braccio [7]i faccia sul' appiccatura della [8]mano · e colla maggiore lũghezza [9]dell' orecchio e · coi · 3 spati, [10]i che è diuiso il uolto, e que[11]sta grossezza ẽtra · 4 volte da[12]la giũtara della mano al fine del go[13]mito; [14]tãto è largo il piè, quãto è [15]lo spatio del ginochio ĩfra · *a* · *b*; [16]tãto è la padella del ginochio, [17]quãto è la gãba ĩfra *r* · *s*.

[18]La minore grossezza della gãba [19]i proffilo ẽtra 6 volte dal di sotto [20]del piè

m n o are equal. The narrowest width of the leg seen in front goes 8 times from the sole of the foot to the joint of the knee, and is the same width as the arm, seen in front at the wrist, and as the longest measure of the ear, and as the three chief divisions into which we divide the face; and this measurement goes 4 times from the wrist joint of the hand to the point of the elbow. [14]The foot is as long as the space from the knee between *a* and *b*; and the patella of the knee is as long as the leg between *r* and *s*.

[18]The least thickness of the leg in profile goes 6 times from the sole of the foot

35. simile he g.
329. 1. dala chalcagnio. 3. chõgivgnie chon.
330. 2. som simili
331. 2. grosseza. 5. ala. 6. chol [illegible]. 7. apichatura. 8. chola . . magiore lũgeza. 9. e co . 3. 10. iche diuiso. 11. grosseza. 14. larghe. 16. padela. 18. grosseza. 19. sotto. 21. chello . . infralla. 22. choda. 23. cholla magiore grosseza del la [illegible]

34. *e f 4 dal cazo.* By reading *i* for *e* the sense of this passage is made clear.

35. 2 is not to be found in the sketch which renders the passage obscure. The two last lines are plainly legible in the facsimile.

330. See the lower sketch, Pl. XIV, No. 1.

331. See Pl. XV. The text of lines 2—17 is to the left of the front view of the leg, to which it refers. Lines 18—27 are in the middle column and refer to the leg seen in profile and turned to the left, on the right hand side of the writing. Lines 20—30 are above, to the left and apply to the sketch below them.

Some farther remarks on the proportion of the leg will be found in No. 336, lines 6, 7.

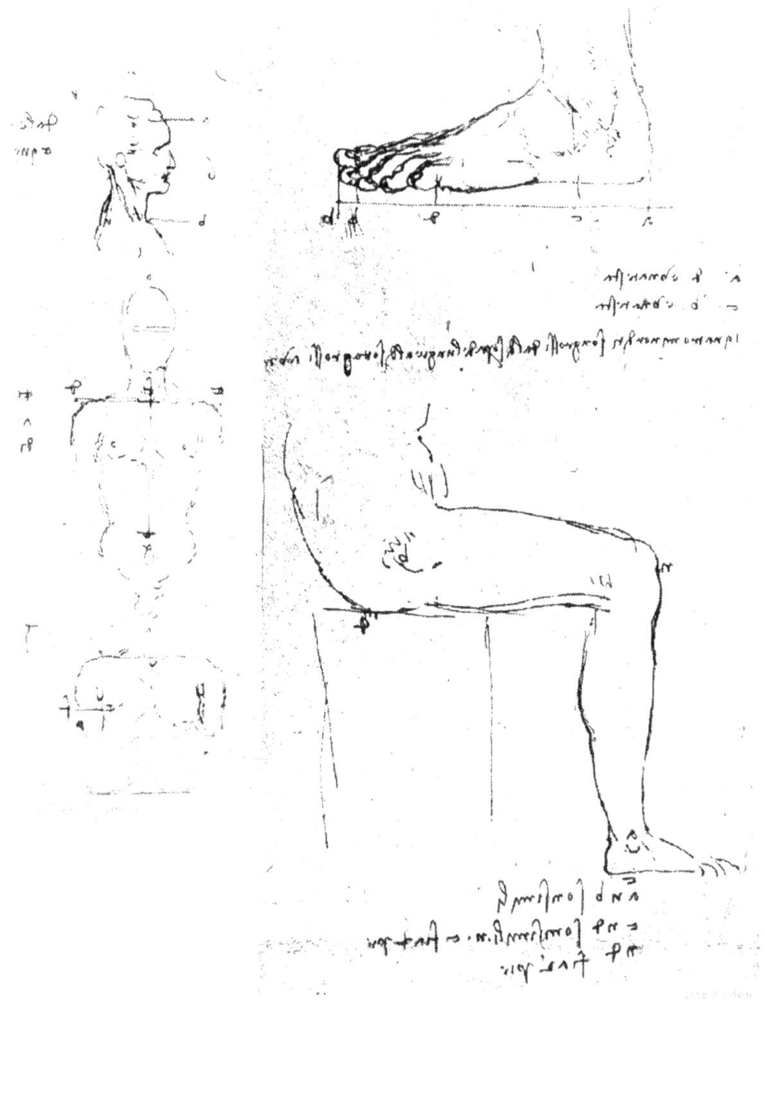

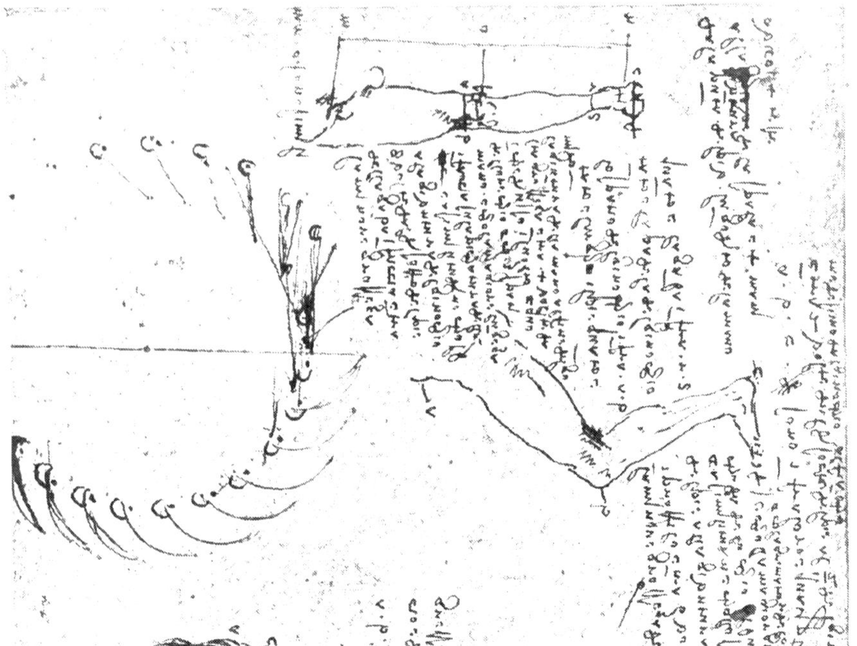

alla givntura del ginochio, [21]e à similitudine collo spatio, ch'è ĩfra la [22]coda del'ochio al buso dell'orechio, [23]e colla maggior grossezza del braccio ĩ profilo, [24]e col lagrimatojo del'ochio al'appiccatura de' capelli

[25]*a b c* sonō ĩfra loro equali per lũghezza *c d* [26]ētra 2 volte dal di sotto del piè al 1/2 del ginochio e quel [27]medesimo dal ginochio al fiãco

[28]*a · b c* sono equali, *a* b | è 2 piedi, [29]cioè dal calcagnio alla pũta del dito [30]grosso

to the knee joint and is the same width as the space between the outer corner of the eye and the opening of the ear, and as the thickest part of the arm seen in profile and between the inner corner of the eye and the insertion of the hair

a b c [*d*] are all relatively of equal length *c d* goes twice from the sole of the foot to the centre of the knee and the same from the knee to the hip

[28] *a b c* are equal, *a* to *b* is 2 feet—that is to say measuring from the heel to the tip of the great toe

W P 6, I*a*]

332.

Se vno s'inginochia, quello stremerà la quarta [2]parte di sua altezza,

[3]Stando l'omo ginochioni colle mani al petto [4]il bellico fia il mezzo di sua altezza e simil[5]mente le punte de' gomiti,

[6]Il mezzo dell'omo che sede, cioè dal sedere alla [7]sommità del capo, fia il braccio di sotto della poppa [8]e 'l di sotto della spalla, essa parte sedēte, [9]cioè dal sedere al di sopra del capo, fia [10]tanto piv che mezzo l'omo, quanto è la [11]grossezza e lunghezza de testiculi.

On the central point of the whole body

In kneeling down a man will lose the fourth part of his height

When a man kneels down with his hands folded on his breast the navel will mark half his height and likewise the points of the elbows.

Half the height of a man who sits—that is from the seat to the top of the head—will be where the arms fold below the breast, and below the shoulders The seated portion—that is from the seat to the top of the head—will be more than half the man's [whole height] by the length of the scrotum

W P 6, I*b*]

333

Il cubito è la quarta parte dell'altezza dell'omo ed è simile alla maggior larghezza delle spalle, [2]dal'una givntura delle spalle all'altra fia due teste [3]e 'l simile fia dalla somītà del petto all'ombelico, [4]dalla detta sōmità al nascimēto del mēbro è vna testa

The relative proportions of the torso and of the whole figure

The cubit is one fourth of the height of a man and is equal to the greatest width of the shoulders From the joint of one shoulder to the other is two faces and is equal to the distance from the top of the breast to the navel [9] From this point to the genitals is a face's length.

W P 6, II*a*]

334

Dalle radici de' capegli alla sōmità del petto *a b* fia la sesta parte dell'altezza dell'omo [2]e questa misura fia simile

The relative proportions of the head and of the torso

From the roots of the hair to the top of the breast *a b* is the sixth part of the height of a man and this measure is equal

24 colagrimator apichatura de "ca pelli" 25 a b c [d] lũgeza 26 disocto equl 27 fiãcho 29 pũda 30 grōssoe chosi

332 2 altɩza 3 cholle 4 belicho mezo alteza essimil 6 mezo chessede 7 chapo fia il br di popa 9 chapo 10 mezo ella 11 ellungeza de testichuli

333 1 chupido ella alteza magior largeza 2 dalluna spalli 3 pecto onbellicho 4 nasscimēto e vna 1

334 1 chapegli petto "a b" fia. 3 [e] tanto è , spalli 4 bellicho ecquesta nasscimēto 6 Il br dove sispicha

332. See Pl VIII, No 2

333 Compare with this the sketches on the other page of the same leaf Pl VIII, No 2

4 *dalla detta somità* It would seem more accurate to read here *dal detto ombilico*

334 The three sketches Pl XIV, No 2 belong to this text

[3]Tanto · è · dall'ultima · parte · delle · spalle · all'altra, quanto è dalla somità dell petto [4]al bellico · e questa · parte · entra · quattro volte · dal di sotto del piè al nascimēto [5]di sotto del naso.

[6]Il braccio, dove si spicca dalla spalla dināzi, entra · 6 uolte · in nello spatio ch'è infra l'uno e l'altro [7]stremo delle spalle · e 3 volte nella testa dell'omo, e quattro nella lunghezza del piè, [8]e tre nella mano dentro e fori.

From the outside part of one shoulder to the other is the same distance as from the top of the breast to the navel and this measure goes four times from the sole of the foot to the lower end of the nose.

The [thickness of] the arm where it springs from the shoulder in front goes 6 times into the space between the two outside edges of the shoulders and 3 times into the face, and four times into the length of the foot and three into the hand, inside or outside.

W. P. 6a II6]

335.

The relative proportions of the torso and of the leg (335—340).

a b c sono equali e son simili allo spatio · ch'è dall'appiccatura del braccio col petto e l'appiccatura [2]del mēbro ·, e lo spatio ch'è dalla pūta de' diti della mano al fopello del braccio, e al mezzo del petto, e sappi [3]che · *c* · *b* · è la terza parte che à la lunghezza dell'omo dalla spalla a terra; [4]*d* · *e* · *f* · son simili infra loro · e son simili alla maggior larghezza · delle spalle.

a b c are equal to each other and to the space from the armpit of the shoulder to the genitals and to the distance from the tip of the fingers of the hand to the joint of the arm, and to the half of the breast; and you must know that *cb* is the third part of the height of a man from the shoulders to the ground; *d e f* are equal to each other and equal to the greatest width of the shoulders.

W. P. 5a]

336.

— Foppel del mēto — [2]fianco — [3]al nascimēto del grosso dito — [4]fin del pescie di dētro della coscia — [5]fin del rilevo del fuso della gāba; [6]la minore grossezza della gāba entra [7]3 nella sua coscia · stando in faccia.

—Top of the chin—hip—the insertion of the middle finger. The end of the calf of the leg on the inside of the thigh.—The end of the swelling of the shin bone of the leg. [6]The smallest thickness of the leg goes 3 times into the thigh seen in front.

W. P. 2a]

337.

The relative proportions of the torso and of the foot.

Il busto · *a* · *b* · fia · nella più sottile parte · uno · pie: e da · *a* · *b* · fiā · 2 piè, che fiā · 2 · quadrati, [2]al cavallo; la piv sottile sua · parte entra · 3 · volte nella lughezza · che fa 3 · quadrati.

The torso *a b* in its thinnest part measures a foot; and from *a* to *b* is 2 feet, which makes two squares to the seat—its thinnest part goes 3 times into the length, thus making 3 squares.

W. P. 7a]

338.

The proportions of the whole figure (338—341).

L'omo a giaciere [2]arriva a $^1/_9$ di sua [3]altezza.

A man when he lies down is reduced to $^1/_9$ of his height.

inello . . ellaltro. 7. spali . . lungeza.

335. 1. dalla . pichatura . . chol . . e lla [b] pichatura. 2. ello . . a fobello . mezo . essapi. 3. ella . . dila largeza dellomo . . atterra. 4. infraloro . . largeza . . spali.

336. 1. fopel. 2. fiancho. 3. nasimēto. 5. fin de. 6. grossezza . . entre.

337. 1. fi "a" nel pi . . i . che fia. 2. chavallo . . lūgeza.

338. 1 diacere 2. ariva. 3. alteza.

335. See Pl. XVI, No. 1.

3. *lunghezza*, in MS. *larghezza*.

336. See Pl. XVII, No. 2, middle sketch.

337. See Pl. VII, No. 2, the lower sketch.

1. *Il busto . . uno piè*. This is less plainly shown in the sketch which accompanies the text than in No. 5. (W. 104). *da a b fiā 2 piè*. For 2 read perhaps $2^1/_2$; but the whole passage is obscure.

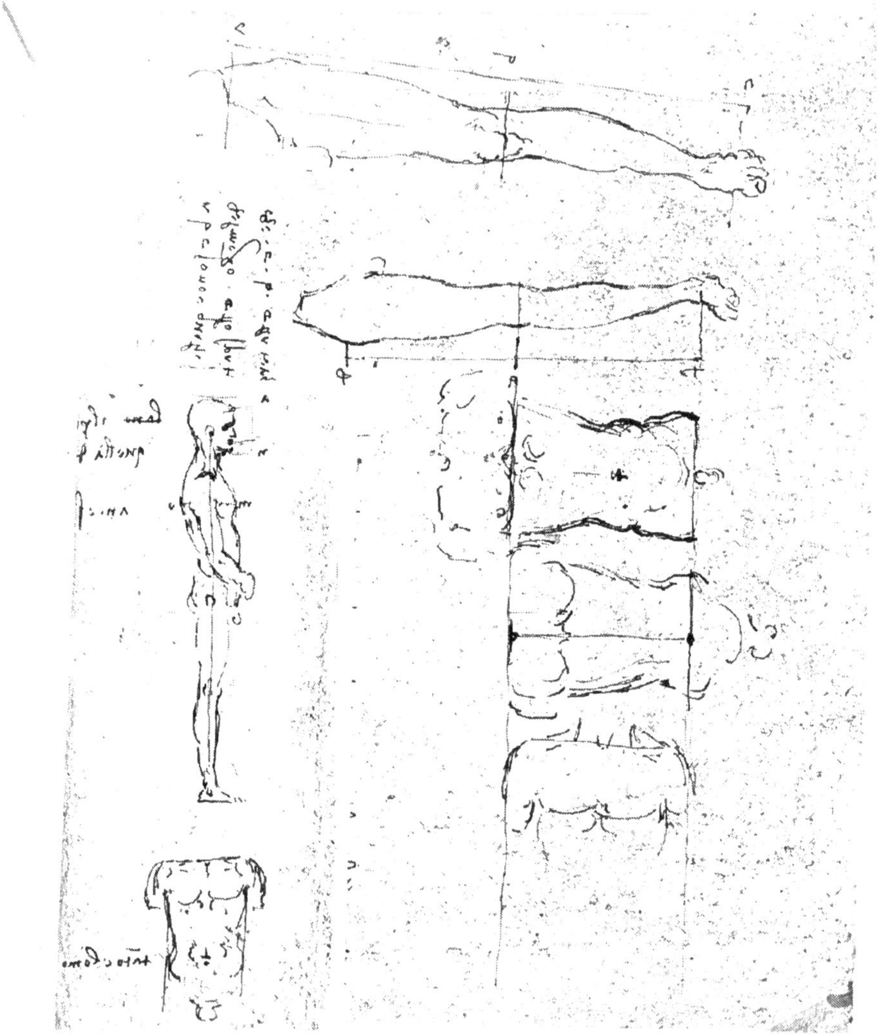

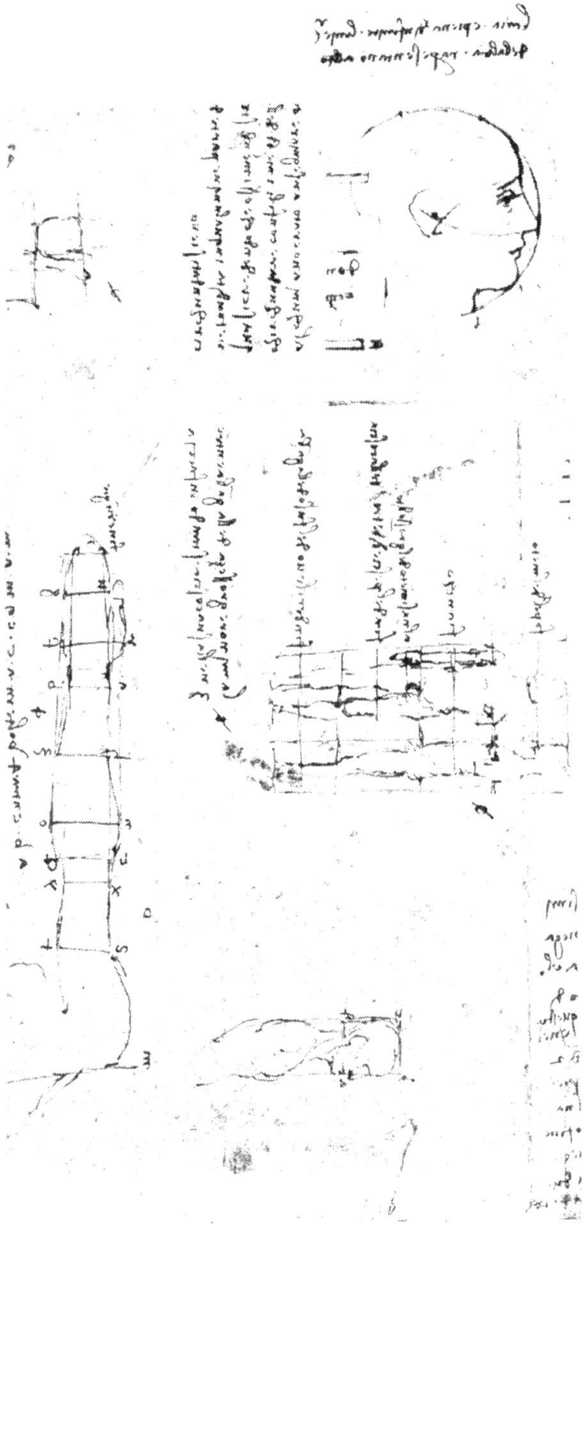

W P 7 b]

339

Il buco dell' orechio, la nascita della spalla, [2]quella del fiãco e del piè son perpẽdiculare linia, [3]*a n* è simile a *m o*

The opening of the ear, the joint of the shoulder, that of the hip and the ancle are in perpendicular lines, *a n* is equal to *m o*

C A 350 a, 1089 a]

340

Dal mento insino al nascimẽto de' capelli si è $^1/_{10}$ parte dalla figura, [2]della giuntura della palma della mano ĩsino alla sommità del dito lungo $^1/_{10}$ parte, [3]dal mẽto alla sommità del capo $^1/_8$ parte, [4]e dalla forcella alla sofnita del petto si è $^1/_5$ parte, [5]e dalla forcella del petto insino alla sommità del capo $^1/_4$ parte, [6]e dal mẽto alle nari del naso $^1/_3$ parte del uolto, [7]e quel medesimo dalle nari al ciglio e dal ciglio al nascimẽto de' capegli, [8]e 'l piè è $^1/_6$ parte, [9]e'l gomito $^1/_4$ parte, [10]larghezza di spalle $^1/_4$ parte

From the chin to the roots of the hair is $^1/_{10}$ of the whole figure From the joint of the palm of the hand to the tip of the longest finger is $^1/_{10}$ From the chin to the top of the head $^1/_8$, and from the pit of the stomach to the top of the breast is $^1/_6$, and from the pit below the breast bone to the top of the head $^1/_4$ From the chin to the nostrils $^1/_3$ part of the face, the same from the nostrils to the brow and from the brow to the roots of the hair, and the foot is $^1/_6$, the elbow $^1/_4$, the width of the shoulders $^1/_4$

W P 5 a]

341

Larghezza di spalle $^1/_4$ del tutto, [2]dalla snodatura della spalla alla mano $^1/_3$, [3]dal taglio del labro di sotto all'omero [4]della spalla uno piè

[5]La maggiore grossezza dell'omo dal petto alla schiena [6]entra 8 volte nell'omo ed è simile allo [7]spatio ch'è dal mẽto alla sofnità del capo

[8]La maggior larghezza è nelle spalle, e entra 4

The width of the shoulders is $^1/_4$ of the whole From the joint of the shoulder to the hand is $^1/_3$, from the parting of the lips to below the shoulder-blade is one foot

The greatest thickness of a man from the breast to the spine is one 8th of his height and is equal to the space between the bottom of the chin and the top of the head

The greatest width is at the shoulders and goes 4

W P 7 b]

342

The torso from the front and back

Tanto è l'omo sotto i bracci quãto lo spatio de' fiãchi

[2]Tanto è l'omo largo ne' fiãchi quãt'è dal sõmo d'essi fiãchi [3]al di sotto delle natiche, stãdo l'omo di pari peso sopra i

The width of a man under the arms is the same as at the hips

A man's width across the hips is equal to the distance from the top of the hip to the bottom of the buttock, when a man stands

339 1 [lane] il puso la nasc spala 2 fiãcho perpẽdichulare 3 ha m
340 1 nassimẽto de chapelli dela 2 dala dela lungho 4 dala forciella dellalla 6 allianari 7 dalanari nasimẽto 9 egomito 10 largeza dispale
341 1 il trezo *written on the margin* largeza 4 spalla ĩ pie 5 magiore grosseza sciena 6 [essimile] 7 somita del chapo 8 largeza [delle] e spalli
342 1 i br quãto 2 sumo 4 somita di 5 spalli 6 mezo infralla

339 See Pl XVI, No 2, the upper sketch
342 The lower sketch Pl XVI, No 2, is drawn by the side of line 1

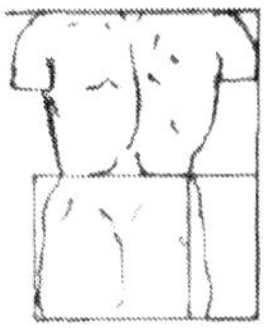

a sua piè, [4]e 'l medesimo spatio · fia da essa soñita de' fiachi alla givntura [5]delle spalle; [6]la cintura overo il di sopra de fiachi fia · in mezzo infra la [7]givntura delle spalle e 'l di sotto delle natiche.

equally balanced on both feet; and there is the same distance from the top of the hip to the armpit. The waist, or narrower part above the hips will be half way between the arm pits and the bottom of the buttock.

Ven. (121) n°1/A

343.

Vitruvius' scheme of proportions.

Vetruuio · architecto mette nella sua · opera · d'architectura [1], che le misure dell'omo sono · dalla · natura [2]distribuite · in questo · modo · cioè · che · 4 diti fa · uno palmo · e 4 palmi · fa · uno pie ·, 6 palmi fa un cubito · 4 [3]cubiti · fa · uno uomo · e 4 · cubiti fa uno · passo · e 24 palmi · fa uno uomo · e queste misure son ne' sua edifiti; [4]Se tu apri tāto le gābe · che tu cali da capo $^1/_{14}$ di tua altezza e apri e alzi tanto le braccia che colle lunghe dita tu tochi la linia della [5]soñità del capo, sappi che 'l cietro delle stremità delle aperte mēbra fia il bellico [6]e lo spatio che si truova infra le gābe, fia triāgolo equilatero.

Vitruvius, the architect, says in his work on architecture that the measurements of the human body are distributed by Nature as follows: that is that 4 fingers make 1 palm, and 4 palms make 1 foot, 6 palms make 1 cubit; 4 cubits make a man's height. And 4 cubits make one pace and 24 palms make a man; and these measures he used in his buildings. If you open your legs so much as to decrease your height $^1/_{14}$ and spread and raise your arms till your middle fingers touch the level of the top of your head you must know that the centre of the outspread limbs will be in the navel and the space between the legs will be an equilateral triangle.

[7]Tanto apre l'omo nelle braccia · quāto · è la · sua · altezza.

The length of a man's outspread arms is equal to his height.

[8]Dal nascimento · de' capegli · al fine di sotto del mento · è · il decimo dell'altezza · del uomo; dal di sotto · del mento · alla · soñità · del capo · è · l'octauo · dell'altezza · dell'omo: dal di sopra · del petto · alla · soñità · del capo · fia il · sexto dell'omo; dal di so[10]pra · del petto al nascimēto de' capegli · fia · la settima · parte · di tutto · l'omo; dalle · tette al di sopra · del capo fia [11]la · quarta · parte · dell'omo: la maggiore · larghezza · delle · spalle · contiene · in se la quarta parte dell'omo ·, dal go[12]mito · alla punta · della · mano · fia la · quinta · parte · dell'omo: da esso · gomito · al termine della · spalla · fia la octaua [13]parte · d'esso omo: tutta · la mano · fia la decima ·

From the roots of the hair to the bottom of the chin is the length of a man's height; from the bottom of the chin to the top of his head is one eighth of his height; from the top of the breast to the top of his head will be one sixth of a man. From the top of the breast to the roots of the hair will be the seventh part of the whole man. From the nipples to the top of the head will be the fourth part of a man. The greatest width of the shoulders contains in itself the fourth part of the man. From the elbow to the tip of the hand will be the fifth part of a man; and from the elbow to the angle of the armpit will be the eighth part of the man. The whole hand will be the tenth part of

343. 1. mette . . chelle. 2. dissstribuite . inquessto . . fa . ī . palmo . . fa ī pie . . fa un chubito. 3. fa ī homo . he. 4. chubidi fa ī passo he . . fa ī homo . equeste. 4. Sstu . . chetu chali da chapo . . alza . . cholle lunge. 5. chapo . . bellicho. 6. ello . . chessi . . infralle ghera . . dissecto. 7. nele . . ella. 8. nasscimento de chapegli . . somi. 9. chapo . he . . pecto . . somita del chapo. 10. secttimo . . ttucto pecto . . nasscimēto de chapegli . . secttima . . chapo. 11. largeza . . spalli chontiene . . se [la oct] la quarta. 12. isspalla. 13. tucta . . nasscie . . mezo. 14. secttima . . socto . . socto.

343. See Pl. XVIII. The original leaf is 21 centimètres wide and 33½ long. At the ends of the scale below the figure are written the words *diti* (fingers) and *palmi* (palms). The passage quoted from Vitruvius is Book III, Cap. 1, and Leonardo's drawing is given in the editions of Vitruvius by FRA GIOCONDO (Venezia 1511, fol., Firenze 1513, 8vo) and by CESARIANO (Como 1521).

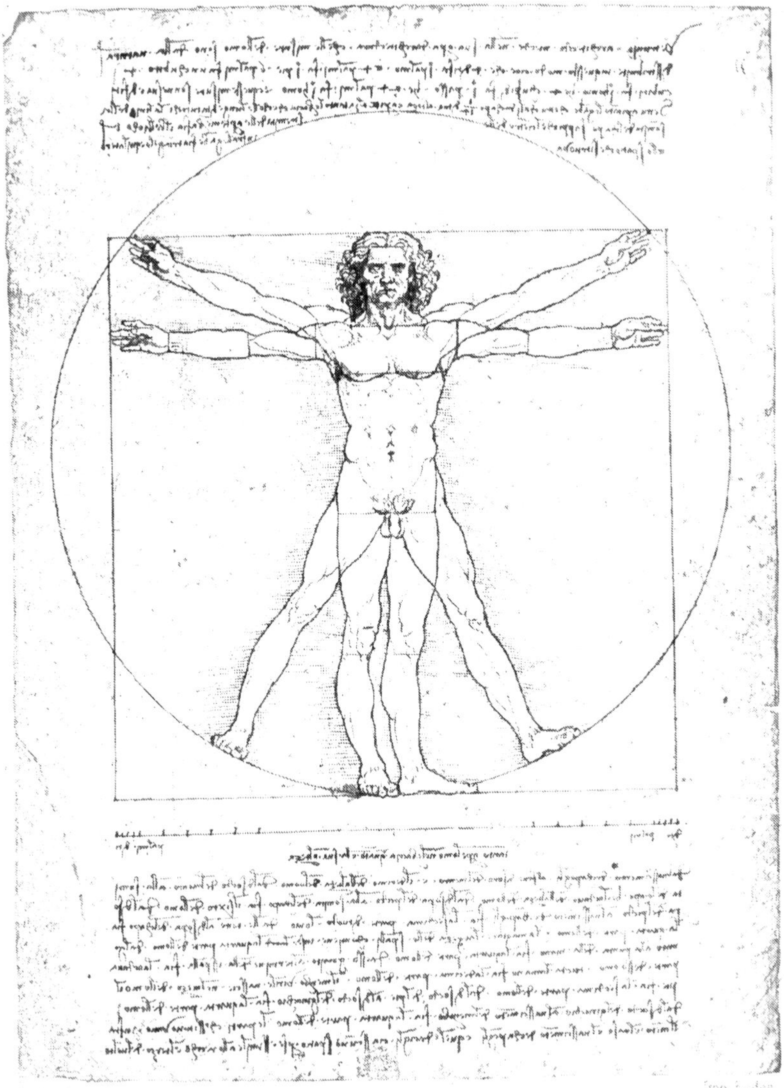

Héliog. Dujardin — Imp. Eudes

parte · dell'omo. il menbro · virile · nascie · nel mezzo dell'omo; il [14] piè · fia la settima · parte · dell'omo; dal di sotto del piè · al di sotto del ginochio · fia · la quarta · parte · dell'omo, [15] dal di sotto · del ginochio al nascimēto del membro · fia · la quarta parte · dell'omo le parti che si truovano infra [16] il mēto e 'l naso e 'l nascimēto de' capegli e quel de' cigli · ciascūno spatio · per se è simile all'orechio ed è 'l terzo del uolto.

the man; the beginning of the genitals marks the middle of the man. The foot is the seventh part of the man. From the sole of the foot to below the knee will be the fourth part of the man From below the knee to the beginning of the genitals will be the fourth part of the man The distance from the bottom of the chin to the nose and from the roots of the hair to the eyebrows is, in each case the same, and like the ear, a third of the face

Ash I; 12 *a*]

344

Da *b a* è una testa e così da *c a*, [2] e questo accade quādo il gomito [3] fa angulo recto.

From *b* to *a* is one head, as well as from *c* to *a* and this happens when the elbow forms a right angle. The arm and head

W P 8 *a*]

345.

Dalla pūta del piv lūgo dito della mano [2] alla giv̄tura della spalla è 4 mani [3] o vuoi 4 teste.

[4] *a · b · c* sono equali e ciascuno [5] intervallo · è 2 teste

From the tip of the longest finger of the hand to the shoulder joint is four hands or, if you will, four faces. Proportions of the arm (345—349)

a b c are equal and each interval is 2 heads.

B 3 *b*]

346

La mano isino doue si cōgivgnie col osso [2] del braccio ētra 4 volte dalla pūta del piv [3] lungo dito isino alla giv̄tura della spalla

The hand from the longest finger to the wrist joint goes 4 times from the tip of the longest finger to the shoulder joint.

W P 4 *a*]

347.

a b c sono equali e son simili al piè e lo spatio ch'è dalla tetta al mamolino, [2] *d e* fia la terza parte di tutto · l'omo ·

f · g è la quarta · parte dell'omo ed è simile a *g · h* · e simile al cubito

a b c are equal to each other and to the foot and to the space between the nipple and the navel *d e* will be the third part of the whole man.

f g is the fourth part of a man and is equal to *g h* and measures a cubit

15 socto chessi 16. nasscimēto de chapegli ciasscūno essimile allorecheel
344 1. e ỉ T cio 2 ecquesto achade
345 1 dala delā 2 dela spala 4 ciaschuno 5 intervalo
346 1 chol
347 1. esson 3 ella essimile ha . essimilo al chupido

344 See Pl XLI, No. 1

345. Lines 1—3 are given on Pl XV below the front view of the leg; lines 4 and 5 are below again, on the left side The lettering refers to the bent arm near the text

347 See Pl XIX, No 1

1 *mamolino* (=*bambino*, little child) may mean here the navel.

W. P 5a]

348.

a b · entra 4 volte in *a · c* · e 9 in *a · m*; ¶la maggiore grossezza del braccio in[3]fra 'l gomito · e la mano entra 6 in *a · m*¶ [4]ed è simile a · *r · f* ·; [5]la maggiore grossezza del braccio · infra la spalla e 'l go[6]mito entra 4 da *c · m* · ed è simile · *h · n · g*; [7]la minore grossezza del braccio sopra 'l gomito *x · y* · non è ra[8]dice quadrata, ma è simile al mezzo dello spatio *h* 3 [9]che si trova infra la givntura del braccio dẽtro [10]e la givntura della mano;

[11]La grossezza del braccio sulla mano [12]entra · 12 volte in tutto il braccio, [13]cioè dalla punta de' diti insino [14]alla givntura della spalla, cioè [15]3 nella mano e 9 nel braccio;

[16]Il braccio piegato è 4 teste,

[17]Il braccio dalla spalla al gomito [18]nel piegarsi crescie [19]di sua lunghezza · cioè la lunghezza [20]dalla spalla al gomito, e esso ac[21]crescimẽto è simile alla gro[22]ssezza del braccio sulla giuntura della mã, [23]quãdo sta in proffilo, e simile [24] allo spatio ch' è dal di sotto del mẽto al ta[25]glio della bocca, e la grossezza delle 2 [26]dita della mã di mezzo, e la grãdezza [27]della bocca, e lo spatio ch' è dalla appicca[28]tura de' capelli alla fronte, e la sommità del [29]capo; Queste cose nominate sõ [30]simili infra loro ma nõ simili al [31]sopra detto accrescimẽto del braccio

[32]Il braccio dal gomito alla mano mai [33]crescie per piegare o dirizarsi,

[34]Il braccio dalla spalla alla givntura [35]di dẽtro quãd'è disteso;

[36]Quando il braccio è disteso *p · n* · è simi[37]le a · *n · a*, E quando si piega [38]*n · a* · sciema $^1/_6$ di sua lũghezza e 'l [39]simile fa · *p · n*; E 'l gomito di [40]fori nel piegarsi crescie $^1/_7$, e questo nel [41]suo piegarsi crescie e ariva alla lũghezza di 2 [42]teste, E 'l

a b goes 4 times into *a c* and 9 into *a m*. The greatest thickness of the arm between the elbow and the hand goes 6 times into *a m* and is equal to *r f*. The greatest thickness of the arm between the shoulder and the elbow goes 4 times into *c m*, and is equal to *h n g*. The smallest thickness of the arm above the elbow *x y* is not the base of a square, but is equal to half the space *h* 3 which is found between the inner joint of the arm and the wrist joint.

[11]The width of the wrist goes 12 times into the whole arm, that is from the tip of the fingers to the shoulder joint; that is 3 times into the hand and 9 into the arm.

The arm when bent is 4 heads.

The arm from the shoulder to the elbow in bending increases in length, that is in the length from the shoulder to the elbow, and this increase is equal to the thickness of the arm at the wrist when seen in profile And the space between the bottom of the chin and the parting of the lips, is equal to the thickness of the 2 middle fingers, and to the width of the mouth and to the space between the roots of the hair on the forehead and the top of the head[29]. All these distances are equal to each other, but they are not equal to the above-mentioned increase in the arm.

The arm between the elbow and wrist never increases by being bent or extended.

The arm, from the shoulder to the inner joint when extended.

When the arm is extended, *p n* is equal to *n a*. And when it is bent *n a* diminishes $^1/_6$ of its length and *p n* does the same The outer elbow joint increases $^1/_7$ when bent; and thus by being bent it increases to the length of 2 heads. And on the inner

349. 2 magiore grore grosseza in I. 3 ella. 4 essimile ha r 5 magore grosseza del br infralla . ego 7 grosseza . br sopral gomito "x y" non 8 mezo "h 3" 9 chessi . . infral [br di dentro] la . . del br 10 ella 11 grosseza br . 12 il br 14 ala . . coe 15 nel br 16 4 T 17 brcio 18 il nel . . cresscie 19 lungeza . lunghera. 20 de dalla . essoa 21 cresscimẽto essimile 22 seza del br sula 23. essimile 25 bocha ella grosseza. 26 mezo ella grandeza. 27 bocha ello . . apicha. 28. chapelli . ella somita 29 nominato. 31 acresimẽdo del br 32. il br 33 cresscie 34 Il br. 36. il bre . . essimi. 37 le ha n a Ecquondo 38 lũgeza 39 Ell e | "questo" 40 cresscie. 41 piegarsi | "cresscie" e . lũgeza 42 dentro ne nel 43. esso br era dal na 44 chollatera al 45 tesste e mezo. 46. $^1/_2$ T e 47 col-

348. Compare Pl. XVII. Lines 1—10 and 11—15 are written in two columns below the extended arm, and at the tips of the fingers we find the words *fine d'unghie* (ends of the nails). Part of the text—lines 22 to 25—is visible by the side of the sketches on Pl. XXXV, No. 1.

29. *Queste cose.* This passage seems to have been written on purpose to rectify the foregoing lines. The error is explained by the accompanying sketch of the bones of the arm.

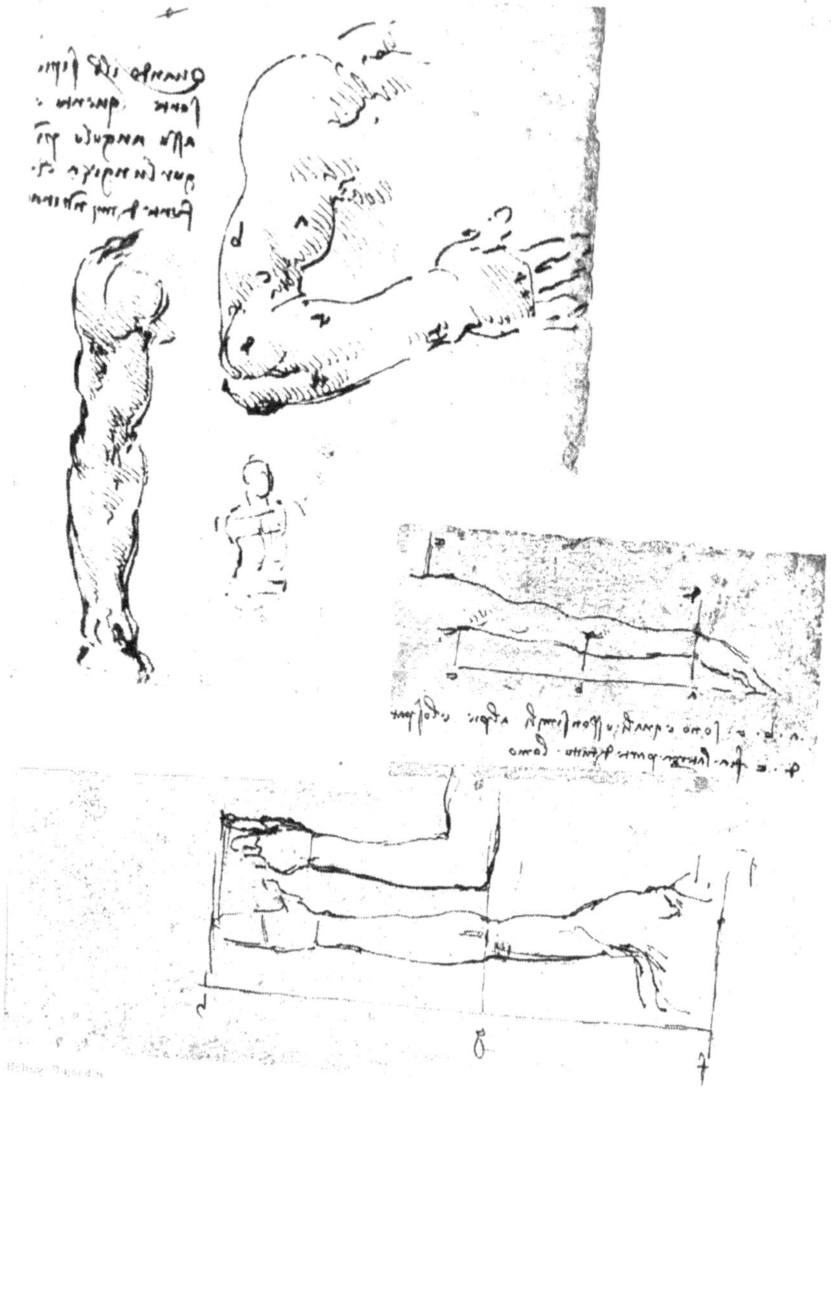

dentro nel suo pie[43]garsi fa che dove esso braccio era dal nas[44]cimento suo collaterale al suo fine[45] colla mano, 2 teste e mezzo, piega[46]to sciema quella $^1/_2$ Testa e torna due, [47]vna dalla givtura al suo fi collaterale, [48]l'altra infino alla mã.

[49]Il braccio piegato avrà 2 teste dal di sopra [50]della spalla al gomito e 2 da esso go[51]mito al nascimẽto de' quatro diti [52]sulla palma della mano; lo spatio, [53]ch'è da esso nascimẽto de' 4 diti al gomito, [54]mai si muta per alcuna mutatione [55]del braccio.

[56]Se questo braccio si dirizzerà, elli calerà il 3° dello [57]spatio ch'è infra *b·n*, e se sia diritto e pie[58]gherassi, crescierà la metà

side, by bending, it is found that whereas the arm from where it joins the side to the wrist, was 2 heads and a half, in bending it loses the half head and measures only two: one from the [shoulder] joint to the end [by the elbow], and the other to the hand.

The arm when folded will measure 2 faces up to the shoulder from the elbow and 2 from the elbow to the insertion of the four fingers on the palm of the hand. The length from the base of the fingers to the elbow never alters in any position of the arm.

If the arm is extended it decreases by $^1/_3$ of the length between *b* and *n*; and if — being extended — it is bent, it will increase

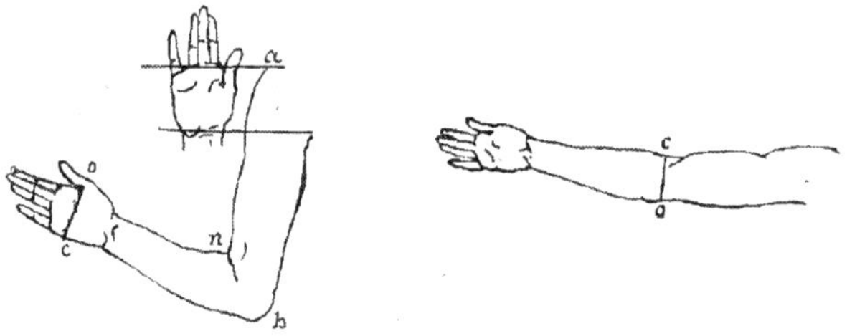

di *o c*; [59]tanto è dalla spalla al gomito, quanto [60]è dal pricipio dentro del grosso dito a esso gomito [61]*a b c*.

[62]La minore grossezza del braccio in proffilo *z·c* entra 6 [63]dal nodello della mano al foppello del gomito disteso [64]e 14 in tutto il braccio e è 42 in tutto l'omo suo; [65]la maggiore grossezza del braccio in proffilo è simile [66]alla maggiore grossezza del braccio in facia; ma l'una [67]è posta nel terzo del braccio dalla givntura alla metà, l'altro [68]nel terzo della givntura alla mano.

the half of *o c*. [59]The length from the shoulder to the elbow is the same as from the base of the thumb, inside, to the elbow *a b c*.

[62]The smallest thickness of the arm in profile *z c* goes 6 times between the knuckles of the hand and the dimple of the elbow when extended and 14 times in the whole arm and 42 in the whole man[64]. The greatest thickness of the arm in profile is equal to the greatest thickness of the arm in front; but the first is placed at a third of the arm from the shoulder joint to the elbow and the other at a third from the elbow towards the hand.

lare. 49. br . . ara 2 T dal. 50. eso. 52. sula. 53. nassimẽto. 54. alchuna. 56. dirizera e chalera. 58. gerassi cressciera. 60. dento . . dito neso. 62. grosseza del br (in profil m . n . entra 6). 63. nodel . . fopilo. 64. bree. 65. magiore grosseza in . . essimile. 66. magiore grosseza del br in. 67. de br dala. 69. la minore grosseza del br \\\\\\ 70. 2 nella magiore del br grosse \\\\\\

59—61. The figure sketched in the margin is however drawn to different proportions.

62—64. The arm sketch on the margin of the MS. is identically the same as that given below on Pl. XX which may therefore be referred to in this place. In line 62 we read therefore *z c* for *m n*.

W. P. 7 *a*]

349.

[2] Tanto è dalla sõmità della spalla alla pūta del gomito, quanto da essa [3] punta · alla givntura delle 4 minor dita colla palma della mano, [4] e ciascuna parte è 2 teste.

[5] *a* · *e* è simile alla palma della mã; *r* · *f* · e · *o* · *g* · son simili a una mezza testa, [7] e ciascuno entra 4 da · *a* · *b* · e da · *b* · *c*: [8] da · *c* · *m* · è $\frac{1}{2}$ testa; *m* · *n* · è $\frac{1}{3}$ testa, ẽtra [9] 6 · in *c* · *b* · e in · *b* · *a*; [10] *a* · *b* · sciema $\frac{1}{7}$ di sua lūghezza, quãdo jl braccio · si [11] distẽde: *c* · *b* · mai · fa mvtatione, [12] *o* · fia senpre · il mezzo infra · *a* · *s*.

[14] *y* · *l* · è la polpa del braccio ed è vna testa, e quãdo · jl braccio si piega . [15] essa polpa diminviscie $\frac{2}{3}$ di sua lūghezza, [16] *o* · *a* in nel piegare · diminviscie $\frac{1}{6}$, e similmente [17] *o* · *r*.

[18] *a* · *b* · è $\frac{1}{7}$ di *r* · *c*; [19] *f* · *s* · si è $\frac{1}{8}$ di · *r* · *c* e ciascuna di queste [20] 2 · misure sono le piv grosse del braccio; [21] *k* · *h* · è la piv sottile parte che sia infra la spalla e 'l gomito [22] ed è $\frac{1}{8}$ di · tutto il braccio · *r* · *c* · [23] *o* · *p* · è $\frac{1}{5}$ di *r* · *l* ·; *c* · *z*, entra 13 · ĩ *r* · *c*.

From the top of the shoulder to the point of the elbow is as far as from that point to the joints of the four fingers with the palm of the hand, and each is 2 faces.

[5] *a e* is equal to the palm of the hand, *r f* and *o g* are equal to half a head and each goes 4 times into *a b* and *b c*. From *c* to *m* is $\frac{1}{2}$ a head; *m n* is $\frac{1}{3}$ of a head and goes 6 times into *c b* and into *b a*; *a b* loses $\frac{1}{7}$ of its length when the arm is extended; *c b* never alters; *o* will always be the middle point between *a* and *s*.

y l is the fleshy part of the arm and measures one head; and when the arm is bent this shrinks $\frac{2}{5}$ of its length; *o a* in bending loses $\frac{1}{6}$ and so does *o r*.

a b is $\frac{1}{7}$ of *r c*. *f s* will be $\frac{1}{8}$ of *r c*, and each of those 2 measurements is the largest of the arm; *k h* is the thinnest part between the shoulder and the elbow and it is $\frac{1}{8}$ of the whole arm *r c*; *o p* is $\frac{1}{5}$ of *r l*; *c z* goes 13 times into *r c*.

Br. Mus. 44 *a*]

350.

The movement of the arm (350—354).

Nelle piegature vltime delle giunture di qualūque [2] mẽbro si sciupa ogni rilieuo in cõcauità, e così [3] ogni concavità dell'ultime dette piegature [4] si fa in colmo, quãdo el mẽbro é nel ultima sua [5] dirittura; e qui spesse volte si fà grãdissimi erro[6] ri chi non à tale sciẽtia e si fida tanto del suo ingegno e nõ ricorre alla imitatione [7] del naturale, e tal varietà si fa piv nel mezzo [8] de' lati che dinãzi, e piv diricto che ne lati.

In the innermost bend of the joints of every limb the reliefs are converted into a hollow, and likewise every hollow of the innermost bends becomes a convexity when the limb is straightened to the utmost. And in this very great mistakes are often made by those who have insufficient knowledge and trust to their own invention and do not have recourse to the imitation of nature; and these variations occur more in the middle of the sides than in front, and more at the back than at the sides.

W. 197]

351.

Quando il braccio si piega in agolo nel suo gomito · genera angolo d'alcuna [2] sorte; quanto esso angolo si farà piv acuto, tanto i mvscoli di dentro [3] a esso angolo si

When the arm is bent at an angle at the elbow, it will produce some angle; the more acute the angle is, the more will the muscles within the bend be shortened; while

349. 1. trezo. 3. cholla. 4. 2 T. 5. essimile. 6. *r* . *f* . he . *o g* . . 1/2 meza. 7. classchuno. 8. 1/2 T m . n . e 1/3 T. a b . en . b. 10. lūgeza . . Il br . si. 12. senpr. 13. [o . y . qua]. 14. ella . . del br ed . . Il br . si. 15. diminviscie e 2/5 di sua lūgeza. 16. inel . . diminviscie 1/2 essimile. 19. sie [l] 1/8 . quesste . . h . . del br. 21. ella . . chessia infralla . . ellomito. 22. il br.

350. 1. gunture. 2. si scrubia. 3. piegature ogni cõca. 4. vita si fa. 6. tale essciẽtia | "e ssi fida tanto del suo ingegno" e no. 7. ettal . . mezo.

351. 1. il br . . gomito eguero — angulo. 2. quento esso angulo . . mvsscoli. 3. asso angolo piv brieuielli musscoli aposit.

349. See Pl. XX where the text is also seen from lines 5—23.

351. See Pl. XIX, No. 2.

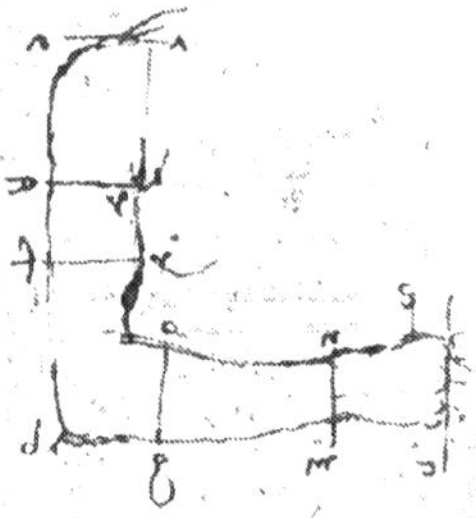

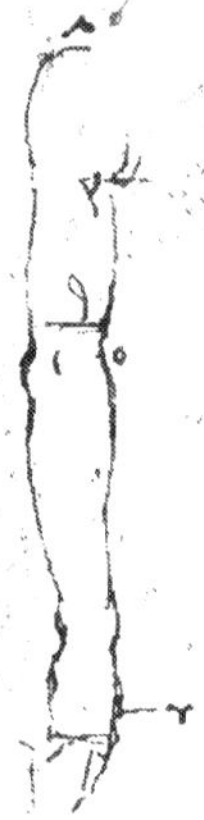

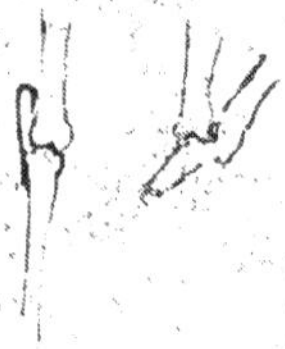

a.b. è 1/7 di r.c

fanno piv brieui, e li muscoli oppositi si faranno di ma[4]ggior lunghezza che in ordinario · come dire nello esenplo, *d c e* [5]forte diminviranno *b n* forte s'allargherà

the muscles outside will become of greater length than before As is shown in the example, *d c e* will shrink considerably, and *b n* will be much extended

Ash I, 2, II *a*]

352

Pittura

[2]Il braccio · dove si uolta tira dirieto la sua spalla a mezzo la schiena

Of painting

The arm, as it turns, thrusts back its shoulder towards the middle of the back.

C A 44 *b*, 137 *b*]

353

[1]10 sono li moti principa[2]li della mano, cioè in [3]dentro, in fori, destro e [4]sinistro, circūvolvbile, [5]in sù e in giù, chiudere [6]e aprire, dilatatione e [7]restrinsione delle sua dita

The principal movements of the hand are 10, that is forwards, backwards, to right and to left, in a circular motion, up or down, to close and to open, and to spread the fingers or to press them together

C A 98 *b*, 308 *a*]

354

Del moto delle dita delle mani

[2]Li moti delli diti sono principali cioè [3]astendere e piegare l'astendere e pie[4]gare si uaria in modi, cioè alcuna [5]volta si piega tutto d'un pezzo sopra la [6]prima giuntura, alcuna volta si piega [7]o dirizza mezzo sopra la 2ª giū[8]tura, e alcuna volta si piega tutto [9]in se e nel medesimo tempo si piega in tut[10]te le sue 3 giunture, e se alle 2 prime [11]giunture sarà proibito il piegamento, [12]allora la 3ª giūtura sarà piegata con mag[13]giore facilità, che ne mai si potrà piega[14]re per se sola, essendo libere l'altre giunture, [15]e essa nō si pieghino tutte le 3 giū[16]ture, Oltre alli· predetti moti ce ne à [17]4 altri principali, de' quali 2 sono fra sù [18]e giù, e 2 altri tra qua e là, e ciascū di que[19]sti è fatto colla sua senplice corda, Di [20]questi ne seguita infiniti altri moti fatti sē[21]pre cō 2 corde, e lasciata vna d'esse corde [22]va ripigliando l'altra, fu fatto le corde [23]grosse di dentro al dito e le sottili di fori, fu [24]fatto le corde di dentro a ogni giūtu[25]ra e di fori no

[26]Della potētia che fā le 3 [27]corde dentro alli diti nelle [28]3 giūture

Of the motions of the fingers

The movements of the fingers principally consist in extending and bending them This extension and bending vary in manner, that is, sometimes they bend altogether at the first joint, sometimes they bend, or extend, half way, at the 2nd joint, and sometimes they bend in their whole length and in all the three joints at once If the 2 first joints are hindered from bending, then the 3rd joint can be bent with greater ease than before, it can never bend of itself, if the other joints are free, unless all three joints are bent Besides all these movements there are 4 other principal motions of which 2 are up and down, the two others from side to side, and each of these is effected by a single tendon From these there follow an infinite number of other movements always effected by two tendons, one tendon ceasing to act, the other takes up the movement The tendons are made thick inside the fingers and thin outside, and the tendons inside are attached to every joint but outside they are not

[26] Of the strength [and effect] of the 3 tendons inside the fingers at the 3 joints

4 gor lungeza chellin 5 he *b n* sallargera
352 mezo sciena
353 3 desstro 4 sinisstro 5 ciudere 7 rosstrinsione
354 1 delli 2 coe 3 asstendere e pieghare eppie 4 ghare coe 5 piegha pezo 6 guntura piegha 7 [mezo] o diriza mezo 2ª gū 8 piegha 9 piegha in tu 10 gunture esse 11 gunture piegamento [il] 12 alora guntura 13 gore che p' a ' 14 gunture 15 3 gū 18 e gu e qua ella 19 effatto 27 ellasciato 23 elle 24 chordi gutu 26 cheffā 28 gūture

354 26 This head line has, in the original, no text to follow

355.

E. 17 a]

The movement of the torso (355—361)

Nota la uariatione della spalla in tutti li mo[2]ti del braccio intra sù e giù, in dentro, infora, [3]indirieto, inãti, e cosi ne' moti revertigi[4]nosi e qualũche altri moti

[5]E 'l simile fa del collo, mani e piedi e petto so[6]pra li fianchi ecc.

Observe the altered position of the shoulder in all the movements of the arm, going up and down, inwards and outwards, to the back and to the front, and also in circular movements and any others.

And to the same with reference to the neck, hands and feet and the breast above the lips &c.

356.

W III]

3 sono li muscoli principali [2]della spalla cioè *b c d*, e due [3]sono li laterali che la movono [4]inãzi e indirieto, cioè *a o*; [5]*a* la move inãzi e *o* la tira [6]indirieto; e insù l'alza *b c d*, [7]insù e inãzi *a b c*, insù e indi[8]rieto *c d o*; e in giù basta [9]quasi il peso di se medesima;

[10]Il muscolo *d* si vnisce col muscolo *c*, quã[11]do il braccio va inanzi, e nel tornare indi[12]rieto il muscolo *b* s'unisce col muscolo *c*.

Three are the principal muscles of the shoulder, that is *b c d*, and two are the lateral muscles which move it forward 2 backward, that is *a o*, *a* moves it forward, and *o* pulls it back, and *b c d* raises it; *a b c* moves it upwards and forwards, and *c d o* upwards and backwards. Its own weight almost suffices to move it downwards.

The muscle *d* acts with the muscle *c* when the arm moves forward; and in moving backward the muscle *b* acts with the muscle *c*.

357.

W A II, 203 b (24)]

DELLE RENI INARCATE.

[2]Le reni inarcate overo schiene — [3]senpre le poppe sõ più basse che [4]le scapule d'essa schiena.

[5]Nelli petti inarcati senpre [6]le poppe sõ più alte che le [7]scapule della schiena.

[7]Dalle reni diritte fiẽ sẽpre [9]trovate le poppe dell'altezza [10]d'esse scapule.

OF THE LOINS, WHEN BENT.

The loins or backbone being bent. The breasts are are always lower than the shoulderblades of the back.

If the breast bone is arched the breasts are higher than the shoulderblades.

If the loins are upright the breast will always be found at the same level as the shoulderblades.

358.

W 215]

a b nervo e tallone nell' alzare [2]del calcagnio s'accostano vn dito [3]l'uno all'altro e nello abbassare [4]si separano vn dito.

a b the tendon and ankle in raising the heel approach each other by a finger's breadth, in lowering it they separate by a finger's breadth

355 1 spella 2 del br. su eggiu 3 chosi 5 chollo. eppiedi e pecto

356 1 musscoli principoli 2 *d* he due 3 chella movano 4 innãzi . coe 8 gu bassta 10 musscolo . . vnissce . musscolo. 11 il [p] brracco . innanzi 12 musscolo *b* sunissce col musscolo *c*

357 1 innarchate 2 innarchate . sciene. 3 chel 4 spatole . . sciena 5. elli pectinarchati 6 chelle 7 spatolo della sciena. 8 delle rene diricte fie 9 trovato 10. desse spatole

358 1 ettallone. 2. chalchagnio [d si superano] "sachostano".

356. See Pl. XXI. In the original the lettering has been written in ink upon the red chalk drawing and the outlines of the figures have in most places been inked over

357. See Pl XXII, No 1

358. See Pl. XXII, No. 2 Compare this facsimile and text with Pl. III, No. 2, and p. 152 of MANZI's edition Also with No 274 of LUDWIG's edition of the Vatican Copy.

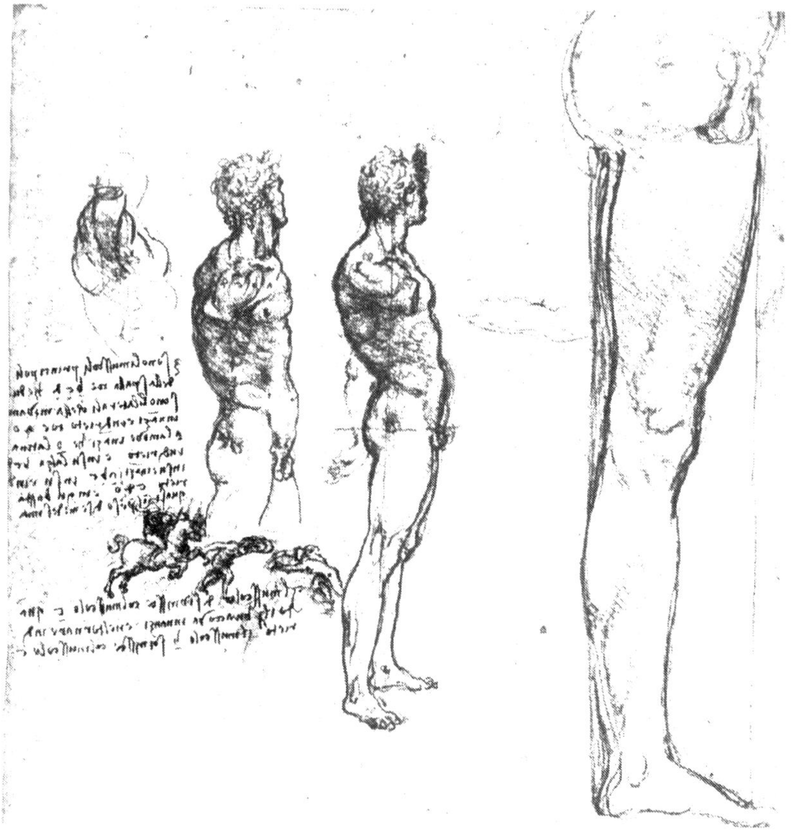

A 2 a]

359

Tāto quāto la parte dello nvdo *d a* diminvìscie pel posare, tāto l'opposita [2] parte crescie cioè tāto quāto la parte *d a* diminvìscie di sua [3] misura l'opposita parte sopra crescie alla sua misura, [4] el bellico mai escie di sua altezza verso il mēbro virile, e questo [5] abassamēto nascie perchè la figura che posa sopra uno piè quel piè si fa ciētro [6] del sopra posto peso essēdo così il mezzo delle spalle ui si dirizza di sopra [7] vsciēdo fori della sua linia perpēdiculare, la quale linia passa per i mezzi super[8]fitiali del corpo, e questa linia si uiene a torcere nella sua superiore stre[9]mità sopra il piè che posa e i liniamēti traversi costretti [10] a equali angoli si fanno coi loro stremi piv bassi ī quella parte che posa [11] come appare in *a b c*

Just so much as the part *d a* of the nude figure decreases in this position so much does the opposite part increase, that is in proportion as the length of the part *d a* diminishes the normal size so does the opposite upper part increase beyond its [normal] size The navel does not change its position to the male organ, and this shrinking arises because when a figure stands on one foot, that foot becomes the centre [of gravity] of the superimposed weight This being so, the middle between the shoulders is thrust above it out of it perpendicular line, and this line, which forms the central line of the external parts of the body, becomes bent at its upper extremity [so as to be] above the foot which supports the body, and the transverse lines are forced into such angles that their ends are lower on the side which is supported. As is shown at *a b c*.

E 3 a]

360

Pictura

[2] Nota nelli moti e attitudini delle [3] figure come si variano le mē[4]bra e li lor sētimēti, perchè le [5] scapule nelli moti delle braccia e spalle ua[6]riano assai la schiena, e di que[7]sto troverai tutte le cause nel [8] libro della mia notomia

Of painting

Note in the motions and attitudes of figures how the limbs vary, and their feeling, for the shoulderblades in the motions of the arms and shoulders vary the [line of the] back bone very much And you will find all the causes of this in my book of Anatomy

Ash I 15 a]

361

Dell'attitudine

[2] La fōtanella della gola cade sopra il piè, e gittādo uno braccio inātì la fōtanella escie d'esso piè, [3] e, se la gāba gitta indireto, la fontanella va inātì, e così si mvta in ogni attitudine

Of [change of] attitude

The pit of the throat is over the feet, and by throwing one arm forward the pit of the throat is thrown off that foot And if the leg is thrown forward the pit of the throat is thrown forward, and so it varies in every attitude

359 1 par dello loposita 2 cresscie cioe [que] tāto diminvissie 3 loposita sopra [cresscie a] cresscie 4 belicho essae altera [ag] overo ecquesto 5 nasscie sopra ī pie 6 chosi spalì diriza 7 vssciēdo perpēdichu lare 8 chorpo ecquesta torciere la 9 posa [ek par] e i chostretti 10 angholi fano [be] coloro quela 11 apare
360 2 neli attitudine 3 fighure chome variano 4 elli perche les 5 spatole nelli delle br \ ua *On the margin* \ esspalli 6 lassciena 7 stro troverai chavsene
361 1 dattitudine 2 chade gittando ī braccio 3 esse

359 See Pl XXII, No 3

E. 10 a] **362.**

The proportions vary at different ages (362—367).

PICTURA.

[2]Descrivi quali sieno li muscoli e quali le [3]corde, che mediante diuersi movimēti di cias[4]cun mēbro si scuoprino o si ascondono o nō [5]faccino nè l'ū nè l'altro, e ricordati che que[6]sta tale actione è inportātissima, e necies[7]sarissima appresso de' pittori e scultori che fā [8]professione di maestri ecc.

[9]E 'l simile farai d'un fanciullo dalla sua na[10]tiuità insino al tenpo della sua decrepitudi[11]ne per tutti li gradi della sua età come infanti[12]a, pueritia, adolescientia e giovētù ecc.

[13]E in tutti discriverai le mutationi delle mēbra [14]e giunture le quali ingrassano o dimagrano.

OF PAINTING.

Indicate which are the muscles, and which the tendons, which become prominent or retreat in the different movements of each limb; or which do neither [but are passive] And remember that these indications of action are of the first importance and necessity in any painter or sculptor who professes to be a master &c.

And indicate the same in a child, and from birth to decrepitude at every stage of its life; as infancy, childhood, boyhood, youth &c.

And in each express the alterations in the limbs and joints, which swell and which grow thinner.

E. 19 b] **363.**

O pictore anatomista guarda che la troppa [2]notitia delli ossi, corde e muscoli nō si[3]a cavsa di farti vn pictore legnioso, col [4]volere che li tua ignivdi mostrino tutti li sē[5]timēsti loro, adūque, volendo riparare a questo, [6]vedi in che modo li muscoli nelli vechi o magri [7]coprino over vestino le loro ossa, e oltre [8]a questo nota la regola come li medesimi mus[9]coli nenpino li spati superfitiali che infra loro s'I[10]terpongono; e quali sono li muscoli [11]di che mai si perde la notitia in alcū grado di grassez[12]za, e quali sō li muscoli delli quali per ogni mi[13]nima pinguedine si perde la notitia delli lor cō[14]tatti, e molte son le volte che di più muscoli se [15]ne fa vn sol muscolo nello ingrassare, e molte [16]sō le volte che nel dimagrare o invechiare d'un sol [17]muscolo se ne fā più muscoli, e di questo tal [18]discorso se ne dimostrerà a suo loco tutte le [19]particularità loro, e massime nelli spati [20]interposti infra le giūture di ciascū mēbro ecc.

O Anatomical Painter! beware lest the too strong indication of the bones, sinews and muscles, be the cause of your becoming wooden in your painting by your wish to make your nude figures display all their feeling. Therefore, in endeavouring to remedy this, look in what manner the muscles clothe or cover their bones in old or lean persons; and besides this, observe the rule as to how these same muscles fill up the spaces of the surface that extend between them, which are the muscles which never lose their prominence in any amount of fatness, and which too are the muscles of which the attachments are lost to sight in the very least plumpness. And in many cases several muscles look like one single muscle in the increase of fat; and in many cases, in growing lean or old, one single muscle divides into several muscles. And in this treatise, each in its place, all their peculiarities will be explained—and particularly as to the spaces between the joints of each limb &c.

362. 2 desscrivi musscholi equali 3. chorde 4 schun . . sisscuoprino ossi asschondono 5 nellūnellaltro e richordati checquesta. 7. di pichtori esschultori cheffā 9 fanciullo [al] dalla 11 chome 12 adolesscientia. 13 tucti disscriverrai 14 e giunture e quale ingrassa oddimagra.

363 1 natomissta ghuarda chella 2 chorde ēmusscholi 3. eno chausa chol 4 chelli ingnivdi mosstrino 5 acquessto 6. musscoli . magri chu 7 obprino vessuno [le osse] le oltri 8 adi quessto . reghola 9 choli . lisspati infralloros sī 10. terponghono E quali . . musscholi 11 alchū 12 ecquali 13 pinghuedine chō 14 tacti . . molte solle muscholi 15 muscholo 17 musscholo , . musscholi ed quessto. 18. disschorso . dimossterra assuo locho 19 partichularita 20. interpossti infralle ciassū 21 Anchora . mancherai della; — di notare *is wanting* 22 predecu

363 DE ROSSI remarks on this chapter, in the Roman edition of the Trattato, p 504: "*Non in questo luogo solo, ma in altri ancora osserverà il lettore, che Lionardo va pungendo quelli che fanno abuso della loro dottrina anatomica, e sicuramente con ciò ha in mira il suo rivale Bonarroti, che di anatomia facea tanta pompa.*" Note, that Leonardo wrote this passage in Rome, probably under the immediate impression of MICHAEL ANGELO's paintings in the Sistine Chapel and of RAPHAEL's Isaiah in Sant' Agostino.

[21] Ancora nõ mancherai [di notare] della varietà che fanno [22] li predetti muscoli intorno alle givture delli mẽ[23]bri di qualũche animale, mediante la diversità de' [24] moti di ciascũ mẽbro, perchè in alcuno lato d'es[25]se giũture si perde integralmẽte la notitia d'essi musco[26]li per causa dell' acciescimẽto o mãcamẽto della car[27]ne, della quale tal muscoli son composti ecc.

Again, do not fail [to observe] the variations in the forms of the above mentioned muscles, round and about the joints of the limbs of any animal, as caused by the diversity of the motions of each limb, for on some side of those joints the prominence of these muscles is wholly lost in the increase or diminution of the flesh of which these muscles are composed, &c.

Ash I 7a]

364

Delle differenti misure ch'è dai putti [2] agli omini

[3] Tra li omini · e i puttinitruovo grã differẽza di lũghezze da l'una all'al[4]tra givtura, imperochè l'omo à dalla giũtura della spalla al gomito [5] e dal gomito alla pũta del dito grosso e da l'vn omero della spalla [6] all'altra due teste per pezzo, e 'l putto n'à una perchè la natura ci cõpone [7] prima la grãdezza della casa dello ĩtelletto che quella delli spiriti [8] vitali

Of the different measurements of boys and men

There is a great difference in the length between the joints in men and boys for, in man, from the top of the shoulder [by the neck] to the elbow, and from the elbow to the tip of the thumb and from one shoulder to the other, is in each instance two heads, while in a boy it is but one because Nature constructs in us the mass which is the home of the intellect, before forming that which contains the vital elements

W 240b]

365.

De' pictura

[2] Quali muscoli sono quelli che si diuidono [3] nello inuechiare o ne' giouani che dimagrano? [4] Quali son li lochi nelle mẽbra vmane doue [5] per nessuna qualità di grassezza mai la carne [6] non cresce nè per nessũ grado di magrezza [7] mai la carne non diminuisce?

[8] Quel che si ricerca in questa dimanda fia [9] trouato in tutte le giunture superfitiali delle [10] ossa, come spalla, gomito, giunture delle mã [11] e delle dita, fianchi, ginochi, cauigli e dita de' piè [12] e simili cose, le quali si diranno ai lochi loro, [13] le maggior grossezze, che acquistino le mẽbra, [14] sono in quella parte del muscolo ch'è più dis[15]tante ai sua fermamẽti

[16] La carne non cresce mai in quella parte del[17]li ossi che son vicini alla superfitie de' mẽbri

Of painting

Which are the muscles which subdivide in old age or in youth, when becoming lean? Which are the parts of the limbs of the human frame where no amount of fat makes the flesh thicker, nor any degree of leanness ever diminishes it?

The thing sought for in this question will be found in all the external joints of the bones, as the shoulder, elbow, wrists, finger-joints, hips, knees, ancle-bone and toes and the like, all of which shall be told in its place The greatest thickness acquired by any limb is at the part of the muscles which is farthest from its attachments

Flesh never increases on those portions of the limb where the bones are near to the surface

musscholi 24 ciasschũ alchuno 25 giũchere musscho 26 accresscimẽto o mãchamẽto 27 musscholi chonpossti
364 1 diferenti 2 elli 3 diferẽza lũgeze 4 spala 5 dallun 6 pezo na l' perche 7 grãdeza intelleto
365 2 musscoli chessi diuidano 3 õne gouani 5 grosseza 6 cresscie magiers 7 diminuissce 8 chessi ricercha 9 guinture 10 gunture 11 chauichi 12 essimile 13 maggor grosseze 14 e in musschulo 15 al 16 cressce

[18]In *b r d a c e f* mai l'accrescimēto o diminutio[19]ne della carne fa troppa differentia; [20]La natura à posto nel moto dell'omo tutte quel[21]le parti dinanti, le quali, percotēdo l'omo, abbia a [22]sentire doglia, e questo si sente ne' fusi del[23]le ganbe e nella fronte e naso, ed è fatto a cō[24]seruatione dell'omo, inperochè se tale dolore [25]nō fussi preparato in essi mēbri, cierto le molte [26]percussioni in tali mēbra riceuute sarebbero causa della [27]lor distrutione.

[28]Descriui perchè l'ossi delle braccia ganbe son doppi in[29]uerso delle mani e de' piedi,

[30]Doue la carne cresce o diminuisce nelle piegature [31]delle menbra.

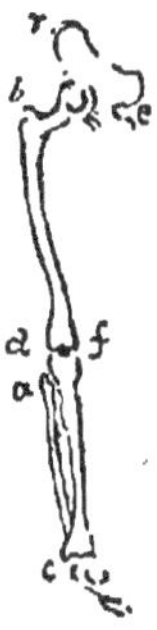

At *b r d a c e f* the increase or diminution of the flesh never makes any considerable difference. Nature has placed in front of man all those parts which feel most pain under a blow, and these are the shin of the leg, the forehead, and the nose. And this was done for the preservation of man, since, if such pain were not felt in these parts, the number of blows to which they would be exposed must be the cause of their destruction.

Describe why the bones of the arm and leg are double near the hand and foot [respectively].

And where the flesh is thicker or thinner in the bending of the limbs.

F 66]

366.

Pictura

[2]Ogni parte d'ū tutto sia proportionata [3]al suo tutto || come se vno homo è di [4]figura grossa e corta che il medesimo [5]sia in se ogni suo mēbro, cioè braccia corte [6]e grosse, mani larghe grosse e corte dita col[7]le sue giūture nel sopra detto modo, e co[8]sì il rimanēte ·, el medesimo intēdo aue[9]re detto delli vniversi animali e piāte [10]così nel diminuire per le proportionalità [11]delle grossezze come nello ingrossarle.

Of painting.

Every part of the whole must be in proportion to the whole. Thus, if a man is of a stout short figure he will be the same in all his parts · that is with short and thick arms, wide thick hands, with short fingers with their joints of the same character, and so on with the rest. I would have the same thing understood as applying to all animals and plants; in diminishing, [the various parts] do so in due proportion to the size, as also in enlarging.

Ash I 7a]

367.

Della cōuentione delle mēbra.

[2]E ancora ti ricordo · che tu abbi grāde auertēza nel dare le mēbra [3]alle figure · che paino, dopo l'essere cōcordāti alla · grādezza del corpo, [4]ācor similmēte all'età, cioè a giovani mēbra cō pochi mvscoli e vene [5]e dilicata superfitie · e rotōde, di grato colore, Ali omini sieno nerbose [6]e piene di mvscoli ·, Ai vechi sieno cō superficie grīze ruvide e venose [7]e nervi molto evidēti.

Of the agreement of the proportion of the limbs

And again, remember to be very careful in giving your figures limbs, that they must appear to agree with the size of the body and likewise to the age. Thus a youth has limbs that are not very muscular not strongly veined, and the surface is delicate and round, and tender in colour In man the limbs are sinewy and muscular, while in old men the surface is wrinkled, rugged and knotty, and the sinews very prominent.

17 chesson 18 la cresscimēto 19 diferentia 20. possto 21 parte abbia as 22. ecquesto si [ue] sente. 23 ennaso ed effatto a chō 24 inperochessi 26 sarē chausa 27. desstructione 28 desscriui . losse . . br 30. cresce o diminuissce

366. 2 tucto. 3 suottutto || chome 4. fighura chorta. 5 br corte. 6 chorte dital chol. 7. le sugiūture . e cho 8 indēde 9 eppiāte 10. chosi 11 grossese chome delle.

367 1 dela 2. ' [chome] e anchora ti richordo chettu 3 ale . . lesere grādeza 4 acor aleta che a. 5 retōde cholore

COML I PUTTINI ÀNO LE GIVNTURE CŌTRARIE ALLI OMINI NELLE LORO GROSSEZZE

[10]I puttı piccolı · àno tutte le gıv̄ture sottılı e lı spatı, postı fra l'una e l'al[11]tra , sono grossı e questo accade perchè la pelle sopra le gıv̄ture è sola sā[12]z'altra polpa ed è dı natura dı neruo che cıgnıe e lega īsıeme lı ossı [13]e la carnosıtà umerosa sı trova fra l'una e l'altra gıvntura [14]ınclusa fra la pelle e l'ossa ma, perchè l'ossa sono pıv grosse nelle gıvntu[15]re che īfra le gıū-ture , la carne nel crescere dell'omo vıene a lascıa[16]re quella superfluıtà che staua fra la pelle e l'osso onde la pelle, s'acco[17]sta pıv all'osso e vıene a sottıglıare le mēbra, e sopra le gıū[18]ture, perchè nō u'è se nō la cartılagınosa e neruosa pelle, nō può dı-sec[19]care, e nō dıseccādo nō dımınuısce , onde per queste ragıonı ı puttını so[20]no sottılı nelle gıūture e grossı ınfra le gıunture come sı [21]vede le gıunture de' dıtı, braccıa e spalle sottılı e concauı busı, e l'omo [22]per lo cōtrarıo essere grosso ī tutte le gıv̄ture, dıta, braccıa, gābe e dove [23]ı puttını ànno ı forı, loro aver dı rılıeuo

HOW YOUNG BOYS HAVE THEIR JOINTS JUST THE REVERSE OF THOSE OF MEN, AS TO SIZE

Little children have all the joints slender and the portions between them are thick, and this happens because nothing but the skin covers the joints without any other flesh and has the character of sinew, connecting the bones like a ligature And the fat fleshiness is laid on between one joint and the next, and between the skin and the bones But, since the bones are thicker at the joints than between them, as a mass grows up the flesh ceases to have that superfluity which it had, between the skin and the bones, whence the skin clings more closely to the bone and the limbs grow more slender But since there is nothing over the joints but the cartilaginous and sinewy skin this cannot dry up, and, not drying up, cannot shrink Thus, and for this reason, children are slender at the joints and fat between the joints, as may be seen in the joints of the fingers, arms, and shoulders, which are slender and dimpled, while in man on the contrary all the joints of the fingers, arms, and legs are thick, and wherever children have hollows men have prominences

Ash I 6 b]

368

The movement of the human figure (368—375)

Modo dı figurare le 18 operatıonı del'-l'omo, [2]fermezza mouımēto, corso, [3]rıtto, appoggıato, [4]a sedere chınato gınochıonı gıacēte, sospeso, [5]Portare esser portato, spīgıere tırare battere, [6]essere battuto ag-gravare e levare

[7][Come debe stare una figura con ū peso ın mano [8]Rıcordotı]

Of the manner of representing the 18 actions of man Repose, movement, running, standing, supported, sitting, leaning kneeling, lying down, suspended Carrying or being carried, thrusting, pulling, striking, being struck, pressing down and lifting up

[As to how a figure should stand with a weight in its hand [8] Remember]

A 28 b]

369

Quello che sıede nō sı può leuare ın pıè, se la parte che dal polo [2]īnanzı nō pesa pıv che quella che da esso polo · ındırıeto, sanza forza dı braccıa,

A sitting man cannot raise himself if that part of his body which is front of his axis [centre of gravity] does not weigh more than that which is behind that axis [or centre] without using his arms

6 chō 7 nerbı 8 chome 9 grosseze 10 pıcholı ellı fralluna ellal 11 ecquesto achade pele essola 13 ella omorosa ellaltra 14 fralla ellossa nele 15 cresscere lascı 16 fralla ellosso 17 assottıglıare le mēbra [e nelle] esopra 18 no po dıse 20 ınfralle 21 esspalı sıttılı elcomo 22 br gābe 23 ano
368 1 operatıone 2 fermeza chorso 3 Rıcto apogıato 4 assedere dıacıēte 6 agravare 7 stare ī figura ımano
369 1 quelo chessıede leuare [dassede] ın 2 brazo 3 quela che locho chonvıene magıore 4 chıoe 6 alchuno

368 8. The orıgınal text ends here

369 See Pl XXII, No 4

Quello che mota i qualunque loco conviene che dia · di se · maggiore · peso dināti al piè piv alto · che dirieto, cioè dināti al polo che dirieto a esso · polo, adūque · l'omo darà di se sēpre · maggiore · peso · inverso · quella · parte dove disidera moversi che in alcuno · altro · loco;

Quello · che piv · corre · piv pende iuerso · il loco doue corre e da di se maggiore peso dinanzi · al polo suo · che dopo; quello che corre alla china fa il suo polo sulle calcagnia, e quello che corre all'erta · lo fa sulle pūte de' piedi ·, e quello che corre alla pianvra lo fa prima ai calcagni e poi nelle · punte de' piedi;

Questo nō porterà il suo peso, se nō ristora colla persona tirata idirieto il peso dinăzi: i modo che sēpre il piè che posa · si troui in mezzo del peso.

A man who is mounting any slope finds that he must involuntarily throw the most weight forward, on the higher foot, rather than behind—that is in front of the axis and not behind it. Hence a man will always, involuntarily, throw the greater weight towards the point whither he desires to move than in any other direction.

The faster a man runs, the more he leans forward towards the point he runs to and throws more weight in front of his axis than behind. A man who runs down hill throws the axis onto his heels, and one who runs up hill throws it into the points of his feet; and a man running on level ground throws it first on his heels and then on the points of his feet.

This man cannot carry his own weight unless, by drawing his body back he balances the weight in front, in such a way as that the foot on which he stands is the centre of gravity.

W. An. III, 176]

370.

Come fa l'omo a levarsi in piedi stādo a sedere in terra piana.

How a man proceeds to raise himself to his feet, when he is sitting on level ground.

F. 85a]

371.

L'omo che camina è piv veloce col capo che co' piedi.

L'uomo che caminādo attraversa tutto un sito piano, va prima alla china e poi altretanto all'erta.

A man when walking has his head in advance of his feet.

A man when walking across a long level plain first leans [rather] backwards and then as much forwards.

S. K. M. II.² 140]

372.

L'omo nel correre dà di se minor peso alle gāmbe che a stare fermo; E similmēte il cavallo che corre sente minor peso dell'omo ch'esso porta, ōde molti si fanno maraviglia che nel corso del cavallo esso

A man when running throws less weight on his legs than when standing still. And in the same way a horse which is running feels less the weight of the man he carries. Hence many persons think it wonderful that, in running, the horse can rest on one single

locho. 7. quelo che . . chore . . locho . . chore magiore. 8. peso [dopo] dinanzi . . quelo che chore. 9. chal chagnia ecquello che chore. 10. ecquello . . chore . . chal chagni. 11. nel. 12. chola persono. 13. unodo . . imezo.

370. 1. allevarsi. 2. assedere.

371. 4. sa [90 sit] tutto. 5. cina.

372. 2. aasta. 4. chorre. 8. regiere. 11. piv he veloce.

371. 3—6. He strides forward with the air of a man going down hill; when weary, on the contrary he walks like a man going up hill.

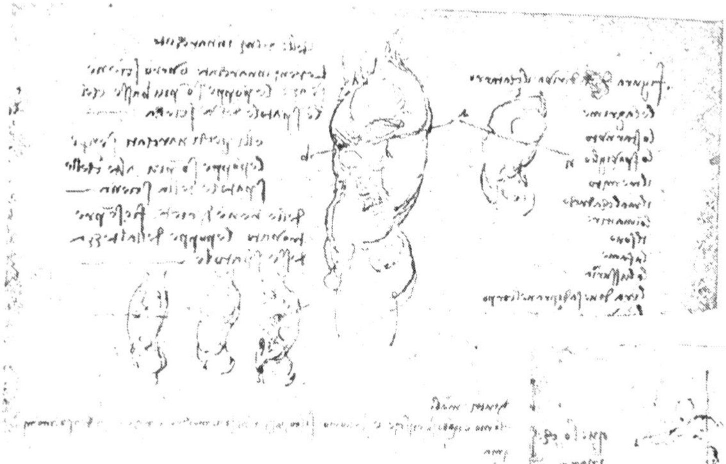

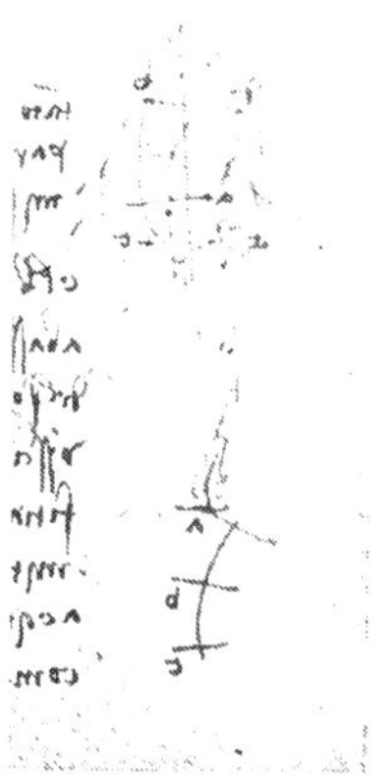

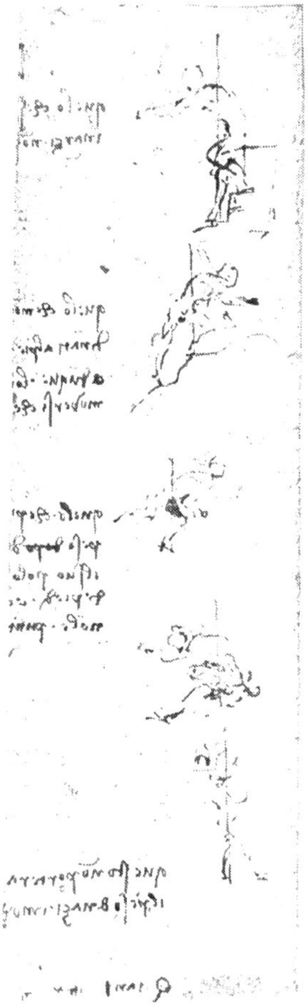

[8]si possa reggere sopra vn sol [9]piede, ōde si dirà, che 'l pe[10]so in moto traversale, qua[11]to piv è veloce, tãto mē pe[12]sa perpendiculare verso il ciētro.

foot. From this it may be stated that when a weight is in progressive motion the more rapid it is the less is the perpendicular weight towards the centre.

M. 55a]

373.

Se vno omo, nel pigliare il suo salto [2]sopra loco stabile, salta 3 · braccia, quã[3]do lui nello spiccare del salto sfu[4]gisse indirieto $^1/_3$ di braccio che manche[5]rebbe esso poi del primo suo salto, e [6]così se lui fussi aumētato $^1/_3$ di [7]braccio quanto accrescierebbe egli del [8]detto salto?

If a man, in taking a jump from firm ground, can leap 3 braccia, and when he was taking his leap it were to recede $^1/_3$ of a braccio, that would be taken off his former leap; and so if it were thrust forward $^1/_3$ of a braccio, by how much would his leap be increased?

C. A. 178a; 536a]

374.

Pictura.

[2]Quãdo l'omo corrēte vol consumare l'inpeto che lo transporta, [3]si prepara a inpetuosità contraria, la qual si gienera col pēdere i[4]dirieto; provasi, perchè se l'impeto trasporta il mobile cō potentia [5]di 4 e 'l mobile vol tornare e cadere indirieto cō potētia di 4, allo[6]ra l'una potentia consuma l'altra a se cōtraria e l'īpeto si cōsuma.

Of drawing.

When a man who is running wants to neutralise the impetus that carries him on he prepares a contrary impetus which is generated by his hanging backwards. This can be proved, since, if the impetus carries a moving body with a momentum equal to 4 and the moving body wants to turn and fall back with a momentum of 4, then one momentum neutralises the other contrary one, and the impetus is neutralised.

W. An. II. 203a]

375.

Quando l'omo vol fermare il suo [2]corso e consumare l'inpeto, nece[3]ssità lo fa pēdere indirieto e fare [4]piccoli e presti passi; [5]senpre il centro del peso dell'omo, che leua [6]l'un de' piedi da terra, resta sopra del centro [7]della pianta del suo piede.

[8]L'uomo che monta sopra le scale [9]dà di se tanto peso inanzi e da costa [10]al più alto piede, che dà contrapeso [11]alla ganba più bassa, onde la fa[12]tica d'essa ganba bassa sol s'astēde [13]in mouere se medesima.

[14]La prima cosa che fa l'omo nel suo mō[15]tare a gradi, esso scarica la gamba che [16]lui vole alzare della grauità del busto che [17]sopra essa ganba si posaua, e ol[18]tre a

When a man wants to stop running and check the impetus he is forced to hang back and take short quick steps. [5]The centre of gravity of a man who lifts one of his feet from the ground always rests on the centre of the sole of the foot [he stands on]. Of walking up and down (375—379).

A man, in going up stairs involuntarily throws so much weight forward and on the side of the upper foot as to be a counterpoise to the lower leg, so that the labour of this lower leg is limited to moving itself.

The first thing a man does in mounting steps is to relieve the leg he is about to lift of the weight of the body which was resting on that leg; and besides this, he gives to

373. 2. locho . . 3 br quã. 3. spichare. 4. gissi . . di br che. 5. del p̊r suo. 6. chosi sellui. 7. br quanto . . acressciere be.
374. 2. chorrēte . . chello. 3. se pr para. 4. sellinpeto. 5. chadere. 6. asse . . cellīpeto.
375. 3. effere. 4. pichole. 5. chelleua. 6. piedi ti terra. 7. piedi. 8. lesscale. 10. piedi. 12. ticha . . sasstēde. 14. chosa. 15. scharicha. 16. bussto. 17. posaua [onde talga] . e ol. 18. adiquesto . . charicha. 22. piedi. 23. appogga. 24. cossca

375. See Pl. XXIII, No. 1. The lower sketch to the left belongs to the four first lines. Lines 5—31 refer to the two upper figures, and the lower figure to the right is explained by the last part of the chapter.

questo carica l'opposita ganba di [19]tutto il resto della quantità dell'omo insieme cō [20]l'altra ganba, dipoi alza la gamba e pone il [21]piè di sopra di quel grado, ove esso si uole leua[22]re: fatto questo esso rende al piede alto tutto [23]l'altro peso del busto e della ganba, e appoggia [24]la mano sopra la coscia e caccia la testa inā[25]zi e fa il mouimēto inuerso la punta del piede [26]superiore, alzando con prestezza il calcagno del pie[27]de inferiore, e con quello inpeto si leua in alto e nel [28]medesimo tenpo distende il braccio, ch'egli appoggiaua sopra [29]il ginochio, il qual distendimēto di braccio spigne il bus[30]to e la testa in alto e cosi dirizza la schiena incur[31]uata;

[32]Quanto il grado, che per l'omo si [33]sale, sarà di maggiore altezza ta[34]to la sua testa sara più i[35]nanzi che 'l piede suo superiore; [36]per pesare [37]più *a* [38]che *b*; [39]quest'o[40]mo non [41]sarà [42]nel [43]grado [44]*m*, [45]mostra [46]la li[47]nia [48]*g f*.

the opposite leg all the rest of the bulk of the whole man, including [the weight of] the other leg; he then raises the other leg and sets the foot upon the step to which he wishes to raise himself. Having done this he restores to the upper foot all the weight of the body and of the leg itself, and places his hand on his thigh and throws his head forward and repeats the movement towards the point of the upper foot, quickly lifting the heel of the lower one; and with this impetus he lifts himself up and at the same time extends the arm which rested on his knee; and this extension of the arm carries up the body and the head, and so straightens the spine which was curved.

[32]The higher the step is which a man has to mount, the farther forward will he place his head in advance of his upper foot, so as to weigh more on *a* than on *b*; this man will not be on the step *m*. As is shown by the line *g f*.

S. K. M. II.[2] 20a]

376.

[2]Dimādo questo [3]peso dell'omo in o[4]gni grado di moto [5]sopra questa scala, [6]che peso esso dà [7]a *b* e a *c*.

[8]Guarda la linia [9]perpendiculare [10]sotto il cētro [11]della gravità [12]dell'uomo.

I ask the weight [pressure] of this man at every degree of motion on these steps, what weight he gives to *b* and to *c*.

[8]Observe the perpendicular line below the centre of gravity of the man.

H.[3] 27a]

377.

Quādo mōti la scala, se poggi le mā [2]sopra le ginochia, tutta la fatica che [3]acquistano le braccia si toglie ali ner[4]vi di sotto le ginochia.

In going up stairs if you place your hands on your knees all the labour taken by the arms is removed from the sinews at the back of the knees.

L. 27b]

378.

Il nerbo che dirizza la gamba, il quale è [2]congiunto colla padella del ginochio, sē[3]te tanto più fatica a leuare l'omo in alto [4]quanto essa gamba è piv piegata, e il mus-

The sinew which guides the leg, and which is connected with the patella of the knee, feels it a greater labour to carry the man upwards, in proportion as the leg is more bent: and the muscle which acts

schacca. 25. effa . . piedi. 26. chon prestera. 27. di. 28. il be chelli apogiaua. 29. di be spigne. 30. ella . . diriza lasschiena. 32. lvmosi. 33. solgie . . magoire altezza. 35. piedi. 31. sarra. 32. nel

376. 1—7 R. 7. ha *b* he a *c*. 8. ghuarda lliua. 9. perpēdichulare.

377. 1—6 R. 1. lasschala se pogi. 2. sopra e ginochia . . fatichs. 3. aquistano.

378. 1. chi. 2. congunto chol [ginoc] la. 3. faticha alleuare . . alto. 4. cimuss. 5. dirizza . . chella la cosscia. 6. conguntione

376. See Pl. XXIII, No. 2. Lines 8—12 are, in the original, written in ink.

377. See Pl. XXIII, No. 3.

379. See Pl. XXIII, No. 4.

[5]colo il quale dirizza l'angolo che fa la coscia [6]nella congiuntione ch'ella fa col busto, è mē [7]difficile e à a leuare māco peso, perchè li mā[8]ca il peso della coscia e oltre a questo à mi[9]glori muscoli perchè son quelli che fāno le na[10]tiche

upon the angle made by the thigh where it joins the body has less difficulty and has a less weight to lift, because it has not the [additional] weight of the thigh itself And besides this it has stronger muscles, being those which form the buttock.

W 3a]

379

Quel che disciēde fa i passi piccoli, perchè [2]il peso resta sopra il piede dirie[3]to, E quel che sale fa li pas[4]si grādi, perchè il suo peso sta sopra [5]il piè dinanzi

A man coming down hill takes little steps, because the weight rests upon the hinder foot, while a man mounting takes wide steps, because his weight rests on the foremost foot

E 15a]

380

Del moto umano.

[2]Quādo tu vuoi fare l'omo motore d'al[3]cuno peso, considera che li moti sono [4]da essere fatti per diuerse linie, cioè o di [5]basso in alto con senplice moto, come [6]fa quel che chinandosi piglia il peso che [7]dirizzandosi vole alzare, O quādo [8]si uole schiacciare alcuna cosa dri[9]eto ouero sospigniere īnāti o voi [10]tirare inbasso con corda che passa per car[11]rucole, Qui si ricorda che 'l peso del[12]l'omo tira tanto quāto il cientro della [13]gravità sua è fori del ciētro del suo sostē[14]tacolo ¶ e [15]a questo s'a[16]giugne la for[17]za che [18]fā le gan[19]be e la schie[20]na piega[21]ta nel suo [22]dirizzarsi ¶

Of the human body in action

On the human body in action (380—388)

When you want to represent a man as moving some weight consider what the movements are that are to be represented by different lines, that is to say either from below upwards, with a simple movement, as a man does who stoops forward to take up a weight which he will lift as he straightens himself Or as a man does who wants to squash something backwards, or to force it forwards or to pull it downwards with ropes passed through pullies [10] And here remember that the weight of a man pulls in proportion as his centre of gravity is distant from his fulcrum, and to this is added the force given by his legs and bent back as he raises himself

Mz 13a (17)]

381.

¶L'uomo ancor lui à ma[2]ggior soma di forza [3]nelle ganbe che nō [4]si richiede al peso suo, e che ciò [5]si è vero, posa in piedi l'o[6]mo sopra la litta e poi metti [7]vn altro homo adosso, e ve[8]drai quanto più si profonda, [9]Di poi li lieua l'omo da dosso [10]e fallo saltare in alto a dirit[11]tura quāto esso può e troue[12]rai la stāpa del suo pie[13]de essersi più profondata nel [14]salto che coll'omo adosso, adū[15]que qui per 2 modi è prouato l'omo [16]aver più forza il doppio che non si richiede a sostenere se medesimo ¶

Again, a man has even a greater store of strength in his legs than he needs for his own weight, and to see if this is true, make a man stand on the shore-sand and then put another man on his back, and you will see how much he will sink in Then take the man from off his back and make him jump straight up as high as he can, and you will find that the print of his feet will be made deeper by the jump than from having the man on his back Hence, here, by 2 methods it is proved that a man has double the strength he requires to support his own body

busto 7 dificile 8 cha cosscia adiquesto 9 musscoli quelle cheffano
379 1 chedisscīede picoli 2 ressta piedi 3 Ecquel chessaglie fallipa 5, dinanza
380 1 de 3 alchuno, chonsidera 5 baso senplici 6. facquel ched 7 Ocquādo 8 isstracinare alchuna chosa 9 sosspigniere 10 chorda per cha 11 ruchola richorda 14 tacholo 17 chef 18 faleghan 19 be esscie 20 piegha 22 dirizarsi

380 10 Compare the sketch on page 198 and on 201 (S K M II[1] 86[b])

382.

C. A. 311 *a*; 1024 *a*]

De pictura.

[2]Se tu ài a figurare vno homo che moui o che leui [3]o tiri o porti vno peso simile al suo, in che modo [4]li debi accociare le ganbe sotto alla sua persona?

Of painting.

If you have to draw a man who is in motion, or lifting or pulling, or carrying a weight equal to his own, in what way must you set on his legs below his body?

383.

A. 30 *b*]

Della · forza · dell'omo.

[2]L'omo ·, tirando · vno · peso · in bilancia · cō se ·, nō può · tirare · se nō tanto · quāto · pesa lui, [3]e s'egli à a leuare · egli leuerà tāto · piv · che nō pesa · quāto · lui avāza · la comvne · forza [4]delli · altri omini [5] la maggior · forza · che possa · fare l'omo · con pari prestezza [6]e movimēto · si è quādo · lui · fermerà · i piedi · sopra · l'una · delle teste · delle bilācie · e pōterà le spalle · in qualche · cosa · stabile: questo · leuerà · dal l'oposita · testa · della · bilācia [7]tāto · peso · quāto lui · pesa · e · tāto · peso · quāto · lui · a forza porta in sulle spalle.

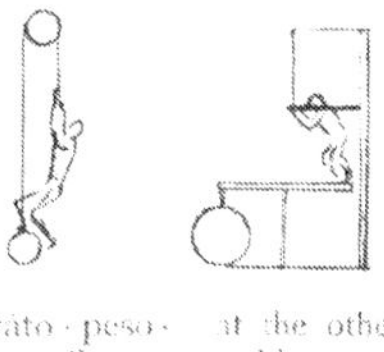

Of the strength of man.

A man pulling a [dead] weight balanced against himself cannot pull more than his own weight. And if he has to raise it he will [be able to] raise as much more than his weight as his strength may be more than that of other men. The greatest force a man can apply, with equal velocity and impetus, will be when he sets his feet on one end of the balance [or lever] and then presses his shoulders against some stable body. This will raise a weight at the other end of the balance [lever], equal to his own weight and [added to that] as much weight as he can carry on his shoulders.

384.

S. K. M. III. 98 *b*]

Nessuno [2]animale può sēplicemēte movere piv peso [3]che sia la soma · che si tro[4]va · fori del cētro del suo sostentaculo.

No animal can simply move [by its dead weight] a greater weight than the sum of its own weight outside the centre of his fulcrum.

385.

S. K. M. I.[2] 7]

Quello che uol · trarre · assai da lunga · coll'arco · debbe [2]tirarsi · tutto insu u piè, leuado l'altro · tato · lontano da [3]quello · che facci debito cōtrapeso alla persona che si gitta [4]fori del primo piè, e non tēga · disteso iteramēte il braccio, [5]e accio chè possa meglio sostenere la fatica, tēga all'arco v̄ legnio che [6]a

A man who wants to send an arrow very far from the bow must be standing entirely on one foot and raising the other so far from the foot he stands on as to afford the requisite counterpoise to his body which is thrown on the front foot. And he must not hold his arm fully extended, and in order that he may be more able to bear the

381. 2. gor sona. li forza [che nō sij]. 3. [richiede] nelle gāba ne nō. 4. cio *is wanting*. 8. sopralabira e pōmeto. 10. stabi. 11. rā esse la. 13. di essersi. 16. richiede assos tenere.
382. 2. afigurare . . chelleni. 3. otiri . . essere. 4. achociare.
383. 2. chōse nōpu. 3. essethalle are . li . . chomvne. 4. magor . . chompari prestezo. 6. lespalli . . chosa. 7. tatanto.
384. 2. p . . 4. chessa la soma chessi truo. 6. sostentachulo.
385. 1. uuol . . dallunga chollarcho. 2. essurā. 3. quello chefacci chessi. 4. disteso. 5. meglio sostenere la . . . techa.

382. In the MS. this question remains unanswered.

383. 7. The stroke at the end of this line finishes in the original in a sort of loop or flourish, and a similar flourish occurs at the end of the previous passage written on the same page. M. Ravaisson regards these as numbers (compare the photograph of page 30[b] in his edition of MS. A). He remarks: *"Ce chiffre 8 et, à la fin de l'alinéa précédent, le chiffre 7 sont, dans le manuscrit, des renvois."*

198'

vso di teneri vada dalla mano alla poppa, e quãdo [7]vuol lassare, subito a ũ tẽpo salti ĩnãti [8]e distẽda il braccio del- [9]l'arco e lassi la corda, [10]e se cõ destrezza [11]farà ogni cosa [12]in un tẽpo, farà as- [13]sai via

strain he must hold a piece of wood which there is in all crossbows, extending from the hand to the breast, and when he wishes to shoot he suddenly leaps forward at the same instant and extends his arm with the bow and releases the string And if he dexterously does every thing at once it will go a very long way

Leic 8a]

386

Quando due omini [2]sono in nelli stremi oppositi d'vn pancone posto in bilancia insieme coll'equal peso delli omini, e che l'ũ di lo[3]ro voglia spiccare vn salto in alto allora esso salto sarà fatto in giù dal suo stremo di pancone [4]e l'omo non si leuerà mai in alto, ma resterà nel suo sito insino che l'opposito omo li ribatte il pãcõ ne' [5]piedi

When two men are at the opposite ends of a plank that is balanced, and if they are of equal weight, and if one of them wants to make a leap into the air, then his leap will be made down from his end of the plank and the man will never go up again but must remain in his place till the man at the other end dashes up the board

W 1a]

387

Dello scaricare il colpo [2]a destra o sinistra

Of delivering a blow to the right or left

C A 344b, 1066a]

388

Perchè l'inpeto nõ si può inmediate consumare ma si\\\\\\[2]endo per qualunche linia, l'inpeto adunque acquistato per la linia [3]*a b c d* si consuma per la linia *d e*, ma non è in tãto che nõ ui res[4]ti parte della sua potẽtia, alla qual potẽtia, aggiunto il moto [5]della linia *d e* colla forza del suo motore, è necessario, che si [6]moltiplichi l'inpeto alla percussione e più che non avrebbe fa[7]tto il senplice inpeto nato dal moto *d e*

[8]L'uomo che à a dare grã percussione colla sua arme [9]si dispone con tutta la sua potentia in contraria parte a quella [10]dov'è il loco che da lui debbe essere percosso, e perchè la cosa [11]che piv si move si fa più potẽte sopra della cosa che tal mo[12]to impedisce

Why an impetus is not spent at once [but diminishes] gradually in some one direction? The impetus acquired in the line *a b c d* is spent in the line *d e* but not so completely but that some of its force remains in it and to this force is added the momentum in the line *d e* with the force of the motive power, and it must follow than the impetus multiplied by the blow is greater that the simple impetus produced by the momentum *d e*

[8] A man who has to deal a great blow with his weapon prepares himself with all his force on the opposite side to that where the spot is which he is to hit, and this is because a body as it gains in velocity gains in force against the object which impedes its motion.

---

6 pop"a" eghuãdo 7 vuo 8 praccio 10 esse chõ destreza 11 fara õni 12 nun
386 2 melli opositi chellundilor 3 spichare allcrara 4 ellomo chello
387 2 essinistra
388 1 linpeto [no] nõ sipo 2 acquisstato 4 sti parte agunto 6 perchussione arebbe 7 senplice [moto] inpeto 8 che a perchussione cholla 9 disspone acquella 10 locho che dallui perchosso perchella 11 chettal 12 inpedissce

386. See Pl XXIV, No 3

387 Four sketches on Pl XXIV, No 1 belong to this passage The rest of the sketches and notes on that page are of a miscellaneous nature

388. 1. The paper has been damaged at the end of line 1 The sketch No 2 on Pl XXIV stands, in the original, between lines 7 and 8 Compare also the sketches on Pl LIV

W. IV]

389

On hair falling down in curls

Nota il moto del liuello [2]dell' acqua, il quale fa a vso [3]de' capelli, che ànno due [4]moti, de' quali l'uno attēde al [5]peso del uello, l'altro al linia[6]mento delle volte, così l'acqua [7]à le sue volte revertigino[8]se, delle quali vna parte attende [9]al inpeto del corso principale, l'al[10]tro attēde al moto incidēte e reflesso

Observe the motion of the surface of the water which resembles that of hair, and has two motions, of which one goes on with the flow of the surface, the other forms the lines of the eddies; thus the water forms eddying whirlpools one part of which are due to the impetus of the principal current and the other to the incidental motion and return flow.

Ash I 29*b*]

390.

On draperies (390—392)

DELLE NATURE DELLE · PIEGHE DE' PANNI

¶[2]Quella parte · della piega · che si trova · piv lontana · dai sua costretti [3]stremi si riducierà più in sua · prima · natura;¶

[4]Naturalmēte ogni · cosa · desidera · mātenersi · in suo · essere; [5]Il panno · perchè è di equale · densità · e spessitudine, sì nel suo [6]rouescio · come nel suo · diritto ·, disidera · di stare · piano: onde [7]quando · lui · è da qualche · piega o falda · costretto · a lasciare [8]essa planitia ·, osserua · la natura · della forza · in quella · parte [9]di se dov' elli è · piv · cōstretto ·, e quella · parte ch' è piv lontana [10]a essi costrignimēti · troverai riducersi · piv alla · prima [11]sua · natura · cioè dello stare disteso · e āpio

OF THE NATURE OF THE FOLDS IN DRAPERY.

That part of a fold which is farthest from the ends where it is confined will fall most nearly in its natural form.

Every thing by nature tends to remain at rest Drapery, being of equal density and thickness on its wrong side and on its right, has a tendency to lie flat; therefore when you give it a fold or plait forcing it to out of its flatness note well the result of the constraint in the part where it is most confined, and the part which is farthest from this constraint you will see relapses most into the natural state, that is to say lies free and flowing

ESĒPLO.

[13]Sia · *a* · *b* · *c* · la piega · del panno · detto di sopra: *a* · *c* · sia il lo[14]co · doue · esso · panno piegato è costretto · io ti pro[15]posi, che Quella · parte · del pāno che era piv lontana · ai costretti stremi [16]si ridurebbe piv · in nella · sua · prima · natura

[17]Adunque · *b* · trouādosi · piv · lontano · da · *a* · *c* · li la piega [17]*a* · *b* · *c* · fia piv · larga · che in nessun altro · suo · loco

EXAMPLE.

Let *a b c* be the fold of the drapery spoken of above. *a c* will be the places where this folded drapery is held fast. I maintain that the part of the drapery which is farthest from the plaited ends will revert most to its natural form.

Therefore, *b* being farthest from *a* and *c* in the fold *a b c* it will be wider there than anywhere else.

389 1. deliello 2 acq"a" 3 chapelli 6. lacq"a". 7 alle reveruertigino 10 refresso

390. 1 piege 2 chessi . chostretti 4 chosa . suo aessere 5 esspesaitudine. 6. riuerscio chome 7 offalda . cosstretto allasciare 9. chōstretto . ecquella. 10 chosstrignimēti 11 āplio. 13 *a b* sia. 14 cho chōstretto 15 chostretti 16 inella. 18 locho

389. See Pl. XXV. Where also the text of this passage is given in facsimile.

390. See Pl. XXVIII, No 6, and compare the drawing from Windsor Pl XXX for farther illustration of what is here stated.

13. *a c sia.* In the original text *b* is written instead of *c*—an evident slip of the pen.

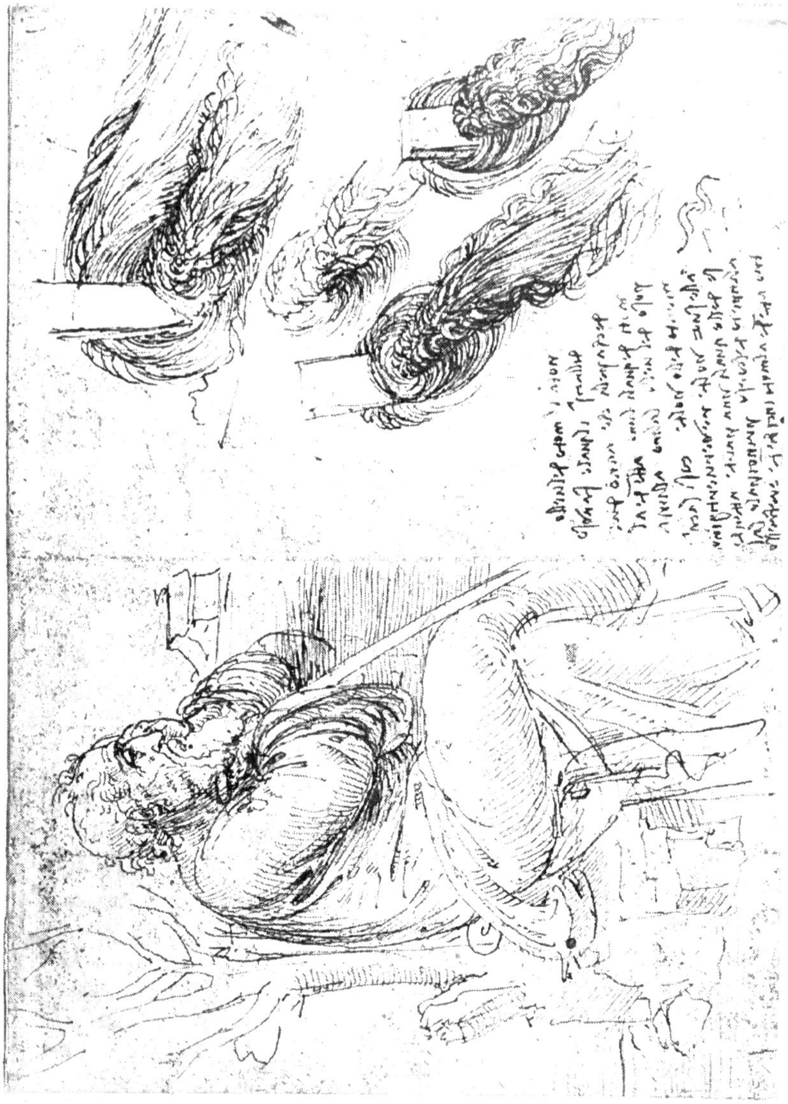

Ash. I. 17 b]

391.

Delle poche pieghe ne' pāni.

[2]Come le figure, essēdo vestite di mātello, nō debono tāto mostrare · lo nvdo [3]che 'l mātello paia ī sulle · carni, se già · tu nō volessi che 'l [4]mātello · fusse · sulle carni, īperochè tu debi pensare che tra 'l mante[5]llo · e le carni sono altre vesti che īpediscono lo scoprire e 'l pare[6]re la forma delle mēbra · sopra il mātello; e quelle mēbra che fai [7]discoprire · fa · le in modo grosse che li apparisca sotto il mātello altre [7]vestimēta, ma solo farai scoprire la quasi uera grossezza delle mēbra [9]a una · nīfa o uno āgielo, i quali si figurano · vestiti di sottili vestimēti [10]sospīti e īpressi dal soffiare de' uēti sopra le mēbra · di dette figure.

Of small folds in draperies.

How figures dressed in a cloak should not show the shape so much as that the cloak looks as if it were next the flesh; since you surely cannot wish the cloak to be next the flesh, for you must suppose that between the flesh and the cloak there are other garments which prevent the forms of the limbs appearing distinctly through the cloak. And those limbs which you allow to be seen you must make thicker so that the other garments may appear to be under the cloak. But only give something of the true thickness of the limbs to a nymph [9] or an angel, which are represented in thin draperies, pressed and clinging to the limbs of the figures by the action of the wind.

Ash. I. 18 a]

392.

Come a uno pāno non si deve dare cōfusione di molte pieghe, anzi ne fa so[2]lamēte doue colle mani o colle braccia sono ritenvte, il resto sia [3]lasciato cadere sēplicemēte doue lo tira sua natura, e nō sia ītra[4]versato lo ignvdo da troppi liniamēti o rōpimēti [di pieghe;

[5]Come i pāni si debō ritrare di naturale, cioè se uorai fare pāno lano usa le [6]pieghe secōdo quello, e se sarà seta o pāno fino o da vilani o di lino o di ue[7]lo, va diuersificādo · a ciascuno · le sue pieghe, e nō fare abito come molti [8]fāno sopra i modelli coperti di carte o corami sottili · che t' īgannerėsti forte.

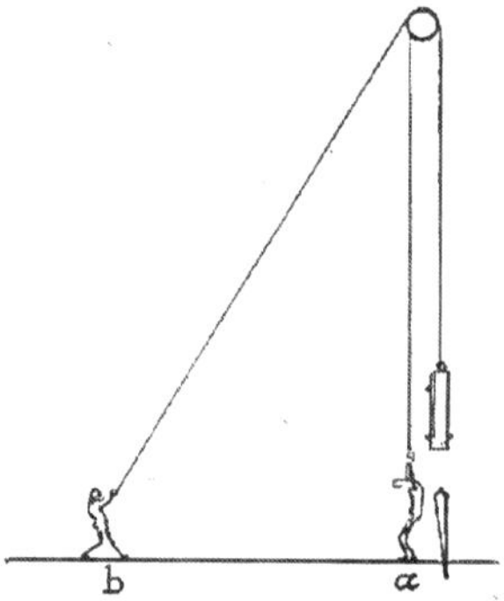

You ought not to give to drapery a great confusion of many folds, but rather only introduce them where they are held by the hands or the arms; the rest you may let fall simply where it is its nature to flow; and do not let the nude forms be broken by too many details and interrupted folds.

How draperies should be drawn from nature: that is to say if you want to represent woollen cloth draw the folds from that; and if it is to be silk, or fine cloth or coarse, or of linen or of crape, vary the folds in each and do not represent dresses, as many do, from models covered with paper or thin leather which will deceive you greatly.

391. 4. fussi sule . . īperochettu . . chettra. 5. elle charni . īpedischano lo scorire. 6. cheffai. 7. fa . lle īmodo . . chelliaparisca. 8. massolo . . grosseza. 9. o ī agielo.

392. 1. a ī pāno nōn si de dare . . piege. 2. cholle . . o cholle. 3. chadere . . e nō sua ītra. 4. lo nvdo . . tropi. 5. coi pani . . pano lano. 6. pege sechōdo . . pano fine. 7. diuersifichādo a ciaschuno . . piege . . come mol. 8. fano . . modeli . chettīganeresti.

391. The little pen and ink drawing from Windsor (W. 102), given on Pl. XXIII, No. 7, clearly illustrates the statement made at the beginning of this passage; the writing of the cipher 19 on the same page is in Leonardo's hand; the cipher 21 is certainly not.

9. *Una nīfa.* Compare the beautiful drawing of a Nymph, in black chalk from the Windsor collection, Pl. XXVI.

Héliog. Dujardin Imp. Eudes

VIII.

Botany for Painters and Elements of Landscape Painting.

The chapters composing this portion of the work consist of observations on Form, Light and Shade in Plants, and particularly in Trees summed up in certain general rules by which the author intends to guide the artist in the pictorial representation of landscape.

With these the first principles of a Theory of Landscape painting *are laid down—a theory as profoundly thought out in its main lines as it is lucidly worked out in its details. In reading these chapters the conviction is irresistible that such a* Botany for painters *is or ought to be of similar importance in the practice of painting as the principles of the Proportions and Movements of the human figure* i. e. Anatomy for painters.

There can be no doubt that Leonardo, in laying down these rules, did not intend to write on Botany in the proper scientific sense—his own researches on that subject have no place here; it need only be observed that they are easily distinguished by their character and contents from those which are here collected and arranged under the title 'Botany for painters'. In some cases where this division might appear doubtful,—as for instance in No. 402*—the Painter is directly addressed and enjoined to take the rule to heart as of special importance in his art.*

The original materials are principally derived from MS. G, *in which we often find this subject treated on several pages in succession without any of that intermixture of other matters, which is so frequent in Leonardo's writings. This MS., too, is one of the latest; when it was written, the great painter was already more than sixty years of age, so we can scarcely doubt that he regarded all he wrote as his final views on the subject. And the same remark applies to the chapters from MSS.* E *and* M *which were also written between* 1513—15.

For the sake of clearness, however, it has been desirable to sacrifice—with few exceptions—the original order of the passages as written, though it was with much reluctance and only after long hesitation that I resigned myself to this necessity. Nor do I mean to impugn the logical connection of the author's ideas in his MS.; but it will be easily understood that the sequence of disconnected notes, as they occurred to Leonardo and were written down from time to time, might be hardly satisfactory as a systematic arrangement of his principles. The reader will find in the Appendix an exact account of the order of the chapters in the original MS. and from the data there given can restore them at will. As the materials are here arranged, the structure of the tree as regards the growth of the branches comes first (394—411) *and then the insertion of the leaves on the stems* (412—419). *Then follow the laws of Light and Shade as applied, first, to the leaves* (420—434), *and, secondly, to the whole tree and to groups of trees* (435—457). *After the remarks on the Light and Shade in landscapes generally* (458—464), *we find special observations on that of views of towns and buildings* (465—469). *To the theory of Landscape Painting belong also the passages on the effect of Wind on Trees* (470—473) *and on the Light and Shade of Clouds* (474—477), *since we find in these certain comparisons with the effect of Light and Shade on Trees* (e. g.: *in No.* 476, 4. 5, *and No.* 477, 9. 12). *The chapters given in the Appendix Nos* 478 *and* 481 *have hardly any connection with the subjects previously treated.*

L 87 b]

393

Alberi

[2]Bassi, [3]alti, [4]rari, [5]spessi cioè di foglie, [6]scuri, [7]chiari, [8]rossi, [9]ramificāti insù, [10]chi diritti all'ochio, [11]chi in giù, [12]gābi biāchi, [13]a chi trapare l'aria [14]a chi no, [15]chi è trito di posta, [16]chi è raro

Trees

Classification of trees

Small, lofty, straggling, thick, that is as to foliage, dark, light, russet, branched at the top, some directed towards the eye, some downwards, with white stems, this transparent in the air, that not, some standing close together, some scattered

I [2] 12 b]

394

Tutti i rami delli alberi in ogni grado della loro [2]altezza givnti insieme sono equali alla gro[3]ssezza del loro pedale

[4]Tutte le ramificationi dell'acque in ogni [5]grado di loro lunghezza , essendo d'equal [6]moto, sono equali alla grossezza del loro [7]principio

The relative thickness of the branches to the trunk (393—396)

All the branches of a tree at every stage of its height when put together are equal in thickness to the trunk [below them]

All the branches of a water [course] at every stage of its course, if they are of equal rapidity, are equal to the body of the main stream

M 78 b]

395

Ogni āno, che i rami delle [2]piante ànno dato fine alla [3]loro maturità, essi ànno [4]cōposto, givti insieme, [5]altrettanta grossezza, quā[6]to è la grossezza del suo pe[7]dale, e in ogni grado della [8]sua ramificatione tu tro-[9]verai la grossezza di detto [10]pedale come è *i k* [11]*g h* *e f* *c d* *a b* [12]tutti saranno equali infra [13]loro, non essendo l'albero stor-[14]piato, altremēti la regola [15]falla

[16]Tutti i rami ànno le di[17]ritture che si dirizzano [18]al ciētro dell'albero *m*

Every year when the boughs of a plant [or tree] have made an end of maturing their growth, they will have made, when put together, a thickness equal to that of the main stem, and at every stage of its ramification you will find the thickness of the said main stem, as *i k*, *g h*, *e f*, *c d*, *a b*, will always be equal to each other, unless the tree is pollard—if so the rule does not hold good

All the branches have a direction which tends to the centre of the tree *m*

393 1—16 R 6 chiari 9 ramifichātu 13 achistrapar laria 14 achinno 15 chi eltrito di posta

394 2 alteza 3 sseza 5 lungeza 6 mo sono grosseza

395 1 ognano che rami 3 maturta 5 grosseza 6 grosseza 7 ella 8 ramifichatione 9 grosseza 10 il pedale come he i k 13 lloro sto "r ' 14 piāti 15 nōfalla 17 chessi dirizano

395 The two sketches of leafless trees one above another on the left hand side of Pl XXVII, No 1, belong to this passage

M 79a]

396

Se la pianta · *n* crescierà alla grossezza [2]di *m*, i sua rami faranno tutta la cōgiūtione [3]*a* · *b* per lo ingrossare de' rami indentro come di [4]fuori.

[5]I rami delle piante fanno [6]in ogni nascimento de' sua [7]ramiculi vna tortura la [8]quale, partorendo il ramo, si [9]viene a biforcare, e detta bifor[10]catura si trova in mezzo a due [11]angoli, de' quali quello sarà [12]piv grosso che sarà dal lato del [13]ramo piv grosso, proportione[14]volmēte, se nō lo guasta l'accidētale.

The law of proportion in the growth of the branches (396—402)

If the plant *n* grows to the thickness shown at *m*, its branches will correspond [in thickness] to the junction *a b* in consequence of the growth inside as well as outside.

The branches of trees or plants have a twist wherever a minor branch is given off; and this giving off the branch forms a fork; this said fork occurs between two angles of which the largest will be that which is on the side of the larger branch, and in proportion, unless accident has spoilt it.

G 34b]

397.

Nessū gobbo [2]è ne rami, che [3]nō ui sia dato a[4]lcun ramo, il [5]quale è mācato;

[6]Crescono più li ramiculi [7]inferiori de' rami del[8]le piāte, che li superio[9]ri, e questo sol nasci[10]e perchè l'umore che li nu[11]triscie, per aver lui gravi[12]tà, è più facilmē[13]te allo ingiù che allo insù, [14]e ancora perchè quelli che vē[15]gono allo īgiù si discostan [16]da l'ōbra ch'è inverso il cētro [17]della piāta; [18]quāto li rami sō [19]più vechi, tanta mag[20]gior diferētia è da [26]li sua ramiculi [22]di sopra a quelli [23]di sotto e i quali sieno del [24]medesimo anno o epoca.

There is no boss on branches which has not been produced by some branch which has failed.

The lower shoots on the branches of trees grow more than the upper ones and this occurs only because the sap that nourishes them, being heavy, tends downwards more than upwards, and again, because those [branches] which grow downwards turn away from the shade which exists towards the centre of the plant. The older the branches are, the greater is the difference between their upper and their lower shoots and in those dating from the same year or epoch.

G. 35a]

398

Delli margini delli [2]alberi.

[3]Li margini delli alberi crescō pi[4]v in grossezza che nō richiede il umo[5]re distribuito che le nutriscie.

Of the scars on trees.

The scars on trees grow to a greater thickness than is required by the sap of the limb which nourishes them.

G 13a]

399

Quella pianta osseruerà [2]il suo accrescimēto cō [3]più diritta linia, la quale [4]genera più minuta ra[5]mificatione

The plant which gives out the smallest ramifications will preserve the straightest line in the course of its growth.

396 1 sella . . cressciera . . grosseza [che] 7 ramichuli. 9. biforchare 10. chatura . mezo 12 chessara. 14 lacidētale
397 1—24 R. 6 crescā 8 chelli 9 ecquesto sol nassci 10. lomore chelli 12 facilmalumē 13 ingu, 14 perche que che vē 15 grno allo 20 gor 22 acquelli 23 e ī qua del. 24 annaepoca.
398 1—5 R. 1 delle margini 3. le . crescā . omo 4 v groseza . . illomo 5 re distrebito chelle nutrisscie
399 1—5 R 2 accresscimēto

396. The sketches illustrating this are on the right hand side of Pl. XXVII, No. 1, and the text is also given there in facsimile

397 The sketch accompanying this in the MS. is so e[illegible]

399. This passage is illustrated by two partly effaced sketches One of these closely resembles the lower one given under No 408, the other also represents short closely set boughs on an upright [illegible]

G. 14 a]

400.

Della ramificatione.

[2] Senpre il principio della ramifi-[3]catione à la linia cētrale della sua gro[4]ssezza, che si dirizza alla linia cētrale [5] della pianta.

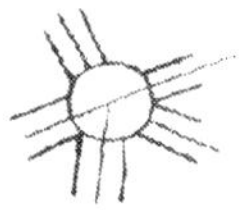

Of the ramification.

The beginning of the ramification [the shoot] always has the central line [axis] of its thickness directed to with the central line [axis] of the plant itself.

G. 37 a]

401.

Senpre li rami nello sepa[2]rarsi dal fusto fāno vna [3] basa con una globosità,[4] come si mostra in *a b c d*.

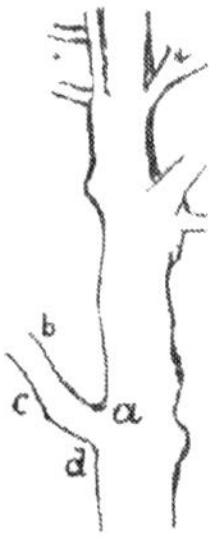

In starting from the main stem the branches always form a base with a prominence as is shown at *a b c d*.

G. 33 a]

402.

Perchè molte volte li legnami nō [2] sō diritti nelle lor uene.

[3] Quādo li rami, che succedono il secōdo anno so[4]pra del ramo dell'anno passato, nō ànno le [5] grossezze simili sopra li rami antecedēti, ma [6] sono dal lato, allora il uigore di quel ramo [7] di sotto si torce al nutrimēto de quel ch'è più al[8]to, ancorachè esso sia vn poco dal lato;

[9] Ma se tali ramificationi avrā equalità [10] nel loro cresciere, le uene del loro fusto [11] sarā diritte e equidistāti in ogni grado d'altez[12]za della loro pianta.

[13] Adūque tu pittore, che non ài tale regole, per [14] fuggire il biasimo delli intēdenti sii vago di [15] ritrare ogni tua cosa di naturale e nō dispre[18]zzare lo studio come fanno i guadagnatori.

Why, very frequently, timber has veins that are not straight.

When the branches which grow the second year above the branch of the preceding year, are not of equal thickness above the antecedent branches, but are on one side, then the vigour of the lower branch is diverted to nourish the one above it, although it may be somewhat on one side.

But if the ramifications are equal in their growth, the veins of the main stem will be straight [parallel] and equidistant at every degree of the height of the plant.

Wherefore, O Painter! you, who do not know these laws! in order to escape the blame of those who understand them, it will be well that you should represent every thing from nature, and not despise such study as those do who work [only] for money.

400. 1—5 R. 3 chatione a [il centro] "la linia cētrale" della. 4. se chessi diriza.
401. 1—4 R. 1. sepr. 2. fano.
402. 3. sucedano. 5. grosseze simile. 7. notrimēto. 8 pucho. 9. Massettale ramificatione ara. 10. nelloro cressciere . . fussto. 11. dalte. 14. sia vagho. 18. zare.

E 6*b*]

403.

Della ramificatione [2]delle piãte.

[3]Le piãte, che assai si dilatano, ànno li angoli [4]delle partitioni che separano le loro ra[5]mificationi tanto più ottusi, quãto el na[6]scimento loro è più basso, cioè più vi[7]cino alla parte più grossa e più vecchia del[8]l'albero: adunqve nella parte piv giova-[9]ne dell'albero li ãgoli delle sua ramificatio-[10]ni sono più acuti.

The direction of growth (403—407)

Of the ramifications of plants.

The plants which spread very much have the angles of the spaces which divide their branches more obtuse in proportion as their point of origin is lower down, that is nearer to the thickest and oldest portion of the tree. Therefore in the youngest portions of the tree the angles of ramification are more acute.

G 32*b*]

404.

Li stremi delle ramificatiõ delle piãte, [2]se nõ sõ superati dal peso de' frutti, si volta[3]no ĩverso il celo quãto è possibile;

[4]Le parti diritte delle lor foglie stanno volte [5]inverso il celo per ricevere il nutrimẽto de[6]lla rugiada che cade la notte;

[7]Il sole dà spirito e vita alle piãte [8]e la terra col-l'umido le notrisce; [9]intorno a questo caso io provai già a [10]lasciare solamẽte vna mi[11]nima radice a vna zucca e quella tenevo [12]nutrita coll'acqua, e tale zucca cõdusse a per[13]fezione tutti li frutti ch'ella, potè poi [14]generare, li quali furono circa 60 z[15]ucche, di quelle lunghe, e posi la mẽte cõ dili[16]gentia a tale vita e cognobbi che la rugiada [17]della notte era quella che col suo umido pe[18]netrava abondantemẽte per l'appi-[19]ccatura delle sua grã foglie al nutrimẽto [20]d'essa piãta colli sua figliuoli—overo uo-[21]va che ànno a producere li sua figliuoli.

[22]La regola delle foglie nate nel ramo vltimo [23]dell'ãno sarà nelli 2 rami fratelli in contra[24]rio moto, cioè che voltandosi intorno il nascimẽ[25]to delle foglie il loro ramo in modo che la 6ª foglia [26]di sopra

The tips of the boughs of plants [and trees], unless they are borne down by the weight of their fruits, turn towards the sky as much as possible.

The upper side of their leaves is turned towards the sky that it may receive the nourishment of the dew which falls at night.

The sun gives spirit and life to plants and the earth nourishes them with moisture. [9] With regard to this I made the experiment of leaving only one small root on a gourd and this I kept nourished with water, and the gourd brought to perfection all the fruits it could produce, which were about 60 gourds of the long kind, and I set my mind diligently [to consider] this vitality and perceived that the dews of night were what supplied it abundantly with moisture through the insertion of its large leaves and gave nourishment to the plant and its offspring —or the seeds which its offspring had to produce—[21].

The rule of the leaves produced on the last shoot of the year will be that they will grow in a contrary direction on the twin branches; that is, that the insertion of the leaves turns round each branch in such a

403 1 delle ramifichatione 3 angholi. 4. partitiõ chesseperano. 6. baso 9 ãgholi . . ramifichatio. 10. achuti
404 4 parte stão 6. rugada che chade 8 ella 9. acquesto 10 allasciare 11. zucha ecquella 12 nutrita 13 fezione 14 circha. 15 ucc 16. attaln . chella rugada. 18 abondamẽte 19 chatura. 20. overo ho. 21. va [delli] che .

403. Compare the sketches on the lower portion of Pl. XXVII, No. 2.

404. A French translation of lines 9—12 was giv [illegible] *Arts*, Oct. 1877; his paper also contains some valuable information as to botanical science in the ancient classical writers and at the time of the [illegible]

nasce sopra la sesta di sotto, e 'l moto [27]del loro voltarsi è, se l'ū volta inuerso la sua cōpagna [28]a destra, l'altra li si volta a sinistra; [29]la foglia è tetta over poppa del ramo o fru[31]to che nasce nell'anno che viene

way, as that the sixth leaf above is produced over the sixth leaf below, and the way they turn is that if one turns towards its companion to the right, the other turns to the left, the leaf serving as the nourishing breast for the shoot or fruit which grows the following year

G 5a]

405

Li rami più bassi delle piā[2]te che fā grā foglie e frutti [3]gravi come noci, fichi e si[4]mili sempre si dirizzano alla [5]terra

[6]Senpre li rami nascono so[7]pra la foglia

The lowest branches of those trees which have large leaves and heavy fruits, such as nut-trees, fig-trees and the like, always droop towards the ground

The branches always originate above [in the axil of] the leaves

G 4b]

406.

I ramiculi superiori delli [2]rami laterali delle piāte [3]costā più al lor ramo mae[4]stro che nō fā quelli di sotto

The upper shoots of the lateral branches of plants lie closer to the parent branch than the lower ones

G 35b]

407.

Senpre li rami più bassi, [2]poich'elli ànno generato [3]l'angolo della lor sepera[4]tione del suo fusto, si pi[5]egano in basso

The lowest branches, after they have formed the angle of their separation from the parent stem, always bend downwards so

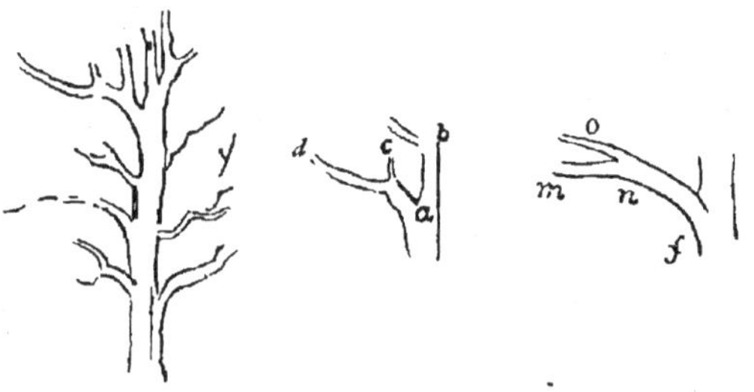

per nō si ser[6]rare adosso alli altri ra[7]mi che sopra lui s'accodano [8]nel medesimo fusto

as not to crowd against the other branches which follow them on the same stem and

figlolı 23 dellano . sarāno 24 coe 25 folie . . chella 26. sessta 27 sellū il suo cōpagno 28 adesstra assinistra. 29 he. 31. nassce il 32 lannō *Lines 29—32 are written in margin.*

405 1—7 R. 2 poglie 3 coci 4 dirizano 6. nassca

406 1—4 R maes 4 que di

407 1—21 R 5 si se 7 sacodano 8 fussto 9 podere 10. chelli nutrissce 11. mosstra 13 affatto [lāgolo] ilato.

e [9]per potere meglio pigliare [10]l'aria che li nustrisce—[11]come mostra l'angolo *b a c* [12]che il ramo *a c* poich'elli [13]à fatto il lato dell'an[14]golo *a c*, si piega in ba[15]sso in *c d* e il ramicu[16]lo *c* si secca per l'essere [17]suo di sottile.

[18]Senpre il ramo maestro va di sotto [19]come mostra il ramo *f* [20]*n m*, che nō va per *f* [21]*n o*.

to be better able to take the air which nourishes them. As is shown by the angle *b a c*; the branch *a c* after it has made the corner of the angle *a c* bends downwards to *c d* and the lesser shoot *c* dries up, being too thin.

The main branch always goes below, as is shown by the branch *f n m*, which does not go to *f n o*.

408.

G. 36a]

The forms of trees (408—411).

L'olmo senpre mette più lun[2]ghezza nelli vltimi rami del me[3]desimo anno che in quelli che [4]sō più bassi, e questo fa la [5]natura, perchè i rami più al[6]ti sō quelli che ànno a cresce[7]re la quatità dell'albero e quel[8]li di sotto ànno a seccare, [9]perchè nascono nell'onbra e il [10]loro accrescimēto sarebbe [11]inpedimēto dello introito [12]de' razzi solari e dell'aria in[13]fra essa ramificatio mae[14]stra di tal piāta.

[15]Li rami maestri inferio[16]ri si piegano piv che i superio[17]ri, per essere più obbliqui che [18]essi superiori e ancora perchè sō [19]maggiori e piv vecchi.

The elm always gives a greater length to the last branches of the year's growth than to the lower ones; and Nature does this because the highest branches are those which have to add to the size of the tree; and those at the bottom must get dry because they grow in the shade and their growth would be an impediment to the entrance of the solar rays and the air among the main branches of the tree.

The main branches of the lower part bend down more than those above, so as to be more oblique than those upper ones, and also because they are larger and older.

409.

G. 36b]

Vniversalmente [2]quasi tutte le rettitu[3]dini delle piāte s'in[4]curvano tenēdo la [5]parte convessa diver[6]so mezzodì, e le loro [7]ramificazioni son [8]più lunghe e grosse e piv [9]spesse a esso mezzodì [10]che a tramōtana, [11]e questo nascie perchè 'l [12]sole tira l'umore in[13] verso quella superfitie del[14]la pianta la quale li è [15]più vicina.

[16]E questo s'os[17]serua se nō [18]li è ocupato [19]il sole dall'al[20]tre piāte.

In general almost all the upright portions of trees curve somewhat turning the convexity towards the South; and their branches are longer and thicker and more abundant towards the South than towards the North. And this occurs because the sun draws the sap towards that surface of the tree which is nearest to it.

And this may be observed if the sun is not screened off by other plants.

410.

G. 51a]

Il ciriegio è di natura dell' a[2]bete nella sua ramifica[3]tione fatta a gradi intor[4]no a

The cherry-tree is of the character of the fir tree as regards its ramification placed

14. piegha. 16. secha per lesere. 17. disutile. 18. Senpre maesstro. 20. ramo f.

408. 2. gghezza neli. 4. ecquesto. 5. perche rami. 6. cressce. 7. eque. 8. anno | asseechare. 9. nasscano. 10. acresscimēto. 15. maesstri. 16. chesuperiori. 18. esse. 19. magori . . vecchi.

409. 1—20 (R). 2. tucte. 3. dine. 6. mezodi ella. 7. ramificazione. 10. attramōtana. 11. ecquesto nasscie. 12. lomore. 16. ecquesto os. 18. ochupato. 19. ecquesto si manifessta. 20. nelle piante chessono. 21. spesse rimāde (?) che ro (?). 22. mettano ogni 3 anni.

410. 1—15 R. [illegible] dal mezo.

lor fusto, e li su[5]a rami nascono a 4 o [6]a cinque o 6 a riscon-tro [7]l'un dell'altro, e la sōma [8]delli stremi ramiculi [9]conpone piramide [10]dal mezzo in [11]sù, e il noce e la quercia [12]dal mezzo in sù cōpone v[13]na mezza spera

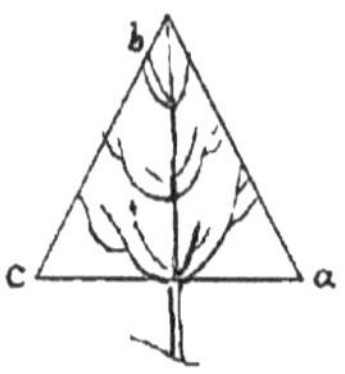

in stages round its main stem, and its branches spring, 4 or five or 6 [together] opposite each other, and the tips of the topmost shoots form a pyramid from the middle upwards, and the walnut and oak form a hemisphere from the middle upwards.

G 88*b*]

411.

Per il ramo del [2]noce che solo è [3]percosso e battu[4]to quād'elli à [5]cōdotto a perfe[6]ctione . .

The bough of the walnut which is only hit and beaten when it has brought to perfection . . .

G 33*a*]

412.

DEL NASCIMĒTO DE' RAMI NELLE PIĀTE

OF THE INSERTION OF THE BRANCHES ON PLANTS

The insertion of the leaves (412—419)

[2]Tale è il nascimēto delle ramificationi delle [3]piāte sopra i lor rami prīcipali qual'è quella de[4]l nascimēto delle foglie sopra li ramiculi del me[5]desimo āno d'esse foglie, le quali foglie ano [6]quattro modi di procce-dere, l'una più alta che l'altra, [7]il primo più vniuersale è, che senpre la sesta di sopra [8]nasce sopra la sesta di sotto, e il secondo [9]è che le 2 terze di sopra sō sopra le due terze di [10]sotto, e 'l terzo modo è che la 3ª di [11]sopra è sopra la 3ª di sotto

Such as the growth of the ramification of plants is on their principal branches, so is that of the leaves on the shoots of the same plant These leaves have [6] four modes of growing one above another The first, which is the most general, is that the sixth always originates over the sixth below [8], the second is that two third ones above are over the two third ones below [10], and the third way is that the third above is over the third below [11]

11 ecquerch 12 mezo 13 meza
411 1—6 R 1 della 2 chessolo he
412 1 nascimēto 2 Tale he il ramichationi 3 quel e quella 4 nasscimēto ramichuli 5 dessimo āno desse foglie le 6 proccedere chellaltro 7 eprimo he chessenpre 8 nassce sessta 9 he che 2 10 hechella 11 essopra

411. The end of the text and the sketch in red chalk belonging to it, are entirely effaced

412 See the four sketches on the upper portion of the page reproduced as fig 2 on Pl XXVII

6 *Quattro modi* (four modes) Only three are described in the text, the fourth is only suggested by a sketch

This passage occurs in MANZI's edition of the Trattato, p 399, but without the sketches and the text is mutilated in an important part The whole passage has been commented on, from MANZI's version, in Part I of the *Nuovo Giornale Botanico Italiano*, by Prof G UZIELLI (Florence 1869, Vol I) He remarks as to the 'four modes' *"Leonardo, come si vede nelle linee sequenti da solo tre esempli Questa ed altre inesattezze fanno desiderare, sia esaminato di nuovo il manoscritto Vaticano"* This has since been done by D KNAPP of Tübingen, and his accurate copy has been published by H LUDWIG, the painter The passage in question occurs in his edition as No 833, and there also the drawings are wanting The space for them has been left vacant, but in the Vatican copy *'niente'* has been written on the margin, and in it, as well as in LUDWIG's and MANZI's edition, the text is mutilated

8 *la sesta di sotto* *"Disposizione 2/5 o 1/5 Leonardo osservò probabilmente soltanto la prima"* (UZIELLI)

9—10 *terze di sotto* *"Intende qui senza dubbio parlare di foglie decussate, in cui il terzo verticello è nel piano del primo"* (UZIELLI)

11 3ª *di sotto* *"Disposizione 1/2"* (UZIELLI)

G 27a]

413.

DESCRITIŌ DELL'OLMO.

[2]Questa ramificatione dell'olmo [3]à il maggiore ramo nella sua frōte, [4]e 'l minore è il primo ed il penvltimo [5]quādo la maestra è diritta;

[6]Il nascimēto da l'una foglia all'al[7]tra è la metà della maggior lūghez[8]za della foglia alquāto māco, [9]perchè le foglie fāno interual[10]lo ch'è circa al 3° della larghez[11]za di tal foglia.

[12]L'olmo à le [13]sue foglie [14]più presso [15]alla [16]cima del suo [17]ramo, che al [18]nascimēto e le [19]lor larghezze [20]poco varia[21]no, e sono risguar[22]dandole di vn me[23]desimo aspetto.

A DESCRIPTION OF THE ELM

The ramification of the elm has the largest branch at the top. The first and the last but one are smaller, when the main trunk is straight.

The space between the insertion of one leaf to the rest is half the extreme length of the leaf or somewhat less, for the leaves are at an interval which is about the 3rd of the width of the leaf.

The elm has more leaves near the top of the boughs than at the base; and the broad [surface] of the leaves varies little as to [angle and] aspect.

G 28a]

414.

Le foglie del noce, conpartite per [2]tutto il ramiculo di quell'anno, [3]sō tanto più distanti l'una [4]dall' altra e cō maggiore nu[5]mero, quāto il ramo, doue [6]tal ramicolo nascie, è più giova[7]ne, e son tāto più vicine ne' [8]loro nascimēti e di minore nu[9]mero, quanto il ramiculo do[10]ve nascono è nato in ramo pi[11]v vechio, nascono li sua fru[12]tti in istremo del suo ramiculo, [13]e li sua rami maggiori son di sotto [14]al lor ramo, doue nascono, [15]e questo accade perchè la grauità del [16]suo umore è più atta a discende[17]re che a mōtare, e per questo li [18]rami che nascō sopra di loro, [19]che vanno inverso il celo, son pi[20]ccoli e sottili, e quādo il ra[21]miculo guarda inuerso il celo, le [22]foglie sue si dilatano [23]dal suo stre[24]mo con eguale partitiō colle lor [25]cime e se 'l ramiculo guarda all'o[26]rizzonte, le foglie restano ispia[27]nate, e questo nasce perchè le foglie [28]universalmente tengono il riverscio [29]loro volto alla terra.

[30]I ramiculi sō [31]tanto mino[32]ri quanto essi na[33]scono più vici[34]ni al nascimē[35]to del ramo che [36]li produce.

In the walnut tree the leaves which are distributed on the shoots of this year are further apart from each other and more numerous in proportion as the branch from which this shoot springs is a young one. And they are inserted more closely and less in number when the shoot that bears them springs from an old branch Its fruits are borne at the ends of the shoots And its largest boughs are the lowest on the boughs they spring from. And this arises from the weight of its sap which is more apt to descend than to rise, and consequently the branches which spring from them and rise towards the sky are small and slender[20], and when the shoot turns towards the sky its leaves spread out from it [at an angle] with an equal distribution of their tips; and if the shoot turns to the horizon the leaves lie flat, and this arises from the fact that leaves without exception, turn their underside to the earth[29]

The shoots are smaller in proportion as they spring nearer to the base of the bough they spring from.

413 3 magore 4 eil p° el il 5 maestra 6 nasscimēto dalluna 7 ella. magor lūge 8 mācho 9 fano 10. large 12—15 Lolmo alle sue foglie piu presso la cima alla 17—23 ramo chellnasscimēto el lor largeze pocho variano di risguardare a vn medesimo asspetto

414 2 anno e. 3 distante lun 4 magiore 6 nasscie . . goua 8 nasscimēti 10. nasscano. 11. nassono 13 elli. magori 14 nascano. 15 ecquesto acade che. 16. omore . . atto . . disscende 20. choli essotili ecquado 22 dilata. eguali 26 rizonte 27 ecquesto nassce chelle. 28 tengano iriverscio. 31. tanto [p] mino 32 ri quanto e na 33 nascā

413 See Pl. XXVII, No 3 Above the sketch and close under the number of the page is the word '*olmo*' (elm).

414 See the two sketches on Pl. XXVII, No 4. The second refers to the passage lines 20—30.

G 16 *b*]

415.

DEL NASCIMẼTO DELLE FOGLIE SO[2]PRA LI SUOI RAMI

[3]Non diminviscie la grossezza di nes[4]sũ ramo dallo spatio, ch'è da foglia [5]a foglia, se nõ quãto è la grossezza [6]del-l'ochio ch'è sù essa foglia, [7]la qual grossezza mãca al [8]ramo, che succiede, insino al[9]l'altra foglia

[10]A messo la natura le foglie delli vlti[11]mi rami di molte piãte in modo, che senpre la se[12]sta foglia è sopra la prima, e così segue [13]successiuamẽte, se la regola non è impe[14]dita, e questo à fatto per 2 vtilita d'e[15]sse piãte, e la prima è perchè, nascendo [16]il ramo e 'l frutto nell'ãno seguẽte dalla [17]gemella vena o ochio ch'è sopra in cõtatto dell'a[18]ppicatura della foglia, l'acqua che bagnia [19]tal ramo possa disciendere a nutrire [20]tal gemella col fermarsi la goccia nella [21]concavità del nascimẽto d'essa foglia, e il [22]secõdo giovamẽto è che, nasciẽdo tali ra[23]mi l'anno seguẽte, l'uno nõ copre l'altro perchè [24]nascono volti a cinque aspetti li 5 rami, [25]e 'l sesto nasce sopra il primo assai remoto

OF THE INSERTION OF THE LEAVES ON THE BRANCHES

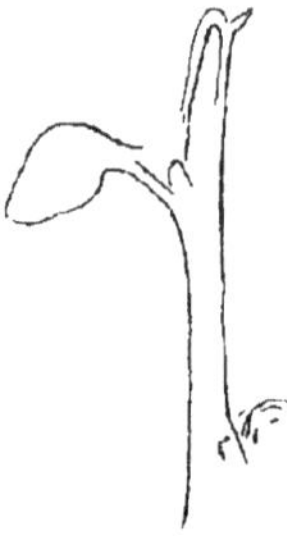

The thickness of a branch never diminishes within the space between one leaf and the next excepting by so much as the thickness of the bud which is above the leaf and this thickness is taken off from the branch above [the node] as far as the next leaf

Nature has so placed the leaves of the latest shoots of many plants that the sixth leaf is always above the first, and so on in succession, if the rule is not [accidentally] interfered with, and this occurs for two useful ends in the plant First that as the shoot and the fruit of the following year spring from the bud or eye which lies above and in close contact with the insertion of the leaf [in the axil], the water which falls upon the shoot can run down to nourish the bud, by the drop being caught in the hollow [axil] at the insertion of the leaf And the second advantage is, that as these shoots develop in the following year one will not cover the next below, since the 5 come forth on five different sides, and the sixth which is above the first is at some distance

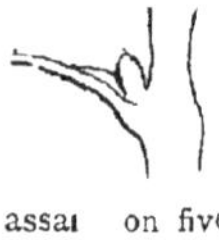

G 30 *b*]

416

DELLE RAMIFICATIÕI DELLE [2]PIÃTE COLLE LORO FOGLIE

[3]Le ramificationi delle piante, alcune [4]come l' olmo sono larghe e sotti[5]li a uso di mano aperta in iscor[6]to, e queste si mostrã nelle lor [7]quãtità di sotto si mostrã dalla par[8]te superiore, e quelle che sõ più al[9]te si mostrã di sotto, e quelle di [10]mezzo in vna parte di sotto e vna [11]di sopra, e la parte di sopra è in istre[12]mo d'essa ramificatione, e que[13]sta parte di mezzo è la più scor[14]tata, che nessuna altra di que[15]lle, che sono volte colle pũte in[16]verso te, e d'esse parti di mez[17]zo dell'altezza della piãta la

OF THE RAMIFICATIONS OF TREES AND THEIR FOLIAGE

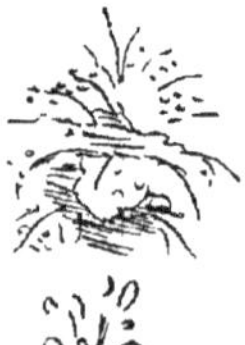

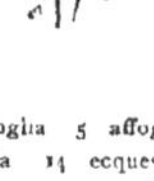

The ramifications of any tree, such as the elm, are wide and slender after the manner of a hand with spread fingers, foreshortened And these are seen in the distribution [thus] the lower portions are seen from above, and those that are above are seen from below, and those in the middle, some from below and some from above The upper part is the extreme [top] of this ramification and the middle portion is more foreshortened than any other of those which are turned with their tips towards you And of those parts of the middle of

415 1—9 R 1 nasscimẽto 3 diminvisscie 4 daffoglia 5 affoglia ella grosseza 7 grosseza mãcha 10 deli 11 rami [delle] di piante che 13 sucessiuamẽte sella 14 ecquesto affatto 15 ella naciendo 16 nellano 17 vena ochio 18 pichatura 20 gocca 21 nasscimẽto 22 govamẽto he che nassciẽdo 24 nasscano asspetti
416 4 essotti 5 ausso 6 ecqueste 8 ecquelle 9 mosstrã ecquelle 11 ella 12, ecquesta 13 mezo ella 15 ches-

pi[18]v lunga sarà inverso li stremi d'e[19]ssi alberi e farà queste tali rami[20]ficatiō come le foglie della felce [21]saluatica · che nasce per l'argine de' fi[22]vmi

[23]Altre ramificatiō sō tonde come [24]son quelle delli alberi che mettono li [25]ramiculi e foglie che la sesta è sopra [26]la prima, altre son rare e tras[27]parēti come il salice e simili.

the height of the tree, the longest will be towards the top of the tree and will produce a ramification like the foliage of the common willow, which grows on the banks of rivers.

Other ramifications are spherical, as those of such trees as put forth their shoots and leaves in the order of the sixth being placed above the first Others are thin and light like the willow and others.

G 29a]

417.

Vedi nel ramo inferiore del sā[2]buco il quale mette le foglie a 2 [3]a due, incrociādo le poste l'u[4]na sopra dell'altra, e se 'l fusto va dirit[5]to inverso il celo, questo ordine nō [6]māca mai, e le maggiori sue foglie [7]sō nella parte più grossa del fusto, [8]e le minori nella parte più sottile, [9]cioè inverso la cima; Ma per torna[10]re al ramo di sotto dico che le foglie [11]delle quali le lor poste aueano a incro[12]ciarsi secondo il ramo di sopra, esse essē[13]do costrette alla legie delle foglie che [14]ànno a voltare la parte del lor diritto [15]inverso il celo per pigliare la rugiada la [16]notte, è necessario che tali poste si pie[17]ghino e nō facciā piv crociamento.

You will see in the lower branches of the elder, which puts forth leaves two and two placed crosswise [at right angles] one above another, that if the stem rises straight up towards the sky this order never fails, and its largest leaves are on the thickest part of the stem and the smallest on the slenderest part, that is towards the top. But, to return to the lower branches, I say that the leaves on these are placed on them crosswise like [those on] the upper branches, and as, by the law of all leaves, they are compelled to turn their upper surface towards the sky to catch the dew at night, it is necessary that those so placed should twist round and no longer form a cross.

G 27b]

418.

Senpre la foglia volgie il suo [2]dritto inverso il cielo acciò pos[3]sa meglio ricevere con tutta la [4]sua superfitie la rugiada che cō len[5]to moto discende dall'aria, e ta[6]li foglie sono in modo cōparti[7]te sopra le loro piāte che l'una oc[8]cupa l'altra il mē che sia possibile [9]col'interzarsi l'una sopra dell'altra, [10]come si uede fare all'edera [11]che copre li muri e tale intreccia[12]mēto serue a due cose, cioè al la[13]sciare l'intervalli che l'aria e 'l sole pos[14]sā penetrare infra loro, la [15]2ª ragione è che le goccie che ca[16]giano della prima foglia possā ca[17]dere sopra la 4ª e la sesta de[18]li altri alberi.

A leaf always turns its upper side towards the sky so that it may the better receive, on all its surface, the dew which drops gently from the atmosphere. And these leaves are so distributed on the plant as that one shall cover the other as little as possible, but shall lie alternately one above another as may be seen in the ivy which covers the walls And this alternation serves two ends; that is, to leave intervals by which the air and sun may penetrate between them The 2nd reason is that the drops which fall from the first leaf may fall onto the fourth or—in other trees—onto the sixth.

sono. 16 parte di me 17 alteza. 18 lungha 19 effara 20 felice 21. nassce 24 mettiano. 25 effolie chella.

417 2 bucho il qualle 3 in cro [sc] ciado. 4 essel fussto va diri 6. māc̄ha mai elle magor sue foglie so 7 fussto 8 elle 9 coe 11 aueano inocro 12 esē 16 notte . posste 17. facia cruciamento

418 2 acco po 4 sua rugada che colen 5 etta. 7 chelluna 9 col rinterzarsi 11 chopre . ettale interza 12 coe 13. chellaria el sole po. 14 loro ellaria la 15 ragione he che. 16 possa. 17 ella sessta

417 See Pl. XXVII, No. 5

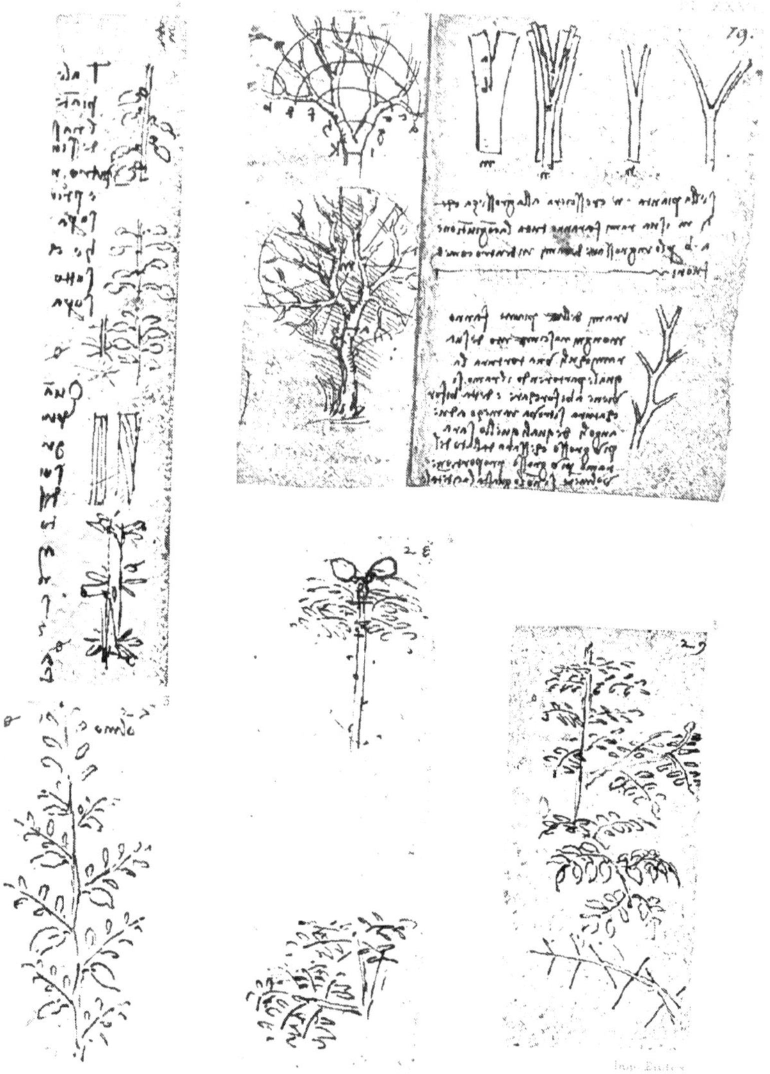

Imp. Ducher

G 33*b*]

419

Ogni ramo e ogni frutto nasce sopra il na[2]scimēto della sua foglia, la quale li scusa ma[3]dre col porgierli l'acqua delle piogge e l'umidi[4]tà della rugiada che li cade la notte di sopra, e [5]molte volte li toglie li superchi calori delli razzi [6]del sole

Every shoot and every fruit is produced above the insertion [in the axil] of its leaf which serves it as a mother, giving it water from the rain and moisture from the dew which falls at night from above, and often it protects them against the too great heat of the rays of the sun

M 77*b*]

420

Light on branches and leaves (420—422)

Quella parte del corpo sarà piv [2]alluminata che fia ferita dal [3]razzo luminoso [4]infra angoli piv equali

That part of the body will be most illuminated which is hit by the luminous ray coming between right angles

G 8*a*]

421

Le piāte giovani · ànno le foglie [2]più tiāsparēti e piv poli[3]ta scorza che le vechie, è in i[4]specie il noce è più chiaro di [5]maggio che di settenbre

Young plants have more transparent leaves and a more lustrous bark than old ones, and particularly the walnut is lighter coloured in May than in September

G 24*a*]

422

Del color acidētale [2]delli alberi

[3]Li colori accidentali delle frō[4]de delli alberi sono 4, cioè ōbra, lu[5]me, lustro e transparētia

Of the accidents of colouring in trees

The accidents of colour in the foliage of trees are 4 That is shadow, light, lustre [reflected light] and transparency

Della dimostratiō [7]delli accidenti

[8]Delle parti accidentali delle [9]foglie delle piāte in lunga distā[10]tia si farà vn misto il quale p[11]artecciperà più di quello ac[12]cidēte che sarà di maggiore figu[13]ra

Of the visibility of these accidents

These accidents of colour in the foliage of trees become confused at a great distance and that which has most breadth [whether light or shade, &c] will be most conspicuous.

G 10*a*]

423

The proportions of light and shade in a leaf (423—426)

Dell' ōbra della foglia

[2]Alcuna volta la foglia à 3 accidēti [3]cioè onbra, lustro e transparētia, [4]come se'l lume fussi in *n* · alla foglia [5]*s*, e l'occhio in *m* che vedrà *a* allumi[6]nato, *b* aōbrato, *c* transparente

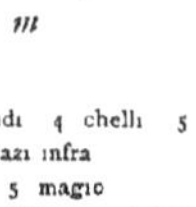

Of the shadows of a leaf

Sometimes a leaf has three accidents [of light] that is shade, lustre [reflected light] and transparency [transmitted light] Thus, if the light were at *n* as regards the leaf *s*, and the eye at *m*, it would see *a* in full light, *b* in shadow and *c* transparent

419 1 onni ongni nassce 2 liscusa 3 ellumidi 4 chelli 5 taglie
420 1 chorpo 3 razo luminoso da [angoli p] 4 razi infra
421 1—5 R 1 govane an 2 trāsparēte 3 chelle 5 magio
422 1—13 R 1 de color 4 ce 5 lusstro ettransparētia 10 il qua p 12 magore
423 1—6 R 1 fogla 2 foglia a 3 coe 5 sellocchia vedera

420 See Pl XXVIII, No 1.

G 10*b*]

424.

La foglia di superfitie cōcava, [2]veduta da riverscio di sotto ī sù, [3]alcuna volta si mostrerà mez[4]za ōbrosa e mezza trāsparēte, [5]come *o·p* sia la foglia e 'l [6]lume *m* e l'ochio *n*, il quale ve[7]drà·*o*·aōbrato perchè il lume [8]nō la percote infra angoli equa[9]li nè da ritto nè da riuerscio; [10]e 'l *p*·fia alluminato da ritto, [11]il quale lume traspare nel suo [12]riverscio.

A leaf with a concave surface seen from the under side and up-side-down will sometimes show itself as half in shade and half transparent. Thus, if *o p* is the leaf and the light *m* and the eye *n*, this will see *o* in shadow because the light does not fall upon it between equal angles, neither on the upper nor the under side, and *p* is lighted on the upper side and the light is transmitted to its under side.

G. 3*a*]

425.

Ancorachè le foglie di pulita [2]superfitie sieno in grā par[3]te d'ū medesimo colore da ritto a [4]loro riverscio, elli accade che [5]quella parte ch'è veduta dall'aria [6]participa del colore d'essa aria, e [7]tanto più pare participar d'esso [8]colore d'aria, quanto l'ochio l'è [9]piv propīquo e la vede più in [10]scorto || e vniversalmēte le sue [11]ōbre si dimostrā più oscu[12]re nel diritto che nel riverscio, [13]per il paragō che lì è fatto da lustri [14]che con tale ōbra cōfinano.

[15]Il riverscio della foglia, ā[16]corachè in se il suo colore sia [17]il medesimo che del diritto, si [18]dimostra di più bel colore, il qua[19]le colore à vn verde participā[20]te di giallo, e questo accade quā[21]do tal foglia è interposta infra

Although those leaves which have a polished surface are to a great extent of the same colour on the right side and on the reverse, it may happen that the side which is turned towards the atmosphere will have something of the colour of the atmosphere, and it will seem to have more of this colour of the atmosphere in proportion as the eye is nearer to it and sees it more foreshortened. And, without exception the shadows show as darker on the upper side than on the lower, from the contrast offered by the high lights which limit the shadows.

The under side of the leaf, although its colour may be in itself the same as that of the upper side, shows a still finer colour—a colour that is green verging on yellow—and this happens when the leaf is placed between

G 2*b*]

426.

l'ochio e 'l lume, che l'alumina [2]dalla opposita parte.

[3]E le sue onbre son [4]nelli medesimi siti che es[5]se erā dalla opposita parte; [6]adūque tu pittore, quando [7]fai li alberi d'apresso, ricordati [8]che, sendo coll'ochio alquāto [9]sotto l'albero, che ti accaderà ve[10]dere le sue foglie dal diritto e da[11]l riuerscio, e le parti diritte [12]sarā tanto più azzurre quāt' elle [13]fiē vedute più in iscorto e una [14]medesima foglia alcuna volta [15]mostra vna parte da ritto e [16]vna da riverscio e per questo ti [17]bisognia farla di due colori.

the eye and the light which falls upon it from the opposite side.

And its shadows are in the same positions as those were of the opposite side. Therefore, O Painter! when you do trees close at hand, remember that if the eye is almost under the tree you will see its leaves [some] on the upper and [some] on the under side, and the upper side will be bluer in proportion as they are seen more foreshortened, and the same leaf sometimes shows part of the right side and part of the under side, whence you must make it of two colours

424 1—12 R. 3 vōta simosstrera. 4 meza trassparēte 6 ellochio. 8. nola. 9 le ne 10. alluminata 11 il qua lume
425 1—21 R 1 anchora chelle 2 grā pa. 4 achade 9. ella. 11 osscu 12 re dal diritto 13 chellefatto dallustri 14. confina. 17 diritto esi 19. colore \\\\\ vn 20 gallo ecquesto achade 21 to tal foglio
426 1—17 R 1 ellume chellalumina 4 [adun] elle 9 achadera 11 e he le parte. 12. azure. 13. e vn 15 mosstra

424 See Pl XXVIII. No. 2 the upper sketch on the page. In the original they are drawn in red chalk.

G 3*b*]

427

Of the transparency of leaves (427—429)

L'onbre che sõ nelle foglie trăspa[2]renti, vedute da riverscio, son quelle [3]medesime ŏbre che son dal diritto d'essa [4]foglia, la quale traspare da riverscio [5]insieme colla parte luminosa, ma [6]il lustro mai può trasparere

The shadows in transparent leaves seen from the under side are the same shadows as there are on the right side of this leaf, they will show through to the underside together with lights, but the lustre [reflected light] can never show through

G 4*a*]

428

Quando l'una verdura è direto all'al[2]tra, li lustri delle foglie e le [3]lor trasparẽtie si dimostrã di maggiore po[4]tẽtia che quelle che cõfinano colla chia[5]rezza del l'aria

[6]E se 'l sole allumina le foglie sanza [7]che s'inframettono infra lui e l'ochio e [8]sanza che esso ochio veda il sole, [9]allora li lustri delle foglie e lor traspa[10]rentie sono eccessive

[11]Molto è utile il fare alcune rami[12]ficationi basse, le quali sienõ scure e cã[13]peggino in verdure alluminate che siẽ [14]alquanto remote [16]dalle verdure oscure vedute di sotto, [17]quella parte è piv oscura ch'è piv vicina [18]all'ochio o ch'è più distãte dal l'aria luminosa

When one green has another [green] behind it, the lustre on the leaves and their transparent [lights] show more strongly than in those which are [seen] against the brightness of the atmosphere

And if the sun illuminates the leaves without their coming between it and the eye and without the eye facing the sun, then the reflected lights and the transparent lights are very strong

It is very effective to show some branches which are low down and dark and so set off the illuminated greens which are at some distance from the dark greens seen below That part is darkest which is nearest to the eye or which is farthest from the luminous atmosphere

G 4*b*]

429

Nõ finger mai foglie transparẽti [2]al sole, perchè son confuse e questo ac[3]cade perchè sopra la trasparẽtia d'una [4]foglia vi si stanpirà l'onbra d'una al[5]tra foglia che li sta di sopra, la qua[6]le ŏbra è di termini spediti e di te[7]rminata oscurità, e alcuna vol[8]ta è mezza o terza parte d'essa [9]foglia che à ŏbra, e così tale ra[10]mificatione è cõfusa ed è da fu[11]gire la sua imitatione

[12]Quella foglia è mẽ trasparente [13]che piglia il lume infra ãgoli più [14]disformi

Never paint leaves transparent to the sun, because they are confused, and this is because on the transparency of one leaf will be seen the shadow of another leaf which is above it This shadow has a distinct outline and a certain depth of shade and sometimes is [as much as] half or a third of the leaf which is shaded, and consequently such an arrangement is very confused and the imitation of it should be avoided

The light shines least through a leaf when it falls upon it at an acute angle

G 8*a*]

430

The gradations of shade and colour in leaves (430—434)

Le ŏbre delle piãte nõ son mai [2]nere, perchè dove l'aria pene[3]tra non può essere tenebre

The shadows of plants are never black, for where the atmosphere penetrates there can never be utter darkness

427 1 dellonbre chessõ 4 quale \\\\\ sspa \\\\ da
428 3 trassparẽtie magore 4 cõfinanno 5 reza 6 essel 7 chessinframettano ellochio 9 lusstri ellor 10 ecesiue 11 fare ver alcune 12 base sure 13 pegino 14 alquando remote dalle prime 15 [che si ẽ] delle verdure osscure 16 delle 17 osscura
429 2 ecquessto 3 chade trassparẽtia 5 chelle sta 12 trassparente
430 1—3 R 3 po

G. 8 b]

431.

Se 'l lume viene da · *m* [2]e l'occhio sia in · *n* · esso [3]ochio vedrà il color[4]e delle foglie *a b* tutte [5]participare del colore [6]dello *m* cioè dell'aria, e 'l [7]· *b c* sarà vedute da [8]riverscio trasparēti [9]cō bellissimo color ver[10]de partecipāte di giallo;

If the light comes from *m* and the eye is at *n* the eye will see the colour of the leaves *a b* all affected by the colour of *m* —that is of the atmosphere; and *b c* will be seen from the under side as transparent, with a beautiful green colour verging on yellow.

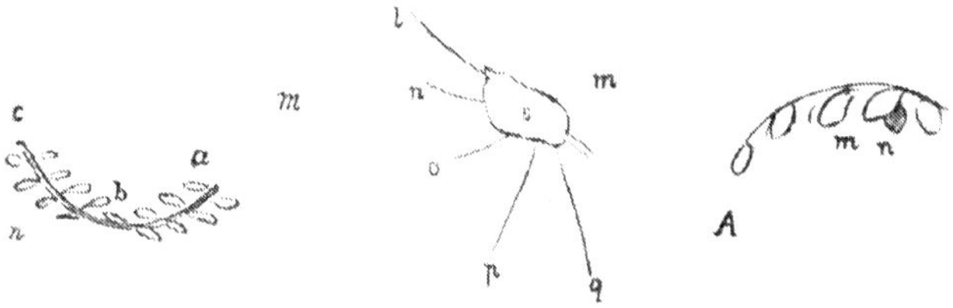

[11]Se *m* · sarà il luminoso [12]alluminatore della foglia · *s* ·, [13]tutti gli occhi che vedranno il [14]riverscio di essa foglia, la ve[15]drà di bellissimo verde chiaro [16]per essere trasparēte;

[17]Molte sō le volte che le poste [18]delle foglie sarā sanza ōbre [19]e ànno il riverscio trasparente [20]e il diritto fia lustro.

If *m* is the luminous body lighting up the leaf *s* all the eyes that see the under side of this leaf will see it of a beautiful light green, being transparent.

In very many cases the positions of the leaves will be without shadow [or in full light], and their under side will be transparent and the right side lustrous [reflecting light].

G. 9 a]

432.

Il salice e altre simili piā[2]te che si tagliano li lor rami [3]ogni 3 o 4 anni, mettono rami [4]assai diritti e la loro ōbra è in[5]verso il mezzo doue nascono [6]essi rami, e inverso li stremi [7]fan poca ōbra per le lor minu[8]te foglie e rari e sottili rami, [9]adunque li rami che si leua[10]no verso il celo avrā poca [11]ōbra e poco rilieuo, e quelli [12]rami, che guardano · dall'orizzōte [13]in giū nascono nella parte [14]oscura dell'ōbra e vēgonsi ris[15]chiarādo appoco insino [16]a loro stremi, e questi mostra[17]no bō rileuo per essere in gra[18]di di rischiaramento in cāpo [19]onbroso.

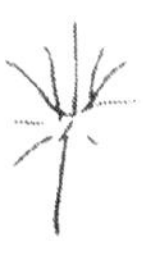

[20]Quella piāta fia meno onbra[21]ta che avrà più rara ramificati[22]one e rare foglie.

The willow and other similar trees, which have their boughs lopped every 3 or 4 years, put forth very straight branches, and their shadow is about the middle where these boughs spring; and towards the extreme ends they cast but little shade from having small leaves and few and slender branches. Hence the boughs which rise towards the sky will have but little shade and little relief; and the branches which are at an angle from the horizon, downwards, spring from the dark part of the shadow and grow thinner by degrees up to their ends, and these will be in strong relief, being in gradations of light against a background of shadow.

That tree will have the least shadow which has the fewest branches and few leaves.

431. 1—R. 2. ellochio. 5. vedera. 6. cioe. 8. trassparente. 13. vedaranno. 14. foglia. 17. chelle. 19. ano. 20. lusstro.

432. 1—22 R. 2. a chessi 3. mett̄. 4 assai . . ellā. 5 mezo . . nasscano. 7. pocha 8. essottili 9. chessi. 10. arā. 11. pocha . . ecquelli. 13. ingiu nascano. 14 osscura . . vēgansi. 15. sciarādo appocho. 16. allora . . ecqueste. 18. risschiaramento 21. ara.

G 10*b*]

433

DELLE FOGLIE OSCURE [2]DINANZI ALLE TRASPARĒTI

[3]Quādo le foglie saranno interposte [4]infra il lume e l'occhio, allora la più vici[5]na all'occhio sarà più scura e la più re[6]mota sarà più chiara, nō cāpeggiādo ne [7]l'aria, e questo accade nelle fogli[8]e che sō dal centro dell'albero [9]ī là cioè inverso il lume

OF DARK LEAVES IN FRONT OF TRANSPARENT ONES.

When the leaves are interposed between the light and the eye, then that which is nearest to the eye will be the darkest, and the most distant will be the lightest, not being seen against the atmosphere, and this is seen in the leaves which are away from the centre of the tree, that is towards the light.

G 28*b*]

434

DE' LUMI DELLE FOGLIE SCURE

[2]I lumi di quelle foglie sarā più del colore del[3]l'aria che in loro si specchia, le quali sono di co[4]lore più oscuro, e questo è causa[5]to perchè il chiaro della parte alluminata coll'oscuro in se conpo[6]ne colore azzurro, e tal chiaro nascie [7]dall'azzurro dell'aria che nella [8]superfitie polita di tal foglie si specchia, ed aumē[9]ta l'azzurro che la detta chiarezza sol generare [10]colle cose oscure

OF THE LIGHTS ON DARK LEAVES

The lights on such leaves which are darkest, will be most near to the colour of the atmosphere that is reflected in them. And the cause of this is that the light on the illuminated portion mingles with the dark hue to compose a blue colour, and this light is produced by the blueness of the atmosphere which is reflected in the smooth surface of these leaves and adds to the blue hue which this light usually produces when it falls on dark objects

DE' LUMI DELLE FOGLIE DI UERDURA TRAENTI AL GIALLO

[13]Ma le foglie di uerdura traēte al giallo nō [14]ànno nello spechiare dell'aria a fare lustro [15]d'azzurro participante, conciosiachè ¶ogni cosa che appari[16]sce nello specchio participa del colore di tale [17]spechio ¶ adunque l'azurro dell'aria spechi[18]ato nel giallo della foglia pare verde, perchè azzurro e gia[19]llo insieme misti cōpongono bellisimo color[20]e verde, adunque verdi gialli sarā li lustri del[21]le foglie chiare traenti al color giallo

OF THE LIGHTS ON LEAVES OF A YELLOWISH GREEN

But leaves of a green verging on yellow when they reflect the atmosphere do not produce a reflection verging on blue, inasmuch as every thing which appears in a mirror takes some colour from that mirror, hence the blue of the atmosphere being reflected in the yellow of the leaf appears green, because blue and yellow mixed together make a very fine green colour, therefore the lustre of light leaves verging on yellow will be greenish yellow

Br M 114*b*]

435.

Sono li alberi infra loro in nelle cāpagnie di varie nature di uerde, in[2] perochè alcuni

A classification of trees according to their colours

The trees in a landscape are of various kinds of green, inasmuch as some verge

433 1—9 R 2 trasparente 3 interposste 4 infralume ellocchio 5 ella 6 cāpegādo 7 ecquesto achade 8 chessō 9 coe

434 1 fogie 3 sisspecohia 4 osscuro ecquesto 5 chiaro "della parte alluminata collosscuro 6 ettal nasscie 7 azurro 8 sisspecchia 9 azurro chella ciareza 10 osscure 14 isspechiare affare lusstro 15 concosiache 18 gallo 'della foglia ' pare 20 verdigalli lusstri

435 1 infralloro inelle 2 alcuno neggregga essimili 3 giallegia e noci vite verdure \\\\\\\\\\\\ 4 giallegiano con

433 See Pl XXVIII, No 2, the lower sketch

negreggiā, come abeti, pini, cipressi, lauri, bussi e simili, [3]alcuni gialleggiā, come sono i noci e peri, viti e verdure \\\\\\ [4]alcuni gialleggiano con oscurità come castagni roveri, [5]alcuni rosseggiano inverso l'autunno come sorbi, melagrani, viti[6]e ciriegi, alcuni biancheggiano come salici, olivi, canne e si[7]mili

[8]Sono l'alberi di uarie figure..

towards blackness, as firs, pines, cypresses, laurels, box and the like. Some tend to yellow such as walnuts, and pears, vines and verdure. Some are both yellowish and dark as chesnuts, holm-oak. Some turn red in autumn as the service-tree, pomegranate, vine, and cherry; and some are whitish as the willow, olive, reeds and the like

Trees are of various forms .

G 12a]

436

Del lume universale allu[2]minatore delle piante

The proportions of light and shade in trees (436—440)

[3]Quella parte della piāta [4]si dimostrerà vestita d'on[5]bre di minore oscurità, [6]la quale fia più remota da[7]lla terra

[8]Provasi, *a p* sia la pi[9]anta, *n b c* sia [10]l'emisperio alluminato, [11]la parte di sotto del·l'albero ve[12]de la terra *p c* cioè la par[13]te *o* , e vede vn poco del[14]l'emisperio in *c d*; Ma la [15]parte più alta nella cōcauità [16] · *a* · è veduta da maggior sōma de[17]ll'emisperio, cioè *b · c* e per que[18]sto (e perchè nō vede la oscurità [19]della terra) resta più allumi[20]nata, Ma se l'albero, è spesso [21] di foglie, come lauro, albatro, bo[22]sso o leccio, allora è variato, [23]perchè ancora [24]che *a* nō veda la [25]terra e' uede la [26]oscurità delle fo[27]glie, diuise da mo[28]lte ōbre [29]la quale os[30]curità riverbe[31]ra insù nelli ri[32]versci delle so[33]praposte foglie, [34]e questi tali al[35]beri ànno l'onbre tā[36]to più oscure, [37]quanto esse sō [38]più vicine al [39]mezzo dell'albero.

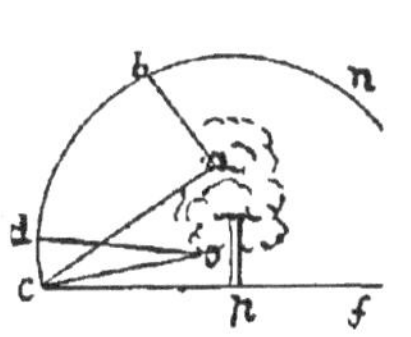

Of a generally distributed light as lighting up trees

That part of the trees will be seen to lie in the least dark shadow which is farthest from the earth.

To prove it let *a p* be the tree, *n b c* the illuminated hemisphere [the sky], the under portion of the tree faces the earth *p c*, that is on the side *o*, and it faces a small part of the hemisphere at *c d*. But the highest part of the convexity *a* faces the greatest part of the hemisphere, that is *b c*. For this reason—and because it does not face the darkness of the earth—it is in fuller light. But if the tree has dense foliage, as the laurel, arbutus, box or holm oak, it will be different, because, although *a* does not face the earth, it faces the dark [green] of the leaves cut up by many shadows, and this darkness is reflected onto the under sides of the leaves immediately above. Thus these trees have their darkest shadows nearest to the middle of the tree.

G 15a]

437.

Dell'onbra della verdura

[2]Senpre l'onbre delle verdure partecipa[3]no dello azzurro e così ogni onbra d'o[4]gni altra cosa, e tanto più ne pi[5]glia quanto ella è più distante dal[6]l'ochio, e meno, quanto ella è più vi[7]cina.

Of the shadows of verdure.

The shadows of verdure are always somewhat blue, and so is every shadow of every object, and they assume this hue more in proportion as they are remote from the eye, and less in proportion as they are nearer.

osscurita come asstagni rove \\\\\\\\\\\\ 5 rossegiano inver laltunno 6. bianchegiano . . salci . essi 8 figure de quali la *here the text breaks off*

436. 1—39 R. 4 dimostera 5 osscurita 6 la qua fia 8 *a b* sia 9 n b c sia [lorizōte o] 11 disō dellalbero 12 coe 13 pocho 14 lemissperio . Malla. 16 magor soma 17 llemissperio coe a c , e pe que 18 osscurita 20. Massellalbero esspesso. 22 ollecco . variato 4. 23 4 perche 28 ōbre [delle vici] 29 [ne] la quale 33 praposste. 34 ecquesti 35 beri allonbre. 36 osscure 39. meza.

437 3 accuro . . ongni 4 chosa ettanto . ne pil 5 ellatre piu distanti 6. ellahc 10 lazurro 12 mosstrano 17 [La cosa

[8]Le foglie, che [9]spechiano [10]l'azzurro del-[11]l'aria, senpre [12]si mostrano [13]all'ochio per ta[14]glio.

The leaves which reflect the blue of the atmosphere always present themselves to the eye edgewise.

DELLA PARTE ALLUMINATA [16]DELLE VERDURE E MŌTI

[18]La parte alluminata si dimostierà [19]piv in lunga distanza del suo na[20]turale colore, la quale sarà allumi[21]nata da più potente lume.

OF THE ILLUMINATED PART OF VERDURE AND OF MOUNTAINS.

The illuminated portion, at a great distance, will appear most nearly of its natural colour where the strongest light falls upon it.

G. 28 *b*]

438.

LI ALBERI CHE SONO ALLUMINATI [2]DAL SOLE E DALL'ARIA.

[3]Li alberi alluminati dal sole e dal-l'aria, avendo [4]le foglie di colore oscuro, sarā da vna parte [5]alluminati dall'aria e per questo tale allu[6]minatione participa d'azzurro, e dall'altra parte [7]saranno alluminati dall aria e dal sole, e quella [8]parte che l'ochio vedrà alluminata dal sole fia lustra.

OF TREES THAT ARE LIGHTED BY THE SUN AND BY THE ATMOSPHERE.

In trees that are illuminated [both] by the sun and the atmosphere and that have leaves of a dark colour, one side will be illuminated by the atmosphere [only] and in consequence of this light will tend to blueness, while on the other side they will be illuminated by the atmosphere and the sun, and the side which the eye sees illuminated by the sun will reflect light.

Ash. I. 4*a*]

439.

DEL FIGURARE UNO SITO SELUAGGIO.

[2]Li alberi e l'erbe, che sono piv ramificati di sottili rami, deono [3]avere minore oscurità d'ōbra quell'albero e quelle erbe, che avrāno maggiori [4]foglie, fieno cagiō di maggiore ōbra.

OF DEPICTING A FOREST SCENE.

The trees and plants which are most thickly branched with slender branches ought to have less dark shadow than those trees and plants which, having broader leaves, will cast more shadow.

E. 18*b*]

440.

PICTURA.

[2]Nella situatione dell'ochio, il qual uede [3]alluminata quella parte delle piante che [4]veggono il luminoso, mai fia veduta al-[5]luminata l'una pianta come l'altra ·, [6] pruovasi e sia l'ochio *c* che vede [7]le due piante

ON PAINTING.

In the position of the eye which sees that portion of a tree illuminated which turns towards the light, one tree will never be seen to be illuminated equally with the other. To prove this, let the eye be *c* which sees

alluminata re] 18 alumina'a si dimosstrerra 19 illungha 20 cholore 21 potente [cholore] lume

438. 3 Deli alberi eddallaria 4 osscuro 5 alluminate alluminate dallaria talle 6 dazurro 7 alluminate ecquella 8 chellochio lusstra

439. 1 Ī sito seluagio 2 li alberi [erbe] ellerbe chessono piv ramifiga[ndi]ti 3 osscurta arāno magiore 4 chagiō di magiore

440. 4 veghano 5 chome 6 essia 8 dicho chettale 9 vedera 11 chome superochecquell albero 12 dimossterra

440. The two lower sketches on the left of Pl. XXVIII, No. 3, refer to lines 21—23. The upper sketch has apparently been effaced by Leonardo himself.

b d, le quali sono allu[8]minate dal sole *a*; dico che tale occhio *c* [9]non vedrà li lumi essere della medesima [10]proportione alla sua ōbra nell'vno albero [11]come nell'altro ·; inperochè quell'albero, ch'è [12]più vicino al sole, si dimostrerà tanto pi[13]v ōbroso che quell che n'è più remo[14]to, quāto l'uno albero è più vicino al cō[15]corso de' razzi solari che vēgono all' ochio [16]che l'altro ecc

[17]Vedi che dell'albero *d* nō si uede dall'occhio *c* [18]altro che ōbra, e dal medesimo occhio *c* si [19]vede l'albero *b* mezzo alluminato e mezzo [20]aōbrato.

[21]L'albero che è veduto sotto: l'ochio vede [22]la cima d'esso albero stare dētro alla cir[23]culatione che fanno li sua rami

[24]Ricordati, o pictore, che tanto sono varie le [25]oscurità dell'onbre in una medesima spe[26]tie di piante, quante son varie le rarità [27]o densità delle loro ramificationi.

the two trees *b d* which are illuminated by the sun *a*, I say that this eye *c* will not see the light in the same proportion to the shade, in one tree as in the other. Because, the tree which is nearest to the sun will display so much the stronger shadow than the more distant one, in proportion as one tree is nearer to the rays of the sun that converge to the eye than the other; &c.

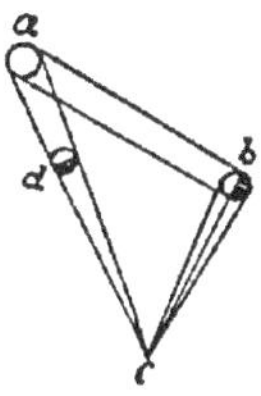

You see that the eye *c* sees nothing of the tree *d* but shadow, while the same eye *c* sees the tree *b* half in light and half in shade

When a tree is seen from below, the eye sees the top of it as placed within the circle made by its boughs[23]

Remember, O Painter! that the variety of depth of shade in any one particular species of tree is in proportion to the rarity or density of their branches.

E 19*a*]

441.

The distribution of light and shade with reference to the position of the spectator (441—443)

Le ōbre delle piāte, poste ne' paesi, nō [2]si dimostrano vestite di se cō [3]medesima situatione nelle piante destre co[4]me nelle sinistre, e massime essendo il sole a [5]destra o a sinistra, provasi per la 4 che di[6]cie ¶li corpi oppachi, interposti infra 'l lume [7]e l'ochio, si dimostrā tutti ōbrosi, e per la 5ª ¶l'o[8]chio interposto infra 'l corpo opaco e lu[9]me vede il corpo opaco tutto alluminato, [10]e per la 6ª ¶l'ochio e 'l corpo opaco, interposto infra le [11]tenebre e'l lume, fia veduto mezzo ōbroso e mezzo lu[12]minoso.

The shadows of trees placed in a landscape do not display themselves in the same position in the trees on the right hand and those on the left; still more so if the sun is to the right or left As is proved by the 4th which says Opaque bodies placed between the light and the eye display themselves entirely in shadow, and by the 5th: The eye when placed between the opaque body and the light sees the opaque body entirely illuminated. And by the 6th: When the eye and the opaque body are placed between darkness and light, it will be seen half in shadow and half in light.

G 9*b*]

442.

Dell'erbe de' prati

Of the herbs of the field.

[1]Delle erbe che pigliā l'onbre delle [3]piāte, che nascono infra esse, quelle [4]che

Of the plants which take a shadow from the plants which spring among them, those

13 checquell 14 al chō 15 chorso . . vēghano 16. chellaltro 18 eddal 19 emezo. 21. Labro. 23 chulatione chelfanno 24 Richordati . . chettanto . le [le ō] 25 [bre] osscurita dellonbre nuna 27 oddensita . . ramifichationi

441 1 posste 2. si [debbō] dimosstrano [circhu] vestite 3. desstre cho 4 sinisstre. 5 desstra o assinisstra . . cheddi, 6. chorpi interpossti 7 ellochio si dimosstra tutte ōbrose 8. interpossto . oppacho ollu 9 oppacho 10 chorpo opacho . . infralle 11 ellume . mezo . . mezo

442 1—21 R 1 delle erbe piglia dellepi 2 3 nasscano esse (quelle *is wanting*) 5 minate . . ellerbe. 6. āonbrate.

441. See the figure on the right hand side of Pl. XXVIII, No. 3. The first five lines of the text are written below the diagram and above it are the last eight lines of the text, given as No. 461

sō di quà dall'ōbra ànno li festuchi allu[5]minati in cāpo ōbroso, e l'erbe, che [6]loro ànno onbrate, [7]āño li festuchi oscuri ī [8]cāpo chiaro, cioè nel cāpo ch'è di là da [9]l'onbra

which are on this side [in front] of the shadow have the stems lighted up on a background of shadow, and the plants on which the shadows fall have their stems dark on a light background, that is on the background beyond the shadow

Delle piāte che sono [12]infra l'ochio e 'l lume

[13]Delle piāte, che sono infra l'ochio e 'l lume, [14]la parte dināti fia chiara, la qual [15]chiarezza fia mista di ramificatiō di fo[16]glie trasparēti (per essere vedute da river[17]scio) cō foglie lustre vedute dal di[18]ritto, e il loro canpo di sotto e dirieto [19]sarà di verdura oscura, per essere aō[20]brata dalla parte dināti della detta piāta, [21]e questo accade nelle piāte più alte dell'ochio

Of trees which are between the eye and the light

Of the trees which are between the eye and the light the part in front will be light, but this light will be broken by the ramifications of transparent leaves—being seen from the under side—and lustrous leaves—being seen from the upper side, and the background below and behind will be dark green, being in shadow from the front portion of the said tree This occurs in trees placed above the eye

G 19*b*]

443.

Dove si de' ritrarre [2]li paesi

[3]Li paesi si debbono ritrarre in modo, che [4]li alberi siē mezzo alluminati e mezzo a[5]ōbrati, ma meglio è farli quādo il so[6]le è occupato da nvvoli, che allora li [7]alberi s'aluminano da lume vniversale [8]del celo e da ōbra vniversale della terra, [9]e questi sō tāto più oscuri nelle [10]lor parti, quāto esse parti sō più pres[11]so al mezzo dell'albero e della terra.

From whence to depict a landscape

Landscapes should be represented so that the trees may be half in light and half in shadow, but it is better to do them when the sun is covered with clouds, for then the trees are lighted by the general light of the sky, and the general darkness of the earth And then they are darkest in certain parts in proportion as those parts are nearest to the middle of the tree and to the earth

G 20*b*]

444

Delle piāte meri[2]dionali

[3]Quādo il sole è all'oriēte, le pi[4]ante meridionali e settētriona[5]li ànno quasi tanto di lume quā[6]to d'ōbra, Ma tāto maggior sō[7]ma di lume quāto esse son pi[8]v occidētali, e tāto ma[9]gior sōma d'ōbra quāto esse [10]sō più oriētali

Of trees to the South

When the sun is in the east the trees to the South and to the North have almost as much light as shadow But a greater share of light in proportion as they lie to the West and a greater share of shadow in proportion as they lie to the East

Delli prati

[12]Stādo il sole all'oriēte, le ver[13]dure de' prati e altre piccole piā[14]te sō di bellissima verdura per esse[15]re trasparēti al sole, il che non ac[16]cade ne' prati occidētali, e le erbe [17]meridionali e settētrionali sō [18]di mediocre bellezza di verdura

Of meadows

If the sun is in the East the verdure of the meadows and of other small plants is of a most beautiful green from being transparent to the sun, this does not occur in the meadows to the West, and in those to the South and North the grass is of a moderately brilliant green

The effects of morning light (441—448)

8 chāpo coe 10 chessono 13 chessono 14 ella qual 15 chiarera di fol 16 trassparēti vedete 17 lusstre 19 osscura 21 ecquesto achade

443 1—11 R 1 si de ritrarre 3 debō chel 4 mezi ēmezo 6. ochupato 9 ecquesti osscuri 10 esse parte pre 11 mezo

444 1—18 R 3 sole he 5 li anquasi 6 Matiāto magor so 8 ettante 9 gor 13 pichole 14 ese 15 sole il ce none a 16 chade. elli 17 essettētrionali

G 21 a]

445.

4 ASPETTI DE' PAESI

[1]Quando il sole è all'oriẽte, tutte [3]le parti alluminate delle piãte sõ [4]di bellissima verdura, e questo ac[5]cade, perchè le foglie alluminate dal [6]sole dẽtro [7]alla metà dell'orizzonte, [8]cioè la metà oriẽtale, sõ [9]trasparẽti ·, [10]e dẽtro al semicircolo occidẽ[11]tale le verdure ànno tristo colore, [12]e l'aria vmida e turba, di color [13]di oscura cenere, per non es[14]sere trasparẽte come la oriẽ[15]tale, la quale è lucida e tã[16]to più quãto essa è più vmida.

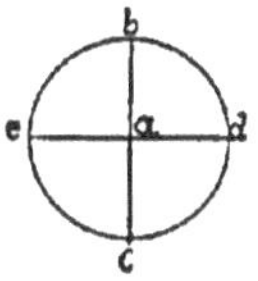

[17]Le õbre delle piãte oriẽtali [18]occupano grã parte della pianta [19]e sono tanto più oscure quãto [20]li alberi sõ più spessi di foglie

OF THE 4 POINTS OF THE COMPASS [IN LANDSCAPES].

When the sun is in the East all the portions of plants lighted by it are of a most lively verdure, and this happens because the leaves lighted by the sun within the half of the horizon that is the Eastern half, are transparent; and within the Western semicircle the verdure is of a dull hue and the moist air is turbid and of the colour of grey ashes, not being transparent like that in the East, which is quite clear and all the more so in proportion as it is moister.

The shadows of the trees to the East cover a large portion of them and are darker in proportion as the foliage of the trees is thicker.

G 21 b]

446.

DEGLI ALBERI ORIẼTALI.

[2]Stãdo il sole all'oriẽte, li alberi ve[3]duti inverso esso oriẽte avran[4]no il lume che li circunderà, d'into[5]rno alle sue õbre, eccetto diuer[6]so la terra, saluo se l'albero nõ fus[7]si stato rimõdo l'anno passato, [8]E gli alberi meridionali e settẽ[9]trionali saranno mezzi õbrosi e mez[10]zi luminosi, e più e mẽ onbrosi[11]o luminosi secõdo che sarã [12]più e meno oriẽtali o occi[13]dẽtali.

[14]L'occhio alto o basso varia [15]le õbre e li lumi nelli alberi, inpero[16]chè, l'ochio alto vede li alberi, cõ po[17]che õbre e il basso con assai õbre.

[18]Tanto sõ varie le verdure [19]delle piãte quãto sõ varie [20]le loro spetie.

OF TREES IN THE EAST.

When the sun is in the East the trees seen towards the East will have the light which surrounds them all round their shadows, excepting on the side towards the earth; unless the tree has been pruned [below] in the past year And the trees to the South and North will be half in shade and half in light, and more or less in shade or in light in proportion as they are more or less to the East or to the West

The [position of] the eye above or below varies the shadows and lights in trees, inasmuch as the eye placed above sees the tree with the little shadow, and the eye placed below with a great deal of shadow.

The colour of the green in plants varies as much as their species.

G 22 a]

447.

DEL'ÕBRE DELLI ALBERI.

[2]Stãdo il sole all'oriẽte, li alberi occi[3]dẽtali all'ochio ‖ si dimostrano di po[4]chissimo rilievo e quasi d'insẽsi[5]bile dimostra-

OF THE SHADOWS IN TREES.

The sun being in the East [to the right], the trees to the West [or left] of the eye will show in small relief and almost imper-

445 1-20 R 1. asspetti 3 parte 4. ecquesto 6. sole [in tutto lonzo] dẽtro . . orizonte 8 coe. 10. gemice ocidẽ 11 an 12 alluria . etturba. 13 osscura cenere [elliari] per nõn e 15 he lucida ettã. 18 ochupano. 19. essono . . osscure
446 1—20 R 1 ãberi 3 aran. 4 chelli 5 eccepto 6. sellalbero non fu. 8 essettẽ 9. sara mez õbrosi 10. i luminos e piu 11 olluminosi secõche. 12 ho occi 14 obbasso. 15 elli
447 1—22 R. 2 oci 4. ecquasi. 5 per lana 7 he molto 11. chauone . . achade chelie 12 multudine . . ellume. 13 vẽ

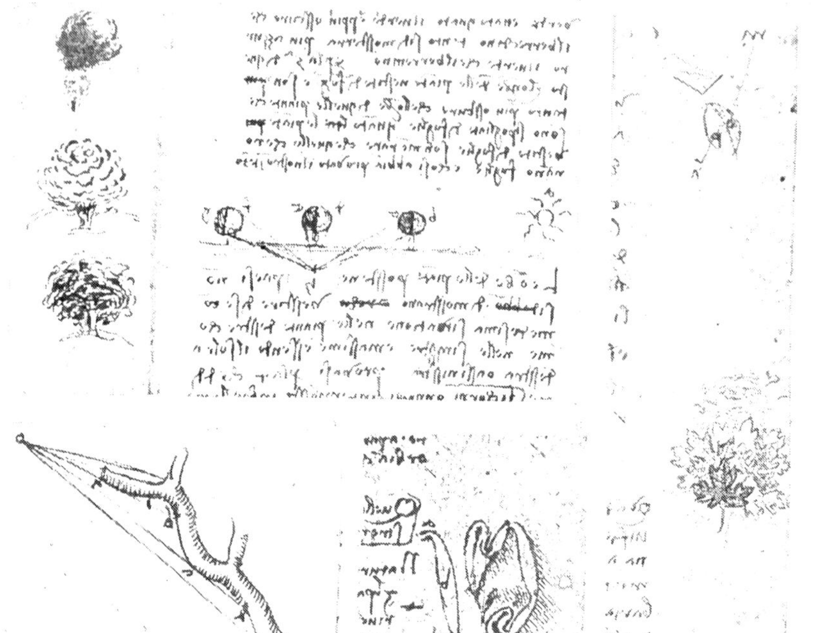

tione, perchè l'aria, che in[6]fra l'occhio e esse piante s'interpone, [7]è molto fvsca, per la 7ª di questo, [8]e sō privati d'ōbra, e bēchè l'ōbra [9]sia in ciascuna diuisiō [10]di ramifi[11]catione, egli accade che le si[12]militudini dell'ōbra e lume, che [13]vēgono all'ochio, sien cōfuse e [14]miste insieme e per la loro piccola [15]figura nō si possano cōprēdere, [16]E li lumi prīcipali sō nelli [17]mezzi delle piāte e le ōbre inver[18]so li stremi, e le loro separationi [19]sō diuise dal'ōbre delli interualli d'esse [20]piāte, quādo le selue sono spesse [21]d'alberi, e' nelli rari termini po[22]co si vedono

ceptible gradations, because the atmosphere which lies between the eye and those trees is very dense [7], see the 7th of this — and they have no shade, for though a shadow exists in every detail of the ramification, it results that the images of the shade and light that reach the eye are confused and mingled together and cannot be perceived on account of their minuteness And the principal lights are in the middle of the trees, and the shadows towards the edges, and their separation is shown by the shadows of the intervals between the trees, but when the forests are thick with trees the thin edges are but little seen

G 22 *b*]

448

Delli alberi oriētali

[2]Stādo il sole all'oriēte, li sua alberi [3]sono oscuri inverso il mezzo e li loro stremi sō luminosi.

Of trees to the east

When the sun is in the East the trees are darker towards the middle while their edges are light

L 87 *a*]

449

Le cose poste nel lume mal si disciernono, [2]ma fra lume e ōbra spicherā bene.

[3]Per ritrare paesi fa che 'l sol sia a mezzodì e volta[4]ti a ponēte o a levāte e ritrai, e se ti volte[5]rai a settētrione, tutte le cose che sarā poste [6]per questa linia fiē sanz' ōbre, e massime quelle [7]che sarā piv propinque all'ōbra del tuo capo, [8]e se ti volterai a mezzodì, ogni cosa per quella [9]linia fia tutto ōbrosa, [10]tutte le piāte, che fiē verso il sole, che avranno per suo [11]canpo l'aria, fieno oscure, e l'altre piā[12]te, che cāpeggieranno in tale oscurità, fiē nere [13]in mezzo e chiare inverso li stremi

Objects in high light show but little, but between light and shadow they stand out well

To represent a landscape choose that the sun shall be at noon and look towards the West or East and then draw And if you turn towards the North, every object placed on that side will have no shadow, particularly those which are nearest to the [direction of the] shadow of your head And if you turn towards the South every object on that side will be wholly in shadow All the trees which are towards the sun and have the atmosphere for their background are dark, and the other trees which lie against that darkness will be black [very dark] in the middle and lighter towards the edges

The effects of midday light

gano 14 pichola 15 possā cōplēdere 17 mezi elle 18 elle lor seperationi 22 vedano
448 1—3 R 3 osscuri mezo chelli
449 1—13 R 1 lecho ello nel discieruano 2 frallume 3 amezo (e volta 4 alleuāte esetti 5 assettatrione chessarā 6 masime quele 8 essetti 10 cheffiē cheārā 11 osscure chelaltre 12 chāpegieranno 13 imezo

447 7 *per la 7ª di questo* This possibly referred to something written on the seventh page of this note book marked *G* Unfortunately it has been cut out and lost

G 25 *b*]

450.

The appearance of trees in the distance (450. 451)

DELLA TRAFORATIŌ [2]DELLE PIĀTE IN SE

[3]La traforatione dell'aria nelli cor[4]pi delle piante e la traforatione [5]delle piāte infra l'aria in lunga [6]distantia non si dimostrano alli occhi, [7]perchè, doue con fatica si conprēde il tutto, [8]con difficultà si conoscono le parti—ma [9]fassi vn misto confuso, il qual parti[10]cipa più di quel ch'è maggior sōma; [11]li traforamēti dell'albero sono di par[12]ticule d'aria alluminata, le quali sō [13]assai minori della piāta, e però pri[14]ma si perdono di notitia che essa pian[15]ta, ma nō resta per questo che esse nō [16]vi sieno, onde per neciessità si fa vn mi[17]sto d'aria e di scuro del' albero onbroso, il [18]quale insieme cōcorre all'ochio che 'l ue[19]de

OF THE SPACES [SHOWING THE SKY] IN TREES THEMSELVES

The spaces between the parts in the mass of trees, and the spaces between the trees in the air, are, at great distances, invisible to the eye; for, where it is an effort [even] to see the whole it is most difficult to discern the parts. — But a confused mixture is the result, partaking chiefly of the [hue] which predominates. The spaces between the leaves consist of particles of illuminated air which are very much smaller than the tree and are lost sight of sooner than the tree, but it does not therefore follow that they are not there. Hence, necessarily, a compounded [effect] is produced of the sky and of the shadows of the tree in shade, which both together strike the eye which sees them.

DELLI ALBERI CHE OCCUPANO LE TRA[21]FORATIONI L'UN DELL'ALTRO

[22]Quella parte dell'albero sarà mē trafora[23]ta, alla quale s'oppone dirietro infra [24]l' albero, e l'aria maggior somma d'altro al[25]bero, come nel albero *a* nō si occupa tra[26]foratione, nè in *b* per nō esservi alberi dirieto: [27]Ma in *c* u'è sol la metà traforata cioè *c o* [28]occupata dall' albero *d*, e vna parte del [29] l'albero *d* è occupata dall'albero *e*, e po[30]co più oltre tutta la traforatione corpo[31]rale delli alberi è persa [32] e sol ui re[33]sta la la[34]terale.

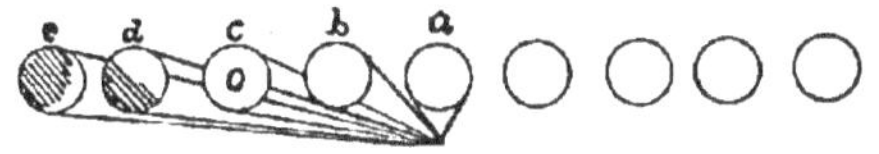

OF TREES WHICH CONCEAL THESE SPACES IN ONE ANOTHER

That part of a tree will show the fewest spaces, behind which a large number of trees are standing between the tree and the air [sky], thus in the tree *a* the spaces are not concealed nor in *b*, as there is no tree behind. But in *c* only half shows the spaces filled up by the tree *d*, and part of the tree *d* is filled up by the tree *e* and a little farther on all the spaces in the mass of the trees are lost, and only that at the side remains.

G 26 *b*]

451.

DE' ALBERI.

[2]Quali termini dimostrano le piāte [3]remote dall'aria che si fa lor cāpo?

[4]Li termini, che ànno le ramificatiō deli al[5]beri coll'aria alluminata, quanto più sō [6]remoti più si fanno in figura tra[7]ēte allo sperico, e quanto più son [8]vicine più dimostrāsi remote da [9]tale spericità, come *a* albero primo, che [10]per essere lui vicino

OF TREES.

What outlines are seen in trees at a distance against the sky which serves as their background?

The outlines of the ramification of trees, where they lie against the illuminated sky, display a form which more nearly approaches the spherical on proportion as they are remote, and the nearer they are the less they appear in this spherical form; as in the first tree *a* which, being near to the eye,

450 4 ella 5 lungha 6. allocchi. 7. faticha si conplēde il tuto. 8 conosce 10. maggor soma co 14 perdano. 16. mis 18. cōcore 20 ochupano 23 sopone 24 ellaria magor. 25 ocupa. 26 nō esser a alberi 27 trofaroto coe 28 occupato 31 deli

451. 2. dimostrino 3 remo dall aria chessi 4 cheāle. 5. collariallumınata 7 spericho 8 dimostrā remote. 9 albero P°

451. The sketch No. 4, Pl. XXVIII, belongs to this passage.

all'ochio, [11]dimostra la vera figura [12]della sua ramificatione, la [13]quale si diminuiscie quasi in *b*, [14]e al tutto si perde in *c*, doue non che li ra[15]mi d'essa pianta si vedono, ma tut[16]ta la pianta cō grā fatica si conosce [17]¶Ogni corpo onbroso, il quale sia di qua[18]lunque figura si voglia, in lunga distā[19]tia pare essere sperico,¶ E questo [20]nascie perchè, s'elli è vn corpo quadra[21]to, in breuissima distātia si perdono li ango[22]li sua, e poco piv si perde più di lati mi[23]nori che restano, e così prima che si [24]perda il tutto si perde le parti per esse[25]re minor del tutto, come l'uomo, ch'è in tal[26]le aspetto, perde prima le ganbe, braccia e tes[27]ta che 'l busto, di poi perde prima li [28]stremi della lunghezza che della larghezza e [29]quādo son fatti equali sarebbe □, se li an[30]goli vi restassino, ma non ui restando è tondo

displays the true form of its ramification, but this shows less in *b* and is altogether lost in *c*, where not merely the branches of the tree cannot be seen but the whole tree is distinguished with difficulty Every object in shadow, of whatever form it may be, at a great distance appears to be spherical And this occurs because, if it is a square body, at a very short distance it loses its angles, and a little farther off it loses still more of its smaller sides which remain And thus before the whole is lost [to sight] the parts are lost, being smaller than the whole, as a man, who in such a distant position loses his legs, arms and head before [the mass of] his body, then the outlines of length are lost before those of breadth, and where they have become equal it would be a square if the angles remained, but as they are lost it is round

I 1 37 *b*]

452

La stanpa dell'onbra di qualūque cor[2]po di uniforme grossezza mai sarà simile [3]al corpo, donde ella nascie

The image of the shadow of any object of uniform breadth can never be [exactly] the same as that of the body which casts it

The cast shadow of trees (452 453)

Br M 114 *a*]

453.

Tutti li alberi, veduti diuerso il sole, sono oscuri verso il [2]mezzo, la quale oscurità fia della figura del suo albero, quādo fia [3]diuiso dalli altri

[4]Le onbre diriuative delli alberi, veduti dal sole, sono oscure quāto quel[5]la del mezzo delli alberi

[6]L'onbra diriuatiua delli alberi, mai fia di minor somma che la somma d'esso al[7]bero, ma fia tanto maggiore quāto il sito dove si taglia fia piv obbliquo īuerso [8]il cētro del mōdo

[9]Quella onbra sarà piv stretta inverso il mezzo dell'albero, del quale il suo albero fia [10]di più rara ramificatione

All trees seen against the sun are dark towards the middle and this shadow will be of the shape of the tree when apart from others

The shadows cast by trees on which the sun shines are as dark as those of the middle of the tree

The shadow cast by a tree is never less than the mass of the tree but becomes taller in proportion as the spot on which it falls, slopes towards the centre of the world

The shadow will be densest in the middle of the tree when the tree has the fewest branches

che 12 le 14 perde c 15 vedino mattu 16 faticha 17 onbro 18 lungha 19 spericho Ecquessto 20 nasscie 21 iunbreuissima perdono 23 nori che resstano 24 parte 26. le essetto perde brci c tes 27 bussto 28 lungeza largeza ec 29 sarebe □, selli

452 2 grosseza Mai 3 nasscie

453 1 osscuri 2 mezo osscurita 4 solessono osscure 5 mezo dellalberi 6 ' chella 7 maffia magore 9 mezo 10 [pi] di piu 11 ogngni mezo tutti 13 obra vesstita parte 14 dacquella 15 ecquesto dacquella

452 See Pl XXVIII, No 5

453 The three diagrams which accompany this text are placed, in the original, before lines 7—11 At the spots marked *B* Leonardo wrote *Albero* (tree) At *A* is the word *Sole* (sun), at *C Monte* (mountain) at *D piano* (plain) and at *E cima* (summit)

[11] Ogni ramo à 'l mezzo dell'onbra di qualunche ramo e per coseguēza di tutto [12] il suo albore.

[13] La figura di qualunche ōbra di ramo o d'albero fia vestita di parti luminose [14] da quella parte, donde viene il lume, la quale alluminatione fia della figura [15] dell'onbre, e questo fia per ispati d'ū miglio da quella il parte che si trova il [16] sole.

Light and shade on groups of trees (453—457).

[17] S'elli accade che alcū nvuolo in alcuna parte aonbra qualche parte de' colli, [18] li alberi sua fanno māca mvtatione che in loco piano, perchè essi alberi su colli [19] son piv spessi di rami, perchè manco mettono per anno che ne' piani, onde essi rami per [20] essere oscuri di natura e per essere pieni d'onbre, le onbre de' nvuoli no li possono [21] piv oscurare, e i piani che si interpongono infra li alberi, che non ānno preso al[22] cuna onbra, forte si transmutano della lor chiarezza, e massimamente quelli [23] che son vari dal verde cioè terreni lauorati o ruine di mōti o loco di sterilità e sasso; [24] dove li alberi confinano coll'aria, essi paiono d'u medesimo colore—[25] se già non fussino molto propinqui e di foglie spesse, come il pino e simili alberi; [26] quādo tu vedrai li alberi per quel uerso che li allumina il sole, tu li vedrai quasi d'una medesima [27] chiarezza · e le ōbre che dentro vi sono fieno occupate dalle foglie alluminate, che infra l'ochio tuo e [28] l'onbre s'interpōgono.

Every branch participates of the central shadow of every other branch and consequently [of that] of the whole tree.

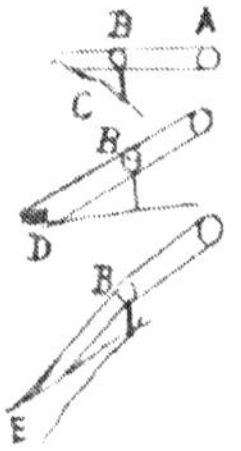

The form of any shadow from a branch or tree is circumscribed by the light which falls from the side whence the light comes; and this illumination gives the shape of the shadow, and this may be of the distance of a mile from the side where the sun is.

If it happens that a cloud should anywhere overshadow some part of a hill the [shadow of the] trees there will change less than in the plains; for these trees on the hills have their branches thicker, because they grow less high each year than in the plains. Therefore as these branches are dark by nature and being so full of shade, the shadow of the clouds cannot darken them any more; but the open spaces between the trees, which have no strong shadow change very much in tone and particularly those which vary from green; that is ploughed lands or fallen mountains or barren lands or rocks. Where the trees are against the atmosphere they appear all the same colour—if indeed they are not very close together or very thickly covered with leaves like the fir and similar trees. When you see the trees from the side from which the sun lights them, you will see them almost all of the same tone, and the shadows in them will be hidden by the leaves in the light, which come between your eye and those shadows.

Alberi vicini.

[29] Li alberi, che infra 'l sole e l'ochio s'interpongono—dopo le onbre, che diuerso il loro cietro si dilatano, [30] si uedrà il uerde delle lor foglie trasparēte, la qual transparētia fia interrotta in molte [31] parti dalle foglie e rami onbrati, che infra te e loro s'interpōgono, o nelle lor parti superiori [32] da molti lustri di foglie fieno accōpagnate.

Trees at a short distance.

When the trees are situated between the sun and the eye, beyond the shadow which spreads from their centre, the green of their leaves will be seen transparent; but this transparency will be broken in many places by the leaves and boughs in shadow which will come between you and them, or, in their upper portions, they will be accompanied by many lights reflected from the leaves.

chessi. 17. achade [illegible] 18. [illegible] "spatio" piani perche. 19. mettano "per anno" che . . esse ramp. 20. lessere ossuri e pere essere le onbr de . . possano. 21. [illegible] . . chessi interpongano infralli. 22. chiareza e massimamente. 23. cor . . lauorati or uine "e" . . loco sterilita essasso sia. 24. paiono. 25. molti. 26. essimili. 26 chelli. 27. ciareza . . elle . . ochupate delle . . infrallochio tuo elōnbre. 28. sinterpongano. 29. li abri . . ellochio sinterpongano . . il suo cietro. 30. trasparēte. 31. parte . . elloro interpōgano . . parte. 32. lusstri. 32. acōpagnate.

29. The heading *alberi vicini* (trees at a short distance) is in the original manuscript written in the

B M 172 *b*]

454.

Li alberi delle canpagnie poco spiccano l'uno dall'altro, perchè le lor parti luminate [2] confinano sopra le luminate dopo loro, e in questo è poco differētia da' lumi a l'ōbre

The trees of the landscape stand out but little from each other, because their illuminated portions come against the illuminated portions of those beyond and differ little from them in light and shade

G 6 *a*]

455

Delli alberi veduti di sotto [2] e cōtro al lume l'un dopo l'al[3]tro vicinamēte · la parte vltı[4]ma del primo sarà transparēte [5] e chiara in grā parte e can[6]peggierà nella parte oscura [7] dell' albero secondo, e così farān tut[8]ti successiuamēte che sarā situ[9]ati colle predette cōditioni

[10] *s* sia il lume, *r* sia [11] l'ochio, *c d n* sia l'albero [12] primo, *a b c* sia il secondo, dico [13] che *r* occhio vedrà la parte [14] *c f* in grā

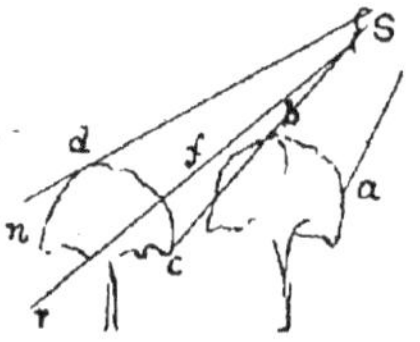

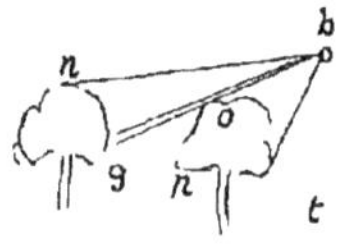

parte trasparēte [15] e chiara per il lume *s*, che la ve[16]de dall' opposita parte, e ve[17]drala in canpo scuro *b c*, perchè [18] tale oscurità è l'onbra dell'albero [19] *a b c*,

[20] Ma se l'occhio è situato in *t* [21] esso vedrà *o p* oscuro nel canpo chi[22]aro *n g*

[23] Delle parti [24] ōbrose traspa[25]rēti delli alberi [26] la più vicina [27] a te è più oscu[28]ra.

Of trees seen from below and against the light, one beyond the other and near together. The topmost part of the first will be in great part transparent and light, and will stand out against the dark portion of the second tree And thus it will be with all in succession that are placed under the same conditions

Let *s* be the light, and *r* the eye, *c d n* the first tree, *a b c* the second Then I say that *r*, the eye, will see the portion *c f* in great part transparent and lighted by the light *s* which falls upon it from the opposite side, and it will see it, on a dark ground *b c* because that is the dark part and shadow of the tree *a b c*

But if the eye is placed at *t* it will see *o p* dark on the light background *n g*

Of the transparent and shadowy parts of trees, that which is nearest to you is the darkest

W VI]

456

Quella parte dell'albero, che campeggia [2] diuerso l'onbra, è tutta d'un colore e do[3]ve li alberi overo rami sō piv spes[4]si ivi è piv scuro, perchè lì māco [5] si stāpa l'aria, Ma dove li ra[6]mi cāpeggiano sopra altri ra[7]mi, quivi le parti luminose [8] si dimostrā piv chiare e le foglie [9] lustre per lo sole che l'allumina

That part of a tree which has shadow for background, is all of one tone, and wherever the trees or branches are thickest they will be darkest, because there are no little intervals of air But where the boughs lie against a background of other boughs, the brighter parts are seen lightest and the leaves lustrous from the sunlight falling on them

454 1 pocho spichano parte 2 pocho diferētia
455 1—28 R 4 del p° sara 6 pegiera osscura 7 albero 2° e tu 8 sucessiuamēte 12 p°, *a b c* sia il 2° dicho 13 vedera 14 gra 15 i lume chella 16 oposita 18 talle osscurita 20 sellochio 21 osscuro 23 parte 24 trasspa 25 rēte deli
456 1—9 R 1 chanpegia 2 ettutta cholore 3 albri[so]overo spe 4 mācho 5 stāpissce 6 cāpegiano 7 parte 8 dimostra chiari 9 chellalumina

G. 27 a]

457.

Nelle copositioni delli alberi frō[2]duti sia auertito di nō replicare [3]troppe volte vn medesimo colore [4]d'una piāta, che canpeggi sopra [5]il medesimo colore dell' altra pi[6]anta, ma varialo cō verdura [7]più chiara o piv oscura o più [8]verde.

In the composition of leafy trees be careful not to repeat too often the same colour of one tree against the same colour of another [behind it]; but vary it with a lighter, or a darker, or a stronger green.

Br. M. 113 a]

458.

On the treatment of light for landscapes (458—465).

Piv bello azzurro ānno i paesi, quādo per li tenpi belli el sole è a mezzodi che in nessuna [2]altra età del dì, perchè l'aria è disgrossata d'umori e risguardando per quell'aspetto tu vedi li al[3]beri belli in verde nei loro stremi e l'onbre inverso il mezzo oscure, e nelle lunghe distantie l'aria che

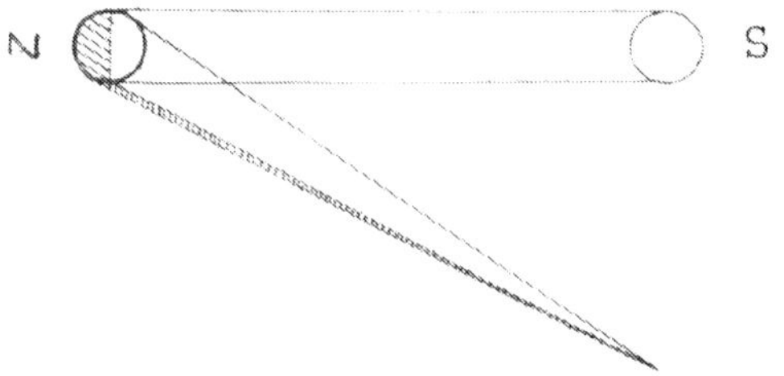

[4]s'interpone infra te e loro si fa piv bella quādo dopo lei è cosa piv oscura, e però l'azzurro è bellissimo.¶ [5]Le cose, vedute per quel uerso che 'l sol'allumina, non ti mostrerā le sue onbre. [6]Ma se tu sei [6]piv basso d'esso sole, tu uedrai quel che dal sole nō fu veduto e ciò sarà tutto onbroso; [7]le foglie delli alberi, che s'interpogono infra te e 'l sole, son di due colori pricipali [8]cioè verde bellissimo, lustro e specchiamēto dell'aria che allumina che nō può essere [9]veduto dal sole, e le onbrose che sol uedono la terra, e le piv oscure che da altro che [10]da oscurità sō circūdate. [11]Molto sono piv belli li alberi infra le

The landscape has a finer azure [tone] when, in fine weather the sun is at noon than at any other time of the day, because the air is purified of moisture; and looking at it under that aspect you will see the trees of a beautiful green at the outside and the shadows dark towards the middle; and in the remoter distance the atmosphere which comes between you and them looks more beautiful when there is something dark beyond. And still the azure is most beautiful. The objects seen from the side on which the sun shines will not show you their shadows. But, if you are lower than the sun, you can see what is not seen by the sun and that will be all in shade. The leaves of the trees, which come between you and the sun are of two principal colours which are a splendid lustre of green, and the reflection of the atmosphere which lights up the objects which cannot be seen by the sun, and the shaded portions which only face the earth,

457. 2. repricare. 7. osscura.

458. 1. accurro . . paessi. 2. dissgressata damori . . rissguardando . [3] asspetto. 3. iaverdi a loro estremi ellonbre . . oscure . . disstantie. 4. infratte ellore . . chosa. 5. chose . . mossterā . . Massetusse. 6. eco sara. 7. chessinterpōgano . . elsole . . di [tre] "2" colori. 8. coe . . lusstro esspecchiamēto . . allumina ch"e" nō potessere. 9. elle onbrose chesol uedano . . elle piv osscure. 10. osscurita. 11. infralle . . chessono . . etc. 12. tusse . . elloro cequesto accade. 13. lisstremi . . trāsparēte.

458. At *S*, in the original is the word *Sole* (sun) and at *N parte di nuvolo* (the side of the clouds).

canpagnie, che sono infra 'l sole e te, [12]che quelli ai quali tu sei infra 'l sole e loro, e questo accade che quelli, che sono diuer[13]so il sole, mostrano inverso li stremi le lor foglie trāsparēti, e chi non è trasparē[14]te, cioè insù li stremi, lustro vero, e che l'onbre sono oscure per[15]chè da niente sono occupate

[16]Li alberi, ai quali tu ti interponi infra 'l sole e loro, non ti si mostreranno se nō [17]col loro chiaro e naturale colore, il quale per se non è molto eccessiuo e oltre a questo al[18]cuni lustri, li quali per non essere in căpo troppo vario dalla loro chiarezza, fieno di poca evidē[19]tia, e se sei piv basso di loro siti, potranno mostrare ancora con quelle parti, [20]le quali il sole nō vide, che fieno onbrose

[21]Pel uēto

[22]Ma se sarai da quella parte, d'onde il uēto spira, tu vedrai li alberi di molto mag[23]giore chiarezza che per altri versi nō uedresti, e questo accade perchè esso vēto di[24]scopre i roversci delle foglie, le quali in tutte sono molto piv biācheggiāti che dal loro [25]diritto, e sopra tutto fieno chiarissime se 'l uento trae da quella regi[26]one, donde si trova il sol di sopra alla quale tu abbi volte le schiene

and the darkest which are surrounded by something that is not dark. The trees in the landscape which are between you and the sun are far more beautiful than those you see when you are between the sun and them, and this is so because those which face the sun show their leaves as transparent towards the ends of their branches, and those that are not transparent—that is at the ends—reflect the light, and the shadows are dark because they are not concealed by any thing

The trees, when you place yourself between them and the sun, will only display to you their light and natural colour, which, in itself, is not very strong, and besides this some reflected lights which, being against a background which does not differ very much from themselves in tone, are not conspicuous, and if you are lower down than they are situated, they may also show those portions on which the light of the sun does not fall and these will be dark.

In the Wind

But, if you are on the side whence the wind blows, you will see the trees look very much lighter than on the other sides, and this happens because the wind turns up the under side of the leaves, which, in all trees, is much whiter than the upper sides, and, more especially, will they be very light indeed if the wind blows from the quarter where the sun is, and if you have your back turned to it

Br M 114 *b*]

459

Quādo il sole è occupato da nvgoli, le cose sono di poca evidētia [2]perchè è poco differentia infra i lumi e l'onbre delli alberi e delli edifiti, per [3]essere alluminati dalla chiarezza dell'aria che circūda ī modo le cose, [4]che poche sono l'onbre e quel[5]le poche si uanno perdēdo in modo che i loi termini se ne vanno ī fumo

When the sun is covered by clouds, objects are less conspicuous, because there is little difference between the light and shade of the trees and of the buildings being illuminated by the brightness of the atmosphere which surrounds the objects in such a way that the shadows are few, and these few fade away so that their outline is lost in haze

G 11 *b*]

460

De' alberi e loro lume

[2]Il uero modo da pratico nel figurare le [3]canpagnie o vo'dire paesi colle sua

Of trees and lights on them

The best method of practice in representing country scenes, or I should

14 coe insulli stremi lusstro [e nelle parte] vero e chellonbe osscure 15 ochupate 16 tutti . elloro mossterranno 17 loro "ciaro e naturale a di quessto 18 lusstri dalloro ciarezza" fieno di pocha 19 tia essesse mos strare parte 20 le quale il son novide cheffieno 21 Masseessarai ma 22 gore chiareza uedressti ecquesto achade vēto dis 23 li quali 24 biāchegiāti 25 essopra dacquella 26 alle lessciene

459 1 ochupato pocha 2 e po diferentia ellonbre 3 dalla grādeza dellaria che circhūda 4 [che pocha diferētia da loro lumi chen] che posono ecque 5 che lor ifumo

460 1—8 R 1 elloro 2 modi 5 ochupato accoche

[4]piante si è dello elegiere che al cielo [5]sia occupato il sole, acciochè esse can[6]pagnie ricevino lume vniversale e nō [7]il particulare del sole, il quale fa l'onbre [8]tagliate e assai differēti dalli lumi

say landscapes with their trees, is to choose them so that the sun is covered with clouds; so that the landscape receives an universal light and not the direct light of the sun, which makes the shadows sharp and too strongly different from the lights.

E 19a]

461.

PICTURA.

[1]Li paesi, fatti nella figuratione del uerno, [3]nō debbono dimostrare le sue mōtagnie azzur[4]re come far si uede alle mōtagnie dell'e[5]state, e questo si prova per la 4ª [6]di questo che dicie ¶Infra le montagnie, vedu[7]te inlūga distantia, Quella si dimostrerà [8]di colore più azzurro, la qual fia ī [9]se più oscura, adūque essendo le piāte [10]spogliate delle lor foglie si dimostrerā [11]di colore più azzurro, la qual fia ī [12]se più oscura, adūque, essendo le piāte [13]spogliate delle lor foglie, si dimostrerā di color [14]berrettino, essendo che le foglie son di color [15]verde, e tāto quāto il uerde è piv oscuro che [16]il berrettino, tanto si dimostrerā più azzur[17]ro il uerde che il berrettino; e per la 2ª di que[18]sto ¶l'onbre delle piāte, uestite di foglie, son [19]tanto più oscure che l'ōbre di quelle piante che [20]sono spogliate di foglie, quāto le piāte, [21]vestite di foglie, son mē rare che quelle che nō [22]ànno foglie, e così abbiā provato il nostro ītēto.

[23]La difinitione [24]del colore azzur[25]ro dell'aria dà [26]sentētia, perchè li [27]paesi sō più az[28]zurri di state che [29]di verno.

OF PAINTING.

In landscapes which represent [a scene in] winter The mountains should not be shown blue, as we see in the mountains in the summer. And this is proved [5] in the 4th of this which says: Among mountains seen from a great distance those will look of the bluest colour which are in themselves the darkest; hence, when the trees are stripped of their leaves, they will show a bluer tinge which will be in itself darker; therefore, when the trees have lost their leaves they will look of a gray colour, while, with their leaves, they are green, and in proportion as the green is darker than the grey hue the green will be of a bluer tinge than the gray. Also by the 2nd of this: The shadows of trees covered with leaves are darker than the shadows of those trees which have lost their leaves in proportion as the trees covered with leaves are denser than those without leaves—and thus my meaning is proved.

The definition of the blue colour of the atmosphere explains why the landscape is bluer in the summer than in the winter.

C A 181 b, 546 b]

462.

DE' PICTURA

[2]Se infra l'ochio e l'orizzonte s'in[3]terpone l'obliquità del colle decli[4]nante inuerso l'ochio, il quale ochio [5]si troui circa il mezzo della altezza d'essa declina[6]tione, al-

OF PAINTING IN A LANDSCAPE.

If the slope of a hill comes between the eye and the horizon, sloping towards the eye, while the eye is opposite the middle of the height of this slope, then that hill will

461 2 fighuratione. 3. dimosstrare 4 chome [le] far . . delles. 5. ecquesto si prova [perche lialberi] per 6. quessto cheddicie [Infralle 7 inllūgha disstantia dimossterra. 8 [piu] di cholore piu . . fia [piv] ī 9. osschura addūque 10. dimossterra. 11 [piu] di cholore . fia piv ī 12 osschura addūque 13 dimosterā di cholor 14 berrectino . . cholli . . color 15 ettāto . eppiu osscuro 16 berrectino . . dimossterra. 18 son [piu] 19. osscuro chellōbre 20. piāte [pri] 22 nano . . echosi 24 cholore 28 di sstāte.

462 2 elloriizonte 3 cholle. 5. cecea il mezo "della alteza" dessa 6. tale [paese] "collo" aquistera. 7 osscurita edequal.

461. 5 6. *Per la 4ª di questo* It is impossible to ascertain what this quotation refers to. *Questo* certainly does not mean the MS. in hand, nor any other now known to us. The same remark applies to the phrase in line 15: *per la 2ª di questo*

462 The quotation in this passage again cannot be verified.

lora tale colle acquisterà 7oscurità in ogni grado della sua longitu8dine, Provasi per la 7a di questo che di9cie quella pianta si dimostrerà più oscu10ra la quale fia veduta piv di sotto, 11la propositione 12è verificata perchè tal colle mostrerà dal mezzo 13in sù tutte le sue piãte nelle parti che sõ 14tanto alluminate dalla chiarezza del cielo quanto la parte che è 15aõbrata dalle oscurità della terra, per la qual co16sa è neciessario che tali piante sieno di medi17ocie oscurità, e da quel sito inverso le radi18ci del colle senpre tali piante vãno rischiarãdo 19per la cõversa della 7a e per essa 7a, e quando tali 20piãte più s'avicinano alla sõmità di 21tal colle, è neciessario a quelle farsi più os22cure, Ma tale oscurità non è proportionata 23alla distantia per la 8a di questo che dicie · 24quella cosa si dimostrerà più oscura che si tro25va in più sottile aria, e per la 10a · quella si dimostre26rà più oscura che confina in cãpo più chiaro

increase in darkness throughout its length. This is proved by the 7th of this which says that a tree looks darkest when it is seen from below, the proposition is verified, since this hill will, on its upper half show all its trees as much from the side which is lighted by the light of the sky, as from that which is in shade from the darkness of the earth, whence it must result that these trees are of a medium darkness And from this [middle] spot towards the base of the hill, these trees will be lighter by degrees by the converse of the 7th and by the said 7th For trees so placed, the nearer they are to the summit of the hill the darker they necessarily become But this darkness is not in proportion to the distance, by the 8th of this which says That object shows darkest which is [seen] in the clearest atmosphere, and by the 10th That shows darkest which stands out against a lighter background

463.

I2 48b]

De' paesi

2I colori oscuri dell'onbre delle mõtagne · 3nelle lunghe distantie pigliano piv bello 4azzurro e più senplice, che nõ fanno le 5loro parti luminose, e di qui nasce quã6do il sasso della mõtagnia rosseggia che le sue 7parti luminose son di bissa, e quãt è piv 8alluminata piv si farà del suo propio co9lore

Of landscapes

The colours of the shadows in mountains at a great distance take a most lovely blue, much purer than their illuminated portions And from this it follows that when the rock of a mountain is reddish the illuminated portions are violet (?) and the more they are lighted the more they display their proper colour

464.

H 2 20a]

Quel loco sarà piv 2luminoso che dalle mõ3tagnie fia più remoto.

A place is most luminous when it is most remote from mountains

465

G 19b]

Õbre e lume delle città

2Quãdo il sole è all'oriéte e l'ochio 3stia sopra il mezzo di una città esso o4chio

Of light and shadow in a town

When the sun is in the East and the eye is above the centre of a town, the eye will

On the treatment of light for views of towns (465—469)

9 dimosstera piu ossci 10 disocto ad 11 dunque |||||||||||||| la proposstione *The word here scratched through and illegible seems to have been* diremo 12 mossteral mezzo 13 in giututte nelle puedi chesso 14 alluminate | "dalla ciarezza" del che 15 osscurita 16 chettali 17 osscurita 18 cholle vano rissiarãdo 19 coversa 7a quando 20 piãte quãto piu somita 21 cholo enneciessario acquelle 22 scure Mattale osscurita 24 dimosstera piu osscura 25 dimosste 26 osscura chãpo

463 2 oscure 3 lunge 4 azurro fanno lele 5 parte 6 chelle 7 parte 8 propie

464 1—3 R

465 1—8 R 1 ellume 2 ellochio 3 mezo 4 vedera 5 mezi 6 mezo 7 onale nella 8 ella

vedrà la parte meridionale d'es[5]sa città aver li tetti mezzo obrosi e [6]mezzo luminosi e così la settetri[7]onale, e la orietale fia tutta obrosa [8]e la occidetale fia tutta luminosa.

see the Southern part of the town with its roofs half in shade and half in light, and the same towards the North; the Eastern side will be all in shadow and the Western will be all in light.

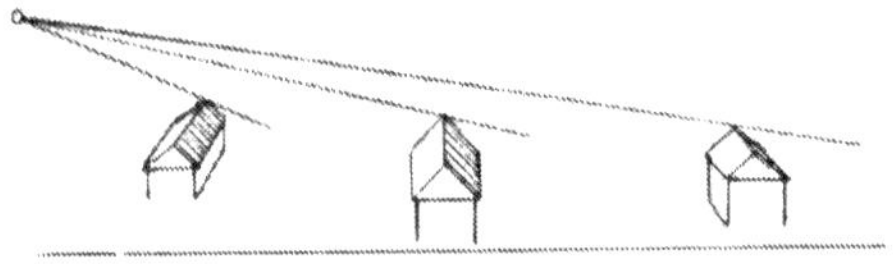

C. A. 157 a; 463 a]

466.

Delle case d'una città, di che si conoscono le diuisioni delle case per il rischiarare che fa i basso la [2]nebbia; se l'ochio e piv alto che le case, li lumi visuali in nello iteruallo ch'è tra [3]casa e casa si uano profondado in nebbia piv grossa, e pero sendo mē trasparēte pare [4]piv biāca, e se le case sono piv alte l'una che l'altra, sēpre si discierne piv il ue[5]ro nell'aria piv sottile, onde le case paiono piv scure quāto piv s'alzano; [6]*n · o · p · q* sieno le qualità dell'aria grossa di umori, *a* sia l'ochio, la casa *b · c* parà piv chiara [7]in fondo e perchè è in aria piv grossa, le linie *c · d · f* parano chiare a uno modo, e bēchè *f* [8]sia piv distāte che *c*, egli è eleuato in aria piv sottile, se le case *b · e* sono d'una me[9]desima altezza, perchè ànno a diuidere per chiarore, variato di nebbia; questo è solo perchè la linia [10]del ochio, che nascie alta, si ua col suo fine profondādo in aria piv bassa e grossa in *d* · [11]che ī · *b*: · e così la linia · *a · f* · si truova piv bassa · ī · *f* · che in · *c*, e la casa *f* · in *e* si truo[12]va dalla linia · *e · k* insino a · *m* · andare piv scura che la sōmità degli ātiposti edifiti.

Of the houses of a town, in which the divisions between the houses may be distinguished by the light which fall on the mist at the bottom. If the eye is above the houses the light seen in the space that is between one house and the next sinks by degrees into thicker mist; and yet, being less transparent, it appears whiter; and if the houses are some higher than the others, since the true [colour] is always more discernible through the thinner atmosphere, the houses will look darker in proportion as they are higher up. Let *n o p q* represent the various density of the atmosphere thick with moisture, *a* being the eye, the house *b c* will look lightest at the bottom, because it is in a thicker atmosphere; the lines *c d f* will appear equally light, for although *f* is more distant than *c*, it is raised into a thinner atmosphere, if the houses *b e* are of the same height, because they cross a brightness which is varied by mist, but this is only because the line of the eye which starts from above ends by piercing a lower and denser atmosphere at *d* than at *b*. Thus the line *a f* is lower at *f* than at *c*; and the house *f* will be seen darker at *e* from the line *e k* as far as *m*, than the tops of the houses standing in front of it.

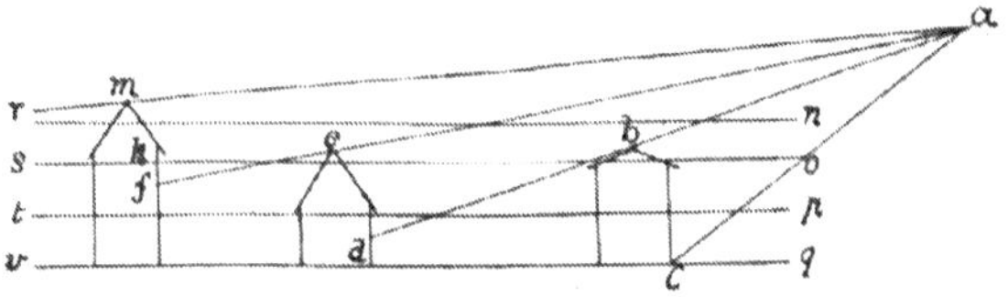

466. 1. dele chessi conocie le diuisioni delle case per risciarare cheffa. 2. chelle . . le lume visuale melo. 3. inebbia. 4. biācha esse. 5. paiono . . nelaria. 6. omori . . ciara. 7. perche en aria . . la linia . . a ī modo. 9. uno altezza . . ciarore nebia . . bui. 10. chol. 11. chosi. 12. ha *m* . . somita.

E 3*b*]

467

DELLE CITTÀ O ALTRI EDIFITII [2] VEDUTI DA SERA O MATTINA NELLA [3] NEBBIA

[4] Delli edifizi veduti in lunga distātia [5] da sera o mattina ī nebbia o aria grossa solo si dimo[6]stra la chiarezza delle lor parti alluminate dal sole [7] che si trova inverso l'orizzonte, e le parti delli [8] detti edifizi, che nō son vedute dal sole, restano quasi del [9] colore di mediocre oscurità di nebbia

OF TOWNS OR OTHER BUILDINGS SEEN IN THE EVENING OR THE MORNING THROUGH THE MIST

Of buildings seen at a great distance in the evening or the morning, as in mist or dense atmosphere, only those portions are seen in brightness which are lighted up by the sun which is near the horizon, and those portions which are not lighted up by the sun remain almost of the same colour and medium tone as the mist

PERCHÈ LE COSE PIÙ ALTE [11] POSTE NELLE DISTĀTIE SON PIÙ OSCU[12]RE CHE LE BASSE ANCORA [13] CHÈ LA NEBBIA SIA VNIFORME Ī GROSSEZZA

[14] Delle cose, poste nella nebbia o altra aria grossa o per [15] vapore o fumo o distantia, quella fia tanto più nota quā[16]to ella sarà più alta, E delle cose d'equale al[17]tezza quella parrà più oscura che campeggia in [18] più profonda nebbia, come accade all'ochio *h* [19] che vedēdo *a b c*, torri d'eguale altezza infra loro, che vede [20] *c* somità della prima torre in *r*, bassezza di due gradi [21] di profondità nella nebbia, e vede la somità della torre [22] di mezzo *b* in vn sol grado di nebbia, adūque *c* somità si [23] dimostra più oscura che la sōmità della torre · *b* ecc

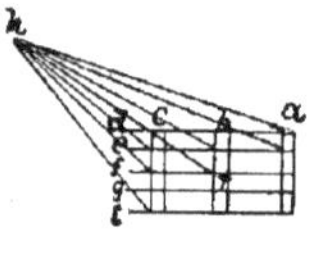

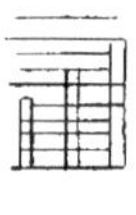

WHY OBJECTS WHICH ARE HIGH UP AND AT A DISTANCE ARE DARKER THAN THE LOWER ONES, EVEN IF THE MIST IS UNIFORMLY DENSE

Of objects standing in a mist or other dense atmosphere, whether from vapour or smoke or distance, those will be most visible which are the highest And among objects of equal height that will be the darkest [strongest] which has for background the deepest mist. Thus the eye *h* looking at *a b c*, towers of equal height, one with another, sees *c* the top of the first tower at *r*, at two degrees of depth in the mist, and sees the height of the middle tower *b* through one single degree of mist Therefore the top of the tower *c* appears stronger than the top of the tower *b*, &c

G 22*b*]

468

DELLI FUMI DELLE CITTÀ

[2] Li fumi sō ueduti melio e più [3] espediti nelle parti oriēta[4]li che nelle occidētali, stādo [5] il sole all'oriēte, e questo [6] nascie per due cavse, e la prima [7] è che il sole traspare colli su[8]a razzi nelle particule di tal [9] fumo e le rischiara e falle [10] evidenti, la secōda è che li [11] tetti delle case, veduti all'o[12]riēte in tal tenpo, sono ōbro[13]si perchè la loro obliquità nō [14] può essere allu-

OF THE SMOKE OF A TOWN

Smoke is seen better and more distinctly on the Eastern side than on the Western when the sun is in the East, and this arises from two causes, the first is that the sun, with its rays, shines through the particles of the smoke and lights them up and makes them visible The second is that the roofs of the houses seen in the East at this time are in shadow, because their obliquity does not allow of their

467 2 dassera ōmattina 3 nebbia [in lungha disstantia] 4 [Le chose che] li veduti lungha disstāua 5 dassera dimos 6 parte 7 chessi elle parte 9 cholore osscurita 11 disstantie osschu 12 chelle ancho 13 chella grosseza 14 chose nebia 15 offumo o disstantia 16 ta ella Eddelle chose 17 osschura e chanpeggia 18 chome achade hallochio e h 19 torre infralloro che ve 23 dimosstra o schura chella

468 1—18 R 3 esspediti parte 5 ecquesto 6 ella p^a 8 rizi partichule 9 elle risciara effalle 14 po 15 achade

minata dal [15]sole, e il simile accade nella [16]poluere e l'una e l'altra è tā[17]to più luminosa quanto ella è più [18]dēsa, ed è più densa inverso il mezzo.

being illuminated by the sun. And the same thing occurs with dust; and both one and the other look the lighter in proportion as they are denser, and they are densest towards the middle.

G. 23a]

469.

Del fumo e polvere.

[2]Stādo il sole all'oriēte, il fumo [3]delle città nō sarà veduto allo [4]occidente, perchè esso no[5]n è veduto penetrato dalli [6]razzi solari, nè veduto ī cāpo [7]scuro, perchè li tetti del[8]le case mostrano all'occhio [9]quella medesima parte che [10]si mostra al sole, e per que[11]sto cāpo chiaro tal fumo po[12]co si uede.

[13]Ma la poluere in simile [14]aspetto si dimostra oscu[15]ra più che 'l fumo per esser lei [16]di materia più densa [17]ch'è 'l fumo, ch'è materia vmida.

Of smoke and dust.

If the sun is in the East the smoke of cities will not be visible in the West, because on that side it is not seen penetrated by the solar rays, nor on a dark background; since the roofs of the houses turn the same side to the eye as they turn towards the sun, and on this light background the smoke is not very visible.

But dust, under the same aspect, will look darker than smoke being of denser material than smoke which is moist.

E. 6b]

470.

The effect of wind on trees (470—473).

Del uēto dipīto.

[2]Nella figuratione del uēto, oltre al pie[3]gare de' rami e il rouersciare le sue [4]foglie inverso lo auenimēto [5]del uēto, si debbe figurare li ra[6]nugolamēti della sottil poluere mista chol[7]la intorbidata aria.

Of representing wind.

In representing wind, besides the bending of the boughs and the reversing of their leaves towards the quarter whence the wind comes, you should also represent them amid clouds of fine dust mingled with the troubled air.

Br. M. 172b]

471.

Descriui i paesi con vēto e con acqua e cō tramōtare e leuare del sole.

VĒTO.

[2]Tutte le foglie che pendevano a terra, nel piegare de' lor ramiculi, insieme con esso [3]ramo a rovesciate si dirizzano col corso de' vēti, e qui la prospettiua loro fa contrario offitio, [4]inperochè, se l'albero è tra te e 'l nascimēto del uēto, le parti delle foglie che son diuerso te [5]danno la lor naturale dimostratione e le opposite, che avevano a volgere le punte in [6]contraria parte, son per lo loro arrovesciamēto volte colle pūte inverso te.

Describe landscapes with the wind, and the water, and the setting and rising of the sun.

THE WIND.

All the leaves which hung towards the earth by the bending of the shoots with their branches, are turned up side down by the gusts of wind, and here their perspective is reversed; for, if the tree is between you and the quarter of the wind, the leaves which are towards you remain in their natural aspect, while those on the opposite side which ought to have their points in a contrary direction have, by being turned over, their points turned towards you.

16. eleuana ele altro ettā. 17. ni piu . . elle piu. 18. mezo.

469. 1—17 R. 6. razi. 7. schuro . . de. 10. mostra. 12. cho. 13. Malla. 14. aspetto si dimostra oscu.

470. 2. figuratione. 3. ghare. 4. auenimēto [delle sue]. 5. foglie] del . . figurare. 6. nughulamēti . . sottil . . ch [illegible]

471. 1. a cq "A" . . elleuare. 2. aterra. 3. dirizano . . equi la prospettiua. 4. [illegible] . . parte . . [illegible] 5. dimostratione elle oposite. 6. arovesclamēto.

C. A. 78a, 228a]

472

L'alberi percossi dal corso de' vẽti si piegano inverso [2]il loco dove tal uẽto si move, e passato che è il uẽto [3]si piegano in contrario moto, cioè nel moto reflesso

Trees struck by the force of the wind bend to the side towards which the wind is blowing, and the wind being past they bend in the contrary direction, that is in reverse motion.

B. M. 277b]

473

¶ Quella parte dell'albero, ch'è piv [2]remota dalla potentia che lo percuote, piv è offesa da essa [3]percussione, perchè è maggiore lieua, onde la natura in questo [4]caso a proveduto collo ingrossarli in quella parte oue [5]piv possono esser offesi, e massime nelli alberi che cresco[6]no in grãde altezza, come abeti e simili

That portion of a tree which is farthest from the force which strikes it is the most injured by the blow because it bears most strain; thus nature has foreseen this case by thickening them in that part where they can be most hurt; and most in such trees as grow to great heights, as pines and the like.

F. 35a]

474

Light and shade on clouds (474—477)

Scriui come li nugoli si cõpongono e come si risol[2]uono, e che causa leua li uapori

Describe how the clouds are formed and how they dissolve, and what cause raises vapour.

W. VI.]

475

Tanto sono le õbre de' nuvoli più chiare [2]quanto essi son piv vicini all'orizzõte

The shadows in clouds are lighter in proportion as they are nearer to the horizon.

B. M. 172b]

476

Quando i nvuoli s'interpongono infra 'l sole e l'ochio tutti li stremi delli [2]loro globi sono chiari e inverso il mezzo sono oscuri,

When clouds come between the sun and the eye all the upper edges of their round forms are light, and towards the middle they

472. 1 perchossi dal chorso pieghino 2 locho eppassato 3 pieghino refresso
473. 2 della chello perchote 3 perchussione magiore 4 chaso chollo 5 possano cressca 6 alteza essimili
474. 1 cõpongano 2 uano
475. 1 chiare 2 vicine orizonte
476. 1 sinterpongano solle ellochio lisstremi 2 globbi mezo osscuri 3 chade 4 datte ecquesto acchade

473. Compare the sketch drawn with a pen and washed with Indian ink on Pl. XL, No. 2. In the Vatican copy we find, under a section entitled *'del fumo'*, the following remark: *Era sotto di questo capitulo un rompimento di montagna, per dentro delle quali roture scherzaua fiame di fuoco, disegnate di penna et ombrate d'acquarella, da uedere cosa mirabile et uiua* (Ed. MANZI, p. 235. Ed. LUDWIG, Vol. I, 460). This appears to refer to the left hand portion of the drawing here given from the Windsor collection, and from this it must be inferred, that the leaf as it now exists in the library of the Queen of England, was already separated from the original MS. at the time when the Vatican copy was made.

475. The drawing belonging to this was in black chalk and is totally effaced.

476. A drawing in red chalk from the Windsor collection (see Pl. XXIX), representing a landscape with storm-clouds, may serve to illustrate this section as well as the following one.

e questo ac[3]cade perchè inverso i superiori detti stremi sono veduti dal sole piv alto [4]di loro e da te piv basso, e questo medesimo accade nelle poste de' rami [5]delle piãte: e ancora si fanno in parte chiari così i nvvoli come li alberi per es[6]sere alquãto transparenti e nelli stremi si mostra piv sottigliezza.

[7]Ma quando l'ochio si trova infra 'l nuvolo e 'l sole, el nugolo fa l'opposito [8]che prima facea, perchè li stremi delle sua globulenze sono oscuri [9]e inverso il mezzo son chiari, e questo accade perchè tu vedi quella par[10]te che ancora il sole vede in faccia e perchè essi stremi ànno del transparẽ[11]te e rendono all'ochio quelle parti che dopo lor s'ascõdono che nõ sendo ve-[12]dute dal sole come le parti che li son volte, è neciessario che sieno al[13]quãto piv oscure; ancora può essere che tu uedi le minvtie d'esse glo[14]bulentie dal lato di sotto, e 'l sole le uede di sopra, e perchè esse nõ sono situate [15]in modo che abbino a rendere chiarezza del sole come prima facea, [16]però sono oscure.

[17]I nuvoli neri, che spesse volte si uegono sopra i chiari e allumina[18]ti dal sole, sono õbrati dalli altri nuvoli che infra loro e 'l sole s'inter[19]pongono.

[20]Ancora le globbosità de' nvuoli, che ãño il sole in faccia, [21]mostrano i sua termini oscuri, perchè campeggiano [22]col canpo chiaro; e che questo sia vero guarderai la sõ[23]mità di tutto il nuvolo ch'è chiara perchè cãpeggia nell'az[24]zurro dell'aria, ch'è piv scura che 'l nuvolo.

are dark, and this happens because towards the top these edges have the sun above them while you are below them; and the same thing happens with the position of the branches of trees, and again the clouds, like the trees, being somewhat transparent, are lighted up in part, and at the edges they show thinner.

But, when the eye is between the cloud and the sun, the cloud has the contrary effect to the former, for the edges of its mass are dark and it is light towards the middle, and this happens because you see the same side as faces the sun, and because the edges have some transparency and reveal to the eye that portion which is hidden beyond them, and which, as it does not catch the sunlight like that portion turned towards it, is necessarily somewhat darker. Again, it may be that you see the details of these rounded masses from the lower side, while the sun shines on the upper side and as they are not so situated as reflect the light of the sun, as in the first instance they remain dark.

The black clouds which are often seen higher up than those which are illuminated by the sun are shaded by other clouds, lying between them and the sun.

Again, the rounded forms of the clouds that face the sun, show their edges dark because they lie against the light background, and to see that this is true, you may look at the top of any cloud that is wholly light because it lies against the blue of the atmosphere, which is darker than the cloud.

W 231a]

477.

De' nuvolo fumo e polvere e fiãme di forno o fornacie ĩfocata.

[2]Il nuvolo nõ mostra le sue globulentie se nõ in quelle parti che son vedute dal sole, e l'altre globosità [3]sono insensibili pel essere lor nelle õbre.

Of clouds, smoke and dust and the flames of a furnace or of a burning kiln.

The clouds do not show their rounded forms excepting on the sides which face the sun, on the others the roundness is imperceptible because they are in the shade.

. posste 5 eanchora . . pere. 6 transsparente . mosstra 7 Ma cquando 8 lisstremi . . globbulenze . osscure 9. mezo chiare ecquesto achade 11 rendano . parte . sasscõde 12 la parte chelli chessieno 13 po . . chettu 15 chellabbino arrendere chiareza 16. osscure 17 enuvoli chesspresse . uegano 18 nvoli infralloro 19 pongano 20. globbosita 21 mosstrano e sua . . osscuri canpegiano 23 cãpegia nella 24 nuvollo

477 1. eppoluere effiãme . . ifochata 2. mosstra . . parte . . ellaltre. 3 per essere. 4. sole he all . elle . . interposto infra-

477. The text of this chapter is given in facsimile on Pls. XXXVI and XXXVII. The two halves of the leaf form but one in the original. On the margin close to lines 4 and 5 is the note *rossore d'aria inverso l'orizonte*—(of the redness of the atmosphere near the horizon). The sketches on the lower portion of the page will be spoken of in No. 668.

137

[4]Se 'l sole è all'oriĉte e le nuvole all'occidente, allora l'ochio, interposto infra 'l sole [5]e 'l nuvolo, vede li termini delle globosità cōponitrici d'esso nuvolo essere scuri [6]e le parti che son circūdate da esse oscurità fieno chiare, E questo nascie [7]perchè li termini delle globosità di tali nuvoli [8]vedono il cielo superiore e laterale, il quale in quel si spechia

[9]E 'l nuvolo e la piāta [10]à le sue parti onbrose [11]sanza dimostrazione [12]d'alcuna globulētia

If the sun is in the East and the clouds in the West, the eye placed between the sun and the clouds sees the edges of the rounded forms composing these clouds as dark, and the portions which are surrounded by this dark [edge] are light And this occurs because the edges of the rounded forms of these clouds are turned towards the upper or lateral sky, which is reflected in them.

Both the cloud and the tree display no roundness at all on their shaded side

C A 346a, 1072a]

478

On images reflected in water

I pittori s'ingānano molte volte [2]faciēdo le acque nelle qua[3]li fanno vedere a loro quel [4]che vede l'omo, Ma l'acqua [5]vede l'obietto per uno lato [6]e l'omo lo uede per l'altro, e [7]spesse volte accade [8]che 'l pittore vedrà [9]vna cosa di sotto e così vn me[10]desimo corpo veduto dināzi [11]e dirieto, di sopra e di sotto, [12]perchè l'acqua gli mostra il simv[13]lacro dell'obietto in un mo[14]do, e l'ochio lo uede in vn altro

Painters often deceive themselves, by representing water in which they make the water reflect the objects seen by the man But the water reflects the object from one side and the man sees it from the other, and it often happens that the painter sees an object from below, and thus one and the same object is seen from hind part before and upside down, because the water shows the image of the object in one way, and the eye sees it in another

E c"]

479

Of rainbows and rain (479 480)

Li colori di mezzo all'arco si mischiano infra loro

[2]L'arco in se nō è nella pioggia, nè etiā nell'ochio che [3]lo vede, benchè si gieneri dalla pioggia, dal sole e dall'ochio [4]L'arco cieleste è senpre veduto da quelli ochi, [5]li quali s'interpōgono infra la pioggia e 'l cor[6]po del sole, adunque stando il sole all'oriente e [7]la pioggia all'occidēte, esso arco si gienera nella piog[8]gia occidētale

The colours in the middle of the rainbow mingle together

The bow in itself is not in the rain nor in the eye that sees it, though it is generated by the rain, the sun, and the eye The rainbow is always seen by the eye that is between the rain and the body of the sun, hence if the sun is in the East and the rain is in the West it will appear on the rain in the West

E o"]

480.

Quando l'aria si converte in pioggia, [2]essa farebbe vacuo, se l'altra aria [3]nō lo proibisce col suo socorso, la [4]quale fa con

When the air is condensed into rain it would produce a vacuum if the rest of the air did not prevent this by filling its place, as

sole 5 vedede deso 6 ella parte chesson circhūdata osschurita Ecquessto 7 tal 8 vedano ellaterale [cir] il śisspcchia 9 ella 10 alle parte 11 dimosstracione 12 dalchuna globbulētia

478 1 singannammolte 2 nelle q 'a 3 allei 4 M"i" laqua 6 ellomo perllaltro es 7 spesse ichade chella 8 [equa ue] chel pitore vedera 9 chosa 10 veduto 13 lacro[nu] dell obietto numo 14 ellochio vede nvn

479 1 cholori di mezo allarcho simistano infrallori 2 Larcho in se nō nella 3 llo 4 Larcho cielesste essenpre dacquelli 5 sinterpōghano infralla 6 alloriente el 7 allocidēte esso archo

480 1 chonverte 2 vachuo sellaltra 3 nollo broibisse chol suo sochorso 4 chon ecque 5 sto he quel nasscie dissta

ipetuoso moto, e que'sto è quel vēto che nascie d'esta[6]te insieme colle furiose pioggie.

it does with a violent rush; and this is the wind which rises in the summer time, accompanied by heavy rain.

G. 37 b]

481.

Of flower seeds.

Tutti li fiori che ueggono il sole, [2]conducono il lor seme, li altri [3]no, cioè quelli che sol uedono la [4]reflessione del sole.

All the flowers which turn towards the sun perfect their seeds; but not the others, that is to say those which get only the reflection of the sun.

6. cholle.

481. 1. ueghano. 2. conducano . . elin. 3. cosequelli . . uedano. 4. refressione.

IX.

The Practice of Painting.

It is hardly necessary to offer any excuses for the division carried out in the arrangement of the text into practical suggestions and theoretical enquiries. It was evidently intended by Leonardo himself as we conclude from incidental remarks in the MSS. (for instance No 110*). The fact that this arrangement was never carried out either in the old MS. copies or in any edition since, is easily accounted for by the general disorder which results from the provisional distribution of the various chapters in the old copies. We have every reason to believe that the earliest copyists, in distributing the materials collected by them, did not in the least consider the order in which the original MS. lay before them.*

It is evident that almost all the chapters which refer to the calling and life of the painter—and which are here brought together in the first section (Nos. 482—508*)—may be referred to two distinct periods in Leonardo's life; most of them can be dated as belonging to the year* 1492 *or to* 1515. *At about this later time Leonardo may have formed the project of completing his* Libro della Pittura, *after an interval of some years, as it would seem, during which his interest in the subject had fallen somewhat into the background.*

In the second section, which treats first of the artist's studio, the construction of a suitable window forms the object of careful investigations; the special importance attached to this by Leonardo is sufficiently obvious. His theory of the incidence of light which was fully discussed in a former part of this work, was to him by no means of mere abstract value, but, being deduced, as he says, from experience (or experiment) was required to prove its utility in practice. Connected with this we find suggestions for the choice of a light with practical hints as to sketching a picture and some other precepts of a practical character which must come under consideration in the course of completing the painting. In all this I have followed the same principle of arrangement in the text as was carried out in the Theory of Painting, thus the suggestions for the Perspective of a picture, (Nos. 536—569*), are followed by the theory of light and shade for the practical method of optics (Nos.* 548—566*) and this by the practical precepts or the treatment of aerial perspective (*567—570*).*

In the passage on Portrait and Figure Painting the principles of painting as applied to a bust and head are separated and placed first, since the advice to figure painters must have some connection with the principles of the treatment of composition by which they are followed.

But this arrangement of the text made it seem advisable not to pick out the practical precepts as to the representation of trees and landscape from the close connection in which they were originally placed—unlike the rest of the practical precepts—with the theory of this branch of the subject They must therefore be sought under the section entitled Botany for Painters.

As a supplement to the Libro di Pittura *I have here added those texts which treat of the Painter's materials,—as chalk, drawing paper, colours and their preparation, of the management of oils and varnishes; in the appendix are some notes on chemical substances. Possibly some of these, if not all, may have stood in connection with the preparation of colours. It is in the very nature of things that Leonardo's incidental indications as to colours and the like should be now-a-days extremely obscure and could only be explained by professional experts—by them even in but few instances It might therefore have seemed advisable to reproduce exactly the original text without offering any translation. The rendering here given is merely an attempt to suggest what Leonardo's meaning may have been.*

LOMAZZO tells us in his Trattato dell'arte della Pittura, Scultura ed Architettura (Milano 1584, libro II, Cap XIV): "Va discorrendo ed argomentando Leonardo Vinci in un suo libro letto da me (?) questi anni passati, ch'egli scrisse di mano stanca ai prieghi di LUDOVICO SFORZA duca di Milano, in determinazione di questa questione, se è più nobile la pittura o la scultura; dicendo che quanto più un'arte porta seco fatica di corpo, e sudore, tanto più è vile, e men pregiata". *But the existence of any book specially written for Lodovico il Moro on the superiority of Painting over sculpture is perhaps mythical. The various passages in praise of Painting as compared not merely with Sculpture but with Poetry, are scattered among MSS. of very different dates.*

Besides, the way, in which the subject is discussed appears not to support the supposition, that these texts were prepared at a special request of the Duke.

I.

MORAL PRECEPTS FOR THE STUDENT OF PAINTING.

G. 25*a*]

482.

NOTITIA DEL GIOVANE DI[2]SPOSTO ALLA PICTURA.

[3]Molti sono li omini che àn desiderio ed amo[4]re al disegnio, ma no dispositione, e questo [5]fia conosciuto nelli putti, li quali sono sē[6]za diligētia e mai finiscono con ōbre le lor co[7]se.

A WARNING CONCERNING YOUTHS WISHING TO BE PAINTERS.

Many are they who have a taste and love for drawing, but no talent; and this will be discernible in boys who are not diligent and never finish their drawings with shading.

How to ascertain the dispositions for an artistic career.

Ash. I. 18*a*]

483.

Il giovane debe · prima · iparare prospettiua, [2]poi le misure d'ogni cosa, [3]poi [disegni?] di mano di bō maestro · per suefarsi a bone mēbra, [4]poi di natura per cōfermarsi le ragioni delle cose ïparate, [5]poi vedere uno tēpo l'opere di mano di diversi maestri, [6]poi · fare · abito · al mettere ï pratica e operare l'arte.

The youth should first learn perspective, then the proportions of objects. Then he may copy from some gōod master, to accustom himself to fine forms. Then from nature, to confirm by practice the rules he has learnt. Then see for a time the works of various masters. Then get the habit of putting his art into practice and work.

The course of instruction for an artist (483—485).

482. 1—7 R. 1. del [pi] govane. 4. ecquesto. 6. ma finiscano.
483. 2. pole . . deni. 3. poi di. 4. chōfermarsi . . dele. 5. tēpo di mano. 6. all . . praticha.

483. The Vatican copy and numerous abridgements all place this chapter at the beginning of the *Trattato*, and in consequence DUFRESNE and all subsequent editors have done the same. In the Vatican copy however all the general considerations on the relation of painting to the other arts are placed first, as introductory.

Ash. I. 28]

484.

ORDO DEL RITRARE.

[2]Ritrai pri[3]ma · disegni · di buono maestro fatto sul' [4]arte e sul naturale · e nõ di pratica, poi [5]di rilievo in cõpagnia del disegnio [6]tratto da esso rilievo ·, poi di buono [7]naturale, il quale debbi mettere i uso.

OF THE ORDER OF LEARNING TO DRAW.

First draw from drawings by good masters done from works of art and from nature, and not from memory; then from plastic work, with the guidance of the drawing done from it; and then from good natural models and this you must put into practice.

Ash. I. 25*b*]

485.

PRECETTI DI PICTURA.

[2]Il pictore debbe prima · suefare · la mano col ritrarre · disegni · di mano di bo maestro [3]e fatta detta · suefationi ·, col givditio del suo precettore ·, debbe di poi suefarsi · col ritrarre [4]cose di rilievo bone · cõ quelle regole che di sotto · si dirà.

PRECEPTS FOR DRAWING.

The artist ought first to exercise his hand by copying drawings from the hand of a good master. And having acquired that practice, under the criticism of his master, he should next practise drawing objects in relief of a good style, following the rules which will presently be given.

Ash. I. 16*a*]

486.

DEL RITRARE.

The study of the antique (486. 487).

[2]Qual è meglio o ritrare di naturale o [3]d'atico, o qual è piv fatica o i proffili [4]o l'onbra · e' lumi?

OF DRAWING.

Which is best, to draw from nature or from the antique? and which is more difficult to do outlines or light and shade?

C. A. 145*b*; 432*a*]

487.

L'imitatione · delle cose antiche · è piv laudabile · che quella delle · moderne.

It is better to imitate [copy] the antique than modern work.

484. 2. del ritrare "di naturale" ritrai. 3. arte sul . . praticha. 5. chõpagnia.
485. 2. chol . . maesstro. 3. e atta . . chol . . chol. 4. chose. 5. chõ.
486. 3. daticho . . faticha.
487. 1. chose . . laldabile chelle.

486. 487. These are the only two passages in which Leonardo alludes to the importance of antique art in the training of an artist. The question asked in No. 486 remains unanswered by him and it seems to me very doubtful whether the opinion stated in No. 487 is to be regarded as a reply to it. This opinion stands in the MS. in a connection—as will be explained later on—which seems to require us to limit its application to a single special case. At any rate we may suspect that when Leonardo put the question, he felt some hesitation as to the answer. Among his very numerous drawings I have not been able to find a single study from the antique, though a drawing in black chalk, at Windsor, of a man on horseback (Pl. LXXIII) may perhaps be a reminiscence of the statue of Marcus Aurelius at Rome. It seems to me that the drapery in a pen and ink drawing of a bust, also at Windsor, has been borrowed from an antique model (Pl. XXX). G. G. ROSSI has, I believe, correctly interpreted Leonardo's feeling towards the antique in the following note on this passage in MANZI's edition, p. 501: "*Sappiamo dalla storia, che i valorosi artisti Toscani dell'età dell'oro dell'arte studiarono sugli antichi marmi raccolti dal Magnifico LORENZO DE' MEDICI. Pare che il Vinci a tali monumenti non si accostasse. Quest' uomo sempre riconobbe per maestra la natura, e questo principio lo stringeva alla sola imitazione di essa.*"—Compare No. 10, 26—28 footnote.

I 79 a]

488

De pittura

[2]Necessaria cosa è al pittore, [3]per essere bon membrificato[4]re nell'attitudine e gesti [5]che far si possono per li nudi, [6]di sapere la notomia de' ner[7]ui, ossi, mvscoli e lacerti, [8]per sapere nelli diuersi moui[9]menti e forze qual neruo [10]o muscolo è di tal mouimēto [11]causa, e solo quelli fare [12]euidenti e ingrossati, e nō [13]li altri per tutto, come mol[14]ti fanno, che per parere giā [15]disegniatore fanno i loro [16]ignvdi legnosi e sanza gra[17]tia che pare a vederli v̄ [18]sacco di noci piv presto che [19]superficie vmana o vero [20]vn fascio di rauanelli più [21]presto che muscolosi nvdi

Of painting

The necessity of anatomical knowledge (488 489)

It is indispensable to a Painter who would be thoroughly familiar with the limbs in all the positions and actions of which they are capable, in the nude, to know the anatomy of the sinews, bones, muscles and tendons so that, in their various movements and exertions, he may know which nerve or muscle is the cause of each movement and show those only as prominent and thickened, and not the others all over [the limb], as many do who, to seem great draughtsmen, draw their nude figures looking like wood, devoid of grace, so that you would think you were looking at a sack of walnuts rather than the human form, or a bundle of radishes rather than the muscles of figures

Ash I 8 b]

489

Come al dipintore è necessario sapere l'a intrī[2]sica forma dell'omo

[3]Quello dipītore, che avrà cognitione della natura de' nervi, mvscoli e lacierti, [4]saprà bene nel movere uno mēbro quāti e quali nerui ne son cagio[5]ne, e quale mvscolo gōfiādo è cagione di raccortare esso nervo e quale corde [6]convertite ī sotilissime cartilagini circondano e raccogliono detto mvscolo e così [7]sarà diuerso e vniversale dimostratore di uari muscoli mediāte i vari effetti delle [8]figure e nō farà come molti che ī diuersi atti sempre fāno quelle medesime [9]cose dimostrare in braccia, schiene, petto, gābe le quali cose nō si debbono mettere īfra i piccioli errori

How it is necessary to a painter that he should know the intrinsic forms [structure] of man

The painter who is familiar with the nature of the sinews, muscles, and tendons, will know very well, in giving movement to a limb, how many and which sinews cause it, and which muscle, by swelling, causes the contraction of that sinew, and which sinews, expanded into the thinnest cartilage, surround and support the said muscle Thus he will variously and constantly demonstrate the different muscles by means of the various attitudes of his figures, and will not do, as many who, in a variety of movements, still display the very same things [modelling] in the arms, back, breast and legs And these things are not to be regarded as minor faults

C A 196 b, 586 b]

490

Dello studio e suo ordine

[1]Dico che prima si debbe imparare le mēbra e sua travagliamēti, e finita [2]tal no-

Of study and the order of study

How to acquire practice

I say that first you ought to learn the limbs and their mechanism, and having this

488 4 giessti 6 di ner 7 mvsscoli ella certi 9 efforze 10 omusscolo he di 11 essolo quelgli 16 inudi essanza 17 vuederi 18 sacho 20 fasscio 21 musscolosi

489 2 sicha 3 ara ellacierti 4 movere ī mēbro ecquali 5 ecqualle sgōfiādo e chagione racortare ecquale 6 sotilissime cartilagine e racholano chosi 8 chome 9 sciene

490 dello studio essuo ordine *is written on the margin* 1 essua 2 seguitale 3 conpone lesstorie 4 accaso 5 coe 6 facia

490 This passage has been published by Dr M JORDAN, *Das Malerbuch des L da Vinci*, p 89, his reading however varies slightly from mine

titia si debbe seguitare li atti secondo li accidenti che accadano all'omo, [3]e 3° conporre le storie, lo studio delle quali sarà fatto dalli atti natura[4]li, fatti a caso mediante li loro accidēti, e por lì mēte per le strade piazze [5]e cāpagnie, e notarli cō brieue discritione di liniamēti, cioè che per una testa [6]si faccia vno o e per uno braccio una linia retta e piegata, e 'l simile si faccia delle gā[7]be e busto, e poi tornādo alla casa fare tali ricordi in perfetta forma, [8]Dice l'aversario che per farsi pratico e fare opere assai ch'elli è meglio che 'l tēpo primo dello [9]studio sia messo in ritrarre vari conponimēti, fatti per carte o muri per di[10]uersi maestri, e in quelli si fa pratica veloce e bono abito, al quale si rispō[11]de che questo abito sarebbe bono, essendo fatto sopra opere di boni componimēti e di [12]studiosi maestri, e perchè questi tali maestri son si rari che pochi se ne trova, è piv [13]sicuro andare alle cose naturali che a quelle d'esso naturale cō grā peggio[14]ramēto imitate e fare tristo abito, perchè chi può andare alla fonte nō vada [15]al uaso

knowledge, their actions should come next, according to the circumstances in which they occur in man And thirdly to compose subjects, the studies for which should be taken from natural actions and made from time to time, as circumstances allow; and pay attention to them in the streets and *piazze* and fields, and note them down with a brief indication of the forms; [5] thus for a head make an o, and for an arm a straight or a bent line, and the same for the legs and the body, [7] and when you return home work out these notes in a complete form. The Adversary says that to acquire practice and do a great deal of work it is better that the first period of study should be employed in drawing various compositions done on paper or on walls by divers masters, and that in this way practice is rapidly gained, and good methods, to which I reply that the method will be good, if it is based on works of good composition and by skilled masters. But since such masters are so rare that there are but few of them to be found, it is a surer way to go to natural objects, than to those which are imitated from nature with great deterioration, and so form bad methods; for he who can go to the fountain does not go to the water-jar.

Ash I. 7*b*]

491.

Quale regola si de' dare a putti pittori.

Industry and thoroughness the first conditions (491—493)

[2]Noi conosciamo chiaramēte che la vista è delle veloci operationi che sia, [3]ed in vn pūto vede īfinite forme: niēte di meno nō cōprende se non una cosa [4]per volta; Poniamo caso tu lettore guarderai in vna occhiata tutta questa [5]carta scritta, e subito giudicherai quella esser piena di uarie lettere, [6]ma non conoscierai in questo tēpo che le lettere sieno, nè che voglino dire, [7]ōde ti bisogna fare a parola a parola verso per uerso, a voler avere [8]notitia d'esse lettere; Ancora se vorai mōtare all'altezza d'uno

What rules should be given to boys learning to paint.

We know for certain that sight is one of the most rapid actions we can perform. In an instant we see an infinite number of forms, still we only take in thoroughly one object at a time. Supposing that you, Reader, were to glance rapidly at the whole of this written page, you would instantly perceive that it was covered with various letters; but you could not, in the time, recognise what the letters were, nor what they were meant to tell Hence you would need to see them word by word, line by line to be able to understand the letters. Again, if you wish to go to the top of a building you must go up step by step; otherwise it will be

. per ībr una . facia 7 ebbussto 8. effare . tēpo p° dello 10. maesstri. 11. te che. 12 maesstri 13 acquelle . pego 14 po . nō \\\\\\\\\

491 1 quella regola. 2 chonosciano chella operatione chessia 3 cōplende se none ī cosa 4 chaso innvna. 5 charta . essubito 6 chonoscierai . volino 7 fare apparola . . versso per 8 Anchora alteza 9 chonuera 10 chosi dicho

Lines 5—7 explained by the lower portion of the sketch No 1 on Pl. XXXI.

edifitio [9]ti converrà salire a grado a grado, latrimēti fia īpossibile peruenire [10]alla sua altezza, così dico a te il quale la natura volgie a questa arte, [11]se vuoi aver vera notitia · delle forme delle cose, comīciarai alle parti[12]cule · di quelle · e non ādare alla seconda, se prima non ài bene nella memoria [13]e nella pratica la prima, E se altro farai, gitterai via il tēpo o vera[14]mēte allūgherai assai lo studio, E ricordoti ch'īpari prima la deligēza [15]che la prestezza

impossible that you should reach the top Thus I say to you, whom nature prompts to pursue this art, if you wish to have a sound knowledge of the forms of objects begin with the details of them, and do not go on to the second [step] till you have the first well fixed in memory and in practice And if you do otherwise you will throw away your time, or certainly greatly prolong your studies And remember to acquire diligence rather than rapidity

Ash I 8a]

492

COME SI DEBE PRIMA INPARARE LA DILIGĒZA [2]CHE LA PRESTA PRATICA

[3]Quando tu disegniatore vorrai fare bono e vtile studio vsa nel tuo disegnia[4]re fare adagio e givdicare īfra i lumi quali e quāti tēghino il primo gra[5]do di chiarezza, e similmēte īfra l'onbre quali sieno quelle che sono più schu[6]re che l'altre e in che modo si mischiano īsieme e le quātità, paragonare [7]l'una choll'altra i liniamēti a che parte si dirizzino, e nelle linie quāta parte [8]d'esse torcie per vno o altro verso, e dove più o meno evidēti e se sia larga [9]o sottile, ed in ultimo che le tue ōbre e lumi sieno uniti sāza tra[10]tti o segni, a uso di fumo E quādo tu avrai fatto la mano e 'l givditio a que[11]sta diligēza verati fatto più presto che tu nō te ne avederai

HOW THAT DILIGENCE [ACCURACY] SHOULD FIRST BE LEARNT RATHER THAN RAPID EXECUTION

If you, who draw, desire to study well and to good purpose, always go slowly to work in your drawing, and discriminate in the lights, which have the highest degree of brightness, and to what extent and likewise in the shadows, which are those that are darker than the others and in what way they intermingle, then their masses and the relative proportions of one to the other And note in their outlines, which way they tend, and which part of the lines is curved to one side or the other, and where they are more or less conspicuous and consequently broad or fine, and finally, that your light and shade blend without strokes and borders [but] looking like smoke And when you have thus schooled your hand and your judgment by such diligence, you will acquire rapidity before you are aware

C A 181b, 546b]

493

VITA DEL PICTORE NE PAESI

[2]Al pittore è neciessario la matematica appartenēte a essa [3]pictura, e la priuatione di cōpagni che son alieni dalli lo[4]ro studi, e ciervello mutabile secondo la uariatione delli [5]obbietti, che dinanti se li oppongono

OF THE LIFE OF THE PAINTER IN THE COUNTRY

A painter needs such mathematics as belong to painting And the absence of all companions who are alienated from his studies, his brain must be easily impressed by the variety of objects, which successively come

The artist's private life and choice of company (493 494)

atte acquesta 11 uolli chose cōmiciati 12 sechonda nonnai memori''a 13 pratucha Esse 14 allūgerai richordoti 15 presteza

492 2 chella praticha 4 . givdichare 5 chiareza essimilmēte qui sieno chessono 6 sinmischano elle 7 chol laltra e drizino 8 dessa e cosi larga 9 ossotile [quando] ed ellumi sāza 10 ossegni arai acque 11 fatta presto nōtte

493 1 pictore [filosafo]ne 2 [la] al pitore le matematiche apartenēte nessa 3 Ella cōpagnie chesson allieni 5 op-

493 In the title line Leonardo had originally written *del pictore filosafo* (the philosophical painter), but he himself struck out *filosofo* Compare in No 363 *pictora notomista* (anatomical painter) The original text is partly reproduced on Pl CI

e remoto da altre cu[6]re, E se nella contẽplatione e difinitione d'ũ caso se ne l'ĩ[7]terpone vn secondo caso come accade, quãdo l'obbietto [8]muove il senso, allora di tali casi si debbe giu[9]dicare quale è di più faticosa difinitione, e quello [10]seguitare insino alla sua vltima chiarezza, e poi [11]seguitare la difinitione dell'altro, E sopra tutto essere [12]di mẽte equale alla natura che à la superfitie dello spechio, [13]la quale si trasmuta in tanti vari colori, quãti sono li [14]colori delli sua obbiecti, e le sue cõpagnie abbino [15]similitudine con lui in tali studi e, nõ le trovando, [16]vsi cõ se medesimo nelle sue cõtemplationi, che [17]in fine nõ troverrà più vtile conpagnia

before him, and also free from other cares [6] And if, when considering and defining one subject, a second subject intervenes—as happens when an object occupies the mind, then he must decide which of these cases is the more difficult to work out, and follow that up until it becomes quite clear, and then work out the explanation of the other [11] And above all he must keep his mind as clear as the surface of a mirror, which assumes colours as various as those of the different objects And his companions should be like him as to their studies, and if such cannot be found he should keep his speculations to himself alone, so that at last he will find no more useful company [than his own]

Ash I 8a]

494

Della vita del pittore nel suo studio

[2]Acciochè la prosperità del corpo nõ guasti quella dello ingegno, [3]il pittore ovvero disegniatore debe essere solitario, e massime quãdo è intẽto [4]alle speculationi e considerationi che continvamente apparẽdo dinãzi [5]agli ochi che danno materia alla memoria d'esser bene riservate, E se tu [6]sarai solo tu sarai tutto tuo, e se sarai acompagniato da uno solo cõpagnio [7]sarai mezzo tuo, e tãto meno quanto sarà maggiore la indiscretione della [8]sua pratica, e se sarai con piv · caderai in più simile incõueniẽte e se [9]tu volessi dire, io farò a mio modo, mi tirerò ĩ parte per potere meglio specu[10]lare le forme delle cose naturali, dico questo potersi mal fare, perchè nõ po[11]tresti fare che spesso nõ prestassi orechi alle lor ciãcie, E, non si potendo servi[12]re a 2 signori, tu faresti male l'ufitio [13]della cõpagnia e peggio l'effetto [14]della speculatione dell'arte e se tu [15]dirai io mi tirerò tãto ĩ parte che le lor [16]parole nõ peruenirãno e nõ mi darãno ĩpacio, io ĩ questa parte ti dico che tu [17]sarai tenvto matto, ma vedi che così faciẽdo tu saresti pur solo, [18]e se

Of the life of the painter in his studio

To the end that well-being of the body may not injure that of the mind, the painter or draughtsman must remain solitary, and particularly when intent on those studies and reflections which will constantly rise up before his eye, giving materials to be well stored in the memory While you are alone you are entirely your own [master] and if you have one companion you are but half your own, and the less so in proportion to the indiscretion of his behaviour And if you have many companions you will fall deeper into the same trouble If you should say "I will go my own way and withdraw apart, the better to study the forms of natural objects", I tell you, you will not be able to help often listening to their chatter And so, since one cannot serve two masters, you will badly fill the part of a companion, and carry out your studies of art even worse And if you say "I will withdraw so far that their words cannot reach me and they cannot disturb me", I can tell you that you will be thought mad But, you see, you will at any rate be alone And if you must have companions

ponghano erremoti 6 Esse chaso 7 chaso achade 8 [di tale i] di tali 9 [e ppiu] e di ecqual 10. seghuitare eppoi 11 siguitare Essopra 13 trassmuta 14 elle 15 collui ennolle 16 vsi chõse cõtemplatione

494 2 Acciochella inciegno 4 isspechulatione e chonsideratione che chontinvamene 5 algli Essettu 6 tussarai esse achompagniato da I solo 7 mezo 8 praticha esse chon chaderai inchõueniẽte esse 9 spechu 10 chose naturale 11 chesspesso prestasi 13 chõpagnia e pegio 14 deli essettu 15 dirai imi chelle 16 queparte chettu 17 maio chosi 18 esse chõpagnia 19 giovare ver chonferimẽto achade spechulo 20 tione

6—11 Leonardo here seems to be speaking of his own method of work as displayed in his MSS and this passage explains, at least in part, the peculiarities in their arrangement pure vorai cōpagnia pigliala del tuo istudio questa [19]ti potrà giovare a aver quel conferimēto che accade dalle varie specula[20]tioni. ogni altra cōpagnia ti potrebbe esser assai dānosa

ship find it in your studio This may assist you to have the advantages which arise from various speculations All other company may be highly mischievous

Ash I 9a]

495

S'EGLI È MEGLIO A DISEGNARE Ī CŌPAGNIA O NO.

[2]Dico e confermo che 'l disegniare ī cōpagnia è molto meglio che solo, per molte ragioni, [3]la prima è che tu ti vergognerai d'essere visto nel numero de' disegniatori essēdo īsofficiēte, [4]e questa vergognia fia cagione di bono studio, secōdariamēte la īuidia bona ti stimv[5]lerà a essere nel nvmero de' piv laudati di te, chè l'altrui lode ti sproneraño, L'altra è che tu piglie[6]rai de' tratti di chi fa meglio di te, e se sarai meglio degli altri farai profito di schifare i man[7]camenti, e l'altrui laude accresceràno tua virtù

OF WHETHER IT IS BETTER TO DRAW WITH COMPANIONS OR NOT

The distribution of time for studying (495—497)

I say and insist that drawing in company is much better than alone, for many reasons The first is that you would be ashamed to be seen behindhand among the students, and such shame will lead you to careful study Secondly, a wholesome emulation will stimulate you to be among those who are more praised than yourself, and this praise of others will spur you on Another is that you can learn from the drawings of others who do better than yourself, and if you are better than they, you can profit by your contempt for their defects, while the praise of others will incite you to farther merits

Ash I 9b]

496

DELLO STUDIARE INSINO QUĀDO TI DESTI [2]O NĀZI T'ADORMĒTI NEL LETTO ALLO SCURO

[3]Ò in me provato essere di nō pocca vtilità, quādo ti truovi allo scuro nel letto [4]andare colla inmaginativa repetēdo i liniamēti superfitiali delle forme [5]per l'adrieto studiate, o altre cose notabili da sottili speculatione cōprese, [6]ed è questo propio uno atto laudabile e vtile a confermarsi le cose nella memoria

OF STUDYING, IN THE DARK, WHEN YOU WAKE, OR IN BED BEFORE YOU GO TO SLEEP

I myself have proved it to be of no small use, when in bed in the dark, to recall in fancy the external details of forms previously studied, or other noteworthy things conceived by subtle speculation, and this is certainly an admirable exercise, and useful for impressing things on the memory

Ash I 8b]

497

DI CHE TĒPO SI DEVE STUDIARE LA ELETIONE DELLE COSE

[2]Le veglie della invernata devono essere da' giovani vsate nelli studi delle [3]cose aparechiate l'estate, cioè tutti li nvdi che

OF THE TIME FOR STUDYING SELECTION OF SUBJECTS

Winter evenings ought to be employed by young students in looking over the things prepared during the summer, that is, all the

495 1 chōpagnia ōno 2 dicho e confermo chōpagnia chessolo 3 chettutti insoficiēte [secondaria sia] 4 ecquesta bonasti stimv 5 laldati lade Laltra chettu 6 esse scifare 7 lalde
496 2 schuro 3 Oime pocha alo 4 chollo 5 chose 6. propio ī atto laldabile chonfirmarsi le chose
497 2 istudi delle 3 chose lastate cioe chettutti lastate, convienti *is wanting in the original.* 4 effare 5 praticha

495 The contradiction by this passage of the foregoing chapter is only apparent. It is quite clear, from the nature of the reasoning which is here used to prove that it is more improving to work with others than to work alone, that the studies of pupils only are under consideration here

497 An injunction to study in the evening occurs also in No 524

ài fatti · l'estate, convienti [4]nducierli · ĩsieme · e fare · cletione · delle migliori mẽbra e corpi [5]di quegli · e metterli · in pratica e bene a mẽte.

drawings from the nude done in the summer should be brought together and a choice made of the best [studies of] limbs and bodies among them, to apply in practice and commit to memory.

DELLE · ATTITUDINI.

[7]Di poi · alla · seguẽte · state farai eletione · di qualchevno che stia bene [8]in su la vita · e che nõ sia · allevato · ĩ givboni ·, a ciò la persona nõ sia strana [9]dalla sua · natura ·, e a quello · farai · fare atti legiadri e galãti e se [10]questo · nõ mostrassi bene · i mvscoli dẽtro ai termini delle mẽbra, nõ mõ[11]t'a niente, bastiti auere · sol da questo · le bone· attitudini, e le mẽbra [12]ricorreggi chõ quelle · che studiasti · la invernata.

OF POSITIONS.

After this in the following summer you should select some one who is well grown and who has not been brought up in doublets, and so may not be of stiff carriage, and make him go through a number of agile and graceful actions, and if his muscles do not show plainly within the outlines of his limbs that does not matter at all. It is enough that you can see good attitudes and you can correct [the drawing of] the limbs by those you studied in the winter.

S. K. M. III 24 *b*]

498.

On the productive power of minor artists (498—501)

Tristo è quel discepolo che [2]non avãza il suo maestro.

He is a poor disciple who does not excel his master

G 25 *a*]

499.

Non è laudabile quel pittore che nõ fa bene [2]se non vna cosa sola, come vno nudo, te[3]sta, panni o animali, o paesi o simili pa[4]rticulari, inperochè non è si grosso in[5]giegnio che, uoltatosi a vna cosa sola e que[6]lla senpre messa in opera, no la facci bene.

Nor is the painter praiseworthy who does but one thing well, as the nude figure, heads, draperies, animals, landscapes or other such details, irrespective of other work; for there can be no mind so inept, that after devoting itself to one single thing and doing it constantly, it should fail to do it well.

Ash. I 10 *a*]

500

COME IL PITTORE NON È LAUDABILE [2]SE QUELLO NON È UNIVERSALE.

[3]D'alcuni · si può chiaramẽte dire · che si ingãnano ·, i quali chiamano bono maestro [4]quello pittore, il quale sol fa bene · una testa · o vna · figura: Cierto non è grã [5]fatto · che studiãdo una sola cosa · il tẽpo · della

THAT A PAINTER IS NOT ADMIRABLE UNLESS HE IS UNIVERSAL.

Some may distinctly assert that those persons are under a delusion who call that painter a good master who can do nothing well but a head or a figure. Certainly this is no great achievement; after studying one

6. atitudine. 8 nõ sia stra 9 acquello esse. 11 dacquesto . attitudine. 12 richoregi chõ studiassti.
498 1 trissto . . dissciepolo. 2. maesstro.
499 1 laldabile 2 none vna 3 ossimili 4 richulare. 5 ecque
500 1 laldabile 2 secquelo 3. alchuni si po . . chessi 4 quelo . . bene ĩ testa . . e non 5 studiãdo ĩ sola chosa . vẽgi

499 In MANZI'S edition (p. 502) the painter G. G. BOSSI indignantly remarks on this passage. "*Parla il Vinci in questo luogo come se tutti gli artisti avessero quella sublimità d'ingegno capace di abbracciare tutte le cose, di cui era egli dotato*" And he then mentions the case of CLAUDE LORRAIN. But he overlooks the fact that in Leonardo's time landscape painting made no pretensions to independence but was reckoned among the details (*particulari*, lines 3, 4).

sua vita che non vēghi a qualche [6]perfectione, ma conosciēdo noi che la pittura abbraccia e contiene in se tutte [7]le cose che produce la natura, e che cōduce l'accidētale operatione delli omini [8]e in vltimo ciò che si può cōprendere cogli ochi, mi pare uno tristo maestro [9]quello che solo una figura fa bene Or nō vedi tu quāti e quali atti sieno solo fac[10]ti da li omini Nō vedi quāti diuersi animali e così albori, erbe, fiori, [11]varietà di siti mōtuosi e piani, fōti, fiumi, città, edifiti publici e privati, [12]strumēti opportuni all'vso vmano, vari abiti e ornamēti e arti, tutte queste [13]cose appartēgono d'essere di pari operazione e bontà vsate da quello [14]che tu vogli chiamare bō pittore

single thing for a life-time who would not have attained some perfection in it? But, since we know that painting embraces and includes in itself every object produced by nature or resulting from the fortuitous actions of men, in short, all that the eye can see, he seems to me but a poor master who can only do a figure well For do you not perceive how many and various actions are performed by men only, how many different animals there are, as well as trees, plants, flowers, with many mountainous regions and plains, springs and rivers, cities with public and private buildings, machines, too, fit for the purposes of men, divers costumes, decorations and arts? And all these things ought to be regarded as of equal importance and value, by the man who can be termed a good painter

Ash I 10b]

501

DELLA TRISTA SCUSATIONE FATTA DA QUELLI CHE FALSAMENTE [2]E ĪDEGNIAMĒTE SI FĀNO CHIAMARE PITTORI

[3]Ecci vna cierta gieneratione di pittori i quali per loro poco studio [4]bisognia che vivino sotto la bellezza d'oro e d'azzurro, i quali cō sō[5]ma stoltitia allegano · nō mettere in opera le bone cose per tristi [6]pagamēti, che saprebbono ancora bē loro fare come vn altro, [7]quādo fussino bene pagati, Or vedi, giēte stolta, nō sāno questi [8]tali tenere qualche opera bona, diciēdo questa è da bō premio [9]e questa è da mezzano, e questa è di sorte, e mostrare d'avere opera [10]da ogni premio

OF THE MISERABLE PRETENCES MADE BY THOSE WHO FALSELY AND UNWORTHILY ACQUIRE THE NAME OF PAINTERS

Now there is a certain race of painters who, having studied but little, must need take as their standard of beauty mere gold and azure, and these, with supreme conceit, declare that they will not give good work for miserable payment, and that they could do as well as any other if they were well paid But, ye foolish folks! cannot such artists keep some good work, and then say this is a costly work and this more moderate and this is average work and show that they can work at all prices?

Ash I 9b]

502.

COME NELLE OPERE D'ĪPORTĀTIA L'OMO NŌ SI DE' FIDARE TĀ[2]TO DELLA SUA MEMORIA CHE NŌ DEGNI RITRARE DI NATURALL

[3]Quello maestro il quale si dessi ad intēdere di potere riseruare ī se tutte le forme [4]e li effetti della natura certo mi parebbe questo essere ornato di molta ignorāza, [5]cōciosia cosa chè detti effetti sono īfiniti, e la memoria nostra non è di tāta capacità [6]che basti. Adūque tu pittore

HOW, IN IMPORTANT WORKS, A MAN SHOULD NOT TRUST ENTIRELY TO HIS MEMORY WITHOUT CONDESCENDING TO DRAW FROM NATURE

Any master who should venture to boast that he could remember all the forms and effects of nature would certainly appear to me to be graced with extreme ignorance, inasmuch as these effects are infinite and our memory is not extensive enough to retain them Hence, O! painter, beware lest the

A caution against one-sided study

acqualche 6 chonociēdo chella chontiene 7 chose 8 chōplendere cholgli pare ī tristo 9 sola ī figura ecquaatti 10 fiori [chāpagnie] 12 tutte que 13 chose apartengano dacquello 14 chettu pitore
501 1 cheffalsa 4 beleza azurro cōso 5 chose 6 chesse perebono anchora chome 7 istolto nō sano
502 3 Quelo maesstro 4 elli parebe 5 chosa dette ella 6 chella chupidita. 7 guadagni chellonore richezze

guarda · che la cupidità del guadagnio nō superi ĩ te l'ono[7]re dell'arte ·, chè il guadagno dell'onore è molto maggiore che l'onore delle richezze, [8]sicchè per queste ed altre ragioni che si potrebbō dire · attenderai · prima col disegnio [9]a dare con dimostratiua forma all'occhio · la intētione, e la ĩuentione fatta ĩ prima [10]nella tua imaginatiua ·, di poi va leuādo e ponēdo tāto che tu ti sadisfaccia, [11]di poi fa acōciare omini vestiti o nudi nel modo che ĩsul opera ài ordinato, [12]e fa che per misura · e grādezza, sotto posto alla prospettiva, che nō passi niēte [13]dell'opera che bene nō sia cōsiliata dalla ragione e dalli effetti naturali, [14]e questa fia la uia da farti onore della tua arte.

lust of gain should supplant in you the dignity of art; for the acquisition of glory is a much greater thing than the glory of riches. Hence, for these and other reasons which might be given, first strive in drawing to represent your intention to the eye by expressive forms, and the idea originally formed in your imagination; then go on taking out or putting in, until you have satisfied yourself. Then have living men, draped or nude, as you may have purposed in your work, and take care that in dimensions and size, as determined by perspective, nothing is left in the work which is not in harmony with reason and the effects in nature And this will be the way to win honour in your art.

G 5*b*]

503.

DELLA VARIETÀ DELLE FIGURE.

How to acquire universality (503—506)

[2]Il pictore debbe cercare d'essere vni[3]uersale, perchè gli manca assai di degnità [4]a fare vna cosa bene e l'altra male, co[5]me molti che solo studiano nello ignu[6]do misurato e proportionato, e nō ricer[7]cā la sua varietà, perchè può vno omo esse[8]re proportionato e essere grosso e cort[9]o o lungo e sottile o mediocre, e chi [10]di questa varietà nō tiene cōto fa senpre [11]le figure sue in stāpa che pare essere tut[12]ti fratelli, la qual cosa merita grā riprēsi[13]one

OF VARIETY IN THE FIGURES

The painter should aim at universality, because there is a great want of self-respect in doing one thing well and another badly, as many do who study only the [rules of] measure and proportion in the nude figure and do not seek after variety, for a man may be well proportioned, or he may be fat and short, or tall and thin, or medium. And a painter who takes no account of these varieties always makes his figures on one pattern so that they might all be taken for brothers, and this is a defect that demands stern reprehension

Ash I 4*a*]

504.

¶COME PER TUTTE VIE SI PUÒ IMPARARE.¶

[2]Questa · benigna · natura ne provede ĩ modo che per tutto [3]il mōdo tu trovi dove imitare.

HOW SOMETHING MAY BE LEARNT EVERYWHERE.

Nature has beneficently provided that throughout the world you may find something to imitate.

G. 5*b*]

505.

DELL'ORDINE DEL FARSI VNIVERSALE.

[2]Facile cosa è a [3]l'omo farsi vniuersale, imperochè tutti [4]li animali terrestri ànno similitudine di mē[5]bra, cioè muscoli nerui e ossa, e [6]nulla si uariano se nō in lūghezza o in [7]grossezza come sarà dimostrato nella

OF THE MEANS OF ACQUIRING UNIVERSALITY.

It is an easy matter to men to acquire universality, for all terrestrial animals resemble each other as to their limbs, that is in their muscles, sinews and bones, and they do not vary excepting in length or in thickness, as

8 ragione chessi . chol 9. chon . ella 10. valleuādo . chettutti 12 effa 14 ecquesta.

503 2 cerchare. 3 Mancha 4 se affare . . ellaltra 5 chessolo . . iniv 7 chā la . perche e po vno 8. chort 9. lungho essottile 11. tu 12 fratelle

504 1. chome per tutti via si po. 2. benignia

505 2 cosa he a chi ssa farsi [vniversale] 3 farsi poi vniuersale inperochetti 4 terrestri ā similitudine di me 5 bra [mussco]

[8]natomia; ecci poi li animali d'acqua che [9]son di molte varietà, delli quali nõ persua-[10]derò il pittore che ui faccia regola, per-[11]chè son quasi d'infinite varietà, e così li [12]animali insetti

will be shown under Anatomy But then there are aquatic animals which are of great variety, I will not try to convince the painter that there is any rule for them for they are of infinite variety, and so is the insect tribe

Ash I 31*b*]

506

PITTURA.

[2]Lo ingiegnio del pittore vol essere a similitudine dello · specchio, il quale senpre [3]si trasmuta nel colore di quella cosa ch'eli à per obietto, e di tãte simili[4]tudini s'enpie · quãte sono le cose che li sono contraposte, Adũque co[5]nosciẽdo tu pittore nõ potere esser bono se nõ sei vniversale maestro di [6]cõtrafare colla tua arte tutte le qualità · delle forme che produce la natura, [7]le quali nõ saprai fare, se nõ le vedi, e ritenerle nella mẽte, Onde andãdo [8]tu per cãpagnie fa che 'l tuo givditio si uolti a vari obietti e di mano ĩ ma[9]no riguardare or questa cosa ora quell'altra, faciẽdo vn fascio di uarie [10]cose elette e scielte infra le mẽ bone, E nõ facci come alcuni pitto[11]ri, i quali, stãchi colla lor fantasia, dismettono l'opera e fãno esercitio [12]col andare a sollazzo, riserbandosi vna stãchezza nella mente, la quale, [13]nõ che veghino, non porgono ĩ mente varie cose, ma spesse volte scontrãdo [14]li amici e parẽti, essendo da quelli salutati, nõ che li vedino o sentino, [15]e non altrementi sono cogniosciuti, come se vi scontrassino altre tãt'aria

PAINTING

The mind of the painter must resemble a mirror, which always takes the colour of the object it reflects and is completely occupied by the images of as many objects as are in front of it Therefore you must know, Oh Painter! that you cannot be a good one if you are not the universal master of representing by your art every kind of form produced by nature And this you will not know how to do if you do not see them, and retain them in your mind Hence as you go through the fields, turn your attention to various objects, and, in turn look now at this thing and now at that, collecting a store of divers facts selected and chosen from those of less value But do not do like some painters who, when they are wearied with exercising their fancy dismiss their work from their thoughts and take exercise in walking for relaxation, but still keep fatigue in their mind which, though they see various objects [around them], does not apprehend them, but, even when they meet friends or relations and are saluted by them, although they see and hear them, take no more cognisance of them than if they had met so much empty air

Ash I 9*a*]

507

DE' GIOCHI CHE DEBONO FARE I DISEGNIATORI

[2]Quando vorete o voi disegniatori pigliare coi giochi qualche utile sollazzo [3]è da vsare senpre cose al proposito della vostra professione, cioè del fare bono [4]giuditio di ochio, del sapere givdicare la uerità delle larghezze e lũghezze delle cose [5]e per suefare lo ingiegnio a simili cose

OF GAMES TO BE PLAYED BY THOSE WHO DRAW.

When, Oh draughtsman, you desire to find relaxation in games you should always practise such things as may be of use in your profession, by giving your eye good practice in judging accurately of the breadth and length of objects Thus, to accustom your mind to such things, let one of

Useful games and exercises (507 508)

coe musscoli 6 seno illũgeza 7 dimostrao 8 dacq''a' 9 deli 10 pichttore

506 2 assimilitudine 3 cholore chosa 4 tudine quãti chose chontraposte cho 5 se nõse 6 cõtraffare cholla 8 chãpagnie 10 esscielte infralle faci chome alchu 11 re i quali stãchi cholla dismettano effano 12 chol assollazo stãcheza 13 no che vegino o porgn ĩ mente varie chose schõtrãdo 14 essentino 15 chogniosciuti chome se li schontrasino altre tãtaria

507 2 choi nutile sollazo 3 chose 4 givdichare largeze ellũgeze chose 5 assimile chose faccia ĩ diuoi 6. chaso

· faccia uno di uoi · una · linia recta [6]a caso su vno mvro · e ciascuno di voi tēga una sottile · festuca o paglia in mano [7]e ciascuno tagli · la sua · alla · lunghezza · che li · pare · la prima linia, stādo · lontani [8]per ispatio di braccia · 10 ·, e poi ciascuno vada · allo esenplo a misurare cō quella la sua [9]givditiale misura· E quello · che piv s'avvicina colla sua misura alla lunghezza de[10]llo esēplo fia superiore e uincitore e acquisti da tutti il premio, che ināzi da uoi [11]fu · ordinato ·, Ancora si debbe · pigliare misure scortate, cioè pigliare uno [12]dardo o altra caña, e riguardare dināzi a se una cierta distātia ·, e ciascuno [13]col suo givditio stimi quāte volte quella misura · entri ī quella distātia, ācora a chi [14]tira meglio una linia di uno braccio, e sia riprovata con filo tirato ·, E simili giochi sono [15]cagione di fare bono jvditio d'ochio, il quale è 'l prīcipale atto della pittura.

you draw a straight line at random on a wall, and each of you, taking a blade of grass or of straw in his hand, try to cut it to the length that the line drawn appears to him to be, standing at a distance of 10 braccia, then each one may go up to the line to measure the length he has judged it to be. And he who has come nearest with his measure to the length of the pattern is the best man, and the winner, and shall receive the prize you have settled beforehand. Again you should take forshortened measures. that is take a spear, or any other cane or reed, and fix on a point at a certain distance, and let each one estimate how many times he judges that its length will go into that distance. Again, who will draw best a line one braccio long, which shall be tested by a thread. And such games give occasion to good practice for the eye, which is of the first importance in painting

Ash I 13a]

508.

Modo d'aumētare e destare lo īgiegnio [2]a varie īuētioni.

[3]Nō resterò però di mettere ītra questi precietti una nova īuētione di specula[4]tione, · la quale · bēchè paia · piccola · e quasi degnia di riso, nōdimeno è di [5]grāde vtilità · a destrare lo ingegno a varie invētioni, e questa · è · se tu [6]riguarderai in alcuni mvri inbrattati di uarie machie o pietre di uari misti, [7]se avrai a īuentionare qualche sito · potrai · li · uedere similitudine di diuersi paesi, [8]ornati di mōtagnie, fiumi, sassi, albori, pianvre, grādi valli e colli [9]in diuersi modi, · ancora vi potrai vedere diuerse battaglie e atti prōti di [10]figure ·, strane arie di uolti · e abiti · e infinite cose ·, le quali potrai ri[11]durre in ītegra · e bona · forma ·, e īterviene ī simili mvri e misti come del suono [12]di cāpane · che ne' loro tochi vi troverai ogni nome e vocabolo che tu ī[13]maginerai

A way of developing and arousing the mind to various inventions.

I cannot forbear to mention among these precepts a new device for study, which, although it may seem but trivial and almost ludicrous, is nevertheless extremely useful in arousing the mind to various inventions. And this is, when you look at a wall spotted with stains, or with a mixture of stones, if you have to devise some scene, you may discover a resemblance to various landscapes, beautified with mountains, rivers, rocks, trees, plains, wide valleys and hills in varied arrangement, or again you may see battles and figures in action, or strange faces and costumes, and an endless variety of objects, which you could reduce to complete and well drawn forms. And these appear on such walls confusedly, like the sound of bells in whose jangle you may find any name or word you choose to imagine

6 suuvno . ciasschuno tēga ī sottile festucha . imano. 7 e ciasschuno talgli . lungeza . chelli 8. di br 10 . . chō 9. Ecquello . . savisina cholla . . lungeza. 10. premio di che, 11 Anchora . schontate 12 pigliare ī. 12 chāna . asse ī cierta. 14 meglio īlinia dī br essia . chon Essimili. 15 chagione

508. 3 precietti ī nova . . spechula 4 pichola 5. longiegmo . . ecquesta . settu 6. mušcli. 7. arai 8 vale e cholli. 11 dure . . del so 12. viroverai . . vocavlo chettu i

II.

THE ARTIST'S STUDIO.—INSTRUMENTS AND HELPS FOR THE APPLICATION OF PERSPECTIVE.—ON JUDGING OF A PICTURE.

Ash. I. 19*b*]

509.

Le stãze overo abitationi piccole raviã lo ingegno et le grãdi lo suiano.

Small rooms or dwellings discipline the mind, large ones weaken it. On the size of the studio.

B. M. 171b]

510.

Quãto piv grosso fia il muro ²minore fia il lume.

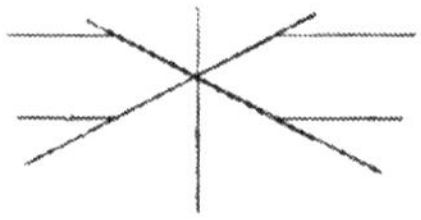

The larger the wall the less the light will be. On the construction of windows (510—512).

B. 20*b*]

511.

Modi di vari lumi dati per varie forme di finestre alle canove: la piv disutile ²è

The different kinds of light afforded in cellars by various forms of windows. The

509. 1. abitatione pichole . . logiĉgnio . lossuiano.
510. 2. ilume.
511. 1. chanove. 2. freda . . pivtile ella . . chalda. 3. ella . . mezana.

511. From a reference to the notes on the right light for painting it becomes evident that the observations made on cellar-windows have a direct bearing on the construction of the studio-window. In the diagram *b* as well as in that under No. 510 the window-opening is reduced to a minimum, but only, it would seem, in order to emphasize the advantage of walls constructed on the plan there shown.

la finestra · *a* · e la piv fredda · la piu vtile e la piv luminosa e piv calda e che vede

least useful and the coldest is the window at *a*. The most useful, the lightest and warmest

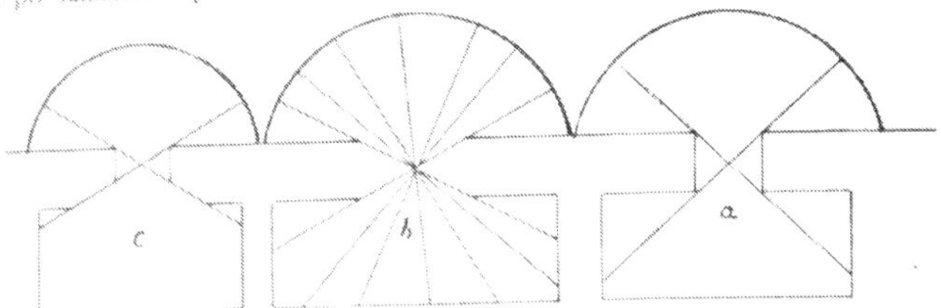

piv · cielo è la finestra · *b*: la finestra · *c* · è di mezzana vtilità.

and most open to the sky is the window at *b*. The window at *c* is of medium utility.

512.

Ash. I. 20a]

FINESTRA DEL PITTORE E SUA CÕMODITÀ.

Il pittore, che vsa imitatione del naturale, debbe · avere · v lume · il quale lui · possa

OF THE PAINTER'S WINDOW AND ITS ADVANTAGE.

The painter who works from nature should have a window, which he can raise

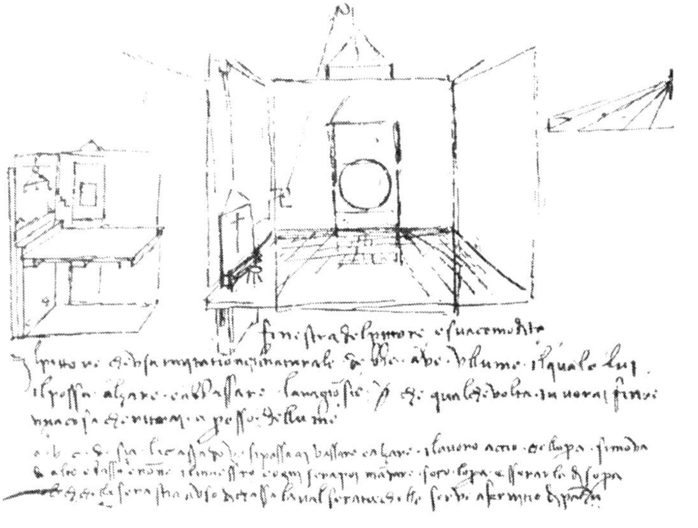

512. 1. comodita. 2. imitatione di naturale . . vilume. 3. il possa . . fnire. 5. chassa . . abassare . . i lauoro . . chellopera. 6. enõne

512. See Pl. XXXI, No. 2. In this plate the lines have unfortunately lost their sharpness, for the accidental loss of the negative has necessitated a reproduction from a positive. But having formerly published this sketch by another process, in VON LÜTZOW'S *Zeitschrift für bildende Kunst* (Vol. XVII, pg. 13) I have reproduced it here in the text. The sharpness of the outline in the original sketch is here preserved but it gives it from the reversed side.

alzare e abbassare, la ragiō si è che qualche volta tu vorai finire [4]vna cosa che ritrai a presso del lume,

[5]*a b c d* sia la cassa, dove si possa abbassare e alzare il lauoro, acciochè l'opera si mova [6]da alto e basso e non il maestro; e ogni sera puoi mādare sotto l'opera e serrarla di sopra, [7]che la sera stia a vso di cassa laqual serrata che le serve a seruitio di pāca

and lower The reason is that sometimes you will want to finish a thing you are drawing, close to the light

Let *a b c d* be the chest on which the work may be raised or lowered, so that the work moves up and down and not the painter. And every evening you can let down the work and shut it up above so that in the evening it may be in the fashion of a chest which, when shut up, may serve the purpose of a bench

Ash I 15*b*]

513.

On the best light for painting (513—520)

¶Quale lume è bono per ritra[2]re di naturale o alto o basso [3]o grāde o piccolo o potēte grā[4]de, o potēte piccolo o grā[5]de debole o piccolo e debole?¶

Which light is best for drawing from nature, whether high or low, or large or small, or strong and broad, or strong and small, or broad and weak or small and weak?

A 23*a*]

514

Della qualità del lume

[2]Il lume grande e alto e nō troppo potente fia quello che renderà le particule de' corpi molto grate

Of the quality of the light

A broad light high up and not too strong will render the details of objects very agreeable

Ash I 2*b*]

515

Come debe essere alto il lume [2]da ritrare di naturale

[3]Il lume da ritrare di naturale vole essere a tramōtana, aciò nō facci [4]mutatione, e se lo fai a mezzodì tieni finestra īpanāta aciò il sole, [5]alluminādo tutto il giorno, quella nō facci mutatione, L'altezza del lume [6]de'essere ī modo · situato che ogni corpo facci tāto lūga per terra la sua [7]ōbra quāto è la sua · altezza

That the light for drawing from nature should be high up

The light for drawing from nature should come from the North in order that it may not vary And if you have it from the South, keep the window screened with cloth, so that with the sun shining the whole day the light may not vary The height of the light should be so arranged as that every object shall cast a shadow on the ground of the same length as itself

il maesstro e poi esserarla 7 loch chella chassa la ualserata chelle pācha
513 3 picholo 4 picholo 5 picolo he debole
514 2 lume partichule de chorpi
515 3 at ramōtana 4 essello fai a mezo di 5 alūminīdo Lalteza 6 imodo faci luga 7 alteza

513 The question here put is unanswered in the original MS

Ash. I. 22]

516

Della qualità · dell'aria [2]al'ōbre e lumi.

[3]Quel corpo · farà maggiore · differēza · dal'ombre ai lumi · che si trove[4]rà · essere · visto · da maggiore · lume ·, come lume di sole o la nocte il [5]lume del foco. e questo · è poco · da usare ĵ pittura, ĵperochè l'opere [6]rimāgono · crude e sanza grazia

[7]Quel corpo ·, che si troverà ĵ mediocre lume, fia in lui poca differēza [8]dai · lumi · all'ombre, e questo accade sul fare della sera o quādo è nuvolo [9]e queste opere sono dolci · e ācci gratia · ōgni qualità di volto, sicchè I ōgni [10]cosa · li stremi sono vitiosi: il troppo lume fa crudo ·, il troppo scuro nō la[11]scia vedere. il mezzano è bono.

The kind of light requisite for painting light and shade.

An object will display the greatest difference of light and shade when it is seen in the strongest light, as by sunlight, or, at night, by the light of a fire But this should not be much used in painting because the works remain crude and ungraceful.

An object seen in a moderate light displays little difference in the light and shade, and this is the case towards evening or when the day is cloudy, and works then painted are tender and every kind of face becomes graceful. Thus, in every thing extremes are to be avoided: Too much light gives crudeness, too little prevents our seeing The medium is best.

De' lumi piccoli.

[12]Ancora · i lumi fatti da piccole finestre fanno grā differēza da lumi al'ōbre ·, e massime se la [14]stāza da quelle · alluminata fia grāde, e questo non è bono a usare

Of small lights.

Again, lights cast from a small window give strong differences of light and shade, all the more if the room lighted by it be large, and this is not good for painting

Ash I 28b]

517.

Pittura.

¶[9] Quella · aria · luminosa · che penetra · e passa · per le · perforate [10]pareti · alle · oscure · abitationi · farà il loco · tanto [11]meno che tenebroso ·, Quanto · essa · perforatura · entra [12]ĵ nelle · pareti · che circūdano · e coprono · il lor pavimento ¶

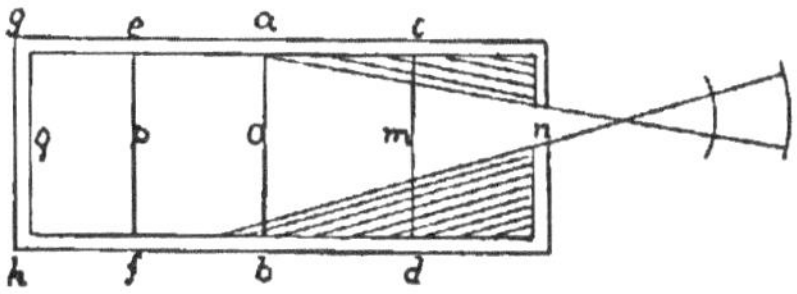

Painting.

The luminous air which enters by passing through orifices in walls into dark rooms will render the place less dark in proportion as the opening cuts into the walls which surround and cover in the pavement.

516. 2. ellumi. 3. diferēza . . chessi 4. magiore . chome 5. ecquesto l e pocho . . ĵpero chellopere. 6 rimāgano . essanza 7. Quell chessi . . mediocle . pocha diferēza 8 ecquesto acade . . nvolo. 9 aci 10. tropo . . il [poco] tropo 11. mezano. 12 pichol. 13 pichole . . fano . diferēza. 14 dacquella aluminata ecquesto

517 1 [Quell'aria luminosa ce per perforate pariete [entra] penetra e pasa 2 inelle osschure abitatione fara 1 illoco 3 tanto . meno che ttenebroso . quāto esso perfo4ramēto entra inelle . pariete che circhun5dano e choprano il pavimēto . Quanto to esso 6 perforamento e minore che lle pariete che circhū7dano e choprano il pavimēto]. — 9. perlle. 10. pariete . . oschure . locho 11 chettenebroso 12 inelle pariete . che circhūdano e choprano . iloro.

A. 2*a*]

518.

QUALITÀ · DI LUME.

[2]Tāto · quanto · *a* · *b* · ētra · in · *c* · *d* · tāte volte è più [3]luminoso · che · *c* · *d* ·, e similemēte · tāte volte · quanto · il [4]pūto *e* entra · in *c* · *d* · tāte uolte · è piv · luminoso che · *c* · *d*, [5]e questo · lume · è bono per quelli che tagliano · lauori sottili.

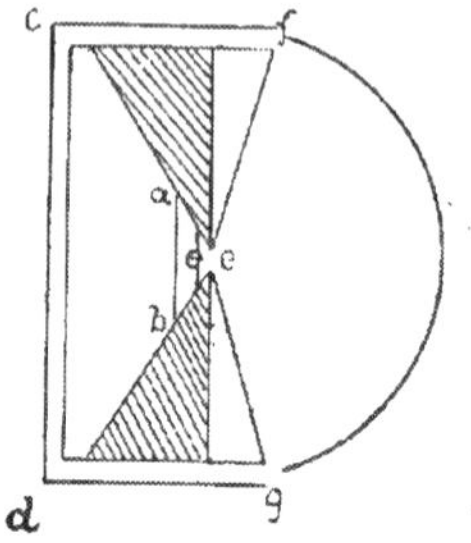

OF THE QUALITY OF LIGHT.

In proportion to the number of times that *a b* goes into *c d* will it be more luminous than *c d*. And similarly, in proportion as the point *e* goes into *c d* will it be more luminous than *c d*; and this light is useful for carvers of delicate work [5].

Ash. I. 18*a*]

519.

¶Come la pittura debe essere vista da una sola finestra, come appare per cagione [2]de' corpi · così fatti;  se tu voli fare in vn altezza vna · palla tonda ti bi[3]sognierà farla lunga · a questa similitudine, e star tāto īdirieto · ch'ella scortādo [4]apparisca · tōda.¶

That the light should fall upon a picture from one window only. This may be seen in the case of objects in this form. If you want to represent a round ball at a certain height you must make it oval in this shape, and stand so far off as that by foreshortening it appears round.

Ash. I. 15*a*]

520.

DELLA · ELETIONE DELL'ARIA [2]CHE DÀ GRATIA AI VOLTI.

[3]Se avrai una corte da potere · a · tua · posta · coprire cō tēda · lina · questo lume fia [4]bono ·, overo quādo voi ritrare vno ritralo a cattivo tēpo o sul fare della sera, [5]faciendo stare il ritratto colla schiena · accosto · a vno · de' mvri d'essa · corte; [6]poni · mēte per le strade · sul fare della

OF SELECTING THE LIGHT WHICH GIVES MOST GRACE TO FACES.

If you should have a court yard that you can at pleasure cover with a linen awning that light will be good. Or when you want to take a portrait do it in dull weather, or as evening falls, making the sitter stand with his back to one of the walls of the court yard. Note in the streets, as evening falls, the faces of the

518. 2. [a. b.] . 3. essimile mēte. 5. ecquesto.
519. 1. da ī sola . . apre . . chagione. 2. chosi . . settu . . alteza. 3. acquesta.
520. 3. arai ī corte. 4. cativo tēpo sol. 5. cholla sciena . achosto. 6. chattivo. 7. dolcieza . . illoro . . arai ī corte. 8. acomodata.

518. M. RAVAISSON in his edition of the Paris MS. A remarks on this passage: *"La figure porte les lettres f et g, auxquelles rien ne renvoie dans l'explication; par conséquent, cette explication est incomplète. La figure semblerait, d'ailleurs, se rapporter à l'effet de la réflexion par un miroir concave."* So far as I can see the text is not imperfect, nor is the sense obscure. It is hardly necessary to observe that *c d* here indicate the wall of the room opposite to the window *e* and the semicircle described by *f g* stands for the arch of the sky; this occurs in various diagrams, for example under 511. A similar semicircle, Pl. III, No. 2 (and compare No. 149) is expressly called *'orizonte'* in writing.

5. For the same reason a window thus constructed would be convenient for an illuminator or a miniature painter.

sera i volti d'omini e done, quado è cattivo tēpo quāta gratia e dolcezza si uede in loro; adūque tu pittore avrai una corte accommodata co mvri tīti in nero cō alquato sporto di tetto sopra esso mvro, e sia larga di braccia 10 e lūga 20 e alta 10, e quādo è sole conviene coprire cō tēla, opur ritrare una opera sul fare della sera quādo è nvuolo o nebbia e questo è perfecta aria.

men and women, and when the weather is dull, what softness and delicacy you may perceive in them. Hence, Oh Painter! have a court arranged with the walls tinted black and a narrow roof projecting within the walls. It should be 10 braccia wide and 20 braccia long and 10 braccia high and covered with a linen awning; or else paint a work towards evening or when it is cloudy or misty, and this is a perfect light.

521.

A. 1a]

Per ritrare uno ignudo di naturale o altra cosa vsa tenere ī mano uno filo con vno piōbo, per potere vedere li scotri delle cose.

To draw a nude figure from nature, or any thing else, hold in your hand a plumb-line to enable you to judge of the relative position of objects.

522.

Ash. I, 6B]

DEL RITRARE VNA COSA.

Fa che, quādo ritrai, che tu moui alcū pricipio di linia che tu guardi per tutto il corpo, che tu ritrai, qualūque cosa si scotri per la dirittura della pricipiata linia.

OF DRAWING AN OBJECT.

When you draw take care to set up a principal line which you must observe all throughout the object you are drawing; every thing should bear relation to the direction of this principal line.

523.

Ash. I, 11a]

DEL MODO DEL RITRARRE UNO SITO CORETTO.

Abbi uno uetro grāde come uno mezzo foglio regale e quello ferma bene dinanzi ali occhi tua, cioè tra l'ochio e la cosa che tu vuoi ritrare, e dipoi ti poni lontano col ochio al detto vetro $^2/_3$ di braccio, e ferma la testa con vno strumēto ī modo nō possi mouere pūto la testa: dipoi serra o ti copri uno ochio, e col pēnello o cō lapis a matita macinata segnia ī sul vetro ciò che di là appare, e poi lucida cō la carta dal uetro e spoluerizzala sopra bona carta e dipignla, se ti piace, vsando bene poi la prospettiva aerea.

OF A MODE OF DRAWING A PLACE ACCURATELY.

Have a piece of glass as large as a half sheet of royal folio paper and set thus firmly in front of your eyes that is, between your eye and the thing you want to draw; then place yourself at a distance of $^2/_3$ of a braccia from the glass fixing your head with a machine in such a way that you cannot move it at all. Then shut or entirely cover one eye and with a brush or red chalk draw upon the glass that which you see beyond it; then trace it on paper from the glass, afterwards transfer it onto good paper, and paint it if you like, carefully attending to the arial perspective.

A IPARARE A FARE BENE UNO POSARE.

Se tu vuoi suefare bene alle rette e bone posature delle figure forma uno quadro over telaro, dētro riquadrato cō fila ifra

HOW TO LEARN TO PLACE YOUR FIGURES CORRECTLY.

If you want to acquire a practice of good and correct attitudes for your figures, make a square frame or net, and square it out

... dāle 10 ... riquādo esso lē coprire. 10. ritrare ī opera ... nebia.

521. ritrare ī inudo ... chosa. 2. mano ī filo chon.

522. 1. 2 chosa ... chetu ... alchū ... i chorpo. 3. chettu ... chosa ... schōtra.

523. 1. ritrarre ī sito. 2. abi ī uetro ... chome ī mezo ... equello. 3. ella. 4. efferma. 5. sera ottutti copri ī ochio e chol.

523. Leonardo is commonly credited with the invention of the arrangement of a plate of glass commonly known as the "vertical plane." Professor E. VON BRÜCKE in his "*Bruchstücke aus der Theorie der bildenden Künste,*" Leipzig 1877, pg. 3, writes on this contrivance. *Unsere Glastafel ist die sogenannte Glastafel des Leonardo da Vinci, die in Gestalt einer Glastafel vorgestellte Bildfläche.*"

l'ochio tuo · e lo nudo che ritrai, [12]e que' medesimi quadri farai sulla carta dove voi ritrare detto nvdo sotti[13]lemēte ·, dipoi poni una pallotta di ciera in vna parte della rete che ti serva [14]per una mira, la quale senpre nel riguardare lo nudo scōtrerai nella fōtanel[15]la della gola, e se fusse volto dirieto scōtrala con uno de' nodi del collo, [16]e queste fila t'isegnierā in tutte le parti del corpo che ī ciascuno atto si tro[17]vano sotto la fontanella della gola, sotto li āgoli delle spalle, sotto le tette, fiā[18]chi e altre parti del corpo; e le linie traverse della rete · ti mostrano [19]quāto è piv alto nel posare sopra una gāba che l'altra, e cosi i fiāchi e le gi[20]nochia e i piedi ·, ma ferma senpre · la rete per linia perpēdiculare, e in effet[21]to · tutte le parti che tu vedi che lo nvdo piglia della rete · fa che 'l tuo nvdo [22]disegniato pigli della rete disegniata; i quadri disegniati possono essere [23]tāto minori che quelli della rete quāto · tu volli · che la tua figura sia minore [24]ch'è la · naturale; dipoi tieni a mēte nello figurare · che farai la regola dello [25]scōtro delle mēbra come te le mostrò la rete ·, la quale debe essere alta [26]3 braccia e mezzo e larga · 3 · distāte da te braccia 7 e presso allo nvdo uno braccio.

with thread; place this between your eye and the nude model you are drawing, and draw these same squares on the paper on which you mean to draw the figure, but very delicately. Then place a pellet of wax on a spot of the net which will serve as a fixed point, which, whenever you look at your model, must cover the pit of the throat; or, if his back is turned, it may cover one of the vertebrae of the neck. Thus these threads will guide you as to each part of the body which, in any given attitude will be found below the pit of the throat, or the angles of the shoulders, or the nipples, or hips and other parts of the body; and the transverse lines of the net will show you how much the figure is higher over the leg on which it is posed than over the other, and the same with the hips, and the knees and the feet. But always fix the net perpendicularly so that all the divisions that you see the model divided into by the net work correspond with your drawing of the model on the net work you have sketched. The squares you draw may be as much smaller than those of the net as you wish that your figure should be smaller than nature. Afterwards remember when drawing figures, to use the rule of the corresponding proportions of the limbs as you have learnt it from the frame and net. This should be 3 braccia and a half high and 3 braccia wide; 7 braccia distant from you and 1 braccio from the model.

6. chō . . matite . . apa. 7. esspolucrezza. 8. airca. 9. affare bene ī. 10. settu . . ai retti e boni posati fo"r"ma ī quadro. 11. telaro . . chō . . ello. 12. sala charta. 13. poni ī balotta . . chetu serva. 14. per ī miera . . scōterai nela fontane. 15. esse fussi . . scōtralo chon. 17. fontanela dela . . dele spali sottotette. 18. chorpo elle . . tīmostrano. 19. sopra ī gāba . . chosi. 20. effe. 21. chettu . . chello. 22. dela . . possano. 23. minore . . chella. 24. checlla . . nelo . . cheffarai. 25. schōtro . . chome. 26. 3 br e mezo ellarga . . datte br 7 . . nvdo ī br.

6. The word *lapis* is never used by Leonardo in the sense of pencil as is shown in the following passage from A. CONDIVI, *Vita di Michel-Agnolo Buonarotti*, Chap. XVIII: "*Ma egli* (Michelangelo in 1495) *non avendo che mostrare, prese una penna (perciocchè in quel tempo il lapis non era in uso) e con tale leggiadria gli gli dipinse una mano, che ne restò stupefatto.*"

10. 11. 13. *quadro . telaro . . rete.* The invention of this contrivance is to be ascribed to LEON BATTISTA ALBERTI who describes it in the first Book '*Della Pittura*.' "*Egli è uno velo sotilissimo tessuto raro, tinto di quale a te piace colore, distinto con fili piu grossi in quanti a te piace paralleli; qual velo pongo tra l'occhio et la cosa veduta, tale che la piramide visiva penetri per la rarità del velo.*" (ed. JANITSCHEK, pg. 101). On this the editor notes (pg. 237): "*Im lateinischen Text betont ausdrücktich Alberti, dass er der Erfinder des* 'Velo' *sei*" („*cujus ego usum nunc primum adinveni*").

This is farther confirmed by VASARI: "*L'anno poi* 1457, *che fu trovato l'utilissimo modo di stampare i libri da GIOVANNI GUITTEMBERG germano; trovò LEON BATTISTA a quella similitudine, per via d'uno strumento, il modo di lucidare le prospettive naturali e diminuire le figure, ed il modo parimente da potere ridurre le cose capricciose, utili all'arte, e bello affatto.*" (Ed. SANSONI, 1878, II, 540).

524.

A. 1⁸]

MODO · DI RITRARE DI NOTTE UNO RILIEUO.

·Fachemetti una carta, non troppa ²lucida, infra rilieuo · e lume e avrai bono ritrare.

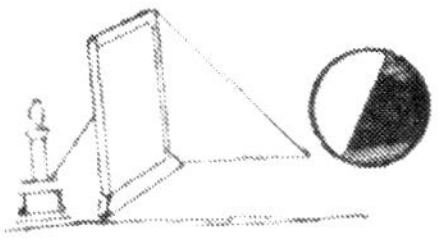

A METHOD OF DRAWING AN OBJECT IN RELIEF AT NIGHT.

Place a sheet of not too transparent paper between the relievo and the light and you can draw thus very well.

525.

A. 1⁸]

Se voli fare · una figura · i sù uno mvro ·, il qual muro sia in iscorto ²e la · figura che ui dipigniérai · paia in propia · forma e spiccata ³da · esso · mvro ·, farai in questo · modo: fa da avere · una · sottile piastra ⁴di ferro · e fali uno piccolo spiraculo nel mezzo · il quale sia ⁵rotodo ·, e accostavi · uno · lume · i modo · che lo tocchi col suo · mezzo, dipoi ⁶poni quello corpo o figura ·, che piv ti piace ·, apresso a detto mvro ⁷i modo · lo tocchi ·, e segnia · la sua · obra i detto mvro e poi la obra e da ⁸lei sua · lumi ·, e fa · che quello che vorà vedere detta · figura · stia ⁹a quello medesimo spiracolo ·, doue stette in prima · il lume. ¹⁰e no ti potrai mai persuadere che detta figura · no sia spiccata dal mvro.

If you want to represent a figure on a wall, the wall being foreshortened, while the figure is to appear in its proper form, and as standing free from the wall, you must proceed thus: have a thin plate of iron and make a small hole in the centre; this hole must be round. Set a light close to it in such a position as that it shines through

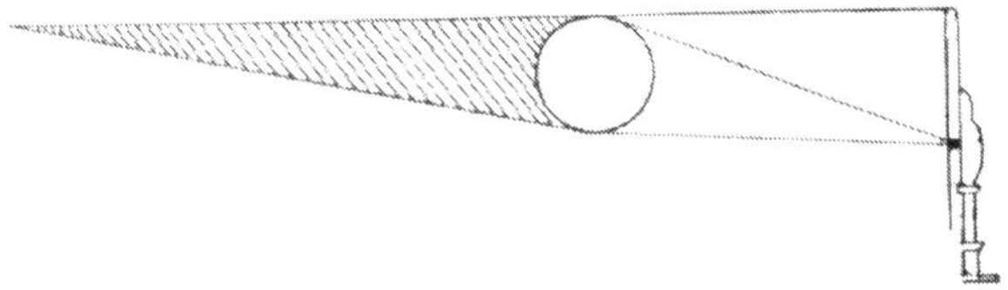

the central hole, then place any object or figure you please so close to the wall that it touches it and draw the outline of the shadow on the wall; then fill in the shade and add the lights; place the person who is to see it so that he looks through that same hole where at first the light was; and you will never be able to persuade yourself that the image is not detached from the wall.

524. 1. notte i rilieuo. 2. fa che metti . . charta nonā tropa. 3. lume ea

525. 1. fare i figura isununo mvro . [m] il. 2. sîla . . easpichata. 3. vedere i . sotile. 4. difere effale i pichole spirachulo nel mezo. 5. rotōlo . e achosta vi i lume . . chello tochi chol suo mezo. 6. quelo chorpo offigura. 7. tochi essegnia 8. effa che quello. 9. [st]a quelo . . spirachōlo . disspichato.

524. Bodies thus illuminated will show on the surface of the paper how the copyist has to distribute light and shade.

525. *uno piccolo spiraculo nel mezzo.* M. RAVAISSON, in his edition of MS. A (Paris), p. 52, reads *nel muro*—evidently a mistake for *nel mezzo* which is quite plainly written; and he translates it *"fait lui une petite ouverture dans le mur,"* adding in a note: *"les mots 'dans le mur' paraissent être de trop. Leonardo a du les écrire par distraction."* But *'nel mezzo'* is clearly legible even on the photograph facsimile given by Ravaisson himself, and the objection he raises disappears at once. It is not always wise or safe to try to prove our author's absence of mind or inadvertence by apparent difficulties in the sense or connection of the text.

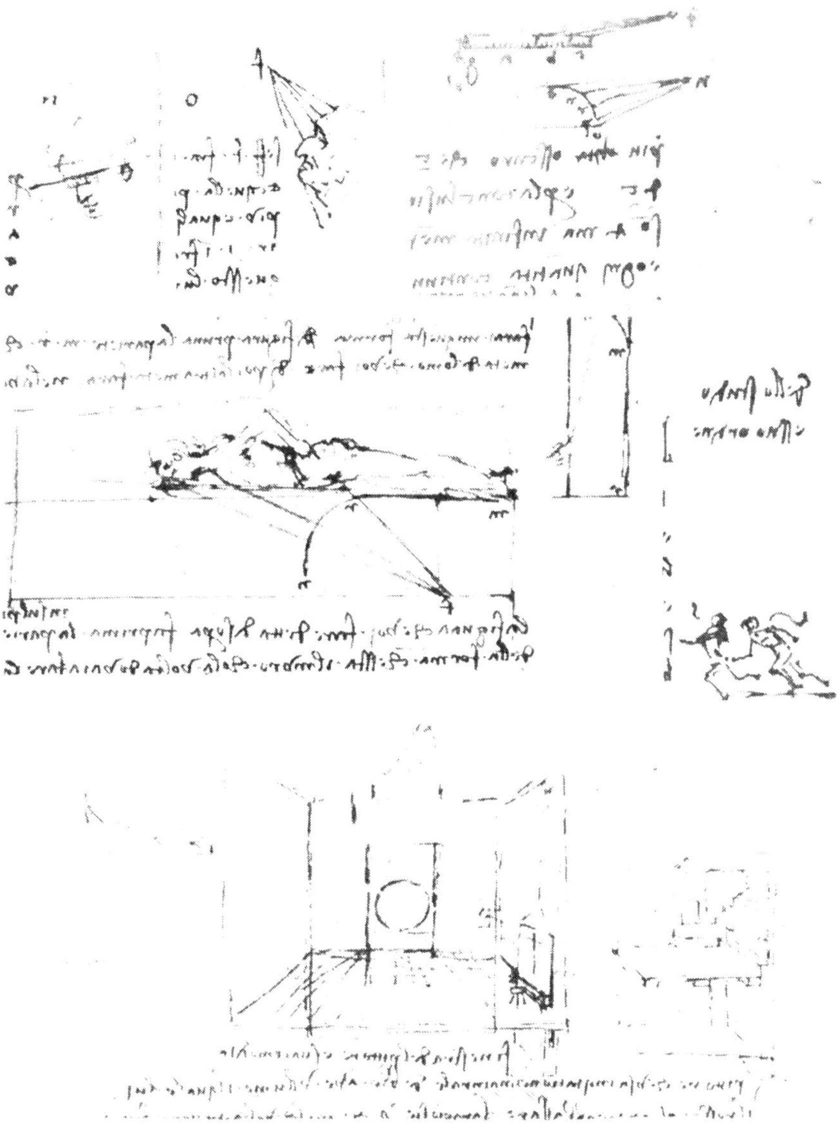

A 38b]

526

A FARE UNA FIGURA IN V̄ MURO DI 12 BRACCIA [2] CHÈ APPARISCA D'ALTEZZA DI 24 BRACCIA

[3] Se voli fare · una figura o altra cosa che apparisca d'altezza di 24 braccia [4] farai in questa forma · figura prima la pariete · *m r* colla [5] metà dell'omo che voi fare dipoi l'altra metà farai nella volta *m n* [6] la figura che voi fare detta di sopra,—fa prima la pariete in sul piā d'una sala [7] della forma che à il mvro colla volta dov'ài a fare la tua [8] figura, dipoi farai dirieto a essa pariete la figura disegniata ī pro[9]ffilo di che grādezza ti piace, e tira tutte le sue linie al pūto *f* [10] e nel modo ch'elle si tagliano sulla pariete *m n* così le figura [11] sul mvro che à similitudine colla pariete, e avrai tutte l'altezze e spor[12]ti della figura, e le larghezze over grossezze che si trovano nel mvro [13] diritto · *m* · *r* ·, faraile in propia forma, imperochè, nel fugire del mvro, [14] la figura diminvisce per se medesima, la figura che va nella volta[15]ti bisognia diminvirla, come se ella fussi diritta, la quale dimi[16]nvitione ti bisognia fare ī sù una sala bē piana e lì sarà [17] la figura che leverai dalla pariete *r n* con le sue vere grossezze [18] e bisogna ridiminuirla in sù una pariete di rilievo e fia bō modo.

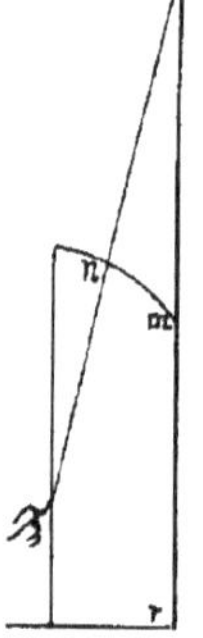

TO DRAW A FIGURE ON A WALL 12 BRACCIA HIGH WHICH SHALL LOOK 24 BRACCIA HIGH

If you wish to draw a figure or any other object to look 24 braccia high you must do it in this way First, on the surface *m r* draw half the man you wish to represent, then the other half, then put on the vault *m n* [the rest of] the figure spoken of above, first set out the vertical plane on the floor of a room of the same shape as the wall with the coved part on which you are to paint your figure Then, behind it, draw a figure set out in profile of whatever size you please, and draw lines from it to the point *f* and, as these lines cut *m n* on the vertical plane, so will the figure come on the wall, of which the vertical plane gives a likeness, and you will have all the [relative] heights and prominences of the figure And the breadth or thickness which are on the upright wall *m n* are to be drawn in their proper form, since, as the wall recedes the figure will be foreshortened by itself, but [that part of] the figure which goes into the cove you must foreshorten, as if it were standing upright, this diminution you must set out on a flat floor and there must stand the figure which is to be transferred from the vertical plane *r n* [17] in its real size and reduce it once more on a vertical plane, and this will be a good method [18]

526 1 affare ī figura 12 br 2 aparissca dalteza 3 fare ī figura chosa che aparischa 24 br 4 forma [di] figura chola 5 nela 6 pariete 'insul sala' 7 chessta cholo 8 laffigura 9 grādeza ettira pupūto f 10 sula. 11 assimilitudine cholla arai alteze esspor 12 largeze grosseze chessi 13 farai 14 le figura diminvite 15 chomesse 16 insuruna 17 dala chon le sue | "vere" grosseze 18 e ridiminuirle insuruna effia

526 See Pl XXXI 3 The second sketch, which in the plate is incomplete, is here reproduced and completed from the original to illustrate the text In the original the larger diagram is placed between lines 5 and 6.

1 2 C A 157[a], 463[a] has the similar heading *'del cresscere della figura'*, and the text begins *"Se voli fare 1 a figura grande* b c" but here it breaks off. The translation here given renders the meaning of the passage as I think it must be understood The MS. is perfectly legible and the construction of the sentence is simple and clear, difficulties can only arise from the very fullness of the meaning, particularly towards the end of the passage

17 *che leverai dalla pariete* r n The letters refer to the larger sketch, No 3 on Pl XXXI

18 Leonardo here says nothing as to how the image foreshortened by perspective and thus produced on the vertical plane is to be transferred to the wall, but from what is said in Nos 525 and 523 we may conclude that he was familiar with the process of casting the enlarged shadow of a squaring net on the surface of a wall to guide him in drawing the figure

Pariete di rilievo, "sur une paroi en relief" (RAVAISSON) *"Auf einer Schnittlinie zum Aufrichten"* (LUDWIG) The explanation of this puzzling expression must be sought in No. 545, lines 15—17

A. 42 a]

527.

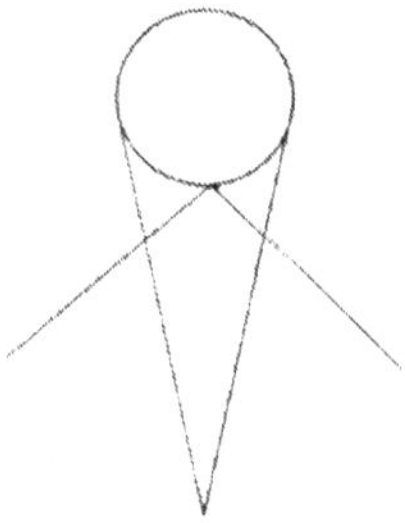

[2]Se uolessi · fare · vna figura di cuba dimostratione in v̄ [3]cantone di mvro ·, fa prima · la cosa i propia · forma e levala ïsulla pariete, [3]ch'essa somigli al cantone dove à essere figurato detto corpo.

If you would to draw a cube in an angle of a wall, first draw the object in its own proper shape and raise it onto a vertical plane until it resembles the angle in which the said object is to be represented.

Ash. I. 4 a]

528.

Perchè la pictura pare meglio [2]nello spechio · che fori?

Why are paintings seen more correctly in a mirror than out of it?

Ash. I. 11 a]

529.

Come lo spechio è 'l maestro de' pittori.

[2]Quãdo voi vedere ·, se la · tua · pittura · tutta ïsieme à conformità colla cosa [3]ritratta di naturale, abbi vno spechio · e favi dẽtro specchiare la cosa viua, e pa[4]ragona la cosa · spechiata · colla tua pittura ·, e cõsidera bene se 'l subietto [5]dell'una · e l'altra similitudine · à · cõformità ïsieme · e sopra tutto lo spechio; [6]lo spechio si de' pigliare · per suo · maestro, cioè · lo spechio · piano, ïpero · ch'ï sulla sua [7]superficie · le cose ãnno similitudine colla pittura ĩ molte parti; cioè tu vedi la [8]pittura fatta sopra a uno piano dimostrare cose che paiono rilevate, e lo spechio [9]sopra uno piano fa quel medesimo; · La pittura è vna sola superfitie e lo specchio [10]quel medesimo ·; La pittura è ïpalpabile ĩ quãto che quello che pare tõdo [11]e spiccato nõ si può circũdare colle mani,

How the mirror is the master [and guide] of painters.

When you want to see if your picture corresponds throughout with the objects you have drawn from nature, take a mirror and look in that at the reflection of the real things, and compare the reflected image with your picture, and consider whether the subject of the two images duly corresponds in both, particularly studying the mirror. You should take the mirror for your guide—that is to say a flat mirror—because on its surface the objects appear in many respects as in a painting. Thus you see, in a painting done on a flat surface, objects which appear in relief, and in the mirror—also a flat surface—they look the same. The picture has one plane surface and the same with the mirror. The picture is intangible, in so far as that which appears round and prominent

527. 1. fugura [chuba] di chuba. 2. chãtone , chosa . . ĩsu pariete.
528. 1. megli. 2. ch' fori.
529. 2. sella . . conformita cholla cossa. 3. abi . . effavi . . speciare. 4. chola. 5. ellaltra . . chõformita . . essopra. 6. maesstro . . ĩ parrechisuta. 7. anno . . chola . . imolte. 8. a ĩ piano . . chose che paiano. 9. sopra ĩ piano paiano fa. 11. esspi-

I understand the concluding lines of this passage as follows: If you draw the upper half a figure on a large sheet of paper laid out on the floor of a room (*sala bè piana*) to the same scale (*con le sue vere grossezze*) as the lower half, already drawn upon the wall (lines 10, 11) you must then reduce them on a '*pariete di rilievo*,' a curved vertical plane which serves as a model to reproduce the form of the vault.

e lo spechio fa il simile, [12] E se tu conosci che lo spechio per mezzo de liniamēti e ōbre e lumi ti fa parere [13] le cose dispiccate e avēdo tu fra i tua colori l'ombre e lumi piv potēti [14] che quelli dello spechio cierto, se li saprai bē comporre īsieme, la tua pitura [15] parrà ācora lei una cosa naturale vista ī vno grāde spechio

cannot be grasped in the hands, and it is the same with the mirror. And since you can see that the mirror, by means of outlines, shadows and lights, makes objects appear in relief, you, who have in your colours far stronger lights and shades than those in the mirror, can certainly, if you compose your picture well, make that also look like a natural scene reflected in a large mirror.

Ash. I 7b]

530.

Del givdicare la tua pittura

[2] Noi sappiamo chiaro · che li errori si conoscono piv in altrui opere che nelle sue, [3] e spesso riprēdendo li altrui piccoli errori ignorerai i tua grādi, et per [4] fugire · simile ignorāza fa che prima sii bono prospectiuo, dipoi abbi in[5] tera notitia delle misure dell' omo e d'altri animali e ācora bono archi[6] tetto cioè ī quāto s'apartiene alla forma delli edifiti e dell'altre co[7] se che sono sopra la terra, che sono īfinite forme, di quāte [8] piv avrai notitia piv fia laudabile la tua operatione, e in quella che tv non ài pratica [9] nō recusare il ritrarle di naturale —ma per tornare alla promessa di sopra [10] dico, che nel tuo dipīgiere che tu debi tenere uno spechio piano e spesso ri[11] guardarai dētro l'opera tua, la quale ui fia veduta per lo contrario e par[12] ratti di mano d'altro · maestro e lì givdicherai meglio l'errori che altri[13] mēti, È ancora bono spesso leuarsi e pigliar un poco d'altro sollaz[14] zo, perchè nel ritornare alle cose tu ài migliore ivditio, chè lo stare [15] saldo sul'opera ti fa forte īgannare, ancora è bono lo alontanarsi, [16] perchè l'opera pare minore e piv sī cōprende in vna occhiata e [17] meglio si conoscie le discordāti e sproportionate mēbra [18] e colori delle cose

Of judging your own pictures

We know very well that errors are better recognised in the works of others than in our own, and that often, while reproving little faults in others, you may ignore great ones in yourself. To avoid such ignorance, in the first place make yourself a master of perspective, then acquire perfect knowledge of the proportions of men and other animals, and also, study good architecture, that is so far as concerns the forms of buildings and other objects which are on the face of the earth, these forms are infinite, and the better you know them the more admirable will your work be. And in cases where you lack experience do not shrink from drawing them from nature. But, to carry out my promise above [in the title]—I say that when you paint you should have a flat mirror and often look at your work as reflected in it, when you will see it reversed, and it will appear to you like some other painter's work, so you will be better able to judge of its faults than in any other way. Again, it is well that you should often leave off work and take a little relaxation, because, when you come back to it you are a better judge, for sitting too close at work may greatly deceive you. Again, it is good to retire to a distance because the work looks smaller and your eye takes in more of it at a glance and sees more easily the discords or disproportion in the limbs and colours of the objects.

chato po circhūdare cholle ello 12 Esse tu mezo ellumi 13 chose dispichate cholori 14 delo chom pore 15 pari lei ī cosa

530 1 givdichare 2 sapiamo chelli chonioscano 3 piccioli 4 sia 5 āchora 6 ali cho | chessono terachessono 8 arai laldabile chettv práticha 9 rechusare allo. 10 dicho chettu tenere ī spechio esspesso 11 guardarai chontrario e parr 12 elli lerori 13 anchora se bono speso pocho sola 14. ale chose tuuai chello 15 anchora īganare 16 chōplende 17 chonoscie le dischordāti 18 cholori

Ash. I. 17a]

531.

Del modo del bene ĩparare a mẽte.

On the management of works (531. 532).

[2]Quãdo tu vorrai · sapere vna · cosa studiata bene a mẽte · tieni questo modo, cioè [3]quãdo · tu ài disegnato vna · cosa medesima tãte volte, che te la · paia avere a mẽte, [4]pruova · a farla · sãza · lo esẽpio · e abbi lucidato sopra vno uetro sottile e pia[5]no · lo esẽplo · tuo e porrai lo · sopra la cosa ·, che ài fatta sãza [6]lo esẽplo, e nota bene dove il lucido non si scõtra col · disegnio tuo e dove truo[7]vi auere errato · li tieni a mẽte di non errare piv, ãzi ritorna allo esẽplo a ritra[8]re tãte volte quella · parte errata che tu l'abbi bene nella imaginatiua, e se [9]per lucidare una cosa tu nõ potessi avere vetro piano, tolli una carta sottilissima [10]di capretto e bene vnta e poi secca, E quãdo l'avrai adoperata a uno disegnio, [11]potrai colla spugnia · cancellarla e fare il secondo.

Of a method of learning well by heart.

When you want to know a thing you have studied in your memory proceed in this way: When you have drawn the same thing so many times that you think you know it by heart, test it by drawing it without the model; but have the model traced on flat thin glass and lay this on the drawing you have made without the model, and note carefully where the tracing does not coincide with your drawing, and where you find you have gone wrong; and bear in mind not to repeat the same mistakes. Then return to the model, and draw the part in which you were wrong again and again till you have it well in your mind. If you have no flat glass for tracing on, take some very thin kidts-kin parchment, well oiled and dried. And when you have used it for one drawing you can wash it clean with a sponge and make a second.

Ash. I. 5a]

532.

Come il pittore debbe esser vago d'udire [2]nel fare dell'opera sua gvditio d'ogni omo.

[3]Ciertamẽ non è · de recusare ·, in mẽtre che l'omo dipignie, il gvditio di ciascuno, [4]iperochè noi conosciamo · che l'omo bẽchè nõ sia · pittore ·, avrà notitia della forma [5]dell' altr' omo e bẽ gvdicherà s'egli è gobbo o à una spalla alta o bassa o s'elli á grã bocca [6]o naso ed altri mãcamẽti; e se noi conosciamo li omini potere con uerità gvdica[7]re l'opere della natura ·, quãto magiormẽte ci conuerrà confessare questi potere [8]gvdicare · li nostri errori, chè sai quãto l'omo s'ingãna nell' opere sua; E se non lo [9]conosci · in te, consideralo in altrui e farai profitto delli altrui [10]errori ·, sicchè sia vago cõ patiẽtia · vdire le altrui · openioni e cõ[11]sidera bene e pẽsa bene · se 'l biasimatore à cagione o no di biasimarti: E se troui di si, [12]raccõcia · e se troui di no · fa la vista no l'avere iteso, o tu li mostra · per ragione — s'elli è [13]omo che tu stimi — la ragione come lui s'inganna.

That a painter ought to be curious to hear the opinions of every one on his work.

Certainly while a man is painting he ought not to shrink from hearing every opinion. For we know very well that a man, though he may not be a painter, is familiar with the forms of other men and very capable of judging whether they are hump backed, or have one shoulder higher or lower than the other, or too big a mouth or nose, and other defects; and, as we know that men are competent to judge of the works of nature, how much more ought we to admit that they can judge of our errors; since you know how much a man may be deceived in his own work. And if you are not conscious of this in yourself study it in others and profit by their faults. Therefore be curious to hear with patience the opinions of others, consider and weigh well whether those who find fault have ground or not for blame, and, if so amend; but, if not make as though you had not heard, or if he should be a man you esteem show him by argument the cause of his mistake.

531. 2. chosa. 3. disegniato ī chosa. 4. affarla . . abi . . sopra ī uetro. 5. poraio. 6. chel. 7. erato . . erare. 8. erata chettu labi . . esse. 9. lucidare ī cosa . . tolli ī carta. 10. secha . . larai a ī disegnio. 10. chāncellarla effare il sechondo.
532. 1. dulcire. 3. ederechusare . . chellomo . . gīvditio di ciaschuno. 4. chonosciamo . . chellomo . . avera. 5. a ī spalla . . osselli . . bocha. 6. machamēti . . ali . . chon . . gīvdicha. 7. chonuera chonfessare. 8. chessai . . Esse nollo. 9. chonsiderato . . effarai. 10. chō . . vdire li . . chō. 11. biasimatore a chagione Esse. 12. rachōcia . esse . . otu. 13. chettu

Ash I 21a]

533

COME NELLE COSE PICCOLE NŌ S'INTĒDE LI ERRORI COME NELLE GRĀDI

[2]Nelle cose di minvta forma nō si può conprendere la qualità del suo errore, [3]come delle grandi, e la ragione si è che, se questa cosa piccola fia fatta a similitudine [4]d'un omo o d'altro animale, le sue parti per la immensa diminvtione nō possono essere ricercate [5]con quello debito fine dal suo operatore che si conuerebbe, ōde nō rimane finita, [6]non essendo finita nō puoi conprēdere i suoi · errori E-senplo Riguarderai da lontano [7]vno omo per ispatio di 300 braccia, e con diligēza gıvdicherai se quello è bello [8]o brutto, o s'eli è mostruoso o di comvne qualità vedrai che con sōmo tuo sforzo nō ti [9]potrai persuadere a dare gıvditio, e la ragione si è che per la sopra detta · distātia questo uomo [10]diminviscie tāto, che nō si può comprēdere le qualità delle particule, ¶e se voli ben vede[11]re detta diminvitione dell'omo sopradetto pōnti vno dito presso. all' ochio vno palmo [12]e tanto alza e abbassa detto dito che la sua superiore stremità termini sotto i piedi della figura [13]che tu riguardi e vedrai · apparire vna incredibile diminuitione, e per questo spesse [14]volte si dubita la forma dell'amico da lontano

HOW IN SMALL OBJECTS ERRORS ARE LESS EVIDENT THAN IN LARGE ONES

On the limitations of painting (533–535)

In objects of minute size the extent of error is not so perceptible as in large ones, and the reason is that if this small object is a representation of a man or of some other animal, from the immense diminution the details cannot be worked out by the artist with the finish that is requisite Hence it is not actually complete, and, not being complete, its faults cannot be determined For instance Look at a man at a distance of 300 braccia and judge attentively whether he be handsome or ugly, or very remarkable or of ordinary appearance You will find that with the utmost effort you cannot persuade yourself to decide And the reason is that at such a distance the man is so much diminished that the character of the details cannot be determined And if you wish to see how much this man is diminished [by distance] hold one of your fingers at a span's distance from your eye, and raise or lower it till the top joint touches the feet of the figure you are looking at, and you will see an incredible reduction For this reason we often doubt as to the person of a friend at a distance

Ash I 25b]

534

PERCHÈ LA PITTURA NŌ PUÒ MAI PARERE [2]SPICCATA COME LE COSE NATURALI

[3]Li pittori spesse volte cadono in disperatione del loro imitare il naturale, [4]vedēdo le loro pitture non avere quel rilievo e quella vivacità che ànno le [5]cose vedute nello spechio, allegādo loro avere colori che per chiarezza [6]o per iscurità avanzano di gran lūga la qualità de'lumi e ōbre della cosa vista [7]nello spechio, accusādo in questo caso la loro igniorāza e nō la ragione ·, perchè [8]nō la conoscono, Impossibile è che la cosa pīta apparisca di tale rilievo [9]che s'assomigli alle cose dello spechio bēchè l'una e l'altra sia in sù

WHY A PAINTING CAN NEVER APPEAR DETACHED AS NATURAL OBJECTS DO

Painters often fall into despair of imitating nature when they see their pictures fail in that relief and vividness which objects have that are seen in a mirror, while they allege that they have colours which for brightness or depth far exceed the strength of light and shade in the reflections in the mirror, thus displaying their own ignorance rather than the real cause, because they do not know it It is impossible that painted objects should appear in such relief as to resemble those reflected in the mirror, although both are seen on a flat surface, unless they are seen

533 1 chome chose pichole erori chome 2 chose chonplendere la qualita [dello errore] del 3 chome ella chesse equesta chosa pichola assimilitudine 4 domo o imensa posono ricierche 5 chon chonucrebbe 6 poi chonprēdere 7 300 br e chon dilegiēza [riguarderai] gıvdicherai secquello ebbello 8 esseli e mosstruoso chomvne vederai chon somo tuo sforto 9 ella decta 10 diminvissce chomprēdere partichule 11 vno [span] palmo 12 ettanto chella dela 13 chettu vederai vno 14 amicho dallontano

534 1 po 2 sichata chome le chose 3 chagiano inaturale 4 ecquella anno 5 chose cholori chiareza 6 chosa 7 acusando chaso 8 chonoschano 8 Inpossibile chella chosa apparischa 9 sasomigli chose benchelluna

vna · superfitie, [10]saluo se fia vista · cõ ũ solo · ochio · e la ragiõ si è, ‡ 2 ‡ ochi che vedono l'una cosa [11]dopo l'altra come · *a* · *b* · che vede *n* · *m* · · *m* · nõ può occupare · interamẽte · *n* · perchè la [12]basa delle linie visuali è si larga · che vede · il corpo secondo dopo · il primo ·, Ma se chiv[13]di vn ochio come · *s* · il corpo *f* occuperà *r* perchè la linia visuale nascie in un solo [14]pũto · e fa basa nel primo corpo, dõde il secondo di pari grãdezza mai fia visto.

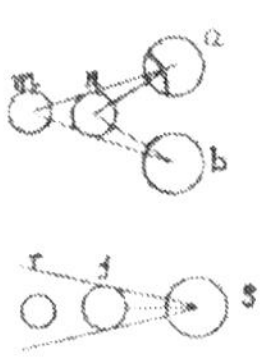

with only one eye; and the reason is that two eyes see one object behind another as *a* and *b* see *m* and *n*. *m* cannot exactly occupy [the space of] *n* because the base of the visual lines is so broad that the second body is seen beyond the first. But if you close one eye, as at *s* the body *f* will conceal *r*, because the line of sight proceeds from a single point and makes its base in the first body, whence the second, of the same size, can never be seen.

Ash. I. 16*b*]

535.

PERCHÈ DI 2 COSE DI PARI GRÃDEZZA [2]PARRÀ MAGGIORE LA DIPĨTA CHE QUELLA DI RILIEVO.

[3]Questa · ragione · nõ fia di facile dimostratione · come molte altre, ma pure [4]m'ĩgiegnierò di sadisfare, se nõ in tutto, in qualche parte; la prospettiva dimi[5]nvita · ci dimostra per ragione ·, che le cose quãto · piv alõtanono dal' ochio [6]piv diminviscono ·, e queste ragioni bẽ sono cõferme dalla · esperiẽza; [7]adũque · le linie visuali che si tronano ĩfra l'obietto · e l'occhio ·, quãdo s'astẽdono [8]alla superfitie della · pittura ·, tutte si tagliano · a uno medesimo termine; E le [9]linie che si truovano ĩfra l'ochio · e la scoltura · sono di uari termini e lũ[10]ghezze: quella linia ch'è piv · lũga · s'astẽde sopra uno mẽbro piv · lõtano che li [11]altri e però quel mẽbro pare minore ·, essẽdovi molte linie più lũghe che [12]l'altre, e per cagione che le molte particule piv lõtane l'una che l'altra essẽ[13]do piv lontane, cõuiene che apparischino minori, apparẽdo minori, vẽgo[14]no a fare per loro diminvire minore tutta la sõma dello obietto; E que[15]sto nõ accadẽdo nella pittura per le linie terminate a vna medesima [16]distãtia cõuiene che sieno sãza

WHY OF TWO OBJECTS OF EQUAL SIZE A PAINTED ONE WILL LOOK LARGER THAN A SOLID ONE.

The reason of this is not so easy to demonstrate as many others. Still I will endeavour to accomplish it, if not wholly, at any rate in part. The perspective of diminution demonstrates by reason, that objects diminish in proportion as they are farther from the eye, and this reasoning is confirmed by experience. Hence, the lines of sight that extend between the object and the eye, when they are directed to the surface of a painting are all intersected at uniform limits, while those lines which are directed towards a piece of sculpture are intersected at various limits and are of various lengths. The lines which are longest extend to a more remote limb than the others and therefore that limb looks smaller. As there are numerous lines each longer than the others— since there are numerous parts, each more remote than the others and these, being farther off, necessarily appear smaller, and by appearing smaller it follows that their diminution makes the whole mass of the object look smaller. But this does not occur in painting; since the lines of sight all end at

sẽsibra sia inmovra. 10. sefia . . chõ . vegano luna chosa. 11. chome . . po . ochupare. 12. nssi . . chorpo sechondo. 13. ochupera . . nasmenvosono. 14. effa . . neprimo chorpo . . sechonda . . grãdeza.

535. perche ‖ duej. 2. grãdeza 2. para . . quela. 5. chelle. 6. diminvischono . eequeste ragione . . cõferme dalla dalla. 7. lini . . chessi . . sastẽdano. 8. ala . . a ĩ medesimo . . Elle. 9. chessi . . ella. 10. geze . quela . . ssastẽde sopra ĩ mebro. 11. quẽmẽbro . . lũga. 12. chagione che ne. 13. apariscino . vẽga. 14. aftare . . soma . . Eeque. 15. achadẽdo

534. This passage contains the solution of the problem proposed in No. 29, lines 10—14. Leonardo was evidently familiar with the law of optics on which the construction of the stereoscope depends. Compare E. VON BRÜCKE, *Bruchstücke aus der Theorie der bildenden Künste*, pg. 69: "*Schon Leonardo da Vinci wusste, dass ein noch so gut gemaltes Bild nie den vollen Eindruck der Körperlichkeit geben kann, wie ihn die Natur selbst giebt. Er erklärt dies auch in Kap. LIII und Kap. CCCXLI* (ed. DU FRESNE) *des* 'Trattato' *in sachgemässer Weise aus dem Sehen mit beiden Augen.*"

Chap. 53 of DU FRESNE's edition corresponds to No. 534 of this work.

diminvitione, adūque le particule [17] nō diminvite nō diminviscono la sōma dello obbietto, e per questo nō [18] diminuiscie la pittura come la scoltura

the same distance there can be no diminution, hence the parts not being diminished the whole object is undiminished, and for this reason painting does not diminish, as a piece of sculpture does

Ash I 4b]

536

COME SI DEBBE PORRE ALTO IL PŪTO

[2] Il pūto debbe essere alto all'altezza dell'occhio d'uno homo comvnale, [3] e l'ultimo della pianura che cōfina col cielo debbe essere fatto all' [4] altezza d'esso termine della terra col cielo, saluo che le [5] mōtagnie che sono libere

HOW HIGH THE POINT OF SIGHT SHOULD BE PLACED

On the choice of a position (536 537)

The point of sight must be at the level of the eye of an ordinary man, and the farthest limit of the plain where it touches the sky must be placed at the level of that line where the earth and sky meet, excepting mountains, which are independent of it

Ash I 25b]

537

DEL MODO DI RITRARE FIGURE PER ISTORIE

[2] Senpre il pittore debbe cōsiderare in nella pariete la quale à a istoriare [3] l'altezza del sito doue vuole collocare le sue figure, e ciò che lui ri[4]trae di naturale a detto proposito, e stare tāto coll'occhio piv basso che la cosa che lui [5] ritrae, quāto detta cosa sia messa in opera piv alta che l'ochio del riguar[6]dante, altremēte l'opera fia reprovabile

OF THE WAY TO DRAW FIGURES FOR HISTORICAL PICTURES

The painter must always study on the wall on which he is to picture a story the height of the position where he wishes to arrange his figures, and when drawing his studies for them from nature he must place himself with his eye as much below the object he is drawing as, in the picture, it will have to be above the eye of the spectator Otherwise the work will look wrong

Ash I 12b]

538

DEL PORRE UNA FIGURA PRIMA NELLA STORIA

[2] La prima figura in nela storia farai tāto minore che 'l naturale, quante braccia [3] tu la figuri lontana dalla prima linia, e poi poni l'altre a cōparatione di quella colla regola di sopra

OF PLACING A FIGURE IN THE FOREGROUND OF A HISTORICAL PICTURE

The apparent size of figures in a picture (538 539)

You must make the foremost figure in the picture less than the size of nature in proportion to the number of braccia at which you place it from the front line, and make the others in proportion by the above rule

nela 17 diminviscano la soma obbieto

536 2 alteza 3 ellultimo chol 4 tera chol chelle 5 chessono

537 2 chōsiderare inella 3 lalteza chollochare eccio chellui 4 istare chollochio chella chosa chellui 5 chosa chellochio

538 1 pore ī figura 2 inella quante br. 3 dala. diquc 4 cola

Tr. 71.

539.

PROSPETTIVA.

[2]Domãdasi · a te pittore · perchè · le figure · da te fatte · [3]in minvta forma · per dimostratione di prospettiva · nõ paiano in [4]pari · dimostratione · di distãtia · grãdi · quãto · le naturali leuate di pari [5]grãdezza alle dipĩte · sopra · la pariete.

[6]E perchè · le cose apparẽti in piccola lontanità · in pari distãtia [7]apparano maggiori che 'l naturale.

PERSPECTIVE.

You are asked, O Painter, why the figures you draw on a small scale according to the laws of perspective do not appear—notwithstanding the demonstration of distance—as large as real ones—their height being the same as in those painted on the wall.

And why [painted] objects seen at a small distance appear larger than the real ones?

Ash. I. 30 b]

540.

The right position of the artist, when painting, and of the spectator (540—547).

DEL RITRARRE.

[2]Quãdo ãi · a ritrarre di [3]naturale · sta · lõtano 3 [4]volte · la grãdezza della [5]cosa che tu ritrai

OF PAINTING.

When you draw from nature stand at a distance of 3 times the height of the object you wish to draw.

Ash. I. 23 b]

541.

DEL RITRARRE DI RILIEVO.

[2]Quello che ritrae · di rilieuo si debbe accõciare in modo · tale · che l' ochio · della figura [3]ritratta · sia · al pari dell'ochio di quello · che ritrae, e questo · si farà a vna testa, [4]la quale · avessi · a ritrarre · di naturale ·, perchè vniversalmẽte · le figure ovvero [5]persone · che scõtri · per le · strade · tutti · ãnno i loro occhi all'altezza · de' tua, [6]e se li facessi · piv alti o piv · bassi · vedresti a · dissimigliare il tuo ritratto.

OF DRAWING FROM RELIEF.

In drawing from the round the draughtsman should so place himself that the eye of the figure he is drawing is on a level with his own. This should be done with any head he may have to represent from nature because, without exception, the figures or persons you meet in the streets have their eyes on the same level as your own; and if you place them higher or lower you will see that your drawing will not be true.

Ash. I. 16 b]

542.

PERCHÈ I CAPITOLI DELLE FIGURE [2]L'UNO SOPRA L'ALTRO È OPERA · DA FUGGIRE.

[3]Questo universale vso, il quale si fa per pittori in nelle faccie delle [4]cappelle è molto da essere ragionevolmẽte biasimato, iperocchè [5]fãno l'una storia ĩ v̄ piano col suo paese · e edifiti, poi s'alzano uno altro [6]grado e fanno una storia e variano il pũto dal primo, e poi la terza [7]e la quarta · in modo, ch'una facciata si uede fatta cõ 4

WHY GROUPS OF FIGURES ONE ABOVE ANOTHER ARE TO BE AVOIDED.

The universal practice which painters adopt on the walls of chapels is greatly and reasonably to be condemned. Inasmuch as they represent one historical subject on one level with a landscape and buildings, and then go up a step and paint another, varying the point [of sight], and then a third and a fourth, in such a way as that on one wall there are 4 points of sight, which is supreme folly in such painters. We know that the

539. 2. atte . . catte fatte [nõ parano in] 3. [spi] inmuta 4. pari. 5. grãdeza. 6. chose . . picula. 7. magiore.
540. 1. ritrare. 2. ai aritrare. 4. grãdeza dela. 5. chosa chetu.
541. 2. achõciare . imodo . . chello chio. 3. equesto. 5. chessachõtri . ano . . alteza. 6. esse . . veresti a disimigliare.
542. 1. [come si di] perche i chapitoli. 3. pe . . inete. 4. chappelle. 5. chol . . po salzano ĩ altro. 6. fanno ĩ storia. 7. ella

punti, [8]la quale è soma stoltitia di simili maestri, noi sappiamo che 'l [9]punto è posto al'ochio del riguardatore della storia, e se tu [10]volessi dire in che modo ò a fare la uita d'uno santo cōpartita [11]in molte storie in vna medesima facia, a questa parte ti rispō-[12]do che tu debi porre il primo piano col pūto all' altez[13]za dell' ochio de riguardatori d'essa storia, e īsù detto piano [14]figura la prima storia grāde [15]e poi, diminvēdo di mano ī ma[16]no le figure e casamēti īsù diuersi colli e pianvre, farai [17]tutto il fornimēto d'essa storia, e 'l resto della faccia ī nella sua [18]altezza farai albori grādi a cōparatione delle figure o āgie[19]li, se fossino al proposito della storia, ovvero vccelli o nvuoli o simi[20]li cose, altrimēti nō te ne īpacciare, ch'ogni tua opera fia falsa

point of sight is opposite the eye of the spectator of the scene, and if you would [have me] tell you how to represent the life of a saint divided into several pictures on one and the same wall, I answer that you must set out the foreground with its point of sight on a level with the eye of the spectator of the scene, and upon this plane represent the more important part of the story large and then, diminishing by degrees the figures, and the buildings on various hills and open spaces, you can represent all the events of the history And on the remainder of the wall up to the top put trees, large as compared with the figures, or angels if they are appropriate to the story, or birds or clouds or similar objects, otherwise do not trouble yourself with it for your whole work will be wrong

A 40*b*]

543

QUELLA COSA FATTA IN PROSPETTIVA AVRÀ [2]MIGLIORE EUIDĒTIA LA QUALE FIA VEDUTA [3]DA LOCO DOV'È FATTA LA SUA VEDUTA

[4]Se vorrai figurare una cosa da presso che faccia l'effetto che fanno le cose naturali, [5]inpossibile fia che la tua prospettiua non apparisca falsa cō tutte [6]le bugiarde dimostrationi e discordāti proportioni che si può ima[7]ginare in vna trista opera, se il riguardatore · d'essa prospettiva nō [8]si truova col suo vedere alla propia distātia e altezza e dirittura de[9]l'ochio over pūto che situasti al fare d'essa prospettiva Onde bisognie[10]rebbe fare una finestra della grādezza del tuo volto o veramēte uno [11]buso, dōde tu riguardassi detta opera, e se così farai sanza dubio nessu[12]no l'opera tua ·, essendo bene accōpagniata d'ōbra e di lumi, farà l'effe[13]tto che fa il naturale, e nō ti potrai fare credere che esse cose sieno [14]dipīte, altremēti nō te ne inpacciare, se già tu nō facciessi la tua ve[15]duta al meno

A PICTURE OF OBJECTS IN PERSPECTIVE WILL LOOK MORE LIFELIKE WHEN SEEN FROM THE POINT FROM WHICH THE OBJECTS WERE DRAWN

If you want to represent an object near to you which is to have the effect of nature, it is impossible that your perspective should not look wrong, with every false relation and disagreement of proportion that can be imagined in a wretched work, unless the spectator, when he looks at it, has his eye at the very distance and height and direction where the eye or the point of sight was placed in doing this perspective Hence it would be necessary to make a window, or rather a hole, of the size of your face through which you can look at the work, and if you do this, beyond all doubt your work, if it is correct as to light and shade, will have the effect of nature, nay you will hardly persuade yourself that those objects are painted, otherwise do not trouble yourself about it, unless indeed you make your view

imodo fatto 8 sapiano 9 essettu 10 dire che āffare duno s̄cō cōpartita 11 imolte storie nvna acquesta 12 chettu porr altu 16 chasamēti 17 dela facia 18 alteza 19 vccello ossimi 20. lle cose īpaciare
543 1 [sē] quella chosa prosspettiva ara 3 locho 4 vorai ī chosa 4 cheffacia cheffa le chose 5 chella prosspettiua aparischa chō 6 dimostratione e disschordāte proportine chessi po 7 prosspettiva 8 chol disstātia e alteza 9 pūto situasti prosspettiva 10 rebe farc ī finestra grādeza veramēte ī 11 esse chosi 12 achōpagniata

543 In the original there is a wide space between lines 3 and 4 in which we find two sketches not belonging to the text It is unnecessary to give prominence to the points in which my reading differs from that of M RAVAISSON or to justify myself, since they are all of secondary importance and can also be immediately verified from the photograph facsimile in his edition

20 volte · lontana, quãto · è · la maggiore larghezza o al[16]tezza · della · cosa · che figuri, e questa · sadisfarà a ogni riguardatore [17]situato · in ogni · cõtraposta · parte · a detta opera.

[18]Se voli · vedere · la pruova · con breuità ·, abbi · uno · pezzo d'asta a similitudine [19]d'una · colonnetta piccola, che sia · alta · otto · grossezze come la colonna [20]sãza basa o capitello ·, dipoi · cõpartisci i sù ũ mvro piano 40 spa[21]ti equali, i quali sieno cõformi ali spati, e sarebbero ĩfra 40 colonne [22]simili alla tua piccola colonna, poi fia stabilita [23]a riscõtro · del mezzo d'essi spati 4 braccia lõtana [24]dal mvro una sottile banda di ferro che abbi nel mezzo · uno piccolo buso rotõdo, [25]della grãdezza d'una grossa · perla, e a questo buso cõgivgni uno lume [26]che tocchi, poi va ponẽdo la tua colonna super ciascũ segnio del muro e se[27]gnia l'õbre, poni la õbra e riguardala pel detto baso del ferro.

at least 20 times as far off as the greatest width or height of the objects represented, and this will satisfy any spectator placed anywhere opposite to the picture.

If you want the proof briefly shown, take a piece of wood in the form of a little column, eight times as high as it is thick, like a column without any plinth or capital; then mark off on a flat wall 40 equal spaces, equal to its width so that between them they make 40 columns resembling your little column; you then must fix, opposite the centre space, and at 4 braccia from the wall, a thin strip of iron with a small round hole in the middle about as large as a big pearl. Close to this hole place a light touching it. Then place your column against each mark on the wall and draw the outline of its shadow; afterwards shade it and look through the hole in the iron plate.

A. 41a]

544.

[2]La cosa · diminvita · debe essere · riguardata a quella medesima [3]distantia · e altezza e dirittura ·, che ponesti · il pũto · del tuo ochio, altremẽti [4]la sciẽtia · non avrà · bono · effetto.

[5]E se nõ uoi o nõ puoi vsare · simile · ragione · per la cagione della pariete [6]dove dipigni, ch'è a essere veduta · da diuerse · persone ·, bisognierebbe diuersi pũti [7]õde sarebbe discordãte · e falsa: põti lõtano · il meno · 10 · volte · la grãdezza della cosa.

¶[8]Il minore · errore · che possi · fare · in questo · caso · siè · che tu · põga · tutte [9]le prime · cose · in propia · forma ·, e in qualũque · parte ti porrai ·, le cose [10]vedute · diminvirãno · per se · medesime, saluo · li spati che si trovano [11]infra corpi · fieno · sanza · ragione ·, imperochè se ti porrai nel mezzo [12]d'una dirittura e riguarderai · molte colonne · collocate sù per · una linia, [13]vedrai · infra pochi intervalli · d'esse colonne le colonne toccarsi, e dopo [14]il toccarsi occuparsi l'una · l'altra in modo tale, che l'ultima colonna [15]apparirà · poco · fori · della · penvltima: adũque l'intervali che si tro[16]vano · infra le coloñe ·

A diminished object should be seen from the same distance, height and direction as the point of sight of your eye, or else your knowledge will produce no good effect.

And if you will not, or cannot, act on this principle—because as the plane on which you paint is to be seen by several persons you would need several points of sight which would make it look discordant and wrong—place yourself at a distance of at least 10 times the size of the objects.

The lesser fault you can fall into then, will be that of representing all the objects in the foreground of their proper size, and on whichever side you are standing the objects thus seen will diminish themselves while the spaces between them will have no definite ratio. For, if you place yourself in the middle of a straight row [of objects], and look at several columns arranged in a line you will see, beyond a few columns separated by intervals, that the columns touch; and beyond where they touch they cover each other, till the last column projects but very little beyond the last but one. Thus the spaces between the

13. cheffa . . chose. 14. faciessi. 15. magiore largeza. 16. tera . della . chossa . cheffiguri ecquesta . sadisffara. 18. chon . . abi . i . pezo dasste assimilitudine. 19. cholonetta pichola chessia alto . . grossez chome la cholona. 20. chapitelo . . chõparusci Isunũ. 21. chõformi . . farebono . . colone. 22. ala . . pichola cholona . . stabilito [^{24} br. lõtano^{24} ĩ tola di fero sottile]. 23. [la quale aci ĩ buso i] arischõtro . del mezo . . 4 br. lõtano. 24. mvro ĩ sottile di fero che abi nel mezo . ĩ pichola . . rotõdo. 25. dela grãdeza . . acquesto . . cõgivgni ĩ lume. 26. tochi . . colona . . esse. 27. pola . . riguardalo.

544. 1. ella. 2. chosa . . acquella. 3. altezza. 4. lassciẽtia . . ara. 5. Esse . . poi . . chagione dela. 6. diuersi . . bisognierebe. 7. sarebe discordãte effalsa . . grãdeza dela. 8. erore . . chesso . . chettu. 9. chose . . porai . . chose. 10. lispati chessi. 11. chorpi . . inperochessetti porai mezzo. 12. cholone . cholochate. 13. vedrai cholone le cholone tocharsi. 14. il tocharsi ochuparsi . . imodo cholona. 15. aparira . pocho . . chessi. 16. cholõne . si perdano intera . mẽte Esse . . dela

si perdono · interamēte; E se il tuo modo della [17]prospettiva fia · bono ·, farà · il medesimo · effetto ·, il quale effetto accade [18]nello · stare · presso alla · linia · dove si posano le coloñe, e questo modo [19]fia sanza gratia, se la cosa figurata . nō fia veduta da uno piccolo buco [20]nel mezzo del quale · sia collocato · il tuo · pūto · del uedere ·, e se cosi [21]farai ·, l'opera tua sarà perfetta e ingannerà i veditori e ueranno le [22]coloñe figurate nella forma qui disotto · figurate.

columns are by degrees entirely lost. So, if your method of perspective is good, it will produce the same effect; this effect results from standing near the line in which the columns are placed. This method is not satisfactory unless the objects seen are viewed from a small hole, in the middle of which is your point of sight; but if you proceed thus your work will be perfect and will deceive the beholder, who will see the columns as they are here figured.

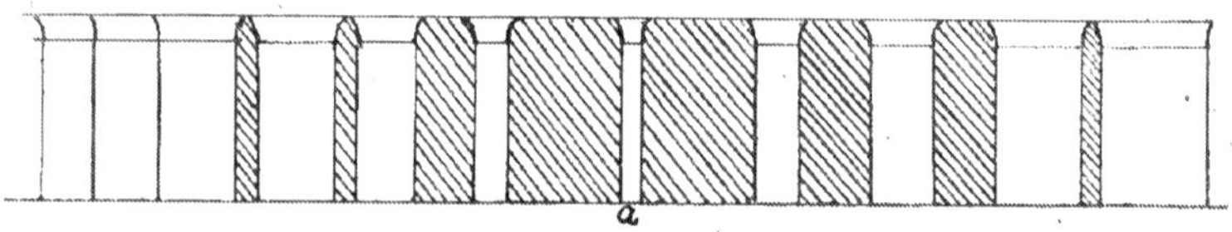

[23]A queste l'ochio è nel mezzo nel pūto · *a* · ed è presso · alle colonne. ¶

Here the eye is in the middle, at the point *a* and near to the columns.

A. 41 *b*]

545.

Se tu nō puoi fare che li omini, che riguardano · la tua opera, [2]stieno · in vn solo · pūto · tirati indirieto · col ochio, quādo figuri [3]la tua opera · al meno . 20 volte la maggiore altezza · o larghezza · della tua · opera, [4]e questa · farà nel mutare · l'ochio del riguardatore si poca varietà [5]che apena · si cōprenderà, e fia · assai laudabile;

If you cannot arrange that those who look at your work should stand at one particular point, when constructing your work, stand back until your eye is at least 20 times as far off as the greatest height and width of your work. This will make so little difference when the eye of the spectator moves, that it will be hardly appreciable, and it will look very good.

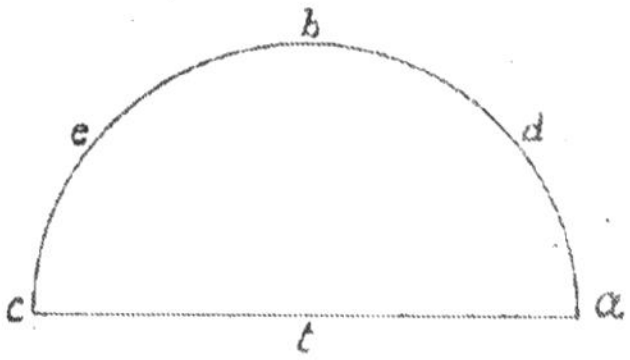

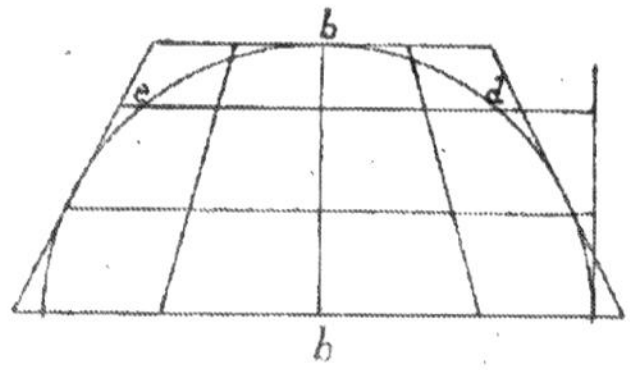

[6]Se 'l punto · sarà · in · *t* · farai · tu le figure poste sul circulo · *d* · *b* · *e* d'una [7]medesima ·

If the point of sight is at *t* you would make the figures on the circle *d b e* all

17. prosspettiva . . achada. 18. nelo . . cholōne ecquesto. 19. chosa . . da ī picholo ochío. 20. mezo . . cholochato . . esse chosi . . inganera. 22. cholōne . . nela. 23. acqueste . . mezo . . cholonne ⁊.
545. 1. ⁊ settu . . poi fare [questo . vedere]. 2. stieno nvn . . chol. 3. il meno magiore alteza olargeza. 4. ecquesta . . mvntare . . pocha. 5. chōplendera effia . . laldabile. 6. circhulo. 7. grādeza . . ciasschuna. 8. vederai. 9. chōplen de cha

544. The diagram which stands above this chapter in the original with the note belonging to it: "a b è *la ripruova* (*a b* is the proof) has obviously no connection with the text. The second sketch alone is reproduced and stands in the original between lines 22 and 23.

grãdezza ·, essendo · ciasscuna · per esso · al pũto · *t* · a vn medesimo modo; [8]poni mẽte · alla figura · disotto · e vedrai · di no, e perchè la farò minore in *b* che ĩ · *d* · *c*.

[9]Chiaro · si cõprende che, collocãdo · 2 cose infra loro · equali, che [10]quella ch'è situata nel terzo · braccio parrà minore che quella ch'è posta [11]nel secondo · braccio; questa cosa è piv disputativa · che da vsarla ·, perchè sei presso.

[12]Tutte le prime cose ·, grãdi o piccole ch' essi sieno, falle in propia forma [13]e se le vedrai di lontano faranno la lor debita dimostratione ·, e se le ved[14]rai · dapresso diminvirano · per loro medesime.

[15]Fa che senpre · la tua pariete ·, sulla quale tu diminvisci le cose [16]vedute, sia fatta della medesima · forma · che il mvro dov'ài [17]a figurare · la medesima · opera.

of one size, as each of them bears the same relation to the point *t*. But consider the diagram given below and you will see that this is wrong, and why I shall make *b* smaller than *d c* [8].

It is easy to understand that if 2 objects equal to each other are placed side by side the one at 3 braccia distance looks smaller than that placed at 2 braccia. This however is rather theoretical than for practice, because you stand close by [11].

All the objects in the foreground, whether large or small, are to be drawn of their proper size, and if you see them from a distance they will appear just as they ought, and if you see them close they will diminish of themselves.

[15]Take care that the vertical plan on which you work out the perspective of the objects seen is of the same form as the wall on which the work is to be executed.

Ash. I. 22*b*

546.

PITTURA.

[2]La grãdezza · della · figura · dipinta · ti debbe mostrare · a che distanza · ell'è veduta; [3]se tu vedi una figura grãde · al naturale sappi ch'ella si dimostra esser presso [4]all'ochio.

OF PAINTING.

The size of the figures represented ought to show you the distance they are seen from. If you see a figure as large as nature you know it appears to be close to the eye.

Ash. I. 3*a*]

547.

DOVE · DEBE STARE QUELLO [2]CHE RIGUARDA · LA PITUTRA.

[2]Poniamo · che · *a* · *b* · sia · la pictura · vista ·, e che · *d* · sia · il lume, [4]Dico, che se ti porrai · infra · *c* · *e* ·, male · cõprenderai la pit-

WHERE A SPECTATOR SHOULD STAND TO LOOK AT A PICTURE.

Supposing *a b* to be the picture and *d* to be the light, I say that if you place yourself between *c* and *e* you will not

cholochãdo . . 2 chose. 10. che quala . . terzo br. para . . queta. 11. sechondo . . chosa . . sepreso. 12. chose grãde. pichole chesi. 13. esse vederai farano . . esse . . vede. 15. chessenpre . . sela . . diminvissci le chose. 17. afigurare

546. 2. grãdeza . . ditebbe. 3. settu . . sapi.

547. 4. Dicho chesse . . porai . . cõpldenderai la pitura. 5. sessia . . vernichata . . ara. 6. effa . . chagione. 7. chõsterai . . razi

545. 8. The second diagram of this chapter stands in the original between lines 8 and 9.

11. Instead of '*se preso*' (= *sie presso*) M. RAVAISSON reads '*sempre se*' which gives rise to the unmeaning rendering: '*parceque toujours* . . .'

15. Compare No. 526 line 18.

tura, [5]e massime · se sia · fatta · a olio o verámēte verniciata ·, perchè avrà lustro [6]e fia · quasi · di natura · di spechio ·, e per questa cagione · quāto piv t'a[7]ccosterai · al pūto *c* ·, meno · vedrai ·, perchè · quivi · risaltano i razzi [8]del lume ·, mādato · dalla · finestra · alla pittura: E se ti porrai infra [9]*e* *d* li fia · bene ·· operata la tua · vista ·, e massime · quāto · più · t' appresserai [10]al punto · *d* ·, perchè quello loco · è meno, · participāte di detta percus[11]sione de' razzi riflessi.

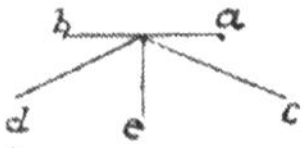

understand the picture well and particularly if it is done in oils, or still more if it is varnished, because it will be lustrous and somewhat of the nature of a mirror. And for this reason the nearer you go towards the point *c*, the less you will see, because the rays of light falling from the window on the picture are reflected to that point. But if you place yourself between *e* and *d* you will get a good view of it, and the more so as you approach the point *d*, because that spot is least exposed to these reflected rays of light.

8. Essetti . porai. 10 locho. 11. razi rifressi.

III.

THE PRACTICAL METHODS OF LIGHT AND SHADE AND AERIAL PERSPECTIVE.

C. A. 126b; 386b]

548.

De' pictura: della oscurità delle ōbre o uoi dire chiarezze de' lumi.

dations ght and hade.

[2] Bēchè li pratici mettino in tutte le cose infuscate, alberi, prati, capelli, barbe [3] e peli di 4 sorti chiarezze nel contrafare vn medesimo colore, cioè [4] prima vn fondamēto oscuro e per 2° vna machia che participa della forma [5] delle parti; 3° una parte più spedita e più chiara, 4° i lumi più che altre parti [6] noti di figura ·; Ma a me pare che esse varietà sieno infinite sopra vna [7] quātità continua, la quale in se è diuisibile in īfinito, e così lo provo: [8] *a g* sia vna quantità cōtinua, *d* sia il lume che l'a[9]llumina; dico per la 4ª che dice ¶che quella parte del [10] corpo alluminato sarà più luminosa che più s'a[11]uicina alla causa che l'allumina; adunque *g* è [12] più oscuro che *c* per tāto quāto la linia *d g* è più lunga che la linia [13] *d c* e per la conclusione che tali gradi di chiarezza o vo'dire di oscurità nō sol [14] sō 4, ma infinitamēte si possono inmaginare, perchè *c d* è quātità cōtinva

Of painting: Of the darkness of the shadows, or I may say, the brightness of the lights.

Although practical painters attribute to all shaded objects—trees, fields, hair, beards and skin—four degrees of darkness in each colour they use: that is to say first a dark foundation, secondly a spot of colour somewhat resembling the form of the details, thirdly a somewhat brighter and more defined portion, fourthly the lights which are more conspicuous than other parts of the figure; still to me it appears that these gradations are infinite upon a continuous surface which is in itself infinitely divisible, and I prove it thus:—[7] Let *a g* be a continuous surface and let *d* be the light which illuminates it; I say—by the 4th [proposition] which says that that side of an illuminated body is most highly lighted which is nearest to the source of light—that therefore *g* must be darker than *c* in proportion as the line *d g* is longer than the line *d c*, and consequently that these gradations of light—or rather of shadow, are not 4 only, but

548. 2. pratichi . . infusscate. 3. cappelli . . sorte chiarere . . coe. 4. osscura. 5. parte 3ª una . . alte parte. 6. ame. 7. chontinua. 8. q[ua]ntita . . chella. 11. chellalumina . . g he. 12. piu [chia] osscuro . . lungha chella. 13. chettali . . ciareza osscurita. 14. possano. 16. delle lūgeze e anno le linie chessattēdā . . ettal. 17. ecquella . . lungeze. 18. chessa tendano

548. 7. See Pl. XXXI. No. I; the two upper sketches.

[15]e ogni quãtità continua è diuisibile in ĩfinito, adunque infinite son le ua[16]rietà delle lũghezze, che ànno le linie che s'astẽdã dal luminoso allo alluminato [¶]e tal fia [17]la proportione delli lumi quale è quella delle lunghezze delle linie infra loro, [18]che s'astendono dal centro del luminoso alle parti d'esso obbietto alluminato.

may be conceived of as infinite, because *c d* is a continuous surface and every continuous surface is infinitely divisible; hence the varieties in the length of lines extending between the light and the illuminated object are infinite, and the proportion of the light will be the same as that of the length of the lines between them; extending from the centre of the luminous body to the surface of the illuminated object.

A. 23 *a*]

549.

COME IL PICTORE SI DEBBE ACCÕCIARE AL LUME · COL SUO RILIEUO.

[2]*a* · *b* · sia la finestra, · *m* · sia · il punto del lume ·, dico che in qualunque · parte il pittore · si stia ·, ch'elli starà [3]bene · pure · che l'ochio · sia · infra · la parte onbrosa · e la luminosa · del corpo · che si ritrae ·, il quale · loco tro[4]verai ·, ponendoti · infra 'l punto · *m* · e la · diuisione che fa · l'onbra · dal lume · sopra il corpo ritratto.

HOW THE PAINTER MUST PLACE HIMSELF WITH REFERENCE TO THE LIGHT, TO GIVE THE EFFECT OF RELIEF.

Let *a b* be the window, *m* the point of light. I say that on whichever side the painter places himself he will be well placed if only his eye is between the shaded and the illuminated portions of the object he is drawing; and this place you will find by putting yourself between the point *m* and the division between the shadow and the light on the object to be drawn.

On the choice of light for a picture (549—554).

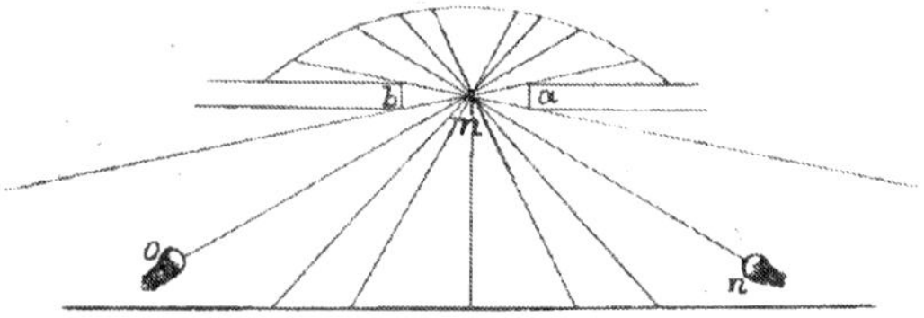

Ash. I. 14 *a*]

550.

COME · L'ÕBRE · FATTE DA LUMI PARTICULARI [2]SI DEONO FUGIRE PERCHÈ SONO Ĩ LORO I FINI SIMILI A PRĨCIPI.

[3]L'onbre, fatte dal sole o altri lumi particulari ·, sono sẽza gratia del cor[4]po · che da quella è accõpagniato, ĩperocchè cõfusamẽte lascia le parti [5]diuise cõ cuidẽte termine d'õbra da lume, e l'õbre sono di pari potẽ[6]tia nel'ultimo che nel prĩcipio.

THAT SHADOWS CAST BY A PARTICULAR LIGHT SHOULD BE AVOIDED, BECAUSE THEY ARE EQUALLY STRONG AT THE ENDS AND AT THE BEGINNING.

The shadows cast by the sun or any other particular light have not a pleasing effect on the body to which they belong, because the parts remain confuse, being divided by distinct outlines of light and shade. And the shadows are of equal strength at the end and at the beginning.

. . parte. *At the beginning of the text the following is written on the margin in five short lines*: dello oscurita delle õbre ouoi dire clareze de lumi.

549. 1. chome . . achõciare . . chol. 2. finesstra . . dicho . . sisstia. 3. chellochio . ella . chorpo chessi . . locho. 4. ella . . cheffa . . chorpo ritracto.

550. 3. chor. 4. dacquella eachõpagniato . . lasscia le parte

Ash. I. 28*]

551.

COME SI DEBE DARE LUME · ALLE · FIGURE.

[1]Il lume · debe · essere usato · secōdo che darebbe il natural sito · dove [2]fingi · essere la tua · figura, cioè se la · figi al sole · fa l'onbre oscure [3]e grā piazze di lumi · e stapi l'ōbre e di tutti i circustāti corpi le loro ōbre [4]in terra; E se la figuri ɉ tristo tepo, fa poca differentia da lumi a ōbra, [5]e sanza fare alcuna altr'ōbra ai piedi, E se la figuri ī casa, fa grā [7]differēza da lumi al'ōbre e ōbra per terra, e se vi figuri finestra īpānata [8]e abitatione biāca, poca differēza da lumi a ōbre; E se ell'è alluminata [9]da foco, farai i lumi rosseggiāti e potēti, e scure l'ōbre, e 'l battimēto del'ōbre [10]per li muri o per terra sia terminato, e quāto più s'alōtana dal corpo [11] piv si faccia, aplo e magno; E se fusse alluminata parte dal foco [12]e parte dall'aria · che quello dell'aria sia più potēte e quello del foco [13]sia quasi rosso, a similitudine di foco ·, E sopra tutto fa · che le tue figure [14]dipīte abbiano il lume grāde e da alto ·, cioè quel vivo che tu ritrai, [15]īperochè le persone che tu · vedi per le strade tutte ànno il lume di sopra e sap[16]pi che non è si gran tuo conosciete · che dadoli i lume di sotto che tu nō [17]durassi fatica a riconoscerlo.

HOW LIGHT SHOULD BE THROWN UPON FIGURES.

The light must be arranged in accordance with the natural conditions under which you wish to represent your figures: that is, if you represent them in the sunshine make the shadows dark with large spaces of light, and mark their shadows and those of all the surrounding objects strongly on the ground. And if you represent them as in dull weather give little difference of light and shade, without any shadows at their feet. If you represent them as within doors, make a strong difference between the lights and shadows, with shadows on the ground. If the window is screened and the walls white, there will be little difference of light. If it is lighted by firelight make the high lights ruddy and strong, and the shadows dark, and those cast on the walls and on the floor will be clearly defined and the farther they are from the body the broader and longer will they be. If the light is partly from the fire and partly from the outer day, that of day will be the stronger and that of the fire almost as red as fire itself. Above all see that the figures you paint are broadly lighted and from above, that is to say all living persons that you paint; for you will see that all the people you meet out in the street are lighted from above, and you must know that if you saw your most intimate friend with a light [on his face] from below you would find it difficult to recognise him.

Ash. I. 15*]

552.

DEL DARE CON ARTIFIZIOSI LUMI E ŌBRE [2]AIVTO AL FINTO RILIEVO DELLA PITTURA.

[3]Nell'aumētare · la pittura nel suo · rilievo vserai fare · infra la finta figura [4]e quella · cosa · visiua, che ricieve la sua · ōbra, · vna linea di chiaro lume che diuida [5]la figura dal oscurato · obietto, e nel medesimo · obietto farai [6]2 parti chiare che mettino

OF HELPING THE APPARENT RELIEF OF A PICTURE BY GIVING IT ARTIFICIAL LIGHT AND SHADE.

To increase relief of a picture you may place, between your figure and the solid object on which its shadow falls, a line of bright light, dividing the figure from the object in shadow. And on the same object you shall represent two light parts which will surround the shadow cast upon the wall

551. 1. ilume. 2. ilume . . darebe. 4. piaze . . stāpisci l'ōbre di. 5. pocha diferentia. 6. casella. 7. diferēza tera esse . . ipanata. 8. diferēza Esse elle. 9. rosegiāti. 10. segnāto. 11. facia āpla e magnia Esse. 12. foco. 13. assimilitudine . . tuto fa chelle. 14. dāso . . chetta. 15. chetto . . ano i lume . . maa. 16. chetto. 17. fatiche a richonoscerlo.

552. 3. Dellaumētare . . infralla. 4. ciaro. 5. farā [chiaro dopo]. 6. imezo. 7. chetta . . chessi. 8. chorpo e massimo . . lebr

552. 6. Compare the two diagrams under No. 565.

in mezzo l'ombra fatta · nel mvro della cōtra-[7]posta figura; e vsa spesso fare quelle mēbra, che tu voi che si partino [8]alquāto dal loro corpo e massime quādo le braccia intraversano il petto, di [9]fare che ifra 'l battimēto dell'ōbra del braccio sul petto e la propria [10]ōbra del braccio · resti · alquāto di lume che paia che passi infra lo spatio ch'è [11]infra 'l petto e 'l braccio, e quādo tu voi che 'l braccio paia piv distāte dal [12]petto tāto piv fa detto · lume maggiore, e senpre fa che tu t'īgiegni [13]d'accomodare i corpi · in cāpi che la parte d'essi corpi ch'è oscura [14]termini in cāpo chiaro ·, e la parte del corpo aluminata termini ī [15]cāpo · scuro.

by the figure placed opposite [6]; and do this frequently with the limbs which you wish should stand out somewhat from the body they belong to; particularly when the arms cross the front of the breast show, between the shadow cast by the arms on the breast and the shadow on the arms themselves, a little light seeming to fall through a space between the breast and the arms; and the more you wish the arm to look detached from the breast the broader you must make the light; always contrive also to arrange the figures against the background in such a way as that the parts in shadow are against a light background and the illuminated portions against a dark background.

G. 31 b]

553.

De situatione.

[1]Ricordati del situare le fi[3]gure, perchè altro è lume e onbra, se [4]vna cosa è in ū loco scuro [5]cō lume particulare, altro [6]vna cosa in loco · chiaro cō [7]lume particular del sole, [8]altro vna cosa in loco scu[9]ro cō lume vniversale della [10]sera o di tēpo nvoloso, [11]e altro il lume vniversale [12]del-l'aria alluminata dal sole.

Of situation.

Remember [to note] the situation of your figures; for the light and shade will be one thing if the object is in a dark place with a particular light, and another thing if it is in a light place with direct sunlight; one thing in a dark place with a diffused evening light or a cloudy sky, and another in the diffused light of the atmosphere lighted by the sun.

G. 19 a]

554.

Del giuditio che ài a fare sopra vn opera [2]d'ū pittore.

[3]Prima è che tu cōsideri le figure s'el-l'ànno [4]il rilievo qual richiede il sito e 'l lume che [5]le allumina; che l'onbre nō siē quel medesi[6]mo nelli stremi della storia che nel mezzo, [7]perchè altra cosa è l'essere circundato dalle [8]ombre, e altro è lo aver le ōbre da vn sol lato; [9]quelle sō circū-date dall'ōbre che sono in[10]verso il mezzo della storia, perchè sono aō[11]brate dalle figure interposte · fra loro [12]e 'l lume; E quelle sono aōbrate da vn sol [13]lato, le quali sono interposte infra lume e [14]la storia, perchè dove nō vedono il lume vedono [15]la storia e ui si rappresēta la scurità d'essa sto[16]ria, e dove nō vedono la storia vedono lo splē[17]dore del lume, e ui si rappresenta la sua chi[18]arezza.

Of the judgment to be made of a painter's work.

First you must consider whether the figures have the relief required by their situation and the light which illuminates them; for the shadows should not be the same at the extreme ends of the composition as in the middle, because it is one thing when figures are surrounded by shadows and another when they have shadows only on one side. Those which are in the middle of the picture are surrounded by shadows, because they are shaded by the figures which stand between them and the light. And those are lighted on one side only which stand between the principal group and the light, because where they do not look towards the light they face the group and the darkness of the group is thrown on them: and where they do not face the group they face the brilliant light and it is their own darkness shadowing them, which appears there.

. . ella. 10. del br . . pal. 11. quāto . . bracio. 12. magiore casenpre fa chettu. 13. dachomodare . . chāpi . . osscura. 14. chāpo . . ella. 15. cāpo chiaro.

553. 1—12 R. 3. altr. lume "e onbra" vise. 4. cosa euii loco s[p]. ro. 5. particulari altr. 8. illoco d. l.

[19]Secōdaria è che 'l seminamēto [20]over cōpartitione delle figure siē cōpar[21]tite secōdo il caso nel quale tu vuoi che [22]sia essa storia; Terza che le figure sieno [23]cō protitudine intēte al lor particulare.

In the second place observe the distribution or arrangement of figures, and whether they are distributed appropriately to the circumstances of the story. Thirdly, whether the figures are actively intent on their particular business.

Ash. I. 7a]

555.

Del dare i lumi.

[2]Dà prima una ōbra vniversale · per tutta la parte cōtenete che nō uede il lume, [3]poi li dà ōbre mezzane e le principali a paragone · l'una · dell'altra ·, [4]e cosi dà il lume cōtenēte di mezzano · lume, dādoli poi i mezzi e prīcipali [5]similmēte a paragone.

Of the treatment of the lights.

First give a general shadow to the whole of that extended part which is away from the light. Then put in the half shadows and the strong shadows, comparing them with each other and, in the same way give the extended light in half tint, afterwards adding the half lights and the high lights, likewise comparing them together.

G. 11 b]

556.

De' ōbra ne' corpi.

The distribution of light and shade (556—559).

[2]Quando figuri le ōbre oscure nelli cor[3]pi ōbrosi, figura senpre la causa di ta[4]le oscurità, e 'l simile farai de' refles[5]si, perchè le ōbre oscure nascono da [6]scuri obbietti e li reflessi da obbi[7]etti di piccola chiarezza, cioè da lumi di[8]minuiti; E tal proportione è [9]dalla parte alluminata de' corpi alla [10]parte rischiarata dal reflesso qua[11]le è dalla causa del lume d'essi cor[12]pi alla causa di tale reflesso.

Of shadows on bodies.

When you represent the dark shadows in bodies in light and shade, always show the cause of the shadow, and the same with reflections; because the dark shadows are produced by dark objects and the reflections by objects only moderately lighted, that is with diminished light. And there is the same proportion between the highly lighted part of a body and the part lighted by a reflection as between the origin of the lights on the body and the origin of the reflections.

Ash. I. 19a]

557.

De' lumi e ōbre.

[2]Ogni parte del corpo e ogni minima particula · che si truova · avere alquāto di rilievo [3]io ti ricordo · che guardi a darli i prīcipali del' ōbre e de' lumi.

Of lights and shadows.

I must remind you to take care that every portion of a body, and every smallest detail which is ever so little in relief, must be given its proper importance as to light and shade.

554. 1—23 R. 3. gudiio . . affare. 3. chetta . . sellanno. 7. ellimegre. 9. chessono. 10. meto. 11. fralloro. 12. Eequelle. 13. lume el. 15. lestoria . . saprese̅ta lasscurita. 17. rapresenta. 18. areza. 19. Secōdaria ne chel. 22. chelle.
555. 2. prima ī ōbra . . chōtenēte. 3. mezane elle. 4. echosi . . chōtenēte di mezano . . mezi.
556. 1—12 R. 2. osscure. 3. osscurita . . refres. 5. nasscā das. 6. elli refressi. 7. pichola chiareza con. 8. Ettal . . eda. 10. alla parte risciarata dal refresso. 12. refresso.
557. 2. de chorpo . . partichula chessi. 3. richordo.

Ash. I. 12 *b*]

558.

Modo del fare alle figure [2] l'ombra cōpagnia del lume e del corpo.

[3] Quādo fai una figura · e tu vogli vedere se l'onbra è cōpagnia del lume, [4] ch'ella nō sia o piv · rossa o gialla che si sia la natura dell'essere del colo[5]re che tu volli aōbrar·, farai cosi: fa ōbra col tuo dito [6] sopra la parte alluminata e se l'ōbra accidentale da te fatta fia simi[7]le al'ōbra naturale fatta dal dito sopra la tua opera, starà bene, [8] e puoi col dito piv presso o piv · lōtano fare ōbre piv scure o piv [9] chiare ·, le quali sēpre paragona colla · tua.

Of the way to make the shadow on figures correspond to the light and to [the colour] of the body.

When you draw a figure and you wish to see whether the shadow is the proper complement to the light, and neither redder nor yellower than is the nature of the colour you wish to represent in shade, proceed thus. Cast a shadow with your finger on the illuminated portion, and if the accidental shadow that you have made is like the natural shadow cast by your finger on your work, well and good; and by putting your finger nearer or farther off, you can make darker or lighter shadows, which you must compare with your own.

Ash. I. 14 *a*]

559.

Del circūdare i corpi [2] cō vari liniamēti d'ōbra.

[3] Fa · che senpre · l'ombre ·, fatte sopra la superfitie de' corpi da uarii obiecti, [4] vsino · ondeggiare cō uari torcimēti mediāte la varietà de' mēbra [5] che fanno l'onbre ·, e della cosa · che ricieve essa ōbra.

Of surrounding bodies by various forms of shadow.

Take care that the shadows cast upon the surface of the bodies by different objects must undulate according to the various curves of the limbs which cast the shadows, and of the objects on which they are cast.

Ash. I. 29 *b*]

560.

De pictura.

[2] I vari paragoni delle uarie qualità d'ōbre e lumi fanno spesse [3] volte [parere] anbiguo e cōfuso al pittore, che vole imitare e cōtrafare le cose, [4] che uede; la ragion si è Questa: se tu vedi vn panno biāco a parte [5] vn nero·, cierto · quella · parte · d'esso paño biāco che cōfinerà · col ne[6]ro · apparirà molto · piv candida · che quella che cōfinasi cō maggi[7]or biāchezza ·, e la ragiō di questo · si prova · nella · mia · prospettiva.

On painting.

The comparison of the various qualities of shadows and lights not infrequently seems ambiguous and confused to the painter who desires to imitate and copy the objects he sees. The reason is this: If you see a white drapery side by side with a black one, that part of the white drapery which lies against the black one will certainly look much whiter than the part which lies against something whiter than itself. [7] And the reason of this is shown in my [book on] perspective.

The juxtaposition of light and shade (560. 561).

558. 2. delume. 3. fai ī figura . ettu. 4. chela . . chessi . . cholo. 5. chettu . . chol. 6. esse . . datte. 8. e poi chol. 9. laquali.

559. 1. circhūdare i chorpi. 2. fa chessenpre . . chorpi . . obiecti. 4. ondegiare. 5. cheffano . . chosa.

560. 2. parachoni . . fano. 3. volte [parere] anbiguo e chōfuso . . chōtrafare. 4. e uede . . settu . . biācho apare. 5. vnero . . biācho che chōñnera . chol. 6. chandida . . quela che chofinassi chō. 7. or biāchera . ella.

560. 7. It is evident from this that so early as in 1492 Leonardo's writing in perspective was so far advanced that he could quote his own statements.—As bearing on this subject compare what is said in No. 280.

Ash. I. 4 a]

561.

DEL' ÕBRA.

[2]Doue · l'õbra cõfina · cõ lume abbi [3]rispetto dov' è piv chiara o scura e do[4]v'ella è piv · o mẽ fumosa iuerso lu[5]me, e sopra tutto · ti ricordo che ne' [6]giovani tu non facci l'onbre termina[7]re come · fa la pietra, perchè la carne [8]tiene vn poco del trasparẽte, come [9]si uede a guardare in una mano che [10]sia posta fra l'ochio [11]e 'l sole, che si vede [12]rosseggiare · e trasparere luminosa; [13]et la parte piv colorita · metterai [14]infra i lumi e l'õbre ·, e se tu voli [15]vedere che obra si richiede alla tua [16]carne faraivi sù un õbra · col tuo [17]dito ·, e secõdo che la · vuoi piv chiara [18]o scura · tieni il tuo dito piv · presso o lõta[19]no dalla · tua pittura e quella cõtrafa.

OF SHADOWS.

Where a shadow ends in the light, note carefully where it is paler or deeper and where it is more or less indistinct towards the light; and, above all, in [painting] youthful figures I remind you not to make the shadow end like a stone, because flesh has a certain transparency, as may be seen by looking at a hand held between the eye and the sun, which shines through it ruddy and bright. Place the most highly coloured part between the light and shadow. And to see what shadow tint is needed on the flesh, cast a shadow on it with your finger, and according as you wish to see it lighter or darker hold your finger nearer to or farther from your picture, and copy that [shadow].

E. 4 a]

562.

DE' CÃPI DELLE FIGURE DE' [2]CORPI DIPINTI.

On the lighting of the background (562—565).

[3]Il canpo, che circũda le figure di qua[4]lunque cosa dipinta, debbe essere piv os[5]scuro che la parte allumina[6]ta d'esse figure e più chiaro che la loro [7]parte õbrosa ecc.

OF THE BACKGROUNDS FOR PAINTED FIGURES.

The ground which surrounds the forms of any object you paint should be darker than the high lights of those figures, and lighter than their shadowed part; &c.

Ash. I. 4 a]

563.

CHE CÃPO DEBE VSARE IL PITTORE [2]ALLE SUA OPERE.

[3]Poichè per isperiẽtia si vede che tutti i corp[4]i sono · circondati · da õbra e lume [5]vuolsi che tu pittore · accomodi ·, che quella parte ch'è alluminata [6]termini ĩ cosa oscura, · e così la parte del corpo · aombrata · termini [7]in cosa · chiara · E questa · regola · darà grãde avmẽto a rilevare [8]le tue figure.

OF THE BACKGROUND THAT THE PAINTER SHOULD ADOPT IN HIS WORKS.

Since experience shows us that all bodies are surrounded by light and shade it is necessary that you, O Painter, should so arrange that the side which is in light shall terminate against a dark body and likewise that the shadow side shall terminate against a light body. And by [following] this rule you will add greatly to the relief of your figures.

561. 2. chõ fina cho . . abi. 3. schura. 5. richordo. 7. chome. 8. pocho . . chome. 11. chessi. 12. rossegiare . ettrasparere. 13. cholorita. 14. ellobre . essettu. 16. charne . . chol. 17. essechõdo . . voi. 18. osschura . . il duo . . presso alõta. 19. quela chõtrafa.

562. 1. chãpi . . fighure. 2. chorpi dipineti. 3. circhũ le fighure di qual. 4. lũche chosa. 5. schuro che [el lume dellef. 6. fighure . . chella. 7. obrosa.

563. 1. chãpo. 2. ale. 3. perrisperietia . . chettutti i chorp. 4. circhondati . . ellume. 5. chettu pitore . achomodi. 6. osschura e chosi . chorpo. 7. chosa . . Ecquesta.

G. 23*b*]

564.

Principalissima parte della pittura son [2]li campi delle cose dipinte; nelli qua[3]li campi li termini delli corpi naturali [4]che ànno in lor curvità convessa senpre [5]si conoscono, e le figure di tali corpi in essi [6]campi, ancorachè li colori de' corpi sieno [7]del medesimo colore del predetto campo, e [8]questo nascie che li termini cõuessi de' [9]corpi non sono alluminati nel medesimo [10]modo, che dal medesimo lume è alluminato [11]il campo, perchè tal termine molte volte sarà [12]più chiaro o più oscuro che esso campo; [13]Ma se tal termine è del colore di tal cam[14]po, sanza dubbio tal parte di pittura proibirà [15]la notizia della figura di tal termine; [16]e questa tale eletione di pittura è da es[17]sere schivata dalli ingiegni de' buoni pictori, [18]conciosiachè la intentione del pictore è di [19]fare parere li sua corpi di quà dai campi, [20]e in nel sopra detto caso accade il contrario [21]nõ che in pictura, ma nelle cose di rilieuo.

A most important part of painting consists in the backgrounds of the objects represented; against these backgrounds the outlines of those natural objects which are convex are always visible, and also the forms of these bodies against the background, even though the colours of the bodies should be the same as that of the background. This is caused by the convex edges of the objects not being illuminated in the same way as, by the same light, the background is illuminated, since these edges will often be lighter or darker than the background. But if the edge is of the same colour as the background, beyond a doubt it will in that part of the picture interfere with your perception of the outline, and such a choice in a picture ought to be rejected by the judgment of good painters, inasmuch as the purpose of the painter is to make his figures appear detached from the background; while in the case here described the contrary occurs, not only in the picture, but in the objects themselves.

Ash. I. 19*a*]

565.

[1]Come si debbe nelle cose ·, che sono · sopra · l'ochio [2]et daccãto ·, le quali · tu uoli · che parino · discoste [3]dal mvro—fare tra l'õbra originale e l'onbra di[4]rivativa uno lume ĩ mezzo, e parrà la cosa dispiccata dal mvro.

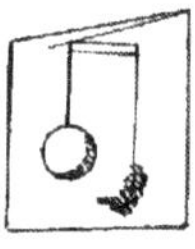

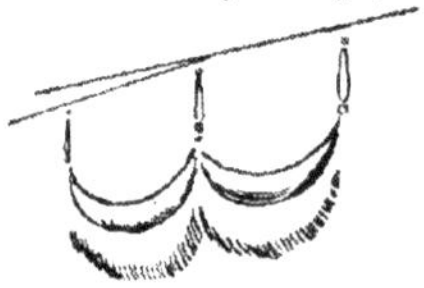

That you ought, when representing objects above the eye and on one side—if you wish them to look detached from the wall—to show, between the shadow on the object and the shadow it casts a middle light, so thatthe body will appear to stand away from the wall.

Ash. I. 15*b*]

566.

Come i corpi biãchi si deono figurare.

[2]Se figurerai uno corpo · biaco esso sia circũdato · da molt'aria, perchè [3]il biãco · non à da se · colore · ma si tignie e trasmvta ĩ parte del co[4]lore ·, che li è per obi-

How white bodies should be represented.

If you are representing a white body let it be surrounded by ample space, because as white has no colour of its own, it is tinged and altered in some degree by the colour of the objects surrounding it. If you see

On the lighting of white objects.

564. 2. chanpi delle chose dipincte. 3. chanpi . . chorpi. 4. chonvessa. 5. chognosschano le . . chorpi. 6. chanpi anchora chelli cholori de chorpi. 7. cholore del predecto chanpo ec. 8. quessto nasscie chelli. 9. chorpi. 11. chanpo. 12. oppiu osschuro . . chanpo. 13. Massettal . . cholore . . chan. 15. fighura. 16. ecquessta . . pictura he. 17. scitata. 18. chonciossia chella . - eddi. 19. chorpi . . da canpi. 20. decto chaso achade il chontrario. 21. chose.

565. 1. chome . . chose chessono. 2. dachato . . tuuuoli . . di sschasto. 3. almvro . . ellonbra. 4. rivativa ĩ lume imezo e para la chosa dispichata.

566. 2. figurerai ĩ corpo biaco circhũdato. 3. dasse coloreñssi tignie frasmuta. 4. se vederai ĩ dona [avere il f] vestita. 5. biãcho infrana . . quela. 6. imodo . . comel. 7. cheffia. 8. razi. 9. azura . . dona . . pa. 10. azurro se nela . . tera visina.

etto· se vedrai una donna vestita [5]di biãco · ĩfra una cãpagnia ·, quella parte di lei che fia veduta [6]dal sole · il suo colore fia chiaro, in modo che darà ĩ parte come [7]il sole noia · alla vista · e quella · parte che fia veduta dalla [8]aria luminosa per li razzi del sole, tessuti e penetrati ĩfra essa, [9]perchè l'aria ĩ se è azzurra ·, la parte della dõna uista da detta aria par[10]rà pẽdere in azzurro; se nella superfitie della terra uicina · fiã [11]prati, · e che la donna si truovi infra 'l prato alluminato dal sole [12]e esso sole, vedrai tutte le parti d'esse pieghe, che posso[13]no essere uiste dal prato, tingersi per razzi reflessi in nel colore d'esso [14]prato, e cosi si ua trasmvtãdo in e' colori de' luminosi e nõ lumino[15]si obietti vicini.

a woman dressed in white in the midst of a landscape, that side which is towards the sun is bright in colour, so much so that in some portions it will dazzle the eyes like the sun itself; and the side which is towards the atmosphere,—luminous through being interwoven with the sun's rays and penetrated by them—since the atmosphere itself is blue, that side of the woman's figure will appear steeped in blue. If the surface of the ground about her be meadows and if she be standing between a field lighted up by the sun and the sun itself, you will see every portion of those folds which are towards the meadow tinged by the reflected rays with the colour of that meadow. Thus the white is transmuted into the colours of the luminous and of the non-luminous objects near it

Ash I 15a]

567.

PERCHÈ I VOLTI DI LÕTANO PAIONO OSCURI.

WHY FACES [SEEN] AT A DISTANCE LOOK DARK

The method of aerial (567—570)

[2]Noi vediamo · chiaro che tutte le similitudini delle · cose evidẽti, [3]che ci sono · per obietto cosi grãdi come piccole, entrano al sẽso per la piccola luce [4]dell' occhio, se per si piccola ẽtrata passa la similitudine della grãdezz adel cielo [5]e della terra ·, essẽdo il uolto dell'omo ĩfra si grã similitudini di cose quasi niẽte per [6]la lõtanità che lo diminvisce, quasi occupa si poco d'essa luce che rimane ĩcõprẽsi[7]bile ·, e avẽdo a passare dalla superfitie alla ĩpressiua per uno mezzo oscuro, cioè il ne[8]rvo voto che pare oscuro ·, quella spetie, nõ sẽdo di colore potẽte, si tignie in quel[9]la oscurità della via, e givta alla ĩpressiua pare oscura: altra cagione nõ si [10]può in nessũ modo · allegare, se quel pũto è nero che sta nella luce · lo è, perch'elli è pieno d'uno [11]omore trãparẽte a vso d'aria e fa l'ufitio che farebbe uno buso fatto in vna asse, e a ri[12]guardarlo pare nero, e le cose viste · per l'aria chiara e scura si cõfvdono nella oscurità.

We see quite plainly that all the images of visible objects that lie before us, whether large or small, reach our sense by the minute aperture of the eye; and if, through so small a passage the image can pass of the vast extent of sky and earth, the face of a man—being by comparison with such large images almost nothing by reason of the distance which diminishes it,—fills up so little of the eye that it is indistinguishable. Having, also, to be transmitted from the surface to the sense through a dark medium, that is to say the crystalline lens which looks dark, this image, not being strong in colour becomes affected by this darkness on its passage, and on reaching the sense it appears dark; no other reason can in any way be assigned. If the point in the eye is black, it is because it is full of a transparent humour as clear as air and acts like a perforation in a board, on looking into it it appears dark and the objects seen through the bright air and a dark one become confused in this darkness.

PERCHÈ L'OMO · VISTO A CIERTA DISTÃTIA NON È CONOSCIVTO

WHY A MAN SEEN AT A CERTAIN DISTANCE IS NOT RECOGNISABLE.

[14]La prospettiva · diminvitiua ci dimostra · che quãto · la cosa · è piv lõtana [15]piv si fa piccola, e se tu riguarderai uno uomo che

The perspective of diminution shows us that the farther away an object is the smaller it looks. If you look at a man at a dis-

11 chella dona . . aluminato. 12. vederai tutte [e de sono] le . pieche che possa 13 no esse . . tigniera per razi refressa nel ch olore. 14 cholori.

567 1 pajano 2 chettutte le similitudine 3 grade . pichola . piciola 4 picola . . dela 5 dela tera chose 6. chello . ocupa . poca . ĩchõprẽsi 7 per ĩ mezo 8 quelle inque 10. po inesũ . alegare . . luce e perchel 11. effa . . farelie ĩ buso fatto nonase 12. elle . chi[illegible] . cõfõde nela 13 nõne 14 chosa. 15 pichola esse .

sia distāte da te · vna bale[16]strata, e porraiti la finestra d'una · piccola agucchia apresso · al' ochio ·, potrai ve[17]dere per quella molti omini mādare le lor similitudini · all' ochio, e in ū medesimo [18]tēpo tutte capirāno ī detta · finestra · ; adūque se l'omo lōtano una balestra[19]ta māda la sua similitudine all' ochio, che occupa una piccola parte d' una fine[20]stra d'agucchia, come · potrai tu in si piccola figura scorgere o vedere il naso [21]o bocca o alcuna particula d'esso corpo, e nō uedēdosi nō potrai [22]conosciere l'omo che nō mostra le mēbra, le quali fanno li omini di diuerse forme.

tance from you of an arrow's flight, and hold the eye of a small needle close to your own eye, you can see through it several men whose images are transmitted to the eye and will all be comprised within the size of the needle's eye; hence, if the man who is at the distance of an arrow's flight can send his whole image to your eye, occupying only a small space in the needle's eye how can you [expect] in so small a figure to distinguish or see the nose or mouth or any detail of his person? and, not seeing these you cannot recognise the man, since these features, which he does not show, are what give men different aspects.

Ash. I. 4a]

568.

COME · LE FIGURE · PICCOLE DEONO [2]PER RAGIONE · ESSER · FINITE.

[3]Dico · che le · cose che apparirāno · di minvta [4]forma · nascierà che · detta cosa fia lontana dall'occhio; essendo così [5]cōuiene ·, che īfra l'ochio e la cosa · sia molta · aria ·, e la molt'aria [6]īpedisce la evidētia della forma · d'essi obbietti, ōde le minute [7]particule · d'essi · corpi · fiano indiscernibili e nō conosciute; Adūque [8]tu · pittore · farai · le piccole · figure · solamēte acciēnate · e nō finite, e se [9]altrimēti · farai ·, cōtrafarai alli effetti della natura tua · maestra; [10]la cosa · rimāe piccola per la · distātia grāde ch'è fra l'ochio e la cosa, [11]la distātia grāde rīchiude · dentro a se di molta aria: la molta aria fa ī se grosso [12]corpo il quale īpediscie · e tolglie all' ochio le minute particule degli obbietti.

THE REASON WHY SMALL FIGURES SHOULD NOT BE MADE FINISHED.

I say that the reason that objects appear diminished in size is because they are remote from the eye; this being the case it is evident that there must be a great extent of atmosphere between the eye and the objects, and this air interferes with the distinctness of the forms of the object. Hence the minute details of these objects will be indistinguishable and unrecognisable. Therefore, O Painter, make your smaller figures merely indicated and not highly finished, otherwise you will produce effects the opposite to nature, your supreme guide. The object is small by reason of the great distance between it and the eye, this great distance is filled with air, that mass of air forms a dense body which intervenes and prevents the eye seeing the minute details of objects.

G. 53b]

569.

D'ogni figura pos[2]ta in lūga distā[3]tia si perde in pri[4]ma la notitia del[5]le parti più mi[6]nute e nell' ulti[7]mo si riservan le [8]parti massime, [9]priuate della no[10]titia di tutti li stre[11]mi, e restano di [12]figura ovale o [13]sperica di termi[14]ni confusi.

Whenever a figure is placed at a considerable distance you lose first the distinctness of the smallest parts; while the larger parts are left to the last, losing all distinctness of detail and outline; and what remains is an oval or spherical figure with confused edges.

homo chessia . . atte. 16. porati . . piciola aguchia. 17. similitudine . . onū. 18. caperano . . ī balestra. 19. ī pichola. 20. daguchia . . pichola. 21. obocha oalchuna . . deso. 22. le chali fano.

568. 1. Chome . . pichole. 3. dicho . . chose [chessiano di pichola] che aparirāno. 4. chosa . . chosí. 5. chēfra . . chosa . . aria ella. 6. la [forma] evidēsia. 7. partichule . . fieno indiscernibile . . chonosciute. 8. pichole. 10. pichola . . chosa. 11. riciude . . asse di molta. 12. tolglie . . partichole.

569. 1. dongni. 2 sta in lūgha distā. 5. lle parte. 7. riserua. 8. parte. 11. resstan. 13. sperícha. 14. chonfusi.

570.

W. An. IV. 218a]

Pictura.

[2]La spessitudine del fumo dall' oriz[3]zonte ingiù è bianca e dall' orizzōte in [4]sù è oscura, e ancora che tal [5]fumo sia in sè d'equal colore, essa equalità si dimostra varia mediante la [7]varietà dello spatio nel qual si trvova.

Of painting.

The density of a body of smoke looks white below the horizon while above the horizon it is dark, even if the smoke is in itself of a uniform colour, this uniformity will vary according to the variety in the ground on which it is seen.

570. 2 lasspessitudine . . ori. 3. biancha . . orizōte. 4. osschura e anchora chettal. 6. dimosstra.

IV.

OF PORTRAIT AND FIGURE PAINTING.

Ash. I. 8a]

571.

DEL MODO DELLO ĨPARARE BENE A CÕPORRE [2]INSIEME LE FIGURE NELLE STORIE.

[3]Quãdo · tu · avrai inparato · bene di prospettiva · e avrai a mẽte tutte le mẽbra [4]e corpi delle · cose, sia vago e spesse volte nel tuo ãdarti a spasso [5]vedere e considerare i siti · e li atti delli omini in nel parlare, in nel cõtẽdere [6]o ridere o zuffare insieme, che atti fieno in loro ·, che atti faccino i circũ[7]stati ·, i spartitori, i veditori d'esse cose ·, e quelli notare cõ brevi se[8]gni in questa forma su un tuo piccolo libretto, il quale tu debi sẽpre por[9]tar cõ teco, e sia di carte tĩte, accio nõ l'abbi a scãcellare ma mutare di vechio [10]in ṽ novo, chè · queste nõ sono cose da essere scãcellate anzi cõ grã diligẽza ri[11]serbate ·, perchè gli sono tãte le ĩfinite forme e · atti delle cose che la memoria [12]nõn è capace a ritenerle, õde queste riserberai come tua autori e maestri.

OF THE WAY TO LEARN TO COMPOSE FIGURES [IN GROUPS] IN HISTORICAL PICTURES.

When you have well learnt perspective and have by heart the parts and forms of objects, you must go about, and constantly, as you go, observe, note and consider the circumstances and behaviour of men in talking, quarrelling or laughing or fighting together: the action of the men themselves and the actions of the bystanders, who separate them or who look on. And take a note of them with slight strokes thus, in a little book which you should always carry with you. And it should be of tinted paper, that it may not be rubbed out, but change the old [when full] for a new one; since these things should not be rubbed out but preserved with great care; for the forms, and positions of objects are so infinite that the memory is incapable of retaining them, wherefore keep these [sketches] as your guides and masters.

Of sketching figures and portraits (571. 572).

571. 1. chõpore. 3. araí . . araì. 4. chorpi . . chose . . esspesse . . ãdarti ossobasso. 5. chonsiderare . . inel . . inel. 7. chose ecquelli. 8. suntuo piciolo. 9. chõtecho essia . . labiaca ciellare. 10. chose . . chãcielate anzichõgra. 11. perche eglie tãte . . chose chella. 12. chapace . . chome tua altori.

571. 8. Among Leonardo's numerous note books of pocket size not one has coloured paper, so no sketches answering to this description can be pointed out. The fact that most of the notes are written in ink, militates against the supposition that they were made in the open air.

Ash. I. 9a]

572.

Del modo del tenere a mēte la forma d'ū volto.

[2]Se uolli avere facilità in tenere a mēte una · aria d'uno volto ·, īpara · prima a mēte [3]di molte teste, occhi, nasi, bocche, mēti · e gole · e colli e spalle: e poniamo caso: j nasi [4]sono di 10 ragioni ·, dritto ·, gobbo, cavo, col rilievo più sù o piv giù che'l mezzo, aquilino, pari ·, simo · e tōdo e acuto; questi [5]sono boni in quāto al proffilo; In faccia i nasi sono di 11 ragioni: equale, grosso in mezzo, [6]sottil' in mezzo, la pv̄ta grossa e sottile nell' appiccatura ·, sottile nel[7]la · pūta e grosso nell' appiccatura ·, di larghe narici · di strette, d'alte e basse, di busi scoperti e [8]di busi occupati dalla pūta, e cosi troverai diversità nelle [9]altre particole, delle quali · cose tu de' ritrare di naturale e metterle a mēte, [10]overo quādo ài a fare uno volto a mēte · porta con teco uno piccolo libretto, doue sieno [11]notate simili fationi ·, e quādo ài dato una ochiata al uolto della persona che uoi [12]ritrare, guarderai poi ī parte quale naso o bocca se le somiglia e fa ui uno piccolo [13]segnio, per riconescierle poi a casa. De' visi mostruosi nō parlo perchè sāza fatica [14]si tēgono a mēte.

Of a method of keeping in mind the form of a face.

If you want to acquire facility for bearing in mind the expression of a face, first make yourself familiar with a variety of [forms of] several heads, eyes, noses, mouths, chins and cheeks and necks and shoulders: And to put a case: Noses are of 10 types: straight, bulbous, hollow, prominent above or below the middle, aquiline, regular, flat, round or pointed. These hold good as to profile. In full face they are of 11 types; these are equal thick in the middle, thin in the middle, with the tip thick and the root narrow, or narrow at the tip and wide at the root; with the nostrils wide or narrow, high or low, and the openings wide or hidden by the point; and you will find an equal variety in the other details; which things you must draw from nature and fix them in your mind. Or else, when you have to draw a face by heart, carry with you a little book in which you have noted such features; and when you have cast a glance at the face of the person you wish to draw, you can look, in private, which nose or mouth is most like, or there make a little mark to recognise it again at home. Of grotesque faces I need say nothing, because they are kept in mind without difficulty.

Ash. I. 6b]

573.

In che modo tu debi fare una testa [2]che le sua parti sieno cōcordāti [3]alle debite diritture.

The position of the head.

[4]Per fare vna · testa che le sua · mēbra · sieno cōcordati al uolta[5]re e piegare d'una testa · tieni · questi modi: tu sai che ochi, ciglia, [6]nari di naso, termini della bocca e i lati del mēto, mascella [7]gote, orechi e tutte parti d'uno volto sono d'equale dirittura

How you should set to work to draw a head of which all the parts shall agree with the position given to it.

To draw a head in which the features shall agree with the turn and bend of the head, pursue this method[5]. You know that the eyes, eyebrows, nostrils, corners of the mouth, and sides of the chin, the jaws, cheeks, ears and all the parts of a face are squarely and straightly set upon the face[8].

572. 2. mēte ī aria. 3. esspalle . . chaso. 4. chavo *col rilievo piu su o piv gu chel mezo aquilino . . achuto. 5. sono di 1[2] ragioni . . imezo. 6. imezo [e grosso nei stremi] la . . essottile nel apichatura. 7. nellapichatura di large anarise . . ebiesse. 8. ochupati . . chosi. 9. partichule . . chose. 10. affare ī volto . . chontecho ī piciolo. 11. simile fatione . equādo . . dato ī ochiata. 12. bocha . . faui ī piciolo. 13. achasa . . faticha. 14. tēgano.

573. 1. fare ī testa. 2. chelle . . sieno [in] chōchordāti. 4. chōcordāti. 5. tussai. 6. anari . . bocha . . masella. 7. volto

573. See Pl. XXX, No. 4, the slight sketch on the left hand side. The text of this passage is written by the side of it. In this sketch the lines seem intentionally incorrect and converging to the right (compare l. 12) instead of parallel. Compare too with this text the drawing in red chalk from Windsor Castle which is reproduced on Pl. XL, No. 1.

5—8. Compare the drawings and the text belonging to them on Pl. IX. (No. 315), Pl. X (No. 316), Pl. XI. (No. 318) and Pl. XII. (No. 319).

[8]poste sopra il uolto; adũque quãdo ài fatto il uolto, fa linie [9]che passino da l'uno canto · dell'ochio · al'altro, e così per la dirittu[10]ra di ciascuno mẽbro, e tratte fori de' lati del uolto le stre[11]mità d'esse · linie, guarda se da destra e da sinistra li spati [12]ĩ nel medesimo paralello · sono equali, Mâ bẽ ti ricordo che tu [13]facci dette linie trarre al pũto della tua veduta.

Therefore when you have sketched the face draw lines passing from one corner of the eye to the other; and so for the placing of each feature; and after having drawn the ends of the lines beyond the two sides of the face, look if the spaces inside the same parallel lines on the right and on the left are equal [12]. But be sure to remember to make these lines tend to the point of sight.

Ash. I, 36]

574.

COME · SI DEBBE CONOSCERE [2]QUAL PARTE DEL CORPO DE' ESSERE [3]PIÙ O MENO LUMINOSA CHE L'ALTRE.

[4]se · *f* · fia · il lume · e la · testa · sarà · il corpo da quello alluminato, [5]e quella · parte · d'essa testa che ricieve · sopra di se il razzo fra · angoli [6]piv equali · sarà · più · alluminata ·, e quella parte · che ricieverà [7]i razzi · ĩfra · ãgoli · meno equali · fia · meno luminosa ·; E fa [8]questo · lume · nel suo ofitio · a similitudine del colpo ·, ĩperochè il [9]colpo · che caderà ĩfra equali · ãgoli · fia · in primo grado di po[10]tentia, e quando caderà · infra diseguali sarà tãto meno potẽte [11]che 'l primo · quãto l'ãgoli · fieno · più · disformi ·; Esẽpli gratia, [12]se gitterai · una · palla · in un · mvro · che l'estremità sieno equi[13]distanti · da te ·, il colpo caderà · ĩfra eguali · ãgoli, E se [14]gitterai la palla ĩ detto muro, stãdo da una delle sue estremità, [15]la palla caderà infra diseguali · angoli ·, e il colpo nõ si [16]appiccherà.

HOW TO KNOW WHICH SIDE OF AN OBJECT IS TO BE MORE OR LESS LUMINOUS THAN THE OTHER.

Let *f* be the light, the head will be the object illuminated by it and that side of the head on which the rays fall most directly will be the most highly lighted, and those parts on which the rays fall most aslant will be less lighted. The light falls as a blow might, since a blow which falls perpendicularly falls with the greatest force, and when it falls obliquely it is less forcible than the former in proportion to the width of the angle. *Exempli gratia* if you throw a ball at a wall of which the extremities are equally far from you the blow will fall straight, and if you throw the ball at the wall when standing at one end of it the ball will hit it obliquely and the blow will not tell. Of the light on the face (574—576).

W. 1]

575.

PRUOVA · E RAGIONE · PERCHÈ INFRA LE PARTI ALLUMINATE [2]SI TROVANO PARTICULE PIV LUMINOSE VNA CHE VN ALTRA.

[3]Poichè provato s'è che ogni terminato [4]lume fa over par che nasca da ṽ sol

THE PROOF AND REASON WHY AMONG THE ILLUMINATED PARTS CERTAIN PORTIONS ARE IN HIGHER LIGHT THAN OTHERS.

Since it is proved that every definite light is, or seems to be, derived from one single

[sop] sono . . diriture. 8. facto. 9. diritu. 10. ciaschuno . . foride [gli] "2" lati. 11. desstra. 12. inel . . eequale . . richordo chettu. 13. faci . . trare . . dela.

574. 1. chonosscere. 2. chorpo. 3. õmeno. 4. seff . f . fia . . ella . . chorpo dacquello. 5. eequella . . razo. 6. eequella. 7. irazi . . Effa. 8. quessto . . assimilitudine del cholpo ĩperoche. 9. cholpo . . chadera. 10. chadera. 12. gitterai ĩ palla. 13. distante atte il cholpo chadera . . E essella. 14. giterai la balla . . da ĩ delle. 15. la pala chadera . . cholpo.

575. 1. infralle parte [l]. 2. [l] si truova partichule. 4. nascha . . quela. . aluminata. 5. dacquello ara . . quale cha. 6. dara

574. See Pl. XXXI. No. 4; the sketch on the right hand side.

575. See Pl. XXXII. The text, here given complete, is on the right hand side. The small circles above the beginning of lines 5 and 11 as well as the circle above the text on Pl. XXXI, are in a paler ink and evidently added by a later hand in order to distinguish the text as belonging to the *Libro di Pittura* (see Prolegomena. No. 12, p. 3). The text on the left hand side of this page is given as Nos. 577 and 137.

punto ·, quella parte allumina[5]ta da quello avrà la sua particula piv luminosa ·, sopra la quale ca[6]derà la linia radiosa fra · 2 · angoli · equali ·, come di sopra si di[7]mostra nelle linie · · *a* · *g* · e così ĩ · *a*. *h* e simile ĩ. *l* · *a* ·, e quella [8]particula della parte alluminata fia mẽ luminosa · sopra la quale la linia [9]ĩcidente ferirà tra · 2 · angoli piv dissimili, come appare ĩ · *b* · *c* · *d*, [10]e per questa via ãcor potrai conosciere le parti priuate di lume, [11]come appare ĩ · *m* · *k*.

[12]Quãdo li angoli, fatti dalle [13]linie ĩcidẽti, sarãno piv [14]equali ĩ quello loco [15]fia · piv · lume, e dove [16]fieno più disequali [17]lì · fia · piv scuro ¶

[18]ancor farò mẽtione [19]della ragiõ della reflessiõ.

point the side illuminated by it will have its highest light on the portion where the line of radiance falls perpendicularly; as is shown above in the lines *a g*, and also in *a h* and in *l a*; and that portion of the illuminated side will be least luminous, where the line of incidence strikes it between two more dissimilar angles, as is seen at *b c d*. And by this means you may also know which parts are deprived of light as is seen at *m k*.

Where the angles made by the lines of incidence are most equal there will be the highest light, and where they are most unequal it will be darkest.

I will make further mention of the reason of reflections

Ash. I. 19 *a*]

576.

Dove si debe [2]fare cadere [3]l'õbra sul uolto.

Where the shadow should be on the face.

W. 1 *a*]

577.

General suggestions for historical pictures (577—581)

Quãdo tu [2]fai vna sto[3]ria · fa · 2 · pũ[4]ti ·, vno dell' occhio [5]e l'altro del lum[6]e el qual fa piv [7]lõtã che puoi.¶

When you compose a historical picture take two points, one the point of sight, and the other the source of light; and make this as distant as possible.

Ash. I 18 *b*]

578

¶ Come le storie nõ debbono · essere · occupate · e cõfuse di molte figure.

Historical pictures ought not to be crowded and confused with too many figures

Ash. I 26 *a*]

579.

Precetti di pittura

[2]Il bozzare delle storie sia pronto ·; e'l mẽbrificare · nõ sia troppo · finito, [3]sia cõtenvto · solamẽte a siti d'esse mẽbra, i quali poi a bell' agio, piacẽdo ti, [4]le potrai finire

Precepts in painting.

Let you sketches of historical pictures be swift and the working out of the limbs not be carried too far, but limited to the position of the limbs, which you can afterwards finish as you please and at your leisure.

anghol chome 7 chosi . essimile 8 alumata lumino qule. 9 angholi . disimili chome apare. 10 ãchor . . cho nosciere . pruate 11 chome apare 14. [p] equali . . locho 16. dixequali 17 pivsschuro 18 anchor 19. rasiõde rifresiõ.

576. 2. lattere

577 4 delochi"o". 5 delum.

578 occhupate e chõfuse

579 2 bozare . mẽbrifichare . . sia [f] tropo 3 chontenuto

579 See Pl. XXXVIII. No 2. The pen and ink drawing given there as No 3 may also be compared with this passage It is in the Windsor collection where it is numbered 101.

Ash I 2 a]

580

¶Sōmo daño è quādo [1]l'opemone avanza l'opera ¶.

The sorest misfortune is when your views are in advance of your work

C A 157 a, 463 a]

581

Del cōporre storie, del nō riguardare le mēbra delle figure nelle storie || come molti fāno che per fare le figure ītere, guastano [2]ī componimēti, e quādo tu fai la figura drieto alla prima fa disegniarla tutta, acciochè le sua [3]mēbra, che vegono apparire fori delle supertitie della prima, cāpino a loro naturale lūghezza e loco

Of composing historical pictures Of not considering the limbs in the figures in historical pictures, as many do who, in the wish to represent the whole of a figure, spoil their compositions And when you place one figure behind another take care to draw the whole of it so that the limbs which come in front of the nearer figures may stand out in their natural size and place

Ash I 17 b]

582.

Come si deono figurare le età dell'omo, cioè īfantia, pueritia, adolesciē[2]tia, giovētù, vecchiezza, decrepitudine

How the ages of man should be depicted that is, Infancy, Childhood, Youth, Manhood, Old age, Decrepitude

How to represent the differences of age and sex (582 583)

Ash I 18 a]

583

Come i vechi debono essere fatti cō pigri e lēti movimēti e gābe piegate [2]nelle ginochia quādo stanno fermo, e piè pari e distāti l'uno dal'altro, sen[3]do declināti ī basso, la testa īnāzi e chinata e le braccia nō troppo distese

[4]Come le dōne si deono figurare con atti vergogniosi, gābe isieme strette, [5]braccia raccolte īsieme, teste basse e piegate ī traverso

[6]Come le vechie si debō figurar ardite e prōte, e con rabbiosi movimēti [7]a uso di furie īfernali, e' movimēti deono apparire piv prōti nelle brac[8]cia e teste che nelle gābe

[9]I putti piccoli con atti prōti e storti, quādo siedono, e nello star ritto [10]atti timidi e pavrosi

Old men ought to be represented with slow and heavy movements, their legs bent at the knees, when they stand still, and their feet placed parallel and apart; bending low with the head leaning forward, and their arms but little extended

Women must be represented in modest attitudes, their legs close together, their arms closely folded, their heads inclined and somewhat on one side

Old women should be represented with eager, swift and furious gestures, like infernal furies, but the action should be more violent in their arms and head than in their legs.

Little children, with lively and contorted movements when sitting, and, when standing still, in shy and timid attitudes.

580 1 somo

581 1 copore nellie fano 2 ichonponimēti ecquādo tuffai le figure ale prime fadidisegniar acciochella 3 vēgano aparire chapinno lūgeza acloco

582 1 leta 2 giuvētu vecieza

583 1 ellōu 2 nele stano 3 eule bracia nōtropo 4 done ati 5 bracia racholte 6 e rabbiosi 7 fure aparire bra. 9 picioli conati segano

582 No answer is here given to this question, in the original MS

583 *braccia raccolte* Compare Pl XXXIII This drawing, in silver point on yellowish tinted paper, the lights heightened with white, represents two female hands laid together in a lap Above is a third finished study of a left hand, apparently holding a veil from the head across the bosom. This drawing evidently dates from before 1500 and was very probably done at Florence, perhaps as a preparatory study for some picture The type of hand with its slender thin forms is more like the style of the *Vierge aux Rochers* in the Louvre than any later works — as the Mona Lisa for instance

Ash. I. 6*a*]

584.

COME LA FIGURA NŌ FIA LAUDABILE [2]SE Ī QUELLA NON APPARISCE ATTO CHE [3]ESPRIMA · LA PASSIONE DELLO SUO UMORE.

Of representing the emotions.

[4]Quella figura è piv [5]laudabile che ne [6]l'atto meglio esprime [7]la passione del suo [8]animo.

COME SI DE' FARE UNA FIGURA IRATA.

[10]Alla · figura · irata · farai · tenere · uno per li capelli, il capo storto a terra, [11]et con uno de' ginochi sul costato ·, e col braccio destro leuare il pugnio [12]in alto: questo · abbi li capelli elleuati ·, le ciglia basse e [13]strette, i dēti stretti e i · 2 stremi da cāto dalla bocca arcati, il collo grosso e dinā[14]zi per lo chinarsi al nimico sia pieno di grize.

COME SI FIGURA UNO DISPERATO.

[16]Al disperato farai dare un coltello e colle mani aversi stracciato [17]i vestimēti, e sia una d'esse mani in opera a stracciarsi la ferita, e farla cō piedi [18]stāti e le gābe alquāto piegate, e la persona similmēte [19]inverso terra cō capelli stracciati e sparsi.

THAT A FIGURE IS NOT ADMIRABLE UNLESS IT EXPRESSES BY ITS ACTION THE PASSION OF ITS SENTIMENT.

That figure is most admirable which by its actions best expresses the passion that animates it.

HOW AN ANGRY MAN IS TO BE FIGURED.

You must make an angry person holding someone by the hair, wrenching his head against the ground, and with one knee on his ribs; his right arm and fist raised on high. His hair must be thrown up, his brow downcast and knit, his teeth clenched and the two corners of his mouth grimly set; his neck swelled and bent forward as he leans over his foe, and full of furrows.

HOW TO REPRESENT A MAN IN DESPAIR.

You must show a man in despair with a knife, having already torn open his garments, and with one hand tearing open the wound. And make him standing on his feet and his legs somewhat bent and his whole person leaning towards the earth; his hair flying in disorder.

Ash. I. 6*b*]

585.

COME DEBI FARE PARERE [2]NATURALE UNO ANIMALE FĪTO.

Of representing imaginary animals.

[3]Tu sai nō potersi fare alcuno animale il quale nō abbia [4]le sue mēbra,—che ciascuno per se à similitudine cō qual[5]cuno · delli altri animali: aduque se voli fare parere [6]naturale uno animale, finto da te ·, diciamo che sia uno serpēte, [7]piglia per la

HOW YOU SHOULD MAKE AN IMAGINARY ANIMAL LOOK NATURAL.

You know that you cannot invent animals without limbs, each of which, in itself, must resemble those of some other animal. Hence if you wish to make an animal, imagined by you, appear natural—let us say a Dragon, take for its head that of a mastiff or hound, with

584. 1. Chome . . laldabile. 2. nōnaparisce. 3. spriema . . dello sommore. 5. laldabile che choni. 6. latto . . spreme. 7. pasione. 9. fare ī. 10. tenere ī per li chapegli il chapo . . attera. 11. chon . . chostato e chol bracio. 12. alu li chapegli. 13. dachāto . . bocha archati il chollo. 14. nimicho. 15. figura ī. 16. darsidun choltello e cholle. 17. sia ī desse . . asstracciarsi . . effarla cho. 18. elle . . ella. 19. tera cho chapegli straciati essparsi.

585. 2. naturale ī. 3. tussai . . alchuno . . abi. 4. assimilitudine chō. 5. chuno. 6. naturale ī . . chessia ī. 7. testa ī . . maschino-

585. The sketch here inserted of two men on horseback fighting a dragon is the facsimile of a pen and ink drawing belonging to BARON EDMOND DE ROTHSCHILD of Paris.

Pl. XXIII.

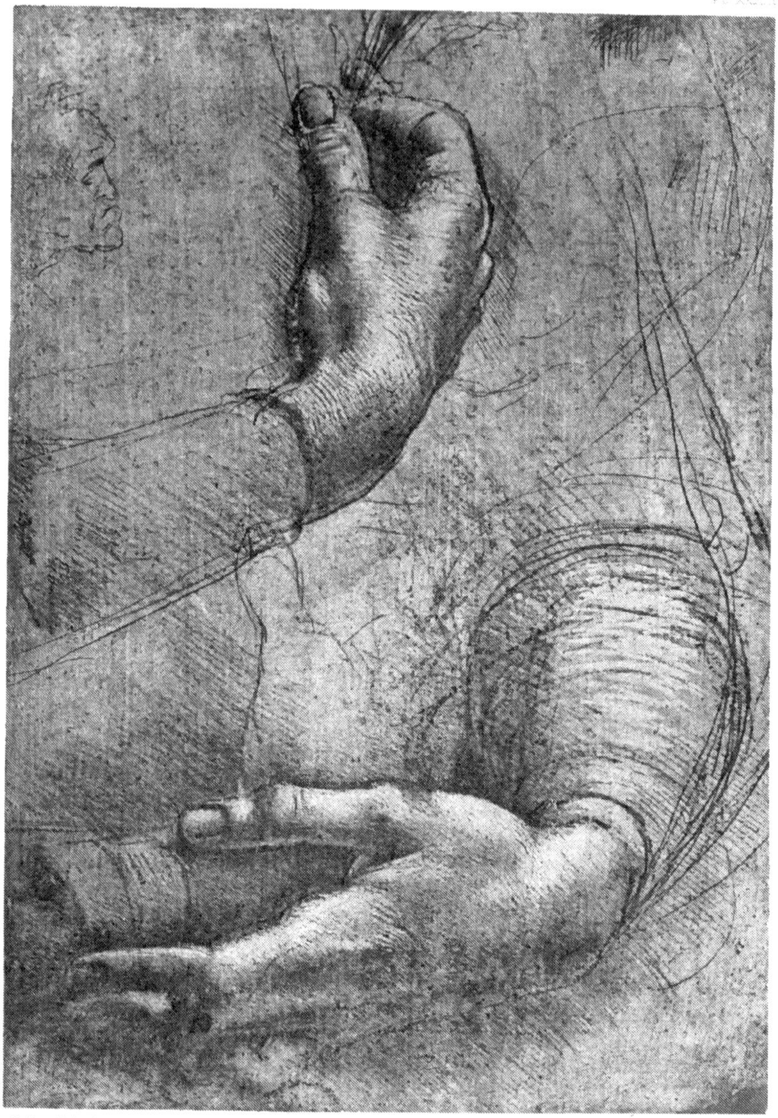

Héliog. Dujardin

Imp. Eudes

testa una di mastino o bracco, e per li ochi di gatta, [8]e per l'orecchie d'istrice, e per

the eyes of a cat, the ears of a porcupine, the nose of a greyhound, the brow of a lion,

lo naso di ueltro, e ciglia da lione e tëpie [9]di gallo vechio, collo di testudine d'aqua.

the temples of an old cock, the neck of a water tortoise.

A. 23a]

586.

DELLO INGÃNO CHE SI RICIEVE NEL GIVDITIO DELLE MĒBRA.

[2]Quel pittore · che avrà · goffe mani · le farà simili nelle sua opere ·, e quel medesimo · l'interuerà · in qualũque [3]mēbro ·, se lũgo · studio nö glielo · uieta: adũque · tu pittore · guarda bene · quella parte · che ài · piv brutta [4]nella · tua · persona · e in quella · col tuo · studio fa bono · riparo ·, ĵperochè se sarai · bestiale · le tue figure · [5]paranno il simile e sanza · ingiegnio ·, e similmëte ogni · parte di bono · e di tristo che ài · in te, si dimo[6]strerà · in parte · in nelle · tue · figure.

OF THE DELUSIONS WHICH ARISE IN JUDGING OF THE LIMBS.

A painter who has clumsy hands will paint similar hands in his works, and the same will occur with any limb, unless long study has taught him to avoid it. Therefore, O Painter, look carefully what part is most ill-favoured in your own person and take particular pains to correct it in your studies. For if you are coarse, your figures will seem the same and devoid of charm; and it is the same with any part that may be good or poor in yourself; it will be shown in some degree in your figures.

The selection of forms (586—591).

Ash. I. 8b]

587.

DELLA · ELETIONE DE' BELLI VOLTI.

[2]Parmi · nö piccola · grazia quella · di quel · pittore · il quale · fa bone arie alle sua

OF THE SELECTION OF BEAUTIFUL FACES.

It seems to me to be no small charm in a painter when he gives his figures a

. . bracho. 8. per li orechie. 9. galo . . cholo.

586. 1. delongãno chessi. 2. ara. 3. sellũgo. 4. enquella chol . . ĵperro . chessessarai. 5. parano . . essanza . essimilmēte . . trissto. 6. sterra . . inelle.

figure [3]la qual gratia ·, chi nõ l'à per natura ·, la può · pigliare · per accidẽtale · studio · in questa · forma; [4]guarda · a torre · le parti bone · di molti · volti belli ·, le quali · belle sieno cõferme [5]piv · per pubblica · fama · che per tuo givditio ·, perchè ti potresti · ingannare · togliẽdo visi [6]che avessino · cõformità · col tuo ·, perchè spesso pare · che simili cõformità ci piacino, [7]e se tu fussi brutto eleggieresti volti nõ belli e faresti brutti volti come molti pittori, che [8]spesso le figure somigliano il maestro ·, sichè piglia · le bellezze come dico, e quelle metti a mẽte.

pleasing air, and this grace, if he have it not by nature, he may acquire by incidental study in this way: Look about you and take the best parts of many beautiful faces, of which the beauty is confirmed rather by public fame than by your own judgment, for you might be mistaken and choose faces which have some resemblance to your own. For it would seem that such resemblances often please us; and if you should be ugly, you would select faces that were not beautiful and you would then make ugly faces, as many painters do. For often a master's work resembles himself. So select beauties as I tell you, and fix them in your mind.

Ash. I. 19a]

588.

Delle mẽbra di che si debe fare · eletione · et di tutte le parti al pro[2]posito · della pittura.

Of the limbs, which ought to be carefully selected, and of all the other parts with regard to painting.

Ash. I. 3a]

589.

In nella eletione delle [2]figure sia più tosto [3]giẽtile che secco o lẽ[4]gnioso.

When selecting figures you should choose slender ones rather than lean and wooden ones.

G. 26a]

590.

MUSCOLI DELLI ANIMALI.

[2]Le cõcavità interposte infra [3]li muscoli nõ debbono essere di [4]qualità che la pelle paja che ve[5]sta due bastoni posti in comũ [6]lor cõtatto come *c*, nec etiam che paiono [7]dua bastoni alquãto remo[8]ssi da tal cõtatto, e che la [9]pelle pẽda in vano cõ curuità la[10]rga come *f*, ma che sia [11]come *i* posato sopra il grasso [12]spũgoso interposto nelli angoli [13]com'è l'angolo *n m o*, il quale an[14]golo nascie dal fin del cõtatto de[15]lli mvscoli, e perchè la pelle nõ può di[16]scẽdere in tale angolo, la natura [17]à riẽpiuto tale angolo di piccola quan[18]tità di grasso spũgoso o vuò dire vi[19]scicoso con vissiche minute pie[20]ne d'aria, la quale in se si cõdensa [21]ossia rarefa secondo lo accrescimen[22]to o rarefatione della sustantia de' [23]muscoli; alora la cõcavità *i* à [24]sempre maggior curvità che 'l muscolo.

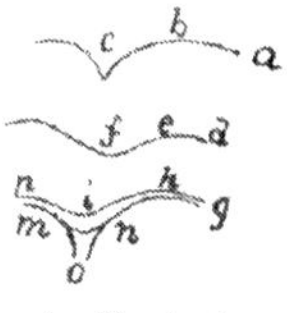

OF THE MUSCLES OF ANIMALS.

The hollow spaces interposed between the muscles must not be of such a character as that the skin should seem to cover two sticks laid side by side like *c*, nor should they seem like two sticks somewhat remote from such contact so that the skin hangs in an empty loose curve as at *f*; but it should be like *i*, laid over the spongy fat that lies in the angles as the angle *n m o*; which angle is formed by the contact of the ends of the muscles and as the skin cannot fold down into such an angle, nature has filled up such angles with a small quantity of spongy and, as I may say, vesicular fat, with minute bladders [in it] full of air, which is condensed or rarefied in them according to the increase or the diminution of the substance of the muscles; in which latter case the concavity *i* always has a larger curve than the muscle.

587. 3. po . . perraccidẽtale. 4. attorre le par bone. 5. perchetti potressti . inganare. 6. chõformita . . chessimil . . piaccino. 7. essettu . . ellegieresti . . effaressi brutti voli. 8. somiglano . . beless.

588. tutte parti.

589. Inella eltetione. 3. secho.

590. 1—24 R. 2. interposste. 3. musscoli. 4. chelia. 5. cõmũ. 6. cõtatto "come c" . . nec chel. 8. echeila. 10. rgha . . f m che.

Ash. I. 13a]

591.

Del serpeggiare e bilico delle · figure · e altri [2]animali.

[3]Qualuque · figura · tu fai ·, o animale giẽtile, ricordati di fugire il legnioso, [4]cioè ch' elle vadino · cõtrapesãdo ossia bilãciando · in modo nõ paia uno pezzo di legno; [5]Quelli che vuoi figurare forti, nõ li fare così, saluo il girare della testa.

Of undulating movements and equipoise in figures and other animals.

When representing a human figure or some graceful animal, be careful to avoid a wooden stiffness; that is to say make them move with equipoise and balance so as not to look like a piece of wood; but those you want to represent as strong you must not make so, excepting in the turn of the head.

Ash. I. 6a]

592.

Della gratia · delle mẽbra.

[2]Le mẽbra del corpo debono essere accomodate cõ gratia · al proposito dello effetto [3]che tu vuoi che facia la figura: e se vuoi far figura · che dimostri · in se leggiadria, [4]debbi fare mẽbra gẽtili e distese · e sanza dimostrare troppi mvscoli e que' pochi, che al [5]proposito · farai dimostrare ·, fa li dolci cioè di poca evidẽza, col' onbre nõ tinte, [6]e le mẽbra ·, massimamẽte le braccia, disnodate, cioè che nessuno mẽ[7]bro nõ ui stia ĩ linia diritta · col mẽbro che si giunge cõ seco · E se 'l fiãco, polo dell' o[8]mo, si trova per lo posare fatto che 'l destro sia piv · alto del sinistro, farai la giũtura della superiore spalla piovere per linia perpẽdiculare sopra al piv eminente [10]oggetto del fianco, e sia essa spalla destra più · bassa che la sinistra, e la fõtanella [11]stia sempre superiore al mezzo della giũtura del piè di sopra · che posi ·, la gãba che nõ posi abbia [12]il suo ginocchio · piv basso che l'altro, e presso all' altra gãba; le latitudini della testa e brac[13]cia sono ĩfinite, però nõ mi estenderò ĩ darne alcuna regola ·, pure che sieno facili [14]e grate, con vari storcimẽti ed i uĩcolamẽti · colle givnture disnodate, acciò nõ paiano [15]pezzi di legno.

Of grace in the limbs.

How to pose figures.

The limbs should be adapted to the body with grace and with reference to the effect that you wish the figure to produce. And if you wish to produce a figure that shall of itself look light and graceful you must make the limbs elegant and extended, and without too much display of the muscles; and those few that are needed for your purpose you must indicate softly, that is, not very prominent and without strong shadows; the limbs, and particularly the arms easy; that is, none of the limbs should be in a straight line with the adjoining parts. And if the hips, which are the pole of a man, are by reason of his position, placed so, that the right is higher than the left, make the point of the higher shoulder in a perpendicular line above the highest prominence of the hip, and let this right shoulder be lower than the left. Let the pit of the throat always be over the centre of the joint of the foot on which the man is leaning. The leg which is free should have the knee lower than the other, and near the other leg. The positions of the head and arms are endless and I shall therefore not enlarge on any rules for them. Still, let them be easy and pleasing, with various turns and twists, and the joints gracefully bent, that they may not look like pieces of wood.

12. neli. 15. mvscoc . . po. 17. picola q"a". 18. tita di rasso spugoso evo. 19. viscice. 21. ossi . . acresscimen. 23. musscoli. 24. senpre magor.

591. 1. del serpegiare epili di delle. 3. tuffai . . richordati . . chõtrapesãdosio . . imodo . . paia ĩ pezo di legnie. 5. Queli . . voi.

592. 2. achomodate chõ. 3. chettu voi cheffacia . . esse voi . . legadria. 4. distesi . . tropi. 5. fali [solamẽte] dolci . . nõtende. 6. bracia. 7. chol . . chessi gugnie cõsecho . Essel. 9. dela . . perpendichulare. 10. ogietto . . hancho essia . . chella . . ella. 11. mezo . . posa . . posa abi. 12. ginochio . . gãba lattitudini . . tessta. 13. astendero. 14. cole. . acio. 15. pizi di legnio.

C A 137 a; 425 a]

593.

Of appropriate gestures (593—600)

La pictura over le figure · dipīte · debbono esser · fatte ī modo tale · che li ri[2]guardatori · d'esse · possino cō facilità · conosciere mediāte · le loro [3]attitudini · il concetto dell'anima · loro ‖ e se tu ài · a fare parla[4]re vn omo · da bene, fa che li atti · sua · sieno conpagni delle bone [5]parole, E similmēte · se tu ài · a figurare · vno uomo · bestiale, fa lo [6]cō movimēti · fieri ·, gittando · le braccia · contro all'auditore, e la testa col [7]petto, sportāti · fori de' piedi ·, accōpagnino · le mani del parlatore, [8]A similitudine · del mvto · che vedēdo 2 parlatori ·, benchè · esso sia pri[9]vato · dell'audito ·, niēte di meno · mediāte li effetti e li atti d'essi parlato[10]ri · lui · cōprēde · il tema · della loro disputa, Io vidi già · ī Firē[11]ze vno sordo · accidētale · jl quale · se tu · li parlaui · forte ·, lui nō ti intē[12]dea ·, e parlādo · piano · sanza sono di voce · lui t'intēdea solo per lo [13]menar · delle · labra; or tu mi potresti dire nō mena le labra vno che parla [14]forte · come · piano, · e menādole · l'uno · come l'altro · nō sarà inteso [15]l'altro · come · l'uno ·; a questa · parte · io lascio dare la sētētia alla [16]sperīētia, fa parlare vno piano e puoi fare ī mēte · le labra.

A picture or representation of human figures, ought to be done in such a way as that the spectator may easily recognise, by means of their attitudes, the purpose in their minds. Thus, if you have to represent a man of noble character in the act of speaking, let his gestures be such as naturally accompany good words; and, in the same way, if you wish to depict a man of a brutal nature, give him fierce movements; as with his arms flung out towards the listener, and his head and breast thrust forward beyond his feet, as if following the speaker's hands Thus it is with a deaf and dumb person who, when he sees two men in conversation —although he is deprived of hearing—can nevertheless understand, from the attitudes and gestures of the speakers, the nature of their discussion I once saw in Florence a man who had become deaf who, when you spoke very loud did not understand you, but if you spoke gently and without making any sound, understood merely from the movement of the lips. Now perhaps you will say that the lips of a man who speaks loudly do not move like those of one speaking softly, and that if they were to move them alike they would be alike understood As to this argument, I leave the decision to experiment; make a man speak to you gently and note [the motion of] his lips.

Ash I. 14 b]

594.

DEL FIGURARE UNO CHE PARLI INFRA PIV PERSONE

[2]Vserai fare quello ·, che tu voi che infra molte persone parli, di considerare la mate[3]ria di che lui · à da trattare: e d'accomo-

OF REPRESENTING A MAN SPEAKING TO A MULTITUDE.

When you wish to represent a man speaking to a number of people, consider the matter of which he has to treat and adapt

593. 1. facte talle chel ri 2 chō conossciere 3 attitudine il chonciecto . . esse . affare 4 dabbene fare chelli . . chonpagni 5 Essimilmēte . settuai . affigurare . . falli. 6 cho chōtro allalditore ella . . chol 7 achōpagnino 8 Assimilitudine 9. auldito . . elli 10. chōprēde la xtema. 11. settu 12 parlādi sollo per 13 labra | "or" tu . . portresti di nō 14 chome chome 15 chome . acquesta 16. seriētua . . piano e po fare [p]ōmēte le labra

594. 1 ī che. 2 vsera quelo chettu 3 lui attrattare e dachomodare. 4 sela materia 5 che cquello . . pigli cole per i 2.

593. The first ten lines of this text have already been published, but with a slightly different reading by Dr M. JORDAN. *Das Malerbuch Leonardo da Vinci's* p 86.

594. The sketches introduced here are a facsimile of a pen and ink drawing in the Louvre which Herr CARL BRUN considers as studies for the Last Supper in the church of *Santa Maria delle Grazie* (see Leonardo da Vinci, LXI, pp. 21, 27 and 28 in DOHME'S *Kunst und Künstler*, Leipzig, Seemann). I shall not here enter into any discussion of this suggestion, but as a justification for introducing the drawing in this place, I may point out that some of the figures illustrate this passage as perfectly as though they had been drawn for that express purpose. I have discussed the probability of a connection between this sketch and the picture of the Last Supper on p. 335. The original drawing is 27 3/4 centimètres wide by 21 high.—The drawing in silver point on reddish paper given on Pl. LII No 1—the original at Windsor Castle—may also serve to illustrate the subject of appropriate gestures, treated in Nos. 593 and 594

dare ī lui · li atti apartenenti a essa materia, [4]cioè · se l'è materia persuasiua · che li atti sieno al proposito, se l'è materia [5]dichia-aratativa per diuerse ragioni, che quello che dice pigli per le dita della [6]mano destra uno dito della sinistra avēdone serrate li 2

his action to the subject. Thus, if he speaks persuasively, let his action be appropriate to it. If the matter in hand be to set forth an argument, let the speaker, with the fingers of the right hand hold one finger of the left hand, having the two smaller ones closed; and

minori, e col viso prōto [7]rivolto uerso il popolo colla bocca alquāto aperta che paia che parli; e, se lui [8]sederà, che paia che si solleui alquāto ritto e inäzi colla testa ·, e se lo fai [9]in piè ·, fa lo alquāto chinarsi col petto e la testa inuerso il popolo, Il [10]quale

his face alert, and turned towards the people with mouth a little open, to look as though he spoke; and if he is sitting let him appear as though about to rise, with his head forward. If you represent him standing make him leaning slightly forward with body and

6. mano "destra" ī dito dela . . serate le . . prō. 7. chola bocha . . che pai che . . esse. 8. soleui . . chola . . esse. 9. fallo . . chol. 10. figurerati. 11. ati . . affare le boche dalchuno vechio . . delle vl. 12. bocha choi sua stremi vasi.

figurerai tacito e attēto, tutti riguardare l'oratore ī uolto co[11]n atti · amiratiui, e fare le bocche d'alcuno vecchio per maraviglia delle v[12]dite sentētie tenere la bocca coi sua stremi · bassi, tirarsi dinetro [13]molte · · pieghe delle guācie ·, e colle ciglia alte nelle giunture le quali creino [14]molte pieghe per la fronte; alcuni sedenti colle dita della mano īsieme tessu[15]te tenersi dētro lo stāco ginochio, altri col'uno ginochio sopra l'altro, [16]sul quale tēga la man, che dētro a se ricieva il gomito del quale la sua [17]mano vada a sostener el mēto barbuto d'alcuno chinato vecchio.

head towards the people These you must represent as silent and attentive, all looking at the orator's face with gestures of admiration, and make some old men in astonishment at the things they hear, with the corners of their mouths pulled down and drawn in, their cheeks full of furrows, and their eyebrows raised, and wrinkling the forehead where they meet. Again, some sitting with their fingers clasped holding their weary knees Again, some bent old man, with one knee crossed over the other, on which let him hold his hand with his other elbow resting in it and the hand supporting his bearded chin.

Ash I 5b]

595.

Della comodità delle mēbra.

[2]Inquāto · alla comodità d'esse mēbra avrai a considerare, che quādo [3]tu vorrai figurare · vno che per qualche accidēte · s'abbia a voltare īdietro [4]o per cāto ·, che tu nō facci movere i piedi e tutte le mēbra ī quella parte dove [5]volta la testa , anzi farai operare cō partire esso svolgimēto in giv[6]ture, cioè quella del piede, del ginochio e fiāco e collo, e se poserai sulla gāba destra [7]farai il ginochio della sinistra piegare ī dētro · e 'l piè suo fia eleuato alquāto di fori, [8]e la spalla · sinistra sia alquāto piv bassa che la destra e la nvca si scōtri a quel [9]medesimo loco dove è volta la noce di fori del piè sinistro ·, e la [10]spalla sinistra sopra la pūta del piè destro in perpēdicolare linia , e sēpre vsa le fi[11]gure che dove si volta la testa che nō ui si uolga il petto, chè la natura per nostra [12]comodità ci à fatto il collo che cō facilità · può seruire a diuerse bande, volendo l'ochio [13]voltarsi in vari siti, e a questo · medesimo sono ī parte obediēti l'altre giūtu[14]re, e se fai l'omo a sedere, e le sue braccia qualche volta s'auessino adoperare [15]ī qualche cosa traversa, fa che · il petto si uolga sopra la givtura del fiāco

Of the disposition of limbs.

As regards the disposition of limbs in movement you will have to consider that when you wish to represent a man who, by some chance, has to turn backwards or to one side, you must not make him move his feet and all his limbs towards the side to which he turns his head. Rather must you make the action proceed by degrees and through the different joints, that is, those of the foot, the knee and the hip and the neck. And if you set him on the right leg, you must make the left knee bend inwards, and let his foot be slightly raised on the outside, and the left shoulder be somewhat lower than the right, while the nape of the neck is in a line directly over the outer ancle of the left foot. And the left shoulder will be in a perpendicular line above the toes of the right foot. And always set your figures so that the side to which the head turns is not the side to which the breast faces, since nature for our convenience has made us with a neck which bends with ease in many directions, the eye wishing to turn to various points, the different joints. And if at any time you make a man sitting with his arms at work on something which is sideways to him, make the upper part of his body turn upon the hips.

. dirieto 13 piege dele guāce echole . . nele givunture. 14. pieghe . sidenti cholle. 15 chol 16 tēgha . asse 17 assostener . vechio

595 2 chomodita . . arai achonsiderare. 3 tu vura . sabi 4 chāto chettu . . faci . tutte mēbra 5 anzi fara farai . . parturi esso sssufolgimēto ī 6. coe quela . . fiācho echollo . esse . sula 8 ella spala . . chella . . nvcha si schōtri. 9. locho. 10. spala . . destro perpēdichulare . . essēpre . . chella . . nosstra. 12. chō . . po diuerse voglido. 13. a voltarsi acquesto . . giutu. 14 seffai . assedere elle . . bracia. 15 chosa . . fiācho

595. 10, 11. Compare Pl. VII, No 5 The original drawing at Windsor Castle is numbered — 104 —

A. 28 *b*]

596.

Quando ritrai li nvdi fa che sempre li ritraga interi, e poi finisci quello mēbro ti pare [2]migliore, e quello coll' altre mēbra metti · in pratica, altremēti faresti vso di non ap[3]piccare · mai · le mēbra bene · insieme.

[4]Non vsar mai fare la testa volta · dove il petto, nè 'l braccio andare come la gāba, [5]e se la testa si uolta · alla spalla destra · fa le sue parti piv basse dal lato sinistro che dal destro, [6]e se fai il petto infori fa che, voltandosi la testa sul lato sinistro, che le parti del lato destro [7]sieno piv alte che le sinistre.

When you draw the nude always sketch the whole figure and then finish those limbs which seem to you the best, but make them act with the other limbs; otherwise you will get a habit of never putting the limbs well together on the body.

Never make the head turn the same way as the torso, nor the arm and leg move together on the same side. And if the face is turned to the right shoulder, make all the parts lower on the left side than on the right; and when you turn the body with the breast outwards, if the head turns to the left side make the parts on the right side higher than those on the left.

W. L. 145 *a*]

597.

De pictura.

[2]Natura de' movimēti nell'omo: [3]nō replicare le medesime actioni nelle menbra dell'omo [4]se la neciessità della loro operatione nō ti costrignie, [5]come si mosstra in *a b*.

Of painting.

Of the nature of movements in man. Do not repeat the same gestures in the limbs of men unless you are compelled by the necessity of their action, as is shown in *a b*.

C. A. 337 *b*; 1026 *b*]

598.

Li moti delli omi[2]ni sieno qual ri[3]chiede la sua degni[4]tà o viltà.

The motions of men must be such as suggest their dignity or their baseness.

C. A. 341 *a*; 1051 *a*]

599.

De pittura.

[2]Fa che la opera s'assomigli allo intēto e alla intē[3]tione, cioè che quādo fai la tua figura che tu [4]pēsi bene chi ella è e quello che tu · vuoi ch'ella faci.

Of painting.

Make your work carry out your purpose and meaning. That is when you draw a figure consider well who it is and what you wish it to be doing.

596. 1. chessepreli ritraga . . finissci quelo. 2. ecquelo chollaltre . . inpraticha . . nōna. 3. pichare. 4. vsar [mi] mai . . bracio . . chome. 5. esse . . allasspalla. 6. esseffai . . sulato . . delato.
597. 3. replichare . . nelle [medesime] menbra. 4. sella . . cōsstrignie.
599. 1. chella hopera sasomigli. 3. chettu . . e cquello chettu. 6. affarlo. 7. vechio ho ū giovane a aparere. 8. efichacia. 9. vechio.

596. In the original MS. a much defaced sketch is to be seen by the side of the second part of this chapter; its faded condition has rendered reproduction impossible. In M. Ravaisson's facsimile the outlines of the head have probably been touched up. This passage however is fitly illustrated by the drawings on Pl. XXI.

597. See Pl. V, where part of the text is also reproduced. The effaced figure to the extreme left has evidently been cancelled by Leonardo himself as unsatisfactory.

De pittura.

[6]Vno medesimo · effetto · a farlo in pittura operare [7]a vn vecchio o u giovane à a apparere tàto di ma[8]ggiore efficacia, quãto il giovane è piv potẽte [9]che 'l uecchio · e simigliãte farai dal giovane al' ĩfante.

Of painting.

With regard to any action which you give in a picture to an old man or to a young one, you must make it more energetic in the young man in proportion as he is stronger than the old one; and in the same way with a young man and an infant.

600.

Ash. I. 13 b]

Del porre le mẽbra.

[2]Le mẽbra, che durano fatica · a farle mvscolose · e quelle che nõ s'adoperano, farai [3]sanza muscoli · e dolci.

Of setting on the limbs.

The limbs which are used for labour must be muscular and those which are not much used you must make without muscles and softly rounded.

Dell' atto delle figure.

[5]Farai · le figure in tale · atto · il quale · sia soffitiẽte · a dimostrare quel che la [6]figura · à · nell' animo: altrimẽte · la tua arte · nõ fia · laudabile.

Of the action of the figures.

Represent your figures in such action as may be fitted to express what purpose is in the mind of each; otherwise your art will not be admirable.

600. 2. faticha affarle myscholose . ecquelle. 3. mvscholi 5. chalia . . altre . mente . laldabile.

V.

SUGGESTIONS FOR COMPOSITIONS

Ash I 4 b]

601

MODO DI FIGURARE UNA BATTAGLIA

[2]Farai prima il fumo dell' artiglieria, mischiato īfra l'aria īsieme · colla polvere mossa [3]dal movimēto de' cavalli e de' cōbattitori , la qual mistione vserai cosi . [4]la polvere perchè è cosa terrestre è pōderosa, e bēchè per la sua sottilità facilmēte [5]si leva e mischia infra l'aria , niētedimeno volētieri ritorna in basso, il suo [6]sōmo motare è fatto dalla parte piv sottile, Adūque li meno fia veduta, [7]e parrà quasi di colore d'aria ·, Il fumo che si mischia infra l'aria [8]īpoluerata , quāto piv s'alza a certa altezza, parrà oscura nuvo[9]la e vedrassi nelle sōmità piv espeditamente [10]il fumo che la polvere, il fumo pederà ī colore alquato azzurro, e la polvere trarà [11]al suo colore , Dalla parte che viene il lume parrà questa mistio[12]ne d'aria fumo e polvere molto più lucida che dall' opposita parte, [13]i cōbattitori quāto · piv fieno īfra detta turbulentia meno si vedrā[14]no, e meno differētia fia dai lor lumi · alle loro · ōbre ,

OF THE WAY OF REPRESENTING A BATTLE.

Of painting battle pieces (601—603)

First you must represent the smoke of artillery mingling in the air with the dust and tossed up by the movement of horses and the combatants And this mixture you must express thus The dust, being a thing of earth, has weight, and although from its fineness it is easily tossed up and mingles with the air, it nevertheless readily falls again It is the finest part that rises highest, hence that part will be least seen and will look almost of the same colour as the air The higher the smoke mixed with the dust-laden air rises towards a certain level, the more it will look like a dark cloud, and it will be seen that at the top, where the smoke is more separate from the dust, the smoke will assume a bluish tinge and the dust will tend to its colour. This mixture of air, smoke and dust will look much lighter on the side whence the light comes than on the opposite side The more the combatants are in this turmoil the less will they be seen, and the less contrast will there be in their lights and shadows Their faces and figures and their appearance, and the musketeers as well as those near them you must make of a glowing red And this glow will diminish in proportion as it is remote from its cause

601 1 figurare ī 2 fumo "dell artileria' misciato infrallaria . cholla 3 chavagli . chōbattitori 4 chosa terestre | "e pō derosa ' e bēche 5 levi misci baso 6 dala 7 chessi 8 alteza 9 la vedcrasi 10 azzuro ella 11 para

Farai rosseggia[15]re i volti e le persone e lor' aria, e li scoppettieri insieme cõ vicini; [16]E detto rossore quãto piv si parte dalla sua cagione piv si perde ·, e le figu[17]re che sono infra · te · e 'l lume, essẽdo lõtane, parrãno scure in campo chia[18]ro ·, e le loro gãbe quãto piv s'appresserà alla terra mẽ fieno vedute, [19]perchè la polvere è lì piv grossa e piv spessa: E se farai caualli [20]corrẽti fori della turba, fa li nvboletti di polvere distãti l'uno dall' altro, [21]quãto può essere lo ĩteruallo de' salti fatti dal cavallo e quello nv[22]volo ·, ch' è · piv lontano da detto · cavallo, mẽ si uegga · anzi sia alto spar[23]so · e raro ·, e 'l piv presso · sia piv euidẽte e minore e piv dẽso: L'aria [24]sia · piena · di saettume di diverse ragioni: chi mõti ·, chi discẽda, [25]qual sia · per linia piana, e le pallotte delli scopietti sieno accõpa[26]gnate da alquãto · fumo dirieto al lor corso · e le prime figure farai [27]poluerose ·, i capelli e ciglia e altri loghi piani atti a sostener la polvere; [28]farai i vĩcitori corrẽti cõ capegli, e altre cose leggiere, sparsi [29]al uẽto colle ciglia · basse

The figures which are between you and the light, if they be at a distance, will appear dark on a light background, and the lower part of their legs near the ground will be least visible, because there the dust is coarsest and densest [19]. And if you introduce horses galloping outside the crowd, make the little clouds of dust distant from each other in proportion to the strides made by the horses; and the clouds which are furthest removed from the horses, should be least visible; make them high and spreading and thin, and the nearer ones will be more conspicuous and smaller and denser [23]. The air must be full of arrows in every direction, some shooting upwards, some falling, some flying level. The balls from the guns must have a train of smoke following their flight. The figures in the foreground you must make with dust on the hair and eyebrows and on other flat places likely to retain it. The conquerors you will make rushing onwards with their hair and other light things flying on the wind, with their brows bent down,

Ash. I. 5 a]

602.

e caccino i cõtrari mẽbri inãzi, cioè · se manderà uno inãzi il piè destro [2]che 'l braccio stãco ãcor lui vẽga inãzi, e se farai alcuna caduta [3]farai il segnio dello · isdruciolare · sù per la polvere condotta ĩ sãguinoso [4]fãgo ·, e dintorno alla mediocre liquidezza della terra farai vedere stampa[5]te le pedate degli omini e cavalli · di lì passati ·, farai alcuno cavallo [6]strascinare morto il suo signore e dirieto a quello lasciare [7]per la · polvere e fãgo il segno dello strascinato corpo; farai i vĩti e battuti [8]pallidi · colle ciglia alte nella lor cõgiũtione e la carne che resta sopra loro [9]sia abbondãte di dolẽti crespe; Le faccie del naso sieno con alquãte grĩze [10]partite in arco

and with the opposite limbs thrust forward; that is where a man puts forward the right foot the left arm must be advanced. And if you make any one fallen, you must show the place where he has slipped and been dragged along the dust into blood stained mire; and in the half-liquid earth arround show the print of the tramping of men and horses who have passed that way. Make also a horse dragging the dead body of his master, and leaving behind him, in the dust and mud, the track where the body was dragged along. You must make the conquered and beaten pale, their brows raised and knit, and the skin above their brows furrowed with pain, the sides of the nose with wrinkles going in an arch from the nostrils to the eyes, and make the nostrils drawn up — which is the cause of the lines of which I speak —, and the lips arched upwards and discovering the upper teeth; and the teeth apart as with crying out

12. oposita. 14. vederã. 15. elle . . dararia elli . . covicini. 16. della . . chagione. 17. chessono . . sure in champo. 19. Esse . . chaualli. 20. corẽti . . falli. 22. chavalo . . uega. 24. ragione. 25. elle ballotte . . schopietti . . achõpa. 26. giate da . . chorso . elle. 27. chapelli . assostencia. 28. corẽti cho chapegli [sparsia] e . . chose legieri. 29. chole.

602. 1. echacci cõtrari . . mandera. 2. stãchoãchor . . esse ffarai alchuna chaduta. 4. alu . . liquideca . . tera . . isstampi. 5. chavalli . . alchuno chavallo. 6. stracinare [il suo chõ] morto . . acquello. 7. effango . . strascinato chorpo . . viũ "e battuti". 8. palidi . . charne. 9. abondãte. 10. archo dale anarisc citerminate nel prencipio . . anari. 11. se alte chagiõ . . archate

601. 19—23. Compare 608. 57—75.

dalle narici e terminate nel prīcipio del-l'occhio, Le nari[11]ci alte, cagiō di dette pieghe, le labra arcate scoprano i dēti di sopra, [12]dēti spartiti in modo di gridare cō lamēto L'una delle ma[13]ni faccia scudo ai pavrosi ochi, voltādo il di dētro iverso il nimico, [14]L'altra stia a terra a sostenere il leuato busto, Altri farai gridāti colla [15]bocca sbarrata e fugiēti· farai molte sorte d'arme īfra i piedi de' cōbatti[16]tori, come scudi rotti, lancie, spade rotte e altre simili cose , farai omini [17]morti, alcuni ricoperti mezzi dalla poluere, altri tutti, La polvere che si [18]mischia coll'uscito sangue cōvertirsi in rosso fango e vedere il sāgue [19]del suo colore correre cō torto corso dal corpo alla poluere, [20]altri morēdo strigniere i dēti, stravolgiere gli ochi, strignere le pugna alla [21]persona e le gābe storte , Potrebbesi vedere alcuno disarmato e abba[22]ttuto dal nimico volgersi al nemico cō morsi e graffi e fare crude[23]le e aspra vēdetta Potresti vedere alcuno cavallo leggiero correre [24]cō i crini sparsi al vēto īfra i nimici e cō piedi fare molto dāno, [25]vedresti alcuno stroppiato cadere ī terra farsi copritura col suo scudo, [26]e 'l nemico chinato in basso far forza di dare morte a quello, [27]potrebbesi uedere molti omini caduti ī vn gruppo sopra uno cavallo morto, [28]Vedrai alcuni vīcitori lasciare il cōbattere e vscire della moltitudine [29]nettādosi colle 2 mani li occhi e le guācie, ricoperte di fāgo, fatto dal lacrima[30]re degli ochi per causa della polvere Vedresti le squadre del soccorso [31]stare piē di sperāza e suspetto cō le ciglia aguzze, faciēdo a quelle ōbra colle mani e riguardare [32]īfra la folta e cōfusa caligine dell'essere attēti al comādamēto del Capi[33]tano, e simile il Capitano col bastone levato e corrēte ī verso il socorso [34]mostrare a quelli la parte dov'è di loro caristia Ed alcū fiume, dentrovi [35]cavalli corrēti, riēpiēdo la circonstāte aqua di turbulēza d'onde, di schiumo [36]e d'acqua cōfusa saltāte īfra l'aria e tra le gābe e corpi de' cavalli [37]E nō fare nessū loco piano se nō le pedate ripiene di sāgue

and lamentation And make some one shielding his terrified eyes with one hand, the palm towards the enemy, while the other rests on the ground to support his half raised body Others represent shouting with their mouths open, and running away You must scatter arms of all sorts among the feet of the combatants, as broken shields, lances, broken swords and other such objects And you must make the dead partly or entirely covered with dust, which is changed into crimson mire where it has mingled with the flowing blood whose colour shows it issuing in a sinuous stream from the corpse Others must be represented in the agonies of death grinding their teeth, rolling their eyes, with their fists clenched against their bodies and their legs contorted Some might be shown disarmed and beaten down by the enemy, turning upon the foe, with teeth and nails, to take an inhuman and bitter revenge You might see some riderless horse rushing among the enemy, with his mane flying in the wind, and doing no little mischief with his heels Some maimed warrior may be seen fallen to the earth, covering himself with his shield, while the enemy, bending over him, tries to deal him a deathstroke There again might be seen a number of men fallen in a heap over a dead horse You would see some of the victors leaving the fight and issuing from the crowd, rubbing their eyes and cheeks with both hands to clean them of the dirt made by their watering eyes smarting from the dust and smoke The reserves may be seen standing, hopeful but cautious, with watchful eyes, shading them with their hands and gazing through the dense and murky confusion, attentive to the commands of their captain The captain himself, his staff raised, hurries towards these auxiliaries, pointing to the spot where they are most needed And there may be a river into which horses are galloping, churning up the water all round them into turbulent waves of foam and water, tossed into the air and among the legs and bodies of the horses And there must not be a level spot that is not trampled with gore

schoprano 12 I dēti imodo chō lamēto [alchuni fara] Luna dele 13 schudo nimicho 14 atterra assostenere i leuato cholla 15 bocha isbarata effugiēte 16 chose 17 alcouni richoperti mezi dala chessi 18 miscia choll chōvertirsi 19 cholore chore chō chorso [super lo chorp] dal corpo 20 signiere 21 elle Potrebesi alchuno 22 nimicho nimicho chō 23 asspra alchuno chavallo legieri chorere 24 cho echo dano 25 alchuno storpiato chadere chopriturо chol schudo 26 nemicho baso ecquello 27 portrebbe ssi chaduti grupo ī chaval 28 vederai alchuni 29 netādosi chole elle ricoperti' fāgho da 30 per lamor della polvere vederesti sochorsi 31 stare | "piē di sperāza e sospetto cho ayuza acquelle chole 32 ed chōfusa chaligine chomādamēto corēte 33 acquelli alchū 35 cavali circhonstate sciuma 36 eddacqua chorp de chavalli 37 I't

603.

G. 15 a]

DELLE ALLUMINATIONI DELLE [2]PARTI INFIME DELLI CORPI CHE INSIEME [3]RESSERO COME LI OMINI IN BATTAGLIE.

[3]Delli omini e cavalli in battaglia travagliati;—[5]le lor parti saran tāto più oscure qua[6]to esse fien più vicine alla terra che li so[7]stiene; E questo si pruova per le parieti [8]de' pozzi i quali si fan tanto più oscure quan[9]to esse più si profondano, e questo na[10]scie perchè la parte più profōda de' pozzi vede [11]ed è veduta da minor parte dell'aria lumi[12]nosa che nessuna altra sua parte.

[13]E li pauimēti [14]del medesimo co[15]lore, che ànno le gā[16]be delli predetti [17]omini e cavalli, fi[18]eno senpre più al[19]luminati infra ā[20]goli equali che [21]le altre predet[22]te gābe ecc.

OF LIGHTING THE LOWER PARTS OF BODIES CLOSE TOGETHER, AS OF MEN IN BATTLE.

As to men and horses represented in battle, their different parts will be dark in proportion as they are nearer to the ground on which they stand. And this is proved by the sides of wells which grow darker in proportion to their depth, the reason of which is that the deepest part of the well sees and receives a smaller amount of the luminous atmosphere than any other part.

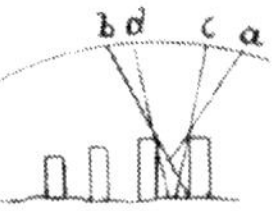

And the pavement, if it be of the same colour as the legs of these said men and horses, will always be more lighted and at a more direct angle than the said legs &c.

604

Ash. I. 17 a]

Of depicting night-scenes.

DEL MODO DEL FIGURARE UNA NOTTE.

[2]Quella cosa che è priuata ĩteramēte di luce è tutta tenebre; essendo la [3]notte · ĩ simile cōditione se tu vi vogli figurare una storia farai · che, [4]essēdovi uno grāde fuoco, che quella cosa ch'è più propiqua a detto fuoco [5]piv si tīga nel suo colore ·, perchè quella cosa ch'è piv vicina all'obietto piv [6]partecipa della sua · natura ·, e faciēdo · il foco pēdere ĩ color rosso [7]farai tutte le cose ·, alluminate da quello, ancora loro rosseggiare, [8]e quelle che sono piv lontane · a detto fuoco piv siē tīte dal colore nero [9]della notte ·; le figure che sono tratte al fuoco · appariscono · scure nella [10]chiarezza d'esso foco, perchè quella parte d'essa cosa che vedi · è tinta dalla oscuri[11]tà della notte e nō dalla chiarezza del foco ·, e quelli che si trovano dai lati [12]sieno mezzi oscuri · e mezzi rosseggiāti, e quelli che si possono vedere dopo [13]e' termini delle fiāme · saranno tutti alluminati · di rosseggiāte lume ĩ cāpo nero ·; ȷn quāto [14]a li atti farai quelli che li sono presso farsi scudo colle mani e cō mātelli ripa[15]ro del superchio · calore · e torti

OF THE WAY TO REPRESENT A NIGHT [SCENE].

That which is entirely bereft of light is all darkness; given a night under these conditions and that you want to represent a night scene,—arrange that there shall be a great fire, then the objects which are nearest to this fire will be most tinged with its colour; for those objects which are nearest to a coloured light participate most in its nature; as therefore you give the fire a red colour, you must make all the objects illuminated by it ruddy; while those which are farther from the fire are more tinted by the black hue of night. The figures which are seen against the fire look dark in the glare of the firelight because that side of the objects which you see is tinged by the darkness of the night and not by the fire; and those who stand at the side are half dark and half red; while those who are visible beyond the edges of the flame will be fully lighted by the ruddy glow against a black background. As to their gestures, make those which are near it screen themselves with their hands and cloaks as a

603. 2. parte corpi insieme. 3. ressco come. 4. charagli in battaglia. 5. parte . . osscure. 6. chelli. 7. Equesto . . pariete. 8. le quali . . osscure q"a". 9. profondano equesto nas. 13. elli. 14. c'so. 15. che à le ghā. 17. omi e charagli. 18. pius. 20. ghali. 22. ghābe.

604. 1. ĩ notte. 2. chosa . . ettutta. 3. ettu . . ĩ storia. 4. sēdovi ĩ . . focho . . propiquo . . focho. 5. cholore . . visina. 6. effaciēdo . il foco . . ĩ cholor. 7. chose aluminate dacquello . . rossegiare [farai]. 8. equelle chessono . . focho . . tīn del. 9. chessono . . focho . . aparisciino scuri. 10. chiareza foco ettinta. 11. chiareza del foco . . chessi. 12. mezi

PL. XXXIV

col uolto ĩ cõtraria parte mostrare fugire [16]quelli piv lõtani farai grã parte di loro farsi colle, mani alli ochi, offesi [17]dal superchio splẽdore

defence against the intense heat, and with their faces turned away as if about to retire Of those farther off represent several as raising their hands to screen their eyes, hurt by the intolerable glare

B M 169 a]

605

Of depicting a tempest (605 606)

Discrivi uno vẽ[2]to terrestre e [3]marittimo [4]Discriui vna [5]pioggia

Describe a wind on land and at sea Describe a storm of rain

Ash I 14 b]

606

Come si dee figurare una fortuna

[2]Se tu uoi figurare una fortuna cõsidera e poni bene i sua effetti, Quãdo [3]il uẽto, soffiãdo sopra la superfitie del mare e della terra, rimove e porta [4]cõ seco quelle cose che nõ sono ferme colla vniuersale massa, e per bẽ [5]figurare questa fortuna farai ĩ prima li nuvoli spezzati e rotti diri[6]zarsi per lo corso del uẽto, accõpagniati da l'arenosa polvere leuata, [7]da liti marini, e rami e foglie leuati per la potẽtia del furore del uẽto [8]sparse per l'aria e ĩ conpagnia di quelle molte altre cose leggiere li alberi [9]e l'erbe piegate a terra, quasi mostrarsi volere seguire il corso de' vẽti [10]coi rami storti fori del naturale corso e cõ le scõpigliate e rouesciate [11]foglie, gli omini che li si trouano parte caduti e rivolti per li panni e per la [12]poluere, quasi sieno sconosciuti, e quelli che restano ritti sieno dopo qual[13]che albero abbracciati a quello, perchè il uẽto nõ li strascini, altri colle [14]mani alli ochi per la polvere chinati a terra ed i panni e capelli diritti [15]al corso del uento, Il mare, turbato e tẽpestoso, sia pieno di ritrosa schi[16]vma ĩfra l'eleuate õde e 'l uẽto levato ĩfra la cõbattuta aria della [17]schivma piv sot-

How to represent a tempest

If you wish to represent a tempest consider and arrange well its effects as seen, when the wind, blowing over the face of the sea and earth, removes and carries with it such things as are not fixed to the general mass And to represent the storm accurately you must first show the clouds scattered and torn, and flying with the wind, accompanied by clouds of sand blown up from the sea shore, and boughs and leaves swept along by the strength and fury of the blast and scattered with other light objects through the air Trees and plants must be bent to the ground, almost as if they would follow the course of the gale, with their branches twisted out of their natural growth and their leaves tossed and turned about [11] Of the men who are there some must have fallen to the ground and be entangled in their garments, and hardly to be recognized for the dust, while those who remain standing may be behind some tree, with their arms round it that the wind may not tear them away, others with their hands over their eyes for the dust, bending to the ground with their clothes and hair streaming in the wind [15] Let the sea be rough and tempestuous and full of foam whirled among the lofty waves, while the wind flings the lighter spray through the stormy air, till it resembles a dense and swathing mist Of the ships that are

osscuri ecquelli possano 13 e termini fiame sarano icãpo 14 quellieli sono comategli aripa 15 chalore chol ulto 16 queli cole mani ali
605 1 ĩ vẽ 2 terrette 4 discriui
606 1 ĩ fortuna 2 figurare ĩ 3 tera 4 cõsecho cholla 5 nvole spezati diri 6 achõpagniati 8 isparsi legieri chose li 9 allera 10 echole 11 pani 12 conoscivti ecqueli 13 abraciati quelli stracini chole 14 [2] mani ali attera chapegli dirito 15 ettẽpestoso sci 16 infralle leuate 17 avvilupata nelia 18 alchuni facci

606 8—11 See Pl XL, No 2
11—15 See Pl XXXIV, the right hand lower sketch

tile, a vso di spessa ed avviluppata nebbia: i navili, che detro [18]vi sono, alcuni se ne faccia colla vela rotta e i brani d'essa uẽtilãdo [19]fra l'aria ĩ cõpagnia d'alcuna corda rotta, alcuni alberi rotti ca[20]duti col navilio intrauersato e rotto ĩfra le tẽpestose õde, cierti omi[21]ni gridati abbracciare il rimanete del navilio, farai li nvuoli cacciati [22]da l'ĩpetuosi venti, battuti nel'alte cime delle mõtagne e fare aquelli avvi[23]luppati, ritrosi, a similitudine dell'õde percosse nelli scogli; l'aria spauẽto[24]sa per le oscure tenebre fatte in nell'aria dalla poluere, nebbia e nvuoli folti.

therein some should be shown with rent sails and the tatters fluttering through the air, with ropes broken and masts split and fallen. And the ship itself lying in the trough of the sea and wrecked by the fury of the waves with the men shrieking and clinging to the fragments of the vessel. Make the clouds driven by the impetuosity of the wind and flung against the lofty mountain tops, and wreathed and torn like waves beating upon rocks; the air itself terrible from the deep darkness caused by the dust and fog and heavy clouds.

G. 6 b]

607.

Figuratione del diluvio.

Of representing the deluge (607—609).

[2]L'aria era oscura per la spessa pioggia, la qual, [3]con obbliqua disciesa, piegata dal trauersal corso [4]de' vẽti, facieva onde di se per l'aria, nõ altramẽti [5]che farsi uegga alla poluere, ma sol si uariaua per[6]chè tale inondatione era traversata dalli liniamẽ[7]ti che fanno le gocciole dell' acqua che disciède; ma [8]il colore suo era tinto dal fuoco, [9]gienerato dalle saette fenditrici e squarciatri[10]cie delli nuvoli, e i vampi delle quali percuotea[11]no e aprivano li grã pelaghi delle riẽpiute [12]valli, li quali aprimẽti mostravano nelli [13]lor vertici le piegate cime delle piante, [14]e Nettuno si vedea in mezzo alle acque col[15]tridẽte e vedeasi Eolo colli sua vẽti rav[16]uilupare notãti piãte diradicate mi[17]ste colle immẽse õde, l'orizzõte con tutto [18]lo emisperio era turbo e focoso per li ricie[19]vuti vanpi delle continue saette, vedeasi [20]li omini e vccielli che riẽpievã di se li gran[21]di alberi, che scoperti dalle dila[22]tate onde cõponitrici delli colli, circũda[23]tori delli grã baratri.

To represent the deluge.

The air was darkened by the heavy rain whose oblique descent driven aslant by the rush of the winds, flew in drifts through the air not otherwise than as we see dust, varied only by the straight lines of the heavy drops of falling water. But it was tinged with the colour of the fire kindled by the thunder-bolts by which the clouds were rent and shattered; and whose flashes revealed the broad waters of the inundated valleys, above which was seen the verdure of the bending tree tops. Neptune will be seen in the midst of the water with his trident, and [15] let Æolus with his winds be shown entangling the trees floating uprooted, and whirling in the huge waves. The horizon and the whole hemisphere were obscure, but lurid from the flashes of the incessant lightning. Men and birds might be seen crowded on the tall trees which remained uncovered by the swelling waters, originators of the mountains which surround the great abysses [23].

W. 158 a]

608.

Diluuio e sua dimostratione [2]in pictura.

[3]Vedeasi la oscura e nvbolosa aria essere conbattuta dal corso di diversi vẽti

Of the deluge and how to represent it in a picture.

Let the dark and gloomy air be seen buffeted by the rush of contrary winds and

chola. 19. rotti cha. 20. chol. 21. abraciare. 22. battute mõtagne e fare acquegli avi. 23. lupati . . assimilitudine . . nelli. 24. ischure . . inell dala . . nebia.

607. 2. osschura. 3. obbliquo disciesso pegħato . . chorso . . notaltromẽti. 5. uegha. 6. deli.. 7. cheffalle ghogeciole . . disscièdc. 8. era [participante del colore] "tinto" del focho. 9. esquartatri. 10. el uapo . . perchotea. 12. mosstravano. 13. pieghate. 14. nechunno . . mezo alla. 15. tridẽde evlo cholli. 16. diradichate. 17. cholle inmẽsse . . chon. 18. emissperio . . effochoso. 19. continvus saetti. 20. cherriẽpievã. 21. che [anchora erano] scoperti. 22. delli de colli circhũda. 23. delle grabalatri.

608. 1. essua dimosstratione . . 2. pictura [cõatti apropiati]. 3. osscura . . chonbattuta . . chorso . . vẽti "cavilupati della cõ-

607. 23. Compare Vol. II. No. 979.

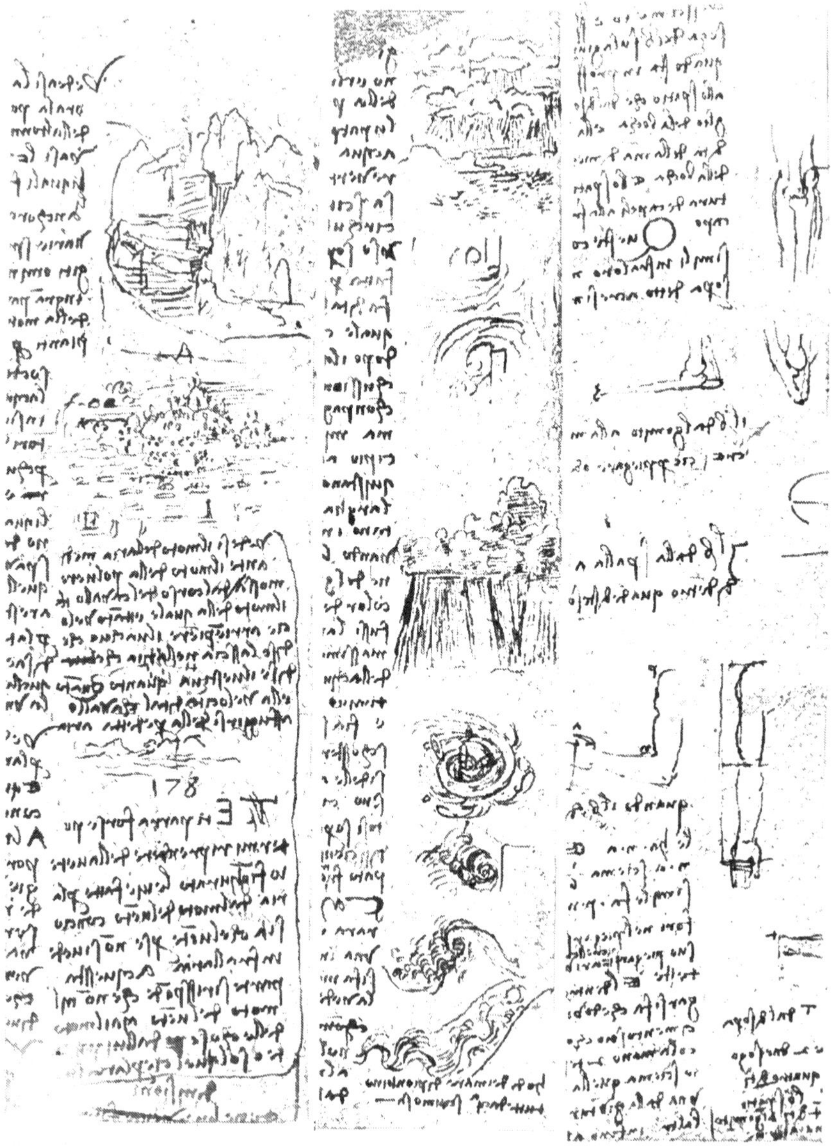

e avviluppati dalla cōtinua pioggia e misti colla gragnuola, li quali or qua ora là portauano infinita ramificatione delle stracciate piante, miste con īfinite foglie; d'intorno vedeasi le antiche piante diradicate e stracciate dal furor de' venti, vedevasi le ruine de' mōti, già scalzati dal corso de' lor fiumi, ruinare sopra i medesimi fiumi e chiudere le loro valli; li quali fiumi rīgorgati allagauano e sōmergieuano le moltissime terre colli lor popoli; ancora avresti potuto vedere nelle sōmità di molti monti essere insieme ridotte molte · varie spetie d'animali, spauētati e ridotti al fin dimesticamēte in cōpagnia de' fuggiti omini e donne colli lor figlioli; E le canpagnie coperte d'acqua mostravā le sue ōde in grā parte coperte di tavole, lettiere, barche, altri vari strumēti fatti dalla neciessità e pavra della morte, sopra li quali era donne, omini colli lor figlioli misti, cō diuerse lamētationi e pianti spaventati dal furor de' venti, li quali con grādissima fortuna rivolgievā l'acque sotto sopra e insieme colli morti, da quella annegati, e nessuna cosa più lieve che l'acqua era che nō fussi coperta di diuersi animali, i quali, fatti tregua, stauano insieme cō paurosa collegatione, infra quali erā lupi, volpi, serpi e d'ogni sorte fugitori dalla morte; E tutte l'onde percuotitricie lor liti conbattevan quelle colle varie percussioni di diuersi corpi annegati, le percussioni de' quali vccideuano quelli, alli quali era restato vita; Alcune congrega-

dense from the continued rain mingled with hail and bearing hither and thither an infinite number of branches torn from the trees and mixed with numberless leaves. All round may be seen venerable trees, uprooted and stripped by the fury of the winds; and fragments of mountains, already scoured bare by the torrents, falling into those torrents and choking their valleys till the swollen rivers overflow and submerge the wide lowlands and their inhabitants. Again, you might have seen on many of the hill-tops terrified animals of different kinds, collected together and subdued to tameness, in company with men and women who had fled there with their children. The waters which covered the fields, with their waves were in great part strewn with tables, bedsteads, boats and various other contrivances made from necessity and the fear of death, on which were men and women with their children amid sounds of lamentation and weeping, terrified by the fury of the winds which with their tempestuous violence rolled the waters under and over and about the bodies of the drowned. Nor was there any object lighter than the water which was not covered with a variety of animals which, having come to a truce, stood together in a frightened crowd—among them wolves, foxes, snakes and others—fleing from death. And all the waters dashing on their shores seemed to be battling them with the blows of drowned bodies, blows which killed those in whom any life remained [19]. You might have

tinua piogia misti cholla gravza" li quali. 4. ramifichatione di "delle stracciate" [varie] piante [le quali] miste chon ifinite. 5. diradichate esstracinate. 6. sopra e . *On the margin is written* "e chiudere le loro valli". 7. righorghati allaghauano essomergieuano cholli. 8. "li" anchora aressti . : ridotto. 9. dimestichamēte. 10 Elle chanpagnie choperte . . mosstravā. 11. choperte. 12. choli . . figlio missti chō. 13. chon. 14. socto . . choli . . dacquella anneghati . . chel. 15. equali [pa] fatti treghua . . ī. 16. cholleghatione . . volpe serpe. 17. della . . perchuotritricie. 18. perchussioni . . anneghati le perchussio . . alliq"a". 19. [t]era . . Alchune chosgreghatione . . aressti, 20. chon arata . . difendeno li picholi . . era

608. This chapter, which, with the next one, is written on a loose sheet, seems to be the passage to which one of the compilers of the Vatican copy alluded when he wrote on the margin of fol. 36: "*Qua mi ricordo della mirabile discritione del Diluuio dello autore.*" It is scarcely necessary to point out that these chapters are among those which have never before been published. The description in No. 607 may be regarded as a preliminary sketch for this one. As the MS. G. (in which it is to be found) must be attributed to the period of about 1515 we may deduce from it the approximate date of the drawings on Pl. XXXIV, XXXV, Nos. 2 and 3, XXXVI and XXXVII, since they obviously belong to this text. The drawings No. 2 on Pl. XXXV are, in the original, side by side with the text of No. 608; lines 57 to 76 are shown in the facsimile. In the drawing in Indian ink given on Pl. XXXIV we see Wind-gods in the sky, corresponding to the allusion to Aeolus in No. 607 l. 15.—Plates XXXVI and XXXVII form one sheet in the original. The texts reproduced on these Plates have however no connection with the sketches, excepting the sketches of clouds on the right hand side. These texts are given as No. 477. The group of small figures on Pl. XXXVII, to the left, seems to be intended for a '*congregatione d'uomini.*' See No. 608, l. 19.

tioni d'uomini avresti potuto vedere, [20] le quali con armata mano difendevano li piccoli siti (che loro erā rimasti) [21] da lioni, lupi e animali rapaci, che quiui cercavā lor salute; O quanti romori [22] spaventevoli si sentivā per l'aria scura, percossa dal furore de' tuoni e delli fulgori da quelli scacciati, — che per [23] quella ruinosamente scorrevano percotēdo ciò che s'opponea al suo corso; O quāti [24] avresti veduti colle propie mani chiudersi li orechi per schifare l'imēsi romori, fatti [25] per la tenebrosa aria dal furore de' uēti misti con pioggia, tuoni cielesti e furore [26] di saette; Altri nō bastando loro il chiudere delli ochi, Ma colle propie mani ponēdo [27] quelle l'una sopra dell'altra, più se li copriuano per nō vedere il crudele stratio fatto del [28] la vmana spetie dall'ira di dio; O quāti lamenti o quāti spavētati si gittavano dalli scogli; [29] Vedeasi le grandi ramificationi delle grā quercie, cariche d'uomini esser portate [30] per l'aria dal furore delli inpetuosi venti; Quante erā le barche volte sotto sopra, [31] e quelle intere e quelle in pezzi esservi sopra giente travagliandosi per loro scampo [32] con atti e movimēti dolorosi pronosticāti di spavētevole morte; [33] Altri con movimēti disperati si toglievano la uita, disperādosi di nō potere sop[34]portare tal dolore, de' quali alcuni si gittavano dalli alti scogli, altri si strī[35]gievano la gola colle propie mani, alcuni pigliavā li propi figlioli e con grā[36]de rapidità li sbattevā interi, alcuni colle propie sue armi si ferivano e vccideā [37] se medesimi, altri gittandosi ginochioni si raccomādauā a dio: o quāte madri piāgie[38]vano i sua annegati figlioli, quelli tenēti sopra le ginocchia, alzando le braccia aperte in[39]verso il cielo e con voci, conposte di diversi vrlamēti, riprēdeuā l'ira delli dei; altri [40] colle mā giunte e le dita insieme tessute mordeuano e cō sanguinosi morsi quel [41] diuoravā, piegandosi col petto alle ginocchia per lo inmēso e insopportabile dolore; [42] Vedeāsi li armēti delli animali come cavalli, buoi, capre, pecore [43] esser già attornitate dalle acque e essere restate in isola nell'alte cime de' mōti già restrigniersi

seen assemblages of men who, with weapons in their hands, defended the small spots that remained to them against lions, wolves and beasts of prey who sought safety there. Ah! what dreadful noises were heard in the air rent by the fury of the thunder and the lightnings it flashed forth, which darted from the clouds dealing ruin and striking all that opposed its course. Ah! how many you might have seen closing their ears with their hands to shut out the tremendous sounds made in the darkened air by the raging of the winds mingling with the rain, the thunders of heaven and the fury of the thunder-bolts. Others were not content with shutting their eyes, but laid their hands one over the other to cover them the closer that they might not see the cruel slaughter of the human race by the wrath of God. Ah! how many laments! and how many in their terror flung themselves from the rocks! Huge branches of great oaks loaded with men were seen borne through the air by the impetuous fury of the winds. How many were the boats upset, some entire, and some broken in pieces, on the top of people labouring to escape with gestures and actions of grief foretelling a fearful death. Others, with desperate act, took their own lives, hopeless of being able to endure such suffering; and of these, some flung themselves from lofty rocks, others strangled themselves with their own hands, other seized their own children and violently slew them at a blow; some wounded and killed themselves with their own weapons; others, falling on their knees recommended themselves to God. Ah! how many mothers wept over their drowned sons, holding them upon their knees, with arms raised spread out towards heaven and with words and various threatening gestures, upbraiding the wrath of the gods. Others with clasped hands and fingers clenched gnawed them and devoured them till they bled, crouching with their breast down on their knees in their intense and unbearable anguish. Herds of animals were to be seen, such as horses, oxen, goats and swine already environed

rimasi) conarmata ma. 21. lione . . cierchav̄a. 22. l'aria "scura" perchossa da dal . . dell fulghoro . . "dacquelli cati ati" *is written in the margin.* 23. ruinosamenti . . [dacq] perchotēdo . . chessoppone alsocorso. 24. aresti . . cholle . . chiudersi . . isscifare. 25. chon . . effurore. 26. basstando . . chiu . . cholle . . ponē. 28. gittavā delli scogli. 29. le . . ramifichationi . . charicha . . portati. 30. dal [chorso] furore. 31. equale intere e quale in peze . . schanpo. 32. pronossticati . . [e dolorosa] morte. 33. Altriui chon . . toglievoila. 34. dolore [alchun] . . delli. 35. gievala ghola cholle . . alchuni . . chon. 36. rapito lissbatteva intera, alchuno cholle . . feria. 37. racomādaua addio. 38. aneghati . . ginocha . . bracia. 39. chon "vo"cie chonposte diderse. 40. cholle . . chelle dite [delle mani] insieme . . morde e chō. 41. pieghandosi chol . . ginochia. 42. vedeasi . . chome chavalli . . chapre pechore. 43. attormitato delle . . resstati . . mōto. 44. resstrigniersi . . ec-

insieme, e quelli del mezzo eleuarsi in alto e caminare sopra delli altri e fare infra loro grã zuffe, de' quali assai ne morivã per carestia di cibo; [46] E già li uccielli si posauan sopra gli omini e altri animali, nõ [47] trovando più terra scoperta che nõ fusse occupata da viuẽti, già la fame, [48] ministra della morte, avea tolto la uita a grã parte delli animali, quando [49] li corpi morti già leuilicati si leuauano dal fondo delle [50] profonde acque e surgievano in alto, E infra le conbattenti onde, sopra le [51] quali si sbattevano l' un nell' altro, e come palle piene di vẽto risaltavã [52] indiretro dal sito della lor percussione, questi si facievã [53] basa de' predetti morti; E sopra queste maladitioni si vedea l'aria [54] coperta di oscuri nuvoli, diuisi dalli serpeggianti moti delle infuriate [55] saette del cielo alluminande or qua or là infra la oscurità [56] delle tenebre.

[57] ¶ Vedesi il moto dell' aria medi[58]ante il moto della poluere, [59] mossa dal corso del cavallo, [60] il moto della quale è tãto velo[61]cie a riẽpiere il uacuo, che [62] di se lascia nell'aria, che [63] di se lo uestiua, quãto [64] è la velocità di tal cavallo [65] a fuggirsi dalla predetta aria.

[66] E ti parrà forse po[67]termi riprendere dell' auere [68] io figurato le uie fatte per l'a[69]ria dal moto del uẽto, concio[70]sia chè 'l uẽto per se nõ si uede [71] infra l'aria; A questa [72] parte si rispõde che non il [73] moto del uẽto, ma il moto [74] delle cose da lui porta[75]te è sol quel che per l'aria si uede. ¶

by the waters and left isolated on the high peaks of the mountains, huddled together, those in the middle climbing to the top and treading on the others, and fighting fiercely themselves; and many would die for lack of food. Already had the birds begun to settle on men and on other animals, finding no land uncovered which was not occupied by living beings, and already had famine, the minister of death, taken the lives of the greater number of the animals, when the dead bodies, now fermented, where leaving the depth of the waters and were rising to the top. Among the buffeting waves, where they were beating one against the other, and, like as balls full of air, rebounded from the point of concussion, these found a resting place on the bodies of the dead. And above these judgements, the air was seen covered with dark clouds, riven by the forked flashes of the raging bolts of heaven, lighting up on all sides the depth of the gloom.

The motion of the air is seen by the motion of the dust thrown up by the horse's running and this motion is as swift in again filling up the vacuum left in the air which enclosed the horse, as he is rapid in passing away from the air.

Perhaps it will seem to you that you may reproach me with having represented the currents made through the air by the motion of the wind notwithstanding that the wind itself is not visible in the air. To this I must answer that it is not the motion of the wind but only the motion of the things carried along by it which is seen in the air.

DIUISIONI.

[77] Tenebre, vento, fortuna [78] di mare, diluvio d'acqua, selue [79] infoccate, pioggia, saette del cie[80]lo, terremoti e ruina di [81] mõti, spianamẽti di città.

[76] THE DIVISIONS.

Darkness, wind, tempest at sea, floods of water, forests on fire, rain, bolts from heaven, earthquakes and ruins of mountains, overthrow of cities.

quelli . . mezo . . chaminare. 45. effare infralloro . . charesstia dicib. 47. fussi ochupata. 48. minisstra 49. leuificliati. 50. essurgievano . . infralle conbattente. 51. fisbattevan . . chome. 52. indireto da sito . . perchussione questi eran [al continuo] si. 53. di . . Essopra. 54. choperta di osscuri . . serpegianti. 55. cielo [le qua] aluminaado . . infralla osscurita. 59. cavallo [il]. 60. ettanto. 61. arriẽpieri in vachuo. 62. lasscia . . che [lui]. 63. se il ucstiua quanto quãto. 64. ella . . chavallo. 65. affuggirsi della. 66. [E] Ti. 68. fighurato. 71. infrallaria Acquessta. 72. rissp̃õde . . nõ ml. 74. chose

76. These observations, added at the bottom of the page containing the full description of the doluge seem to indicate that it was Leonardo's intention to elaborate the subject still farther in a separate treatise.

81. *Spianamenti di città* (overthrow of cities). A considerable number of drawings in black chalk, at Windsor, illustrate this catastrophe. Most of them are much rubbed; one of the least injured is reproduced at Pl. XXXIX. Compare also the pen and ink sketch Pl. XXXVI.

[82]¶Vēti revertiginosi [83]che portano acqua, [84]rami di piāte e omini infra l'aria¶

[85]¶Rami stracciatti da vēti [86]misti col corso de' vē[87]ti con giente di sopra.¶

[88]¶Piāte rotte cariche [89]di gente.¶

[90]¶Navi rotte in pezzi [91]battute in iscogli.¶

[92]Delli armēti, [93]grādine, [94]saette, [95]vēti re[96]vertigino[97]si.

[98]Gente che siē sopra piāte che nō si possō sostenere | alberi e scogli, torri, colli piē di gēte, barche, tavole, madie [99]e altri strumēti da natare | colli coperti d'uomini e donne e animalj e saette da nvuoli che alluminīo le cose.

Whirlwinds which carry water [spouts] branches of trees, and men through the air.

Boughs stripped off by the winds, mingling by the meeting of the winds, with people upon them.

Broken trees loaded with people.

Ships broken to pieces, beaten on rocks.

Flocks of sheep. Hail stones, thunderbolts, whirlwinds.

Peoble on trees which are unable to to support them; trees and rocks, towers and hills covered with people, boats, tables, troughs, and other means of floating. Hills covered with men, women and animals; and lightning from the clouds illuminating every thing.

W. 158 b]

609.

Descritione del diluuio.

[2]Sia inprima figurata la cīma d'un aspro monte con alquanta valle circustante [3]alla sua basa, e ne'lati di questo si ueda la scorza del terreno leuarsi insieme [4]colle minute radici di piccoli sterpi e spogliar di se grā parte delli circūstanti scogli, [5]ruvinosa disciēda di tal dirupamēto con turbolenza del corso vada percuotēdo e scalzando [6]le ritorte e globulenti radici delle grā piāte, e quelle ruinando sotto sopra, e le mō[7]tagnie denudandosi scoprino le profonde fessure fatte in quelle dalli antichi [8]terremoti, e li piedi delle mōtagnie sieno in gran parte rincalzate vestite [9]delle rvine delli arbusti precipitati da lati dell'alte cime de'predetti [10]mōti, i quali siē misti cō fango, radici, rami d'alberi cō diuerse foglie infusi infra esso fango [11]e terra e sassi, E le ruine d'alcuni monti sien disciese nella profondità [12]d'alcuna valle, e faccisi argine della ringorgata acqua del suo fiume, la quale ar[13]gine già rotta scorra con grādissime onde, delle quali le massime percuoti[14]no e ruinino le mura delle città e uille di tal valle, E le ruine degli alti edifiti [15]delle predette città levino grā poluere, l'acqua si leui in alto in forma di fumo, o di ravvi[16]luppati nuvoli si movino contro alla disciendēte pioggia; Ma la ringorgata [17]acqua si vada

Description of the deluge.

Let there be first represented the summit of a rugged mountain with valleys surrounding its base, and on its sides let the surface of the soil be seen to slide, together with the small roots of the bushes, denuding great portions of the surrounding rocks. And descending ruinous from these precipices in its boisterous course, let it dash along and lay bare the twisted and gnarled roots of large trees overthrowing their roots upwards; and let the mountains, as they are scoured bare, discover the profound fissures made in them by ancient earthquakes. The base of the mountains may be in great part clothed and covered with ruins of shrubs, hurled down from the sides of their lofty peaks, which will be mixed with mud, roots, boughs of trees, with all sorts of leaves thrust in with the mud and earth and stones. And into the depth of some valley may have fallen the fragments of a mountain forming a shore to the swollen waters of its river; which, having already burst its banks, will rush on in monstrous waves; and the greatest will strike upon and destroy the walls of the cities and farmhouses in the valley [14]. Then the ruins of the high buildings in these cities will throw up a great dust, rising up in

[p] dallui. 77. denebre. 78. saluc. 79. infochate. 80. lo [ruin] teremoti. 83. porrtano. 84. infralla"ria". 86. corsorso. 90. nave . . pezi. 91. isscogli. 94. saetti. 98. chessiē . . posō scotenere | albri esscogli. 99. notare . colli [de] . . chose.

609. 1. desscritione. 2. fighurato . . asspro vale circhustante. 3. basa [e di questo] ēne . . lasscorza . terеno. 4. pichol . . esspogliar . . "circūstanti" scogli [alla pioggia]. 5. disscīēda di . . deruppamēto chon turbole del chorso . . parchotēdo esschalzando. 6. E gluppolente . . ecquelle . . elle. 7. inquelli. 8. elli . . rinchalzate vestiti. 9. albussti . . dellalalalte . . prede. 10. equali . . missti fangho . . fangho. 11. etterra essassi Elle . . dalchuni . . dissciese. 12. dalchuna effaccisi . . ringhorghata. 13. chon . . perchuti. 14. ruino . . delli Elle. 15. della predetta citti . . laquasi . . ravi. 16. lupali . . dissciendette Malla ringhorghata . . 17. pelagho . . asse . . chon. 18. perchotendo errisaltando . . cholla fangho. 19. sciu-

609. The sketches on Pl. XXXV 3 stand by the side of lines 14 to 54.

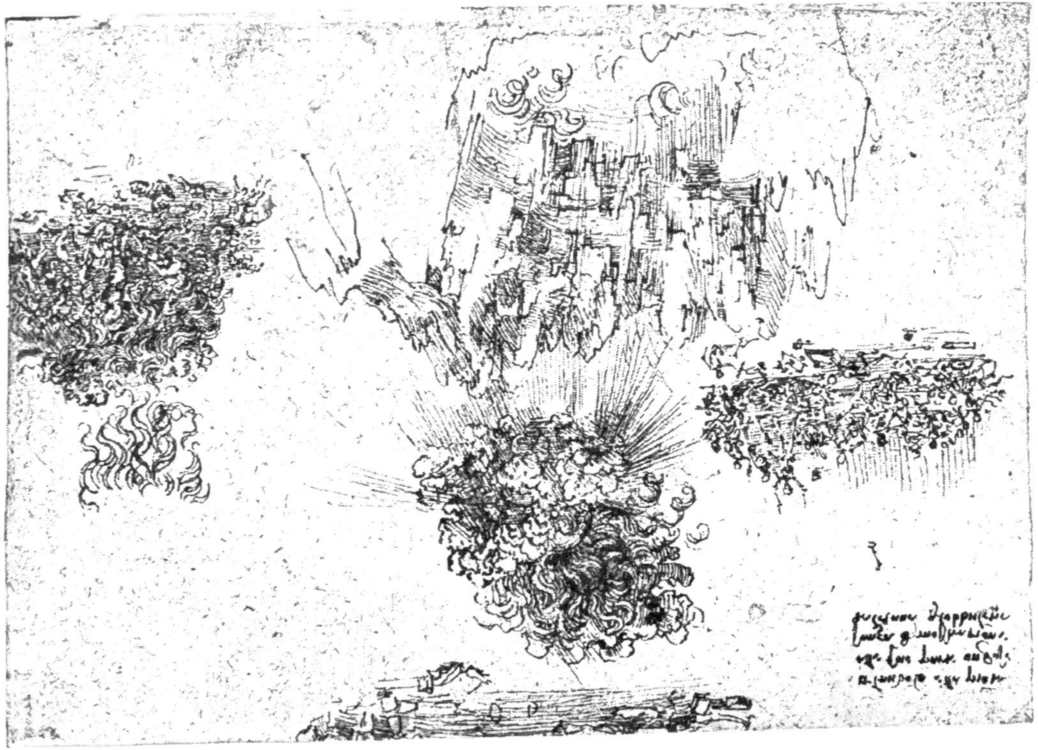

raggirando pel pelago, che dētro a se la rinchiude, e con ritrosi [18]revertiginosi in diuersi obbietti percuotendo e risaltando in aria colla fango[19]sa schiuma, poi ricadendo e faciendo reflettere in aria l'acqua percossa; E le onde [20]circulari che si fuggono dal loco della percussione, caminando col suo inpeto in tra[21]verso sopra del moto dell'altre onde circulari, che contra di loro si muovono e dopo la [22]fatta percussione risalgono in aria sanza spiccarsi dalle lor base; E all'uscita, che l'acqua [23]fa di tal pelago, si uede le disfatte onde distendersi inverso la loro vscita, dopo la [24]quale, cadendo over disciēdendo infra l'aria, acquista peso e moto inpetuoso, [25]dopo il quale, penetrando la percossa acqua, quella apre e penetra con furore alla per[26]cussione del fondo, dal quale poi reflettēdo risalta inverso la superfitie del pelago, ac[27]compagnata dall'aria che con lei si somerse, e questa resta nella uscita colla schiu[28]ma mista cō legniami e altre cose più lievi che l'acqua, intorno alle quali si da prī[29]cipio all'onde che tanto più crescono in circuito, quāto più ac[30]quistano di moto, el qual moto le fa tāto più basse quanto ell'acquistano più [31]larga basa, e per questo sono poco evidenti nel lor consumamēto; Ma se l'onde riperco[32]tono in vari obbietti, allora elle risaltano in dirietro sopra l'auenimento dell'altre onde, osser[33]vando l'accrescimēto della medesima curvità ch'elle l'avrebbero acquistato nell'oservatio[34]ne del già principiato moto; Ma la pioggia nel disciēdere de' sua nvuoli è del medesimo [35]color d'essi nvuoli, cioè della sua parte ōbrosa, se già li razzi solari nō li penetrassino, il che se cosl [36]fusse, la pioggia si dimostrerebbe di minore oscurità che esso nuvolo, e se li gran pesi delle [37]massime ruine delli grā monti o d'altri magni edifiti ne' lor ruine percuoteranno li grā pelaghi [38]dell'acque, allora risalterà gran quātità d'acqua infra l'aria, il moto della quale sarà fatto per cō[39]trario aspetto a quello che fecie il moto del percussore dell'acque, cioè l'angolo della reflessiō, [40]e fia simile all'angolo della incidetia; Delle cose portate dal corso delle acque quella si dis[41]costerà più dalle opposite riue che fia più

shape like smoke or wreathed clouds against the falling rain. But the swollen waters will sweep round the pool which contains them striking in eddying whirlpools against the different obstacles, and leaping into the air in muddy foam; then, falling back, the beaten water will again be dashed into the air. And the whirling waves which fly from the place of concussion, and whose impetus moves them across other eddies going in a contrary direction, after their recoil will be tossed up into the air but without dashing off from the surface. Where the water issues from the pool the spent waves will be seen spreading out towards the outlet; and there falling or pouring through the air and gaining weight and impetus they will strike on the water below piercing it and rushing furiously to reach its depth; from which being thrown back it returns to the surface of the lake, carrying up the air that was submerged with it; and this remains at the outlet in foam mingled with logs of wood and other matters lighter than water. Round these again are formed the beginnings of waves which increase the more in circumference as they acquire more movement; and this movement rises less high in proportion as they acquire a broader base and thus they are less conspicuous as they die away. But if these waves rebound from various objects they then return in direct opposition to the others following them, observing the same law of increase in their curve as they have already acquired in the movement they started with. The rain, as it falls from the clouds is of the same colour as those clouds, that is in its shaded side; unless indeed the sun's rays should break through them; in that case the rain will appear less dark than the clouds. And if the heavy masses of ruin of large mountains or of other grand buildings fall into the vast pools of water, a great quantity will be flung into the air and its movement will be in a contrary direction to that of the object which struck the water; that is to say: The angle of reflection will be equal to the angle nf incidence. Of the objects car-

ma . . richadendo effeciendo refrettera . . perchossa Elle. 20. circhulari chessi fugghano del locho . . perchussione chaminando chol. 21. circhulara . . choutra . . movano. 22. perchusione risaliano . . spicharsi . . Ellusscita chellacq"a". 23. pelagho . . disfacte . . vsscitt. 24. chadendo . . dissciēdendo infrallaria acquissta. 25. perchossa. 26. chussion . . refceliedo . . pelagho. 27. chonpagnlata . . chon . . ecquessta ressta nella vissci cholla sciu. 28. chol . . chose . . lieve chellacquo. 29. allonde [che chol suo] chettauto . . cresschano [quāto] in circhuita. 30. piu [bassa]. 31. largha . . poche . . chonsumamēto Masse . . riperchо. 32. tano . . dirieto. 33. lacresscimēto . . churvita . . arebbe. 34. Malla . . dissiēdero. 35. seggia . . penetrassi . . chosi. 36. fussi . . dimossterrebbe . . osschurita . . hesselli . . della ma. 37. perchoteranno. 38. infrallariael . . perchō. 39. asspecto acquello cheffecie . . perchussore . . langholo . . refresiō. 40. anghelo grave over di maggior quantità, Li ritro[42]si delle acque nelle sue parti sono tanto più veloci quanto elle son più vicine al [43]suo cientro, La cima delle onde del mare discende dinãzi alle lor base, battendosi e confregã[44]dosi sopra le globulentie della sua faccia, e tal confregatione, trita in minute particule della [45]disciendente acqua la qual, con vertendosi in grossa nebbia, si mischia nelli corsi de' uẽti a modo di ravilup[46]pato fumo e revolutiõ di nuvoli, e la leva al fine infra l'aria e si cõuerte ĩ nvuoli [47]Ma la pioggia, che discende infra l'aria, nell' essere conbattuta e percossa dal corso de' uenti, si fa [48]rara o densa, secondo la rarità o densità d'essi venti, e per questo si gienera infra l'aria [49]vna inondatione di trasparẽti, fatti dalla discesa della pioggia, che è vicina all'ochio che [50]la vede, L'onde del mare, che percuotono l'obliquità de'monti che collui confinano, saranno schiumose, [51]con uelocità contro al dosso de'detti colli, e nel tornare, indirieto si scõtrano [52]nell'auenimẽto della secõda onda, e dopo il grã loro strepito tornã con grãde inõdatione [53]al mare, donde si partirono, Gran quantità di popoli d'uomini e d'animali diuersi si uedea scaciati [54]dall' accrescimẽto del diluuio inverso le cime de'monti, uicine alle predette acque.

[55]Onde del mare di Piombino [56]tutta d'acqua schiumosa

[57]Dell'acqua che risalta, [58]de vẽti di Pionbino a Piõbino || ritrosi, di uẽti e di pioggia cõ rami e alberi misti coll' aria || votamẽti dell'acqua che piove [59]nelle barche

ried down by the current, those which are heaviest or rather largest in mass will keep farthest from the two opposite shores The water in the eddies revolves more swiftly in proportion as it is nearer to their centre The crests of the waves of the sea tumble to their bases falling with friction on the bubbles of their sides, and this friction grinds the falling water into minute particles and this being converted into a dense mist, mingles with the gale in the manner of curling smoke and wreathing clouds, and at last it, rises into the air and is converted into clouds But the rain which falls through the atmosphere being driven and tossed by the winds becomes rarer or denser according to the rarity or density of the winds that buffet it, and thus there is generated in the atmosphere a moisture formed of the transparent particles of the rain which is near to the eye of the spectator The waves of the sea which break on the slope of the mountains which bound it, will foam from the velocity with which they fall against these hills, in rushing back they will meet the next wave as it comes and and after a loud noise return in a great flood to the sea whence they came Let great numbers of inhabitants—men and animals of all kinds—be seen driven [54]by the rising of the deluge to the peaks of the mountains in the midst of the waters aforesaid

[55]The wave of the sea at Piombino is all foaming water[58]

Of the water which leaps up from the spot where great masses fall on its surface Of the winds of Piombino at Piombino Eddies of wind and rain with boughs and shrubs mixed in the air. Emptying the boats of the rain water

C A 78*a*, 228*a*]

610

Of depicting natural phenomena (610 611)

Lo immẽso furore del uẽto cacciato [2]dalle ruine de'mõti sopra le incluse spe-

The tremendous fury of the wind driven by the falling in of the hills on the caves

delcorso 41 schosstera delle oposite cheffia retro 42 acque [quello e piu veloce] nlle parte tanto velocie 43 suo cientro la cima Delle dissciende [la cima] "dinãci confreghã 44 globbulentie ettal confreghatione partichula 45 dissciente miscia 46 nvuoli [o diseda nebbia] e la invuoli 47 Malla infrallaria perchossa 48 eddensa oddensita venti [chella perchotano] e quessto infrallari a 49 innondatione [di sottile] di trassparẽti dal dissciẽso 50 perchote monti [chell] che chollui sarrano "sciumose 51 chõ [velocie moto per la] con cholli sisscõ 52 sechõde 53 eddanima scaciere 54 accresscimẽto 55 hõde 56 sciumosa 57 risalta

55 56 These two lines are written below the bottom sketch on Pl XXXV, 3. The MS Leic being written about the year 1510 or later, it does not seem to me to follow that the sketches must have been made at Piombino, where Leonardo was in the year 1502 and possibly returned there subsequently (see Vol II Topographical notes).

610 See the sketches and text on Pl XXXVIII, No 1 Lines 1—16 are there given on the left

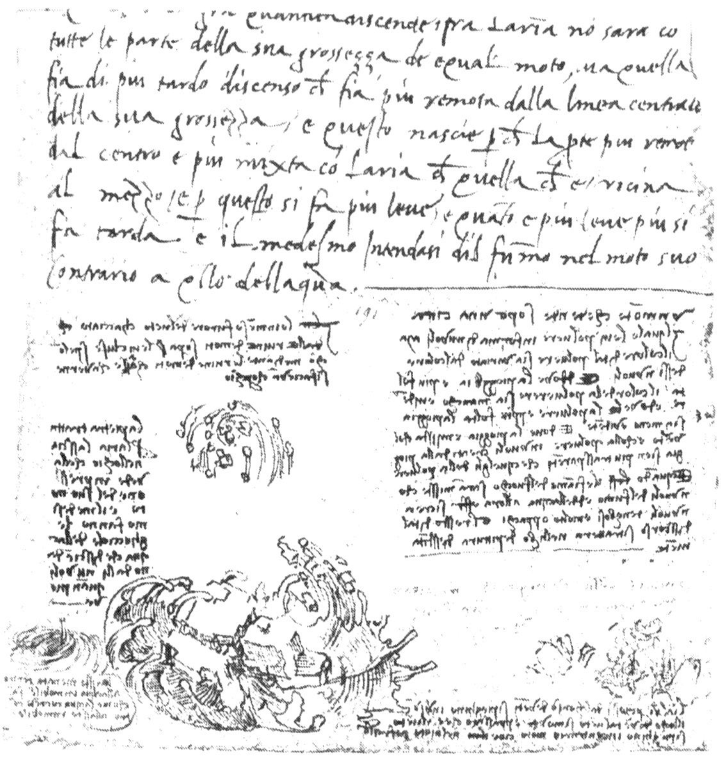
... quando non ascende sopra l'aria no sara co
tutte le parte della sua grossezza de equale moto, ma quella
fia di piu tardo discenso et fia piu remota dalla linea centrale
della sua grossezza, e questo nascie per la parte piu remota
dal centro e piu mixta co l'aria et quella ch'e vicina
al mezzo et p questo si fa piu leve, e quanto e piu leve piu si
fa tarda e il medesimo intendasi del fumo nel moto suo
contrario a quello dellaqua.

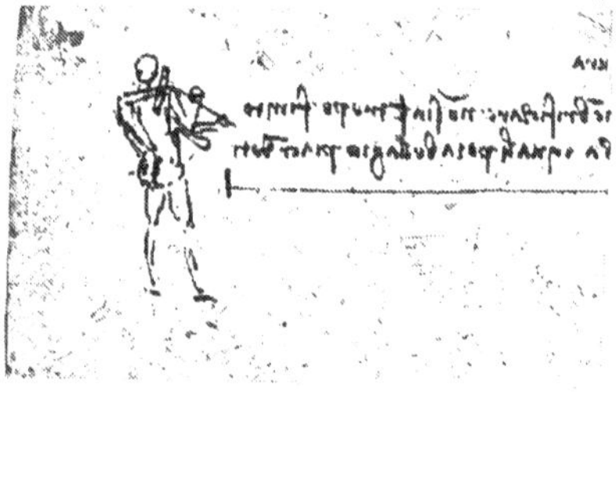

lò[3]che mediante le ruine de' mōti che a caverne [4] si facievā coperchio.

[5] La pietra, tratta [6] per l'aria, lascia [7] nell'ochio che la [8] vede inpressi[9]one del suo mo[10]to, e il medesi[11]mo fanno le [12] gocciole dell'ac[13]qua che disciēdo[14]no dalli nuvoli [15] quādo pio[16]ve.

[17] Vn mōte cadente sopra vna città [18] il quale levi polvere in forma di nuvoli, ma [19] il colore di tal polvere sia variato dal colore [20] d'essi nvuoli; E dove la pioggia è più fol[21]ta, il color della poluere sia manco euidē[22]te, e dove la poluere è più folta, la pioggia [23] sia meno evidēte; E dove la pioggia è mista col [24] vēto e colla poluere, i nuvoli creati dalla piog[25]gia sien più trasparēti che quelli della poluere; [26] E quādo le fiam̄e del fuoco sarā miste con [27] nvuoli del fumo e dell'acqua, allora si creā [28] nvuoli tenebrosi e molto oppachi; e 'l resto di tal [29] discorso si tratterà nel libro de pittura distesa[30]mēte.

within—by the falling of the hills which served as roofs to these caverns.

A stone flung through the air leaves on the eye which sees it the impression of its motion, and the same effect is produced by the drops of water which fall from the clouds when it [16] rains.

[17] A mountain falling on a town, will fling up dust in the form of clouds; but the colour of this dust will differ from that of the clouds. Where the rain is thickest let the colour of the dust be less conspicuous and where the dust is thickest let the rain be less conspicuous. And where the rain is mingled with the wind and with the dust the clouds created by the rain must be more transparent than those of dust [alone]. [26] And when flames of fire are mingled with clouds of smoke and water very opaque and dark clouds will be formed [28]. And the rest of this subject will be treated in detail in the book on painting.

C. A. 152 a; 451 a]

611.

Vedeuasi giēte, che cō gran sollecitu[2]dine apparecchiavā uettovaglia [3] sopra diuerse sorte di navili fatti bre[4]vissimi; dell'onde nō si dimo[5]stravano in que'luoghi dove le te[6]nebrose pioggie colli lor nuvoli [7] reflettevano.

[8] Ma doue li uāpi gienerati dalle [9] celesti saette reflettevano, si ve[10]devano tanti lustri fatti da' simvla[11]cri de' lor vampi, quāte erā l'ō[12]de, che alli ochi de' circustāti poteā [13] reflettere.

[14] Tanto crescieva il nvmero de' si[15]mulacri fatti da uāpi delle saette so[16]pra l'onde dell'acqua, quanto cre[17]scieva la distātia delli ochi lor ris[18]guardatori.

People were to be seen eagerly embarking victuals on various kinds of hastily made barks. But little of the waves were visible in those places where the dark clouds and rain were reflected.

But where the flashes caused by the bolts of heaven were reflected, there were seen as many bright spots, caused by the image of the flashes, as there were waves to reflect them to the eye of the spectator.

The number of the images produced by the flash of lightning on the waves of the water were multiplied in proportion to the distance of the spectator's eye.

del [sito dove chadano li grā pesi perchussori delle acque]. 58. chollaria.

610. 1. [li n] lo . . chacciato. 2. moti. 3. cha "a"sse chaverne. 4. choperchio. 6. lasscia. 7. chella. 12. ghucciole. 13. disscīēda. 15. quā piv. 17. chadende. 20. Eddove. 21. poluerere . . maucho. 22. dove [le] . . eppiu. 23. missta chol. 24. cholla. 25. trassparēti checquelgli. 26. Ecquādo [le] lo . . fuocho . . misstecho. 27. eddeli. 28. ressto. 29. disscorso. . . desstīta.

611. 2. aparecchiavā. 4. dellonde "nō" [pocho] si dimos. 6. cholli. 7. refrettevano. 9. cielesste . . refrette. 10. deva . . lusstri. 12. ali . . circhusstāti. 13. refrectere. 14. scresscievano. 16. cres. 17. disstātia. 18. ghardatori. 19. diminuiva [no quāto

hand side, 17—30 on the right. The four lines at the bottom on the right are given as No. 472. Above these texts, which are written backwards, there are in the original sixteen lines in a larger writing from left to right, but only half of this is here visible. They treat of the physical laws of motion of air and water. It does not seem to me that there is any reason for concluding that this writing from left to right is spurious. Compare with it the facsimile of the rough copy of Leonardo's letter to Ludovico il Moro in Vol. II.

26—28. Compare Pl. XL, 2—the drawing in Indian ink on the left hand side, which seems to be a reminiscence of his observations of an eruption (see his remarks on Mount Etna in Vol II).

[19]E così diminuiva [20]tal numero di simulacri, quãto [21]più s'auicinavano agli ochi che li [22]vedeano, com'è provato nella difi-[23]nitione dello splendore della luna [24]e del nostro orizzõte marittimo, [25]quãdo il sole ui reflette cõ sua [26]razzi, e che l'ochio, che ricieve tal re[27]flessione, sia lontano dal predetto mare.

So also the number of the images was diminished in proportion as they were nearer the eye which saw them [22], as it has been proved in the definition of the luminosity of the moon [23], and of our marine horizon when the sun's rays are reflected in it and the eye which receives the reflection is remote from the sea.

più sil. 20. [facie] tal nume. 24. nosstro . . marictimo. 25. qua quãdo . . refrette cho. 26. razi. 27. fre ione.

611. 22. 23. *Com'è provato.* See Vol. II, Nos. 874—878 and 892—901.

Heliog. Dujardin

VI.

THE ARTIST'S MATERIALS.

S. K. M. II.[1] 9]

612.

Of chalk and paper (612—617).

Per fare pūte da colorire a secco; la [2]tēpera cō vn po' di ciera e nō la secca, [3]la qual ciera disoluerai, cō acqua, [4]che, tenperata la biacca, essa acqua stilla-[5]ta se ne vada in fumo e rimāga la [6]ciera sola, e farai bone pūte; Ma sap[7]pi che bisogna macinare i co[8]lori colla pietra calda.

To make points [crayons] for colouring dry. Temper with a little wax and do not dry it; which wax you must dissolve with water: so that when the white lead is thus tempered, the water being distilled, may go off in vapour and the wax may remain; you will thus make good crayons; but you must know that the colours must be ground with a hot stone.

F. 96a]

613.

Il lapis se disfa in vino e in aceto o in acqua[2]vite, e poi si può ricōgiugnere cō colla dolce.

Chalk dissolves in wine and in vinegar or in aqua fortis and can be recombined with gum.

S. K. M. III. 53a]

614.

Carta da disegnare [2]nero collo sputo.

[3]Togli poluere · di galla · e di vetriolo · e polue[4]rizza ·, e spandi · sopra · carta a vso · di uerni[5]ce poi · scriui cō pēna intīta nello [6]sputo ·, e farai · nero · come · inchiostro.

Paper for drawing upon in black by the aid of your spittle.

Take powdered gall nuts and vitriol, powder them and spread them on paper like a varnish, then write on it with a pen wetted with spittle and it will turn as black as ink.

612. 1. assecho. 2. cōvpo di . . cascero (?). 3. acque. 4. biacha . . stila. 6. effara . . Massa. 8. cholla.
613 1. ilapis . . acq"a". 2. vte . . ricōgugnere.
614. 2. choliossputo. 4. rizza esspandi . . charta. 5. pena. 6. effarai . . inchiosstro.

Br M 174 a]

615.

Se uoi fare lettere scortate, tira la [2]carta in telaio e disegnia e poi ta[3]glia tali lettere e fa passare i razzi [4]solari per tali spiracoli sopra vn altra car[5]ta tirata, e poi rifa li angoli mācati.

If you want to make foreshortened letters stretch the paper in a drawing frame and then draw your letters and cut them out, and make the sunbeams pass through the holes on to another stretched paper, and then fill up the angles that are wanting.

C. A 71 b; 209 b]

616

Questa carta si debbe tigniere di [2]fumo di cādela tēperato cō colla dolce, [3]e poi inbrattare sottilmēte la foglia di [4]biacca a olio, come si fa alle lettere ī [5]istāpa, e poi stampare nel modo co[6]mune, e così tal foglia parrà aōbrata [7]ne' cavi e alluminata nelli rilieui, il [8]che interuiene qui al contrario.

This paper should be painted over with candle soot tempered with thin glue, then smear the leaf thinly with white lead in oil as is done to the letters in printing, and then print in the ordinary way Thus the leaf will appear shaded in the hollows and lighted on the parts in relief, which however comes out here just the contrary.

F 56 a]

617.

Molto fia bella la carta biāca fissa [2]fatta di mistura e latte di gichero colato, [3]e fatta tal carta e poi inumidita e pie[4]gata e avviluppata a caso e mista colla mi[5]stura e così lasciata seccare, Ma se la [6]rōpi auāti ch'ella invmidisca accade a [7]modo di lasagne, e poi inumidisci [8]e avviluppa e poi metti in mistura e lascia [9]seccare, ancora se tal [10]carta sarà vestita di biāco fisso e tras[11]parēte e sardonio, e poi sia inumidi[12]ta accio non faccia angoli, e poi sia avviluppa[13]ta intrāsparēte forte, e come l'è ferma, [14]sega la grossa 2 dita, e lascia secca[15]re, Ancora se fai cartone fisso di [16]sardonio, e seccalo e poi [17]lo metti infra 2 carte di papiro [18]e lo rōpi dentro cō martel di legno, col pu[19]gno, poi apri cō diligenza tenēdo ferma [20]per piano [21]la carta [22]di sotto a[23]cciochè li pez[24]zi rotti nō [25]si sconpa[26]gnino, po[27]i abbi

Very excellent will be a stiff white paper, made of the usual mixture and filtered milk of an herb called calves foot; and when this paper is prepared and damped and folded and wrapped up it may be mixed with the mixture and thus left to dry, but if you break it before it is moistened it becomes somewhat like the thin paste called *lasagne* and you may then damp it and wrap it up and put it in the mixture and leave it to dry; or again this paper may be covered with stiff transparent white and *sardonio* and then damped so that it may not form angles and then covered up with strong transparent size and as soon as it is firm cut it two fingers, and leave it to dry, again you may make stiff cardboard of *sardonio* and dry it and then place it between two sheets of papyrus and break it inside with a wooden mallet with a handle and

615 2 po 3 effa pasare 5 agoli macati
616 1 quessta charda 4 biacha 5 nistāpa stanpire 6 chosi . pāra. 8. interuene il
617 1 biācha 2 falta . . ellatte . gichero colato. 3. eppoi 4 avilupata achaso 5 lassciata sechare Massella. 6. achaso 8 aviluppa po ellascia 9 sechare . settal 10 biācho ettras. 11 essardonio . poi inumidi 12 acco no facca anoli e poi . aviluppa 14 lasscia secha 15 seffai 16. essechalo epoi ī la picha info) 17 [glio] lo . . palpiro 18 ello

616. This text, which accompanies a facsimile impression of a leaf of sage, has already been published in the *Saggio delle Opere di L. da Vinci*, Milano 1872, p. 11. G. Govi observes on this passage: "*Forse aveva egli pensato ancora a farsi un erbario, od almeno a riprodurre facilmente su carta le forme e i particolari delle foglie di diverse piante, poichè (modificando un metodo che probabilmente gli era stato insegnato da altri, e che piu tardi si legge ripetuto in molti ricettarii e libri di segreti), accanto a una foglia di Salvia impressa in nero su carta bianca, lasciò scritto Questa carta . . .*

Erano i primi tentativi di quella riproduzione immediata delle parti vegetali, che poi sotto il nome d'Impressione Naturale, fu condotta a tanta perfezione in questi ultimi tempi dal signor de Hauer e da altri."

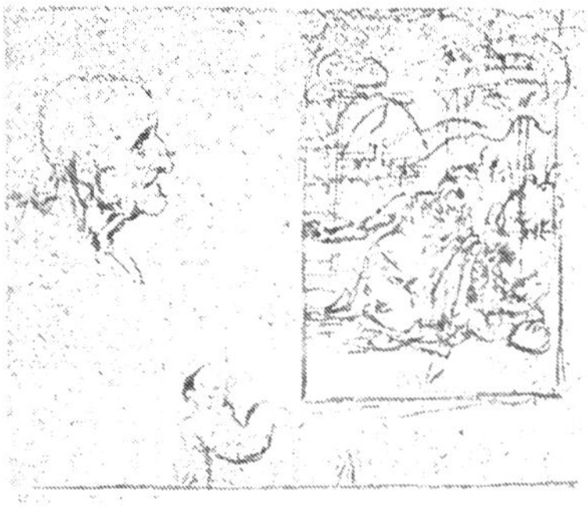

vna [28]carta in[29]collata cal[30]da, e appicca [31]la sopra tut[32]ti essi pez[33]zi, e lascia [34]fermare, [35]poi la uol[36]ta sotto so[37]pra e da di [38]transparē[39]te più vol[40]te nello spa[41]tio, ch'è tra [42]li pezzi ve[43]rsādo og[44]ni volta, [45]poi di ne[46]ro e poi [47]di bianco [48]fisso, e co[49]sì lascia o[50]gni volta se[51]ccare, po[52]i la spiana [53]e pulisci.

then open it with care holding the lower sheet of paper flat and firm so that the broken pieces be not separated, then have a sheet of paper covered with hot glue and apply it on the top of all these pieces and let them stick fast, then turn it upside down and apply transparent size several times in the spaces between the pieces, each time pouring in first some black and then some stiff white and each time leaving it to dry, then smoothe it and polish it

C A 258a, 784a]

618

Per fare verde bello | togli il uerde e mescola [2]colla mūmia | e farai l'ōbra più scura, poi per farla [3]più chiaro verde e oquria e per più chiara verde [4]e giallo e pe' lumi giallo ischietto, di poi togli [5]verde e curcuma ǰsieme, e vela sopr' o[6]gni cosa, [7]per fare v̄ rosso bello togli cinabrese o mattita [8]o oquria arsa pell'ōbre scure e pelle più [9]matita e minio, e pe' lumi minio solo, poi vela [10]cō lacca bella [11]per fare olio buono a dipigniere | Vna parte d'olio [12]vna di prima dirinentia e una di seconda.

On the preparation and use of colours. (618—627)

To make a fine green take green and mix it with bitumen and you will make the shadows darker Then, for lighter [shades] green with yellow ochre, and for still lighter green with yellow, and for the high lights pure yellow, then mix green and turmeric together and glaze every thing with it To make a fine red take cinnabar or red chalk or burnt ochre for the dark shadows and for the lighter ones red chalk and vermilion and for the lights pure vermilion and then glaze with fine lake To make good oil for painting One part of oil, one of the first refining and one of the second

C A 70a, 207a]

619

¶ Onbra nera adopera [2]lume, biacca, giallo, verde, minio e lacca, [3]Onbre mezzane, togli l'ombra di sopra [4]e mescola colla detta īcarnazione arre[5]cādovi vn poco di giallo e vn po' di uerde, e alle [6]volte della lacca, [7]per avere l'onbre togli verde e lacca nell'ōbre mezzane ¶

Use black in the shadow, aud in the lights white, yellow, green, vermilion and lake Medium shadows, take the shadow as above and mix it with the flesh tints just alluded to, adding to it a little yellow and a little green and occasionally some lake, for the shadows take green and lake for the middle shades

H 2 46b]

620

Farai bella oquria se terrai il modo [2]che si tiene a fare la biacca

You can make a fine ochre by the same method as you use to make white

23 cioche li pe 26 appi 30 apica 44 poi di dine 50 chate 53 pulisca
618 1—12 P 1 emēsscola 2 cholla mūmia effarai isscura poi per \\\ a 3 eoquria e per 4 issciетto 5 churchuma ǰ sieme cheuela 6 chosa 8 o oquria isscure e pelle piu chan 9 emminio eppellumi 10 chō 11 parce 12 dirinentia sechonda
619 1 nera e oqurie (?) 2 biaccha gialla ellacha 3 mezane 4 ēmesschola cholla īchazione arripi 5 ēdovi pocho 6 laccha 7 lonbre o verde ellacche mezane enella
620 1 oquria settierai 2 chessi affare biaccha

618 and 619 If we may judge from the flourishes with which the writing is ornamented these passages must have been written in Leonardo's youth.

C. A. 70 *b*; 207 *b*]

621.

GIALLO BELLO.

[2]Disolui risagallo a vno sorbimẽto con acqua [3]forte.

BIANCO.

[5]Metti la biacca in vn tegame, che ui sia g[6]rossa vna corda per tutto, e lasci[7]a la stare 2 di al sole e al sereno, e fa [8]che la mattina quando il sole a rasciutto [9]la rugiada della notte ...

A FINE YELLOW.

Dissolve realgar with one part of orpiment, with aqua fortis.

WHITE.

Put the white into an earthen pot, and lay it no thicker than a string, and let it stand in the sun undisturbed for 2 days; and in the morning when the sun has dried off the night dews.

Tr. 78]

622.

Per fare rosso ĩ nero per ĩcarnatione: [2]togli rubini di Rocca Nova o granati e mischia un attimo; ancora il bolo [3]armeno è bono ĩ parte.

To make reddish black for flesh tints take red rock crystals from Rocca Nova or garnets and mix them a little; again armenian bole is good in part.

L. 92 *a*]

623.

La õbra fia verde terra bruciata.

The shadow will be burnt ‚terra-verte'.

A. 88]

624.

PROPORTIONE DI COLORI.

[2]Se una oncia di nero · misto · con vna õcia di biacca · fanno uno grado di scurità ·, quãti gradi [3]di scurità · farà 2 õcie di nero sopra una oncia di biacca?

THE PROPORTIONS OF COLOURS.

If one ounce of black mixed with one ounce of white gives a certain shade of darkness, what shade of darkness will be produced by 2 ounces of black to 1 ounce of white?

W. P. 5 *a*]

625.

¶Ricuocere nera ·, gialla uerdegiãte nel fine azzurra.¶

Remix black, greenish yellow and at the end blue.

F. 96 *b*]

626.

Verde rame e aloe o fiele o curcuma fa [2]bel verde, ancora il zafferano o l'opimẽto [3]bruciato, ma dubito che in brieue nõ di-uẽga nero; [4]azzurro, oltramarino e giallo di

Verdigris with aloes, or gall or turmeric makes a fine green and so it does with saffron or burnt orpiment; but I doubt whether in a short time they will not turn

621. 2. risalghallo . . sorpimeto chon acq for. 4. biancho. 5. biaccha nvm teghame. 6. chorda . . ellasce. 7. effa. 8. chella . . rasscintto. 9. rugada.

622. 1. forubini di rocha . . miscia chollattimo. 3. amenio.

623. 1. brucata.

624. 1. cholori. 2. se ĩ onchia . . chon . . biacha fannogrado . . schurita. 3. schurita . . sopra [2] ĩ . . biacha.

625. 1. richuocere. 2. azura.

626. 3. brucato . . diuẽgha. 5. ssti . . con. 6. Lacha . . fa . . azurro.

uetro insieme mi[5]sti fanno verde bellissimo in fresco, cioè in muro.
[6]Lacca e verderame · fà bon òbra allo azzurro a o[7]lio.

black. Ultramarine blue and glass yellow mixed together make a beautiful green for fresco, that is wall-painting. Lac and verdigris make a good shadow for blue in oil painting.

S. K. M. II.[1] 95 a]

627.

Macina il verderame colorato molte volte insie[2]me cō sugo di limō, e guardalo dal giallorino.

Grind verdigris many times coloured with lemon juice and keep it away from yellow (?).

A. 1 a]

628.

A PREPARARE IL LEGNIAME PER DIPĪGNIERE SU;

[2]Il legnio sarà d'arcipresso o pero o sorbo o noce, il quale salderai cō ma[3]stico e tremētina secōda destillata · e biacca o vuoi calcina, e metti ī telajo [4]ī modo possa cresciere e discresciere secōdo l'umido o secco; dipoi [5]li da con acquavite ·, che vi sia dentro disoluto, arsenico o solimato 2 [6]o 3 volte, di poi da olio di lino bolito in modo peni[7]tri per tutto, e inanzi si freddi fregalo bene con v̄ panno in modo parrà [8]ascivtto ·, e dalli di sopra verniceliquida e biacca colla stecca, poi laua [9]con orina, quādo è ascivtta ·; e poi spoluerezza e proffila [10]il tuo disegnio sottilmēte e da di sopra l'imprimitura di 30 parti di uerde[11]rame e vna di uerderame e 2 di giallo.

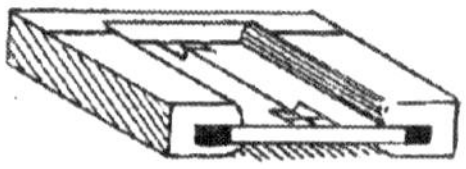

TO PREPARE A PANEL FOR PAINTING ON.

Of preparing the panel.

The panel should be cypress or pear or service-tree or walnut. You must coat it over with mastic and turpentine twice distilled and white or, if you like, lime, and put it in a frame so that it may expand and shrink according to its moisture and dryness. Then give it [a coat] of aqua vitae in which you have dissolved arsenic or [corrosive] sublimate, 2 or 3 times. Then apply boiled linseed oil in such a way as that it may penetrate every part, and before it is cold rub it well with a cloth to dry it. Over this apply liquid varnish and white with a stick, then wash it with urine when it is dry, and dry it again. Then pounce and outline your drawing finely and over it lay a priming of 30 parts of verdigris with one of verdigris with two of yellow.

S. K. M. III. 52 b]

629.

Olio.

[2]Fa olio di semēza di senape, · e se lo [3]voi fare cō piv facilità mischia la ma[4]cinata semēza · con olio di linseme, [5]e metti ogni cosa sotto'l torchio.

Oil.

The preparation of oils (629—634).

Make some oil of mustard seed; and if you wish to make it with greater ease mix the ground seeds with linseed oil and put it all under the press.

627. 1. chollarata. 2. guardallo.
628. 2. ilegnio . . ossorbo . . qua. 3. sticho . . destilata . ebiacha ovoi . . chalcina. 4. cressciere e discressciere sechōdo . . ossecho. 5. chon acq"a" vite . . disoluuto . . sollimato. 6. da [vernice] olio . . imodo. 7. cnāzi [z] si . . chonv̄panimodo para. 8. biacha cola stecha po. 9. chōn . . assciutta . . spoluereza. 10. lanprimiera.
629. 2. senapi essello. 3. voi . . mista. 5. ōni sottol torchio f.

628. M. Ravaisson's reading varies from mine in the following passages: 1. *opero allor* [?] *bo* [*alloro?*] = "*ou bien de* [*laurier*]."
6. *fregalo bene con un panno.* He reads *pane* for *panno* and renders it. "*Frotte le bien avec un pain de façon* [*jusqu'à ce*] *qu'il etc.*
7. *colla stecca po laua.* He reads "*polacca*" = "*avec le couteau de bois* [?] *polonais* [?]."

K.3 32 b]

630.

A TORRE ODORE ALL'OLIO.

[2] Togli l'olio forte e mettine 10 [3] boccali in ū uaso, e fa vn segnio nel [4] vaso secondo l'altezza dell'olio, e poi v'a[5]gugni uno boccale d'aceto e fallo tā[6]to bollire che l'olio diminuisca in[7]sino alla bassezza del fatto segno, [8] e così sarai certo l'olio essere tor[9]nato nella prima quātità e l'aceto essere [10] se ne ito tutto in fumo e portato [11] ne con seco tutto il tristo odore, e'l [12] simile credo farebbe all' olio di no[13]ce e ogni altro olio che auesse tri[14]sto odore.

TO REMOVE THE SMELL OF OIL.

Take the rank oil and put ten pints into a jar and make a mark on the jar at the height of the oil; then add to it a pint of vinegar and make it boil till the oil has sunk to the level of the mark and thus you will be certain that the oil is returned to its original quantity and the vinegar will have gone off in vapour, carrying with it the evil smell; and I believe you may do the same with nut oil or any other oil that smells badly.

C. A. 4 b; 21 a]

631.

Perchè le noci · sono fasciate da una cierta bucciolina che uiene della natura de . . . . ., [2] se tu non le spogli quando ne fai l'olio, quel mallo tigne l'olio, e quando lo metti [3] in opera quel mallo si parte dall'olio e viene in sulla superficie della pittura, [4] e questo è quel che la fa cambiare.

Since walnuts are enveloped in a thin rind, which partakes of the nature of . . ., if you do not remove it when you make the oil from them, this skin tinges the oil, and when you work with it this skin separates from the oil and rises to the surface of the painting, and this is what makes it change.

C. A. 70 b; 207 b]

632.

PER FAR RINUENIRE COLORI SECCHI A OLIO.

[2] Se vuogli far rinuenire i colori secchi a olio, [3] tiegli i molle nella maestra del sapone [4] una notte, e col dito · gli rimena con detta [5] maestra ·, e versa in un bicchiere e laualo cō [6] l'acqua e in questo modo riavrai i colori che si [7] seccano, Ma fa che ogni colore riuenuto abbi [8] il suo bicchiere di per se, dandogli il suo colore di ma[9]no ī mano che tu gli rinvieni, e fa che sieno molli, [10] e quando li uolessi adoperare attēpera e tu li laua [11] cō acqua 5 o · 6 volte con aqua di pozzo, e lascia posare; [12] se la maestra · s'intorbida con alcuni colori [13] fa la passare per feltro.

TO RESTORE OIL COLOURS THAT HAVE BECOME DRY.

If you want to restore oil colours that have become dry keep them soaking in soft soap for a night and, with your finger, mix them up with the soft soap; then pour them into a cup and wash them with water, and in this way you can restore colours that have got dry. But take care that each colour has its own vessel to itself adding the colour by degrees as you restore it and mind that they are thoroughly softened, and when you wish to use them for *tempera* wash them five and six times with spring water, and leave them to settle; if the soft soap should be thick with any of the colours pass it through a filter.

630. 1. Atorre . . ne io. 3. bochali nū. 4. vaso 2° lalteza. 5. gugni ī bochale . . effallo. 6. cheliolio diminuissca. 7. bassexa. 9. nella p° quātita ellaceto. 13. auessi

631. 1—4 *written from the left to the right.* 1. fassciate . . cierta "bucciolina" che ɐ natura de ||||||. 2. sette. 3. qul . . dalloc. 4. equessto . . chella fa chanbiare.

632. 1. per rinuenire cholori. 2. far *is wanting;* cholori. 3. maesstra. 4. echol . . chon. 5. maesstra . . inum . . ellaualocho. 6. equessto . . riarai i cholori chessi. 7. sechano . . onicholore. 8. cholore. 9. chettu . . effa chessieno molie. 10. ettu. 11. coaque o . . chon aqua di pozo ellasscia. 12. sella masstra . . chon . . cholore. 13. falla.

632 and 634. The same remark applies to these sections as to No. 618 and 619.

S. K. M. III. 85 *a*]

633.

OLIO.

Semēza di senepa · pesta con olio di lino.

OIL.

Mustard seed pounded with linseed oil.

C. A. 108 *b*; 339 *b*]

634.

. . . . di fuori della catinella piv · basso 2 dita che non è il piano dell' olio ·, e falla [2]entrare nel collo d'una anpolla e lasciala stare, e tutto · l'olio così se partirà da quel latte, [3]verrà · in questa · anpolla · e sarà · chiaro · come cristallo ·, e cō questo macina · i tua colori, [4]e ogni bruttura e viscosità · rimarrà insieme cō quell' acqua || sappi che tutti gli oli che sono [5]creati ne' semi · o frutti sono chiarissimi di lōr natura, ma il colore giallo che tu vedi in loro nō nascie se nō [6]dal non · saper lo trarre fuori; il fuoco o caldezza di sua natura à forza di farli [7]pigliare colore; piglia la sperienza da licori o gomme d' albori · i quali, se tengono di ragia, in breue [8]tenpo si rassodano, perchè v'è dentro più caldezza che non è nell' olio, e col lungo tenpo [9]pigliano vn cierto giallo che pende in nero, ma l'olio perchè non è si caldo nō fa questo, [10]benchè alquanto si rassodi in sedimento tutta via si fa più bello, [11]e 'l cambiare dell' olio, che fa nel dipigniere, non nascie se non è da vn cierto fūgo, di natura del mallo, [12]il quale è incorporato in quella bucciollina che chiude dentro a se la noce ·, la quale · essendo · pesta [13]insieme colle noci e perch' egli è di natura quasi simile all'olio si mescola con esso ed è si sottil cosa [14]ch' egli à forza di penetrare e uscire · sopra a tutti i colori ·, e questo è quella cosa ch'egli fa mutare, · [15]e se tu · volessi · che l'olio sapessi di buono e non ĭgrossassi ·, mettivi dentro vn poco di canfora, [16]fondata al lēto fuoco, e mescolasi col'olio bene e mai non si rassodi.

. . . . outside the bowl 2 fingers lower than the level of the oil, and pass it into the neck of a bottle and let it stand and thus all the oil will separate from this milky liquid; it will enter the bottle and be as clear as crystal; and grind your colours with this, and every coarse or viscid part will remain in the liquid. You must know that all the oils that have been created in seads or fruits are quite clear by nature, and the yellow colour you see in them only comes of your not knowing how to draw it out. Fire or heat by its nature has the power to make them acquire colour. See for example the exudation or gums of trees which partake of the nature of rosin; in a short time they harden because there is more heat in them than in oil; and after some time they acquire a certain yellow hue tending to black. But oil, not having so much heat does not do so; although it hardens to some extent into sediment it becomes finer. The change in oil which occurs in painting proceeds from a certain fungus of the nature of a husk which exists in the skin which covers the nut, and this being crushed along with the nuts and being of a nature much resembling oil mixes with it; it is of so subtle a nature that it combines with all colours and then comes to the surface, and this it is which makes them change. And if you want the oil to be good and not to thicker, put into it a little camphor melted over a slow fire and mix it well with the oil and it will never harden.

633. 2. sēmemēza.

634. 1. ellaltr |||||| nda . . chatinella . . effalla. 2. ellentrare nell chollo . . ellascia lasstare ettutto . . chossi . . perera da quellatte. 3. quessta . . essara . . chome crisstallo . ecchō quessto . . e tua cholori. 4. visscìosita . . chō . . chettutti . . chessono. 5. neserai offrutti . . "di lor natura" ma . . gallo chettu vedilōro no nasscie sēnnō. 6. saperllo . . fuocho o chaldezza . . afforza. 7. cholore . . lassperienza dallichori o ghomme . . equali setteughono di ragie in brieue. 8. chaldeza chennon . . ecchol [tenp] lugho. 9. cheppende . . mallolic . . chaldo . . quessto. 10. [esseno] bench . . inse dimeno cuttavia. 11. chambiare . . cheffa . . nasscie sennon . . fugho. 12. el . . inchorporato . . asse . . pessta. 13. cholle epperch . . chon . . chosa. 14. usscire . . attutti i cholori . ecquesto ecqualla chosa. 15. essettu . . chellolio . . sapessi . . enona ĭgrossasi . . pocho dichanfora. 16. alleto fuocho emmesscola . . chol . . emmai (?) . . rassoda.

S. K. M. I.[2] 5]

635.

On varnishes [or powders] (635—637).

[VERNICE.

[2]Tolli cipresso ·, e quello · destilla · e abbi · vna brocca [3]grāde · e lì · metti · detta destillatione · cō tanta · acqua [4]che parsii l'anbra ·, e tura · ben di sopra · in modo nō [5]ui spiri ·. e quādo · è disoluta · arrogi in detta cosa [6]della detta · stilatione · i modo sia · liquida · a tuo modo, [7]e sappi che le carabe è liquore d'arcipresso].

VARNISH [OR POWDER].

Take cypress [oil] and distil it and have a large pitcher, and put in the extract with so much water as may make it appear like amber, and cover it tightly so that none may evaporate. And when it is dissolved you may add in your pitcher as much of the said solution, as shall make it liquid to your taste. And you must know that amber is the gum of the cypress-tree.

[VERNICE.

[9]E perchè la vernice · e gomma di ginepro ·, se stilerai · [10]il ginepro, potrai disoluere in questa stilatione detta [11]vernice · nel modo . detto disopra].

VARNISH [OR POWDER].

And since varnish [powder] is the resin of juniper, if you distil juniper you can dissolve the said varnish [powder] in the essence, as explained above.

S. K. M. I.[2] 8]

636.

[VERNICE.

[2]Intacca vn ginepro · e dalli · l'acqua · a piedi, e quello [3]liquore · mischia · con olio di noce · e avrai vernice perfetta fatta [4]di vernice d'anbra · bella · e buona · per eciellētia [5]fallo · di magio · over d'aprile].

VARNISH [OR POWDER].

Notch a juniper tree and give it water at the roots, mix the liquor which exudes with nut-oil and you will have a perfect varnish [powder], made like amber varnish [powder], fine and of the best quality make it in May or April.

G. 46 b]

637.

VERNICE.

[2]Mercurio cō giove e venere, fattone il pa[3]stello, sia colla sagoma corretto [4]al continuo insino che mercurio [5]si separi integralmēte da giove e venere.

VARNISH [OR POWDER].

Mercury with Jupiter and Venus,—a paste made of these must be corrected by the mould (?) continuously, until Mercury separates itself entirely from Jupiter and Venus.

B. 2 b]

638.

On chemical materials (638—650).

Ricordo come · l'acqua vite racoglie i se tutti i colori e odori [2]de' fiori, e se uoi fare azzurro metti ui fiordalisi e per rosso solani.

Note how aqua vitae absorbs into itself all the colours and smells of flowers. If you want to make blue put iris flowers into it and for red solanum berries (?)

635. 2. ecquello . . bocca. 3. elli meti. 4. parea lanbraetura . . imodo. 5. disoluata arogi. 6. atuo. 7. essapi chele carabe darci plesso. 9. goma.
636. 2. intacha . . acquello. 3. ara.
637. 1. vernice dellogna. 2. merchurio chō giove "evenere" . . il pas. 3. saghoma correcto. 4. al chontinuo . . merchurio.
638. 1. chome . . tu[t]ti cholori edori 2. azuro . . fiocarusi e . . solaci.

637. Here, and in No. 641 *Mercurio* seems to mean quicksilver, *Giove* stands for iron, *Venere* for copper and *Saturno* for lead.

W. XIII.]

639.

Sale fatto di sterco vmano bruciato [2]e calcinato e fattone liscia ·, e que[3]lla · dissecca al lēto fuoco e tutti li ster[4]chi in simile modo fanno sale e quelli [5]sali destillati · sono molto · penetrāti.

Salt may be made from human excrement burnt and calcined and made into lees, and dried by a slow fire, and all dung in like manner yields salt, and these salts when distilled are very pungent.

Tr. 49]

640.

¶L'aqua del mare, gocciolata dal fango over tera arzila, [2]lassia ī quella ōgni salsedine.¶ [3]¶Le lane, messe alle spōde del navilio, sorbiscono l'acqua dolce.¶ [4]Se stilli cō cāpana, l'aqua marina fia ī principale ecielēza, [5]e adattādo vn fornello alla sua cucina quelle medesime [6]legnie che cuociono, stilleranno vna grā quantità d'acqua, [7]se la cāpana fia grāde.

Sea water filtered through mud or clay, leaves all its saltness in it. Woollen stuffs placed on board ship absorb fresh water. If sea water is distilled under a retort it becomes of the first excellence and any one who has a little stove in his kitchen can, with the same wood as he cooks with, distil a great quantity of water if the retort is a large one.

G. 53 a]

641.

Sagoma.

[2]La sagoma sia di uenere overo di giove [3]o saturno è spesso rigittata in grēbo [4]alla madre sua; E sia adoperata con [5]sottile, e'l sagomato sia [6]venere e giove inpastato sopra vene [7]re; Ma prima proverai uene[8]re e mercurio misto cō giove e tieni [9]modo che mercurio se ne fugga[10]poi in volgili bene in modo che [11]venere o giove sinnectuti ui sottilissimamē[12]te quanto sia possibile.

Mould (?).

The mould (?) may be of Venus, or of Jupiter and Saturn and placed frequently in the fire. And it should be worked with fine emery and the mould (?) should be of Venus and Jupiter impasted over (?) Venus. But first you will test Venus and Mercury mixed with Jove, and take means to cause Mercury to disperse; and then fold them well together so that Venus or Jupiter be connected as thinly as possible.

W. VIII.]

642.

Sal nitro, [2]vitriolo, [3]cinabro, [4]allume, iamene [5]sal ammoniaco, [6]mercurio, sullimato, [7]salgemma, [8]sal arcali, [9]sal comune, [10]allume di roco [11]allume scisso, [12]arsenico, [13]sullimato, [14]risagallo, [15]tartero, [16]orpimēto, [17]verderame.

Nitre, vitriol, cinnabar, alum, salt ammoniac, sublimated mercury, rock salt, alcali salt, common salt, rock alum, alum schist (?), arsenic, sublimate, realgar, tartar, orpiment, verdegris.

639. stercho. 2. chalcinato effatto neliscia ecque. 3. disecha . . focho ettutti lisster. 5. desstilati.

640. 1. cholate . . tera arzila. 2. lassia ī quela . . salsendine. 3. tesse . . spōte sorbisschono lacq"a". 4. stili chō . . lacq. 5. e dattādo . . fornelo . . chusina. 6. chochano . stilerano . . dacqa. 7. chapana.

641. 1. saghoma. 2. saghoma. 3. essaturno esspesso. 4. Essia . . chon is. 5. olgirams soctile. 6. inpassato sopra erē. 7. ev Ma . . proverrai. 8. merchurio missto . . ettieni. 9. merchurio . . fugghe. 10. ppoi invulghana. 11. oggieve siinnectuti ui soctilissimamē.

642. 2. vitrolo. 4. allume iamene. 5. armoniacho. 7. salgemme. 8. arkalai. 9. rocho. 12. arsenicho. 13. risalghallo.

641. See the note to 637.

5. *olgirams* and 6, 7. *erēnev*. The apparent unmeaning of these words is solved, if we read them backwards: *olgirams* = *smariglio*; *erēnev* = *venere*.

643.

H 1 88 *b*]

¶ Pece oncie 4, [2] cera nova oncie 4, [3] incieso oncie 2, [4] olio rosato oncia una.¶

Pitch four ounces virgin wax, four ounces incense, two ounces oil of roses one ounce.

644.

H 3 88 *b*]

Oncie 4 cera nova, [2] oncie 4 pece greca, [3] oncie 2 incēso, [4] oncia una olio rosato, [5] fōdi prima cera e olio, [6] poi la pece greca, [7] poi l'altre cose in polvere

Four ounces virgin wax, four ounces Greek pitch, two ounces incense, one ounce oil of roses, first melt the wax and oil then the Greek pitch then the other things in powder.

645.

Br M 139 *a*]

Il uetro assottigliato si taglia [2] con forbici, il quale posto so[3]pra le tarsie d'osso dorate o [4] d'altri colori, tu le puoi legare [5] insieme coll'osso e poi met[6]tere, e resterà cō lustro che [7] nō si frāge nè cōsuma col fre[8]garsi con mano.

Very thin glass may be cut with scissars and when placed over inlaid work of bone, gilt, or stained of other colours you can saw it through together with the bone and then put it together and it will retain a lustre that will not be scratched nor worn away by rubbing with the hand.

646.

S K M III 53 *a*]

AD AQUARE IL UINO [2] BIĀCO · E FARSI NERO.

[3] Fa polverizare · la galla e stare 8 · dì in [4] vino bianco ·, e così · fa disoluere il [5] vitriolo · nell'acqua ·, e fa ben posare e rischi[6]arare l'acqua e 'l uino ognivno per se e bē co[7]lare, e quādo con essa · acqua adac[8]querai · il uino · bianco ·, esso si farà [9] vermiglio.

TO DILUTE WHITE WINE AND MAKE IT PURPLE.

Powder gall nuts and let this stand 8 days in the white wine; and in the same way dissolve vitriol in water, and let the water stand and settle very clear, and the wine likewise, each by itself, and strain them well; and when you dilute the white wine with the water the wine will become red

647.

S K. M. III 55 *a*]

Metti la marchesita [2] in acqua forte, e se fa [3] verde ·; sappi · che à [4] in se rame, [5] tralo cō sal nitro [6] e sapone tenero.

Put marcasite into aqua fortis and if it turns green, know that it has copper in it. Take it out with saltpetre and soft soap.

648.

L. 2 *a*]

Il cavallo bianco si può ismachia[2]re col ferretto di spagna o acqua for[3]te overo col merdocco leuare il pe[4]lo nero al bianco cō rottorio, forzare [5] a terra.

A white horse may have the spots removed with the spanish haematite or with aqua fortis or with . . . . . Removes the black hair on a white horse with the singeing iron. Force him to the ground.

643 1. ō 4 2 ō 4 3 ōciēso ō 2. 4 ō l̄
644 1—7 R 1. ō 4 2 ō 4 grecha. 3 ō 2 4. ō l̄ 5. primo 7 chose
645. 4 tulle poi comrame
646 2 effarassi. 3 esstare. 4. chosi 5. nellacq"a" effa . rissci 6. lacq"a" 7 ecquādo chon.
647. 2 acq"a" . . esse tralo. 6. essavō
648 1 po issmachia. 2 ferretto disspagna o acq"a". 3. merdocho 4 al nere e "bianco" cōrattorio sorzare 5 attera.

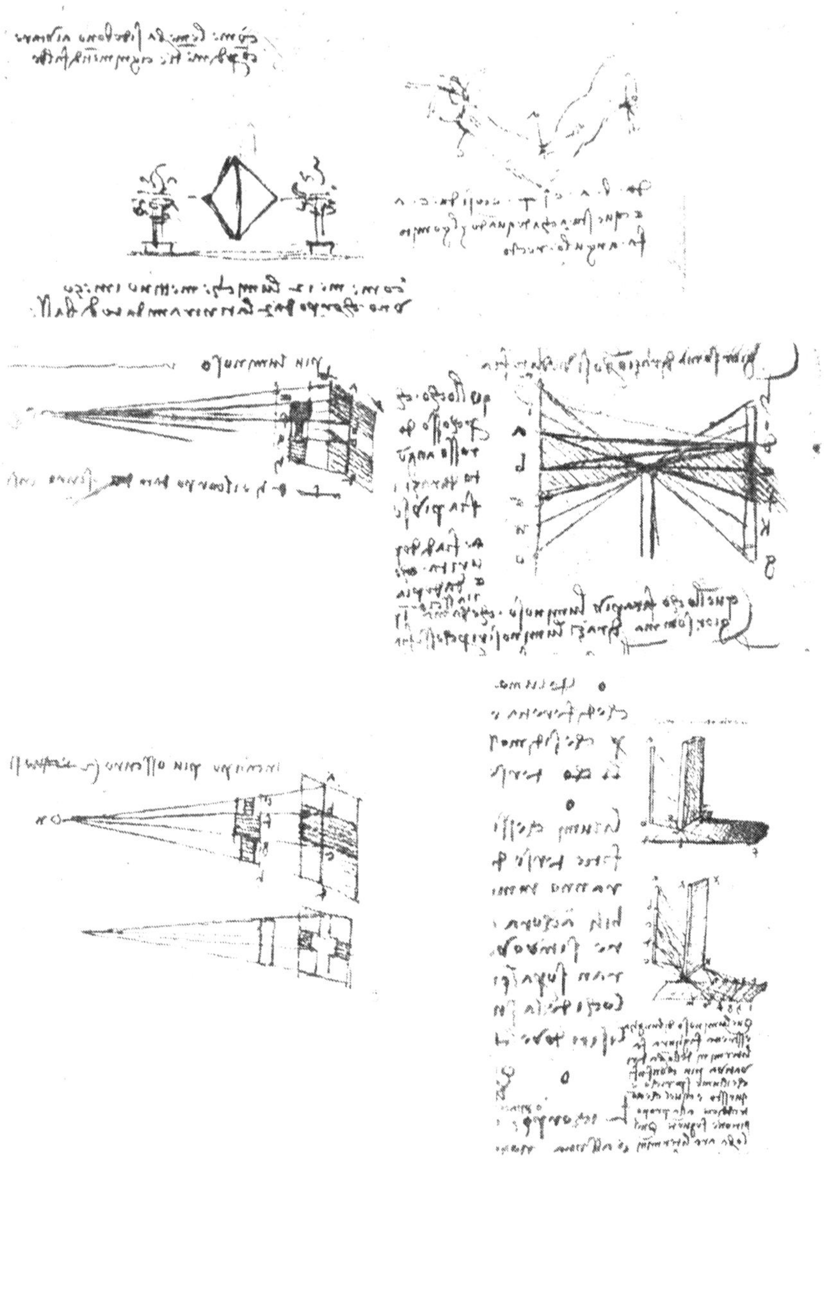

S. K. M. I.[2] 5]

649.

Fuoco.

[2]Se volessi · fare · vn fuoco che sēza · dāno · infocherebbe · vna sala, [3]farai · così: profuma · prima · la · sala · con spesso · fumo [4]d'incēso · o d'altra · cosa · odorifera ·, di poi · buffa; overo [5]farai bolendo · andare infumo libre 10 d'acquavite, [6]ma fa che la sala · sia · bē serrata e gitta poluere [7]di vernice · infra detti · fumi, che sarà · il polverio [8]assai be sostenvto · dai fumi, di poi entra subito [9]con vna torcia · a presso · ī detta · sala · e subito ogni [10]cosa s'infocherà.

Fire.

If you want to make a fire which will set a hall in a blaze without injury do this: first perfume the hall with a dense smoke of incense or some other odoriferous substance: It is a good trick to play. Or boil ten pounds of brandy to evaporate, but see that the hall is completely closed and throw up some powdered varnish among the fumes and this powder will be supported by the smoke; then go into the room suddenly with a lighted torch and at once it will be in a blaze.

S. K. M. I.[2] 8]

650.

Fuoco.

[2]Tolli · quella · superfitie · gialla, ch'ànno · i pomi · rāci, [3]e quelli · destilla · al limbico ·, che sarà · detta · stilatiō [4]perfetta.

Fire.

Take away that yellow surface which covers oranges and distill them in an alembic, until the distillation may be said to be perfect.

[Fuoco.

[6]Serra · bene · vna camera · e abbi · vna · piastra [7]di rame o di ferro · īfocata ·, e spruzzavi · suso · dua boccā[8]li d'acqua · vite · a poco · per uolta ·, in modo · si converta in fumo, [9]di poi fa · etrare · vno con un lume, e subito vedrai [10]la camera īfocarsi a vso d'ū vāpeggiare cieleste e nō [11]farà alcuna lesione · a persona.

Fire.

Close a room tightly and have a brasier of brass or iron with fire in it and sprinkle on it two pints of aqua vitae, a little at a time, so that it may be converted into smoke. Then make some one come in with a light and suddenly you will see the room in a blaze like a flash of lightning, and it will do no harm to any one.

649. 1. fuocho. 2. focho . . infocherebe. 3. chosi . . chonispesso. 5. dacq"a". 6. serata. 9. chon . . apreso . . essubito ōni.
650. 1. fuocho. 3. ecquelli allimbicho chessara. 5. fuocho. 6. chamera. 7. fero . . espluzavi su so dua bocha. 8. dacq"a" . a pocho . . imodo si chonverta ifum"o". 9. chonū. 10. chamera īfocharsi . vāpegiare. 11. alchuna.

VII.

PHILOSOPHY AND HISTORY OF THE ART OF PAINTING.

S. K. M. III. 19 b]

651.

The relation of art and nature (651. 652).

Cosa bella mortal passa e nõ d'arte.

What is fair in men, passes away, but not so in art.

Ash. I. 15 b]

652.

COME CHI SPREZZA LA PITTURA · NÕ [2]AMA · LA FILOSOFIA NE LA NATURA.

[3]Se tu · sprezzerai · la pittura ·, la quale · è sola · imitatrice · di tutte l'opere evidẽti di natura, [4]per certo · tu sprezzerai una sottile · invẽtione · la quale cõ filosofica e sottile specula-[5]tione · cõsidera tutte le qualità delle forme: mare e siti, piãte, animali, erbe e fiori, le [6]quali sono · cĩte d'onbra · e lume; e veramẽte questa è sciẽtia, e legittima · figliuo[7]la di natura ·, perchè la pittura · è partorita da · essa natura ·; ma per dire piv corretto [8]diremo nipote di natura ·, perchè tutte le cose evidẽti sono state partorite dalla natura,

HE WHO DESPISES PAINTING LOVES NEITHER PHILOSOPHY NOR NATURE.

If you contemn painting, which is the only imitator of all visible works of nature, you will certainly despise a subtle invention which brings philosophy and subtle speculation to the consideration of the nature of all forms—seas and plains, trees, animals, plants and flowers—which are surrounded by shade and light. And this is true knowledge and the legitimate issue of nature; for painting is born of nature—or, to speak more correctly, we will say it is the grandchild of nature; for all visible things are

652. 1. spreza. 2. nella. 3. settio . isprezerai. 4. ciertu . tu sprezerai Ī . . filosoficha . . spechula. 5. essiti. 6. ellume . . questa [arte e] e . . figli. 7. coretto. 8. direno . . chose. 9. chose . . dimãderano.

delle quali cose partorite · è nata la pittura, · adūque rettamēte la dimāderemo nipote di natura, parēte di dio.

produced by nature, and these her children have given birth to painting. Hence we may justly call it the grandchild of nature and related to God.

Ash. I. 16b]

653.

Come la pittura avāza tutte l'opere vmane per sottile speculationi appartenenti · a quella.

L'occhio · che si dice finestra dell'anima è la prīcipale · via, dōde il comvne · sēso può piv copiosa· e magīficamēte · cōsiderare · le īfinite opere di natura ·, e l'orechio è il secōdo il quale si fa nobile · per le cose racōte, le quali à veduto l'ochio ·; se uoi istoriografi o poeti · o altri mattematici nō ui aveste col'ochio viste le cose, male le potreste riferire per le scritture, e se tu poeta figurerai · una storia colla pittura della penna, el pittore col pennello la farà di piv facile sadisfatione e mē tediosa a essere cōpresa: se tu dimāderai la pittura muta poesia, ācora il pittore potrà dire del poeta · orba pittura ·; or guarda quale è più dannoso morbo o cieco o mvto; se 'l poeta è libero come 'l pittore nelle īuētioni, le sua fintioni · nō sono di tāta sadisfatione ali omini quāto le pitture, perchè se la poesia s'astēde colle parole a figvrare forme, atti e siti, il pittore si move colle propie similitudini delle forme a cōtrafare esse forme; or guarda qual'è piv propīquo all'omo · o 'l nome d'omo o la similitudine d'esso omo; il nome dell'omo si uaria ī uari paesi e la forma non è mvtata se nō da morte.

That painting surpasses all human works by the subtle considerations belonging to it.

Painting is superior to poetry (653. 654).

The eye, which is called the window of the soul, is the principal means by which the central sense can most completely and abundantly appreciate the infinite works of nature; and the ear is the second, which acquires dignity by hearing of the things the eye has seen. If you, historians, or poets, or mathematicians had not seen things with your eyes you could not report of them in writing. And if you, O poet, tell a story with your pen, the painter with his brush can tell it more easily, with simpler completeness and less tedious to be understood. And if you call painting dumb poetry, the painter may call poetry blind painting. Now which is the worse defect? to be blind or dumb? Though the poet is as free as the painter in the invention of his fictions they are not so satisfactory to men as paintings; for, though poetry is able to describe forms, actions and places in words, the painter deals with the actual similitude of the forms, in order to represent them. Now tell me which is the nearer to the actual man: the name of man or the image of the man. The name of man differs in different countries, but his form is never changed but by death.

Ash. I. 16a]

654.

E se il poeta · serue al sēso per la uia del'orechio, il pittore per ochio, piv degnio senso; ma io nō uoglio da questi tali altro · se nō che uno bono pittore figuri il furore d'una battaglia e che 'l poeta ne scriua uno altro ·, e che sieno messi i publico di cōpagnia, vedrai i veditori doue piv si fermerāno, doue piv cōsedererano, doue si darà piv laude e quale sadisfarà meglio; cierto la pittura, di grā lunga piv utile e

And if the poet gratifies the sense by means of the ear, the painter does so by the eye—the worthier sense; but I will say no more of this but that, if a good painter represents the fury of a battle, and if a poet describes one, and they are both together put before the public, you will see where most of the spectators will stop, to which they will pay most attention, on which they will bestow most praise, and which will satisfy them best. Undoubtedly painting being by a long way the more intelligible and beau-

653. 3. apartēente. 4. locchio [si dice essere la prima e prīcipale ma] chessi. 6. chōsiderare . . ellorechio. 7. istogriorafi. 8. auessi . . potresti. 9. scritture [le quali scriture so nate dalla pittura] essettu. 10. ỉ storia cola . . pena . . penelo. 11. cōplesa. 12. pitore potra [della crittura dire] dire. 13. danosa mo[s]rso. 15. sella. 16. cole . . essiti . . cole. 17. similitudine dele. 19. ella.

bella, piv piacerà, poni scritto il no[7]me di dio in ṽ loco e ponui la sua figura a riscōtro, vedrai quale fia piv [8]reverita, se la pittura abbraccia ī se tutte le forme della natura, voi no[9]n avete se non i nomi i quali non sono vniversali come le forme, se voi [10]avete li effetti delle dimostrationi, noi abbiamo le dimostrationi delli effetti, [11]tolgasi uno poeta che discriva · le bellezze d'una doña al suo inamorato, [12]tolsi uno pittore che la figuri, vedrai dove la natura volgerà piv [13]il givdicatore innamorato ·, cierto il cimēto delle cose dourebbe lascia[14]re dare la sētentia alla speriētia voi avete messa la pittura īfra [15]l'arti mecaniche, cierto se i pittori fussino atti al laudare collo scriue[16]re l'opere loro come voi, io dubito nō giacerebbe ī si uile cognome, [17]se uoi la chiamate mecanica, perchè è prima manvale che le mani figur[18]ano quel che truovano nella fantasia, voi scrittori disegniate colla penna [19]manualmēte quello che nello īgiegnio vostro si truova , e se voi [20]diceste essere mecanica perchè si fa a prezzo chi cade ī questo errore, [21]se errore si può chiamare piv di uoi ? se voi legiete per li studi, nō andate voi [22]a chi piv vi premia? fate voi alcuna opera sāza qualche premio? Bē[23]chè questo nō dico per biasimare simili openioni, perchè ogni fatica [24]aspetta premio, e potrà dire uno poeta, io farò una fintione che significa [25]cose grādi, questo medesimo farà il pittore, come fecie Apelle [26]la calūnia, se voi diceste la poesia è piv eterna, per questo dirò [27]essere piv eterne le opere d'un calderaio, chè 'l tēpo piv le cōserua [28]che le vostre o nostre opere, mēte di meno è di poca fātasia, [29]e la pittura si può, dipigniēdo sopra rame cō colori di uetro, fare [30]molto piv eterna, noi per arte possiamo essere detti nipoti a dio, [31]se la poesia s'astēde ī filosofia morale , è questa ī filosofia naturale, [32]se quella descrive l'operationi della mēte, questa cōsidera quello che la [33]mēte opera ne mouimēti: se quella spavēta i popoli colle īfernali [34]fitioni ·, questa colle medesime cose in atto fa il simile pōga si il [35]poeta a figurare una bellezza, vna fierezza , una cosa nefāda e brutta, [36]vna mostruosa col pittore , faccia a suo modo come vole trasmv[37]tationi di

tiful, will please most Write up the name of God [Christ] in some spot and set up His image opposite and you will see which will be most reverenced Painting comprehends in itself all the forms of nature, while you have nothing but words, which are not universal as form is, and if you have the effects of the representation, we have the representation of the effects Take a poet who describes the beauty of a lady to her lover and a painter who represents her and you will see to which nature guides the enamoured critic Certainly the proof should be allowed to rest on the verdict of experience You have ranked painting among the mechanical arts but, in truth, if painters were as 'apt at praising their own works in writing as you are, it would not lie under the stigma of so base a name If you call it mechanical because it is, in the first place, manual, and that it is the hand which produces what is to be found in the imagination, you too writers, who set down manually with the pen what is devised in your mind And if you say it is mechanical because it is done for money, who falls into this error—if error it can be called—more than you? If you lecture in the schools do you not go to whoever pays you most? Do you do any work without pay? Still, I do not say this as blaming such views, for every form of labour looks for its reward And if a poet should say "I will invent a fiction with a great purpose," the painter can do the same, as Apelles painted Calumny If you were to say that poetry is more eternal, I say the works of a coppersmith are more eternal still, for time preserves them longer than your works or ours, nevertheless they have not much imagination [29] And a picture, if painted on copper with enamel colours may be yet more permanent We, by our arts may be called the grandsons of God If poetry deals with moral philosophy, painting deals with natural philosophy Poetry describes the action of the mind, painting considers what the mind may effect by the motions [of the body] If poetry can terrify people by hideous fictions, painting can do as much by depicting the same things in action Supposing that a poet applies himself to represent beauty, ferocity, or a base, a foul

654 1 esse 2 che ī 3 ī altro sieno me 4 vederai 5 lalde 7 rischōtro vederai 8 abraccia dela 9 enomi 10 abbiano deli 11 ī poeta belleze dona 12 tolsi ī vederai voltera 13 dourebe 15 larte mechaniche laldare 16 diacierebbe 17 ciamate mechanicha chelle 18 disegniādo cola 19 quelo nelo vstro esse 20 dicessi mechanicha prezo chade erore 21 erore si po 22 alchuna 23 faucha 24 pora dire ī faro ī significha. 25 grāde 26 caluma dicessi. 27 eterno lopere 28 pocha 29 ella sipo 30 posiano deu 31 sella ecquesta 32 secquela loperatione mētuque considera ucella cella 33 secquella cole 34 chole 35 affigurare una fiereza ī 36. assuo 37 sadisfacci 38 chonformita colla cosa vua chella iganato

forme, che il pittore nõ sadisfacci piv, nõ s'è egli uiste [38]pitture auere tãta cõformità colla cosa uiva ch'ell'ã ĩgãnato [39]homini e animali?

or a monstrous thing, as against a painter, he may in his ways bring forth a variety of forms, but will the painter not satisfy more? are there not pictures to be seen, so like the actual things, that they deceive men and animals?

Ash I 10a]

655

COME LA SCOLTURA È DI MINORE ĨGEGNIO [2]CHE LA PITTURA E MÃCANO IN LEI MOLTE PARTI NATURALI.

[3]Adoperãdomi io nõ meno in iscultura che ĩ pittura e faciẽdo l'una [4]e l'altra in vn medesimo grado, mi pare cõ piccola ĩputatione potere [5]dare sẽtẽntia, quale sia di maggiore ingiegnio e difficoltà e perfectio[6]ne l'una che l'altra, Prima la scoltura è sottoposta a cierti lumi, [7]cioè di sopra, e la pittura porta per tutto cõ seco lume e õbra, [8]E lume e õbra è la ĩportãtia adũque della scoltura, lo scultore ĩ questo caso è ajvtato [9]dalla natura del rilievo ch'ella gienera per se, e 'l pittore per accidẽtale arte [10]lo fa ne'lochi dove ragionevolmẽte lo farebbe la natura, lo scultore non si [11]può diversificare nelle varie nature de'colori delle cose, la pittura [12]nõ mãca in parte alcuna, le prospettive delli scultori nõ paio[13]no niẽte vere, quelle del pittore paiono a cẽtinaja di miglia [14]di là dall'opera, La prospettiva aerea è lõtana da lor opera, [15]nõ possono figurare i corpi trãsparẽti, nõ possono figurare i lu[16]minosi, nõ linie reflesse, nõ corpi lucidi come spechi e simili [17]cose lustrãti, nõ nebbie, nõ tẽpi oscuri e infinite cose che nõ [18]si dicono per nõ tediare, ciò che l'à è ch'ella è piv resistẽte al tenpo, ben[19]chè à simil resistẽtia la pittura, fatta sopra rame grosso coperto [20]di smalto biãco e sopra quello dipĩto cõ colori di smalto e rimesso [21]ĩ foco e fatto cuocere, questa per eternità avãza la scoltura, Potrà [22]dire che doue fanno uno errore nõ esser facile il raccõciare, questo è [23]tristo argomẽto a volere provare che una ismemoratagine inremediabile [24]faccia l'opera piv degnia, ma io dirò bene che

THAT SCULPTURE IS LESS INTELLECTUAL THAN PAINTING, AND LACKS MANY CHARACTERISTICS OF NATURE.

Painting is superior to sculpture (655 656)

I myself, having exercised myself no less in sculpture than in painting and doing both one and the other in the same degree, it seems to me that I can, without invidiousness, pronounce an opinion as to which of the two is of the greatest merit and difficulty and perfection. In the first place sculpture requires a certain light, that is from above, a picture carries everywhere with it its own light and shade. Thus sculpture owes its importance to light and shade, and the sculptor is aided in this by the nature, of the relief which is inherent in it, while the painter whose art expresses the accidental aspects of nature, places his effects in the spots where nature must necessarily produce them. The sculptor cannot diversify his work by the various natural colours of objects, painting is not defective in any particular. The sculptor when he uses perspective cannot make it in any way appear true, that of the painter can appear like a hundred miles beyond the picture itself. Their works have no aerial perspective whatever, they cannot represent transparent bodies, they cannot represent luminous bodies, nor reflected lights, nor lustrous bodies—as mirrors and the like polished surfaces, nor mists, nor dark skies, nor an infinite number of things which need not be told for fear of tedium. As regards the power of resisting time, though they have this resistance [19], a picture painted on thick copper covered with white enamel on which it is painted with enamel colours and then put into the fire again and baked, far exceeds sculpture in permanence. It may be

655 2 chella r mãcha illei 3 pittura effaciẽdo 4 ellaltra nv plchola 5 magiore dificulta 7 chõsecho 8 Ellume ella chaso e ivtato 9 chela 11 diversifichare 12 mãcha alchuna paia 13 pitore paiono a cẽtinara 14 dallor 15 possano i chorpi possano 16 refresse chorpi chome essimili 17 soschuri chose 18 dichano Cio chela chele piv 19 assimil 20 essopra chõ 21 chocere 22 fano ĩ erore rachõciare 23 che ĩ

655 19 From what is here said as to painting on copper it is very evident that Leonardo was not acquainted with the method of painting in oil on thin copper plates, introduced by the Flemish

lo ingiegnio del [25]maestro fia piv difficile a raccōciare che fa simile errori, che non è a ra[26]cōciare l'opera da chi l'à guastata.

said that if a mistake is made it is not easy to remedy it; it is but a poor argument to try to prove that a work be the nobler because oversights are irremediable; I should rather say that it will be more difficult to improve the mind of the master who makes such mistakes than to repair the work he has spoilt.

Ash. I 11 *b*]

656.

Noi sappiamo · bene che quello ·, che sarà pratico e bono, nō farà simili [2]erron ·, anzi cō bone regole · andrà leuādo tanto poco per volta che bē cō[3]ducerà sua opera; · ācora lo scoltore, se fa di terra o ciera, puo leuare [4]e porre ·, e quādo è terminata · cō facilità · si gitta di brōzo ·, e questa [5]è l'ultima operatione e la piv permanēte ch'abbi la scultura · Imperocchè [6]quella ch'è sola di marmo è sottoposta alle ruine, e nō lo brōzo, adūque [7]quella · pittura, fatta ī rame che si può, come dissi della pittura, levare e porre [8]è pari al brōzo, che quādo facievi quell'opera prima di ciera, ancor si poteva [9]leuare e porre; se questa scoltura di brōzo è eterna, questa di rame [10]e di uetro è etternissima; se 'l brōzo rimane nero e brutto, questa è piena [11]di uari e vaghi colori e d'infinite varietà, della quale com'è di sopra ·; [12]e se tu volessi dire solamēte della pittura fatta ī tauola, di questa son io [13]cōtēto dare la sētētia colla scultura, diciēdo così, come la pittura [14]è piv bella e di piv fantasia e piv copiosa, è la scoltura piv dura[15]bile ·; altro nō à; la scoltura · cō poca fatica mostra quel che nel[16]la pittura · pare cosa miracolosa; a far parere palpabile [17]cose īpalpabili, rileuate le cose piane, lontane le cose vicine; [18]in effetto la pittura è ornata d'infinite speculationi che la scultura nō le adopera.

We know very well that a really experienced and good painter will not make such mistakes, on the contrary, with sound rules he will remove so little at a time that he will bring his work to a good issue. Again the sculptor if working in clay or wax, can add or reduce, and when his model is finished it can easily be cast in bronze, and this is the last operation and is the most permanent form of sculpture. Inasmuch as that which is merely of marble is liable to ruin, but not bronze. Hence a painting done on copper which as I said of painting may be added to or altered, resembles sculpture in bronze, which, having first been made in wax could then be altered or added to; and if sculpture in bronze is durable, this work in copper and enamel is absolutely imperishable. Bronze is but dark and rough after all, but this latter is covered with various and lovely colours in infinite variety, as has been said above; or if you will have me only speak of painting on panel, I am content to pronounce between it and sculpture; saying that painting is the more beautiful and the more imaginative and the more copious, while sculpture is the more durable but it has nothing else. Sculpture shows with little labour what in painting appears a miraculous thing to do, to make what is impalpable appear palpable, flat objects appear in relief, distant objects seem close. In fact painting is adorned with infinite possibilities which sculpture cannot command.

24 facia. 25 dificile . . cheffa . erori. 36 cōuare lopera dacquello guasta *4*.

655 1 *4* noi sappiano . checquello . chessara praticho 2 erori pocho . chō. 3. anchora la scholtura seffa di tera occiera po 4 pore . . ecquesta. 5. ellultima . . ella abi. 6. chessola. 7. chessipo chome ti di della pitura . . pore. 8 quella prima lopera 9 pore . . brōza. 10 brōso 12 essettu 13 cholla. 14 ella 15 pacha fatucha . . chel 16 chosa . . affar. 17 īpalpabile. 18. effecto . . speculatione chella

painters of the XVIIth century. J. LERMOLIEFF has already pointed out that in the various collections containing pictures by the great masters of the Italian Renaissance, those painted on copper (for instance the famous reading Magdalen in the Dresden Gallery) are the works of a much later date (see *Zeitschrift für bildende Kunst*. Vol. X pg. 333, and. *Werke italienischer Master in den Galerien von München, Dresden und Berlin* Leipzig 1880, pg. 158 and 159.—Compare No. 654, 29.

330'

K 3 30*b*]

657

Aphorisms (657—659)

Pittura

[2]Li omini e le parole [3]son fatti, e tu pitto[4]re nō sapiēdo adopera[5]re le tue figure, tu [6]se' come l'oratore che [7]nō sa adoperare le pa[8]role sue.

Of painting

Men and words are ready made, and you, O Painter, if you do not know how to make your figures move, are like an orator who knows not how to use his words

W A IV 152*a*]

658

Quando il poeta cessa del figurare colle parole [2]quel che in natura è in fatto, allora il poeta nō [3]si fa equale al pittore, perchè se il poeta, la[4]sciando tal figuratione, e' descrive le parole or[5]nate e persuasive di colui a chi esso vole fare par[6]lare, allora egli si fa oratore e non è più poeta nè è pittore, e se lui [7]parla de' celi, egli si fa astrologo e filosofo, e te[8]ologo parlando delle cose di natura o di dio, ma [9]se esso ritorna alla figuratione di qualunche co[10]sa e' si farebbe emulo al pittore, se potesse soddi[11]sfare all'ochio in parole come fa il pittore

As soon as the poet ceases to represent in words what exists in nature, he in fact ceases to resemble the painter, for if the poet, leaving such representation, proceeds to describe the flowery and flattering speech of the figure, which he wishes to make the speaker, he then is an orator and no longer a poet nor a painter And if he speaks of the heavens he becomes an astrologer, and philosopher, and a theologian, if he discourses of nature or God. But, if he restricts himself to the description of objects, he would enter the lists against the painter, if with words he could satisfy the eye as the painter does

Ash I 15*b*]

659

Se tu saprai ragionare e scrivere la dimostratione delle forme, [2]il pittore le farà che parrāno animate con ōbre e lumi, cōponitori dell'aria de' volti, [3]della quale tu nō puoi agivgniere colla pēna dove s'agivgnie col penello

Though you may be able to tell or write the exact description of forms, the painter can so depict them that they will appear alive, with the shadow and light which show the expression of a face, which you cannot accomplish with the pen though it can be achieved by the brush.

C A 139*a*, 419*a*]

660.

On the history of painting (660 661)

Come la pittura va d'età in età declinando e pèdèdosi, [2]quādo i pittori non ànno per autore · altro che la fatta pittura

[4]Siccome il pittore avrà la sua pittura di poca eccielenza, se quello piglia per autore [5]l'altrui pitture, ma s'egli · jnparerà dalle cose naturali farà bono frutto, [6]come vedemo in ne' pittori dopo i romani, i quali senpre imitarono l'uno dall'altro [7]e di età

That painting declines and deteriorates from age to age, when painters have no other standard than painting already done

Hence the painter will produce pictures of small merit if he takes for his standard the pictures of others. But if he will study from natural objects he will bear good fruit, as was seen in the painters after the Romans who always imitated each other and so their art constantly declined from age to age After

657 1—8 R 2 elle 3 ettu 4 opera

658 2 facto 4 desscrive 6 oratore "e non e piu poeta ne' e no pictore essellui 7 asstrolagho e filosafo ette 8 olagho 9 potessi cos 10 sodidi 11 ochio \\\\\) parole

659 1 settu esscrivere 2 ellumi 3 poi chol

660 1 chome va "deta in eta' dechnando 2 ano per altore altore chella 3 chome la pittura 4 si chome ara pocha secquello altore 5 massegli chose 6 chome ine imitorono 7 andaro dechinatione vene 5 [ēstado chōtēto alo suo maestro non avēdo] nato i mōu · 9 abitato chapre essimil assimile 10 super \ capre de

in età · senpre andava · detta arte ī declinatione ; dopo questi · venne Giotto Fiorētino, [8]il quale [nō è stato cōtēto allo imitare l'opere di Cimabue suo maestro] nato ī mōti [9]soletari, abitati solo da capre e simil bestie, — questo, sēdo volto · dalla natura · a simile arte, [10]comīciò a discegniare sopra i sassi li atti delle capre delle quali lui era guardatore; [11]e così comīciò a fare tutti li animali che nel paese si trovavā in tal modo, che questo dopo molto [12]studio avāzò nō che i maestri della sua età, [13]ma tutti quelli · di molti secoli passati ·, dopo · questo · l'arte [14]ricadde, perchè tutti imitavano [15]le fatte pitture ·, e così di secolo ī secolo ādò declinādo īsino [16]a tāto, che Tomaso fiorētino, cognominato Masacio, mostrò con opera perfetta co[17]me quelli che pigliavano per autore altro che la natura, · maestra dei maestri, [18]s'afaticavano īuano · ; [19]così voglio dire di queste cose matematiche, · che quegli che solamēte studiano [20]li autori · e nō le opere di natura ·, sō per arte nipoti e nō figlioli d'essa natura, mae[21]stra di boni autori; O della sōma stoltitia di quelli i quali biasimano · coloro che [22]īparano dalla natvra ·, lasciādo stare li autori discepoli d'essa natura!

these came Giotto the Florentine who—not content with imitating the works of Cimabue his master—being born in the mountains and in a solitude inhabited only by goats and such beasts, and being guided by nature to his art, began by drawing on the rocks the movements of the goats of which he was keeper. And thus he began to draw all the animals which were to be found in the country, and in such wise that after much study he excelled not only all the masters of his time but all those of many bygone ages. Afterwards this art declined again, because everyone imitated the pictures that were already done, thus it went on from century to century until Tomaso, of Florence, nicknamed Masaccio, showed by his perfect works how those who take for their standard any one but nature—the mistress of all masters—weary themselves in vain. And, I would say about these mathematical studies that those who only study the authorities and not the works of nature are descendants but not sons of nature the mistress of all good authors. Oh! how great is the folly of those who blame those who learn from nature [22], setting aside those authorities who themselves were the disciples of nature.

661

Ash I 18a]

Come la prima pittura fu sol d'una linia, la quale circūdaua [2]l'ōbra dell'omo, fatta dal sole ne'mvri.

That the first drawing was a simple line drawn round the shadow of a man cast by the sun on a wall.

662.

S K M III 48a]

The painter's scope.

Il dipintore disputa e gareggia [2]colla natura.

The painter strives and competes with nature.

[quali] le 11 affare tuti 12—22 *are written in a parallel column* 12 studio avazo [tutti i ma] . . dela 13 queli secholi 14 richade [insinom] perche tutti [pigliavano per altore] imitavano. 15 chosi di sechol ī seculo ādo diclinādo 16. attāto che "to" maso "fiorētino" cognominato masacio . chon cho. 17 quelgli . . altore chella. 18 iuano 19 chosi , chose matematice 20 altori . . le opre . soprarteni potienō figlioli 21 altori . . di soma . . queli . . choloro 22 altori

661. 1 circhūtaua

662. 1 garegia. 2 ̄cola.

660 22. *lasciando stare li autori.* In this observation we may detect an indirect evidence that Leonardo regarded his knowledge of natural history as derived from his own investigations, as well as his theories of perspective and optics Compare what he says in praise of experience (Vol II; *XIX*).

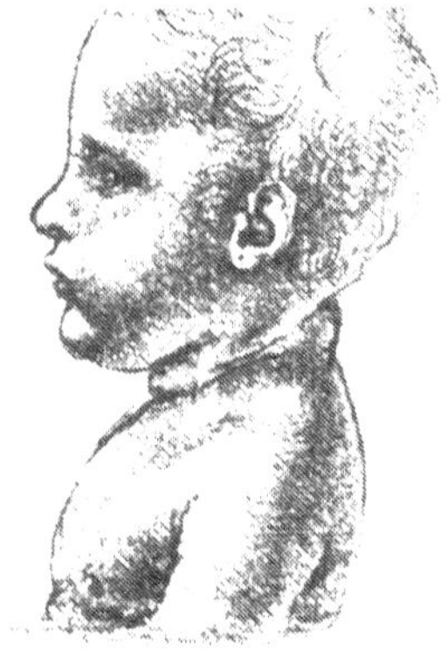

X.

Studies and Sketches for Pictures and Decorations.

An artist's manuscript notes can hardly be expected to contain any thing more than incidental references to those masterpieces of his work of which the fame, sounded in the writings of his contemporaries, has left a glorious echo to posterity. We need not therefore be surprised to find that the texts here reproduced do not afford us such comprehensive information as we could wish. On the other hand, the sketches and studies prepared by Leonardo for the two grandest compositions he ever executed: The Fresco of the Last Supper in the Refectory of Santa Maria delle Grazie at Milan, and the Cartoon of the Battle of Anghiari, for the Palazzo della Signoria at Florence—have been preserved; and, though far from complete, are so much more numerous than the manuscript notes, that we are justified in asserting that in value and interest they amply compensate for the meagerness of the written suggestions.

The notes for the composition of the Last Supper, which are given under nos. 665 *and* 666 *occur in a MS. at South Kensington, II*[2]*, written in the years* 1494—1495. *This MS. sketch was noted down not more than three or four years before the painting was executed, which justifies the inference that at the time when it was written the painter had not made up his mind definitely even as to the general scheme of the work; and from this we may also conclude that the drawings of apostles' heads at Windsor, in red chalk, must be ascribed to a later date. They are studies for the head of St. Matthew, the fourth figure on Christ's left hand—see Pl. XLVII—, the sketch (in black chalk) for the head of St. Philip, the third figure on the left hand—see Pl. XLVIII—, for St. Peter's right arm—see Pl. XIL, and for the expressive head of Judas which has unfortunately somewhat suffered by subsequent restoration of outlines,—see Pl. L. According to a tradition, as unfounded as it is improbable, Leonardo made use of the head of Padre Bandelli, the prior of the convent, as the prototype of his Judas; this however has already been contradicted by Amoretti "Memorie storiche" cap. XIV. The study of the head of a criminal on Pl. LI has, it seems to me, a better claim to be regarded as one of the preparatory sketches for the head of Judas. The*

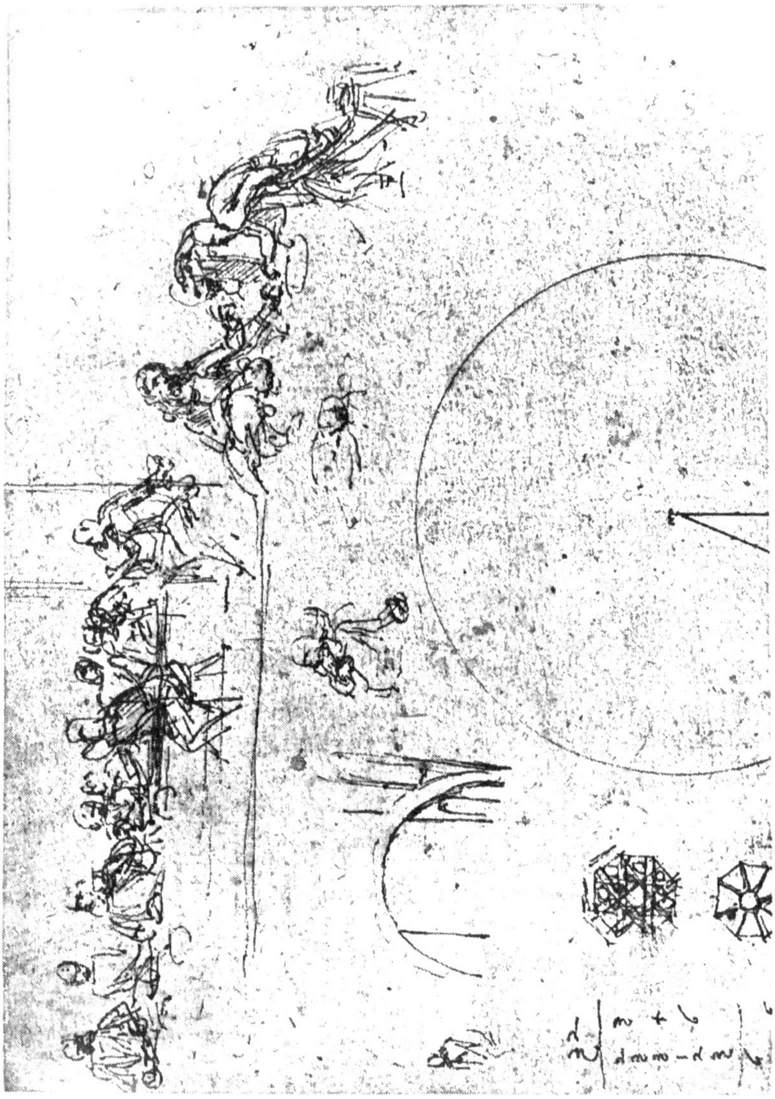

Windsor collection contains two old copies of the head of St. Simon, the figure to the extreme left of Christ, both of about equal merit (they are marked as Nos. 21 and 36)—the second was reproduced on Pl. VIII of the Grosvenor Gallery Publication in 1878. There is also at Windsor a drawing in black chalk of folded hands (marked with the old No. 212; No. LXI of the Grosvenor Gallery Publication) which I believe to be a copy of the hands of St. John, by some unknown pupil. A reproduction of the excellent drawings of heads of Apostles in the possession of H. R. H. the Grand Duchess of Weimar would have been out of my province in this work, and, with regard to them, I must confine myself to pointing out that the difference in style does not allow of our placing the Weimar drawings in the same category as those here reproduced. The mode of grouping in the Weimar drawings is of itself sufficient to indicate that they were not executed before the picture was painted, but, on the contrary, afterwards; and it is, on the face of it, incredible that so great a master should thus have copied from his own work.

The drawing of Christ's head, in the Brera palace at Milan was perhaps originally the work of Leonardo's hand; it has unfortunately been entirely retouched and re-drawn, so that no decisive opinion can be formed as to its genuineness.

The red chalk drawing reproduced on Pl. XLVI is in the Accademia at Venice; it was probably made before the text, Nos. 664 and 665, was written.

The two pen and ink sketches on Pl. XLV seem to belong to an even earlier date; the more finished drawing of the two, on the right hand, represents Christ with only St. John and Judas and a third disciple whose action is precisely that described in No. 666, l. 4. It is hardly necessary to observe that the other sketches on this page and the lines of text below the circle (containing the solution of a geometrical problem) have no reference to the picture of the Last Supper. With this figure of Christ may be compared a similar pen and ink drawing reproduced on page 297 below on the left hand; the original is in the Louvre. On this page again the rest of the sketches have no direct bearing on the composition of the Last Supper, not even, as it seems to me, the group of four men at the bottom to the right hand—who are listening to a fifth, in their midst addressing them. Moreover the writing on this page (an explanation of a disk shaped instrument) is certainly not in the same style as we find constantly used by Leonardo after the year 1489.

It may be incidentally remarked that no sketches are known for the portrait of "Mona Lisa", nor do the MS. notes ever allude to it, though according to Vasari the master had it in hand for fully four years.

Leonardo's cartoon for the picture of the battle of Anghiari has shared the fate of the rival work, Michael Angelo's "Bathers summoned to Battle": Both have been lost in some wholly inexplicable manner. I cannot here enter into the remarkable history of this work; I can only give an account of what has been preserved to us of Leonardo's scheme and preparations for executing it. The extent of the material in studies and drawings was till now quite unknown. Their publication here may give some adequate idea of the grandeur of this famous work. The text given as No. 669 contains a description of the particulars of the battle, but for the reasons given in the note to this text, I must abandon the idea of taking this passage as the basis of my attempt to reconstruct the picture as the artist conceived and executed it.

I may here remind the reader that Leonardo prepared the cartoon in the Sala del Papa of Santa Maria Novella at Florence and worked there from the end of October 1503 *till February* 1504, *and then was busied with the painting in the Sala del Consiglio in the Palazzo della Signoria, till the work was interrupted at the end of May* 1506. *(See Milanesi's note to Vasari pp.* 43—45 *Vol. IV ed.* 1880.*) Vasari, as is well known, describes only one scene or episode of the cartoon—the Battle for the Standard in the foreground of the composition, as it would seem; and this only was ever finished as a mural decoration in the Sala del Consiglio. This portion of the composition is familiar to all from the disfigured copy engraved by Edelinck. Mariette had already very acutely observed that Edelinck must surely have worked from a Flemish copy of the picture. There is in the Louvre a drawing by Rubens (No.* 565*) which also represents four horsemen fighting round a standard and which agrees with Edelinck's engraving, but the engraving reverses the drawing. An earlier Flemish drawing, such as may have served as the model for both Rubens and Edelinck, is in the Uffizi collection (see Philpots's Photograph, No.* 732*). It seems to be a work of the second half of the XVIth century, a time when both the picture and the cartoon had already been destroyed. It is apparently the production of a not very skilled hand. Raphael Trichet du Fresne,* 1651, *mentions that a small picture by Leonardo himself of the Battle of the Standard was then extant in the Tuileries; by this he probably means the painting on panel which is now in the possession of Madame Timbal in Paris, and which has lately been engraved by Haussoullier as a work by Leonardo. The picture, which is very carefully painted, seems to me however to be the work of some unknown Florentine painter, and probably executed within the first ten years of the XVIth century. At the same time, it would seem to be a copy not from Leonardo's cartoon, but from his picture in the Palazzo della Signoria; at any rate this little picture, and the small Flemish drawing in Florence are the oldest finished copies of this episode in the great composition of the Battle of Anghiari.*

In his Life of Raphael, Vasari tells us that Raphael copied certain works of Leonardo's during his stay in Florence. Raphael's first visit to Florence lasted from the middle of October 1504 *till July* 1505, *and he revisited it in the summer of* 1506. *The hasty sketch, now in the possession of the University of Oxford and reproduced on page* 337 *also represents the Battle of the Standard and seems to have been made during his first stay, and therefore not from the fresco but from the cartoon; for, on the same sheet we also find, besides an old man's head drawn in Leonardo's style, some studies for the figure of St. John the Martyr which Raphael used in* 1505 *in his great fresco in the Church of San Severo at Perugia.*

Of Leonardo's studies for the Battle of Anghiari I must in the first place point to five, on three of which—Pl. LII 2, *Pl. LIII, Pl. LVI—we find studies for the episode of the Standard. The standard bearer, who, in the above named copies is seen stooping, holding on to the staff across his shoulder, is immediately recognisable as the left-hand figure in Raphael's sketch, and we find it in a similar attitude in Leonardo's pen and ink drawing in the British Museum—Pl. LII,* 2—*the lower figure to the right. It is not difficult to identify the same figure in two more complicated groups in the pen and ink drawings, now in the Accademia at Venice—Pl. LIII, and Pl. LIV—where we also find some studies of foot soldiers fighting. On the sheet in the British Museum —Pl. LII,* 2—*we find, among others, one group of three horses galloping forwards: one*

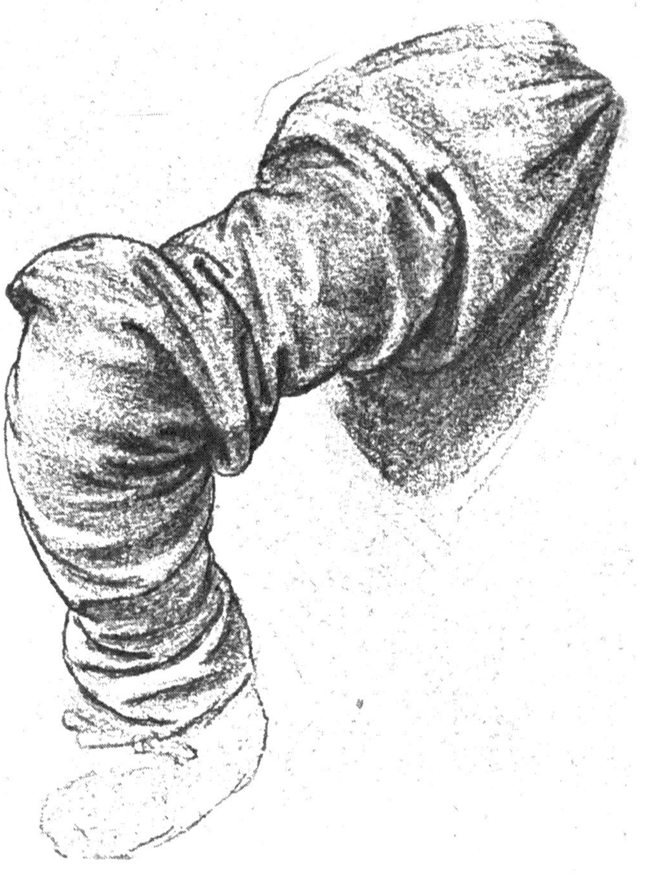

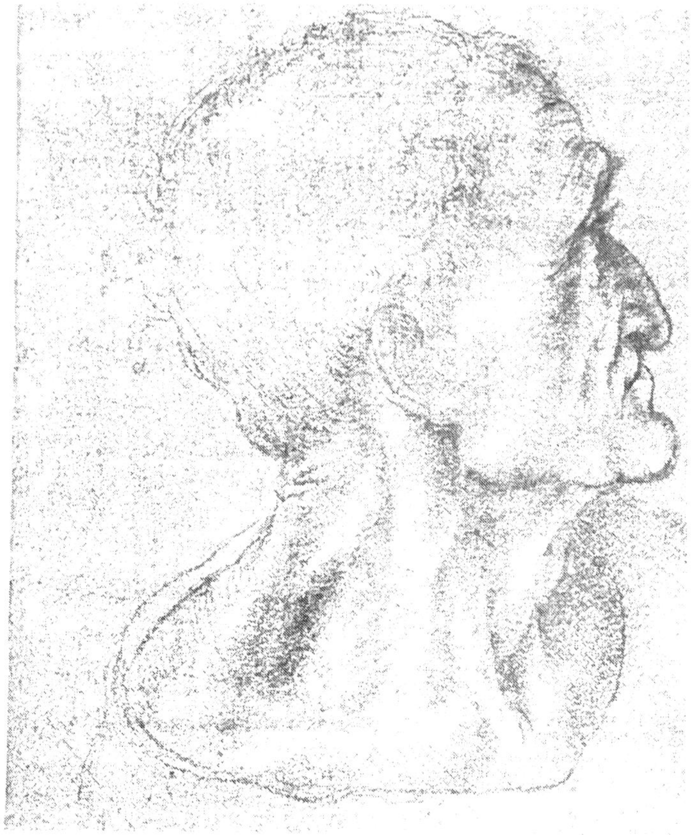

horseman is thrown and protects himself with his buckler against the lance thrusts of two others on horseback, who try to pierce him as they ride past. The same action is repeated, with some variation, in two sketches in pen and ink on a third sheet, in the Accademia at Venice, Pl. LV; a coincidence which suggests the probability of such an incident having actually been represented on the cartoon. We are not, it is true, in a position to declare with any certainty which of these three dissimilar sketches may have been the nearest to the group finally adopted in executing the cartoon.

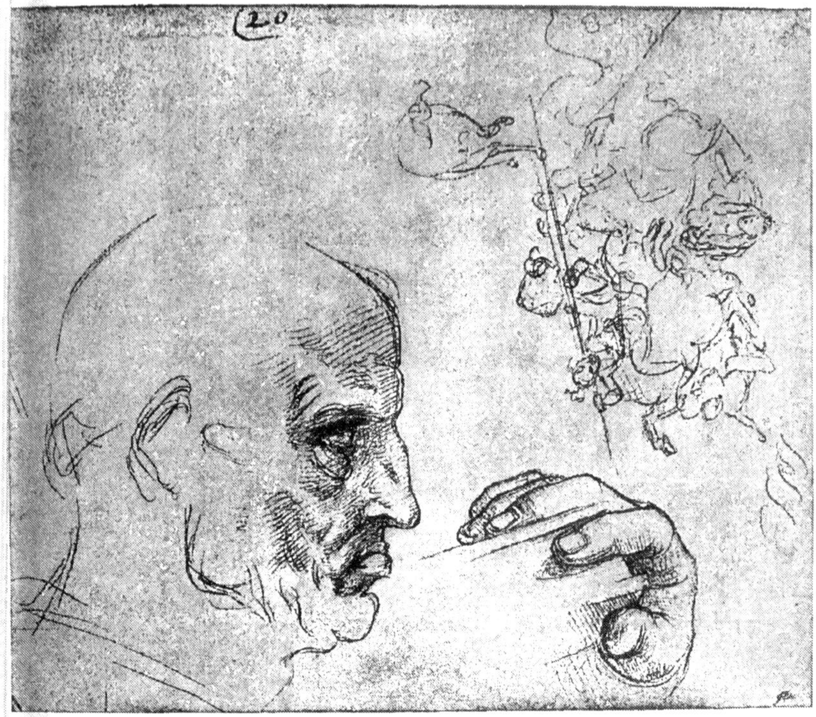

With regard, however, to one of the groups of horsemen it is possible to determine with perfect certainty not only which arrangement was preferred, but the position it occupied in the composition. The group of horsemen on Pl. LVII is a drawing in black chalk at Windsor, which is there attributed to Leonardo, but which appears to me to be the work of Cesare da Sesto, and the Commendatore Giov. Morelli supports me in this view. It can hardly be doubted that da Sesto, as a pupil of Leonardo's, made this drawing from his master's cartoon, if we compare it with the copy made by Raphael—here reproduced,

for just above the fighting horseman in Raphael's copy it is possible to detect a horse which is seen from behind, going at a slower pace, with his tail flying out to the right and the same horse may be seen in the very same attitude carrying a dimly sketched rider, in the foreground of Cesare da Sesto's drawing.

If a very much rubbed drawing in black chalk at Windsor—Pl. LVI—is, as it appears to be, the reversed impression of an original drawing, it is not difficult to supplement from it the portions drawn by Cesare da Sesto. Nay, it may prove possible to reconstruct the whole of the lost cartoon from the mass of materials we now have at hand which we may regard as the nucleus of the composition. A large pen and ink

drawing by Raphael in the Dresden collection, representing three horsemen fighting, and another, by Cesare da Sesto, in the Uffizi, of light horsemen fighting are a farther contribution which will help us to reconstruct it.

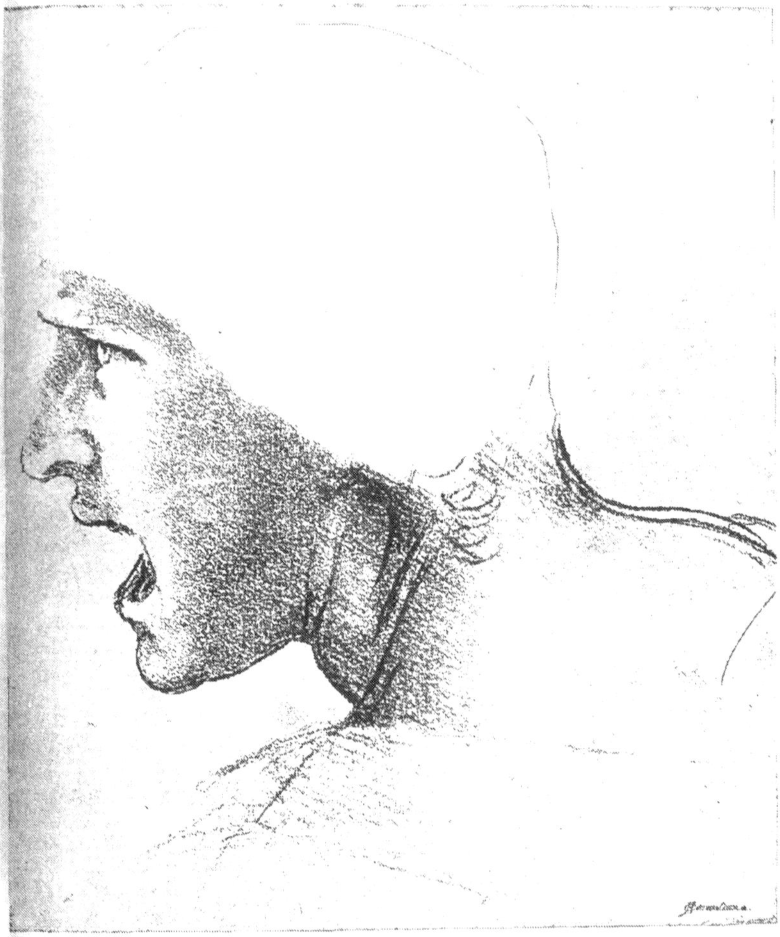

The sketch reproduced on Pl. LV gives a suggestive example of the way in which foot-soldiers may have been introduced into the cartoon as fighting among the groups of horsemen; and I may here take the opportunity of mentioning that, for reasons which

it would be out of place to enlarge upon here, I believe the two genuine drawings by Raphael's hand in his "Venetian sketch-book" as it is called—one of a standard bearer marching towards the left, and one of two foot-soldiers armed with spears and fighting with a horseman—to be undoubtedly copies from the cartoon of the Battle of Anghiari.

Leonardo's two drawings, preserved in the museum at Buda-Pesth and reproduced on pages 338 and 339 are preliminary studies for the heads of fighting warriors. The two heads drawn in black chalk (pg. 338), and the one seen in profile, turned to the left, drawn in red chalk (pg. 339), correspond exactly with those of two horsemen in the scene of the fight round the standard as we see them in Madame Timbal's picture and in the other finished copies. An old copy of the last named drawing by a pupil of Leonardo is in MS. C. A. 187b; 561b (See Saggio, Tav. XXII). Leonardo used to make such finished studies of heads as those, drawn on detached sheets, before beginning his pictures from his drawings—compare the preparatory studies for the fresco of the Last Supper, given on Pl. XLVII and Pl. L. Other drawings of heads, all characterised by the expression of vehement excitement that is appropriate to men fighting, are to be seen at Windsor (No. 44) and at the Accademia at Venice (IV, 13); at the back of one of the drawings at Buda-Pesth there is the bust of a warrior carrying a spear on his left shoulder, holding up the left arm (See Csatakèpek a XVI—lk Századból összeállította Pelszky Károly). These drawings may have been made for other portions of the cartoon, of which no copies exist, and thus we are unable to identify these preparatory drawings. Finally I may add that a sketch of fighting horse and foot soldiers, formerly in the possession of M. Thiers and published by Charles Blanc in his "Vies des Peintres" can hardly be accepted as genuine. It is not to be found, as I am informed, among the late President's property, and no one appears to know where it now is.

An attempted reconstruction of the Cartoon, which is not only unsuccessful but perfectly unfounded, is to be seen in the lithograph by Bergeret, published in Charles Blanc's "Vies des peintres" and reprinted in "The great Artists. L. da Vinci", p. 80. This misleading pasticcio may now be rejected without hesitation.

There are yet a few original drawings by Leonardo which might be mentioned here as possibly belonging to the cartoon of the Battle; such as the pen and ink sketches on Pl. XXI and on Pl. XXXVIII, No. 3, but we should risk too wide a departure from the domain of ascertained fact.

With regard to the colours and other materials used by Leonardo the reader may be referred to the quotations from the accounts for the picture in question given by Milanesi in his edition of Vasari (Vol. IV, p. 44, note) where we find entries of a similar character to those in Leonardo's note books for the year 1505; S. K. M. I² (see No. 636).

That Leonardo was employed in designing decorations and other preparations for high festivals, particularly for the court of Milan, we learn not only from the writings of his contemporaries but from his own incidental allusions; for instance in MS. C. 15b (1), l. 9. In the arrangement of the texts referring to this I have placed those first, in which historical personages are named—Nos. 670—674. Among the descriptions of Allegorical subjects two texts lately found at Oxford have been included, Nos. 676 and 677. They are particularly interesting because they are accompanied by large sketches which render the meaning of the texts perfectly clear. It is very intelligible that in other cases, where

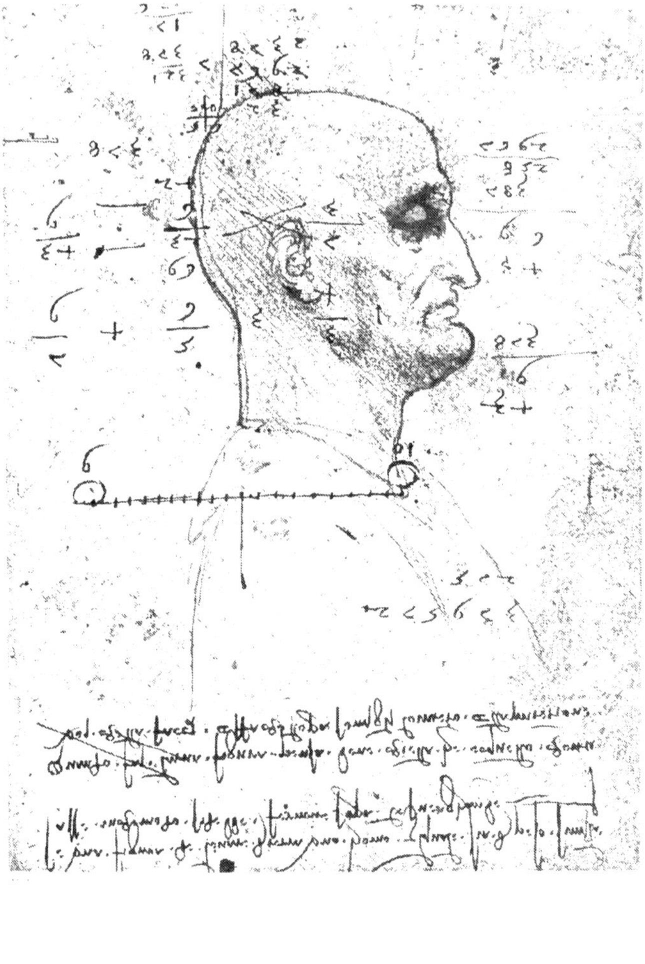

there are no illustrative sketches, the notes must necessarily remain obscure or admit of various interpretations. The litterature of the time affords ample evidence of the use of such allegorical representations, particularly during the Carnival and in Leonardo's notes we find the Carnival expressly mentioned—Nos. 685 *and* 704 *Vasari in his Life of Pontormo, particularly describes that artist's various undertakings for Carnival festivities. These very graphic descriptions appear to me to throw great light in more ways than one on the meaning of Leonardo's various notes as to allegorical representations and also on mottoes and emblems—Nos* 681—702 *In passing judgment on the allegorical sketches and emblems it must not be overlooked that even as pictures they were always accompanied by explanations in words. Several finished drawings of allegorical compositions or figures have been preserved, but as they have no corresponding explanation in the MSS they had no claim to be reproduced here The female figure on Pl XXVI may perhaps be regarded as a study for such an allegorical painting, of which the purport would have been explained by an inscription*

F. U. 1151 446

663.

...bre 1478 | jcomīciai le 2 vergini Marie.

[In the autumm of] 1478 I began the two Madonna [pictures]. On Madonna pictures.

663. 1. Jchomīciai . . Vergine.

663. Photographs of this page have been published by BRAUN, No. 439, and PHILPOT, No. 718.

1. *Incominciai.* We have no other information as to the two pictures of the Madonna here spoken of. As Leonardo here tells us that he had begun two Madonnas at the same time, the word *'incominciai'* may be understood to mean that he had begun at the same time preparatory studies for two pictures to be painted later. If this is so, the non-existence of the pictures may be explained by supposing that they were only planned and never executed. I may here mention a few studies for pictures of the Madonna which probably belong to this early time; particularly a drawing in silver-point on bluish tinted paper at Windsor—see Pl. XL, No. 3—, a drawing of which the details have almost disappeared in the original but have been rendered quite distinct in the reproduction; secondly a slight pen and ink sketch in the Codex VALLARDI, in the Louvre, fol. 64, No. 2316; again a silver point drawing of a Virgin and child drawn over again with the pen in the His de la Salle collection also in the Louvre, No. 101. (See Vicomte BOTH DE TAUZIA, *Notice des dessins de la collection His de la Salle, exposés au Louvre.* Paris 1881, pp. 80, 81.) This drawing is, it is true, traditionally ascribed to Raphael, but the author of the catalogue very justly points out its great resemblance with the sketches for Madonnas in the British Museum which are indisputably Leonardo's. Some of these have been published by Mr. HENRY WALLIS in the Art Journal, New Ser. No. 14, Feb. 1882. If the non-existence of the two pictures here alluded to justifies my hypothesis that only studies for such pictures are meant by the text, it may also be supposed that the drawings were made for some comrade in VERROCCHIO's atelier. (See VASARI, Sansoni's ed. Florence 1880. Vol. IV, p. 564): *"E perchè a Lorenzo piaceva fuor di modo la maniera di Lionardo, la seppe così bene imitare, che niuno fu che nella pulitezza e nel finir l'opere con diligenza l'imitasse più di lui."* Leonardo's notes give me no opportunity of discussing the pictures executed by him in Florence, before he moved to Milan. So the studies for the unfinished picture of the Adoration of the Magi—in the Uffizi, Florence—cannot be described here, nor would any discussion about the picture in the Louvre *"La Vierge aux Rochers"* be appropriate in the absence of all allusion to it in the MSS. Therefore, when I presently add a few remarks on this painting in explanation of the Master's drawings for it, it will be not merely with a view to facilitate critical researches about the picture now in the National Gallery, London, which by some critics has been pronounced to be a replica of the Louvre picture, but also because I take this opportunity of publishing several finished studies of the Master's which, even if they were not made in Florence but later in Milan, must have been prior to the painting of the Last Supper. The original picture in Paris is at present so disfigured by dust and varnish that the current reproductions in photography actually give evidence more of the injuries, to which the picture has been exposed than of the original work itself. The wood-cut given on p. 344, is only intended to give a general notion of the composition. It must be understood that the outline

and expression of the heads, which in the picture is obscured but not destroyed, is here altogether missed. The facsimiles which follow are from drawings which appear to me to be studies for "*La Vierge aux Rochers.*"

1. A drawing in silver point on brown toned

paper of a woman's head looking to the left. In the Royal Library at Turin, apparently a study from nature for the Angel's head (Pl. XLII).

2. A study of drapery for the left leg of the same figure, done with the brush, Indian ink on greenish paper, the lights heighten ed with white.

Th.]

664.

Bernardo di Bandino's Portrait.

Berrettina di tanè,	A tan-coloured small cap,
2 farsetto di raso nero,	A doublet of black serge,
3 cioppa nera foderata,	A black jerkin lined
4 giubba turchina foderata	A blue coat lined,
5 di gole di volpe,	with fur of foxes' breasts,
6 e'l collare della givbba	and the collar of the jerkin
7 soppannato di velluto appicchiet-	covered with black
8 tato nero e rosso;	and white stippled velvet.
9 Bernardo di Bandino	Bernardo di Bandino
10 Baroncigli;	Baroncelli;
11 calze nere.	black hose.

664. 1. berettino. 4. giupba. 5. di ghole di gholpe. 6. chollare. 7. appicci. 8. lato . . errosso. 10. baroncigli. 11. chalze.

The original is at Windsor, No. 223. The reproduction Pl. XLIII is defective in the shadow on the upper part of the thigh, which is not so deep as in the original; it should also be observed that the folds of the drapery near the hips are somewhat altered in the finished work in the Louvre, while the London copy shows a greater resemblance to this study in that particular.

3. A study in red chalk for the bust of the Infant Christ—No. 3 in the Windsor collection (Pl. XLIV). The well-known silver-point drawing on pale green paper, in the Louvre, of a boy's head (No. 363 in REISET, *Notice des dessins, Ecoles d'Italie*) seems to me to be a slightly altered copy, either from the original picture or from this red chalk study.

4. A silver-point study on greenish paper, for the head of John the Baptist, reproduced on p. 342. This was formerly in the Codex Vallardi and is now exhibited among the drawings in the Louvre. The lights are, in the original, heightened with white; the outlines, particularly round the head and ear, are visibly restored.

There is a study of an outstretched hand—No. 288 in the Windsor collection—which was published in the Grosvenor Gallery Publication, 1878, simply under the title of: "No. 72 Study of a hand, pointing" which, on the other hand, I regard as a copy by a pupil. The action occurs in the kneeling angel of the Paris picture and not in the London copy.

These four genuine studies form, I believe, a valuable substitute in the absence of any MS. notes referring to the celebrated Paris picture.

664. These eleven lines of text are by the side of the pen and ink drawing of a man hanged—Pl. LXII, No. 1. This drawing was exhibited in 1879 at the *Ecole des Beaux-Arts* in Paris and the compilers of the catalogue amused themselves by giving the victim's name as follows: "*Un pendu, vêtu d'une longue robe, les mains liées sur le dos . . . Bernardo di Bendino Barontigni, marchand de pantalons*" (see *Catalogue descriptif des Dessins de Maîtres anciens exposés à l'Ecole des Beaux Arts*, Paris 1879; No. 83, pp. 9—10). Now, the criminal represented here, is none other than Bernardino di Bandino Baroncelli the murderer of Giuliano de' Medici, whose name as a coadjutor in the conspiracy of the Pazzi has gained a melancholy notoriety by the tragedy of the 26th April 1478. Bernardo was descended from an ancient family and the son of the man who, under King Ferrante, was President of the High Court of Justice in Naples. His ruined fortunes, it would seem, induced him to join the Pazzi; he and Francesco Pazzi were entrusted with the task of murdering Giuliano de' Medici on the fixed day. Their victim not appearing in the cathedral at the hour when they expected him, the two conspirators ran to the palace of the Medici and induced him to accompany them. Giuliano then took his place in the chancel of the Cathedral, and as the officiating priest raised the Host—the sign agreed upon—Bernardo stabbed the unsuspecting Giuliano in the breast with a short sword; Giuliano stepped backwards and fell dead. The attempt on Lorenzo's life however, by the other conspirators at the same moment, failed of success. Bernardo no sooner saw that Lorenzo tried to make his escape towards the sacristy, than he rushed upon him, and struck down Francesco Nori who endeavoured to protect Lorenzo. How Lorenzo then took refuge behind the brazen doors of the sacristy, and how, as soon as Giuliano's death was made known, the further plans of the conspirators were defeated, while a terrible vengeance overtook all the perpetrators and accomplices, this is no place to tell. Bernardo Bandini alone seemed to be favoured by fortune; he hid first in the tower of the Cathedral, and then escaped undiscovered from Florence. Poliziano, who was with Lorenzo in the Cathedral, says in his 'Conjurationis Pactianae Commentarium': "*Bandinus fugitans in Tiphernatem incidit, a quo in aciem receptus Senas pervenit.*" And Gino Capponi in summing up the reports of the

665.

S. K. M. II² 141]

Notes on the Last Supper (665—668)

Vno che beveua e lasciò [3]la zaina nel suo sito e volse la testa inverso il propositore.

[4]Vn altro tesse le dita delle sue mani insieme [5]e co rigide ciglia si uolta al compagnio, [6]l'altro colle mani aperte mostra le palme di quelle [7]e alza le spalle inverso li orecchi e fa la bocca della [8]maraviglia;

One who was drinking and has left the glass in its position and turned his head towards the speaker.

Another, twisting the fingers of his hands together turns with stern brows to his companion [6]. Another with his hands spread open shows the palms, and shrugs his shoulders up his ears making a mouth of astonishment [8].

665 2. vno che [poleua bere e per] beveua elasscio. 5. cho. 6. cholle. 7. lesspalli inver . . effa la bocha. 9. ecquello.

numerous contemporary narrators of the event, says: "*Bernardo Bandini ricoverato in Costantinopoli, fu per ordine del Sultano preso e consegnato a un Antonio di Bernardino dei Medici, che Lorenzo aveva mandato apposta in Turchia: così era grande la potenza di quest' uomo e grande la voglia di farne mostra e che non restasse in vita chi aveagli ucciso il fratello, fu egli appiccato appena giunto*" (*Storia della Repubblica di Firenze II*, 377, 378). Details about the dates may be found in the *Chronichetta di Belfredello Strinati Alfieri*: "*Bernardo di Bandino Bandini sopradetto ne venne preso da Gostantinopoli a dì* 14. *Dicembre* 1479 *e disaminato, che fu al Bargello, fu impiccato alle finestre di detto Bargello allato alla Doana a dì* 29. *Dicembre MCCCCLXXIX che pochi dì stette.*" It may however be mentioned with reference to the mode of writing the name of the assassin that, though most of his contemporaries wrote Bernardo Bandini, in the *Breve Chronicon Caroli Petri de Joannis* he is called Bernardo di Bandini Baroncelli; and, in the *Sententiae Domini Matthaei de Toscanis*, Bernardus Joannis Bandini de Baroncellis, as is written on Leonardo's drawing of him when hanged. Now VASARI, in the life of *Andrea del Castagno* (Vol. II, 680; ed. Milanesi 1878), tells us that in 1478 this painter was commissioned by order of the Signoria to represent the members of the Pazzi conspiracy as traitors, on the façade of the Palazzo del Podestà—the Bargello. This statement is obviously founded on a mistake, for Andrea del Castagno was already dead in 1457. He had however been commissioned to paint Rinaldo degli Albizzi, when declared a rebel and exiled in 1434, and his adherents, as hanging head downwards; and in consequence he had acquired the nickname of Andrea degl' Impiccati. On the 21th July 1478 the Council of Eight came to the following resolution: "*item servatis etc. deliberaverunt et stantiaverunt Sandro Botticelli pro ejus labore in pingendo proditores flor. quadraginta largos*" (see G. MILANESI, *Arch. stor. VI* (1862) p. 5 note.

As has been told, Giuliano de' Medici was murdered on the 26th April 1478, and we see by this that only three months later Botticelli was paid for his painting of the "*proditores*". We can however hardly suppose that all the members of the conspiracy were depicted by him in fresco on the façade of the palace, since no fewer than eighty had been condemned to death. We have no means of knowing whether, besides Botticelli, any other painters, perhaps Leonardo, was commissioned, when the criminals had been hanged in person out of the windows of the Palazzo del Podestà to represent them there afterwards in effigy in memory of their disgrace. Nor do we know whether the assassin who had escaped may at first not have been provisionally represented as hanged in effigy. Now, when we try to connect the historical facts with this drawing by Leonardo reproduced on Pl. LXII, No. I, and the full description of the conspirator's dress and its colour on the same sheet, there seems to be no reasonable doubt that Bernardo Bandini is here represented as he was actually hanged on December 29th, 1479, after his capture at Constantinople. The dress is certainly not that in which he committed the murder. A long furred coat might very well be worn at Constantinople or at Florence in December, but hardly in April. The doubt remains whether Leonardo described Bernardo's dress so fully because it struck him as remarkable, or whether we may not rather suppose that this sketch was actually made from nature with the intention of using it as a study for a wall painting to be executed. It cannot be denied that the drawing has all the appearance of having been made for this purpose. Be this as it may, the sketch under discussion proves, at any rate, that Leonardo was in Florence in December 1479, and the note that accompanies it is valuable as adding one more characteristic specimen to the very small number of his MSS. that can be proved to have been written between 1470 and 1480.

665. 666. In the original MS. there is no sketch to accompany these passages, and if we compare them with those drawings made by Leonardo in preparation for the composition of the picture—Pl. XLV, XLVI—, (compare also Pl. LII, 1 and the drawings on p. 297) it is impossible to recognise in them a faithful interpretation of the whole of this text; but, if we compare these passages with the finished picture (see p. 334) we shall see that in many places they

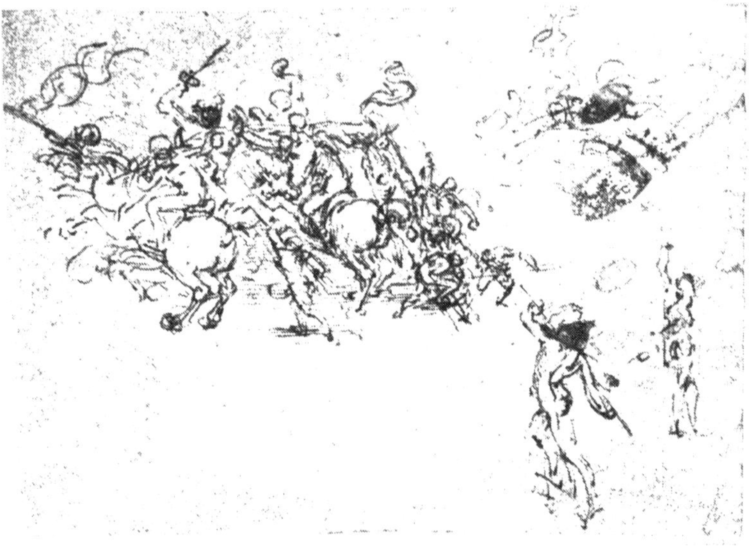

[9] Vn altro parla nell' orechio all' altro, e quello che [10] l'ascolta si torcie inverso lui e gli porgie li orechii, [11] tenendo vn coltello nel' una mano e nell' altra il pa[12]ne mezzo diuiso da tal coltello, [13] l'altro nel uoltarsi tenendo vn coltello in mano versa [14] con tal mano vna zaina sopra della tavola

[9] Another speaks into his neighbour's ear and he, as he listens to him, turns towards him to lend an ear [10], while he holds a knife in one hand, and in the other the loaf half cut through by the knife [13] Another who has turned, holding a knife in his hand, upsets with his hand a glass on the table [14]

S K M II² 1b]

666.

L'altro posa le mani sopra della tavola e guarda, [2] l'altro soffia nel boccone, [3] l'altro si china per uedere il propositore e fassi [4] ōbra colla mano alli ochi, [5] l'altro si tira indirieto a quel che si china e [6] vede il propositore infra 'l muro e 'l chinato

Another lays his hand on the table and is looking Another blows his mouthful. [3] Another leans forward to see the speaker shading his eyes with his hand [5] Another draws back behind the one who leans forward, and sees the speaker between the wall and the man who is leaning [6]

S K M II² 78b]

667.

CRISTO

[2] Giovā cōte , quello del ca[r]dinale del Mortaro.

CHRIST

Count Giovanni, the one with the Cardinal of Mortaro

V A X 8]

668.

Filippo, Simone, Matteo, Tome, Jacopo maggiore, Pietro, [2] Filippo, Andrea, Bartolomeo

Philip, Simon, Matthew, Thomas, James the Greater, Peter, Philip, Andrew, Bartholomew

10 porcie orechicō 11 choltello 12 mezo 13 inman 666 2 bochone 3 effassi 5 acquel chessi he 6 cinato

667 1—3 R 1 crissto 2 del cha 668 1—2 R 1 Matteo [tōme], tōme magore 2 filipo

coincide For instance, compare No 665, l 6—8, with the fourth figure on the right hand of Christ The various actions described in lines 9—10, 13—14 are to be seen in the group of Peter, John and Judas, in the finished picture however it is not a glass but a salt cellar that Judas is upsetting

In No 666 Line 1 must refer to the furthest figure on the left, 3, 5 and 6 describe actions which are given to the group of disciples on the left hand of Christ

6. *chinato* I have to express my regret for having misread this word, written *cinato* in the original, and having altered it to "*ciclo*" when I first published this text, in 'The Academy' for Nov 8, 1879 immediately after I had discovered it, and subsequently in the small biography of Leonardo da Vinci (Great Artists) p 29

667 As this note is in the same small Manuscript as the passage here immediately preceding it, I may be justified in assuming that Leonardo meant to use the features of the person here named as a suitable model for the figure of Christ The celebrated drawing of the head of Christ, now hanging in the Brera Gallery at Milan, has obviously been so much restored that it is now impossible to say, whether it was ever genuine We have only to compare it with the undoubtedly genuine drawings of heads of the disciples in Pl XLVII, XLVIII and L, to admit that not a single line of the Milan drawing in its present state can be by the same hand

668 See Pl XLVI The names of the disciples are given in the order in which they are written in the original, from right to left, above each head The original drawing is here slightly reduced in scale, it measures 39 centimètres in length by 26 in breadth.

669.

C. A. 73 a; 214 a]

Fiorentini
[2]Neri di Gino Capponi
[3]Bernardetto de' Medici.

Niccolò da Pisa
Conte Francesco,
Micheletto,
[4]Pietro Giãpaolo
[5]Guelfo Orsino,
[6]Ms. Rinaldo delli Albizzi

[7]Cominciasi dal'oration di Niccolò Piccinino a sol[8]dati e fuori usciti Fiorentini tra quali est ms. Rinaldo delli Albizzi e altri Fiorentini; [9]Di poi si faccia come lui prima mõtò a cavallo [10]armato; e tutto lo esercito li andò direto, [11]40 squadre di cavalli, [12]2000 pedoni andavano con lui; [13]E'l Patriarca la mattina di buon'ora montò [14]in su un monte per scoprir il paese, cioè colli, [15]campi, e valle irrigata da uno fiume, [16]e uide dal Borgo a San Sepolco venire [17]Niccolò Picinino con le genti con gran polvere, [18]e scopertolo tornò al campo delle genti e parlò loro; [19]Parlato ch'ebbe pregò Dio ad mani giunte, comparì [20]una nugola, dalla quale usciva san Piero che parlò [21]al Patriarca; [22]500 cavalli furono mandati dal Patriarca per impe[23]dire o raffrenare lo impeto nimico; [24]Nella prima schiera Francesco, figliuolo di Niccolò Picci[25]nino, venne il primo ad investire il ponte, [26]ch'era guardato dal Patriarca e Fiorentini; [27]Dopo il ponte da mano sinistra mandò fanti [28]per impedire li nostri, i quali ripugnavano, [29]de' quali era capo Micheletto, il quale quel dì [30]per sorte aveva in guardia lo esercito; [31]Qui, ad questo ponte si fa una

Florentines
Neri di Gino Capponi
Bernardetto de' Medici

Niccolò da Pisa
Conte Francesco
Micheletto,
Pietro Gian Paolo
Guelfo Orsino,
Messer Rinaldo degli Albizzi

Begin with the address of Niccolò Piccinino to the soldiers and the banished Florentines among whom are Messer Rinaldo degli Albizzi and other Florentines. Then let it be shown how he first mounted on horseback in armour; and the whole army came after him—40 squadrons of cavalry, and 2000 foot soldiers went with him. Very early in the morning the Patriarch went up a hill to reconnoitre the country, that is the hills, fields and the valley watered by a river; and from thence he beheld Niccolò Picinino coming from Borgo San Sepolcro with his people, and with a great dust; and perceiving them he returned to the camp of his own people and addressed them. Having spoken he prayed to God with clasped hands, when there appeared a cloud in which Saint Peter appeared and spoke to the Patriarch.—500 cavalry were sent forward by the Patriarch to hinder or check the rush of the enemy. In the foremost troop Francesco the son of Niccolò Piccinino[24] was the first to attack the bridge which was held by the Patriarch and the Florentines. Beyond the bridge to his left he sent forward some infantry to engage ours, who drove them back, among

669. 1—63 *written from left to right.* 1. fiorent"ini" Nic"o". 2. gino Caponi . . franc"o". 3. Bernardecto d'. 4. giãpaulo. 5. Ghuelfo orsino. 6. albizi. 7. Comintisi . . nico. 8. Fior"ni" . albizi. 13. Patriarcha . . bonahora. 14. In susũ monte. 19. Parlato hebbe . . giunte chon. 21. Patriarcha. 22. Patriarcha. 26. Patriarcha. 32. Vinsono. 33. hastorre. 37. vinsono.

669. This passage does not seem to me to be in Leonardo's hand, though it has hitherto been generally accepted as genuine. Not only is the writing unlike his, but the spelling also is quite different. I would suggest that this passage is a description of the events of the battle drawn up for the Painter by order of the Signoria, perhaps by some historian commissioned by them, to serve as a scheme or programme of the work. The whole tenor of the style seems to me to argue in favour of this theory; and besides, it would be in no way surprising that such a document should have been preserved among Leonardo's autographs.

2—7. *Neri di Gino Capponi* and *Bernardetto de' Medici* were the *Commissari* of the Florentine Republic.

Nicolò da Pisa, compare line 44.

Conte Francesco, see line 24.

Micheletto Sforza Attendolo, see line 29. He and *Pier Giampaolo Orsino* were Captains together of the Lombard troops.

13. *Il Patriarcha*, Cardinal Scarampi, Patriarch of Aquileia, Legate of the Papal see.

16. *Borgo San Sepolcro.* On a map drawn by Leonardo and reproduced on Pl. CXIII *borgo a sã sepolcro* is to be read near the upper margin to the left between a view of a town and a sketch of the windings of the Tiber. Below somewhat more to the left is the word '*Anghiari*,' the name of the village where the battle was fought.

20. *Usciva San Piero.* The battle took place on St. Peter and St. Paul's day, June 29th, 1440.

gran pugna, [32]Vinsero li nostri e lo inimico è scacciato, [33]Qui Guidoe Astorre suo fratello, signore di [34]Faenza, con molte genti si rifeciono e resta[35]urarono la guerra, e urtarono tanto forte [36]le genti Fiorentine, che ricuperarono il ponte e [37]vennero sino ad li padiglioni, contro a quali [38]venne Symonetto con 600 cavalli ad urtare [39]li inimici, e li cacciò un altra volta dal [40]luogo, e riacquistarono il ponte, e drieto [41]a lui venne altra gente con 2000 cavalli, [42]e così lungo tempo si combattè variamente, et [43]dipoi il Patriarca per disordinare lo inimico, mandò [44]Niccolò da Pisa innanzi e Napoleone Orsino, [45]giovane senza barba, e drieto a costoro [46]gran moltitudine di gente, e qui fu fatto [47]un altro gran fatto d'arme, In questo tempo [48]Niccolo Piccinino spinse innanzi il restante delle [49]sue genti, le quali feciono un'altra volta incli[50]nare i nostri, e se non fusse stato che il Patriarca [61]si mise innanzi e con parole e fatti non avesse rite[52]nuto que' capitani, sarebbono iti li nostri in fuga, [52]Fece il Patriarca piantare certe artiglierie [54]al colle, colle quali sbaragliava le fanterie delli [55]nimici, e fu questo disordine tanto che Niccolò [56]cominciò a rivocare il figliuolo e tutte le sue [57]genti, e si misero in fuga verso il borgo, [58]e qui si fece una grande strage d'uomini, [59]nè si salvarono se non li primi che fuggirono [60]o si nascosero Durò il fatto d'arme fino al [61]tramontar del sole e 'l Patriarca attese[62]a ritirare le genti, e seppellire li morti [63]e da poi ne fece uno trofeo

whom was their captain Micheletto [29] whose lot it was to be that day at the head of the army Here, at this bridge there is a severe struggle, our men conquer and the enemy is repulsed Here Guido and Astorre, his brother, the Lord of Faenza with a great number of men, re formed and renewed the fight, and rushed upon the Florentines with such force that they recovered the bridge and pushed forward as far as the tents But Simonetto advanced with 600 horse, and fell upon the enemy and drove them back once more from the place, and recaptured the bridge, and behind him came more men with 2000 horse soldiers And thus for a long time they fought with varying fortune But then the Patriarch, in order to divert the enemy, sent forward Niccolò da Pisa [44] and Napoleone Orsino, a beardless lad, followed by a great multitude of men, and then was done another great feat of arms At the same time Niccolò Piccinino urged forward the remnant of his men, who once more made ours give way, and if it had not been that the Patriarch set himself at their head and, by his words and deeds controlled the captains, our soldiers would have taken to flight The Patriarch had some artillery placed on the hill and with these he dispersed the enemy's infantry, and the disorder was so complete that Niccolò began to call back his son and all his men, and they took to flight towards Borgo And then began a great slaughter of men, none escaped but the foremost of those who had fled or who hid themselves The battle continued until sunset, when the Patriarch gave his mind to recalling his men and burying the dead, and afterwards a trophy was erected

H 3 50 a]

670

L'ermellino col sangue, [2]Galeazzo tra tēpo trāquillo [3]e effigie di fortuna

Ermine with blood Galeazzo, between calm weather and a representation of a tempest

Allegorical representations referring to the duke of Milan (670—673)

43 Patriarcha 46 facio 50 fussi Patriarcha 51 fatti havesse. 53 Patriarcha 57 missero 60 nascosono 61 Patriarcha 63 ne fe

670 1—3 R 1 sange 3 effigi:ri di

670 Only of the beginning this text is legible, the writing is much effaced and the sense is consequently obscure It seems to refer like the following passage to an allegorical picture

2 *Galeazzo* probably here means Gian Galeazzo Maria Sforza, whose tragical death took place in the year when this MS was written His father Galeazzo Maria—who succeeded Francesco, the founder of the Sforza family—had been murdered in 1476 and his mother, Bona of Savoy, held the regency during the youth's minority, he was imprisoned in 1494 by his uncle Lodovico il Moro and probably poisoned by his orders

671.

H.3 40b]

Il Moro cogl' ochiali [2]e la invidia colla falsa ĩ[3]famia dipĩta, e la [4]givstitia nera pel [5]Moro.

[6]La fatica colla vite [7]ĩ mano.

Il Moro with spectacles, and Envy depicted with False Report and Justice black for il Moro.

Labour as having a branch of vine [*or* a screw] in her hand.

672.

I.2 90b]

Il Moro in figura di uẽtura [2]colli capelli e panni e mani inãzi, e messer [3]Gualtieri cõ riverẽte atto lo pi[4]glia per li panni d'abasso, venẽdo[5]li dalla parte dinãzi.

[6]ãcora la povertà in figura spa[7]ventevole corra dirieto a vn giovanetto [8]e'l Moro lo copra col lembo della [9]vesta, e colla verga dorata [10]minacia tale mostro

[11]Erba colle ra[12]dici in sù per u[13]no che fusse [14]in sul finire; [15]la roba e la [16]gratia.

[17]Delle taccole e storne[18]lli

[19]Quelli che si fideranno [20]abitare appresso di lui, che [21]sarãno grã turbe, questi tut[22]ti morirãno di crudele mor[23]te, e si vedrã i padri e le [24]madri d'insieme colle sue [25]famiglie esser da crudeli anima[26]li divorati e morti.

Il Moro as representing Good Fortune, with hair, and robes, and his hands in front, and Messer Gualtieri taking him by the robes with a respectful air from below, having come in from the front [5]

Again, Poverty in a hideous form running behind a youth Il Moro covers him with the skirt of his robe, and with his gilt sceptre he threatens the monster.

A plant with its roots in the air to represent one who is at his last;—a robe and Favour.

Of tricks [*or* of magpies] and of burlesque poems [*or* of starlings].

Those who trust themselves to live near him, and who will be a large crowd, these shall all die cruel deaths; and fathers and mothers together with their families will be devoured and killed by cruel creatures.

673

I.2 91a]

Era più nero · ch'un calabrone, [2]gli ochi auea · rossi com' ũ foco ardẽte [3]e cavalcaua sopra vn grã rõzone, [4]largo sei spanne e lungo · piv di 20 [5]cõ sei giganti · attaccati · all'arcione, [6]e vno ĩ mano: che rodea col dẽte, [7]e dirieto · li uenivano porci cõ zãne [8]fori della bocca forse dieci spanne

He was blacker than a hornet, his eyes were as red as a burning fire and he rode on a tall horse six spans across and more than 20 long with six giants tied up to his saddle-bow and one in his hand which he gnawed with his teeth. And behind him came boars with tusks sticking out of their mouths, perhaps ten spans.

671 1—7 R 1 choglochiali 2 ellaũidia cholla 3 ella

672 17—26 R panni "e mani" . meser 3 gualtieri conriverẽte 7 cora avgiovanetto 8 lenbo delle 9. vesa echolla. 10. minacci dale 12 dice 13 cheffussi 15 ella 17 tachole 19 Quelle lichessi 21 gra turbe quesitu 22 crudeli mo 23 le essi vedra . elle 24 chelle 25 eser da crudele "anima"

673 1 hera . , chuchalabrone. 2. chomũfocho 3 chaualchaua . gã 4 se . ellungo 5. cõse . attachati allarcone 6 ĩmano chello rodea chol. 7 uenia zane 8 bocha

672. 1—10 have already been published by *Amoretti* in *Memorie Storiche* cap XII He adds this note with regard to Gualtieri. "*A questo M Gualtieri come ad uomo generoso e benefico scrive il Bellincioni un Sonetto* (*pag.* 174) *per chiedergli un piacere; e 'l Tantio rendendo ragione a Lodovico il Moro, perchè pubblicasse le Rime del Bellincioni; ciò hammi imposto, gli dice: l'humano fidele, prudente e sollicito executore delli tuoi comandamenti Gualtero, che fa in tutte le cose ove tu possi far utile, ogni studio vi metti.*" A somewhat mysterious and evidently allegorical composition—a pen and ink drawing—at Windsor, see Pl. LVIII, contains a group of figures in which perhaps the idea is worked out which is spoken of in the text, lines 1—5.

11. Above this line in the MS. is a small indistinct sketch of a plant, evidently intended to illustrate this remark

Br. M. 250 a]

674.

Allegorical representations (674—678).

Sopra dell' elmo fia una · mezza · palla la quale · à significatione · dello nostro emisperio, in forma di mŏdo, [2]sopra il quale fia uno paone colla coda distesa che passi la groppa, riccamĕte ornato, e ogni ornamĕto [3]che al cavallo s'apartiene sia di peñe di paone · in căpo d'oro, a significatione dalla bellezza che risulta della gra[4]tia che viene da quello che ben serue.

Above the helmet place a half globe, which is to signify our hemisphere, in the form of a world; on which let there be a peacock, richly decorated, and with his tail spread over the group; and every ornament belonging to the horse should be of peacock's feathers on a gold ground, to signify the beauty which comes of the grace bestowed on him who is a good servant.

[5]Nello scudo uno spechio [6]grăde a significare che, chi [7]bĕ uol fauore, si spechi nelle sue [8]virtù.

[9]Dall' opposita parte fia similmĕte collocata la fortezza [10]colla sua colonna ĭ mano, vestita di biăco che significa . . .

[11]E tutte coronate, e la prudĕtia con 3 occhi; [12]la sopraveste · del cavallo fia di senplice oro tessuto, [13]seminata di spessi ochi di pagoni, e questo s'intĕde per tutta [14]la sopraveste dell cavallo · e dell'omo; e 'l cimiero dell'omo [15]e'l suo torchione di peñe di paŏ · in campo d'oro;

[16]Dal lato · sinistro fia vna rota, il ciĕtro della quale [17]fia collocato al ciĕtro della coscia dirieto del cauallo [18]e al detto ciĕtro apparirà la prudĕtia vĕstita di rosso per la carità sedĕte [19]in focosa qua-

On the shield a large mirror to signify that he who truly desires favour must be mirrored in his virtues.

On the opposite side will be represented Fortitude, in like manner in her place with her pillar in her hand, robed in white, to signify. . . And all crowned; and Prudence with 3 eyes. The housing of the horse should be of plain cloth of gold closely sprinkled with peacock's eyes, and this holds good for all the housings of the horse, and the man's dress. And the man's crest and his neck-chain are of peacock's feathers on golden ground.

On the left side will be a wheel, the centre of which should be attached to the centre of the horse's hinder thigh piece, and in the centre Prudence is seen robed in red, Charity sitting in a

674. 1. meza . . assignifichatione . . nosstro emissperio. 2. cholla choda disstesa chi . . richamĕte. 3. pene . . chăpo . . assignifichatione . . belleza . della. 4. dacquello chi . . della. 5. schudo. 6. assignificare. 9. oposita . . chollochata la forteza. 10. cholla . . chollona . . biăcho . . significha. 11. tutti . . chon. 12. chavallo. 13. disspessi . . ecquesto. 14. sopravesste . . chavallo. 15. pene doro di pao . in chaupo. 17. cholochata . . chauallo. 18. [per la carita] e al rosso "per la carita". 16. fochosa

driga e vn ramicello di lauro i man a significatione della speraza, che nascie dal ben seruire.

Messer Antonio Grimani venetiano, copagno d'Antonio Maria.

fiery chariot and with a branch of laurel in her hand, to signify the hope which comes of good service.

[21]Messer Antonio Grimani of Venice companion of Antonio Maria[23].

675.

B. 3?]

A la fama si de' dipigniere tutta la persona piena di ligue in scanbio di penne, e i forma di uccello.

Fame should be depicted as covered all over with tongues instead of feathers, and in the figure of a bird.

676.

Ox. 24]

Piacere e dispiacere fannosi binati, perchè mai l'uno è sanza l'altro come se fussin appiccati, voltasi le schiene perchè sò cotrari.

Fango, oro.

Se piglierai il piacere sappi che lui à dirieto a se chi, ti porgierà tribolatione e petimeto.

Questo si è il piacere isieme col dispiacere e figuransi binati, perchè mai l'uno è spiccato dal altro; fañosi colle schiene voltate, perchè son contrari l'uno al'altro; fañosi fondati sopra vn medesimo

Pleasure and Pain represent as twins, since there never is one without the other; and as if they were united back to back, since they are contrary to each other.

[6]Clay, gold.

If you take Pleasure know that he has behind him one who will deal you Tribulation and Repentance.

[9]This represents Pleasure together with Pain, and show them as twins because one is never apart from the other. They are back to back because they are opposed to each other; and they exist as contraries in

chadriga [illegible] e un [illegible] lauro [illegible] 20. nascie. 21. Meser antonio gri. 22. chõpagno.

675. 2. penne [illegible] forma di ucciello.

676. [illegible] 7. piacie sa piche lui [chi] adrieto . asse chitti. 9. chol disspiacere . . ma luno [illegible] dal altro. 10. fano si cholle . . chontrari . . fanosi. 11. v medesimo. 12. faticha chol. 13. chola chana . . . [illegible]

674. *Meser Antonio Gri.* His name thus abbreviated is, there can be no doubt, Grimani. Antonio Grimani was the famous Doge who in 1499 commanded the Venetian fleet in battle against the Turks. But after the abortive conclusion of the expedition —Ludovico being the ally of the Turks who took possession of Friuli—, Grimani was driven into exile; he went to live at Rome with his son Cardinal Domenico Grimani. On being recalled to Venice he filled the office of Doge from 1521 to 1523. *Antonio Maria* probably means Antonio Maria Grimani, the Patriarch of Aquileia.

676. The pen and ink drawing on Pl. LIX belongs to this passage.

7. *oro. fango*: gold, clay. These words stand below the allegorical figure.

8. *tribolatione.* In the drawing caltrops may be seen lying in the old man's right hand, others are falling and others again are shewn on the ground. Similar caltrops are drawn in MS. Tri. p. 98 and underneath them, as well as on page 96 the words *triboli di ferro* are written. From the accompanying text it appears that they were intended to be scattered on the ground at the bottom of ditches to hinder the advance of the enemy. Count Giulio Porro who published a short account of the Trivulzio MS. in the "*Archivio Storico Lombardo*", Anno VIII part IV (Dec. 31, 1881) has this note on the passages treating of "*triboli*": "*E qui aggiungerò che anni sono quando venne fabbricata la nuova cavallerizza presso il castello di Milano, ne furono trovati due che io ho veduto ed erano precisamente quali si trovano descritti e disegnati da Leonardo in questo codice*".

There can therefore be no doubt that this means of defence was in general use, whether it were originally Leonardo's invention or not. The play on the word "*tribolatione*", as it occurs in the drawing at Oxford, must then have been quite intelligible.

9—22. These lines, in the original, are written on the left side of the page and refer to the figure shown on Pl. LXI. Next to it is placed the group of three figures given in Pl. LX No. 1. Lines 21 and 22, which are written under it, are the only explanation given.

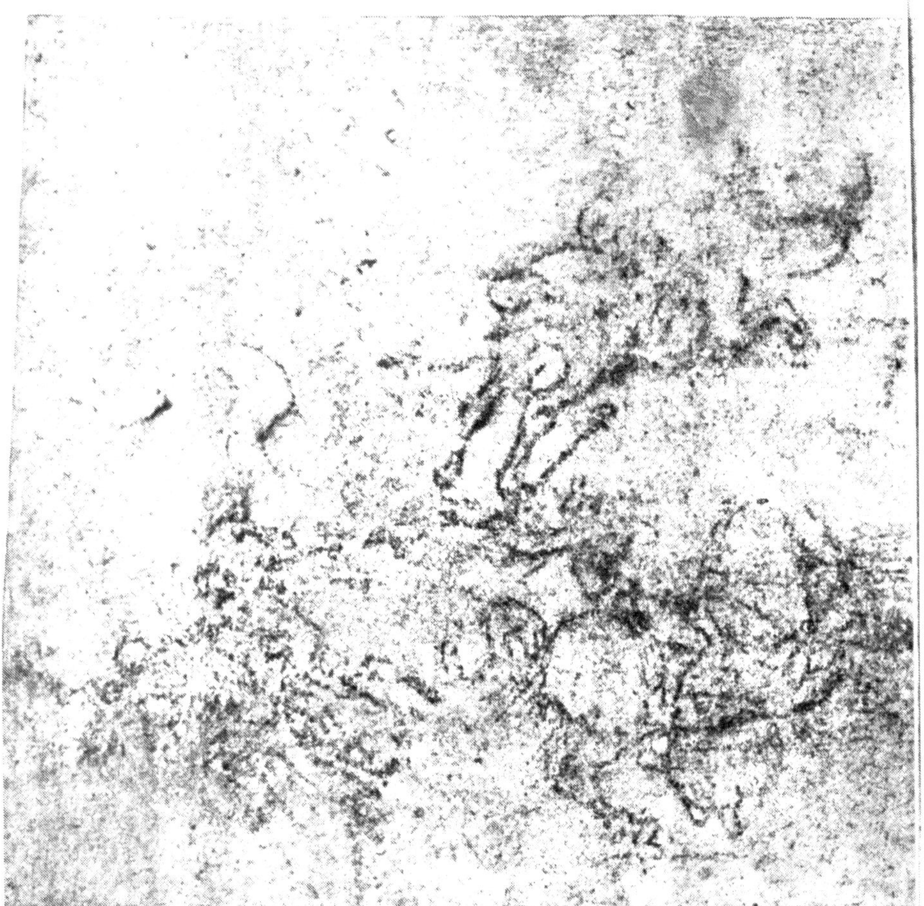

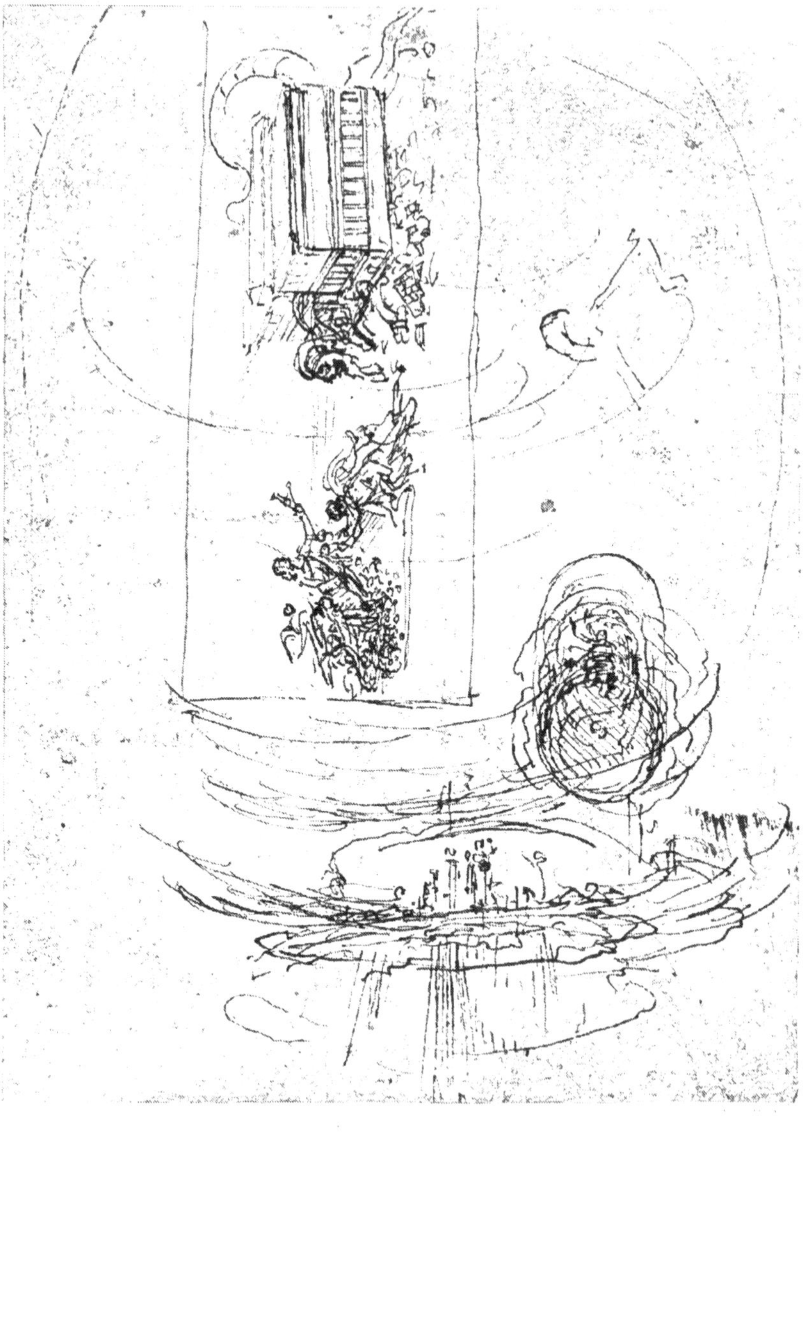

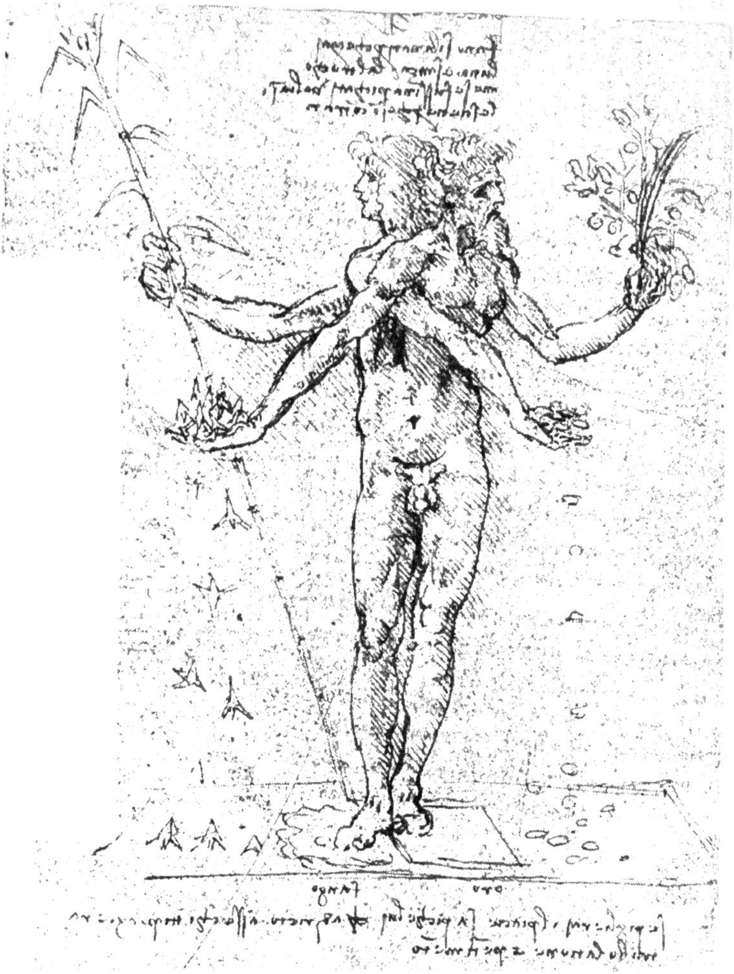

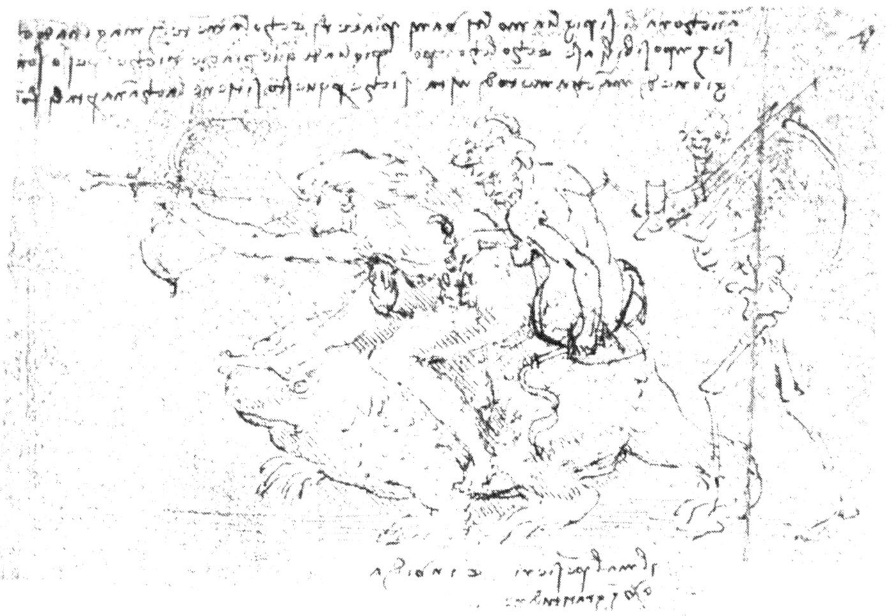

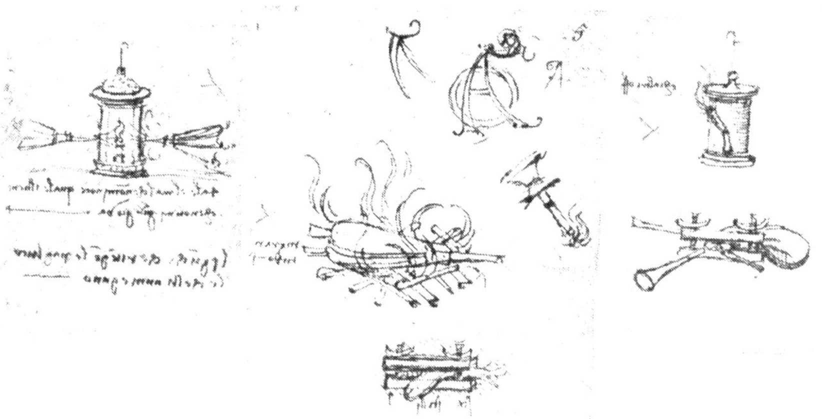

corpo, perchè ãno vn medesimo fondamẽto, jperochè 'l fondamẽto del piaciere [12]si è la fatica col dispiacere, il fondamẽto del dispiaciere si sono i vari e lascivi [13]piacieri; E però qui si figura colla canna nella mä destra ch'è vana e sẽza forza, [14]e le pvnture fatte con quella sõ uenenose; mettõsi j Toscana al sostegnio [15]de' letti, a significare che quivi si fãno j vani sogni e quivi si consuma [16]grã parte della vita, quiui si gitta di molto vtile tempo, cioè quel della mattina, [17]chè la mẽte è sobria e riposata e così il corpo atto a ripigliare nove fatiche; [18]ancora lì si pigliano molti vani piaceri e colla mẽte jmaginãdo co[19]se jmpossibili a se, e col corpo pigliãdo que' piacieri che spesso son ca[20]gione di mãcamẽto di uita, sichè per questo si tiene la cãna per tali fõdamenti.

[21]Il mal pẽsiero è ĩvidia [22]over jgratitudine.

the same body, because they have the same basis, inasmuch as the origin of pleasure is labour and pain, and the various forms of evil pleasure are the origin of pain. Therefore it is here represented with a reed in his right hand which is useless and without strength, and the wounds it inflicts are poisoned. In Tuscany they are put to support beds, to signify that it is here that vain dreams come, and here a great part of life is consumed. It is here that much precious time is wasted, that is, in the morning, when the mind is composed and rested, and the body is made fit to begin new labours; there again many vain pleasures are enjoyed; both by the mind in imagining impossible things, and by the body in taking those pleasures that are often the cause of the failing of life. And for these reasons the reed is held as their support.

Evil-thinking is either Envy or Ingratitude.

Ox. 2 b]

677.

Questa ĩvidia si figura colle fiche verso jl cielo, [2]perchè, se potesse, vserebbe le sue forze cõtro a dio; [3]fassi colla maschera j volto di bella dimostratio[4]ne; fassi ch'ella è ferita nella vista da palma [5]e olivo; fassi ferito l'orechio di lavro e [6]mirto a significare che vittoria e verità [7]l'offendono; fassi le vscire molti fvlgori, [8]a significare il suo mal dire; fassi magra [9]e secca, perch'è sempre j continuo strvgimẽto, [10]fassi le jl core roso da vn serpẽte ẽfian[11]te; fassi le vn turcasso, e le freccie [12]lingue, perchè spesso cõ quelle offẽde; [13]fassi le vna pelle di liopardo, perchè quello [14]per invidia ãmazza il lione, con ĩgãno; [15]fassi le vn uaso ĩ mano piẽ di fiori e si[16]a quello piẽ di scorpioni e rospi e altri [17]veneni; fassi le cavalcare la morte, [18]perchè la invidia, nõ morẽdo, mai languisce [19]a signo-

Envy must be represented with a contemptuous motion of the hand towards heaven, because if she could she would use her strength against God; make her with her face covered by a mask of fair seeming; show her as wounded in the eye by a palm branch and by an olive-branch, and wounded in the ear by laurel and myrtle, to signify that victory and truth are odious to her. Many thunderbolts should proceed from her to signify her evil speaking. Let her be lean and haggard because she is in perpetual torment. Make her heart gnawed by a swelling serpent, and make her with a quiver with tongues serving as arrows, because she often offends with it. Give her a leopard's skin, because this creature kills the lion out of envy and by deceit. Give her too a vase in her hand full of flowers and scorpions and toads and other venomous creatures; make her ride upon death, because Envy, never dying, never tires of ruling. Make her bridle, and load her with divers kinds

fo ||||||. 14. choquele . . mettãsi J toscana. 15. significhare . . fano . . chonsuma. 16. dela . . tẽpo . . dela mati ||||. 17. soblia . . chosi il chorpo. 18. anchora . . piglia . . chola . . cho. 19. jposibili . . chol chorpo . . cha. 20. mãchamẽto . . chãna . . fõdam"ẽ". 21. pẽsieri.

677. 1. chole . . jl cie ||||. 2. potessi vserebe . . chõtro a ||||||. 3. fasi cola . . bela dimostr |||||. 4. chele ferita . . vissta da pal ||||||. 5. lavro |||||. 6. assignificare . . vettoria eve ||||||. 7. fassele vsscire molte folgore. 8. assignificare . . fassimage ||||||. 9. essecha . . strugimẽ ||||||. 10. fasse. 11. turchasso che le frecie. 12. speso chõquela. 13. fasse . . pele . . chuel ||||. 14. amaza . . chon ĩ gano. 15. fasse . . fioriess ||||. 16. acqueli . . rosspical ||||||. 17. fassele chavalchare la mo |||||. 18. lanvidia . . mai lan |||||||||. 19. asigniore giare fasse . . briglia c ||||. 20. cha e charicha . . diversi . . 21. tuti . . dela. 24. que.

reggiare; fassi le la briglia[20]carica di diverse armi perchè [21]tuti strumētı della morte.

[22]Tolerare.

[23]ſtolerabile.

[24]Subito che nascie la uirtù, quel[25]la partoriscie contra se la invidia, [26]e prima · fia · il corpo sēza · l'ō[27]bra che la virtù · sanza · la invidia

of arms because all her weapons are deadly.

Toleration.

Intolerable

No sooner is Virtue born than Envy comes into the world to attack it, and sooner will there be a body without a shadow than Virtue without Envy.

Br. M 231 b]

678.

Quādo si apre il paradiso di [2]Plutone alor stā diavo[3]li che son in dodici olle, [4]a vso di bocche īfernali ·, [5]quiui sia la morte, [6]le furie, [7]cenere, [8]molti putti nudi che piāgino; [9]e uiui fochi fatti di vari colori....

When Pluto's Paradise is opened, then there may be devils placed in twelve pots like openings into hell. Here will be Death, the Furies, ashes, many naked children weeping, living fires made of various colours....

I 2 59 a]

679.

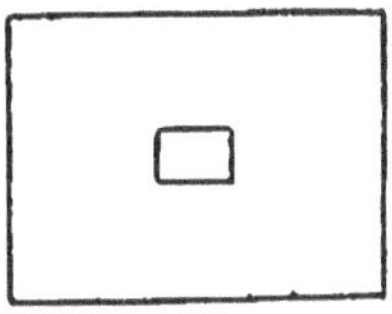

Arrangement of a picture

Joanes Battista	S. Agostino	John the Baptist	Saint Augustin
[2]San Piero	Paolo	Saint Peter	Paul
[3]Elisabetta Nostra Doña	Sta Chiara	Elisabeth Our Lady	Saint Clara.
[4]Bernardino	Lodovico	Bernardino	Louis
[5]Bonaventura	Antonio da Padua	Bonaventura	Anthony of Padua.
[6]Sto Francesco		Saint Francis.	

[6]Francesco,
[7]Antonio, giglio e libro,
[8]Bernardino col Gesù,
[9]Lodovico co 3 gigli nel petto, cō corona a piedi,
[10]Bonavētura cō serafini,
[11]Sta Chiara col tabernaculo,
[12]Elisabetta cō corona di regina.

Francis,
Anthony, a lily and book,
Bernardino with the [monogram of] Jesus,
Louis with 3 fleur de lys on his breast and the crown at his feet,
Bonaventura with Seraphim,
Saint Clara with the tabernacle,
Elisabeth with a Queen's crown.

25 partoriscie chontra. 26. chorpo 27 chella . lanvidia

678. 1. sapre. 3. liche sonco dodici olle 4 boce 7 cennere 8 piāghino 10. *the leaf is here distroyed, only the words* vino bolē *in the middle of the line have remained legible*

679 *The five names on the right side* Jo baita &c. *and lines 7 to 12 are written from left to right None of the names have capital initial letters* 1—6 iob[a]ti' ta . saostino nostra dona sca ciara . lodovco . franc"o" . Padu 'a" 7 franc"o" 9 peto cō coronna piedi 1 co 11 ciara

677. The larger of the two drawings on Pl LXI is explained by the first 21 lines of this passage L. 22 and 23, which are written above the space between the two drawings, do not seem to have any reference to either L. 24—27 are below the allegorical twin figure which they serve to explain

679. The text of the first six lines is written within a square space of the same size as the copy here given. The names are written in the margin following the order in which they are here printed. In lines 7—12 the names of those saints are repeated of whom it seemed necessary to point out the emblems

680. This has already been published by AMORETTI *Memorie storiche* cap. XVI. His reading varies somewhat from that here given, *e. g.* l. 5 and 6 *Certi Sangirolami in su d'una figura;* and instead of l 13. *Un San Bastiano.*

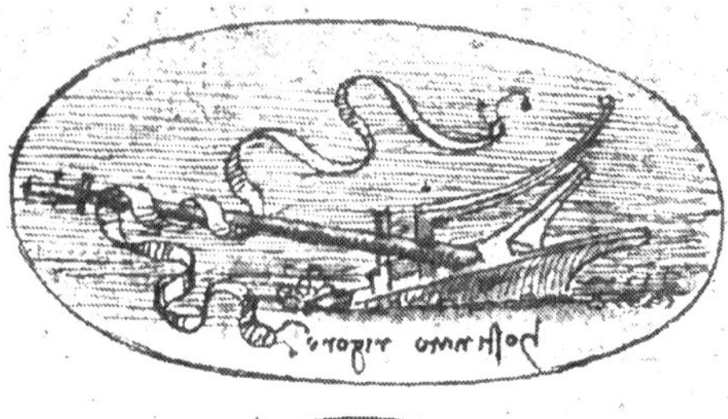

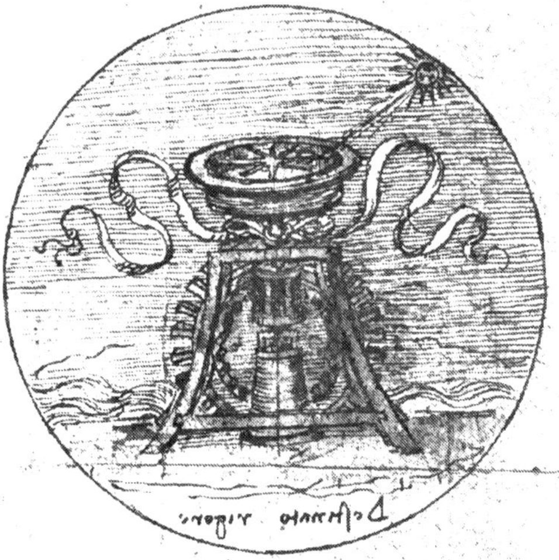

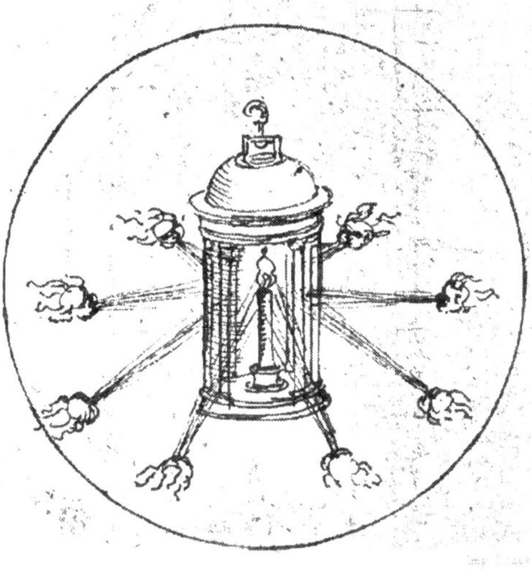

C. A. 317 a; 959 a]

680.

Una testa in faccia di giouane
2 cō una bella capellatura,
3 Molti fiori ritratti di naturale,
4 vna testa ĩ faccia riccivta,
5 cierti sã Girolami,
6 misure d'una figura,
7 disegni di fornegli,
8 vna testa del Duca,
9 Molti disegni di gruppi,
10 4 disegni della tavola di sãto angielo,
11 vna storietta di Girolamo da Fegline,
12 vna testa di Cristo fatta di penna,
13 8 sã Bastiani,
14 Molti cōponimēti d'ãgioli,
15 vn calcidonio,
16 vna testa ĩ proffilo cō bella capellatura,
17 cierti coppi di prospettiva,
18 cierti strumēti per navili,
19 cierti strumēti d'acqua,
20 vna testa ritratta d'Atalãta che alzava il uolto,
21 la testa di Geronimo da Fegline,
22 la testa di Giã Francesco Borso,
23 molte gole di vechíe,
24 molte teste di vechi,
25 molti nvdi ĩteri,
26 molte bracia ganbe piedi e attitudini,
27 vna nostra donna finita,
28 vn' altra quasi ch'è in proffilo,

List of drawings.

A head, full face, of a young man with fine flowing hair,
Many flowers drawn from nature,
A head, full face, with curly hair,
Certain figures of Saint Jerome,
[6] The measurements of a figure,
Drawings of furnaces.
A head of the Duke,
[9] many designs for knots,
4 studies for the panel of Saint Angelo
A small composition of Girolamo da Fegline,
A head of Christ done with the pen,
[13] 8 Saint Sebastians,
Several compositions of Angels,
A chalcedony,
A head in profile with fine hair,
Some pitchers seen in (?) perspective,
Some machines for ships,
Some machines for waterworks,
A head, a portrait of Atalanta raising her face;
The head of Geronimo da Fegline,
The head of Gian Francisco Borso,
Several throats of old women,
Several heads of old men,
Several nude figures, complete,
Several arms, eyes, feet, and positions,
A Madonna, finished,
Another, nearly in profile,

680. *Lines 1 and 2 are written from left to right and upside down.* 1. nvna tessta . . gouane. 4. tessta. 5. sãgirolami. 6. msure . . fighura. 8. ducha. 11. girolamo da feghine. 12. di xpõ fatta. 13. basstiani. 14. chõponimēti. 15. chalcidonio. 16. tessta . . chõ . . chapellatura. 17. choppi di prosspettiva. 19. dacq"a". 20. tessta . . dattalãta. 21. tessta de ieronimo da feglino. 22. tessta di giãfranciessco. 23. ghole. 24. moltesste. 25. ĩtegri. 26. attitudine. 27. nosstra. 28. qusi chẽ proffilo. 29. tessta di nosstra . . vãcielo. 30. tessta . . chol meto lũgho. 31. tessta di zĩghana. 32. tessta

9. *Molti disegni di gruppi.* VASARI in his life of Leonardo (IV, 21, ed. MILANESI 1880) says: "*Oltrechè perse tempo fino a disegnare* gruppi *di corde fatti con ordine, e che da un capo seguissi tutto il resto fino all' altro, tanto che s'empiessi un tondo; che se ne vede in istampa uno difficilissimo e molto bello, e nel mezzo vi sono queste parole: Leonardus Vinci Accademia*". *Gruppi* must here be understood as a technical expression for those twisted ornaments which are well known through wood cuts. AMORETTI mentions six different ones in the Ambrosian Library. I am indebted to M. DELABORDE for kindly informing me that the original blocks of these are preserved in his department in the Bibliothèque Nationale in Paris. On the cover of these volumes is a copy from one of them. The size of the original is $23^1/_2$ centimètres by $26^1/_4$. The centre portion of another is given on p. 361. G. GOVI remarks on these ornaments (*Saggio* p. 22): "*Codesti gruppi eran probabilmente destinati a servir di modello a ferri da rilegatori per adornar le cartelle degli scolari* (?). *Fregi somigliantissimi a questi troviamo infatti impressi in oro sui cartoni di vari volumi contemporanei, e li vediam pur figurare nelle lettere iniziali di alcune edizioni del tempo.*"

Dürer who copied them, omitting the inscription, added to the second impressions his own monogram. In his diary he designates them simply as "*Die sechs Knoten*" (see THAUSING, Life of A. Dürer I, 362, 363). In Leonardo's MSS. we find here and there little sketches or suggestions for similar ornaments. Compare too G. MONGERI, *L'Arte in Milano*, p. 315 where an ornament of the same character is given from the old decorations of the vaulted ceiling of the Sacristy of S. Maria delle Grazie.

680. 17. The meaning in which the word *coppi*, literally pitchers, is here used I am unable to determine; but a change to *copie* seems to me too doubtful to be risked.

29 la testa di nostra donna che va in cielo,
30 vna testa d'ū uechio col mēto lūgo,
31 una testa di zīgana
32 vna testa col capello ī capo,
33 vna storia di passione fatta in forma,
34 vna testa di putta cō treccie rānodate,
35 vna testa con bruna cōciatura.

Head of Our Lady ascending into Heaven,
A head of an old man with long chin,
A head of a gypsy girl,
A head with a hat on,
A representation of the Passion, a cast,
A head of a girl with her hair gathered in a knot,
A head, with the brown hair dressed.

Mottoes and Emblems (681—702)

W 243]

681.

Ostinato rigore.
2 Destinato rigore.

Stubborn rigour.
Doomed rigour.

W. L. 198a]

682

¶Inpedimento nō mi piega,
2 ogni īpedimēto è distrutto dal rigore,
3 nō si · uolta chi a stella è fisso.

Obstacles cannot crush me
Every obstacle yields to stern resolve
He who is fixed to a star does not change his mind

W. L 198b]

683.

L'edera è di lunga vita

Ivy is [a type] of longevity.

W P 11a]

684

Vertià il sole
2 bugia maschera
3 innocētia
4 malignità
5 ¶Il foco distrugie la
6 bugia, cioè il sofistico, e
7 rende la uerità, scacciādo
8 le tenebre ¶
9 Il foco è da essere messo per cōsuma-
10 tore d'ogni sofistico e scopri-
11 tore e dimostratore di uerità,
12 perchè lui è luce, scaccia-
13 tore delle tenebre occultatri-
14 ci d'ogni essentia.

Truth the sun.
falsehood a mask
innocence,
malignity.
Fire destroys falsehood,
that is sophistry, and
restores truth, driving out
darkness.
Fire may be represented as the destroy of all sophistry, and as the image and demonstration of truth; because it is light and drives out darkness which conceals all essences [or subtle things]

chol chapello ī chapo. 33 vnasstoria 34 tessta . chō tregie ranodate 35 tessta bruna chōciatura.
681 1 hostinato
682 1 nomi piegha. 2. ōnipedimēto. 3. asstella elfisso
683. 1 lungha.
684. 2 mascera 5 distrugie [la] la 6 coe 7 scacādo 10 soffisticho e escōpri 12 lui [sca] e luce scacca. 13 ochultatri.

681 See Pl. LXII, No. 2, the two upper pen and ink drawings. The originals, in the Windsor collection are slightly washed with colour The background is blue sky; the plough and the instrument with the compass are reddish brown, the sun is tinted yellow.

682. This text is written to elucidate two sketches which were obviously the first sketches for the drawings reproduced on Pl. LXII, No. 2

683. In the original there is, near this text, a sketch of a coat wreathed above the waist with ivy.

684 See Pl. LXIII L. 1—8 are in the middle of the page, L 9—14 to the right below; L 15—22 below in the middle column. The rest of the text is below the sketches on the left. There are some other passages on this page relating to geometry.

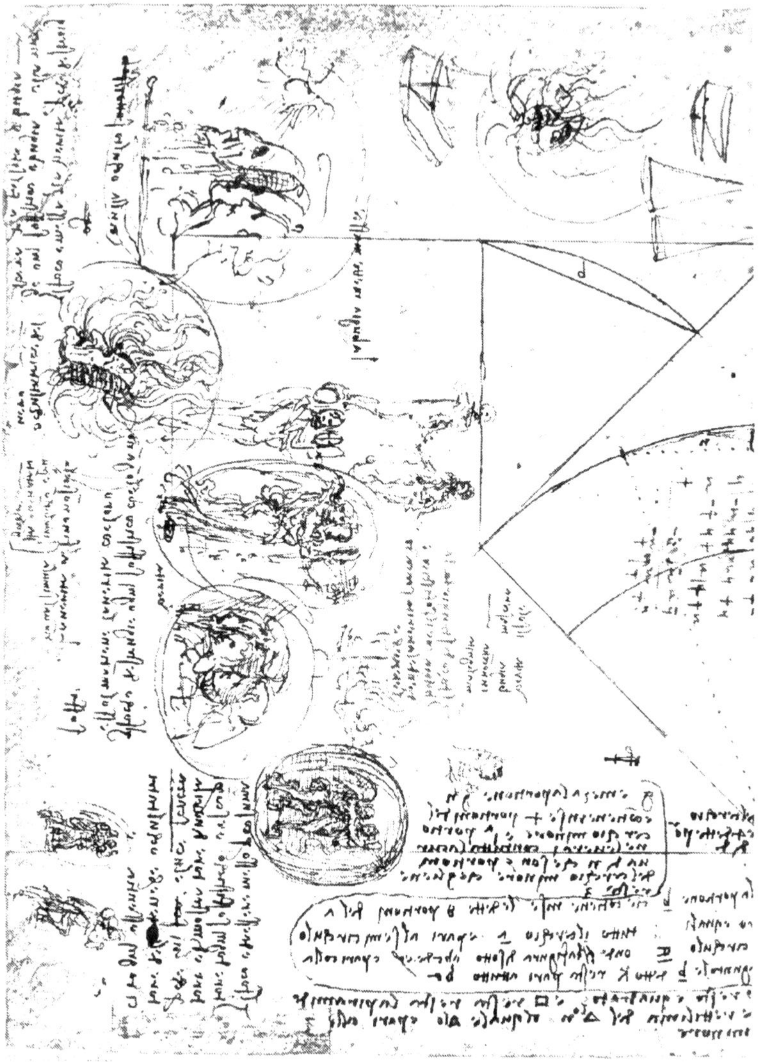

VERITÀ.

16 Il foco destrugie ogni soffistico cioè lo ĩgãno,
17 e sol mãtiene la verità cioè l'oro.
19 La uerità al fine nõ si cela;
20 nõ ual simulatione; ¶ Simulatiõ è fru-
21 strata avanti a tãto
22 giudice. ¶
23 la bugia mette maschera;
24 ¶ nulla occulta sotto il sole.
25 Il foco è messo per la verità, perchè destrug-
26 ge ogni soffistico e bugia, e la ma-
27 schera per la falsità e bugia, —
28 ocultatrice del uero. —

TRUTH.

Fire destroys all sophistry, that is deceit;
and maintains truth alone, that is gold.
Truth at last cannot be hidden.
Dissimulation is of no avail. Dissimulation is to no purpose before so great a judge.
Falsehood puts on a mask.
Nothing is hidden under the sun.
Fire is to represent truth because it destroys all sophistry and lies; and the mask is for lying and falsehood which conceal truth.

W. P. 11 *b*]

685.

Prima privato di moto che stanco
2 di giouare.
7 2 6 13
3 ¶ mancherà primae il moto ch'l giouamẽto;
4 prima morte che | nõ mi stãco nel giouare
5 stanchezza; | è motto da carnovale;
6 nõ mi satio di seruire; | sine lassitudine.
7 tutte le opere
8 nõ sõ per istancarmi;
9 mani nelle quali fio-
10 ccã ducati e pietre pre-
11 tiose, queste mai si stã-
12 cano di seruire, ma
13 tal seruitio è sol per sua
14 vtilità e non è al no- | non mi stanco
15 stro proposito; | nel giovare.
16 naturalmẽte
17 natura così mi dispone;

Movement will cease before we are weary
of being useful.
Movement will fail sooner than usefulness.
Death sooner than weariness. | I am never weary of being useful,
In serving others I cannot do enough. | is a motto for carnval. Without fatigue.
No labour is
sufficient to tire me.
Hands into which
ducats and precious
stones fall like snow; they
never become tired by serving,
but this service is only for its
utility and not for our own benefit. | I am never weary of being useful.
Naturally
nature has so disposed me.

Ash. I. 1 *a*]

686.

Sia fatto ĩ mano alla ĩgratitudine;
2 il legnio · nutrica il foco che lo cõsuma

This shall be placed in the hand of Ingratitude.
Wood nourishes the fire that consumes it.

16. focho . . coe lõgãno. 17. essol. 18. soffi. 19. nõ ual simula. 21. sta. 22. gudice. 23. mette massce. 24. ochulta. 25. [og]. 26. messa. 27. oni . . ella. 28. scera. 29. ochultatrice.
685. 1. stancho. 2. di digouare. 3. gouameto. 4. govare. 10. chaducati. 12. gauo. 13. essol. 14. nonee al nos . . stancho. 15. gorare.
686. 1. fa"to" imano. 2. ilegnio notricha il focho.

687.

Br. M. 173 a]

PER LA INGRATITUDINE.

²Quando apparisce il sole che scaccia le tenebre in comvne, tu spegni il lume che te le scaciava in particulare ⁴a tua necessità e commodità.

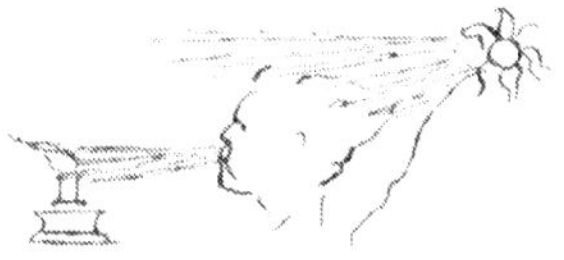

TO REPRESENT INGRATITUDE.

When the sun appears which dispels darkness in general, you put out the light which dispelled it for you in particular for your need and convenience.

688.

W. 18]

Di qua Adā e di là Eva;
²o miseria vmana, di quāte cose per danari ti fai seruo!

On this side Adam and Eve on the other;
O misery of mankind, of how many things do you make yourself the slave for money!

689.

H.3 41 b]

Così si se²para la trista vni³tione.

Thus are base unions sundered.

690.

H.3 53 a]

Cōstantia nō comicia, ma è quel ²che persevera.

Constancy does not begin, but is that which perseveres.

691

H.3 70 a]

Amor Timor e Reverentia, questo ²scrivi in tre sassi; de' serui.

Love, Fear, and Esteem,—
Write these on three stones. Of servants.

692.

H.2 16]

Prudentia fortezza.

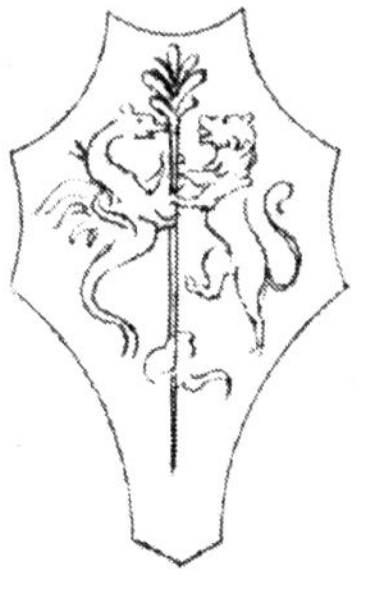

Prudence Strength.

687. 2. aparisce . . chesscancia. 3. ilume chettellescaciava in particul. 4. attua neciessita.
688. 1. adā . . evā. 2. chose 689. 1—3 R. 2. pera. 690. 1—2 R. 2. ce. 691. 1—2 R. 692. R. forteza.

688. See Pl. LXIV. The figures of Adam and Eve in the clouds here alluded to would seem to symbolise their superiority to all earthly needs.

689. A much blurred sketch is on the page by this text. It seems to represent an unravelled plait or tissue.

690. A drawing in red chalk, also rubbed, which stands in the original in the middle of this text, seems to me to be intended for a sword hilt, held in a fist.

H.[2] 13 a]

693.

La fama sola si leva al cielo, [2]perchè le cose virtuose sono amiche [3]a dio; [4]La infamia sottosopra figurare si [5]debbe, perchè tutte le sue operationi [6]sō contrarie a dio e inverso l'inferi [7]si dirizzano.

Fame alone raises herself to Heaven, because virtuous things are in favour with God. Disgrace should be represented upside down, because all her deeds are contrary to God and tend to hell.

H.[2] 15 b]

694.

Corta libertà.

Short liberty.

H.[1] 40 a]

695.

Nessuna cosa è da temere più che sozza fama; [2]Questa sozza fama è nata da uita.

Nothing is so much to be feared as Evil Report. This Evil Report is born of life.

H.[1] 40 b]

696.

Per nō disobbidire.

Not to disobey.

693. 1. la famasola essi leva. 2. chose vertudiose sono miche. 5. tutte sue. 7. dirizano.
695. 1. chosa edatteme "piu chella" quāto soza. 2. soza.
696. R. disubidire.

S. K. M. II²; 1 b]

697.

Abbero tagliato che rimette
30
40
1200
²ancora spero;
³falcon
⁴tenpo.

A felled tree which is shooting again.
30
40
1200
I am still hopeful.
A falcon,
Time.

F. 6 a]

698.

La verità fa qui che la ²bugia affligge le ligue ³bugiarde.

Truth here makes Falsehood torment lying tongues.

M. 4 a]

699.

Tale è 'l mal che nō mi noce qual è il bene ²che non mi giova.

Such as harm is when it hurts me not, is good which avails me not.

M. 4 b]

700.

Chi altri offende, se nō sicura.

He who offends others, does not secure himself.

M. 5 a]

701.

Ingrati²tudo.

Ingratitude.

C. A. 67 b; 203 b]

702.

I pēsieri si voltano alla sperāza.

One's thoughts turn towards Hope.

697. 2. anchora. 698. 1. chella. 2. alrigue. 3. bugarde 699. 2. nommi [gi] giova. 700. sichura. 702. (R).

697. 1. *Albero tagliato.* This emblem was displayed during the Carnival at Florence in 1513. See VASARI VI, 251, ed. MILANESI 1881. But the coincidence is probably accidental.

699. See Pl. LX, No. 2. Compare this sketch with that on Pl. LXII, No. 2. Below the two lines of the text there are two more lines: *li giechi (giunchi) che ritēgō le paglucss (pagliucole) chelli (che li) anniegano.*

700. See Pl. LX, No. 3.

701. See Pl. LX, No. 4. Below the bottom sketches are the unintelligible words "*sta stilli.*" For "*Ingratitudo*" compare also Nos. 686 and 687.

702. By the side of this passage is a sketch of a cage with a bird sitting in it.

C. A. 228 *b*; 687 *b*]

703.

Uccello della comedia.

A bird, for a comedy.

Ornaments and Decorations for feasts (703—705.)

L² 1 *b*]

704.

VESTA DA CARNOVALE.

[2] Per fare vna bella veste tagli tela sottile e dale [3] vernice odorifera, fatta da olio di tremẽtina e [4] vernice in grana ĩ colla stanpa traforata [5] e bagnata, acciò nõ si appicchi, e questa stãpa [6] sia fatta a gruppi, i quali poi siẽ riẽpivti [7] di miglio nero e 'l cãpo di miglio biãco.

A DRESS FOR THE CARNIVAL.

To make a beautiful dress cut it in thin cloth and give it an odoriferous varnish, made of oil of turpentine and of varnish in grain, with a pierced stencil, which must be wetted, that it may not stick to the cloth; and this stencil may be made in a pattern of knots which afterwards may be filled up with black and the ground with white millet[7].

Mz. 10 *a* (14)]

705.

Porterassi neve [2] distante ne lochi [3] caldi, tolta dall' al[4] te cime de' monti, [5] e si lascierà ca[6] dere nelle feste [7] alle piazze nel [8] tenpo dell' estate.

Snow taken from the high peaks of mountains might be carried to hot places and let to fall at festivals in open places at summer time.

703. ocel. 704. 2. dalle. 3. in grane e o | colla. 5. acio non sia pi[illegible]chi. 6. posieriẽpivti.
705. 3. chaldi . . dellal. 5. essi. 7. delle piaze. 8. dellastate.

703. The biographies say so much, and the author's notes say so little of the invention attributed to Leonardo of making artificial birds fly through the air, that the text here given is of exceptional interest from being accompanied by a sketch. It is a very slight drawing of a bird with outspread wings, which appears to be sliding down a stretched string. Leonardo's flying machines and his studies of the flight of birds will be referred to later.

704. Ser Giuliano, da Vinci the painter's brother, had been commissioned, with some others, to order and to execute the garments of the Allegorical figures for the Carnival at Florence in 1515—16; VASARI however, is incorrect in saying of the Florentine Carnival of 1513: *"equelli che feciono ed ordinarono gli abiti delle figure furono Ser Piero da Vinci, padre di Lionardo, e Bernardino di Giordano, bellissimi ingegni."* (See MILANESI's ed. Vol. VI, pg. 251.)

7. The grains of black and white millet would stick to the varnish and look like embroidery.

REFERENCE TABLE TO THE NUMERICAL ORDER OF THE CHAPTERS.

I.

GENERAL INTRODUCTION TO THE BOOK ON PAINTING.

1. Leic. 22 *b*.
2. F. 2 *b*.
3. W. An. III. 163 *b*.
4. Br. M. 1 *a*.
5. F. 23 *a*.
6. Br. M. 32 *b*.
7. W. An. IV. 167 *a*.
8. C. A. 146. II *a*; 436 *a*.
9. C. A. 117 *b*; 361 *b*.
10. C. A. 117 *b*; 361 *b*.
11. C. A. 115 *a*; 357 *a*.
12. C. A. 117 *b*; 361 *b*.
13. C. A. 200 *a*; 594 *a*.
14. Ash. I. 17 *b*.
15. E. 80 *b*.
16. G. 53 *b*.
17. E. 79 *b*.
18. C. A. 218 *b*; 648 *a*.
19. G. 8 *a*.
20. C. A. 75 *a*; 219 *a*.
21. C. A. 117 *b*; 361 *b*.
22. C. A. 337 *b*; 1026 *b*.
23. Ash. I. 13 *a*.
24. E. 17 *b*.
25. C. A. 136 *b*; 412 *b*.
26. C. A. 339 *a*; 1033 *a*.
27. H.[2] 85 *a*.
28. Tr. 74.
29. W. An. IV. 153 *b*.
30. C. 7 *b* (9).
31. H.[2] 38 *a*.
32. H.[3] 40 *a*.
33. H.[2] 43 *b*.
34. Ash. I. 12 *a*.
35. L. 41 *b*.
36. S. K. M. II.[1] 1 *a*.
37. I.[1] 19 *b*.
38. I.[1] 20 *a*.
39. C. A. 200 *a*; 594 *a*.

II.

LINEAR PERSPECTIVE.

40. Ash. I. 22 *b*.
41. A. 38 *b*.
42. C. A. 130 *a*; 398 *a*.
43. Tr. 68.
44. Ash. III. 27 *b*.
45. Br. M. 131 *b*.
46. Br. M. 132 *a*.
47. W. L. 145. C. *b*.
48. Ash. I. 21 *a*.
49. G. 37 *a*.
50. A. 3 *a*.
51. C. A. 84 *b*; 245 *a*.
52. A. 10 *a*.
53. C. 27 *b*.
54. C. A. 201 *a*; 597 *a*.
55. A. 36 *b*.
56. A. 37 *a*.
57. A. 37 *b*.
58. A. 27 *a*.
59. W. 232 *b*.
60. C. A. 136 *b*; 412 *b*.
61. Ash. I. 22 *b*.
62. W. L. 146 *a*.
63. Ash. I. 27. II *a*.
64. C. A. 100 *b*; 313 *a*.
65. C. A. 136 *a*; 412 *a*.
66. W. L. 145. B. *a*.
67. C. A. 176 *b*; 531 *b*.
68. Ash. I. 32 *b*.
69. A. 9 *b*.
70. C. A. 133 *b*; 404 *b*.
71. D. 8 *a*.
72. C. A. 201 *b*; 598 *b*.
73. W. L. 145. D. *b*.
74. Br. M. 221 *b*.
75. Br. M. 220 *a*.
76. Br. M. 171 *b*.
77. W. L. 145. B. *b*.
78. W. L. 145. B. *a*.
79. W. L. 145. D. *b*.
80. W. L. 145. C. *b*.
81. W. L. 115. D. *b*. *a*.
82. C. A. 123 *b*; 380 *b*.
83. A. 1 *b*.
84. Br. M. 220 *a*.
85. A. 10 *b*.
86. A. 38 *a*.
87. W. L. 145. C. *b*.
88. A. 9 *b*.
89. G. 53 *b*.
90. G. 13 *b*.
91. H.[2] 33 *a*.
92. Ash. I. 12 *a*.
93. A. 8 *b*.
94. A. 10 *b*.
95. C. A. 1 *a*; 1 *b*.
96. C. A. 142 *b*; 425 *b*.
97. S. K. M. II.[2]; 63 *a*.
98. A. 11 *a*.
99. Ash. I. 12 *b*.
100. A. 8 *b*.
101. C. A. 41 *a*; 132 *a*.
102. Ash. I. 12 *b*; 31.
103. S. K. M. II.[2]; 16 *b*.
104. C. A. 130 *b*; 398 *b*.
105. H.[2] 28 *b*.
106. G. 29 *b*.
107. E. 16 *b*.

108. F. 16a.
109. Br. M. 62a.

III.

SIX BOOKS ON LIGHT AND SHADE.

GENERAL INTRODUCTION.

110. Br. M. 171a.
111. C. A. 246a; 735a.
112. Ash. I. 6b.
113. K.[3] 25b.
114. K.[3] 26a.
115. M. 80a.
116. M. 79b.
117. E. 3b.
118. G. 3b.
119. Ash. I. 15b.
120. W. L. 145. D.a.
121. W. 232b.
122. Ash. I. 14a.
123. C. 14b.
124. Br. M. 248b.
125. Ash. I. 13b.
126. Br. M. 171a.
127. Br. M. 170b.
128. C. A. 111 b; 335a.
129. A. 8b.

FIRST BOOK ON LIGHT AND SHADE.

130. W. L. 146a.
131. C. 8a.
132. Ash. I. 3a.
133. Ash. I. 3b.
134. H.[2] 42b.
135. E. 31b.
136. Br. M. 171a.
137. W. I.
138. Ash. I. 20b.
139. Ash. I. 20a.
140. Ash. I. 20a.
141. C. 10a.
142. Ash. I. 12a.
143. Br. M. 171a.
144. Tr. 20.
145. Ash. I. 17a.
146. Tr. 29.
147. Ash. I. 28b.

SECOND BOOK ON LIGHT AND SHADE.

148. Ash. I. 22a.
149. Ash. I. 21b.
150. C. A. 46b; 144a.
151. C. A. 130b; 398b.
152. H.[2] 18a.
153. E. 17a.
154. S. K. M. II.[2] 76b.
155. G. 32a.
156. E. 15a.
157. E. 32b.

THIRD BOOK ON LIGHT AND SHADE.

158. W. 232b.
159. E. 32b.
160. C. 7b.
161. E. 31a.
162. E. 32a.
163. H.[2] 28b.
164. Ash. I. 6a.
165. Br. M. 170b.
166. E. 31a.
167. Br. M. 170b.
168. Tr. 28.
169. Ash. I. 25a.
170. W. II.
171. Ash. I. 25; 1a.
172. Br. M. 170b
173. Ash. I. 24a.
174. C. 21a.
175. K.[3] 31b.
176. Ash. I. 15a.
177. Tr. 22.
178. C. A. 30a; 115a.
179. C. A. 201a; 597a.
180. C. 8b.
181. Br. M. 170b.
182. Ash. I. 5b.
183. W. L. 145. Aa.
184. C. A. 174a; 523a.
185. Br. M. 245a.
186. Br. M. 248b.
187. C. A. 187. II.a; 502a.

FOURTH BOOK ON LIGHT AND SHADE.

188. I. 37b.
189. C. A. 184b; 555b.
190. A. 1a.
191. C. A. 237. II. 715b.
192. C. A. 124a; 383a.
193. C. A. 363a; 1136a.
194. C. A. 146b; 434a.
195. W. 232b.
196. Ash. I. 5b.
197. E. 31b.
198. E. 32a.
199. Ash. I. 13b.
200. C. A. 30b; 96b.
201. Tr. 29.
202. Ash. I. 28b.

FIFTH BOOK ON LIGHT AND SHADE.

203. Ash. I. 3a.
204. W. 232b.
205. Ash. I. 21a.
206. H.[2] 28b.
207. Br. M. 93b.
208. S. K. M. III. 37b.
209. W. 232b.
210. C. A. 139b; 419b.
211. E. 2b.
212. E. 30b.

SIXTH BOOK ON LIGHT AND SHADE.

213. C. 7a.
214. A. 64b.
215. C. 5a.
216. C. 4b.
217. C. 4a.
218. C. 3b.
219. C. 3a.
220. C. 2b.
221. C. 2a.

IV.

PERSPECTIVE OF DISAPPEARANCE.

222. E. 80a.
223. E. 80b.
224. Ash. I. 23a.
225. E. 79b.
226. L. 77b.
227. Br. M. 115a.
228. H.[2] 23a.
229. C. 12a.
230. E. 15a.
231. Br. M. 188a.
232. H.[2] 1a.
233. C. A. 175b, 520b.
234. A. 8b.
235. A. 2a.
236. Ash. I. 21a.
237. E. 17a.
238. E. 3a.
239. Ash. I. 25b.
240. E. 32b.
241. I.[1] 17b.
242. I.[1] 18a.
243. C. A. 124b; 383b.
244. F. 22a.
245. Ash. I. 3b.
246. C. A. 124a; 383a.
247. G. 12b.
248. C. A. 174a; 383a.
249. A. 64b.

250.	C 24a
251.	C 23a
252	C 5a
253	C. 1b
254	C 1a.
255	C. 14b.
256	C 14a
257	C 21b
258	C 12a
259	C 8b
260	C 8b.
261	C. 13b
262	C 10a

V

THEORY OF COLOURS.

263	G 37a
264.	E. 32b
265	W 232b
266	Br M 211b
267.	Ash. I 2a.
268	E 17a
269	W 240b
270.	W. L 145 Ba.
271	C A 178a, 536a
272	C A. 44b, 137b
273	C A. 187 II² 562a
274	W. L 145 Db.
275	Ash I 22a.
276.	W. L 145 Ca
277.	F. 23a.
278	F 75a
279	C A 192b, 571b
280.	C A 181b, 546b
281.	A 19b.
282.	A 20a.
283	Ash. I 3a
284.	Ash I 2b.
285	Ash I 9b.
286	E 18a
287	W An IV 232b.
288.	W L. 145 Ab.

VI.

PERSPECTIVE OF COLOUR AND AERIAL PERSPECTIVE

289	C 12b
290.	C. 13a
291.	Ash. I. 17b.
292	W. 232b
293	Ash I 25b
294	Ash I 13a.
295	Ash I 10a
296	Tr 75
297	W. 3
298	Ash. I. 17a
299	Ash. I. 17b
300	Leic 4a
301.	Leic. 36a
302	F. 18a.
303	C 18a
304	H.² 29b
305	Br. M 169a
306	G. 53b
307	L. 75b

VII.

ON THE PROPORTIONS AND ON THE MOVEMENTS OF THE HUMAN FIGURE

308	H¹ 31b
309	C. A 157a, 463a
310.	W. P. 2a
311	A 62b
312	A 63a
313	W P 119a.
314	W. P. 7a
315	Ven Ac. IV 16.
316	W P. 12
317	W P 5a.
318	W P 3 Ia
319	Tur 7
320.	Tur. 11
321	W P. 3 II
322	W P 1b
323	W. P. 8a
324	W P 1a.
325	W. P 4b
326	W P 7a
327.	W P. 3 IIa.
328	W P 7a
329	B 3b.
330	W. P. 7a
331.	W P 8a
332	W P. 6 Ib
333	W P 6 Ib.
334.	W P 6 IIa
335	W P 6 IIb
336	W P. 5a.
337.	W P 2a
338	W P. 7a
339	W. P 7b
340.	C. A 350a, 1089a
341	W. P 5a
342	W P. 7b
343	Ven. (121) nº .A[1]
344	Ash I 12a.
345	W. P. 8a.
346	B. 3b.
347	W. P. 4a.
348	W. P 5a
349	W. P 7b
350.	Br M 44a
351	W. 197.
352.	Ash. I. 25 IIa
353	C. A. 44b; 137b.
354	C A 98b, 308a.
355.	E 17a
356	W. III
357	W. A. II 203b (24)
358	W 215
359	A 29a
360	E 3a
361	Ash. I. 15a.
362	E. 20a
363	E 19b
364	Ash I 7a.
365	W 240b
366	E 6b
367	Ash I 7a.
368	Ash I 6b
369	A 28b
370.	W. A III 167b
371	F 83a
372	S K M II² 14a
373	M 55a
374	C. A. 178a, 536a
375	W A II 203a.
376	S. K M II² 20a
377	H² 27a
378	L 27b.
379	W 3a
380	E. 15a.
381	M² 13a.
382	C. A 341a, 1052a.
383	A. 30b
384	S K. M. III 58b.
385.	S K. M. I² 7.
386	Leic. 8a
387	W. 1a.
388	C A 344b, 1066a
389	W IV.
390	Ash I 29b
391.	Ash. I. 17b
392	Ash I¹ 8a.

VIII

BOTANY FOR PAINTERS AND ELEMENTS OF LANDSCAPE PAINTING.

393	L 87a.
394	L¹ 12b
395	M. 78b
396	M 79a.
397	G. 34b.
398	G. 35a.
399	G. 13a.
400.	G. 14a.

401.	G. 37a.
402.	G. 33a.
403.	L. 6b.
404.	G. 32b.
405.	G. 5a.
406.	G. 4b.
407.	G. 35b.
408.	G. 36a.
409	G. 36b.
410.	G. 51a.
411.	G. 88b.
412.	G. 33a.
413.	G. 27a.
414.	G. 28a.
415.	G. 16b.
416.	G. 30b.
417.	G. 29a.
418.	G. 27a.
419.	G. 33b.
420.	M. 77b.
421.	G. 8a.
422.	G. 24a.
423.	G. 10a.
424.	G. 10b.
425.	G. 3a.
426.	G. 2b.
427.	G. 3b.
428.	G. 4a.
429.	G. 4b.
430.	G. 8a.
431.	G. 8b.
432.	G. 9a.
433.	G. 10b.
434.	G. 28b.
435.	Br. M. 114b.
436.	G. 12a.
437.	G. 15a.
438.	G. 28b.
439.	Ash I. 4a.
440.	E. 18b.
441.	E. 19a.
442.	G. 9b.
443.	G. 19b.
444.	G. 20b.
445.	G. 21a.
446.	G. 21b.
447.	G. 22a.
448.	G. 22b.
449	L. 87a.
450.	G. 25b.
451.	G. 26b.
452.	L.[1] 37b.
453.	B. M. 114a.
454.	B. M. 172b.
455.	G. 6a.
456.	W. VI.
457.	G. 27b.
458.	B. M. 113b.
459.	B. M. 114b.
460.	G. 11b.
461.	E. 19a.
462.	C. A. 181b; 546b.
463.	I.[1] 48a.
464.	H.[2] 20a.
465.	G. 19b.
466.	C. A. 157a; 463a.
467.	E. 3b.
468.	G. 22b.
469.	G. 23a.
470.	E. 6b.
471.	B. M. 172b.
472.	C. A. 78a; 228a.
473.	B. M. 277b.
474.	F. 35a.
475.	W. VI.
476.	B. M. 172b.
477.	W. 231.
478.	C. A. 346a; 1072a.
479.	E. 0'.
480.	E. 0''.
481.	G. 37b.

IX.

THE PRACTICE OF PAINTING.

I. MORAL PRECEPTS FOR THE STUDENT OF PAINTING.

482.	G. 25a.
483.	Ash. I. 18a.
484.	Ash. I. 2b.
485.	Ash. I. 25b.
486.	Ash. I. 10a.
487.	C. A. 145a; 431a.
488.	L. 79a.
489.	Ash. I. 8b.
490.	C. A. 196b; 586b.
491.	Ash. I. 7b.
492.	Ash. I. 8a.
493.	C. A. 181b; 546b.
494.	Ash. I. 8a.
495.	Ash. I. 9a.
496.	Ash. I. 9b.
497.	Ash. I. 8b.
498.	S. K. M. III. 24b.
499.	G. 25a.
500.	Ash. I. 10a.
501.	Ash. I. 10b.
502.	Ash. I. 9b.
503.	G. 5b.
504.	Ash. I. 4a.
505.	G. 5b.
506.	Ash. I. 31b.
507.	Ash. I. 9a.
508.	Ash. I. 13a.

II. THE ARTIST'S STUDIO.—INSTRUMENTS AND HELPS FOR THE APPLICATION OF PERSPECTIVE.—ON JUDGING OF A PICTURE.

509.	Ash. I. 19b.
510.	B. M. 171b.
511.	B. 20b.
512.	Ash. I. 29a.
513.	Ash. I. 15b.
514.	A. 23a.
515.	Ash. I. 2b.
516.	Ash. I. 2a.
517.	Ash. I. 28b.
518.	A. 2a.
519.	Ash. I. 18a.
520.	Ash. I. 15a.
521.	A. 1a.
522.	Ash. I. 6b.
523.	Ash. I. 11b.
524.	A. 1b.
525.	A. 42b.
526.	A. 38b.
527.	A. 42a.
528.	Ash. I. 4a.
529.	Ash. I. 11a.
530.	Ash. I. 7b.
531.	Ash. I. 11b.
532.	Ash. I. 9b.
533.	Ash. I. 21a.
534.	Ash. I. 25b.
535.	Ash. I. 16b.
536.	Ash. I. 4b.
537.	Ash. I. 25b.
538.	Ash. I. 12b.
539.	Tr. 71.
540.	Ash. I. 4a.
541.	Ash. I. 25b.
542.	Ash. I. 19b.
543.	A. 40b.
544.	A. 41a.
545.	A. 41b.
546.	Ash. I. 22b.
547.	Ash. I. 3a.

III. THE PRACTICAL METHODS OF LIGHT AND SHADE AND AERIAL PERSPECTIVE.

548.	C. A. 196b; 586b.
549.	A. 23a.
550.	Ash. I. 14a.
551.	Ash. I. 2b.
552.	Ash. I. 14a.
553.	G. 33b.
554.	G. 19a.

555	Ash I 7a
556	G 11b
557	Ash. I 19a.
558.	Ash I 12b
559.	Ash I 14a
560	Ash. I 29b
561.	Ash I 4a
562	E. 4a.
563	Ash I 4a
564	G 23b
565.	Ash I 19a
566.	Ash I. 15b
567.	Ash I 15a.
568	Ash. I. 4a
569	G 53b
570.	W. A IV. 218b
	IV. OF PORTRAIT AND FIGURE PAINTING
571	Ash. I. 8a
572.	Ash. I. 9a
573	Ash I. 6b
574	Ash I. 3b
575	W. I
576	Ash I 19a
577	W. I
578	Ash I. 18a
579	Ash. I 26a.
580	Ash. I 2a.
581	C A 157a, 463a
582	Ash I. 17b
583	Ash I 18a
584	Ash I. 6a
585	Ash. I. 6b
586	A 23a
587	Ash I 8b
588	Ash I. 19a.
589	Ash I 2a.
590.	G. 26a.
591	Ash. I 13a
592	Ash I. 6a.
593.	C A 137a, 415a
594	Ash. I 14b
595.	Ash. I 5b
596	A. 28b
597	W. L. 145a
598	C A 337b, 1026b
599	C. A. 341a, 1051a.
600.	Ash. I 15b.
	V. SUGGESTIONS FOR COMPOSITION.
601	Ash I 4b
602.	Ash I. 3a
603.	G 15a.
604.	Ash I. 17a.
605.	Br M 169a
606	Ash I 14b
607.	G 6b.
608.	W 158a.
609	W. 158b.
610.	C A 78a; 228a
611	C A 152a, 451a
	VI THE ARTIST'S MATERIALS.
612	S K. M II' 0'
613	F. 96a
614	S K. M. III 53a
615	Br M 174a
616	C A. 71b, 209b
617	F. 56a
618	258a, 784a
619	70a, 207a
620.	II^2 46b
621	C. A 70b, 207b
622	Tr 78
623	L 92a
624	A 8b
625	W. P 5a.
626	F. 96b
627	S K. M II^1 95a
628	A. 1a
629	S K. M III 52b.
630.	K 3 32b
631	C A 46 11b
632	C A 70b, 207b
633.	S K M III 85a.
634	C A 108b, 339b
635	S K. M I^2 5
636	S. K M L^2 8
637	G 46b.
638	B 2b.
639	W XIII
640.	Tr. 49
641	G 53a
642	W VIII.
643	II^1 18b.
644	H 3 88b
645.	Br M 139a
646	S. K M III 53a.
647.	S K M III. 55a.
648	L 2a
649.	S. K. M. I.^{2} 5
650	S K M, 1 2 8
	VII PHILOSOPHY AND HISTORY OF THE ART OF PAINTING
651	S. K M III 19b
652.	Ash I. 15b.
653.	Ash. I 16b.
654	Ash I. 16a.
655.	Ash I. 10b
656	Ash. I. 11a
657	K.3 30b
658.	W A. IV 152a
659.	Ash. I 18a.
660	C. A. 139a, 419a.
661	Ash I 18a
662.	S. K. M III 48a
	X. STUDIES AND SKETCHES FOR PICTURES AND DECORATIONS.
663	F U. 115, 446.
664.	Th
665	S K. M.^{2}, 2a
666	S. K M II^2, 1b.
667	S. K. M II^2, 78b
668.	V A. X. 8
669	C A. 75a, 214a.
670	H.3 50a
671	II^2 40b
672.	J.^{2} 90b
673	J^2 91a
674	Br M. 250a.
675	B. 3b
676	Ox 2a
677	Ox 2b
678	Br M 231b
679	J^2 59a.
680	C A 317a, 959a
681	W. 243
682	W L 198a.
683	W L 198b
684	W P. 11a
685	W P. 11b
686	Ash. I 1a
687	Br. M. 173a.
688	W. IX
689.	H 3 51b
690.	H.3 53a.
691.	H 3 70a
692	H.^{2} 1b
693.	H^2 13a
694.	H.^{2} 15b
695	H.^{1} 40a
696	H.^{1} 40b
697	S. K M. II^2 1b.
698	F. 0"
699	M. 4a
700.	M. 4b.
701.	M. 5a
702.	C A. 67b, 203b
703	C. A. 228b, 687b.
704.	J^2 1b
705	Mz. 10a

PRINTED

FOR

SAMPSON LOW, MARSTON, SEARLE & RIVINGTON

LONDON

BY

W. DRUGULIN ORIENTAL AND OLD-STYLE PRINTER

LEIPZIG.

CPSIA information can be obtained
at www.ICGtesting.com
Printed in the USA
LVHW080540080822
725407LV00003B/22

9 781298 532367